ICSA

STUDY TEXT

Professional Paper 15

Company Secretarial Practice

New in this September 2000 edition

- Electronic Communications Act 2000
- Developments in role of Financial Services Authority
- Changes in Listing Rules
- All-employee share plans

FOR 2001 EXAMS

BPP Publishing
September 2000

First edition 1994
Sixth edition September 2000

ISBN 0 7517 5139 1 (previous edition 0 7517 5029 8)

British Library Cataloguing-in-Publication Data
A catalogue record for this book
is available from the British Library

Published by

BPP Publishing Limited
Aldine House, Aldine Place
London W12 8AW

www.bpp.com

Printed in England by DA COSTA PRINT
35 – 37 Queensland Road
London N7 7AH

We are grateful to the Institute of Chartered Secretaries and Administrators for permission to reproduce in this text the syllabus and syllabus commentary of which the Institute holds the copyright.

We are also grateful to the Institute of Chartered Secretaries and Administrators, the Association of Chartered Certified Accountants, and the Chartered Institute of Management Accountants for permission to reproduce past examination questions. The suggested solutions have been prepared by BPP Publishing Limited.

Page

HOW TO USE THIS STUDY TEXT

Aims of this Study Text

To provide you with the knowledge and understanding, skills and application techniques that you need if you are to be successful in your exams

This Study Text has been written around the official ICSA **Company Secretarial Practice** syllabus

- It is **comprehensive**. We do not omit sections of the syllabus; the examiner may examine any part of the syllabus from any angle - and you do not want to be left high and dry.
- It keeps you **up-to-date** in developments in company secretarial practice, the way in which the examiner is designing questions and relevant legislation, etc.
- It is **on-target**. We do not include any material which is not examinable. You can therefore rely on the BPP Study Text as the stand-alone source of all your information for the exam, without worrying that any of the material is irrelevant.

To allow you to study in the way that best suits your learning style and the time you have available, by following your personal Study Plan

You may be studying at home on your own until the date of the exam, or you may be attending a full-time course. You may like to read every word, or you may prefer to skim-read and devote the remainder of your time to question practice. Whatever your approach, you will find the BPP Study Text meets your needs in designing and following your personal Study Plan.

To tie in with the rest of the BPP Effective Study Package to ensure you have the best possible chance of passing the exam

Recommended period of use	Elements of the BPP Effective Study Package
3-12 months before exam	**Study Text** Use the Study Text to acquire knowledge, understanding, skills and the ability to use application techniques.
↓	
1-3 months before exam	**Practice & Revision Kit** Read the helpful checklists which are provided for each topic area in the Kit. Then try the numerous examination questions, for which there are realistic suggested answers.

Settling down to study

By this stage in your career you are probably very experienced at learning and taking exams. But have you ever thought about *how* you learn? Let's have a quick look at the key elements required for effective learning.

Key element of learning	**Using the BPP Study Text**
Motivation	You can rely on the comprehensiveness and technical quality of BPP material. You've chosen the right Study Text - so you're in pole position to pass your exam!
Clear objectives and standards	Do you want to be a prizewinner or simply achieve a pass? Decide.
Feedback	Work through the examples in this text and do the Exercises and Test your knowledge quizzes. Evaluate your efforts critically - how are you doing?
Study Plan	You need to be honest with yourself about your progress - don't be over-confident, but don't be negative either. Make your Study Plan (see below) and try to stick to it. Focus on the short-term objectives - completing two chapters a night, say - but beware of losing sight of your study objectives.
Practice	Use the Test your knowledge quizzes and Chapter roundups to refresh your memory after you have completed your initial study of each chapter.

These introductory pages let you see exactly what you are up against. But however you study, there are two things you should do.

- **Read through the syllabus** and **syllabus commentary;** these will help you to identify areas you have already covered, perhaps at a lower level of detail, and areas that are totally new to you.
- **Study the examination paper section,** where we show you the format of the exam and analyse the recent papers, **including the one set in June 2000**.

Developing your personal Study Plan

Preparing a Study Plan (and sticking closely to it) is one of the key elements in learning success. First you need to be aware of your style of learning. There are four typical learning styles. Consider yourself in the light of the following descriptions and work out which you fit most closely. You can then plan to follow the key study steps in the sequence suggested.

Learning styles	Characteristics	Sequence of key study steps in the BPP Study Text
Theorist	Seeks to understand principles before applying them in practice	1, 2, 3, 5, 6, 7, 8, 9, 10, 11, 12 (4 continuous)
Reflector	Seeks to observe phenomena, thinks about them and then chooses to act	
Activist	Prefers to deal with practical, active problems; does not have much patience with theory	1, 2, 8/9 (read through), 6, 7, 10, 3, 4, 8/9 (full attempt), 11, 12 (5 continuous)
Pragmatist	Prefers to study only if a direct link to practical problems can be seen; not interested in theory for its own sake	8/9 (read through), 2, 6, 7, 10, 1, 3, 4, 8/9 (full attempt), 11, 12 (5 continuous)

Key study steps

We have broken the learning process down into a series of key steps, which you can apply to each chapter in turn. We list them here in the order which seems to work best for **theorists** and **reflectors**. If you are an **activist** or a **pragmatist** you may prefer to use a different sequence. The various options are summarised after the table of steps. Tackle the chapters in the order you find them in the Study Text. Taking into account your individual learning style, follow these key study steps for each chapter.

Key study steps	Activity
Step 1 *Chapter topic list*	Study the list. Each numbered topic is a numbered section in the chapter.
Step 2 *Introduction*	Read through it. It is designed to show you *why* the topics in the chapter need to be studied - how they lead on from previous topics, and how they lead into subsequent ones.
Step 3 *Explanations*	Proceed methodically through the chapter, reading each section thoroughly and making sure you understand. Where a topic has been examined, we state the month and year of examination against the appropriate heading. You should pay particular attention to these topics.
Step 4 *Note taking*	Take brief notes if you wish, avoiding the temptation to copy out too much.
Step 5 *Examples*	Follow each through to its solution very carefully.
Step 6 *Case examples*	Study each one, and try to add flesh to them from your own experience - they are designed to show how the topics you are studying come alive (and often come unstuck) in the real world.

Key study steps	Activity
Step 7 *Exercises*	Make a very good attempt at each one in the chapter. These are designed to put your knowledge into practice.
Step 8 *Solutions*	Check yours against ours, and make sure you understand the reasons why they may differ.
Step 9 *Chapter roundup*	Work through it very carefully, to make sure you have grasped the major points it is highlighting.
Step 10 *Test your knowledge quiz*	When you are happy that you have covered the chapter, use the Test your knowledge quiz to check how much you have remembered of the topics covered. The answers are in the paragraphs in the chapter that we refer you to.
Step 11 *Illustrative questions*	Either at this point, or later when you are thinking about revising, make a full attempt at the question(s) suggested at the very end of the chapter. You can find these at the end of the Study Text, along with the answers so you can see how you did.

Learning style approaches

Learning style	Sequence of key study steps in the BPP Study Text
Theorist Reflector	1, 2, 3, 5, 6, 7, 8, 9, 10, 11, (4 continuous)
Activist	1, 2, 7/8 (read through), 5, 6, 9, 3, 7/8 (full attempt), 10, 11 (4 continuous)
Pragmatist	7/8 (read through), 2, 5, 6, 9, 1, 3, 7/8 (full attempt), 10, 11 (4 continuous)

Next you should complete the following checklist.

Am I motivated? (a) ☐

Do I have an objective and a standard that I want to achieve? (b) ☐

Am I a theorist, a reflector, an activist or a pragmatist? (c) ☐

How much time do I have available per week, given: (d) ☐

- The standard I have set myself
- The time I need to set aside later for work on the Practice and Revision Kit
- The other exam(s) I am sitting, and (of course)
- Practical matters such as work, travel, exercise, sleep and social life?

Now:

- Take the time you have available per week for this Study Text (d), and multiply it by the number of weeks available to give (e). (e) ☐
- Divide (e) by the number of chapters to give (f). (f) ☐
- Set about studying each chapter in the time represented by (f), following the key study steps in the order suggested by your particular learning style.

This is your personal Study Plan.

Moving on...

However you study, when you are ready to embark on the practice and revision phase of the BPP Effective Study Package, you should still refer back to this Study Text, both as a source of reference (you should find the index particularly helpful for this) and as a refresher (the Chapter roundups and Test your knowledge quizzes help you here).

And remember to keep careful hold of this Study Text - you will find it invaluable in your work.

SYLLABUS

Objective

To develop an understanding of the company secretary's role in putting into practice statutory provisions and Stock Exchange Regulations, and observing established and best practice.

	Covered in Chapter
Governance	
An understanding of how limited companies are governed and the respective roles of the company secretary, directors, shareholders and other parties.	
Company secretary	
Role of the company secretary; qualifications and duties as an officer of the company; powers; core and additional duties. Relationship with directors. Offences under the Companies Act.	1, 3
Directors	
Role of directors, including the chairman and non-executive directors. Appointment, retirement, resignation and removal of directors. Shadow and Alternate directors. Conflicts of interest. Disqualification of directors. Penalties. Offences under the Companies Act. Directors' share dealing, Model Code and insider dealing. Company records and service agreements. Directors' Report.	2, 3, 18
Auditors	
Appointment and remuneration of auditors; resignation of auditors; their rights and duties.	2
Meetings	
Law, practice and procedure in respect of annual general meetings, and extraordinary general meetings, class meetings, board of directors' meetings, board committee meetings. Written resolutions.	4 – 9
Shareholders	
Shareholders' rights and obligations.	4, 12
Best practice	
The continuing debate about best practice in company governance; Combined Code appended to the Stock Exchange Listing Rules	3
Share registration	
An understanding of the role of a company's registrar and the principles and procedures involved in share registration.	
Register of members, share registration and transfer procedures	
Register of members. Procedures under the CREST system.	15, 18 – 22
Types of transfer forms and transfer registration procedures. Issue of share certificate. Stamp Duty and Stamp Duty Reserve Tax. Procedures for dealing with lost share certificates, including indemnity.	
Payment of dividends and interest. Scrip dividends and dividend reinvestment plans. Lost dividend warrants, unclaimed dividends and untraceable shareholders.	
New issues: methods of bringing securities to listings. Sub-division of shares. Allotment letters, renunciation, application for registration, splitting and consolidation.	

	Covered in Chapter
Employee share schemes	
An understanding of the main types of approved employee share schemes (including profit-sharing, savings related, and employee share trusts) and the main types of approved company option and incentive schemes. Rules and procedures relating to such schemes including price fixing, appropriation of shares, share option certificates, exercising options. Disclosures and approvals.	23
Incorporation and company compliance	
An understanding of the constitution and organisation of a limited company.	
Company formation	
Types of company. Procedures for registration and subsequent procedures. Company names and business names. The registered office. Accounting reference date. Seal. First board meeting and other actions necessary to form a company. Elective regime.	10, 11
Memorandum and articles	
Drafting and altering Memorandum and Articles. Table A Regulations (1985 version in particular).	11
Loan stock	
Procedures for issue of loan stock. Trust deeds. Procedures for conversion and redemption of loan stock. Debentures, fixed and floating charges. Registration of charges. Convertible securities.	13
Statutory registers and statutory returns	
Maintaining the statutory registers and making them available for inspection. Preparing and filing documents at Companies House. Annual returns. The preparation and content of an Annual Report. Registered Office.	14, 15
Stock Exchange and regulatory requirements	
General understanding of the rules regarding applications for listings (including an appreciation of the prospectus and listing particulars), and knowledge of the practical procedures involved. The regulatory structure under the Financial Services Act 1986 – (basic legislative background, general concepts, their application etc.). Ten statements of Principle issued by SIB. The implications of having a primary or secondary overseas listing.	3, 16, 17
The guidelines of investing institutions such as the Association of British Insurers and National Association of Pension Funds. The procedures in respect of take-overs, mergers and schemes of arrangement. The principles of the City Code on Takeovers and Mergers. Timetabling and other arrangements. Verification procedures.	
Registration consequences of take-overs, demergers and other capital events.	

SYLLABUS EXPANSION

Note that the following points are made in the ICSA's syllabus booklet.

'All modules are based on English and EU derived law and practice, except where national alternatives are shown.'

'Students are expected to keep abreast of changes in the law affecting the modules which they are studying. However, a detailed knowledge of new legislation will not be examined within six months of the passing of the relevant Act.

The ICSA provides the following further guidance in the Company Secretarial Practice Qualifying Pack.

Governance (Broad)

An understanding of how the company secretary, directors, shareholders and others fit together in a limited company. The following six sections focus on constituent parts of that understanding.

Company Secretary (Full)

Detailed knowledge of appointment and dismissal and duties of company secretary as set out in Companies Act 1985. Understanding of the role of the company secretary as proposed by the Combined Code and the ICSA.

Directors (Full)

Detailed knowledge of appointment and dismissal of directors and their duties, rights and responsibilities as set out in the Companies Act 1985, Table A articles of association, the Listing Rules and the Combined Code. Understanding of best practice and current debate about governance as it applies to directors.

Auditors (Full)

Detailed knowledge of procedures for appointing and dismissing auditors and their rights and responsibilities in the area of governance. The financial aspects of an auditor's work do not form part of the syllabus.

Meetings (Full)

Detailed knowledge of legal requirements affecting company meetings as set out in the Companies Act 1985 and Table A plus a good understanding of best practice, principally as regards conduct and calling of general meetings and good boardroom practice.

Shareholders (Full)

Candidates are expected to have a detailed knowledge of shareholders' rights as regards the company and its directors as set out in the Companies Act 1985 and Table A and to have an understanding of the current debate about the influence (or lack of influence) of shareholders over the company in which they hold shares.

Best Practice (Full/Broad)

Detailed knowledge of generally-accepted codes of best practice (for example the Combined Code) and some insight into the current debate about corporate governance (issues such as remuneration, stakeholders etc).

Share Registration (Broad)

Candidates are expected to understand the role of a registrar and to have an overview of CREST and certificated registration.

Register of members, share registration and transfer procedures (Full)

Detailed knowledge of work of a registrar and the registrar's relationship with individual shareholders; procedures involving a private company's certificated shares; and an understanding of the mechanics of CREST.

Employee Share Schemes (Full)

Detailed knowledge of those employee share schemes approved by the Inland Revenue. Candidates are not expected to follow closely the ongoing debate about executive remuneration and incentive plans.

Incorporation and Company Compliance/Company Formation (Full)

Candidates are expected to know in detail the procedure for forming new companies; to be able to make simple judgements about suitable types of company; and to identify decisions required of subscribers and directors in forming a company.

Memorandum and Articles (Full)

Detailed knowledge of the standard memorandum of association and the provisions of Table A articles and of the procedures for adopting and subsequently altering the memorandum and articles.

Loan Stock (Broad)

An understanding of the traditional forms of loan stock sufficient to answer questions about their administration and record-keeping. Candidates are not expected to have a sophisticated understanding of the different forms of company indebtedness.

Statutory Registers (Full)

Detailed knowledge of registers required to be kept by the Companies Act 1985, returns to Companies House, content of directors' report, and procedures surrounding the registered office.

Stock Exchange and Regulatory Requirements (Full/Broad)

Detailed knowledge of the continuing obligations including the model code for share dealing. (Full)

An understanding of the general principles involved in applications for listing, the ABI and NAPF guidelines, and the City Code on Takeovers and Mergers and an understanding of the practical procedures affecting the company secretary. (Broad)

That part of the syllabus dealing with the Financial Services Act 1986 will not be examined while the Government is overhauling financial regulation in the UK.

Grades

The 'grades' are Full, Broad, and Intermediate, and are explained more fully below.

Full

This grade refers to sections of syllabuses where you must be familiar with the whole area. Questions can be expected on topics in this category in each examination diet.

Broad

A general overview of topics within this area is expected. While you are not expected to answer full questions on topics indicated as 'Broad', you will be expected to make reference to 'Broad' topics within answers to questions categorised under the 'Full' designation.

Intermediate

This category corresponds to topics which, while not pivotal to a full understanding of the module, may assist in interpretation of a topic categorised as 'Full' or 'Broad'.

THE EXAMINATION PAPER

Paper requirements and format

Section A: 12 compulsory short answer questions. 40 marks available in total.

Section B: 3 questions from a choice of 5. Each question carries 20 marks.

Questions in both Sections A and B will be drawn from across the syllabus.

Key features of students' abilities to be demonstrated

- Awareness of legal requirements and regulatory frameworks
- Awareness of individual and organisational obligations and needs
- Effective means of minimising the risk of non compliance
- Application of given procedures
- Appreciation of the implications of non compliance with legal and regulatory requirements

Analysis of papers

June 2000

Section A

1. 12 short answer questions

Section B

2. Savings-related share option scheme
3. Death of shareholder; change of name; dividend mandate
4. Removal of director; political donations; procedures at board meetings
5. Point of order; show of hands; powers of chairman
6. Appointment of director; payment for shares; payment of dividends

December 1999

Section A

1. 12 short answer questions

Section B

2. CREST
3. Shareholdings; company office
4. Directors' transactions
5. Types of company; company finance
6. Notice

June 1999

Section A

1. 12 short answer questions

Section B

2. Chairman; re-election of directors; board committee
3. Documents filed on incorporation; elective and written resolutions; registers; agenda for first board meeting
4. Rights issue; missing share certificate
5. Good corporate governance practice
6. Shareholder rights to convene meetings and propose resolutions.

December 1998

Section A

1. 12 short answer questions

Section B

2. Minutes of board meeting
3. Gifts of shares; garnishee order; register of members
4. Public access to company records
5. Rights issue
6. Polls; proxies; corporate representatives; membership

June 1998

Section A

1. 12 short answer questions

Section B

2. Directors' report
3. Nominee shareholdings; savings-related option schemes; joint holdings in executorship
4. Proceedings at annual general meeting
5. Share dealings by listed company director
6. Appointment and resignation of directors and secretary; accounting reference date

Specimen paper

Section A

1. 12 short answer questions

Section B

2. Convening of board meeting; directors' interests
3. Share schemes; disclosure of directors' remuneration
4. Rotation of directors; purchase of own shares
5. Procedures for incorporation; location of registered office; company name; paperwork
6. Dividend reinvestment plans

Assume Table A has been adopted.

Part A
Governance

Chapter 1

THE COMPANY SECRETARY

This chapter covers the following topics.

Introduction

This chapter introduces the company secretary and describes his duties in outline. These will be amplified in later chapters of this Study Text, so it is a good idea to come back to this chapter and re-cap when you have worked through the rest of the text.

1 APPOINTING A COMPANY SECRETARY 6/98

1.1 Every company must have a secretary, but a **sole director cannot** also be a secretary.

1.2 A **corporation** may be a secretary to a company. However, Company A cannot have Company B as its secretary if Company B has a sole director who is also the sole director of Company A: s 283.

1.3 Single member private companies (see Chapter 7) must also have a secretary who is not the sole director/member.

Qualifications of a company secretary **Specimen paper, 6/00**

1.4 The directors of a *public* company must take all reasonable steps to secure that the secretary is suitably qualified for his post by his knowledge and experience and who fulfils one of a number of criteria.

(a) On the 22 December 1980 he held the office of **secretary, assistant** or **deputy secretary** of the company.

(b) For at least three out of the five years preceding his appointment as secretary, he held the **office of secretary** of a company other than a private company.

(c) He is a **barrister, advocate** or **solicitor**, called or admitted in any part of the United Kingdom.

(d) He is a **member** of any of the following bodies:

- Institute of Chartered Secretaries and Administrators
- Institute of Chartered Accountants in England and Wales
- Institute of Chartered Accountants in Scotland
- Institute of Chartered Accountants in Ireland
- Institute of Cost and Management Accountants
- Chartered Association of Certified Accountants
- Chartered Institute of Public Finance and Accountancy

(e) He is a person who, by virtue of previous offices held, appears to the directors to be **capable** of discharging the functions required of the secretary.

There are no equivalent requirements for private companies, but larger or more complex private companies should recruit secretaries of similar qualifications and experience to those of public companies.

1.5 Two or more persons, such as a partnership, may be appointed **joint secretaries**. A company may also appoint a **deputy** or **assistant secretary**, who assists or acts in place of the secretary: s 283. The secretary may also be a director (though not a sole director).

1.6 The term '**officer**' includes the secretary.

Notification to the registrar 6/98

1.7 The registrar should be notified as follows.

(a) When the company is formed, **particulars** of the **first secretary** must be given in the papers delivered to the registrar: s 10(2)(b) (**Form 10** - see Appendix 1). Whenever there is a **change of secretary**, notice must be given to the registrar within 14 days: s 288(2) (Form **288b** notifying resignation, Form **288a** a new appointment; Form 288c any other change in particulars - see Appendices 15 to 17).

(b) Particulars of the secretary must be included in the **register** of **directors** and **secretary**, and in the **annual return**: s 288(1) and Sch 15.

2 DUTIES OF THE COMPANY SECRETARY

2.1 Company legislation makes reference to certain specific duties of the company secretary but does not provide a general definition of what the company secretary should do. The secretary's precise duties will vary according to the size of company. The most important duties, however, will be in the following areas.

Arranging meetings of the board of directors

2.2 The secretary's most important tasks in this area are likely to be the following.

(a) **Issuing** the **agenda** in advance

(b) **Collecting** or **preparing** the **papers** that the meeting has to consider, and ensuring that anyone outside the board who needs to attend will be available

(c) **Attending** the **meeting** and **ensuring** that **proper procedures** are **followed**. These include ensuring the meeting is quorate

(d) **Drafting** and **circulating** the **minutes**

(e) **Communicating** the **decisions** to the **staff** of the company or to outsiders, for instance a refusal to approve the transfer of shares

Signing and authentication of documents

2.3 The secretary will normally be responsible for **completing** and **signing** the **annual return** of the company. Various other statutory documents to be delivered to the Registrar, such as an application for re-registration of the company as limited or unlimited (ss 51(4) and 49(4)) may be signed by the secretary or a director. In addition the secretary's signature may be used when the seal is affixed, or where a deed is created. S41 authorises the secretary to authenticate any document requiring authentication by the company.

The company seal

2.4 If the company has a seal (it is not compulsory), the secretary will normally be responsible for its custody. The secretary should keep a record of all documents to which the seal is affixed, normally in a **register of sealings**.

Maintaining the statutory registers

2.5 The register that is likely to take up the most time is the **register of members**. Unless the work is contracted to outside Registrars, the secretary will enter transfers of shares and be responsible for issuing share certificates. In addition the following registers also have to be maintained.

- Register of charges
- Register of directors and secretaries
- Register of directors' interests and debentures of the company
- For public companies, a register of interests in the voting shares
- The minute book of proceedings of meetings of the company

General administrative duties

2.6 In addition the secretary may act as the general administrator and head office manager. Possible examples of duties under this heading include the following.

(a) Ensuring **compliance** with the company's **memorandum** and **articles**, and other statutory and regulatory requirements such as the Listing Rules

(b) **Communicating** with **shareholders**

(c) If the company does not have a separate accounts department, **maintaining** the **accounting records** required by s 221, and preparing the directors' report and accounts

(d) **Corresponding** with **legal advisers**, tax authorities, trade associations etc

(e) **Administering** the **office**, dealing with staff matters, office equipment, pensions and employee share schemes

Independence of the secretary

2.7 Whatever the duties of the secretary, the secretary's **ultimate loyalty** must be to the company. This may mean the secretary coming into conflict with for example a director or even the chairman.

2.8 If, for example, one of the directors has a clear **conflict of interest** between his duties to the company and his personal interests, the company secretary should ensure that the board minutes reflect the conflict. If the conflict precludes a director from voting and being counted in the quorum at the board meeting, the proper procedure should be followed. * eg. Bridgwater college FD = secretary.

2.9 Sir John Harvey-Jones has commented that it is the secretary who does as much as anybody to set the whole atmosphere of the board. Thus Sir John believes that the appointment of secretary is a key one. It is, he thinks, more important than that of any director.

2.10 Others have recognised the importance of the role of the secretary. The Cadbury Code of Corporate Governance (which we will discuss in detail in Chapter 3) required the directors to appoint a capable company secretary. They should ensure that the secretary is not removed without the **consent** of the **whole board**. The Code reinforces the point that the secretary has a key role in ensuring board procedures are properly followed.

ICSA statement of best practice

2.11 The ICSA have published a Statement of best practice on reporting lines for the company secretary. The key points are as follows.

(a) The company secretary is **responsible** to the **board**, and should be **accountable** to the board through the chairman on all matters relating to his duties as an officer of the company (the core duties).

(b) If the company secretary has other executive or administrative duties beyond the core duties, he should **report** to the **chief executive** or such other director to whom responsibility for the matter has been delegated.

(c) The company secretary's **salary**, share options and benefits should be **settled** (or at least noted) by the **board** or remuneration committee on the recommendation of the chairman or chief executive.

3 LEGAL POSITION OF THE COMPANY SECRETARY 12/99

3.1 At one time the functions of the secretary were merely as described above, and he dealt with them strictly in accordance with instructions given to him. The law therefore treated him as a mere subordinate, lacking authority to enter into contracts or to speak for the company.

3.2 It followed that the company was not bound by the actions of the secretary, if they had not been expressly authorised, since the secretary had no apparent authority as the company's agent implied from holding the office of secretary. In *Ruben v Great Fingall Consolidated 1906*, the company denied that its secretary had ostensible authority to issue a share certificate. In *Houghton & Co v Nothard, Lowe & Wills 1928* the company repudiated a letter written by the secretary, on the grounds that the secretary (as such) had no authority to commit the company (in a somewhat unusual situation).

3.3 However, under agency law if a person is employed in a capacity in which he does certain things for his principal, he has **ostensible** or **apparent** authority to bind his principal by such actions on his behalf, unless the principal has denied him that authority and the other party has notice of the restriction. In 1971 the Court of Appeal applied this principle and recognised that it is a normal function of a company secretary to enter into contracts connected with the *administration* of the company.

> *Panorama Developments (Guildford) Ltd v Fidelis Furnishing Fabrics Ltd 1971*
> *The facts:* B, the secretary of a company, ordered cars from a car hire firm, representing that they were required to meet the company's customers at London Airport. Instead, he used the cars for his own purposes. The bill was not paid, so the car hire firm claimed payment from B's company.
>
> *Decision:* B's company was liable, for he had apparent authority to make contracts such as the present one, which were concerned with the administrative side of its business. The decision recognises the general nature of a company secretary's duties. The court also said that, if the issue had arisen, it might not have treated the secretary as having apparent authority to make *commercial* contracts such as buying or selling trade goods, since that is not a normal duty of the company secretary.

3.4 These principles apply mainly to large companies, in which there is a considerable volume of administrative work, for which the secretary is well fitted by reason of his experience, training and role as the principal channel of communication between the board and the management and professional advisers of the company.

Offences under the Companies Acts

3.5 In the context of the liability of the company secretary, a number of general duties conferred upon the officers of the company clearly fall within the secretary's ambit because they are administrative matters. If not carried out, they will therefore result in the secretary being **liable**. Examples of these matters are the registers of members and of directors and their interests, the register of charges, and the various returns to the Registrar.

3.6 Liability is generally only imposed where the secretary is in default, ie where he knowingly and wilfully authorises or permits the default. Generally speaking, if the directors have appointed a qualified secretary, there can be no excuse for such a person to allow a default to continue as soon as he knows of the default. Moreover there can be little excuse for such a person if he allows himself to remain ignorant in an attempt to avoid liability.

3.7 A few examples of offences and their penalties are listed below. The 'statutory maximum' means, in England and Wales, the prescribed sum under s 32 of the Magistrates' Court Act 1980, and in Scotland the prescribed sum under s 289B of the Criminal Procedure (Scotland) Act 1975.

Section No	*Offence*	*Penalty*
122(2)	Company failing to give notice to registrar of reorganisation of share capital	Fine: $^1/_5$ of statutory maximum
191(4	Refusal of inspection or copy of register of debentureholders etc	Fine: $^1/_5$ of statutory maximum
221(5) or 222(4)	Company failing to keep accounting records	On indictment: 2 years imprisonment or a fine or both Summary: 6 months imprisonment or the statutory maximum or both
288(4)	Default in complying with section 288 (keeping register of directors and secretaries, refusal of inspection).	Fine: the statutory maximum
363(3)	Company with share capital failing to make annual return	The statutory maximum
382(5)	Company failing to keep minutes of proceedings of company and board meetings etc	$^1/_5$ of statutory minimum
450	Destroying or mutilating company documents; falsifying such documents or making false entries; parting with such documents or altering them or making omissions	On indictment: 7 years imprisonment or a fine or both Summary: 6 months imprisonment, or the statutory maximum fine or both.

(The statutory maximum is £5,000.)

3.8 The offences for which directors may be held liable are discussed in Chapter 2.

Exercise

What was the significance of the *Panorama Developments* case?

Solution

See paragraph 3.3.

---

4 FUTURE ROLE OF THE COMPANY SECRETARY

4.1 One recommendation of the current review of company law was the abolition of the requirement for private companies to have a company secretary.

4.2 ICSA has argued strongly against this proposal. An article on its website sets out its views.

Loss of accountability

4.3 The proposal will mean that **only one person** need be **involved** in the management of the company; in addition the company need not be audited if it is small enough. The article points out that an individual, maybe based offshore and without any independent oversight, would be able to set up a limited company with a UK accommodation address, and with little chance of being **held to account** if things did go wrong.

Role of the secretary

4.4 The article argues that a qualified company secretary is responsible for **protecting** the **probity** of the organisation. He or she is a guard against the directors acting in their own interest rather than those of the company; an important aspect of the role is to remind directors of their responsibilities. The secretary also acts to **protect** the **interests** of **third party shareholders** and other **stakeholders**, and is also responsible for interpreting the decisions of the board and ensuring they are implemented throughout the company.

Omission

4.5 Under the current Companies Act, the secretary (as an officer of the company) is held responsible for well over a hundred **breaches** of law. The proposals envisage that the responsibilities currently devolved upon the secretary will in future be devolved upon the directors, but the article points out that the directors' **priorities** and **areas of expertise** may not be in the areas of governance and compliance.

Governance

4.6 The article argues that if a secretary is appointed when a company is formed, this should mean that the principles of compliance and good governance are **embedded** in the company's procedures from the start, and these aspects will be of critical importance as the company grows towards listing.

Conclusion

4.7 The article proposes that the requirements concerning the company secretary in the Companies Act should be strengthened and the following requirement should apply to all companies:

> 'Every company and its director(s) should have recourse to the advice and support of a named, UK resident company secretary, suitably qualified to assist the directors in safeguarding the rights, advancing the interests and meeting the obligations of the company and to provide the necessary advice and guidance to the directors as to their obligations and responsibilities under company law and regulation, the company's constitution and governance best practice.'

Chapter roundup

- Every company must have a secretary (separate from a sole director) and for a plc the secretary must be **suitably qualified** for the position.
- The secretary's duties include the following
  - Dealing with members and directors' queries
  - Making suitable arrangements for meetings
  - Drafting agendas for meetings and resolutions
  - Minuting meetings
  - Ensuring records and registers are up to date (whether he delegates this task or not)
  - Ensuring registration of appropriate forms with the Registrar of Companies
  - Acting as general administrator and head office manager
- The company secretary is responsible for his own actions as an **officer** of the company and in particular as regards his normal and statutory duties.
- Notice of his **appointment** or a **change** of secretary must be **notified** to the **registrar**.

Test your knowledge

1 What are the statutory rules on the appointment of a company secretary? (see paras 1.1 - 1.4)

2 Describe the normal duties and status of a secretary of a medium-sized company. (2)

3 What is the fine for failing to make an annual return? (3.7)

Now try illustrative question 1 at the end of the Study Text

Chapter 2

DIRECTORS

This chapter covers the following topics.

1 Who and what is a director?

2 The role of directors

3 Appointment of directors

4 Company records and service agreements

5 Ceasing to be a director

6 Directors' powers and duties

7 Annual accounts and auditors

8 The directors' report

9 Directors' interests, contracts and loans

10 The chairman

Introduction

This chapter discusses the role of directors. Again, some of the topics will be developed further in later chapters.

You will have studied directors as part of your *Corporate Law* studies, so this chapter may be revision for some of you. Do not forget, however, that this paper is concerned less with legal principles *per se* than with their application in a practical context, particularly the impact on the company secretary.

You should pay particular attention to Section 8 on the directors' report.

1 WHO AND WHAT IS A DIRECTOR? **6/00**

1.1 A company, as an abstract 'entity', cannot manage itself. Accordingly it is a basic requirement of company law that a company shall have at least one director; a public company is required to have a minimum of at least two directors: s 282.

1.2 The same person **cannot** be both the **sole director** of a company and its **secretary**: s 283. In practice most companies have at least two directors and, in that situation, there is no objection to one of the directors also being appointed secretary, but when documents are to be signed by a director *and* by the secretary, they must be signed by two different persons. There is no objection to a corporate body being a director of a company, but in that situation its functions as director are performed by an individual acting for it.

1.3 Company law imposes a number of duties on directors as individuals, but the law also regards the **board** of two or more directors as a group which takes collective decisions, if necessary by voting at a **board meeting**.

Who is a director?

1.4 There is no comprehensive definition of a company director, but any person who occupies the position of director is treated as such: s 741. The test is one of **function**. The director's function is to take part in making decisions by attending meetings of the board of directors; anyone who does that is a director, whatever he may be called. A person who is given the title of director, eg 'sales director' or 'director of research', to give him status in the company structure, is not a director in company law unless, by virtue of his appointment, he is a member of the board of directors.

Shadow directors

6/00

1.5 As the legal responsibilities (and the disclosures required) of company directors can be burdensome, a person might seek to avoid them by not accepting formal appointment as a director, but using his power, eg as a major shareholder, to manipulate the acknowledged board of directors.

1.6 To counter that method of avoiding legal rules, it is provided (in several statutory rules) that a person (other than a professional advisor merely acting in that capacity, such as an accountant or solicitor) is to be a 'director' for legal purposes if the board of directors is accustomed to act in accordance with his directions or instructions. In connection with the rules on loans to, and transactions with, directors, such a person is called a '**shadow director**': s 741(2). This may catch loans between holding and subsidiary companies.

1.7 The definition of shadow directors is important as they may be **liable** under the Insolvency Act 1986 for **wrongful trading**: *Re Hydrodam (Corby) Ltd 1994*. A shadow director may also suffer **disqualification** under the Company Directors Disqualification Act 1986.

1.8 Controlling shareholders, including holding companies, may be at risk of being classified as shadow directors. However it is necessary to show that the directors act on their directions. It would not be enough just to show that the directors or some of them are their nominees: *Kuwait Asia Bank FC v National Mutual Life Nominees Ltd 1990*.

Alternate directors

6/99

1.9 An **alternate director**, who may or may not be an existing director, is a person who is appointed to **act on behalf of**, and in the place of, a **director**. The alternate is appointed by a director under the company's articles of association. Where a company has adopted Table A articles they provide, at articles 65-69, that any director may appoint an alternate, providing that the alternate is willing to act and is approved by the rest of the board. The alternate is appointed in writing by the appointor; that notice of appointment is then submitted to the board who must then approve the appointment by board resolution.

1.10 Since an alternate director is appointed to carry out the functions of the director who appoints him, it follows that he **discharges** all the **duties** of a director including attending and voting at board meetings. It also therefore follows that the appointor can limit the functions of the alternate, for example, voting on specific topics only. If the alternate attempts to act outside the functions delegated to him he may be in breach of duty since although he is classified as an 'alternate', he is nevertheless a director within the meaning of the Companies Act and is subject to the same duties and liabilities as an ordinary director. All the requirements for notifying Companies House, entries in registers and declarations of interests (discussed later in this text) also apply to alternate directors.

1.11 Table A articles provide that in order to be able to carry out his functions an alternate is entitled to **receive notice** of all directors' meetings and meetings of committees of directors, and to attend and vote at those meetings if his appointor is not personally present. An alternate is not entitled to receive any remuneration for his services.

1.12 Alternates, as already described, act for their appointor but they are not the agent of their appointor and are alone responsible for their own acts and defaults. A form of appointment is given below.

Draft form of appointment

The Directors [Date]

.... [Ltd] [plc]

I hereby given notice to the company that I have appointed .... of [address] [who is also a director of this company]* to be my alternate as a director. I ask the directors to approve this appointment and confirm your approval to me.

* to be included only where the alternate is an existing director.

Executive and non-executive directors

1.13 A director may also be an **employee**, usually a member of the management, of his company. Since the company (represented by the board, of which he is a member) is also his employer, there is potential conflict of interest which in principle a director is required to avoid.

1.14 To make it possible for an individual to be both a director and an employee, the articles (Table A Article 84) usually make **express provision** for it, but prohibit the director from voting at a board meeting on the terms of his own employment. If the articles permit, a director may also have some connection with the company, say as a consultant or professional adviser, and earn remuneration from the company in that capacity. The Combined Code (discussed in Chapter 3) contains provisions about the remuneration of directors of listed companies.

1.15 Directors' **service agreements** are **open to inspection** by members, and any service agreement which the company is not free to terminate within five years is only valid in that respect if approved in general meeting. The Combined Code suggests that the contracts of directors of quoted companies should not generally exceed **one year.**

1.16 Directors who have additional management duties as employees may be distinguished by special titles such as 'Finance Director'. Except in the case of a managing director, however, any such title does not affect their personal legal position. They have two distinct positions:

(a) As a **member** of the **board** of directors

(b) As a **manager** (usually working full time) with management responsibilities as an employee

1.17 On the other hand, a director who is '**non-executive**' (as are many directors of public companies) only acts as a member of the board of directors. The role of the non-executive director must depend on the circumstances of the company. In some cases, he contributes business experience gained by his activities outside the company; in others, he finds it necessary to restrain the working directors, especially if he considers that their projects will expose the company to risks of adverse trading, insolvency, or even illegality.

1.18 A non-executive director has the **same legal responsibilities** as any other director, and may press his point if he deems it necessary. Working directors generally welcome and respond to his efforts, if he plays his part with good sense and goodwill.

Managing director

1.19 If the articles so provide (Table A Article 84), the board may appoint one or more directors to be managing directors. A managing director (MD) does have a special position, and has **wider apparent powers** than any other director. Duties may also be delegated to a committee consisting of one or more directors.

1.20 A director need not be a British national nor be resident in the UK, but nationality is one of the particulars of a director to be recorded in the register of directors: s 289(1).

2 THE ROLE OF DIRECTORS

2.1 The role of directors and their function in and duties to a company are topical subjects on which there is much debate. We shall briefly consider two aspects - the code of practice on non-executive directors recommended by the Stock Exchange in 1987 and the statement of best practice on the role and duties of directors issued by the Institutional Shareholders' Committee (ISC) in 1991.

Code of practice on non-executive directors

2.2 A *Code of Recommended Practice on Non-Executive Directors* was published in April 1987 by Pro-Ned. Its adoption was 'warmly recommended' by the Stock Exchange, for non-listed companies it represents good practice. The aim of the code was to achieve a proper balance between independent non-executive directors and other directors.

> 'Effective boards are essential to the success of British business. In quoted companies, boards are more likely to be fully effective if they are comprised both of able executive directors and strong, independent non-executive directors.'

2.3 Among others, the code makes the following points:

(a) An **independent non-executive** director is one who:

(i) Has **not** been **employed** in an **executive** capacity by the company on whose Board he or she sits within the last five years

(ii) If a **professional advisor**, is not retained by the company (whether personally, or through his or her firm) on a continuing or regular basis

(iii) Is **not** (whether personally or through his or her employer) a **significant customer** of or supplier to the company

(b) In larger quoted companies where the turnover is £50 million or more or whose employees number 1,000 or more, the board should normally include at least **three independent non-executive directors** (who should comprise about **one third** of the board). In smaller quoted companies, the number of non-executive directors should be appropriate to the size of the board and the company's resources.

(c) The main tasks of the non-executive director are to:

- Contribute an **independent view** to the Board's deliberations
- Help the Board provide the company with **effective leadership**
- Ensure the **continuing effectiveness** of the directors and management
- Ensure high standards of **financial probity** on the part of the company

(d) In order to succeed in these tasks, the non-executive directors need to enjoy the **full support** of the **chairman,** and need to be provided with the necessary information in sufficiently good time to enable them to consider it properly.

(e) Non-executive directors should be consulted on **major issues** of **audit** and **control** and on the appointment, dismissal and remuneration of directors. Where appropriate committees are established (such as an Audit Committee or an Appointments and Remuneration Committee); these should comprise mainly non-executive directors.

(f) Non-executive directors should normally be **appointed** for a **specific term,** subject to re-election by rotation as for other directors.

2.4 The code recommends that listed and AIM companies not yet complying with it should do so within a 'reasonable period of time'.

2.5 The National Association of Pension Funds and the Association of British Insurers issued guidance in July 1999 on criteria for determining whether a non-executive director is independent. The guidance states that the non-executive director should be assumed to be independent unless he or she:

(a) Was **formerly an executive**

(b) Is or has been **paid by** the company in any capacity other than as a non-executive director

(c) Is a **trading partner**, or is or was connected to an organisation that trades with the company

(d) Has been a non-executive director for **nine** or **more years**

(e) Is **closely related** to an executive director

(f) Has been awarded **share options**, performance-related pay or is a pension scheme member

(g) **Represents** a **controlling** or significant **shareholder**

(h) Has recently been **appointed** by **other** than **formal process** (generally this would mean following a recommendation to the board by a nomination committee)

(i) Has **cross-directorships** with another executive director

(j) Is **deemed** by the company **not** to be **independent**

Statement of best practice on directors **6/00**

2.6 The Institutional Shareholders' Committee (ISC) is formed by representatives of a group of large institutional investors, such as pension funds and insurance companies. They have substantial stakes in many large quoted firms and plan to exert pressure as a body of shareholders in diverse companies.

2.7 The aim of the statement of best practice is to summarise the views of institutional shareholders and to help companies in structuring and running their businesses. As a general principle it states that all directors (both executive and non-executive) should have equal responsibility in leading the company and should always act in the company's best interest.

2.8 It supports the Pro-Ned code of practice and adds to it that:

(a) Non-executive directors should be **independent** and **impartial**, and therefore should not participate in incentive schemes in the company, nor should they be compensated for loss of office.

(b) The number and calibre of non-executive directors should be sufficient for them to carry **significant weight** with the board.

(c) Non-executive directors should acknowledge a duty to **monitor** the **board's performance** and report any shortcomings to the shareholders.

(d) **Other directorships** in the same industry should only be taken by non-executive directors with the **board's approval**.

2.9 The statement also concerns itself with two other significant areas: the appointment and removal of directors, and their remuneration.

Appointment and removal of directors

2.10 The statement recommends, over and above the statutory rules in this area, that:

(a) There should be a **maximum** as well as a minimum number of directors stated in the articles.

(b) The roles of **chairman** and **chief executive** should **not** be **combined.**

(c) Companies should **avoid confusion** over referring to non-board members as 'directors'.

(d) Each director's ability should be signified in **brief biographical details** included in the annual report.

(e) The articles should provide for **dismissal** of a director:

  (i) By **written resolution** of all or a substantial percentage of his fellow directors, to be validated at a general meeting

  (ii) By **fellow directors** following his failure to attend a certain number of board meetings

Directors' remuneration

2.11 Over and above the legal rules on directors' service contracts, the statement recommends that:

(a) The contracts should **not run** for **more than three years.**

(b) The contracts should **prevent** the **involvement** of executive directors in similar companies unless board approval is obtained.

2.12 The statement recommends that each company should have a **compensation committee** to approve service contracts and directors' remuneration, including options and bonus schemes. This should consist largely or (ideally) solely of non-executive directors, so that executives are excluded from the process of awarding their own pay rises. In addition, the statement calls for disclosure in the accounts of:

(a) **How** executive directors' remuneration is **decided** upon

(b) The **details** of any *ex gratia* or **compensation** payments made (there should be no confidentiality agreement on this)

(c) A **summary** of all **incentive schemes** operating

3 APPOINTMENT OF DIRECTORS — Specimen paper, 6/98, 6/99, 12/99, 6/00

3.1 On formation of a company it must give **particulars** of the first directors, signed by them to signify their consent: s 10(2). On the formation of the company those persons become the first directors: s 13(5). This is so even if the articles name other persons or make some other provision for appointing the first directors; s 13 overrides the articles, if they differ. The same procedure applies to the appointment of the first company secretary.

3.2 Once a company has been formed, any appointment of directors in addition to, or in replacement of, previous directors is made as the **articles provide**. Most companies follow Table A in providing for co-option of new members by existing directors, and election of directors in general meeting. The articles may exclude retirement by rotation, or permit some person (say the holding company or a major shareholder) to appoint one, several or all directors. It is a matter of choosing whichever procedure is convenient.

3.3 Table A Articles 73 - 80 on retirement and re-election of directors ('rotation') provides as follows:

(a) Every year, **one third** (or the number nearest to one third) shall retire; at the first AGM of the company they all retire.

(b) **Retiring directors** are **eligible** for re-election.

(c) Those retiring shall be those in **office longest** since their last election.

(d) If directors fail to agree who should retire and be offered for re-election, the question should be decided **by lot.**

(e) A director shall be **deemed** to be **re-elected,** unless the meeting decides otherwise.

(f) The directors themselves may fill a **casual vacancy** by **co-option**. Such an appointee must **stand for re-election** at the next AGM after his appointment, and does not count in determining the one-third to retire by rotation. This provision is contained in the Stock Exchange articles of association for a listed company. The company in general meeting may also elect new directors.

(g) A **managing director**, or other director holding executive office, is **not subject** to **retirement by rotation** and is excluded in reckoning the one-third in (a) above.

3.4 In addition, if a director retires because he reaches the age of 70, and he retires at a general meeting other than the one he would normally have retired at, he is not counted in reckoning who is to retire by rotation.

Exercise

The board of Teddy PLC has the following directors at the start of its AGM on 31 December 20X7.

	Age	When last elected/re-elected
Mr Timothy	42	31 December 20X4
Mr Paul	64	31 December 20X5
Mr Henry	70	31 December 20X6
Mr Maurice	38	31 December 20X6
Mr Edgar	34	31 December 20X6
Mr Gordon	43	2 May 20X7
Mr Edward	41	2 May 20X7

At the board meeting on 2 May 20X7 Mr Gordon and Mr Edward were appointed to fill casual vacancies and Mr Timothy was appointed managing director. The company's articles follow Table A as regards rotation of directors; the articles do not contain any provision about re-appointing directors who are over the statutory age limit. Which directors would be due for re-election at the AGM on 31 December 20X7?

Solution

Mr Gordon and Mr Edward must stand for re-election since they have been appointed during the year.

Mr Henry must stand for re-election as he has reached the age of 70, and Teddy PLC is a public company with no provision in its articles for automatic appointment of directors who are 70.

Calculation of who is to retire by rotation excludes Mr Gordon, Mr Edward, Mr Henry and Mr Timothy (who, as managing director, is not subject to re-election), thus leaving three directors. One of these must therefore retire by rotation. As Mr Paul has been in office the longest, it must be him.

3.5 When the appointment of directors is proposed at a general meeting of a public company, a **separate resolution** should be proposed for the election of each director: s 292. This is to prevent a weak candidate from securing election jointly with a candidate for whom there is stronger support. The rule may be waived only if a resolution is unanimously passed to that effect.

3.6 A company may, by its articles or a separate agreement, permit a director to **assign**, ie **transfer**, his office to another person. Any such transfer is valid only if approved by special resolution passed in general meeting (s 308), but no such approval is required if the articles provide that a director *on retiring* may nominate a director in his place - which is the better way to achieve the desired result.

3.7 Listed companies should notify the Stock Exchange Company Announcements Office of the following information for any new director:

(a) Details of any **other directorships** of publicly quoted companies held in the last five years indicating which are still held

(b) Where relevant, details of any **unspent criminal convictions**, involvements in **insolvency** proceedings, **public criticisms** by statutory or regulatory authorities, or **disqualification** as a director

3.8 **Notification** of **appointment** should be made to the Companies Announcement Office without delay and at the latest by the **end** of the **business day** following the decision or receipt of notice about the change by the company. The details can either be included as part of the notification of appointment, or should be sent separately to the Companies Announcement Office within 14 days of the appointment becoming effective.

4 COMPANY RECORDS AND SERVICE AGREEMENTS — Specimen paper

4.1 Even if a newly appointed director is a colleague already well known to him, the secretary should write to him to ask for certain information required for company records and, as appropriate, to provide information. These matters include the following.

(a) The director should sign **Form 288** a (a notice of appointment of director or secretary - see Appendix 15) before it is sent to the registry, within 14 days of his appointment. It may be necessary to ask him for information required to complete the 'particulars' which the form must contain. The same information should be entered in the register of directors and secretary: ss 288-9.

Details of any subsequent change in particulars, for example a change in address, should be sent to the registry on **Form 288c** (Change of particulars for directors or secretary - see Appendix 17).

(b) It is useful to obtain a **specimen signature** from the director. Directors are not normally now authorised signatories of cheques drawn on the company's bank account, but if there is to be the arrangement in this case, a specimen should be obtained and sent to the bank.

(c) Many companies have no **share qualification**, so they do not require directors to be shareholders of the company as provided in Table A. If there is a prescribed shareholding in the articles, however, the director should be informed of it and reminded that he has a limited period (two months, unless the articles fix a shorter time: s 291) in which to become the 'registered' holder of his qualification shares.

(d) The director should provide information of **his interest (if any) in shares or debentures** *of the company*, for entry in the relevant register kept under s 325. The same information is given in the directors' report on the accounts: Sch 7 paragraphs 2A and 2B. The director should be reminded of his obligation to give notice to the company of any change in his interest, within 3 working days: Sch 13 para 22. His interest for this purpose includes that of his spouse and minor children: s 327.

(e) If the director has **other business interests**, which is especially likely if he is a non-executive director, he should be asked to write to the company giving general notice that he is to be regarded as interested in any contract which the company may make with other named companies of which he is a director or shareholder, and with any firm in which he is a partner. In this way he will, as far as the notice goes, comply with s 317 (disclosure of directors' interests in contracts). Failure to do so deprives him of the benefit of the relieving provisions of the articles: Table A Article 85. Matters of this kind can easily be overlooked later on under the pressure of some urgent transaction.

(f) **UK Listing Authority** and **Stock Exchange rules** require directors of listed companies to submit information about their directorships.

4.2 In a more general way, the secretary should, by letter or in conversation, act as follows.

(a) Discover how the director wishes to have his **fees paid**, eg by transfer to his bank account; in this connection the company may need particulars of his PAYE coding (which will follow by notice from the Inland Revenue) and his National Insurance contributions. He may well be paying the maximum NI contributions already, or may possibly be exempt if he is aged 65 or more.

(b) Supply him with a **copy** of the **memorandum** and **articles**, and of any other documents, such as debenture trust deeds (which may impose restrictions on the amount which the board can borrow). He may also wish to have a copy of the latest report and accounts, for reference.

(c) Gather any **other particulars** necessary; for instance the Stock Exchange and the ISC urge companies to include in their annual reports the identity of directors who act in a non executive role, together with a short biographical note on each.

Directors' service agreements 6/98, 12/99

4.3 If a director is to work as a manager in the company's business, it is generally useful to him, and to the company, if the basic terms of his employment are set down in a formal **service agreement**, which should preferably be drafted by the company's solicitors. Apart from other considerations, the service agreement (if properly drafted) will also constitute the notice of terms of employment which the company is required to give to an employee under the Employment Protection (Consolidation) Act 1978 s 1.

4.4 Any agreement which cannot be terminated by the company without penalty within five years requires approval by the company in general meeting: s 319 or alternatively by informal agreement of all members, provided they have had the opportunity to consider the contract: *Wright v Atlas Wright Europe Ltd 1999.* However the provisions of the articles should also be considered. If for example the articles require the board to approve a service contract, there must be evidence that the board as a whole has **approved the contract**, otherwise it will not be binding: *UK Safety Group v Heane 1998.* If it is submitted for approval, a memorandum of its terms must be available for inspection at the registered office, during the 15 days before the general meeting and at the meeting itself: s 319(5).

4.5 Apart from setting out the remuneration, pension rights, holiday and sick pay entitlement of the director, it may be useful to **define** his **duties** (or to state that they shall be such as the board may decide from time to time), and to impose on him, for a limited period, a reasonable restraint against joining a competitor company.

4.6 A company must **make available** for **inspection** by members a copy, or particulars (if there is no written service agreement), of contracts of employment between the company or a subsidiary and a director of the company: s 318. There are two exceptions to the general rule:

(a) If the contract requires the director to work wholly or mainly outside the UK, only brief particulars, ie the director's name and the duration of the contract, need be given.

(b) If the contract will expire, or if the company can terminate it without compensation, within a year, no copy or particulars need be kept available for members' inspection.

4.7 The copy or particulars must be available either at the **registered office** or at the **principal place of business** in England.

4.8 The **AGM notice** must include a note giving the **time and place** for **inspection**, or stating, if that is the case, that there are no directors' service contracts (Listing Rules Section 21 paragraph 9(c)).

4.9 Prescribed particulars of **directors' remuneration** must be given in the accounts, as must particulars of any **compensation** for **loss of office**, and directors' pensions: Sch 5 Pt 5.

Directors' service agreements and the Listing Rules

4.10 Under the Listing Rules, anyone can inspect **directors' service contracts** at the registered office of the company **during normal business hours** on each business day and at the place of the annual general meeting for at least 15 minutes prior to and during the meeting.

4.11 The information available must include the following:

(a) The name of the **employing company**

(b) The **date of** the contract with the unexpired term and details of any notice period

(c) Full **particulars** of the directors' **remuneration** including salary and other benefits

(d) Any **commission** or **profit sharing** arrangements

(e) Any **compensation** payable for early termination

(f) Any other matters to enable investors to estimate the **possible liability** of the company upon early termination of the contract

4.12 The Annual Report must contain details of the **unexpired term** of any director who is standing for re-election at the next annual general meeting. It must also contain details of any service contract with a notice period in **excess of one year**, or where **compensation** for loss of office **exceeds one year's salary** plus benefits in kind.

5 CEASING TO BE A DIRECTOR 6/98, 12/99, 6/00

5.1 A director may always vacate his office by **resignation** (Table A Article 81 providing for resignation by notice in writing given to the company), or by **not offering** himself for re-election when his previous term of office ends under the rotation rules. In addition, there are statutory provisions for **removal** from office and for **disqualification**.

Removal of directors

5.2 The articles may provide for the removal of a director from office. For example, some company articles provide that a director may be removed from office by **extraordinary resolution** passed in general meeting, or even by a **resolution** of the **board of directors**. These provisions are to permit a company to dismiss a director without observing the formalities of the statutory procedure of ss 303 - 304. But if the director also has a service agreement he may still be entitled to compensation for the breach by his dismissal. 75% majority

Beneficiary of a trust protects his interests

5.3 In addition to any provisions of the articles for removal of directors, a director may be removed from office by **ordinary resolution** of which **special notice** has been given: s 303. On receipt of the special notice, the company must **send a copy** to the director, who may require that a memorandum of reasonable length shall (unless it is defamatory) be issued to members; he also has a right to address the meeting at which the resolution is considered: s 304.

5.4 This statutory power of removal **overrides** the articles and any service agreement (though the director may claim damages for breach of the agreement). The power is, however, limited in its effect in the following ways.

(a) A member who gives special notice to remove a director cannot insist on the inclusion of his resolution in the notice of a meeting, unless he qualifies by representing members who either have **one twentieth** of the **voting rights**, or are at least **100** in number with shares on which an average of at least **£100** has been **paid up**: s 376.

(b) A director may be irremovable if he has **'weighted' voting rights**, and can prevent the resolution from being passed: *Bushell v Faith 1970*. But if the company is listed, it may not adopt devices such as 'weighted' voting rights to block the general legal power to remove directors by ordinary resolution.

(c) A director may also be irremovable if at least **one member** of **all classes** of shareholder must be present to constitute a quorum. Hence if all shareholders of one class refuse to attend they can prevent a director's removal. The court will not over-ride the class rights by using s 371 to convene a meeting despite their absence: *BML Group Ltd v Harman & Another 1994*.

5.5 The dismissal of a director may also entail payment of a substantial sum to settle his claim for **breach of contract**, if he has a service agreement, but shareholders can prevent the company becoming committed to a long-term service agreement with a director, since a service contract of more than five years must be approved in general meeting: s 319.

Disqualification of directors **12/98, 6/99**

5.6 A person cannot be appointed a director, or continue in office, if he is or becomes disqualified under the **articles** or **statutory rules** as explained below.

5.7 The articles often embody the statutory grounds of disqualification, and add some optional extra grounds. Table A Article 81 provides that a director must vacate his office if:

(a) He is **disqualified** by the **Companies Acts** or any rule of law (eg if he ceases to be the registered holder of qualification shares).

(b) He becomes **bankrupt** or enters into an arrangement with his creditors.

(c) He becomes of **unsound mind.**

(d) He **resigns**.

(e) He is **absent** for a period of **six consecutive months** from board meetings held during that period, without obtaining leave of absence, and if the other directors resolve that he shall on that account vacate office. 'Is absent' is usually taken to include involuntary absence, eg due to illness, and to cause the six months' period to run from the latest meeting which the director attended.

5.8 No person may be appointed a director of a public company, or of a private company which is a subsidiary of a public company, if at the time of his appointment he has attained the age of 70. The rules (s 293) are as follows.

(a) A director shall in such a case **vacate his office** at the conclusion of the next AGM after attaining 70, and is **not to** be **automatically re-elected** as a retiring director.

(b) There are two exceptions to (a) above as follows.

 (i) If the **appointment** was made **in general meeting**, as a resolution of which **special notice** had been given, stating the age of the director

 (ii) If **excluded** by the **articles**

(c) Directors should **disclose** their **ages** to the company for the purposes of this rule: s 294.

5.9 A director who becomes **bankrupt** is disqualified (until he obtains his discharge) from **acting** as a director except with the leave of the court; he may be disqualified by the articles from holding office altogether.

5.10 The Company Directors Disqualification Act 1986 also provides for disqualification (for up to 15 years) by court order, on various grounds such as the following:

(a) Conviction of offences involving **serious dishonesty**
(b) **Neglect** of **statutory duties** as a director
(c) **Irresponsibility** leading to insolvency of the company

The DTI maintains a register of disqualification orders. Relevant offences now include insider dealing: *R v Goodman 1993* (discussed below).

Action after a change of directors

5.11 Whenever a director vacates office, no matter whether he retires, resigns, is removed from office or is disqualified, the following action should be taken.

(a) An **entry** should be made in the **register of directors and secretary**, and in the register of directors' interests in shares and debentures, to record that on a specified date he ceased to be a director: ss 288 and 325.

(b) **Notice** (**Form 288b** - see Appendix 16) should be given to the registrar within 14 days: s 288. Companies House has claimed that a director's **resignation** is not effective until they have received Form 288b.

(c) If the company's **letterhead** shows the names of the directors (this is optional but any list must show *all* the directors), the **director's name** should be **deleted** on each company letter issued, until it is economic to reprint a new stock: s 305.

5.12 Other matters which may, depending on the circumstances, require attention are as follows.

(a) If the company is listed, **notice** must be given to the **Stock Exchange**, which will pass it on to the press through the Regulatory News Service. Companies may use public relations agents to prepare their own release for the press.

eg. Iceland. Malcolm Walker resigned as MD. shares @ 52 each. Malcolm sold holding for ≈ £13m. then price halved.

(b) If the director was an authorised signatory of cheques drawn on the company's bank account, the **bank should** be **informed**.

(c) The **director's fees**, which accrue from day to day (Table A Article 82), should be **paid up to** the date on which he vacated office, and the appropriate tax form supplied to him.

(d) If the director was an employee under a fixed term service agreement, it may be necessary to **negotiate a settlement** of his claim for premature termination of his employment contract. He is not, however, entitled to any fees (payable under the articles) in lieu of notice, and he may only have **non-contractual compensation** for loss of office if it is properly sanctioned in general meeting.

Defective appointment of a director

5.13 It is sometimes discovered at a later stage that a director was not validly appointed, or that he was required to vacate office (for instance on attaining age 70 or because he ceased to hold his **qualification** shares). It is provided by statute (s 285) that the **acts** of a director shall be **valid despite** the discovery of a **defect** of appointment or qualification. The rationale of this is that 'the wheels of business will not go round smoothly unless it may be assumed that that is in order which appears to be in order'.

5.14 However the courts have tended to apply this principle as narrowly as possible, and it is by no means clear how a particular court will react to a given set of facts. It is therefore best in most cases to obtain legal advice, and perhaps to pass a resolution in general meeting to validate retrospectively the acts of the directors.

5.15 There is not always a problem over this situation. If, for example, the quorum for board meetings is two, and only one of three directors was not properly appointed (or in office), the decision of a meeting at which the other two directors were present would normally be valid. Of course, if there was *no* quorum without him, or if he acted in an individual capacity, the validity of the decision or action would depend on his personal position.

6 DIRECTORS' POWERS AND DUTIES

6.1 The directors, acting collectively at board meetings, have such powers of management over the company's business and property as the articles may give them. The usual position is as follows.

(a) The directors may exercise all the powers of the company itself, subject to the following limitations.

(i) The CA reserves certain decisions to the **company in general meeting** (eg an increase of authorised capital: s 121(4)), or requires the directors to obtain authorisation from a general meeting (eg to allot shares: s 80).

(ii) The articles may **limit the directors' powers** (eg to borrow money - see (b) below), or **confer** a **power** on the **general meeting** (eg to declare a final dividend, Table A Article 102) or to fix the directors' remuneration (Table A Article 82)).

(iii) Table A Article 70 provides that a **special resolution** passed in general meeting shall be a direction binding on the directors for the future, but not invalidating what they have already done. This article is discussed further in Chapter 4.

(b) It is usual, and essential in the case of a listed company, for the articles to impose on the directors a **limit** to the amount which they may **borrow** without the sanction of a general meeting.

(c) The directors may **delegate powers** to **committees** (Table A Article 72) 'consisting of one or more directors'. If the articles are worded to permit non directors to be co-opted to such committees, and the company is listed, the Stock Exchange (in its Listing Rules) requires that there shall always be an effective majority of directors to take a decision of such a committee. This right has become important as a result of the reports on corporate governance and their emphasis on board committees.

6.2 It should also be remembered that the directors' exercise of their powers is limited to actions performed in **good faith** in the **interests** of the company, and for a proper purpose. To some extent the company in general meeting, after proper disclosure, may relax the principles in particular cases.

6.3 A listed company must conform to Stock Exchange requirements, which may entail a related party transaction being approved at a general meeting even if s 320 of the Companies Act 1985 does not apply. (A related party transaction is a transaction with a director or a substantial shareholder or contractual arrangement with a controlling shareholder. The various 'classes' of transaction under Stock Exchange regulations, with the procedures relating to them, are described in the chapters on the securities industry.)

Directors' duties

6.4 Directors' duties are mainly matters to be studied in the context of *Corporate Law*. The remainder of this chapter deals with some specific matters, for which the Companies Act 1985 expressly requires due performance by the directors as a board. Failure to attend to these matters can lead to disqualification as a director by a court order, under the Company Directors Disqualification Act 1986.

Offences under the Companies Act

6.5 We have seen that a company secretary may be liable under the Companies Act for breaches of administrative provisions since those are his area of responsibility. Directors however are responsible for compliance with all aspects of the Companies Act. Hence directors are subject to sanctions under the Companies Act for a very wide range of offences, which can be grouped under the following general headings.

(a) Failure to **file information** with the Registrar of Companies

(b) Failure to **respond** to **members' requests** for information including copies of the memorandum or articles, or minutes of the general meeting

(c) **Breaches** of the regulations relating to **company names**, including failing to change the company's name on direction from the Registrar and trading under a misleading name

(d) Offences in connection with **share issues** including directors exercising a power of allotment without having received the necessary authority

(e) Contravention of the rules relating to **consideration for shares**

(f) A public company doing business or exercising powers contrary to **s 117**

(g) Breaches of the **capital maintenance** rules including a public company failing to convene a meeting on serious loss of capital

(h) Failure to have the **certificates required** by s 185 ready following allotment or transfer of shares

(i) Failure to **keep** and preserve proper **accounting records**, and other offences relating to the statutory financial statements and audit

(j) Failure to **maintain** or update the **registers** or other documentation required by the Companies Act

(k) **Invalid acting** as a director

(l) Failure by directors to **disclose notifiable interests**

(m) **Improper dealing** in shares by directors

(n) Breaches of the rules relating to **loans to directors**

(o) Failure to **publicise properly** the company's **name**

(p) Offences relating to company meetings including **failure** to **give notice** to members and **improper proceedings**

(q) Breaches of orders imposing **restrictions** on **share dealing**

(r) **Fraudulent trading**

(s) Offences relating to **company dissolution**

(t) Breaches of the regulations relating to **overseas companies**

(u) **False statements** in **prospectuses**

6.6 Specific offences will be referred to in detail throughout this text.

6.7 Financial penalties are generally either the **statutory maximum** (£5,000) or one fifth of the statutory maximum (£1,000). Certain offences can however be punished by a **prison sentence**. These include making false or deceptive statements, or making certain statements (such as a declaration of solvency under s 173) without having reasonable grounds. Breaches of various of the capital maintenance regulations can also result in a jail term.

7 ANNUAL ACCOUNTS AND AUDITORS

7.1 The basic principle is that the directors must in respect of each accounting reference period of the company:

- **Prepare** a **balance sheet** and profit and loss account (s 226)
- **Lay accounts** for the period before the company in general meeting (s 241)
- **Deliver** to the registrar a copy of those accounts (s 242)

7.2 The information to be given in the accounts, their format, and other matters of form and content are regulated mainly by s 226 and Sch 4. There is an overriding requirement that the accounts shall give a **true and fair view**; additional data must be given to supplement the statutory prescribed figures if, without those additions, the accounts would not give a true and fair view.

Accounting reference date and period — 6/98, 12/98

7.3 The accounts must be **made up** to a date which falls within the period **seven days** before or after the end of the accounting reference period: s 223. The **accounting reference period** is fixed to begin on the day after the end of the previous period, and to end on the company's chosen accounting reference date: s 224.

7.4 Any new company will automatically have the last day of the month in which it is incorporated as its accounting reference date. For example, a company incorporated on 17 July 2000 will automatically have an accounting reference date of 31 July. Its first accounts therefore will be made up to 31 July 2001.

7.5 Any company can alter its accounting reference date by filing **form 225** including a new company which may wish to alter the date automatically fixed for it on incorporation. Accounting periods can be shortened but there are restrictions on extending the period.

(a) No accounting period can be extended so that it **exceeds 18 months.**

(b) **Five years** must elapse before **another extension** is permitted unless it is to bring it into alignment with other group companies within the European Economic Area, by order of the court or with the specific approval of the Secretary of State.

(c) No **alteration** to the date is permitted **after** the **relevant date** for the **filing** of accounts for that year has been passed.

7.6 The **seven days' grace** before or after the chosen recurrent annual date is to permit a company, if it wishes, to make up its accounts to, for example, the last working day on or before 31 December, or for a period of exactly 52 weeks. These rules prevent what was a common practice of altering the final date of successive accounting periods so as to impede comparison or delay publication.

7.7 The directors must also **lay** the **annual accounts**, together with the directors' and auditor's reports, before members in **general meeting** (unless a private company has dispensed with this requirement under s 252): s 241. It must deliver a copy to the registrar, within a maximum period reckoned from the date to which the accounts are made up: s 242. The standard permitted interval between the end of the accounting period and the issue of accounts is **seven** months for a public, and **ten** months for a private, company. Either is entitled to claim an extension of three months if it carries on business or has interests abroad: s 244.

7.8 Failure to comply with ss 241 and 242 leads to the directors at the end of the period being guilty of an offence, which may lead to a fixed fine or a daily default fine. A director may defend himself by showing that he took all reasonable steps to ensure compliance. The company may also be liable to a penalty under civil proceedings. The court may order that default be remedied: s 242(3).

7.9 There are certain reliefs and special provisions relating to the following.

(a) The **first accounts of a company following its incorporation.** Broadly, the first accounts may cover any period of 6-18 months: thereafter the accounts follow the normal annual cycle: s 224.

(b) An **unlimited company**. Unless it is the subsidiary or holding company of a limited company, or is controlled by a consortium of limited companies, it need not deliver to the registrar a copy of its accounts: s 254. That its accounts need not be made available for public inspection at the registry is one of the principal advantages of an unlimited company.

(c) A **small or medium-sized company** (as defined) need not deliver to the registrar full accounts, but only an abbreviated version to permit confidentiality: s 246.

7.10 The accounts must be **audited**, and the auditor's report must be attached to the copies issued to members, delivered to the registrar or published; a company which is 'dormant' or qualifies for audit exemption on grounds of size may exclude this requirement: ss 235, 233 and 250. The accounts must be accompanied by a **directors' report** which is considered further in Section 8 of this chapter.

Circulation of accounts

7.11 Each member and debentureholder is entitled to be sent a **copy** of the **annual accounts**, together with the directors' and auditor's reports, at least 21 days before the meeting before which they shall be laid: s 238(1). Anyone else entitled to receive notice of a general meeting, including the company's auditor, should also be sent a copy. At any other time any member or debentureholder is entitled to a copy free of charge within seven days of requesting it: s 239(1).

Summary financial statements 12/99

7.12 A listed public company may prepare a summary financial statement (SFS) to be circulated to members instead of the full accounts, provided its constitution allows: s 251(1). The summary may be sent to any member who has **expressly agreed** to receive any such a statement.

7.13 The summary must also be sent to any member who has **failed to respond** to a notice from the company enquiring whether the member wishes to continue to receive full accounts. This notice may either be as part of a package sent out one year to members containing the full accounts and summary financial statements, or in advance of sending out the full financial statements.

Laying the accounts before members in general meeting

7.14 The accounts must be laid before members in general meeting (unless, as mentioned above, s 252 has been used). It is usual to deal with the accounts at each year's Annual General Meeting, but it is not obligatory to do so; the accounts may be considered at an Extraordinary General Meeting (as for example when the accounts are not ready at the time when the AGM must be held, to comply with AGM rules).

7.15 When the accounts are laid before a general meeting, it is common practice to propose a resolution that they be **'adopted'** or approved. (It is more correct to word the resolution so that the company in general meeting merely 'receives' the accounts prepared and approved by the directors.) This gives the members present an opportunity of asking pertinent questions, making criticisms or suggestions etc. The approval of the accounts is regarded as a **vote of confidence** in the directors, though even if the accounts are not 'adopted', they are still the accounts and their validity is not affected.

7.16 We have seen that **every member** of a company (and also every **debentureholder**) is **entitled** to **receive** a **copy** of the accounts, but only those members who are entitled to attend general meetings are able to take part in the discussion of the accounts.

Group accounts

7.17 A **holding company** which has one or more subsidiary undertakings must **lay group accounts** before members, and deliver them to the registrar. These are normally **consolidated accounts**, in which the financial position of the holding company and subsidiary undertakings is presented as an integrated set of figures: s 227.

Appointment of auditors 12/99

7.18 The first auditor of a new company is appointed by the **directors** to hold office until the conclusion of the first general meeting at which the accounts are considered: s 385. The directors or the company in general meeting may also appoint an auditor to fill a casual vacancy: s 388.

7.19 In the ordinary way the **members** appoint the auditor at each **general meeting** at which the accounts are considered, to hold office until the next such meeting, that is to audit and report on the accounts to be prepared for that subsequent meeting. If the members fail to appoint an auditor at the general meeting at which the accounts are considered, the company must, within seven days of the meeting, give notice to the Secretary of State who has power to appoint an auditor: s 387.

7.20 Where a private company has elected, under s 252, to dispense with the laying of accounts before the company in general meeting, the auditor must be appointed by a general meeting:

(a) **Within a period** of **28 days** (the 'time for appointing auditors') after the date on which the annual accounts are sent to members

(b) If **notice** has been given under s 253(2) **requiring** the **laying** of **accounts** before the general meeting, from the conclusion of the meeting: s 385A

The auditor so appointed holds office from the end of the 28 day period (or the conclusion of the meeting) until the end of the time for appointing auditors for the next financial year.

7.21 The auditor who is in office when the election is made remains so until the end of the time for appointing auditors for the next financial year (unless the general meeting decides otherwise). The auditor in office when the election ceases to have effect remains in office until the conclusion of the next general meeting at which accounts are laid.

7.22 A private company may **dispense** with the **obligation** to **appoint** an auditor annually, by elective resolution in accordance with s 379A. In this case the auditor shall be deemed to be re-appointed for each succeeding financial year whilst the election is in force: s 386. This will be so unless:

(a) The company is 'dormant' and therefore can resolve under s 250 to exempt itself from the obligation to submit audited accounts.

(b) A resolution has been passed under s 393 to terminate the auditor's appointment (see below).

7.23 When the election ceases, the auditor remains in office until the conclusion of the next general meeting at which accounts are laid, or until the end of the 'time for appointing auditors' for the next financial year.

Termination of an auditor's appointment 12/98

7.24 An auditor may be **removed** from office before the expiry of his appointment by passing an ordinary resolution in general meeting: s 391. **Special notice** to the company is required: s 391A. An auditor may **resign** his appointment by giving notice in writing to the company delivered to the registered office: s 392. Alternatively he may simply decline to offer himself for re-election.

7.25 Where a private company has **dispensed** with the annual appointment of auditors under s 386 any member of the company may deposit **notice in writing** at the registered office proposing that the appointment of the company's auditors be brought to an end: s 393. No member may deposit more than one such notice in any financial year of the company.

7.26 The directors must then **convene** a **general meeting** for not more than 28 days after the date of the giving of the notice, and propose a suitable resolution for termination of the auditors' appointment: s 393(2). If the motion is passed, the auditor is not deemed to be re-appointed when otherwise he next would be; if the notice was deposited within 14 days of sending the annual accounts to the members, any deemed re-appointment for the following financial year ceases to have effect: s 393(3). Private companies may alternatively use written resolutions to change auditors.

7.27 In his notice of resignation or on ceasing to hold office for any reason (s 394) the auditor must deposit at the company's registered office either:

(a) A statement that there are **no circumstances** connected with his resignation which he considers should be brought to the notice of members or creditors of the company

(b) A **statement** disclosing what those **circumstances** are

7.28 In the case of resignation, the statement shall be deposited along with the notice of resignation; in the case of failure to seek re-appointment, it shall be deposited not less than 14 days before the time allowed for next appointing auditors. In any other case, the time limit is 14 days after ceasing to hold office: s 394(2).

7.29 On receiving the auditor's notice of resignation the company must send a copy of it to the registrar: s 392 (3).

7.30 If the auditor's notice contains a statement of circumstances the company must also **send** a copy to **every person entitled to receive a copy** of the accounts: s 392 (3). S 394 (3) provides similar requirements where the statement of circumstances is not in connection with an auditor's resignation. The auditor is required to send to the Registrar a copy of the statement of circumstances. The only exception to this rule is if the auditor's statement contains what is considered to be defamatory matter. If it does, the company or any other aggrieved person can apply to the court to stop the statement being read out at the General Meeting, or sent to the Registrar.

7.31 An auditor who includes in his statement of resignation a statement of the circumstances connected with it must:

(a) **Requisition** an **Extraordinary General Meeting** at which he will explain his reasons

(b) **Attend** and speak at any **meeting** at which his **resignation** or the **appointment** of his **successor** is to be **considered**: s 392A

Duties and powers of auditors

7.32 The statutory duty of auditors is to report to the members whether the accounts give a **true and fair view** and have been **properly prepared** in accordance with the Companies Act: s 235. To fulfil this duty, the auditors must carry out such investigations as are necessary to form an opinion as to whether:

(a) **Proper accounting records** have been **kept** and proper returns adequate for the audit have been received from branches.

(b) The **accounts** are in **agreement** with the **records**: s 237.

(c) The information given in **the directors' report** is **consistent** with the **accounts**: s 235(3).

If the auditors are satisfied on these matters they need not be mentioned in the report.

7.33 Auditors have wide statutory powers to enable them to obtain whatever information they may require for the purpose of their audit. In particular they may inspect books and records and call on officers of the company for **information or explanations**: s 389A. It is a criminal offence for an officer of a company to make a false statement to an auditor if it is misleading, false or deceptive in a material particular and is made knowingly or recklessly (with indifference as to its truth): s 389A(2).

8 THE DIRECTORS' REPORT — 6/98, 6/00

8.1 Attached to every balance sheet there must be a directors' report (s 234). (The Companies Act 1985 allows small companies exemption from delivering a copy of the directors' report to the Registrar of companies.) CA 1985 states specifically what information must be included in the directors' report (as well as what must be shown in the accounts themselves or in notes to the accounts as we saw above).

8.2 The directors' report is largely a **narrative report**, but certain figures must be included in it. The purpose of the report is to give the users of accounts a more complete picture of the state of affairs of the company. Narrative descriptions should help to 'put flesh on' the skeleton of details provided by the figures of the accounts themselves. However, in practice the directors' report is often a rather dry and uninformative document, perhaps because it must be verified by the company's external auditors, whereas the chairman's report need not be.

8.3 The directors' report is expected to contain a **fair review** of the development of the business of the company during that year and of its position at the end of it. No guidance is given on the form of the review, nor the amount of detail it should go into.

8.4 S 234 CA 1985 also requires the report to show the amount, if any, recommended for *dividend*.

8.5 Other disclosure requirements are as follows.

(a) The **principal activities** of the company in the course of the financial year, and any significant changes in those activities during the year

(b) Where significant, an estimate should be provided of the **difference between the book value of land held as fixed assets and its realistic market value**

(c) Information about the company's policy for the employment for **disabled persons**

  (i) The policy for giving fair consideration to applications for jobs from disabled persons

  (ii) The policy for continuing to employ (and train) people who have become disabled whilst employed by the company

  (iii) The policy for the training, career development and promotion of disabled employees

  (Companies with fewer than 250 employees are exempt from (c).)

(d) The names of persons who were **directors** at any time during the financial year.

(e) For those persons who were directors at the year end, the **interests of each** (or of their spouse or infant children) in shares or debentures of the company:

  (i) At the beginning of the year, or at the date of appointment as director, if this occurred during the year

  (ii) At the end of the year

  If a director has no such interests at either date, this fact must be disclosed. (The information in (e) may be shown as a note to the accounts instead of in the directors' report.)

(f) **Political and charitable contributions** made, if these together exceeded more than £200 in the year, giving:

  (i) Separate totals for political contributions and charitable contributions

  (ii) The amount of each separate political contribution exceeding £200, and the name of the recipient (see below).

(g) Particulars of any **important events** affecting the company or any of its subsidiaries which have occurred since the end of the financial year (significant 'post-balance sheet events')

(h) An indication of likely **future developments** in the business of the company and of its subsidiaries

(i) An indication of the activities (if any) of the company and its subsidiaries in the field of **research and development**.

(j) Particulars of **purchases** (if any) of *its own shares* by the company during the year, including reasons for the purchase

(k) Particulars of **other acquisitions of its own shares** during the year (perhaps because shares were forfeited or surrendered, or because its shares were acquired by the company's nominee or with its financial assistance)

8.6 Small private companies are allowed certain exemptions from the above disclosure requirements. In addition, small private companies, if they file abbreviated accounts at Companies House, do not need to include a directors' report in the accounts that are filed.

8.7 A further requirement relating to the directors' report is contained in the Employment Act 1982. The requirement relates to any company employing on average more than 250 people each week. The directors of such a company must state in their report what action has been taken during the financial year to introduce, maintain or develop arrangements aimed at:

(a) **Employee information**, providing employees systematically with information on matters of concern to them

(b) **Employee consultation**, consulting employees or their representatives on a regular basis so that the views of employees can be taken into account in making decisions which are likely to affect their interest

(c) **Employee involvement**, encouraging the involvement of employees in the company's performance through an employees' share scheme or by some other means

(d) **Company performance**, achieving common *awareness* on the part of all employees of the financial and economic factors affecting the performance of the company

8.8 These provisions do not mean that any such action must be taken, only that if it is taken it must be disclosed in the directors' report. Moreover, wide discretion is granted to the directors in deciding what needs to be disclosed, since no definition is given of such terms as 'matters of concern to them' or 'decisions which are likely to affect their interests'. For listed companies however, the Combined Code (discussed in Chapter 3) contains a number of disclosure requirements, particularly the requirement for the board to present a balanced and understandable assessment of the company's position and prospects.

Creditor payment policy 6/00

8.9 A recent amendment to CA 1985 requires companies to disclose details of the company's policy on the **payment of creditors**. This disclosure requirement applies if:

(a) The company was at any time during the year a **public company**.

(b) The company did **not** qualify as a **small or medium-sized** company under s 247 and was at any time within the year a member of a group of which the parent company was a public company.

8.10 The directors' report needs to state, with respect to the financial year immediately following that covered by the report whether:

(a) I respect of some or all of its suppliers (ie those classified as 'trade creditors') it is the company's policy to follow any **code or standard on payment practice**, and if so, the name of the code or standard, and the place where information about, and copies of, the code or standard can be obtained.

(b) In respect of some or all of its suppliers, it is the company's policy to:

(i) **Settle the terms of payment** with those suppliers when agreeing the terms of each transaction

(ii) Ensure that those suppliers are **made aware** of the terms of payment

(iii) **Abide** by the terms of payment

8.11 **Where** the company's policy is **not as mentioned** in either of the two paragraphs above, in respect of some or all of its suppliers, the report should state **what its policy is** with respect to the payment of those suppliers. If the company's policy is different from different suppliers or classes of suppliers, the directors' must identify the suppliers or classes of suppliers to which the different policies apply.

Political donations

8.12 In response to a recommendation by the Committee of Standards on public life, the DTI has published a consultation document that recommends that companies should be **required** by **statute** to have any form of political donation, including sponsorship and donations in kind, **approved beforehand** by their shareholders and disclosed in their accounts. If approval is not obtained, proposed sanctions include criminal penalties and making directors repay the donations.

Listing Rules

8.13 The Listing Rules contain additional disclosures for the directors' report of listed companies.

(a) Details of **significant** (greater than 3%) **holdings** in the company's shares at a date not more than one month before the date of notice of the general meeting at which the accounts are laid

(b) **Changes in directors' interests** in shares and directors' options to subscribe between the period-end and a date not more than one month before the date of notice of the general meeting at which the accounts are laid

(c) The Listing Rules' Combined Code also contains disclosures about corporate governance and directors' remuneration; these are discussed further in Chapter 3.

Laying management accounts before the directors

8.14 The need for directors to **consider management** accounts, however, is apparent in the following two areas.

(a) Under the statutory grounds (Company Directors' Disqualification Act 1986 Sch 1 paragraph 6) for disqualification of directors, 'responsibility for the causes of the company becoming insolvent' is attributed to the directors. It is from the management accounts that signs of trouble may be gleaned.

(b) The statutory grounds for making directors personally liable for wrongful trading (s 214 IA), states that they 'ought to have concluded that there was no reasonable prospect that the company would avoid going into insolvent liquidation'. Again the management accounts should allow them to reach such a conclusion.

8.15 The Combined Code states that boards should be supplied with **sufficient information** to enable them to discharge their duties. Much of this information will be supplied by **management**, but directors may need to make further enquiries of other sources if necessary.

8.16 If the company has a finance director or chief accountant, it may not be the personal duty of the company secretary to produce up to date financial statements to the board at its meetings. He should certainly arrange the dates and business of each meeting, however, with a view to proper consideration of such material.

9 DIRECTORS' INTERESTS, CONTRACTS AND LOANS

Specimen paper, 12/99

9.1 A director may have an interest (as a private individual or as an owner or representative of another business) in a contract with his own company. For example, a director may personally own a freehold property which he rents to the company.

9.2 There are three possible objections to a director making, or being interested in, a contract with his own company as follows.

(a) He may be obtaining a **personal advantage** from his position as director.

(b) There may be a **conflict of interest** which may affect his judgement.

(c) By concealment of his interest he may **induce** the **other directors**, or the shareholders, to **approve transactions** which they might have rejected if they had known of his interest.

On the other hand, exceptions should be possible in proper cases.

Declaration of directors' interests

9.3 The main statutory safeguard is a requirement that a director shall always '**declare the nature of his interest**', direct or indirect, in a contract or proposed contract with the company: s 317. The disclosure must be made to the **first meeting** of the directors at which the contract is considered, or (if later) at the **first meeting held after** the director becomes **interested** in the **contract**.

9.4 The purpose of the rule on giving notice is to ensure that the other directors will deal with the contract in the knowledge that the director concerned has an interest. There must be no concealment. Failure to give notice is a criminal offence for which the director may be fined; he will then **lose the benefit** of any relieving provisions in the articles, the company may award the contract, and the director may have to account for any secret profit.

9.5 A director who does give notice is not thereby relieved of his duty to avoid a conflict of interest, but the standard articles (Table A Article 94) grant wide exemptions, and permit a director to be interested in a contract provided he observes the following two regulations.

(a) He **discloses** the **nature** of his **interest** as required by s 317.

(b) He **does not vote** and is not **reckoned** as one of the **quorum** of directors at the board meeting which approves the contract. There are certain exceptions to this:

   (i) A resolution to give a guarantee, security or indemnity to the director, for instance if he has lent the company money, or incurred some obligation on its behalf

   (ii) A resolution to give a guarantee, security or indemnity to a third party in respect of an obligation for which the director has assumed a personal responsibility, such as to give security to the company's bank, in respect of an overdraft for which a director has previously given the bank his own personal guarantee

   (iii) A director's interest arising from his subscribing for, or underwriting, an issue of the company's securities

   (iv) A resolution relating to a retirement benefits scheme, which has been, or is to be, approved for tax purposes by the Inland Revenue

9.6 Many companies have articles which deal differently with these matters. In particular, the 1948 Table A Article 84 extends the exceptions (matters on which the interested party may vote) to:

(a) Directors' contracts of employment

(b) Contracts in which directors have an interest as shareholder in another company which is the other party to the transaction

9.7 It is essential to consider the exact terms of the articles in any such case if it is material whether or not the director who has an interest may be counted in the quorum and vote. If he abstains from voting on a matter in which he is interested, that fact should be recorded in the minutes.

9.8 It is also worth noting that the interest of anyone **connected** with a director is treated as the interest of the director himself, for the purpose of Article 94. So, for example, a director could not vote on a resolution which would, directly or indirectly, benefit his spouse or his partner in another business enterprise.

9.9 It is good practice for directors to give an **annual declaration** of their interests, even though this does not alleviate their duty to disclose new interests in the meantime.

Substantial and material property transactions

9.10 The shareholders' approval is required for any contract (or arrangement) by which the company buys from or sells to a director of the company or of its holding company or a person connected with any such director property which exceeds **£100,000** in value or (if less) exceeds **10 per cent** of the company's **net assets** (subject to a **minimum** of **£2,000** value): s 320.

9.11 If this approval is not obtained the contract is **voidable** by the company (or alternatively it may seek an indemnity) and the director (or person connected with him) is accountable to the company for any gain and liable to indemnify the company for any loss: s 322. Other directors who approved the transaction may be similarly liable.

9.12 If the company is a subsidiary and the contract is made with a director of a holding company (or a person connected with him) approval must be obtained at a general meeting of the holding company. 'Connected person' is explained later.

9.13 A company must **disclose** in the annual accounts any contract or **arrangement** with the company (or a subsidiary) in which a director, directly or through a connected person, had an interest which was '**material**'. The other directors may decide that a director's interest in a contract is not material for disclosure. Contracts of a value not exceeding £1,000 or (if greater) not exceeding one per cent of the company's assets (subject to a maximum of £5,000) are exempt from this disclosure requirement: s 232 and Sch 6.

Loans to directors **6/98**

9.14 Every company is prohibited by s 330 (subject to certain exceptions) from:

(a) **Making a loan** to a director of the company, or of its holding company

(b) **Guaranteeing** or **giving security** for a loan to any such director

(c) **Taking an assignment** of a loan etc which, if made originally by the company, would have been contrary to (a) and (b)

(d) **Providing a benefit** to another person, as part of an arrangement by which that person enters into a transaction forbidden to the company itself by rules (a), (b) or (c)

9.15 There are the following general exceptions (in ss 334 and 336-338) to the rules above.

(a) A company may make a loan, or give a guarantee or security in respect of a loan, to a director who is also its **holding company**: s 336.

(b) A company may make a loan to a director to **enable him** to **perform his duties**, provided that the loan is **approved** in general meeting, before or afterwards. If the loan is made before approval is obtained, it must be approved at or before the next AGM; it must be repaid within six months of that AGM, if not so approved: s 337. The company must be informed of the purpose of the expenditure, the amount of funds to be supplied and the extent to which the company is liable in the transaction to be entered into by the director.

(c) A company whose ordinary business is the **lending of money** etc may make a loan to a director in the **ordinary course of its business**, and on the same terms as it would accord to any other borrower: s 338.

(d) A company may make a loan to a director **not exceeding £5,000**: s 334. "De minimus Rule"

(e) **Group** companies, even when there is relevant company status, may **lend to each other**: s 333. A holding company may lend to directors of its subsidiaries, provided they are neither directors of, nor connected with directors of, the holding company.

9.16 Additional rules apply to '**relevant companies**', which include any public company, and any private company which is a member of a group which includes a public company. These public company rules also extend to private companies associated with a public company by membership of the same group.

(a) The **exceptions** described in (b) and (c) above are limited to a maximum of £10,000 and £100,000, although a bank is only restricted to £100,000 if it is for a residence

(b) There are **restrictions** on **indirect means** of enabling a director to obtain goods or services on credit, by transactions called 'quasi-loans' and 'credit transactions'; for example, if the company arranges with a credit card company to issue a credit card to a director, on terms that the company will settle the monthly account for his purchases, that is a 'quasi-loan'

(c) A **company transaction** with a **third party** who is 'connected' with one of its directors is subject to the same rules as apply to its transactions with a director himself.

9.17 A person is **connected** with a director of a company if:

(a) He or she is the **spouse**, or child under 18, of the director.

(b) It is a **company** in which the director and any other persons 'connected' with him together **own** at **least one fifth** of the equity share capital (or control at least one fifth of the votes).

(c) He or she is a **trustee** of a trust of which the director or persons connected with him are beneficiaries.

(d) He or she is a **partner** in a firm in which the director or another person connected with him is also a partner.

Compensation for loss of office

9.18 Even if a director has no contract which entitles him to fees in lieu of notice or other terminal payment, he may receive **non-contractual compensation** for loss of office paid to him voluntarily. Any such compensation is lawful only if **approved** by members of the company in general meeting after proper disclosure has been made to *all* members, whether voting or not. There are three recognised types of compensation payment:

(a) A direct payment of compensation made by the company (s 312)

(b) A payment made to directors in connection with the purchase of the company's business or its winding up (s 313)

(c) A payment made when a takeover bidder has made an offer to the general body of shareholders with a view to gaining control or acquiring one third at least of the votes (and in other related situations): s 314

9.19 If the takeover bidder buys the directors' shares at a higher price than is offered to other shareholders the excess is treated as a compensation payment: s 315.

9.20 If a director receives an unauthorised payment from a third party he holds it in trust for the company (in a sale of the business) or for the shareholders (in a takeover bid).

9.21 Any payment made in connection with a **purchase** of the **business** or a **takeover bid** within the three year period running from one year before to two years after the relevant transaction is treated as a compensation payment to which these rules apply: s 316(1). However a *bona fide* payment by way of **damages** for **breach of contract**, or by way of **pensions** in respect of past services, is **not affected**: s 316(3).

9.22 Compensation paid to directors for loss of office is distinguished from any payments made to directors **as employees**, for example to settle claims arising from the premature termination of the service agreements. These are contractual payments which do not require approval in general meeting: *Taupo Totara Timber Co v Rowe 1977*. Hence ss 312-315 only apply to uncovenanted payments. This is discussed further in Chapter 14.

Directors' dealings in company securities

9.23 A director has a duty to give notice to the company of his interest, and of any change in it; the company has a duty to enter this information in a register, which is held at the registered office and is open to inspection by the public. This is discussed further in chapter 14.

9.24 A director (and a spouse or child under 18 of a director) is **prohibited** from dealing in **options**, ie the right to buy or sell listed shares of the company, or of any other company of the group: s 323. This ban applies to dealings in existing options (which are traded as described in the later chapter on the securities industry). It **does not prohibit** a director from obtaining from the company an **option** to subscribe for its shares, which is the essential feature of share option schemes.

9.25 The prohibition of '**insider dealing**' (contained in Part V of the Criminal Justice Act 1993) applies to directors, who are treated as *insiders* by reason of their position as directors. The offence is discussed in detail in Chapter 17.

9.26 A listed company is required to adopt rules on dealings in its securities which are no less exacting than the **Model Code** (in the Listing Rules). The code is described in more detail below.

The Model Code for securities transactions by directors of listed companies

Specimen paper, 6/98

9.27 Under the Model Code, listed companies are required to have rules about their securities transactions which are **at least as stringent** as the Model Code.

General principles

9.28 The freedom of directors and certain employees of listed companies is restricted by statute (the Criminal Justice Act 1993), by common law and by the requirement of the Listing Rules that listed companies adopt and apply a code of dealing based on the Model Code.

9.29 The Code imposes restrictions above and beyond those that are imposed by law. Its purpose is to ensure that directors, certain employees and persons connected with them do not abuse, and place themselves above suspicion of abusing, price sensitive information in periods leading up to an announcement.

Rules

9.30 (a) A director must not deal in any securities of the listed company on **considerations** of a **short term nature**.

(b) A director must not deal in any securities of the listed company during a '**close period**'. A close period is:

(i) The period of **two months** immediately **preceding** the **preliminary announcement** of the company's annual **results** or, if shorter, the period from the relevant financial year end up to and including the time of the announcement

(ii) If the company reports on a **half-yearly** rather than a quarterly basis, the period of **two months** immediately **preceding** the **announcement** of the half-yearly **results** or, if shorter, the period from the relevant financial period end up to and including the time of the announcement

(iii) If the company reports on a **quarterly basis**, the period of **one month** immediately **preceding** the **announcement** of the quarterly **results** or, if shorter, the period from the relevant financial period end up to and including the time of the announcement. (See paragraph (i) for the position in the final quarter.)

(c) A director must not deal in any securities of the listed company at any time when he is in possession of **unpublished price-sensitive information** in relation to those securities, or otherwise where clearance to deal is not given.

(d) A director must not deal in any securities of the listed company without **advising** the **chairman** (or one or more other directors designated for this purpose) in advance and **receiving clearance**. In his own case, the chairman, or other designated director, must advise the board in advance at a board meeting, or advise another designated director, and receive clearance from the board or designated director, as appropriate.

(e) A director must not be given clearance to deal in any securities of the listed company during a prohibited period. A 'prohibited period' means:

(i) Any **close period**

(ii) Any period when there exists any matter which constitutes **unpublished** price **sensitive information** in relation to the company's securities (whether or not the director has knowledge of such matter) and the proposed dealing would (if permitted) take place after the time when it has become reasonably probable that an announcement will be required in relation to the matter

(iii) Any period when the person responsible for the clearance otherwise has reason to believe that the **proposed dealing** is in **breach** of this code.

(f) A **written record** must be maintained by the company of the receipt of any advice received from a director under (d) and of any clearance given. Written confirmation from the company that such advice and clearance (if any) have been recorded must be given to the director concerned.

(g) In **exceptional circumstances**, where it is the only reasonable course of action, clearance may be given for a director to **sell** (but not to purchase) securities when he would otherwise be prohibited from doing so only because the proposed sale would fall within a close period.

(h) Where a director is acting as a **trustee**, the provisions of the Code apply as if he were dealing on his own account.

(i) Directors should seek to prohibit dealing during prohibited periods by connected persons. **Connected persons** in this context are:

(i) As defined by s 346

(ii) Investment managers acting for a director or a person connected with a director

(j) The prohibition on dealing in listed securities during close periods also applies to **unlisted** securities that are convertible into **listed** securities.

(k) Companies can make **formulaic awards** of options or shares to directors or employees under employees' share schemes during a close period. The awards are permissible provided that they are in accordance with the **terms** of the **scheme**, and where failure to make the award could alert the market to the existence of **price-sensitive discussions.**

(l) Directors' remuneration may be paid in shares. However, a director may not join a share scheme during a **prohibited period** unless he is **newly appointed** to the board. The terms of participation may not be changed during a close period.

(m) Companies may not **purchase** or redeem any of their **own securities** during a period when a director would be **prohibited** from dealing. The exception is that the price or value of the securities not be substantially affected by the publication of the information giving rise to the prohibited period, or a share buy-back is to be completed in accordance with specific terms announced in an open period.

10 THE CHAIRMAN

10.1 The directors of a company may appoint one of their number to be chairman of the board of directors: he then presides at every directors' meeting which he attends, unless for some reason he is unwilling to do so.

10.2 If there is no chairman of the board, or if the appointed chairman is unwilling to preside at a meeting, or fails to attend within **five minutes** of the intended start of the meeting, the directors present may appoint another director to be chairman of that particular meeting. The same procedure applies to **general meetings**, at which the chairman of the board of directors will normally preside. If *no* director is present and willing to act as chairman within fifteen minutes of the intended start of the meeting, the **members** present can choose one of themselves to act as chairman.

10.3 Unless the articles provide otherwise, the appointment of chairman is for an indefinite period. The chairman vacates office if:

- He **resigns** (though continuing to be a director).
- He **ceases** to be a **director.**
- He is **removed** by the **board**, which may remove him at any time.

10.4 The chairman of the board of directors is a figurehead, frequently engaged in public relations activities on behalf of the company, presenting a favourable image of the company to customers, other business contacts and the general public. He also has other functions, not least to ensure that there is harmony between individual directors (such as the managing director and the rest of the board). It is his duty to ensure as far as possible that the board functions smoothly and efficiently, and to do this he must:

- Keep in **regular**, if informal, **contact** with the managing director
- Discuss **potential disagreements** with other directors
- Try to **resolve difficulties**, if possible, outside board meetings

10.5 The chairman presides at meetings of the board, and is responsible for the following:

(a) Ensuring that the **functions** of the board are carried out

(b) Ensuring that the **meeting proceeds** in an **efficient manner**, without unnecessary or irrelevant discussion, and with a reasonable cross-section of views being heard

(c) Providing an **agenda** for the board meetings (and any necessary documentation, although the secretary would handle the paperwork)

(d) Making sure all directors are **properly briefed** on issues arising at board meetings

The chairman of the board usually presides at general meetings of the company as well. His role as chairman of a meeting is discussed further in the following chapter.

Chapter roundup

- Directors manage the company's affairs, are the principal officers of the company and are often held personally responsible for the dealings of the company.
- Directors should pay close attention to their **statutory powers** and those **powers** conferred or limited by the memorandum or articles.
- There must be at least **two directors** (unless it is a private company which may have one director but such a director cannot also be the secretary). Such directors must be **capable** of holding the position.
- **Appointment** and **retirement** are generally covered by the **articles**, that is retirement and re-election by rotation of directors: Table A Articles 73-80.
- Detailed records of the directors should be kept and **registered** (within 14 days of appointment) at the Companies Registry.
- Directors should always **disclose** all **interests** they have in the company which may affect the company. A detailed record should be kept of these interests. If the director fails to disclose he may be held personally liable to the company or shareholders.
- Matters which must be disclosed include the following.
  - **Service contracts** - they must not be fixed, with no right to terminate for more than five years, unless they are approved by resolution
  - **Interests in shares** or debentures (including associated personal interests)
  - **Interests in substantial property transactions** or contracts with the company (including associated persons)
  - **Loans** to directors

  If a director is unsure whether a matter needs to be disclosed he should make disclosure just in case.
- **Removal** of a director may be governed by the articles, but a director may be removed at any time by **ordinary resolution** with special notice being given and giving the director a right to respond and defend his position: s 303-304. If the company removes a director from his office this may be in breach of his contract. Care should be taken to follow procedures for removal set down by the **contract** and notice should be taken of any financial entitlement the director may have as a result of loss of office and possible breach of contract.
- Note of any changes must be made in the company register of directors and secretaries and filed at Companies House on Forms 288a - 288c.
- The directors' powers are generally set out by the **articles** but are subject to limitations imposed by **statute**, such as the ability of shareholders to resolve to empower or limit the powers and duties of the directors, and the Stock Exchange Listing Rules.
- In general the directors are responsible for ensuring that the company complies with its **statutory duties**, such as producing annual accounts to be laid before the board and the company. The directors must **report** to the company setting out a review of the development of the company during and at the end of the company's financial year, and give recommendations on the application, retention and distribution of profits.

Test your knowledge

1 Explain the terms (a) 'shadow director'; (b) 'alternate director'; and (c) 'non-executive director'. (see paras 1.6, 1.9, 1.17)

2 How are the directors of a newly formed company appointed in the first instance? (3.1)

3 Explain the Table A provisions on retirement of directors. (3.3)

4 How may a member discover the terms of employment of a working director of the company? (4.6)

5 Indicate the practical constraints on action by a single shareholder to secure the dismissal of a director. (5.4, 5.5)

6 What action should be taken by the secretary following the resignation of a director of a public company? (5.11, 5.12)

7 What are the limits on the management powers of the directors? (6.1 - 6.3)

8 Outline the statutory rules on accounting reference dates. (7.3 - 7.6)

9 Give three matters which should be mentioned in the formal directors' report issued with the accounts. (8.3 - 8.5)

10 What disclosures are required (a) by the director to the board; and (b) in the accounts, about a director's interest in a contract with the company? (9.4 - 9.5, 9.13)

11 In what circumstances may a company make a loan to one of its directors? (9.15)

12 How far is a director of a listed company restricted in his dealings in shares of the company? (9.26 - 9.30)

Now try illustrative question 2 at the end of the Study Text

Chapter 3

CODES OF PRACTICE AND GUIDELINES

This chapter covers the following topics.

1 Corporate Governance: Cadbury, Greenbury and Hampel

2 Future developments in corporate governance

Introduction

The previous syllabus guidance notes gave the following guidance on this area, which remains relevant. 'Whilst a thorough knowledge and understanding of the law and company secretarial procedures is required, students should also understand the purpose of the law and procedures, and be able to assess the potential consequences of failure to follow the correct procedures in relation to the company, its officers and shareholders, etc. Particular emphasis will also be placed on relevant codes of practice, eg Committee on the Financial Aspects of Corporate Governance and guidelines, eg those issued by investor bodies such as the National Association of Pension Funds and Association of British Insurers which compliment the legal and regulatory requirements, and which listed companies in particular are expected to follow. These voluntary codes and guidelines are frequently amended to reflect current practice and changing circumstances.'

The new syllabus places similar emphasis on this area.

You should note that the Cadbury and Hampel codes have already been mentioned in Chapters 1 and 2 in connection with secretary and directors respectively. You should also note that other codes of practice, such as the ICSA's code of good boardroom practice are covered where appropriate elsewhere in this Study Text.

1 CORPORATE GOVERNANCE: CADBURY, GREENBURY AND HAMPEL 6/99

1.1 Your syllabus requires you to have some knowledge of topical issues relating to corporate governance. This area has developed over the last few years with the various corporate governance committees, culminating in the publication of the Stock Exchange's Combined Code on corporate governance.

Cadbury committee

1.2 The first major development during the 1990s in corporate governance was the Cadbury committee. This was set up in May 1991 because of the lack of confidence which was perceived in financial reporting and in the ability of auditors to provide the assurances required by the users of financial statements.

Corporate governance

1.3 The Cadbury committee reported in December 1992. Its report went beyond purely financial matters and made recommendations about corporate governance in general. Cadbury defined corporate governance as 'the system by which companies are directed and controlled'.

Code of Best Practice

1.4 This was aimed at the directors of all UK plcs, but the directors of all companies were encouraged to use the Code for guidance.

Get Cadbury report

1.5 The major provisions of the Cadbury report were as follows. (You should try and read the whole of the report).

Board of directors

1.6 The report stressed the importance of the board of directors meeting on a **regular basis**, retaining full control over the company and monitoring executive management. Certain matters such as major acquisitions or disposals of assets, should be **referred** automatically to the **board**. The chairman's role in good corporate governance is crucial. There should be a **clear division of responsibilities** at the head of a company, with no one person having complete power. Generally this would mean the posts of chairman and chief executive being held by different people; if they were held by the same person there should be a **strong independent element** on the board.

Non-executive directors

1.7 The report saw non-executive directors as important figures because of the **independent judgement** they brought to bear on important issues. There should be at **least three non-executive** directors on the board, a **majority** of whom should be **independent** of management and free from any other relationship that might compromise independence. They should be formally appointed by a **nomination committee**, which should itself have a majority of non-executive directors.

Executive directors

1.8 The report contained provisions about the length of service contracts and disclosure of remuneration which were developed further in the Greenbury and Hampel reports (see below).

The audit committee

1.9 The audit committee was seen by the Cadbury committee as a key board committee. The audit committee should **liase** with **internal** and **external auditors**, and provide a forum for both to express their concerns. The committee should also **review** half yearly and annual **statements**.

Accounts

1.10 The Cadbury committee stressed the importance of the board presenting a **balanced** and **understandable assessment** of the company's position. The directors should **explain** their **responsibilities** for preparing accounts. Statements should also be made about the company's ability to continue as a **going concern**, and the effectiveness of its **internal controls**.

Greenbury report

Specimen paper, 6/98

1.11 In July 1995 the Greenbury committee's report on directors' remuneration was published. The report developed a number of recommendations of the Cadbury committee. Greenbury stressed the importance of the role of the **remuneration committee**, which the report recommended should consist entirely of non-executive directors.

1.12 The Greenbury report also established a Code of Best Practice. The code's recommendations can be grouped under four main headings.

The remuneration committee

1.13 The most important recommendation was that the board should set up a remuneration committee of non-executive directors to **determine** the company's **general policy** on the **remuneration** of **executive directors and** specific remuneration packages for each director. The non-executive directors on the committee should have no personal interests other than as shareholders, no conflicts of interest and no day-to-day involvement in running the business. The remuneration committee chairman should be available to answer questions at the AGM.

Disclosures

1.14 The report suggested that a report on **remuneration policy** should be included or attached to the annual accounts. The report on remuneration should give details of the company's policy on the remuneration of executive directors including:

- Remuneration levels
- Comparator companies
- Main components of remuneration
- Performance criteria and measurement
- Pension provision
- Contracts of service
- Compensation for loss of office

1.15 The remuneration committee should consider whether shareholders should approve this policy at each AGM.

1.16 The remuneration report should also contain details of the **remuneration packages** of **individual directors** including basic salary, benefits-in-kind, bonuses and long-term incentives. Details should also be given of individual entitlement to share options, and pensions entitlements earned during the year.

1.17 In addition **service contracts** with notice periods **greater than one year** should be **disclosed**, and the **reasons** for longer notice periods explained. **Incentive schemes** should be **performance-related** and shareholders should be invited to approve long-term incentive schemes.

Remuneration policy

1.18 The report emphasised that the remuneration committee should consider the **wider pay scene**, and should provide packages sufficient to attract, retain and motivate directors of sufficient quality. Performance-related elements should reconcile the interests of directors and shareholders.

1.19 The remuneration committee should consider the level and form of rewards in the light of performance criteria set. Matters to be carefully considered would include the terms of share option schemes, the phasing of rewards, and the pension consequences of various elements of the remuneration package. Share options should not be issued at a discount.

Service contracts and compensation

1.20 The report generally favoured notice and contract periods of less than one year, though up to two years may be acceptable in certain circumstances. **Periods longer** than **two years** should only be set in **exceptional circumstances**, for example initial contracts necessary to attract directors from outside.

1.21 In general remuneration committees should take a tough line over dismissal for unsatisfactory performance, and also mitigation of compensation by directors. Committees should consider phasing of compensation payments over a period, and stopping them when the director starts a new job.

1.22 A 1999 survey by the Department of Trade and Industry indicated that many listed companies were failing to comply with a number of the recommendations originally aired in the Greenbury report. In particular:

(a) A significant number of remuneration committees did not consist solely of independent non-executive directors; a few had executive directors as members. The government has proposed that all quoted companies should be required to have a **committee** composed solely of **independent non-executive directors,** the **chairman** should be **prohibited** from being a member, and the committee should have access to **independent professional advice**.

(b) Disclosure about the **linkage** between **performance** and **remuneration** was insufficiently clear in most accounts. Further disclosure requirements including objectives and comparisons with other companies were proposed.

(c) **Compensation for loss of office commitments** and arrangements should be disclosed in listed company accounts.

(d) Not many companies were putting their remuneration report to the vote in the accounts. The government was considering a range of options to ensure shareholder approval, including a compulsory **vote** on the **remuneration report** and remuneration **policy,** or **annual re-election** of directors or the chairman of the remuneration committee.

The Hampel report

1.23 The Hampel committee was set up in 1996 to carry out the following tasks:

(a) Conduct a review of the Cadbury code and its implementation to ensure that the original purpose is being achieved, proposing amendments to and deletions from the code as necessary

(b) Keep under review the role of directors, executive and non-executive, recognising the need for board cohesion and the common legal responsibility of all directors

(c) Be prepared to pursue any relevant matters arising from the Greenbury report

(d) Address as necessary the role of shareholders and auditors in corporate governance issues

(e) Deal with any other relevant matters

1.24 The Hampel committee produced a final report in January 1998. The committee followed up matters raised in the Cadbury and Greenbury reports, aiming to **restrict** the **regulatory burden** on companies and **substituting principles for detail** whenever possible. The introduction to the report also states that whilst the Cadbury and Greenbury reports concentrated on the prevention of abuses, Hampel was equally concerned with the positive contribution good corporate governance could make.

1.25 The introduction to the report pointed out that the primary duty of directors is to shareholders, to **enhance** the **value** of **shareholders' investment** over time. Relationships with other stakeholders were important, but making the directors responsible to other stakeholders would mean there was no clear yardstick for judging directors' performance.

1.26 The Hampel committee was also against treating the corporate governance codes as sets of prescriptive rules, and judging companies by whether they have complied ('box-ticking'). The report stated that there may be **guidelines** which will normally be appropriate but the differing circumstances of companies meant that sometimes there are valid reasons for exceptions.

1.27 The Hampel report sets out principles of corporate governance. The major recommendations of the report were as follows.

Directors

1.28 The committee stressed that executive and non-executive directors should continue to have the same duties under the law. The committee stated that the roles of **chairman** and **chief executive** should generally be **separate**, but whether or not the roles of chairman and chief executive are combined, a **senior non-executive director** should be **identified**. **Non-executive directors** should make up **at least one third** of the **board**. The report also stressed the importance of monitoring director performance with all directors submitting themselves for **re-election at least once every three years**, and boards assessing the performance of individual directors and collective board performance.

Directors' remuneration

1.29 In common with the Cadbury and Greenbury reports, the Hampel committee saw the remuneration committee as the key mechanism for setting the pay of executive directors. Remuneration committees should develop policy on remuneration and devise reasonable remuneration packages for individual executive directors. The committee believed that boards should try to reduce directors' contract periods to one year or less. The accounts should include a **general statement** on **remuneration policy**, but the committee saw no need for this statement to be the subject of an AGM vote. (As discussed above, the government is considering making a vote on remuneration at the AGM compulsory).

Shareholders and the AGM

1.30 The major recommendations of the committee were that shareholders should be able to **vote separately** on each **substantially separate issue**; and that the practice of 'bundling' unrelated proposals in a single resolution should cease. Companies should **propose** a **resolution** at the AGM relating to the **report and accounts**. Notice of the AGM and related papers should be sent to shareholders at least 20 working days before the meeting. Institutional shareholders should adopt a considered policy on voting shares which they control.

Accountability and audit

1.31 The Hampel committee stressed, as the Cadbury committee had, the importance of the **audit committee**. However, whilst the report stated that directors should report on internal control, the committee did not believe that the directors should be required to report on the effectiveness of controls. Auditors should **report privately** on internal controls to directors. Directors should maintain and review controls relating to all relevant control objectives, and not merely financial controls.

Comments on the Hampel report

1.32 Reaction to the Hampel report has been mixed. Some commentators have welcomed the emphasis on common-sense guidance and the primary need to generate returns for shareholders.

1.33 However other commentators have criticised the Hampel report for stating that the debate on accountability has obscured the first responsibility of a board, to enhance the prosperity of a company over time. Critics have argued that **accountability** and **prosperity** should be seen as **compatible**. Hampel's emphasis on principles rather than detailed guidelines has also come in for adverse comment. Some critics have commented that the principles set out in the Hampel report are so broad that they are of little use as a guide to best corporate governance practice.

1.34 In addition Hampel has been criticised for:

(a) Dropping the Cadbury requirement for the board to report publicly on the effectiveness of internal controls

(b) Also dropping the requirement for the auditors to report publicly on the statement made by the board

(c) Paying insufficient attention to the needs of stakeholders other than shareholders

1.35 Within hours of publication of the Hampel report the Government responded by announcing that a major review of company law would be carried out. This can be seen as a direct contradiction of Hampel's plea to give the voluntary approach more time to work.

Stock Exchange requirements

1.36 Hampel proposed combining the various best practices, principles and codes of Cadbury, Greenbury and Hampel into one single 'supercode'. The Stock Exchange has issued a **Combined Code** on corporate governance, which was derived from the recommendations of the Cadbury, Greenbury and Hampel reports. In June 1998 the Stock Exchange Listing Rules were amended to make compliance with the new code obligatory for listed companies for accounting periods ending after 31 December 1998. The major elements of this code are listed in Appendix 23 of this Text.

1.37 The Combined Code requires listed companies to include in their accounts:

(a) A narrative statement of how they **applied** the **principles** set out in the Combined Code. This should provide explanations which enable their shareholders to assess how the principles have been applied.

(b) A statement as to whether or not they **complied throughout** the **accounting period** with the provisions set out in the Combined Code. Listed companies that did not comply throughout the accounting period with all the provisions must specify the provisions with which they did not comply, and give **reasons** for **non-compliance**.

2 FUTURE DEVELOPMENTS IN CORPORATE GOVERNANCE

Reporting on internal control

2.1 In September 1999 a working party from the Institute of Chartered Accountants in England and Wales published further guidance on internal controls **Internal Control Guidance for Directors on the Combined Code** (the Turnbull report).

2.2 The working party suggested that the system of internal control should be **embedded** in the **operations** of the company, be **appropriate** for the company, include procedures for **reporting** any major **control weaknesses**, and **remain relevant** in the changing business environment.

2.3 The guidance points out that the control system can only provide reasonable assurance against a company failing to meet its business objectives or all material losses, frauds or breaches of laws and regulations.

2.4 The report recommends that when assessing the effectiveness of internal control, boards should consider the following:

(a) The **nature** and **extent** of the **risks** which face the company and which it regards as **acceptable** for the company to bear within its particular business

(b) The **threat** of such **risks becoming** a **reality**

(c) If that happened, the company's ability to **reduce** the **incidence** and **impact** on the business

(d) The **costs and benefits** related to operating relevant controls

2.5 In order to be able to carry out an effective review, boards should regularly receive and review reports on internal control, concentrating.

(a) What the **risks** are and how they have been **identified, evaluated** and **managed**

(b) The **effectiveness** of the internal control system in the management of risk

(c) Whether **actions** are being taken to **reduce** the risks found

(d) Whether the results indicate that **internal control** should be **monitored more extensively**

2.6 The board should disclose as a minimum in the accounts, the existence of a **process** for **managing risks**, how the board had **reviewed** the **effectiveness** of the process and that the **process accords** with the **ICAEW's guidance**. The board should also disclose:

(a) An **acknowledgement** that they are responsible for the company's system of internal financial control and reviewing its effectiveness

(b) An **explanation** that such a system is designed to **manage** rather than eliminate the risk of **failure** to **achieve business objectives,** and can only provide **reasonable** and not absolute **assurance** against material misstatement or **loss**

(c) A **summary** of the process that the **directors** (or a board committee) have **used to review the effectiveness** of the system of internal financial control and consider the need for an internal audit function if the company does not have one. There should also be disclosure of the process the board has used to deal with **material internal control aspects** of **any significant problems** disclosed in the annual accounts

(d) **Information** about those **weaknesses** in internal financial control that have resulted in material losses, contingencies or uncertainties which require disclosure in the financial statements or the auditor's report on the financial statements.

2.7 The statement should be based on an annual assessment of internal control which should confirm that the board has considered **all significant aspects** of internal control. In particular the assessment should cover:

(a) The **changes** since the last **assessment** in **risks** faced, and the company's **ability** to **respond** to **changes** in its business environment

(b) The **scope** and **quality** of management's monitoring of risk and internal control, and of the work of internal audit, or consideration of the need for an internal audit function if the company does not have one

(c) The **extent** and **frequency** of reports to the board

(d) **Significant controls**, **failings** and **weaknesses** which have or might have material impacts upon the accounts

(e) The **effectiveness** of the **public reporting** processes

2.8 An article by Robin Johnson in August 1999's *Chartered Secretary* highlighted how the Turnbull committee's recommendations might affect the work of a company secretary. The article warns that failure by directors to consider risk management may lead to negligence claims and criminal liability.

2.9 The article emphasises that companies will need to carry out an internal risk audit, focusing on contractual relationships and how risk is managed in relation to customers, suppliers, regulators, employees or consumers. The audit should consider how risk is **managed** and **controlled**, and whether the **risks** that are being run are **acceptable** (how probable it is that they will crystallise, what would happen if a major risk occurred and the cost of controlling and minimising the risk). Audits should be conducted by appropriately senior staff, who should have access to non-executive directors and the audit committee.

2.10 Once the audit team has reported, a programme of risk minimisation and control should be implemented; this will involve systems training, communication and constant identification of opportunities and risks.

2.11 The debate on the extent to which companies and their auditors should report of the effectiveness of internal controls is likely to continue over the next few years.

Institutional shareholders

2.12 The Association of British Insurers (ABI) and the National Association of Pension Funds (NAPF) have issued guidance on how institutional shareholders should exercise their votes. The guidance focuses on the concept of '**responsible voting**', defined as the application of informed decisions reached within a framework of a considered corporate governance policy based on the Stock Exchange's Combined Code. However responsible voting represents only part of the dialogue that should exist between institutional members and boards.

2.13 The guidance suggests that in general boards should be **positively supported** unless there are good reasons for not doing so. This will therefore mean that boards should be concerned if they are not receiving support. Institutional shareholders should communicate early to boards an intention to vote against a proposal, to maximise the chances of a satisfactory solution to the problems involved.

2.14 The guidance also emphasises the importance of the **remuneration report** as a means of communicating the principles upon which remuneration will be determined (particularly the link with performance) and compensation upon termination of employment. Performance criteria should be demanding, linked to enhanced shareholder value and measured against a benchmark which will normally be based on the performance of directors of other comparable companies.

2.15 A particular concern is the **compensation** given on **early termination** of contracts, as this is seen on some occasions as rewarding failure, or giving compensation even though the individual soon starts a new job. The guidance suggests that compensation should be **phased over** the **length** of the **notice period**, with payments ceasing when the individual begins new employment.

2.16 The ABI has itself recently issued a statement of principles on share incentive schemes. As well as emphasising the need for challenging performance criteria, the guidance also stresses the importance of disclosure, including **disclosure** of **performance** criteria and the **policy** for **granting share options**. The costs of the scheme to shareholders should also be disclosed; companies should show the maximum value of shares that could possibly be allocated, the expected value, and the maximum dilution of share capital.

2.17 A NAPF committee has recommended enhanced use of **electronic voting** and **communication**. This, together with written voting instructions, control of votes delegated to agents and review by boards of institutional voting, should increase the level of voting by institutions, and also enhance their contribution.

Company law reform

2.18 The government is considering corporate governance issues as part of its wide-ranging review of company law, with the object of producing new legislation sometime early in the twenty-first century.

2.19 One issue certainly under consideration is to make certain of the recommendations of the corporate governance reports legally binding. Wider issues are also being considered, particularly the role of stakeholders. The Company Law Review Steering Group suggested two possible approaches:

(a) Relying on current principles, but with certain changes in the law and an expansion of disclosure requirements

(b) Allowing or requiring directors to balance shareholder interests against those of other stakeholders

---

Exercise

Keep your eyes open for developments in this area, particularly how companies annual reports and accounts are reflecting the new requirements.

Chapter roundup

- **Corporate governance** is an important and topical issue.
- The **Cadbury Report** makes recommendations on the following subjects.
  - The board
  - Non-executive directors
  - Executive directors
  - Audit committees
  - Internal controls
  - Interim reports, auditors' fees, rotation of audit partners, reporting to regulatory authorities
- The **Greenbury Report** focuses on executive directors' remuneration, which should be determined by a remuneration committee. Disclosures in the accounts should include details of each director's remuneration package and the company's overall remuneration policy.
- The **Hampel Report** makes recommendations on the following subjects.
  - Directors
  - Directors' remuneration
  - Shareholders
  - Accountability and audit
- The Stock Exchange's **Combined Code** has united the recommendations of the Cadbury, Greenbury and Hampel reports, and has been appended to the London Stock Exchange's Listing Rules.
- Future developments in corporate governance will focus on reviews of internal control and institutional shareholders, amongst other topics.

Test your knowledge

1 Why was the Cadbury Committee set up? (see para 1.2)

2 What were the main provisions of the Cadbury code in relation to the board of directors? (1.6)

3 What details does the Greenbury report suggest should be given in the accounts concerning (a) the company's remuneration policy; (b) the remuneration of individual directors? (1.15, 1.17)

4 What were the main provisions of the Hampel report in relation to the annual general meeting? (1.30)

5 What corporate governance details does the Stock Exchange require to be included in a listed company's accounts? (1.37)

6 What should a board review of internal control consider? (2.4)

7 What disclosure requirements about internal control did the Turnbull committee propose? (2.6)

When you have worked through Chapter 4
try illustrative question 3 at the end of the Study Text

Chapter 4

THE DISTRIBUTION OF POWER

This chapter covers the following topics.

1 The company as a legal person

2 Control over directors' powers

3 Importance of the general meeting

4 The binding effect of a majority decision: minority protection

5 Procedural safeguards for the minority

6 The memorandum and articles of association

Introduction

The law and procedure of company meetings has developed from the more general principles covered in your studies for the *Administration of Corporate Affairs* paper. It is, however, a two-way interaction, since many of the general principles have themselves been tested and refined in the context of company meetings.

There are several different types of company meeting, as explained in Chapter 5. The purpose of this chapter is to put company general meetings, that is meetings of the members of companies, in the context of company structure.

A meeting is a means of arriving at a decision, so we must look at:

(a) How powers of decision are distributed within the structure of a company; and

(b) The extent to which decisions of general meetings of companies in particular can determine the policy and future conduct of the company.

Most of these aspects should be familiar to you from your *Corporate Law* studies.

1 THE COMPANY AS A LEGAL PERSON

1.1 Perhaps the most celebrated case in company law, *Salomon v Salomon & Co Ltd 1897*, established that a **company** is a **separate legal entity**, *distinct* from:

- Members (even if one of them owns practically all its shares)
- Directors who manage its affairs and take many of its decisions
- Employees
- Creditors, even if they are also shareholders and/or directors and/or employees

1.2 Although a company is a separate legal 'person', however, it is an abstraction with no mind of its own: other persons connected with it must make the decisions required by the company's affairs. Such persons must be formally connected with the company in a particular way, notably as shareholders or directors. Unlike the case of a partnership, a proprietorial interest in a company does not imply a general right to take part in its management or to act as its agent.

1.3 As will be explained below, the ultimate power of decision is given to members assembled in general meeting. But, especially if the company has a large number of members, it is not practicable to **manage** a company by taking all the decisions in general meeting. Thus every company must have at least one director (s 282) and a public company must have two. Most companies have two or more directors.

1.4 As a company usually has a number of members (a public company *must* have at least two) and usually has two or more directors, a number of practical questions arise within each group, and in their relations with each other, as to the existence and distribution of decision making powers.

(a) How are **powers allocated** between members and directors?

(b) How are the **directors appointed** and what power have members to control or dismiss them?

(c) How are **disputes** among members or among directors to be **resolved**?

2 CONTROL OVER DIRECTORS' POWERS

2.1 The division of powers between the members of the company in general meeting and the directors is well defined.

(a) Both the Companies Act and the articles of association of the company allow the **general meeting** exclusive power to make major changes in the company, such as:

(i) An **alteration** of its **objects** or capital (in the memorandum of association)

(ii) An **alteration** of the **articles** themselves

(b) Other powers are delegated to the **directors**: one of the most important is the power to borrow money for the company, and thereby to incur heavy financial liabilities. A number of other important transactions are within the powers delegated to the directors, but require them to obtain **approval** from a general meeting. S 80, for example, provides that 'The directors of a company shall not exercise any power of the company to allot relevant securities, unless they are... authorised to do so by: (a) the company in general meeting; or (b) the company's articles.'

Limitation on directors' powers

2.2 As we have noted above, legislation and the articles of the company may place limits on the way in which the directors may exercise the power of the company.

2.3 There are also common law principles which constrain the directors' exercise of their powers. They must:

(a) Act in what they consider to be the **best interests of the company** (not blatantly in the exclusive interest of a third party, as in *Re Lee, Behrens & Co 1932*)

(b) Exercise their powers **for the purposes for which those powers were given to them**

2.4 A single shareholder may call the directors to account if they disregard these principles, although the general body of shareholders in general meeting may release the directors from the constraints of the 'proper purpose' doctrine.

Bamford v Bamford 1969
The facts: The directors allotted shares for the purpose of altering the balance of votes in general meeting, to frustrate a takeover bid which they honestly considered detrimental to the interests of the company. However, an allotment of shares *should* be made to augment the resources of the company or otherwise to promote its development: the allotment made in this case was not for a 'proper purpose'. A resolution was passed in general meeting to ratify what the directors had done. Some shareholders challenged the validity of the allotment by court action.

Decision: The resolution was a valid ratification of the allotment of the shares.

2.5 The powers delegated to directors by the standard form of article **cover** the **general management** of the business. Table A Article 70 provides that 'the business of the company shall be managed by the directors, who may exercise all the powers of the company', subject to:

- The provisions of the Companies Act
- The memorandum and articles of association
- Any directions given by *special* resolution

2.6 No change in the memorandum or articles, nor directions given by special resolution, can be made to have 'retrospective effect': they may impose a new limit on the directors' powers, but they cannot invalidate what the directors have already done (while they did have the necessary power).

Control of directors by the general meeting over directors

2.7 The directors are not 'agents' to whom the shareholders may give directions. The directors derive their **authority** from the **constitution** of the company and, so long as they conform to the relevant limits on their powers, as described above, the shareholders may not interfere with what they do: *Salmon v Quin & Axtens Ltd 1909*. The company is the principal, not the shareholders. However this does not preclude the majority acting in its own right to safeguard the company: *Marshall's Valve Gear Co Ltd v Manning Wardle & Co Ltd 1909*.

2.8 What then are the powers of the general meeting to control the directors? The general meeting is, after all, an assembly of those who *own* the company!

(a) It has always been possible to **alter** the **articles** by special resolution (s 9). In this way, the members may make a permanent change in the directors' constitutional powers for future transactions.

(b) The meeting's power to issue a **specific direction** by special resolution (as mentioned above) is really a development of that principle: it is normal practice to give directors authority by such a resolution, if there is any doubt about possible conflict with the articles. The resolution is as effective for its immediate purpose as an explicit and permanent alteration of the articles.

2.9 A more general sanction, to induce the directors to conform to the views of a majority in general meeting, is the statutory power (s 303) which allows the members:

- **Remove** any **director** from office by ordinary resolution
- **Appoint another director** in his place

The procedure of s 303 is cumbersome. To induce a change of management policy by a change of the management itself may in any case be unduly drastic - but directors do not usually allow their differences with shareholders to reach this point. Either the directors modify their policy, or they resign. In this indirect fashion the general meeting can still impose its wishes.

3 IMPORTANCE OF THE GENERAL MEETING

3.1 There is a striking contrast between the theory and the practice of company general meetings. In theory the general meeting of members is the forum in which the proprietors of the company may:

- Call the directors to account
- Remove them from office if they no longer command confidence
- Curtail their powers by alteration of the articles
- Resolve any differences between shareholders themselves, by discussion and vote

Small company meetings

3.2 In practice the general meetings of most companies are brief and perfunctory proceedings. If it is a meeting of a small private company, it is likely that the same individuals are both shareholders and directors. Indeed it is now possible under the Companies (Single Member Private Limited Companies) Regulations 1992 for the sole member director to constitute a meeting (see Chapter 5). In such cases, it is often left to the auditors to prepare the formal documents required for the annual general meeting: these are then presented for signature, and there is really no meeting at all.

3.3 Company law has had to recognise that there is no logical reason for disregarding an **informal consensus** of members as a substitute for a general meeting in the sense of a formal assembly - the '**assent principle**'. On the same principle, any irregularities of meeting procedure may be disregarded.

3.4 Note that, to apply this principle, virtual unanimity is essential. No dissenting member, even if he or she is a very small minority, may be deprived of the right to insist on the proper procedure for convening and conducting a meeting.

3.5 The idea of consensus has been taken a stage further by the Companies Act 1989, which introduced the concept of '**unanimous written resolutions**' for *private* companies together with the right to dispense with holding an AGM by means of an elective resolution (see Chapter 8 on resolutions for a full discussion of these provisions).

Large company meetings

3.6 At the other extreme, a large public company may have tens of thousands of shareholders. But they too may regard the general meetings of their company as a tedious formality and rarely bother to attend them.

3.7 In a typical case, the press representatives and company staff present at a general meeting of a public company outnumber the shareholders. The chairman may take the opportunity to report progress since the end of the latest complete financial year: If there are questions, the chairman - with staff and records at hand - is well prepared to rebut or sidestep the point. Once the accounts have been disposed of, the rest of the routine AGM business is soon completed. At the end, a shareholder rises to move a vote of thanks to the board.

3.8 Even public companies may, however, run into stormy weather at their general meetings. The shareholders may be prepared to support their board of directors only so long as the profits - and therefore the dividends - are satisfactory. The directors of a company which has been doing badly may have a rough passage at the next AGM and may even find that there is opposition to the re-election of those directors who are due to retire by rotation on this occasion. In these circumstances, the meeting is *not* a mere formality. Resolutions put to the vote on a show of hands may have to be put to the overriding test of a real vote on a poll. At every stage the chairman should ensure that the **correct procedure** is followed. It falls to him to maintain order in face of protests from shareholders etc., and he may be required to give instant rulings on points of order.

3.9 If there is a continuing battle within a public company between the directors and their supporters, and a rival group which wishes to oust them from control, the general meetings are the battlefield on which each side resorts to legal and procedural moves to attack the other. Meetings of this kind draw a much larger attendance, and are much more difficult to guide and keep in order. Years ago it was said of a particular public company, which was split into rival factions, that outsiders sometimes bought just one share as a means of securing admittance to meetings, which had acquired the renown and entertainment value of a gladiatorial contest.

3.10 It should be apparent, therefore, that the elaborate and normally unused safeguards of meeting procedure do have their uses: you should treat them seriously in your answer to exam questions, even if your own experience of meetings leads you to take them with a 'pinch of salt'.

4 THE BINDING EFFECT OF A MAJORITY DECISION: MINORITY PROTECTION

4.1 Like *Salomon's* case, the case below established a basic principle of company law and control of a company.

> *Foss v Harbottle 1843*
> *The facts:* Harbottle and other directors had sold land to the company for development at inflated prices. The directors so mismanaged the company that it declined into complete confusion. Foss, who spoke for a group of shareholders, tried to get a general meeting held, so that the company might call the directors to account. But he was unable to do so. He then applied to the court, as a shareholder who had suffered loss, to assert the company's rights against the directors.
>
> *Decision:* The action should be dismissed, since only the *company* was competent to sue to assert or safeguard its rights. Individual shareholders should bring their complaint before a general meeting with a view to obtaining a *majority decision* for the company to take action. However 'general principles of justice and convenience' might permit exceptions, being cases where a minority of shareholders would be allowed to sue on behalf of the company.

4.2 It is not appropriate here to review the exceptions to the rule in *Foss v Harbottle* in all their complexity. However it is useful to consider what constraints are placed on the power of the majority, voting in general meeting, to **impose** a decision which is binding on the company and on any of its members who may disagree with it. How far is the minority protected against an 'interested' or unscrupulous majority?

4.3 Case law recognises a number of limitations to the principle of majority control (the rule in *Foss v Harbottle*) and in those cases permits a minority to bring legal proceedings. The decisions are not entirely consistent, but the principles include the following.

(a) No majority vote can be effective to sanction an act of the company which is **ultra vires** or **illegal**. This used to be the position as regards an *ultra vires* act under s 35, although s 35(3) now allows the possibility of ratification of an *ultra vires* act by special resolution.

(b) If the law or the company's articles require that a **special procedure** shall be observed, such as a special resolution for alteration of the articles, the majority must observe that procedure and their decision is invalid if they do not do so.

(c) A majority decision is binding only if it is obtained by a **sufficient number of votes validly cast**. In particular, votes may not be used for fraudulent purposes (and if those who control the company use their control to defraud it, the minority may bring legal proceedings against the fraudulent majority).

(d) If the company under majority control deprives a member of his **individual rights** of **membership**, he may sue the company to enforce his rights.

These principles were considered in detail as part of your Corporate Law Studies.

Exercise

Explain the effect of a decision taken by a company in general meeting.

Solution

Under the rule in *Foss v Harbottle 1843* a decision of the company in general meeting taken by the appropriate majority is a valid decision of the company binding on the company and all its members, insofar as the matter is within the competence of a general meeting to decide it.

However a majority decision in general meeting is only valid if it is *intra vires* the company and lawful, and if the meeting is properly convened and conducted. Moreover a majority decision is not valid if it amounts to a fraud on the company: *Cook v Deeks 1916*.

The first requirement of a meeting is that it shall be properly convened. The power to call meetings is generally exercised by the directors, under powers given by the articles. In special circumstances however it may be convened by members, by the court or by the DTI.

To convene the meeting notice of 21 or 14 days is required according to the nature of the meeting and of the business. There is a procedure by which all or a large majority of members may waive these periods of notice.

The notice issued to members must give adequate information of the business to be conducted; in particular, the text of any special or extraordinary resolution must be set out in full: s 378. For the removal of a director and the removal of an auditor or the appointment of a new auditor special notice to the company is also required. If the formal notice convening the meeting does not adequately disclose the nature of the business, additional information must be supplied, usually in an accompanying circular: *Kaye v Croydon Tramways Co 1898*.

At the meeting a quorum must be present and any resolution, if it is to be valid, must be passed by the required majority. For a special or extraordinary resolution a three quarters majority of votes cast is required: s 378.

5 PROCEDURAL SAFEGUARDS FOR THE MINORITY

5.1 As was suggested earlier, the elaborate safeguards of meetings procedure may be helpful to an oppressed minority.

General meetings

5.2 The first major safeguard is the general principle that once in every year, every company shall hold **an annual general meeting** (AGM). However, s 366A allows a *private* company to pass an **elective resolution dispensing** with the need to hold the AGM, unless required to do so by a member. This is dealt with in detail in Chapter 6. In addition, members who have at least 10 per cent of the paid-up share capital may require the directors to convene an extraordinary general meeting (EGM). The court, the Department of Trade and Industry or the auditors may in appropriate circumstances intervene to enforce the convening of a general meeting. The directors must therefore normally face their critics at least once a year - sometimes more often.

5.3 Much of the procedure for convening a general meeting is concerned with achieving three other safeguards: notice, proxies and minutes. These points will be discussed at length in later chapters.

6 THE MEMORANDUM AND ARTICLES OF ASSOCIATION

6.1 Because a company is an 'artificial person', with its powers of decision allocated between members in general meeting and the board of directors, it needs a written constitution to make things clear. This constitution takes the form of the memorandum and articles of association.

6.2 The rules on the conduct of company meetings (including board meetings) are contained in the **articles**. These matters will be considered in detail in later chapters, with particular regard to Table A (model articles of a company limited by shares).

6.3 The legal capacity of the company (what is within its powers) is defined by the **objects clause** of the **memorandum of association** (discussed in your corporate law studies).

6.4 Although most companies have not yet taken advantage of the fact, the Companies Act 1989 now entitles a company to be registered with a 'general' objects clause, so that the company's object is to carry on business as a general commercial company.

6.5 In addition, the Act now provides that a company's acts cannot be challenged on the ground of lack of capacity, and that a person acting in good faith is entitled to treat the company as bound, even if in fact the directors' powers are limited: ss 35(1) and 35A.

6.6 With respect to the internal operation of the *ultra vires* rule, it is still open to a member to bring a court action to rescind a potentially *ultra vires* act: s 35(2). It is also open to members to ratify such an act by special resolution: s 35(3).

Indoor management rule: Turquand's case

6.7 A different, but related, problem arises when:

(a) A transaction is within the **capacity of** a company (*intra vires*)

(b) The memorandum or articles of association (usually the articles) require that some **internal authorisation** shall be obtained, usually by approval of the transaction at a general or board meeting.

So far as the **company** is concerned, the proper authorisation must be given, since the written constitution requires it; directors who act without it may be liable to compensate the company for any loss which it may have suffered.

6.8 The third party dealing in good faith with the company, through its board of directors, is usually safeguarded under the rule laid down in the *Turquand* case or now under s 35 of the Companies Act.

> *Royal British Bank v Turquand 1856*
> *The facts:* The company's articles of association authorised the directors to borrow such sums of money as the company in general meeting might by resolution authorise. A resolution was passed which authorised the directors to borrow but did not specify any sum of money. The directors, relying on this defective resolution, borrowed £2,000 from the bank. The company went into liquidation and the liquidator denied liability to repay the loan.
>
> *Decision:* The bank must be presumed to be aware of the need for authorisation of the loan, but it was also entitled to assume that proper authorisation had been given, since it had no means of checking whether the resolution was adequate for its purpose and no grounds for supposing that it was not. This has become known as the 'indoor management' rule, since a third party should be protected from the effects of a breakdown in indoor management procedure of which he could not be aware.

6.9 The rule in *Turquand's* case is often applied to the proceedings of company meetings. A person dealing with a company is entitled to assume, unless he knows or has reason to suspect the contrary, that a necessary decision was given at a meeting duly convened, with a quorum, and otherwise in order.

Chapter roundup

- When discussing company meetings it is important to bear two things in mind: firstly, that the company as a **separate legal** entity **cannot take decisions** itself, and secondly that power to make its decisions is divided between its **managers** (the directors) and its **owners** (the shareholders).
- **General meetings** of shareholders have certain important **powers**, such as to remove directors, but they are not the place for day-to-day operational decisions.
- **Majority decisions** in general meetings are **binding** on the company but there are limitations on that power which serve to protect the **interests** of **minorities**. It should be remembered that the protection is not extensive, and that the principle of majority control (the *Foss v Harbottle* rule) is a powerful one.

Test your knowledge

1 What principle was established by the decision in Salomon's case? (see para 1.1)

2 Give examples of company decisions which must be taken in general meeting. (2.1)

3 How are the directors sometimes constrained in the exercise of the powers delegated to them? (2.2 - 2.5)

4 How may the members of a company in general meeting influence the exercise of their powers by the directors? (2.7 - 2.9)

5 What is the rule in *Foss v Harbottle*? Give examples of some exceptions to it. (4.1, 4.3)

6 What changes to the *ultra vires* rule are made by the Companies Act 1989? (6.4 -6.5)

7 What is the rule in *Turquand's* case and how is it applied? (6.8, 6.9)

Now try illustrative question 3 at the end of the Study Text

Chapter 5

TYPES OF COMPANY MEETING

This chapter covers the following topics.

Introduction

Company meetings may be the following types:

(a) Annual general meeting (AGM)
(b) Extraordinary general meeting (EGM)
(c) Class meeting (meeting of holders of a class of shares in the company)
(d) Board (of directors) meeting
(e) Board committee meeting
(f) Meeting of contributories or of creditors in liquidation

An annual general meeting (AGM), extraordinary general meeting (EGM) and a class meeting are all meetings of members, or of some members, of a company. They are described in this chapter.

Meetings of boards of directors and of committees of the board, have many special features. Accordingly, these types of meeting are studied in later chapters of this Study Text.

1 THE NATURE OF A COMPANY MEETING

1.1 Company law does not provide - because it does not need - its own definition of a meeting. The main point is that a meeting requires the presence of **at least two individuals** who are entitled to take part in the proceedings: *Sharp v Dawes 1876*.

1.2 It has also been held (*Re Sanitary Carbon Co 1877*) that **one member** present in a dual capacity, that is in person and as proxy for others, does **not constitute** a meeting. Likewise, a meeting ceases to 'exist' if all the members leave except one: *Re London Flats Ltd 1969*.

One person as a meeting

1.3 However, in laying down and applying this basic principle, the courts have always recognised that a 'meeting' may bear 'a special meaning under the constitution of a company': *Re James Prain & Sons Ltd 1947*. The Companies Act also has to provide for exceptional circumstances in which one person may be treated as a meeting.

1.4 The recognised exceptions are as follows.

(a) A meeting of the **holders** of a **class of shares** in a company (a 'class meeting') may consist of one person, if he holds all the shares of the class: *East v Bennett Bros Ltd 1911*. However, there are statutory provisions on a *quorum* at a class meeting, which we will consider later.

(b) The **Department of Trade and Industry**, in ordering that an AGM be held, may **direct that** one member present in person or by proxy shall be deemed to constitute a meeting: s 367.

(c) The **court** also has statutory power, in ordering that a meeting be held, to direct as in (b) above: s 371.

(d) There may be a meeting attended by one person if the company is a **single member private company** (s 370A), as provided by the Companies (Single Member Private Limited Companies) Regulations 1991.

The powers referred to in (b) and (c) enable the directing authority to get round the difficulty which arises if for example one of the two members refuses to attend meetings in order to prevent them being held.

1.5 The general principle that a meeting by its nature requires the presence of at least two people should be distinguished from the requirement of a **quorum** for the meeting, as described in detail in Chapter 7. A quorum is often fixed at two (Table A Article 40), but it may be fixed at some higher level. In exceptional cases, where one person may constitute a company meeting, the quorum can obviously not be more than one.

1.6 It is accepted, for example, that the articles of association may fix (or permit) a quorum of one director at a board meeting. This is unavoidable, since a private company need not have more than one director: s 281.

1.7 A meeting, for these purposes, means a meeting face-to-face. A telephone conversation or even a conference call is not a meeting. However, see below for concessions for private companies.

2 THE ANNUAL GENERAL MEETING (AGM) — 6/99, 12/99, 6/00

2.1 Generally every company is required to hold one AGM in each calendar year and to specify it as the AGM in the notice convening the meeting: s 365. However:

(a) The first AGM may be held at any time **within 18 months** of incorporation, so not necessarily in the calendar year of incorporation, or even in the next following year.

(b) There may be **an interval of up to 15 months** between the AGM of one year and of the next.

2.2 As an example, if a company is formed on 31 October 20X0, it need not hold its first AGM until 31 March 20X2 (within eighteen months). If it does hold its first AGM on that date, it must hold its next AGM in 20X3 (the next calendar year) - but is permitted to delay it until 30 June 20X3 (15 months later).

2.3 Note that the 15 month permitted interval between successive AGM does *not* allow a company to omit a calendar year altogether. If, for example, an AGM is held on 15 December 20X2, there must be another one in 20X3 (before the fifteen months is up).

2.4 The articles (Table A Article 37) empower the directors to call general meetings. If a company fails to hold an AGM as required, the directors, as officers of the company in default, are liable to a fine.

2.5 If there is default in holding an AGM, the Department of Trade and Industry may, on the application of a member of the company, call (or direct the calling of) the meeting, giving any additional directions it considers expedient: s 367.

2.6 If, under these directions, an AGM is held a year late (in the calendar year following that in which it should have been held), it does not rank as the AGM of that year as well, unless:

(a) The company **passes a resolution** to that effect at the meeting.

(b) A **copy** of the resolution is **delivered** to the Companies Registry within 15 days after its passing.

Without such a resolution, the company must hold a second AGM as the actual AGM of that year (in addition to the one carried over from the previous year).

2.7 It is possible to call an EGM whenever necessary or useful, but the normal practice is to defer non-urgent special business until the AGM. Accordingly, the AGM is the one occasion in a normal year when the directors must appear before shareholders and give an account of their stewardship of the company.

Dispensing with the AGM

2.8 The regulations on the holding of an AGM are released by s 366A for **private companies** (as part of a wider scheme of deregulation in this area). A private company may pass an **elective resolution** (discussed in detail in Chapter 8 on resolutions and minutes) to dispense with the holding of the AGM. *Any* member can, however, require the holding of an AGM in any particular year in which the resolution is in force, by giving notice to the company not more than three months before the end of the year: s 366A(3).

2.9 If the resolution ceases to be in force, the company is not obliged to hold an AGM if less than three months of that year remain.

3 THE EXTRAORDINARY GENERAL MEETING (EGM)

3.1 Any general meeting which is not described in the notice as an AGM is an EGM. There can usually be only one AGM in each calendar year, so *any* general meeting held after the AGM for the year - even if it transacts business which is normally done at an AGM - *must* be an EGM.

3.2 The directors have power in their discretion to call an EGM at any time, and as often as they may decide (Table A Article 37). In practice, they only call an EGM if there is urgent business which cannot conveniently be left for the next AGM.

3.3 As explained below, there are circumstances in which the directors are *required* to call an EGM for a specific purpose but, unlike an AGM, there is no continuing timetable requiring EGMs at set intervals.

Business of an EGM

3.4 An EGM may transact **whatever business** is set out in the notice of the meeting as being the reason for the meeting.

3.5 There are some differences between AGMs and EGMs in the period of notice required, and the detail given in the notice. These are explained in Chapter 6 on convening company general meetings.

3.6 In any of the following circumstances, the directors are required by law to convene an EGM:

(a) On the **requisition** (order) of members who hold at least **one tenth** of the shares carrying voting rights

(b) On the **requisition of an auditor** who resigns in certain circumstances

(c) In public company, **within 28 days** of the directors becoming aware that the net assets of the company are half (or less) of its called-up share capital

(d) In compliance with an **order** of the **court**

We will consider each of these circumstances in turn.

EGM requisitioned by members 6/99

3.7 Members who hold at least **one tenth** of the **paid-up share capital** carrying voting rights at a general meeting (or, if there is no share capital, representing one tenth of the voting rights) may deposit at the registered office a requisition, signed by all of them, requiring the directors to convene an EGM: s 368. (Several copies, each signed by one member, are also acceptable.) The requisition must state '**the objects of the meeting**'; it is usual to set out the text of the resolution(s) which the requisitionists propose to move at the EGM.

3.8 The directors are then required 'forthwith duly to convene' an EGM for the stated objects (to which the directors may add other resolutions if they wish).

3.9 The directors must issue notices to convene the EGM **within 21 days** of the deposit of the requisition. If they do not the requisitionists, or a majority of them representing more than half their total voting rights, may **themselves** convene the meeting, to be held **within three months** of the date of deposit of the requisition. In this case:

(a) The requisitionists may recover from the directors any **reasonable expenses** which they have incurred through the directors' default.

(b) The business of the EGM must be **confined** to the purposes stated in the requisition.

3.10 The Companies Act 1985 now provides in s 368(8) that 'the directors are deemed not to have duly convened a meeting if they convene a meeting for a date more than 28 days after the date of the notice convening the meeting'.

3.11 The most common reason for a requisition under s 368 is a move to remove the directors from office (by an ordinary resolution, of which special notice is required, under s 303). If the meeting wants a change of policy, it may recognise that directors who oppose it are unlikely to carry it out effectively: a change of directors is therefore the first step. There is, however, no limit on the business for which an EGM may be requisitioned.

EGM on resignation of the auditor

3.12 If the company's auditor ceases to hold office for *any* reason, he is required (s 392 and 394) to state in his notice of resignation whether there are any **circumstances** which he considers should be brought to the notice of members or of creditors of the company. If there *are* such circumstances, they will usually include a serious disagreement between the directors and the auditor over matters relating to the accounts.

3.13 If the auditor's notice of resignation discloses that there are such circumstances he may, with his notice, **deposit a requisition** calling on the directors to convene an EGM to receive and consider the auditor's explanation of the circumstances of his resignation: s 392(A).

3.14 The directors are then required to issue a notice **within 21 days** of the deposit of the requisition, to convene an **EGM to be held within 28 days** from the issue of that notice.

EGM on the financial situation of a public company

3.15 Directors of a public company have an obligation to convene an EGM as a result of becoming aware that the **net assets** have fallen to or below the value of **half the called-up share capital**: s 141.

3.16 The directors must issue the notice to convene the meeting **within 28 days** of becoming aware of the financial situation described. The meeting must be called for a date not more than **56 days** from the date on which the directors became aware of it.

3.17 The actual business of the meeting, under s 142, is not prescribed. In practice, the directors would no doubt take the initiative by laying before the meeting their view of the financial situation and prospects, with any proposals which they may wish to make.

3.18 S 142 does not refer to the company becoming **insolvent** (unable to pay its debts as they fall due): the company may have lost up to half the shareholders' capital but it may still be able to pay off its debts.

3.19 **Prospective insolvency** of any company, public or private, does however force the directors to convene an EGM to put the company into **creditors' voluntary liquidation**. If the directors do not take proper action in such a situation, they may be disqualified from being company directors or made liable for the company's debts on account of wrongful trading (s 214 Insolvency Act 1986).

Checklist: timetable for directors required to convene an EGM

EGM requisitioned by:	*Time limit for notice:*	*Time limit for meeting:*
Members (convened: directors)	21 days of requisition	28 days after the date of the notice
Members (convened: selves)	-	3 months of requisition
Resigning auditor	21 days of requisition	28 days of notice
Financial situation	28 days of awareness	56 days of awareness

EGM by order of the court

3.20 The court has an inherent power to order a general meeting of a company to be held. It will not usually interfere in a dispute between directors and shareholders, by ordering a meeting to resolve it: the shareholders have their own power to requisition a meeting. The court may, however, **encourage** the holding of a meeting as the best solution to a problem before it, for example to approve a director's action that is not for proper purposes: *Hogg v Cramphorn 1967.*

3.21 The court has a general **statutory power** (s 371):

(a) To **order** that a general meeting be held

(b) To **give directions** for the conduct of the meeting, such as fixing a quorum of one, in any case where it is 'impracticable' to hold the meeting in the normal way

The court generally uses this power to order that meetings be held when there is only one member available or willing to attend, and there is no other way of getting a quorum: the meeting could not otherwise be held.

3.22 Any person may apply to the court under s 371; it is not a right confined to members and directors. The court also has specific power (s 425) to order that a meeting or meetings be held to consider a scheme of arrangement, as discussed below.

Exercise

When is a company compelled to call an extraordinary general meeting?

Solution

Members of a company who hold not less than one tenth of the company's paid up share capital carrying voting rights, may requisition the holding of a extraordinary general meeting. As this is a public company it must have a share capital and the alternative qualification does not arise. The directors are then required within 21 days of the deposit of the requisition to issue a notice convening the meeting to transact the business specified in the requisition, for a date not more than 28 days hence: s 368.

An auditor who resigns giving reasons for his resignation may requisition an extraordinary general meeting so that he may explain to members the circumstances of his resignation: s 392A.

If the net assets of a public company are reduced to less than half in value of its called-up share capital, it is the duty of the directors to convene (within 28 days of becoming aware of this situation) an extraordinary general meeting to consider what, if any, steps should be taken: s 141.

The Department of Trade (s 367) and the court (s 371) have statutory power in certain circumstances to direct that a meeting shall be held.

4 CLASS MEETINGS 12/99

4.1 Class meetings are of two kinds.

(a) If the company has more than one class of share, for example if it has 'preference' and 'ordinary' shares, it may be necessary to call a meeting of the holders of one class of shares, to approve a **proposed variation** of the rights attached to their shares.

(b) Under the procedure for a '**scheme of arrangement**' (s 425), the holders of shares of the same class may nonetheless be divided into *separate classes* (for whom separate meetings are required) if the scheme proposed will affect each group differently (this is illustrated later). A scheme of arrangement would also entail class meetings if the scheme affects more than one class of shares.

Variation of class rights

4.2 The **rights** of a class of shares are usually defined by the articles of association. Accordingly, a **variation** of those rights is effected by a resolution passed in general meeting. The holders of a class of shares, however, might be voted down by holders of shares of other classes in a general meeting or have no votes at all in general meeting, as is sometimes the case with preference shares. To protect them, it is always provided that no variation may be made unless the class whose rights are to be varied has given its consent.

4.3 In the ordinary way, therefore, there is:

(a) A **preliminary class meeting** to agree to the variation
(b) A **full general meeting** of the company to make the variation

4.4 For convenience, the two meetings may take place in the same room and one immediately after the other. The class members will simply have to disregard the presence of non-members, who may await the larger meeting to follow - provided that they take no part in the class meeting itself: *Carruth v Imperial Chemical Industries Ltd 1937.*

4.5 Until recently it was the practice to include in the articles of association (1948 Table A Article 4) a procedure for obtaining the **preliminary consent** of a class to the variation of its rights. (Many companies still have articles in this form.) The articles would provide that a decision in favour of the variation, binding on all members of the class, may be given by:

(a) The consent, in writing, of the holders of at least three quarters of the shares of the class

(b) An extraordinary resolution passed (by a three quarters majority of votes cast) at a separate meeting of the holders of shares of the class

Alternative (b) is generally preferred, since the votes of members of the class who do not attend, or who abstain from voting, are disregarded: the majority need not be three-quarters of the whole number of shares of the class, only of **votes cast**.

4.6 This procedure only applies to an **explicit alteration** or reduction of express rights of a class of shares (indirect alteration, by changes to other classes of shares, or by the issue of more shares of the same class, does not require a consent of the class). Even if the consent is given by the required majority, a 15 per cent minority may appeal against it to the court. These, however, are mainly topics of *Corporate Law* rather than procedure at company meetings.

4.7 Some companies do not have the standard 'class consent' or 'variation' procedure in their articles:

(a) They may have no such procedure in the articles at all, or something different.

(b) They may define the class rights in the memorandum of association, with or without:

(i) A variation procedure
(ii) A statement that the rights are entrenched and unalterable

These alternatives are not common but they can cause practical problems.

4.8 To simplify the position, s 125 of the 1985 Act sets out the standard procedure (as in paragraph 4.5 above) with some improvements of detail. In particular, it is provided that:

(a) **Alteration** of the **articles** of association, in order to introduce class consent procedure, or to modify the existing procedure, **is itself a variation of class rights**, for which consent is required.

(b) Where class rights are attached to shares by the memorandum and there is provision in the memorandum or articles for variation of rights, both s 125 and the procedure must be followed if the resolution contains authority for allotment under s 80 or reduction of share capital under s 134. This means that *all* variations of these two types must have a 75% majority, whatever the constitution of the company states.

(c) If the rights of a class of shares are defined by the **memorandum**, and neither the memorandum nor the articles contain a variation procedure, a variation requires the consent of all members of the **company** (not just of the class).

4.9 In effect, whatever is in the articles (if anything) will generally be the operative procedure (though there are some technical exceptions). If the articles are silent (do not contain a variation procedure) s 125 will make the standard procedure applicable.

4.10 Since s 125 is available to any company (unless it is replaced by existing provisions of the company's articles), the 1985 Table A does not contain a variation procedure. Companies with articles in the 1985 form simply come under s 125 instead.

4.11 Whichever method is used, if the holders of at least **15 per cent** of the preference shares vote against, or withhold their consent from, the proposal, they may within 21 days **apply** to the **court** under s 127 for a cancellation of the variation on grounds of unfair prejudice. It is difficult to prove that a variation accepted by a large majority is prejudicial, unless there is evidence that the majority were not concerned with the interests of the class, but were seeking advantages to themselves as members of another class: *Re Holders Investment Trust Ltd 1971*. In this case the objection was raised when the court was asked to approve the reduction of capital under s 135.

Quorum for a class meeting

4.12 Under s 125 the standard general meeting rules, on issuing notices and on voting, apply to a class meeting. However the **quorum** for a class meeting is fixed at **two persons** who hold, or represent by proxy, at least one third in nominal value of the issued shares of the class. If no quorum is present, the meeting is adjourned (under the standard adjournment procedure for general meetings). When the meeting resumes, the quorum is *one* person (who must still hold at least one third of the shares).

4.13 As you may have gathered, if all the shares of the class are held by one person (as in *East v Bennett Bros Ltd 1911*) the simplest procedure is to obtain the written consent of that person. The 'class meeting' need not then be held.

Chapter roundup

- There is no strict legal definition of a meeting. It may be defined as an 'assembly of people for a lawful purpose.'
- Except under certain circumstances, at **least two persons** are required for a meeting.
- Every company must hold an **annual general meeting** in each calendar year and must specify it as an AGM in the notice convening the meeting.
- Any meeting not described in the notice as an AGM is an EGM (extraordinary general meeting). There are certain circumstances in which an EGM *must* be held.
    - On **requisition** of **members** holding at least one tenth of the shares carrying voting rights
    - On **requisition** of an **auditor** who resigns in certain circumstances
    - In a public company **within 28 days** of the directors becoming aware that the company's **net assets** are **half (or less)** of its called up share capital
    - By order of the court.
- There are two types of class meeting:
    - Where a company has **more than one class of share**
    - Under a **scheme of arrangement**

Test your knowledge

1 What are the different types of meeting which a company (or part of it) may hold? (see introduction)

2 In what circumstances may one person only form a quorum for a company meeting? (1.4, 1.5)

3 What is the statutory timetable for holding an AGM? (2.1)

4 In what circumstances are directors required to convene an EGM? (3.6)

5 How may EGM requisitionists overcome a failure of the directors to convene an EGM as required? (3.9)

6 What was the loophole by which directors may have frustrated a requisition (by shareholders) for an EGM and how has it been closed? (3.10)

7 In what circumstances may the court order that an EGM be held? (3.21, 3.22)

8 How may the necessary consent of the holders of a class of shares be obtained for a variation of the rights attached to their shares? (4.5, 4.8)

Now try illustrative question 4 at the end of the Study Text

Chapter 6

CONVENING A COMPANY GENERAL MEETING

This chapter covers the following topics.

1 The decision to convene a general meeting

2 Authority to issue notice

3 Persons to whom notice must be sent

4 Form and service of notice

5 Required period of notice

6 Content of notice

Introduction

Company law imposes stringent requirements for the convening of a general meeting. (The same rules are applied by s 125(6) to class meetings.) The purpose of these rules is to ensure that members are given sufficient advance notice of a meeting and of the business which it will transact to enable them to:

(a) Decide whether to attend

(b) Arrange to be free to do so

(c) Appoint proxies to represent them in their absence

(d) Consult with other members to formulate a common approach to the business of the meeting

(e) Consider the views expressed by financial commentators (if it is a public company whose affairs attract comment in the press)

1 THE DECISION TO CONVENE A GENERAL MEETING

1.1 The directors may call general meetings, according to the articles of association (Table A Article 37).

1.2 There are a number of situations in which the directors *must* call a general meeting, as described in the previous chapter.

(a) An **AGM** should be held **once in each calendar year** (unless an election under s 366A has been made) and within 15 months of the previous AGM (with a special timetable for the first AGM of a newly incorporated company): s 365.

(b) On the requisition of **one tenth of the members** (typically measured by holdings of voting shares) or of an auditor who has resigned, the directors must convene an EGM: s 368 and 391.

(c) In various circumstances the **court may order** that a meeting be held: the order would normally be addressed to the directors.

1.3 There are a number of 'fall-back' provisions covering possible difficulties in obtaining the authority of the board of directors for convening a general meeting.

(a) The articles may provide (Table A Article 37) that if there is no quorum within the UK for a board meeting to convene a general meeting, a **single director or member** may call the general meeting. (You may note that in articles which follow the 1948 Table A Article 49, the power to call a meeting in these circumstances is given to a single director or to *two* members.)

(b) If the articles do *not* make suitable provision, statutory power to convene a meeting is given to:

- **Two members** holding at least **one tenth** of the **issued share capital**
- **One twentieth** of the **members**, if the company has no share capital: s 370(3)

(c) If there is default in holding an AGM, any member may apply to the **Department of Trade and Industry**, which may give directions for calling the meeting: s 366.

(d) If it is 'impracticable' to call or conduct a general meeting in the manner prescribed by the Act or the articles, the **court** may **give directions** that it be called, held and conducted in any manner the court thinks suitable (for instance with a quorum of one): s 371.

Application may be made to the court by a director or by a member entitled to attend and vote at the meeting. The court may also intervene 'of its own motion', but in practice someone (there is no restriction as to who it may be) would bring the matter before the court. For example, the personal representatives of a decreased shareholder might do so.

1.4 The main purpose of ss 367 and 371 is to provide a way of holding a meeting where there is only one surviving member, or only one member is willing to attend the meeting: the quorum in these cases may be fixed at one.

1.5 If it becomes necessary to cancel or postpone a meeting, the correct procedure may be as follows.

(a) If the notice to convene the meeting has not yet been issued, the **board of directors** may simply **meet** and rescind their earlier decision to call a general meeting, since that decision has not yet been implemented.

(b) If the notice to convene the meeting has been issued, the meeting **must be held as arranged**. It is possible to start the meeting by proposing a resolution for its immediate adjournment - and to send an informal notice to members that this will be done, so that they do not waste time in coming to the meeting. However the important point is that a meeting, once convened by notice, cannot be cancelled or postponed unless permitted by the articles: *Smith v Paringa Mines Ltd 1906*.

2 AUTHORITY TO ISSUE NOTICE

2.1 It is usually the duty of the secretary of the company to **prepare** and **issue a notice** to convene a meeting. However he has no authority, by virtue of his position, to act without the authority of the board of directors.

2.2 If a notice is issued without the proper authority, but every member attends the general meeting, the notice may still be considered valid.

2.3 If a member objects that the notice was not issued with proper authority, he should make his objection clear as soon as possible; a delay of, say, six months may be taken as acquiescence.

2.4 The secretary may properly issue the notice, without authority from the board, if the DTI or the court has ordered that the meeting be held.

3 PERSONS TO WHOM NOTICE MUST BE SENT

Specimen paper

3.1 Membership of a company does not always carry the right to vote at general meetings.

(a) **Preference shares** often carry **no voting rights**, or only limited rights to vote in special circumstances.

(b) It is possible to issue **non-voting ordinary shares**.

If there is no right to vote, the definition of the rights attached to the shares usually also states that they give no right to receive notice of the meeting or even to attend.

3.2 In recognition of these possibilities, the Companies Act 1985 does not give every member of a company the right to receive notices of general meetings. It simply provides (s 370(2)) that, unless the articles otherwise provide, notice of a general meeting shall be sent to every member.

3.3 Among non-members, the **auditor** (s 391) and, if the articles so provide, **personal representatives** of deceased members (Table A Article 31) are entitled to receive the notice.

3.4 There may be a practical problem here if a company, especially a large public company, issues the notice of its AGM bound in the same booklet as the copy of its annual accounts. Every member has a statutory right (s 238(1)) to receive a copy of the accounts, even if he is not entitled to the notice of general meetings.

3.5 The usual solution is to add a footnote to the notice, in the booklet, to the effect that:

(a) It is sent for information only to members not entitled to attend.
(b) It does not confer a right to attend.

Failure to give notice of meeting

3.6 Failure to give notice of a meeting to a person entitled to it invalidates the proceedings of the meeting, unless one of the relieving provisions applies.

3.7 The person to whom notice should have been given cannot:

(a) **Waive** the **right** to notice

(b) **Relieve** the company of its obligation to give notice, for instance by indicating in advance that he will not attend

3.8 Although the case below relates to a club, not to a company, it is the leading case on this point for companies as well as other bodies.

Young v Ladies Imperial Club 1920
The facts: The Duchess of Abercorn informed the chairman that she would no longer attend meetings of the committee of which she was a member. The committee, at a meeting of which notice was not given to the Duchess, expelled Mrs Young from membership of the club, on account of disparaging remarks which she had made about it. The issue was whether the expulsion was valid.

Decision: The expulsion was invalid since notice had not been sent to a member of the committee (the Duchess). The Court of Appeal contemplated that the obligation to give notice does not apply when (a) the member is beyond summoning distance or possibly (b) when he is too ill to attend or to communicate his views to the committee by letter.

It is not the practice to rely on the possible exceptions recognised by the court. Both are too uncertain to be usable.

3.9 If the *articles* make exceptions to the entitlement rules, these become part of the 'contract' (s 14) which exists between the company and the members, and are therefore effective. Table A provides that:

(a) '**Accidental omission**' to give notice to a member who is entitled to it shall **not invalidate** the proceedings of the meeting: Article 39. *Re West Canadian Collieries Ltd 1962* allowed the Articles to be applied to the malfunction of an addressograph machine. However *Musselwhite v C H Musselwhite & Sons Ltd 1962* did not allow the provision to operate in the case of a company which had sent notice to the purchaser of shares who had not yet been entered on the register of members.

(b) A member whose address on the register of members is not within the UK may give the company a **UK address** at which notices may reach him. Otherwise, such a member is not entitled to receive notices: Article 111.

3.10 Although a member cannot 'let the company off the hook' by waiving his entitlement to notice, the articles provide that he will be deemed to have received notice if he is present at the meeting, in person or by proxy: (Table A Article 113). No harm has been done.

3.11 If there is a change in the holder of shares on the register, any notice given to a previous holder (who was entitled to it at the time) is taken to have been given to the new holder as well: Table A Article 113.

Exercise

Explain in detail who is entitled to receive notices of general meetings of a public limited company.

Solution

The articles of association of the company will determine who is entitled to receive notice of company annual general meetings. Table A (and therefore the articles of the majority of companies) provide that notice should be given to every member of the company. An exception to this provision is a member who is outside the United Kingdom (although he can be supplied with a notice if he has provided an address for this purpose within the UK).

Table A Art 116 provides that the administrators or the executors of a deceased member must be given notice of general meetings; the same is true for the trustee in bankruptcy of a member. This is the case despite the fact that they may not be entitled to vote at the meeting.

It is usual for the articles to provide that notice of general meetings should be given to the holders of shares that entitle their holder to attend the meeting and vote at it. This means that the holders of shares which do not carry voting rights (as is the case, for example, with non-voting ordinary shares or preference shares) are not entitled to a notice of the meeting.

There is a potential problem with this arrangement, in that the notice of a meeting of a larger company will often be included in (generally at the back of) the accounts and the directors report; this must be sent to every member or debentureholder. People not entitled to notice will therefore receive copies of it as part of a larger document. To avoid this problem, it is usual to include an explanatory note in the document, to the effect that it is for information only in the case of those who are not entitled to receive it.

Finally, by statute, it should be remembered that the auditors of the company have a right to receive notices.

The strictness of the notice regulations can be ameliorated to a certain extent by the inclusion of Article 39, which provides that the proceedings of a meeting shall not be invalidated by reason of an 'accidental omission' to give notice to a person entitled to receive it. This is, however, not the powerful protection it might at first seem; there is a body of case law which applies a somewhat restricted definition to an accidental omission:

---

4 FORM AND SERVICE OF NOTICE

4.1 A notice issued to convene a company general meeting must be in writing: s 369 (although a notice calling a meeting of directors need not be: Table A Article 111).

4.2 Although members may agree to accept short notice they cannot agree to relieve the company of its obligation to give a **written notice**. The articles of association cannot override s 369.

4.3 The method of serving notice is usually prescribed by the articles of association. If the articles are silent, the provisions of Table A are to be applied on that point: s 370(2). In fact, the articles invariably *do* prescribe how notice shall be given, and in most cases *do* follow the model of Table A.

4.4 Article 112 provides that a notice may be either:

(a) **Delivered** to the member **personally**; or
(b) **Sent by post** (or delivered by hand) to the member's registered UK address

4.5 The articles may in addition provide for giving notice by newspaper advertisement, if that is appropriate. It will be necessary to advertise like this if the company has issued share warrants. These are 'bearer' documents; the current holders' details appear neither on the warrants nor on the registers, so the company has no means of knowing who holds warrants.

Notice by post

4.6 Evidence that a **notice** was **correctly addressed** and **posted** is treated as **conclusive** evidence that the notice was duly given: Table A Article 114. As an additional safeguard, it is usually provided (Table A Article 39) that non-receipt of a notice (for example, if it has been properly sent, but got lost in the post) is not to invalidate the proceedings of the meeting.

4.7 For the purpose of reckoning the period of 'clear days' notice which is required, it is assumed that a notice which has been posted will be delivered within a given time.

(a) The **1948 Table A** (Article 131) assumed that a notice would arrive within **24** hours of posting.

(b) The **1985 Table A** (Article 115) is nearer reality in assuming delivery within **48** hours of posting.

4.8 The articles do not usually require the company to use first class post, but the court would be unsympathetic to a company which sent notices by second class post and then insisted that they must be deemed to be served within 24 (or even 48) hours of posting.

Notice by fax

4.9 Notice sent by facsimile transmission ('fax') fulfils the requirement for written notice under s 369 but is not covered by Article 112 (personal delivery or delivery by post). In addition, transmission by fax cannot be conclusive evidence of giving notice under Article 115, nor is it covered by Article 39, which states that non-receipt of a properly posted letter does not invalidate a meeting.

4.10 However, where a document is not required by *law* (not regulation) to be delivered personally, fax transmission is good service provided it can be shown that the document was received, complete and legible, by the person to whom it was sent: *Hastie & Jenkerson v MacMahon 1990*.

4.11 There still remains the problem of the intended recipient denying receipt; sending a fax is not conclusive evidence of notice under Article 114. This problem can probably only be remedied by altering the articles so that sending a properly addressed fax is conclusive evidence.

4.12 The Electronic Communications Act 2000 (discussed further in Chapter 14) will amend Table A to allow the use of fax and other electronic means of communication, such as e-mail. New companies will be able to adopt a Table A that permits electronic communications; any contrary provisions in existing articles (such as Article 112) will be overridden without the need for the company to change its articles. (ICSA recommends that companies do change their articles as soon as convenient, but the Act will allow them to use electronic communications before changing their articles).

Special cases

4.13 There are standard provisions (Table A Articles 112 and 116) for serving notice in special cases.

(a) If more than one person holds shares jointly, notice to all holders is effected by duly **giving notice** to the **'senior' holder** - the one who is named first on the register. Joint holders sometimes split their holdings and have each smaller holding registered with a different sequence of names, so that *each* person is entitled to a notice as first-named holder of one portion.

(b) If a member has died, his **personal representatives** may give notice to the company, requiring it to send notices of meetings to them, addressed as they require and at a UK address. Until this is done, the company is discharging its obligation if it continues to send notices to the member as usual. The same procedure applies to a bankrupt member and his trustee.

5 REQUIRED PERIOD OF NOTICE 12/99

5.1 The standard period of notice (s 369) is:

(a) **21 days:**

- For an AGM
- For a meeting at which a special resolution (s 378(2)) is to be passed

(b) **14 days** in any other case; except that

(c) **7 days' notice** suffices for an unlimited company

5.2 The articles of association may set longer periods than these statutory minima, and the actual notice given may be longer still (since there is no maximum period of notice). Note, however, that under s 369 the articles are void if they attempt to provide for shorter periods of notice than these.

5.3 The articles invariably require that the period of notice be reckoned to **exclude** the day on which the **notice** is deemed to **be received** and the day of the **meeting**. Table A (1948) Article 50 puts it this way, but the expression **clear days** (used in the 1985 Table A Article 38) is a briefer way of saying the same thing.

5.4 Unless the notice is served personally, the company should make allowance - according to the articles - for time in the post before notice is deemed to be served. 1985 Table A articles state that notice shall be deemed to be given **48 hours** after being posted (Article 115). **First class post** should be used.

5.5 For example, if the secretary posts notices for an AGM (requiring 21 clear days) on 1 March, he should allow 48 hours in transit so that notice is to be served on 3 March. The next day (4 March) is the first of the 21 clear days of notice, which expires on 24 March. The AGM may properly be held on the following day (25 March).

March		
1		date of posting
2	48 hrs	
3		date of service
4-24		21 days' notice
25		date of meeting

5.6 If the articles do not specify how a period of notice is to be reckoned, case law indicates that it must be done on a 'clear days' basis.

Waiver of period of notice 12/98

5.7 There is provision in s 369 for the **waiver** of the statutory period of notice (though not, as we have said, of the notice itself). The waiver may be given:

(a) For an AGM, by **all members** entitled to attend and vote

(b) For an EGM, by a **majority** of members who:

(i) Together hold at **least 95 per cent** of the **shares** giving the right to attend and vote; or

(ii) **Represent 95 per cent** of **voting rights**, if there is no share capital; or

(iii) In the case of a private company which has passed an elective resolution to this effect, by **less than 95%** of the shares giving the right to attend and vote (or 95% of the capital), but not by less than 90% in either case: s 369(4)

5.8 The waiver is actually expressed (s 369(3)) in terms of acceptance of 'shorter notice' of the meeting - or a particular item of business - than the standard period. No form of waiver is prescribed. It may therefore be oral, and it may be given in advance of the meeting, at the meeting, or after it.

5.9 In practice, however, it is usual, and prudent, to add a **standard form of waiver** at the foot of the notice of the meeting and ask the members to sign it. Then there is a record of the waiver and sufficient evidence that members understand what the situation is when they attend the meeting in question.

5.10 Although it is always better to get a signed waiver, it is not absolutely necessary to do so if *all* the shareholders are present at an AGM.

Use of the waiver

5.11 Small companies in which the shareholders are also the directors often find it convenient to use the waiver procedure to complete the routine business of an AGM very swiftly.

(a) The directors first resolve to convene the AGM (and the chairman signs the minutes of a board meeting to that effect).

(b) In theory, each shareholder should receive his own copy of the notice - but his presence at the meeting makes it unnecessary, since he is *deemed* to have received notice.

(c) A single copy of the notice of AGM is produced, with an attached waiver, which is signed by the members. For example:

> 'We, being all the members of ABC Ltd, hereby agree to waive the statutory period of 21 days' notice of the Annual General Meeting and consent to holding the said meeting forthwith for the purpose of transacting the business of the meeting as set out in the above notice.'

(d) The meeting is held, and the chairman signs the formal minutes which have been prepared in advance.

(e) On the same occasion two directors may sign the annual accounts, submitted to the meeting (s 238). The preliminary board meeting may also have approved the accounts and authorised their signature, if this had not been done previously.

(f) A director and the secretary sign the annual return (s 365(2)).

(g) The annual accounts and the annual return are sent to the Companies Registry.

6 CONTENT OF NOTICE 12/99

6.1 There is no single prescription for the content of notice of a company general meeting.

(a) Certain **statutory points**, and any requirements in the **articles** of association, should be observed.

(b) Convenience dictates that the notice should also serve as a **skeleton agenda**.

(c) There is an overriding requirement that any notice shall fairly disclose the purpose of the meeting and avoid 'trickiness'.

Content of notices

6.2 The following items should be included:

(a) **Date, time** and **place** of the meeting

(b) Whether the meeting is an **extraordinary** general meeting, or **annual** general meeting: s 366C

Agenda?

(c) Details of the **business** to be transacted

(d) **Identification** and the full text of **special** or **extraordinary resolutions**: s 378 (1) and (2)

(e) **Identification** of **elective resolutions** and statement of their **terms**: s 379A (2)

(f) Details of **special notice** (if not given separately)

(g) Members' **right** to appoint **proxies**, including a statement that a proxy need not be a member of the company;

(h) (i) The name and a printed signature of the secretary as the officer who issues the notice; and

(ii) The authority for its issue

6.3 General secretarial practice has developed a form of notice which is convenient and in general use. An example is given below.

Knowe Shadi Dealers Limited

ANNUAL GENERAL MEETING

Notice is hereby given that the sixth annual general meeting of the company will be held at [place] on [date] at [time] for the following purposes:

1 To receive the report of the directors and the accounts for the year ended [date] and to declare a dividend.

2 To elect directors in place of those retiring.

3 To reappoint the auditors and to authorise the directors to fix their remuneration.

4 To consider and if thought fit pass the following resolution which will be proposed as a special resolution:

THAT the articles of association of the company be altered by omitting therefrom Article 93

By order of the board

Dated .... J Smith

Registered Office Secretary

[address]

A member entitled to attend and vote at the meeting is entitled to appoint a proxy to attend and vote instead of him. A proxy need not be a member of the company.

Nature of business

6.4 If the articles follow the 1985 Table A (Article 38) they will specify that:

> 'The notice shall specify the time and place of the meeting and the general nature of the business to be transacted and, in the case of an annual general meeting, shall specify the meeting as such.'

6.5 However many companies still have articles in the form of the 1948 Table A (Article 50):

> 'The notice shall .... specify the place, the day and the hour of the meeting and, in case of *special business*, the general nature of that business.'

6.6 If we refer to Article 52:

> 'All business shall be deemed *special* that is transacted at an extraordinary general meeting, and also all that is transacted at an annual general meeting, with the exception of declaring a dividend, the consideration of the accounts, balance sheets, and the reports of the directors and auditors, the election of directors in place of those retiring, and the appointment of, and the fixing of the remuneration of, the auditors.'

"ordinary/usual business"

6.7 The effect of articles in the 1948 Table A form is that routine AGM business concerning accounts, dividends, directors and auditors (which is conventionally referred to as 'ordinary' or 'usual' business) need not be specified in an AGM notice - though the same items, included in an EGM notice, would become 'special business'. The 1985 Table A indirectly recognises this, requiring that the 'general nature' of *all* business of every general meeting shall be specified in the notice.

6.8 You should note the difference between 'special' and 'ordinary' business in any case, since exam questions have required an understanding of them.

Other contents of notice

6.9 The AGM notice of a listed company (one which has issued securities which are listed on the Stock Exchange) is required to show, in a footnote, the **time** and **place** at which **copies** of **directors' service agreements** may be inspected.

6.10 The company is required to give the **address** of its **registered office**, identified as such, on its 'business letters': s 351. In case a notice of a general meeting might be considered to fall into this category, it is wise to include the address, as shown in the example.

6.11 More detail of the business may be included if the company wishes.

(a) The amount of the **proposed dividend** might be added, though the directors' report issued with the accounts will disclose the figure.

(b) It is also common to expand the '**re-election**' of directors' item to show the names of the directors who retire.

6.12 Notices to holders of securities that have been admitted to CREST must include a time to be specified in the notice of the meeting for calculating attending and voting entitlements. This time may not be more than 48 hours before the meeting.

Adequate disclosure

6.13 There is an overriding requirement that the notice shall disclose 'the general nature of the business' to be done at the meeting, and sometimes a literal compliance with technical rules does not suffice. It has been said that the business 'must be stated fairly; it must not be stated so as to mislead': *Kaye v Croydon Tramways Co 1898*.

6.14 One form of disclosure is to set out in the notice of the meeting the **full text of the resolutions to be proposed**. The requirements on this point are as follows.

(a) If a resolution is a **special** or an **extraordinary** resolution, it is a statutory rule (s 378) that the text shall be set out **in full** in the notice. (This has further implications, relating to amendments, which are considered in Chapter 8.)

(b) If it is an **ordinary resolution, but not of a routine nature** (so that it would be 'special business' under articles in the 1948 Table A form) it is standard procedure to set out in the notice the **full text** of the resolution.

(c) If it is an **ordinary resolution of a routine nature** it is not necessary or usual to set out the text in full. It is standard procedure to indicate its subject.

Additional information

6.15 It is not necessary to supplement a notice of a meeting with an explanatory circular. However it may be advisable to disclose fairly what is the purpose of the meeting. There is also a growing number of specific requirements for the issue of a circular or at least recognition that one *may* be issued.

(a) In convening a meeting or meetings to consider a **scheme of arrangement** (s 425) the directors are required to issue an 'explanatory statement' which among other things discloses how the scheme affects their personal interests: s 425.

(b) In seeking approval for *an* **issue of equity securities** for cash (otherwise than on a rights issue basis) the directors are required to issue a statement on various points, including their reasons: s 95(5).

(c) A prescribed minimum fraction of the membership may require the company (at their expense) to circulate a **memorandum** of 1,000 words or less on the business of a forthcoming meeting: s 375. A director threatened with removal from office (s 303) and an auditor (in specified circumstances) may also require the company to issue an explanatory memorandum from them to the members, as long as it is of reasonable length and not defamatory in character.

(d) If a company has securities listed on the Stock Exchange it must issue an **explanatory circular** with the notice of any meeting which is to do business other than routine AGM business. The circular must be submitted in draft form to the Stock Exchange for advance approval.

6.16 Where a circular is issued, it is treated as part of the notice of the meeting, so that the two documents are to be read together.

6.17 Another method of providing information to members in preparation for a general meeting is to make documents **available for inspection** at the company's office, or some other address(es) mentioned in the notice of the meeting. A statutory example of this is where there is a proposed contract for the off-market purchase of own shares (s 164). This procedure is not an adequate substitute for an explanatory circular, where that is required by law or Stock Exchange regulations.

6.18 Note the practical distinction between large public and small private companies. The former need to keep up a flow of communication between directors and shareholders, whether the business of the meeting is special or ordinary: a 'chairman's statement' or 'directors' review of the year's operations' may be sent as a supplement to the annual accounts, issued with the most routine AGM notice. It would be pointless, on the other hand, for the two directors of a private company to issue an explanatory circular to themselves as the sole shareholders.

Notice of Meeting

Notice is hereby given that the 1998 Annual General Meeting of BAA plc will be held in the Fleming and Whittle Rooms at The Queen Elizabeth II Conference Centre, Broad Sanctuary, Westminister, London SW1 on **Thursday 9 July 1998 at 11.15am** to transact the following business.

Resolutions

1 To receive the reports of the directors and auditors and the accounts for the year ended 31 March 1998

2 To declare the following directors appointed by the board since the last Annual General Meeting:

3 M J Roberts

4 B J Collie

5 J L Hoerner

To reappoint the following director retiring by rotation:

6 J R F Walls

Details of the directors proposed for reappointment are given in the Annual Report and Annual Review 1997/98.

7 To reappoint Deloitte & Touche as auditors and to authorise the directors to determine their remuneration.

To consider the following special resolutions:

8 The directors be and they are hereby authorised, pursuant to section 95(1) of the Companies Act 1985 and in place of all existing authorities which are hereby revoked, to allot equity securities (as defined in section 94 of that Act) for cash as if section 89(1) of that Act did not apply to such allotment provided that this power shall be limited to:

(a) The allotment of equity securities in connection with a rights issue in favour of the holders of ordinary shares where the equity securities respectively attributable to the interests of all such shareholders are proportionate (as nearly as may be) to the respective numbers of ordinary shares held by them subject to such exclusions or other arrangements as the directors may think necessary or expedient in relation to fractional entitlements or as a results of legal or practical problems arising under the laws of any territory, or requirements of any recognised regulatory body or stock exchange in any territory; and

(b) The allotment (otherwise than pursuant to sub-paragraph (a) above) of equity securities up to an aggregate nominal valued of £52,750,000, being 52,750,000 ordinary shares of £1 each, such authority to expire on the date of the next Annual General Meeting after the passing of this resolution, save that the company may before such expiry make an offer or agreement which would or might require equity securities to be allotted after such expiry and the directors may allot equity securities in pursuance of such offer or agreement as if the said authority had not expired.

Resolution 8 renews an existing authority given to the directors each year to allot shares for cash to persons other than existing shareholders up to a maximum of 5% of the company's issued share capital. This authority gives the directors flexibility to take advantage of business opportunities as they arise and the 5% limit ensures that existing shareholders' interests are protected.

9 The company be and it is hereby unconditionally authorised and in place of all existing authorities which are hereby revoked to make market purchases (as defined in section 163(3)) of the Companies Act 1985) of the company's ordinary shares up to an aggregate of 52,750,000 shares at a price per share (exclusive of expenses) of not less that £1 and not more than 5% above the average of the market values for those shares for the five business days immediately before the date of purchase, such authority (unless previously revoked or renewed) to expire on the date of the next Annual General Meeting after the passing of this resolution save that the company may before such expiry make a contract to purchase shares which would or might require to be executed wholly or partly after such expiry and may make a purchase of shares pursuant to such contract as if the said authority had not expired.

Resolution 9 renews an existing authority for the company to make market purchases of its own shares up to a maximum of 5% of its issued share capital. This authority would only be used if the purchase would improve the company's earnings per share and be in the best interests of shareholders generally.

By order of the board

Rachel Rowson
Secretary
22 May 1998

Registered offices
130 Wilton Road
London SW1V 1LQ

Notes

1 Shareholders are entitled to appoint a proxy or proxies to attend the meeting and, on a poll, vote on their behalf. A proxy need not be a shareholder.

2 Directors' service agreements are available for inspection during normal business hours at the company's registered office and at The Queen Elizabeth II Conference Centre from 10.00 am on 9 July 1998 until the end of the Annual General Meeting.

Chapter roundup

- It is the role of the directors to decide to **convene** general company meetings, although in some circumstances this responsibility can fall to a single director, to members, to the court or to the DTI.
- The secretary sends the **notice** for a meeting and must be careful to send it to all the persons entitled to receive it. Notice can be waived.
- Notice must be served in accordance with **statute** and with the company's regulations; in particular the **correct period of notice** is crucial.
- The content of the notice is not strictly controlled by law, though the secretary should be careful not to miss anything out.

Test your knowledge

1 Who may call the AGM of a company? (see paras 1.1, 1.3)

2 What procedure should be adopted if it is decided to postpone the business for which a meeting has already been called? (1.5)

3 What is the effect of failure to send notice of a meeting to a person entitled to it? (3.6)

4 What are the standard methods, provided by Table A, for serving notices of meetings? (4.4)

5 What are the required periods of notice for general meetings of companies? (5.1)

6 Explain and illustrate what is meant by 'clear days' notice'. (5.3)

7 How may the prescribed period of notice be waived? (5.7 - 5.8)

8 Mention two points which would be found in an AGM notice. (6.2)

9 Explain the distinction between ordinary and special business of a company general meeting, which is found in some articles. (6.5 - 6.6)

10 In what circumstances would the full text of a resolution be included in the notice? (6.14)

11 When may an additional circular be issued with the notice? (6.15)

Now try illustrative question 5 at the end of the Study Text

Chapter 7

CONDUCT OF COMPANY GENERAL MEETINGS

This chapter covers the following topics.

Introduction

The proceedings of a general meeting are only valid and binding on its members if the meeting has been properly:

(a) *Convened:* the previous chapter dealt mainly with the procedure for convening general meetings by the issue of notice

(b) *Constituted:* to constitute a meeting there must be present:

(i) a chairman properly appointed; and
(ii) a sufficient number of persons to constitute a quorum

(c) *Conducted:* a general meeting must pay particular attention to the procedure by which it arrives at its decisions

This chapter is concerned with requirements (b) and (c).

1 THE CHAIRMAN **6/98, 6/99**

1.1 The articles of association (Table A Articles 42 - 43) provide that at a general meeting:

(a) The **chairman** of the board of directors (if any) shall **preside**. (The manner in which a board appoints its chairman is described in Chapter 2).

(b) If the chairman of the board is not present within 15 minutes of the time fixed for the start of the meeting, or if he is unwilling to act, the **directors** may **appoint** one of themselves to be chairman of the general meeting.

(c) If no director is present within 15 minutes of the time for starting the meeting, or if there is no director present who is willing to take the chair, the **members** present may **elect one** of themselves to be chairman of the meeting.

1.2 If the articles do not make these provisions for the appointment of a chairman, the members present at each meeting have a **statutory power** to elect a chairman for the meeting: s 370(5). This is merely a 'fall-back' provision which is rarely applied, as the articles invariably do provide for a chairman.

1.3 If the chairman has been appointed under the regulations, which is the normal case, he can only be removed under the regulations: the meeting cannot usually vote him out of the chair. But a meeting which has properly chosen its own chairman may similarly remove him, by carrying a vote of no confidence and electing another chairman.

1.4 If there is some irregularity in the election of a chairman, objection should be made at once. (In particular, you might note that a person cannot chair a meeting while his own election as chairman is being debated and voted on; he must vacate the chair for the required period. The minutes should state that someone else was 'in the chair' for the point.) If the meeting proceeds under such a chairman, it will be taken to have waived the irregularity, and to have acquiesced in his appointment.

Powers of a chairman 6/00

1.5 The Companies Act 1985 does not define the powers and duties of a chairman of a general meeting. He has common law powers and duties, which may be varied or augmented by the articles of association. Table A provides that:

(a) As regards adjournment:

(i) The chairman **may** (with the **consent** of a meeting at which a quorum is present) and **must** (if **so directed** by the meeting) adjourn the meeting (Article 45).

(ii) If the meeting is **inquorate**, there is **automatic adjournment** (Article 41).

(iii) There may be a **residual power** in the chairman to adjourn if the provisions set out in the articles are inadequate or inappropriate; this is suggested by the following case. This is illustrated by *Byng v London Life Association 1989* discussed below.

In addition to his limited powers under the articles, the chairman has common law powers to adjourn the meeting for a short time to prevent or quell disorder;

(b) As regards voting:

(i) The chairman has a **casting vote** (Article 50).

(ii) In case of dispute as to a **right to vote**, the **decision** of the chairman is final and conclusive (Article 58).

(iii) In a vote on a show of hands, a **declaration** of the result by the chairman is **conclusive**, unless a **poll** is duly **demanded** (Article 47). This is statutory (s 378(4)) when he declares the vote on a special or an extraordinary resolution.

(iv) The chairman (among others) may **demand a poll** (Article 46). If a demand is made for a poll, it may only be withdrawn with the chairman's consent (Article 48). The chairman decides on the arrangements for holding a poll (Article 49).

General duties of the chairman 6/00

1.6 The chairman's general duties, which arise from the common law interpretation of his position, include the following.

(a) He should satisfy himself:

(i) The meeting has been **duly convened** by notice.

(ii) It is **quorate at the start** and, if the articles so require, **throughout** the meeting. If it is not, or ceases to be, quorate he must declare it adjourned.

(b) He should do all that he can to **maintain order**. If a member's behaviour is so disruptive that the business of the meeting cannot reasonably be continued, the chairman may adjourn the meeting or expel the member. Expulsion can have serious consequences; hence first the member should be warned of the threat of expulsion and asked to behave properly.

Marshall v Tinnelly 1937 illustrates that the chairman does have powers to order the removal of a member if the member is behaving in a disorderly fashion. In *Lucas v Mason 1875* the stewards expelled a member without instructions from the chair. The court held that the stewards exercised their own judgement and not that of the chairman, who could not be held liable.

(c) He should **guide** the **meeting through** its **business** in the sequence of the agenda, or in whatever modified order the meeting agrees on.

(d) He should give reasonable opportunities for the **expression** of **different points** of **view,** keeping members to the business under discussion, and discouraging provocative, irrelevant or long-winded speeches.

(e) He should give immediate **rulings on any points of order** which may be raised.

(f) He should **ascertain** the '**sense** of the meeting' by putting each motion to the vote in a proper order and manner, and declaring the result.

Points of order 6/00

1.7 Once a meeting has commenced or 'proceeded to' business, and especially if that business includes binding decisions, it is essential to ensure that:

- The proceedings of the meeting are valid.
- The members are protected from the 'manipulation' of procedure by any party.

This is why the observance of the standing orders or regulations is so important. If any member finds or suspects some irregularity in the convening, constitution or conduct of the meeting, he can submit an objection to the chairman. This is called a **point of order.**

1.8 A point of order may be raised by any member (even if he has already spoken in the debate), at any time and without notice. The person speaking at the time must allow himself to be interrupted, and sit down. A point of order is not generally open to discussion, but the chairman may invite brief remarks from other members.

1.9 The decision on any allegations of irregularity rests with the chairman: his ruling must be immediate, and should be accepted by the meeting. (Legal proceedings may be instituted after the meeting to have a chairman's ruling annulled, but this is only likely if it can be proved that the chairman was not acting in good faith, and that hardship was caused by his ruling.)

1.10 The point of order is disposed of by the chairman's decision, and the member who was interrupted by it may simply resume, unless of course the ruling has been against his right to speak.

1.11 Common objections which may be raised as point of order include the following:

(a) A **defect** in the **convening** or **constitution** of the meeting. There has been insufficient notice, or lack of quorum.

(b) Other **breach** of the regulations. A motion has not been seconded as required, a member is attempting to speak or vote without the right to do so, the chairman is attempting to adjourn without the meeting's consent etc.

(c) A **defect** in the **motion** or **amendment** before the meeting. It is beyond the scope of the notice, or outside the power or terms of reference of the meeting (ultra vires).

(d) The use of **improper language**.

2 DRAFTING AN AGENDA FOR A GENERAL MEETING 12/99

2.1 The agenda will vary according to the type and formality of the meeting and the particular business to be discussed. A typical agenda might include the following.

(a) **Membership**: an optional item allowing the chairman to introduce new members or allude to retirements or resignations

(b) **Apologies for absence**

(c) **Minutes of the last meeting:** read out, or previously circulated

(d) **Matters arising** from the minutes

(e) **Business of the present meeting**: presentation of reports, resolutions etc. as appropriate. This will usually include:

(i) Chairman's report on progress and performance
(ii) Treasurer's report, presentation of accounts and other financial reports
(iii) Declaration of dividends (if any)
(iv) Election of officers
(v) Appointment of auditors, and fixing of their remuneration

(f) **Any other business**

(g) **Date of the next meeting**

3 QUORUM 6/99

3.1 To recapitulate on the important principles explained in earlier chapters:

(a) As a **general principle** (to which company law makes some exceptions) the nature of a meeting requires the *presence* of at least two persons entitled to take part in the proceedings: *Sharp v Dawes 1876.*

(b) The **articles of association** may fix a minimum number of persons whose presence is required to constitute a meeting - a 'quorum'. It may only be one person in those cases where the law permits one person to constitute a meeting; it may also be more than the normal minimum of two.

Standard quorum

3.2 The standard **quorum** under the articles (Table A Article 40) is expressed as follows.

> 'Two persons entitled to vote upon the business to be transacted, each being a member or a proxy for a member or a duly authorised representative of a corporation, shall be a quorum.'

3.3 If the articles make no provision for a quorum, the standard now is **two members** personally present: s 370(4).

3.4 Although most companies have a quorum provision in one or other of these simple forms, it is possible to adopt a special quorum, being one which requires a quorum to include a named shareholder or shareholders who between them hold a prescribed minimum proportion of the issued share capital.

3.5 For a class meeting the quorum may be fixed by the articles. Otherwise, it is **two persons** holding or representing by proxy at least one-third in nominal value of the issued shares of the class.

Reckoning the quorum: Table A Article 40

3.6 Even if the quorum may include proxies (Table A Article 40, quoted above) the overriding legal principle still applies: the presence of two persons is required to constitute a **meeting**. One member who is present in a dual capacity (in person and as proxy for other(s), as in *Re Sanitary Carbon Co 1877*) does not constitute a meeting: he is counted as only one person. In addition the articles must specify if proxies are to be included; if not, only members entitled to vote will be computed in determining whether a quorum is present: *Henderson v Louttit 1894*.

3.7 If the quorum is more than two, however, one person present in a dual capacity may be counted in terms of the members whom he represents as proxy - provided that at least one other person is present, so that a meeting exists.

3.8 The current Table A formula (Article 40) expressly mentions that a '**duly authorised representative** of a corporation' may be counted in reckoning a quorum. The directors of another company (or other corporate body) may resolve to authorise any person to act as its representative at a general or a class meeting of a company: s 374. The representative is not a proxy, but he has all the rights given to a member present in person.

3.9 The Table A formula (Article 40) also requires that only 'persons entitled to vote' at the meeting may be reckoned in the quorum. As a rule, and unlike a directors' meeting, a member may vote at a general meeting even if he has a personal interest in the matter on which the vote is taken: *North-West Transportation Co v Beatty 1887*.

3.10 The following circumstances would, however, bring the 'entitlement' restriction into play.

(a) A member may be **holding only one class of shares**, typically preference shares, which carry a right to attend a general meeting but not to vote at it, on some business at least. As an example, preference shares might give the right to vote at general meetings only on a resolution to vary the rights of the shares or to put the company in liquidation. A preference shareholder could be counted in the quorum for *that* business, but not for other business (if any) of the meeting, since he was not entitled to vote on it.

(b) On a resolution to allow the company to **purchase** its **own shares** by 'off-market' purchase, the would-be vendor may not:

   (i) Vote on a show of hands; nor

   (ii) In voting on a poll, cast the votes attached to shares which he is to sell: ss 164(5) and 174(2).

   He could not be counted in the quorum for that item of business. (If he *does* vote, and the resolution is passed - when it would not have been passed without his votes - the resolution is ineffective.)

Mustering and maintaining a quorum

3.11 Table A Article 40 also provides that:

> 'No business shall be transacted at any meeting unless a quorum *is present*.'

This means that at every stage of the meeting there must be a quorum for the business then under consideration.

3.12 If a meeting begins with a quorum but:

(a) Persons forming part of the quorum leave the meeting, reducing the number present to less than the quorum, before the business is completed

(b) Persons present are disqualified from voting on an item of business, leaving insufficient voting members to make a quorum for that item

the meeting becomes '**inquorate**', and cannot continue.

3.13 The above formula differs from the corresponding Article 53 of the 1948 Table A, which is still found in the articles of many companies. The 1948 formula is:

> 'No business shall be transacted at any general meeting unless a quorum of members **is present at the time when the meeting proceeds to business**.'

It has been held (in *Re Hartley Baird Ltd 1955*) that, when this form of words is used, a quorum is only necessary at the start of the meeting: the meeting may continue despite the subsequent 'loss' of the quorum. In the absence of any reference in the articles, it should be presumed that a quorum has to be present throughout the meeting.

The effect of inquorate meetings

3.14 If a meeting is inquorate, it must be adjourned. The standard formula is (Table A Article 41) as follows:

> 'If such a quorum is not present within half an hour from the time appointed for the meeting, or if during the meeting such a quorum ceases to be present, the meeting shall stand adjourned to the same day in the next week at the same time and place or to such time and place as the directors may determine.'

3.15 Again there are differences between the 1985 formula above and the 1948 wording, which still appears in the articles of many companies:

> 'If within half an hour from the time appointed for the meeting a quorum is not present **the meeting, if convened upon the requisition of members, shall be dissolved;** in any other case it shall stand adjourned to the same day in the next week, at the same time and place or to such other day and at such other time and place as the directors may determine [and if at the adjourned meeting a quorum is not present within half an hour from the time appointed for the meeting, the members present shall be a quorum].'

The words which have been emboldened prevent the company from wasting time and money on fruitless meetings: a meeting requisitioned by the members is clearly pointless if they do not even bother to turn up.

3.16 The absence of a quorum will generally invalidate the proceedings. It has, however, been held that if a board meeting which is inquorate resolves to convene a general meeting, and that meeting is properly held, its proceedings will not be made invalid by the defect in the meeting which convened it.

4 PROXIES **Specimen paper, 12/98, 12/99**

4.1 S 372(1) provides that, in the case of any company which has a share capital, any member of a company entitled to attend and vote at a meeting of it is entitled to appoint another person (whether a member or not) as his proxy to attend and vote instead of him.

4.2 To bring this right to the attention of members, s 372(3) requires that in every notice calling a meeting of the company must appear, with reasonable prominence, a statement that a member entitled to attend and vote is entitled to **appoint a proxy**, or where that is allowed, one or more proxies to attend and vote instead of him, and that a proxy need not also be a member.

4.3 S 372 also provides for the following limitations and modifications of the right to appoint a proxy.

(a) At a general meeting of a **private** company, a proxy has a statutory right to **speak** at the meeting. At a general meeting of a **public** company he may **only speak if the articles so provide** (or if the chairman allows him to do so).

(b) A member of a **private** company may **not appoint more than one proxy** unless the articles permit him to do so.

(c) A proxy has **no right** to **vote** on a **show of hands,** unless the articles permit him to do so. He does, however, have the same rights as the member whom he represents to demand or to join in a demand for a **poll**, on which he *is* entitled to vote: s 372. We will look briefly at each of these points.

4.4 The statutory right given to members of *public* companies to appoint two or more proxies recognises the fact that shares of large public companies are often held in the names of nominee companies (typically those set up by banks or by stockbrokers to meet the needs of their clients). Such a nominee shareholder may represent more than one beneficial owner, and may therefore be instructed to vote for a resolution, by some clients, and against it, by others.

4.5 No right is given under s 383 to proxies to see the minutes of a meeting they attend. Table A Article 59 allows a member to 'appoint more than one proxy to attend on the same occasion', and it does not confine this right to members of *public* companies alone.

4.6 If the articles do give proxies a right to vote on a show of hands, a member who is present both in his own right and as proxy for another member has only one vote on a show of hands - he cannot hold up both hands at once!

4.7 Companies limited by guarantee usually have no share capital, so the statutory provisions above do not apply to them. The articles of such companies:

- Refer to the Table A regulations as not applying to the company (Table C Article 1)
- Usually do confer some right to appoint proxies (Table C Article 8)

4.8 The same statutory rules on proxies apply to class meetings as to general meetings. Remember a 'duly authorised representative of a corporation' is not a proxy (see Section 3).

Form of proxy cards

4.9 Any written form of appointment will suffice, unless the articles specify a form which *must* be used: *Isaacs v Chapman 1916*. Table A Article 61, in providing a recommended form of proxy card (see below) also permits 'a form as near thereto as circumstances allow or any other form which is usual or which the directors may approve.'

4.10 In the case of public companies, it is standard practice to issue, with the notice of a general meeting, a printed **proxy card** in the form of:

- A postcard, pre-stamped and addressed to the company
- A page of the AGM documents which can be detached and folded into envelope size

The shareholder is invited to fill in the particulars in the blank spaces and to appoint the chairman of the meeting (or any other director) to be his proxy at the meeting. He may insert the name of some other person as his proxy if he wishes.

4.11 A *listed* company is required by the Stock Exchange to issue '**two-way proxies**', on which the member can give instructions to his proxy as to **how he is to vote on each resolution**. If the member does not give written or verbal instructions the proxy is authorised to vote as he sees fit.

4.12 Note that this is not postal voting, since there may not be a poll for the proxy to vote on. Where there are contentious matters to be decided, however, and a poll is likely to be held, the issue of proxy cards enables shareholders to use their votes without having to attend the meeting in person.

4.13 The articles may require formalities, such as the signature of another person as witness to the member's signature on a proxy card. Proxies which do not comply with those requirements should be rejected as invalid: *Harben v Philips 1883*.

4.14 The modern trend is to avoid undue formality; the Table A Article 60/61 form of proxy card does not require anything more than the signatory's signature and the date, by way of execution.

Table A Article 60: standard form of proxy card

"PLC/Limited

I/We, , of , being a member/members of the above-named company, hereby appoint of , or failing him, of , as my/our proxy to vote in my/our name[s] and on my behalf at the annual/extraordinary general meeting of that company to be held on 20 , and at any adjournment thereof.

Signed on 20 ."

Table A Article 61: standard form of two-way proxy card

"PLC/Limited

I/We, , of , being a member/members of the above-named company, hereby appoint of , or failing him, of , as my/our proxy to vote in my/our name[s] and on my behalf at the annual/extraordinary general meeting of that company to be held on 20 , and at any adjournment thereof. This form is to be used in respect of the resolutions mentioned below as follows:

Resolution No 1 *for *against

Resolution No 2 *for *against.

*Strike out whichever is not desired.

Unless otherwise instructed, the proxy may vote as he thinks fit or abstain from voting.

Signed this day of 20 ."

Use of proxy cards

4.15 As proxy cards are completed and returned, it is useful to:

(a) **Check them** immediately **against** the **register of members**, in case a transfer of shares has been registered since the card was issued

(b) **Scrutinise them** for correct formal completion

4.16 A schedule of votes, for and against each resolution on a proxy vote, is prepared: this saves time if there is a vote on a poll at the meeting. Moreover, if a demand for a poll is made, the chairman **may disclose** the number of **proxy votes**, for and against, which have been lodged *before* the poll is taken; the demand might then be withdrawn. If a poll is taken, the Chairman should disclose the number of proxy votes lodged for and against the motion as part of the announcement of the result of the poll.

4.17 If it is found necessary to reject a proxy card the company should at once **inform** the **shareholder**; he may still have time to send in a correct proxy card.

4.18 There are two statutory rules (s 372) designed to prevent abuse of this procedure.

(a) The articles may fix a **time** by which proxy cards must be returned (usually to the registered office or the transfer office) in order to be valid. However the article is *void* (under s 372) if the deadline set is more than 48 hours before the meeting.

(b) Proxy cards (or any other invitation to appoint proxies) may only be issued at the company's expense if they are sent to **all members** entitled to receive notice of, and to vote at, the meeting.

4.19 The proxy card is usually so worded that it may be used at the resumption of an adjourned meeting, if the original meeting is adjourned.

4.20 The articles (eg Table A Article 62) may provide for the delivery of proxy cards in the interval between the meeting and a poll, if it is to be held on a later occasion.

(a) If the poll is to be taken 48 hours after it is demanded, proxies should be deposited at **least 24 hours** before the poll.

(b) If the poll is to be taken within 48 hours of the demand, proxies should be delivered to the chairman or secretary, or to any director, **at** the **meeting** at which the poll was demanded.

Otherwise, the appointment will not be valid.

4.21 Unless a standard proxy card is very elaborately worded, it cannot anticipate all the possible amendments to the resolution(s) set out in the notice of the meeting. If a substantial amendment is carried, the proxy's authority to vote is unaffected - but he no longer has instructions as to how he should vote. He should exercise his discretion in whatever fashion he honestly believes is likely to reflect the wishes of his appointor.

Revocation of a proxy and change in instructions

4.22 The appointment of a proxy is not irrevocable, nor does it prevent the member from deciding to attend the meeting and vote in person. If he *does* **attend in person** his presence is an automatic and effective **cancellation** of the authority given to his proxy. Hence in a vote on a poll it is always necessary to check the list of members who have voted in person against the list of proxy voters, to ensure that the same shares have not inadvertently been voted twice.

4.23 To avoid confusion or fraud over revocation, the articles (Table A Article 63) require that **revocation is effective** only if **written notice** of it is delivered to the company before the time when the vote is taken.

4.24 The appointment of a proxy is also terminated by the **death or insanity** of the appointor. In this case, also, a vote cast by the proxy is nonetheless valid, unless the company has had notice of the termination of his authority before the vote is taken.

4.25 A member can also **change** the **instructions** given to a proxy after the card has been deposited, provided the card has been deposited within the specified time limits.

BAA

00006124310

Form of proxy

If you wish to vote at the 1998 Annual General Meeting of BAA plc but are unable to attend in person, you may appoint a proxy to act on your behalf by completing this form.

hereby appoint the Chairman of the meeting

If you wish to appoint someone other than the Chairman as your proxy, delete the words 'the Chairman of the meeting' and insert the full name of your proxy

as my proxy to attend and, on a poll, vote on my behalf at the Annual General Meeting of BAA plc to be held at 11.15 am on 9 July 1998 and at any adjournment thereof.

Please tell your proxy how to vote by ticking the appropriate box opposite each resolution listed below. If you do not give any specific instructions your proxy may vote or abstain at his/her discretion as he/she may on any other resolution that may be proposed at the meeting.

	For	Against
Resolution 1 To receive the reports and accounts for the year ended 31 March 1998	☐	☐
Resolution 2 To declare a final dividend	☐	☐
Resolution 3 To reappoint Mr M J Roberts as a director	☐	☐
Resolution 4 To reappoint Mr B J Collie as a director	☐	☐
Resolution 5 To reappoint Mr J L Hoerner* as director	☐	☐
Resolution 6 To reappoint Mr J R F Walls as a director	☐	☐
Resolution 7 To reappoint the auditors and authorise the directors to determine their remuneration	☐	☐
Resolution 8 To authorise the directors to allot shares for cash	☐	☐
Resolution 9 To authorise the company to purchase its own shares	☐	☐

Signature .... Date 1998

To be valid this form of proxy must be signed and received at the address overleaf not less that 48 hours before the time appointed for holding the meeting. In the case of joint holders any one holder may sign. In the case of a corporation the form must be under seal or under the hand of a duly authorised officer.

If you wish, you may send this form in an envelope to: IRG plc (BAA Proxies), FREEPOST, Beckenham, Kent BR3 4BR

Completion and return of this form of proxy does not prevent a shareholder from attending the meeting and voting in person in which case any votes cast by the proxy will be excluded.

5 VOTING

5.1 Some companies issue shares which:

(a) Do **not carry a right to vote** at all

(b) Carry a right to vote only on **specified issues**

(c) Allocate votes on a '**weighted**' basis. Weighted shares can effectively mean that for example articles cannot be changed or a director can never be removed from office: *Bushell v Faith 1970*

5.2 The standard voting procedure for individual members is set out in Table A Article 54:

> 'Subject to any rights or restrictions attached to any shares, on a show of hands every member who .... is present in person .... shall have one vote and on a poll every member shall have one vote for every share of which he is a holder.'

Voting on a show of hands **6/00**

5.3 A poll may be demanded even before there is a vote on a show of hands (Table A Article 46). However it is usual for the chairman to take a vote on a show of hands as the first step.

(a) He **calls** on those **members present** in person (*not proxies* unless the articles permit them to vote at this stage) **to vote,** by raising their hands (one hand per member): first those 'For' and then those 'Against' the motion.

(b) The chairman makes a **visual count** and declares the motion carried or lost, as the case may be. This declaration is conclusive (Table A Article 47) unless a poll is then duly demanded. Remember if a poll is demanded, the Chairman can disclose the number of proxies if taking a poll would produce the same result as the vote on a show of hands.

(c) The chairman is **not obliged** to **declare** the **exact number** of **votes** which he reckons have been cast either way. If his declaration is challenged as inaccurate, he may take the vote again (though he is not obliged to) in order that a careful recount may be made of votes for and against.

You should note that unless the **articles provide otherwise** there is **no legal requirement** for **resolutions** to be **seconded**: *Re Horbury Bridge Coal Co 1879*.

5.4 The term casting vote refers to a second vote exercisable by the chairman of a meeting **in addition** *to* his own vote as a member (*Nell v Longbottom 1894*), where there is an equality of votes. The right to a casting vote is derivable only from statute or the regulations of the body concerned as in Table A Article 50. In circumstances where the chairman does not have a right to vote because he is not a voting member he cannot assume the right to a casting vote in the event of an equality of votes: *Weakley v AUEW 1975*.

5.5 The chairman has complete discretion as to how he uses his casting vote. However, it can be argued that the function of a chairman's casting vote is to unlock a deadlocked meeting, enabling it to proceed with the next business. The chairman should therefore use the casting vote **against** the resolution, because a majority has not supported the motion.

5.6 Alternatively the Chairman may abstain from using the casting vote and simply declare a **tied vote**: the **resolution** is then **lost**, since it has not been carried by a majority of votes.

Special situations regarding voting

5.7 The articles usually make provision for a number of special situations affecting voting.

(a) The **personal representatives** of a deceased member, on production of the official 'grant of representation' to the company, may be registered as shareholders in their own right. But unless and until they do so, the articles (Table A Article 31) usually disqualify them from voting, since they are not members.

(b) If shares are registered in the **joint names** of two or more persons, the '**senior' joint holder** - the one whose **name appears first** in the register - may vote, in person or by proxy, to the exclusion of the others: Article 54.

(c) If a member has been found **mentally incapable** of managing his own affairs by a competent UK court under the Mental Health Act 1983, the directors may accept appropriate formal evidence of the legal authority of the person in charge of the member's property, and permit him to cast the votes of the member's shares: Article 55.

(d) If a member is in **arrears in payment of sums due on shares,** he may not cast the votes attached to those shares, either at a general or at a class meeting: Article 56.

(e) If any question arises over a member's right to vote, the **chairman's decision at the time is final and conclusive**. A vote admitted at the time of the meeting must remain valid: Article 57.

Exercise

Outline the requirements relating to proxy cards for general meetings of public companies.

Solution

The purpose of the proxy system is to enable a member of a company to use his votes, on a poll, without having to attend the general meeting in person. The proxy system is particularly valuable to members of large public companies, since few of them find it convenient to attend general meetings. A proxy has the same right to demand a poll as the member whom he represents (s 373(2)), and on contentious matters there is no difficulty in obtaining a vote on a poll, in which proxy votes are effective.

Companies which are listed on The Stock Exchange are required to issue 'two-way' proxy cards to the members for all general meetings. The member fills in the card, instructing his proxy how to vote on each resolution. On this basis, it is most convenient to appoint the chairman of the meeting to vote on a poll as proxy for absent members, but in accordance with their precise instructions. It is not a postal voting system; but it has much the same effect.

Companies may fix a time by which proxy cards must be received at a specified address (usually the registered office or transfer office) if they are to be valid and usable. To prevent attempts to *frustrate* the use of proxy cards, the latest time for receipt of proxy cards may not be earlier than 48 hours before the time fixed for the meeting: s 372(5). If the poll is not held at the meeting itself, the articles (Table A Art 62) may also permit members to send in proxies *after* the meeting - but still 24 hours before the time appointed for holding the poll.

By this means the company has a reasonable time before the meeting in which to scrutinise the proxy forms received, to ensure that they are correct and valid. The articles usually provide that proxy cards must be in a specified form (or as near thereto as is practicable). But this is not usually a material point since most members make use of the printed proxy cards sent to them by the company. They must, however, be correctly executed as required by the articles.

It is usual to draw up lists of proxy cards, showing (a) the members who are voting in this way, (b) the number of votes to be cast on a poll, and (c) how many are 'For' and 'Against' each resolution.

---

6 POLLS 12/98

6.1 If a **poll** is duly **demanded**, the result of a **vote** on a **show of hands lapses** and is replaced in due course by the result of the poll.

6.2 A proxy has the same right (or weight) as the member whom he represents, in making or supporting a demand for a poll: s 372.

6.3 The articles specify who may demand a poll. But to avoid excessive restrictions, it is provided (s 373) that a **provision** of the articles is **invalid** if it tries:

(a) To **exclude** the **right** to **demand a poll** at a general meeting, except on the election of a chairman or the adjournment of the meeting (so a poll *may* be demanded on any issue, except these)

(b) To set a **minimum** level of demand for a poll, at:

(i) **More than five members** who are entitled to vote (less than five *may* demand a poll)

(ii) A member or members who represent **at least one tenth** of the **total voting rights** of all members entitled to vote (less than one tenth *may* demand a poll)

(iii) A member or members who hold shares giving a right to vote, and which are **paid up to** at **least one tenth** of the total which has been paid up on such shares (holders of less than this paid up value *may* demand a poll)

6.4 The articles may in fact grant wider rights to demand a poll than the above statutory limits. Table A Article 46 does require (ii) and (iii) of (b) above, the one tenth principle, 'subject to the provisions of the Act' (which disallow it). Table A, however, also provides that:

(a) A **poll may** be **demanded** on the **election** of a **chairman** and the adjournment of the meeting - provided (for obvious practical reasons) that it is taken 'forthwith' and not postponed: Table A Article 51.

(b) **Two** (instead of the statutory five) members entitled to vote, and also the **chairman**, are given the right to demand a poll: Article 45.

6.5 It has been held that if the chairman is thus given a right to demand a poll, he should use his initiative and exercise that right, if he believes (knowing what proxy votes are available) that the result of a poll will be different from the result of a show of hands.

Poll procedure

6.6 The articles (Table A Articles 49, 51 and 52) usually spell out in some detail the timetable etc for a poll, but leave the chairman a wide discretion in settling the arrangements, which must vary according to the needs of the occasion. In outline:

(a) Except for a poll on the election of a chairman and the adjournment of the meeting, which must be held immediately, the **poll** may be **held** at **once**, or at the end of the **meeting**, or on a **later day** (but not more than 30 days after it is demanded).

(b) The chairman may decide **where** and **when** the poll is to be held, and the result declared.

(c) If the poll is to be held at the **end** of the meeting, the **meeting** may **continue** with its other business before proceeding to the poll.

(d) **No notice** need be given of a poll, if the **time** and **place** are **announced** at the **meeting** where the demand is made. In any other case **seven days' clear notice** must be given.

(e) The chairman may decide on the **method** to be used, and may appoint **scrutineers**, who need not be members.

(f) If the poll is *not* taken immediately, **additional proxy cards** may be **deposited** to authorise proxy voting at the poll, as discussed earlier.

Scrutineers

6.7 The chairman usually does exercise his power to appoint scrutineers, who:

- **Conduct** the **poll**
- **Examine** the **votes cast**
- **Present** a **signed report** to the chairman, so that he may declare the result

Generally the total votes for and against would be declared; it would not be normal practice to reveal how individual members voted, although this information is not confidential.

6.8 It is normal practice either to appoint the company's auditors as scrutineers, or to ask each of the opposed groups of members to nominate one representative so that the chairman may appoint them to act jointly as scrutineers.

6.9 As explained above, the company's preliminary checking of proxy cards as they are received may save the scrutineers a great deal of work, and perhaps make it feasible to hold the poll at the end of the meeting, rather than on a later day.

6.10 The responsibility for ensuring that only valid votes, whether cast in person or by proxy, are accepted rests on the scrutineers.

Voting on a poll

6.11 There are two generally accepted methods of voting on a poll, both of which require a written record of how many votes are cast and by whom, which the scrutineers can verify at leisure before reporting the result.

(a) **Voting lists**: two sheets are laid out on separate tables in different parts of the room, each suitably headed with the text of the resolution and the word 'For' or 'Against'. The sheets are ruled in columns, which are headed to require that each person voting shall give:

   (i) The name of the member whose votes are cast

   (ii) The number of votes cast

   (iii) The signature of the voter, as a member, proxy, or authorised representative of a corporate member

(b) **Ballot papers**: these are individual papers distributed to voters, which they complete (with particulars as described in (a) above) and hand in.

6.12 Voting lists facilitate a rapid count, but their use may require that a large number of persons at a meeting have to get up and find the appropriate list to sign before going back to their seats. If the poll is not held at the meeting, but on a later day (with, say, two hours allowed for voters to come in and cast their votes) there is less risk of tumult and confusion than if the same method is used for a poll at the meeting itself.

6.13 If the ballot paper method is used, there should be stewards to distribute and collect in the papers from those at the meeting, who in this case remain seated. If the ballot paper method is preferred, the papers should be prepared in bulk before the meeting.

7 FORMAL OR PROCEDURAL MOTIONS

7.1 Within the limits set by its regulations, the meeting may determine its own course of business. There are various motions which can be put forward in order to regulate or facilitate the business of the meeting: these are known as 'formal' or procedural motions. (They may also be known as 'interruptive' motions).

7.2 Like any other, a procedural motion cannot be moved by anyone who has already spoken in the debate which it interrupts. Nor is it subject to amendment (to avoid pointless wrangling).

7.3 The meeting may resolve that it does not wish to listen to more discussion on a particular question, or to continue its session at all at that stage. A procedural motion may be passed in order to **cut short** the **debate** and bring the meeting to a conclusion.

7.4 There is however sometimes a risk that a majority of members will resort to procedural motions to stifle debate on an embarrassing subject, or one on which they may not wish to disclose their unpopular views. On the other hand, if a party in a meeting wishes to hold off the vote, or 'play for time' while it gathers support etc, a procedural motion may be used to delay business, say by shelving the debate until a later date. A motion used in such a way is called a dilatory motion.

7.5 The chairman has a **general power** to **reject** a **procedural motion** if he considers that:

- It is designed to **hinder** the **progress** of business.
- It is **against** the **regulations** laid down for the meeting.
- It will **prevent adequate discussion**, and the expression of minority views.

7.6 He will often be bound by the regulations in this respect.

7.7 The most drastic procedural step is to require that the motion shall, without further debate, be finally disposed of. For this purpose there are two types of procedural motion:

- Previous question
- Closure

Previous question: 'that the question be not now put'

7.8 The **previous question** motion is 'that the previous question be not now put', the 'previous question' being the original or substantive motion under debate when the procedural motion came up.

(a) If 'previous question' is **carried**, the **debate** on that motion is ended **without** a **vote**.

(b) If 'previous question' is put and **rejected**, the motion must **immediately** be put to the vote, without further debate. (This is because the **rejection** of a motion that 'the previous question be **not now** put' is a double negative, implying that the meeting has decided that the original or substantive motive **shall now** be put to the vote forthwith.)

7.9 Either way, the debate is ended immediately, so the chairman should not allow a 'previous question' motion if there has not yet been sufficient debate to allow the meeting to come to a considered decision.

Closure: 'that the question be now put'

7.10 The **closure** motion is 'that the question be now put'.

(a) If it is carried, the motion previously under debate is put to the vote, without further discussion.

(b) If a closure motion is rejected, however, the debate continues.

7.11 This is a fairer method than 'previous question', since the debate is allowed to continue if that is the wish of the majority. The chairman may himself move to 'close' the debate, with the meeting's consent.

Other procedural motions

7.12 There are a number of other procedural motions by which debate is avoided or cut short for the time being, while still leaving open the possibility of resuming it later. Other procedural motions include the following.

(a) 'That the **meeting proceed to the next business**'.

This motion may be put to the meeting without discussion at the end of any speech. If it is passed, the item - whether a motion or amendment - is simply dropped, and the meeting proceeds to the next item on the agenda.

(b) 'That the **motion be referred back to the committee**'.

This 'reference back' motion is suitable if the meeting considers that a report or recommendations of a committee are unsatisfactory in their present form, and should be reviewed.

(c) 'That the **debate be adjourned**'.

This is sometimes a useful means of interrupting a long debate, to enable the meeting to deal rapidly with some more urgent matter or to cool heated tempers.

(d) 'That the meeting **postpone consideration** of the subject' or 'That the motion lie on the table'.

These motions are generally appropriate if the meeting does not wish to start a discussion of a matter at that session.

If any of these motions is put to the vote and *rejected*, the debate simply continues (or not, as the case may be).

8 ADJOURNMENT

8.1 We have already considered the power to adjourn a meeting above. To recapitulate briefly:

- The basic power to adjourn rests with the **meeting** itself (Table A Article 45).
- There is **automatic adjournment** if the meeting is **inquorate** (Article 41).
- The chairman has **certain inherent powers** to adjourn.

8.2 The chairman has a right to adjourn the meeting because of **disorder**. This right, though, must be used appropriately.

John v Rees 1969
The facts: This was a meeting of a constituency political party, following an acute controversy in which the MP had just been expelled by the national executive of the party. In the course of heated and noisy argument there was 'bodily contact, but no real violence'. The chairman proposed a motion, of which no prior notice had been given, that the constituency party should continue to act in accordance with its constitution. When he failed to obtain acceptance of his motion, he adjourned sine die. The meeting however continued and passed a resolution to disaffiliate from the national party.

* sine die: adjourn without giving a date for reconvening.

Decision: 'The first duty of the chairman is to keep order if he can', and if he cannot, 'to make earnest and sustained efforts to restore order'. It is proper for him to 'summon to his aid any officers or others whose assistance is available', but if this fails and 'people are put in fear' (more than 'mere punching and jostling') the chairman should adjourn. In doing so he should act in good faith, so that order may be restored and the meeting may continue. An adjournment for, say, 15 minutes would be appropriate - but an adjournment sine die, or to a later day, is likely to frustrate the purpose of the meeting and is more than would be required for a restoration of order.

8.3 The chairman also has the power to adjourn where the meeting is unable to proceed because the place where the meeting is to be held is **inadequate** for the number of members who wish to attend. This power too must be exercised reasonably.

Byng v London Life Association 1989
The facts: The annual general meeting of the company was duly convened at the Barbican Cinema in London. Due to the number of people attending, overflow rooms were used and the proceedings were linked by audiovisual technology. This failed halfway through, leaving approximately 1,000 angry members outside the meeting. Matters became difficult and the chairman walked out, declaring that the meeting would reconvene at the Cafe Royal that afternoon.

Decision: The chairman had the inherent power to adjourn the meeting but he exercised it unreasonably since the people who attended at the Barbican could not necessarily attend at the Cafe Royal in the afternoon. This would prevent them from voting since proxies could not be lodged in time. Hence the proceedings of the adjourned meeting were invalid.

8.4 However, suspension of business so that a poll may be taken is *not* an adjournment. After the poll the meeting may resume its unfinished business without formality over the interruption - as is the case with points of order.

8.5 The distinction is important because if the new meeting is a continuation of the previous meeting and there has not been an adjournment, **new proxies cannot** be **appointed**. If however adjournment has occurred, Article 62 allows the appointment of new proxies.

> *Jackson v Hamlyn 1953.*
> *The facts:* A resolution to adjourn was put to the meeting and carried on a show of hands. A poll was then demanded and according to the company articles of association had to be taken forthwith. Since the company had only limited use of the room in which the meeting was being held, the chairman announced that the poll would be taken, and that if the result of the poll was against adjournment he would hold the meeting again the following week.
>
> *Decision:* The chairman had acted correctly. The court said that the resumed meeting would be a continuation of the original meeting and not an adjourned meeting.

8.6 Other Table A rules incidental to adjournment include the following.

(a) The adjournment may be to a **specified time** and **place**, or *sine die*.

(b) If the adjournment is for 14 days or more, it is necessary to give at least **seven clear days' notice** of 'the time and place of the adjourned meeting and the general nature of the business to be transacted'. Otherwise, a fresh notice need not be issued: Article 44.

(c) An **adjourned meeting** may only transact the **uncompleted business** of the original meeting: Article 44.

(d) If a **poll is demanded** on a motion for adjournment, it must be **taken immediately**: Article 51.

9 PRACTICAL CONSIDERATIONS

9.1 The following practical considerations are particularly relevant for company meetings.

Availability of directors

9.2 The secretary of a company of any size will need to ensure the chairman and directors are available on the proposed date.

Facilities for the AGM of a large company

9.3 A **suitable venue** must be booked in good time for the meeting. In practice, an estimate is made of the numbers likely to attend and a room booked according to this estimate which is usually slightly exaggerated.

9.4 The room must be set up for the meeting. The seating and other arrangements may include the following.

(a) There may be a **long table** at one end (possibly on a raised dais on which the directors are seated in pre-arranged places, with the chairman in the centre and the secretary alongside him or her.

(b) It may be necessary to install a **public address** (microphone) system if the room is very large.

(c) It may often be necessary to set aside a **lobby area** for shareholders to be registered.

(d) The general suitability of the **premises** and its **facilities** will obviously vary according to the size and type of meeting.

Paperwork

9.5 Meetings inevitably generate a large amount of 'paperwork' for the secretary, along with the other general administrative duties required before, during and after the meeting. The various documents and other material that must be prepared, and either issued to members or brought to a meeting, include the following.

(a) **Notice and agenda**. A notice and/or agenda will be issued in advance, with any attached papers that may be necessary.

(b) **Chairman's agenda**. The chairman will need a special agenda. This should include

(i) Information about the contents of **each resolution** - for example the contents of the accounts, or comparisons of dividends with previous years

(ii) **Procedural information,** the type of resolution each agenda item will need and the procedures to be followed if a poll is required

(iii) An indication of the **degree of opposition** that is expected on each resolution and also detail of how proxies have voted

(c) **Reports and accounts**, which are the main business of an annual meeting.

(d) **Proxy forms**. Proxy forms (or cards) may also be sent out with the notice of the meeting, if the regulations allow for proxy voting: alternatively, the notice may state how and from whom a proxy form may be obtained.

(i) Once they have been filled in and returned by members, they will have to be **checked** against the **Register of Members** to ensure the persons who sent them are entitled to cast the number of votes claimed.

(ii) The secretary will have to check they have been **completed correctly**.

(iii) They will also have to be **summarised** for the chairman (who usually 'casts' the proxy votes as directed).

(iv) The proxies should be **brought** to the **meeting**, preferably listed under, or bundled into, 'For' and 'Against', for ease of reference. Lists of members and proxies will also have to be prepared for checking admittance and voting rights at the meeting. Where proxy forms are sent out with the AGM notice they will usually need to be returned 48 hours before the meeting.

(e) **Polling lists or voting papers.** If it is anticipated that a poll will be demanded on some issue, and will be taken immediately, polling lists or individual voting papers should be prepared in advance.

(f) **Press announcements**. There may be publicity to arrange, including the reservation of space in newspapers for publication of advance information of the meeting in summary form.

9.6 The secretary should generally bring to the meeting any papers he expects *may* be required for reference at the meeting, for example, a copy of the report and accounts, if not already circulated, and may need to bring other papers for distribution.

Admission of the press to company general meetings 6/98

9.7 'The Press' includes representatives of all news and broadcasting media: TV, radio, newsagency, newspapers and journals etc.

9.8 The Press are often admitted to AGMs, particularly those of the larger plcs. However they have **no right to attend** unless they are shareholders, proxies or corporate representatives. If they attend in any of these capacities they do not have the automatic right to bring cameras or recording machines into the meeting; this is probably a matter for the chairman's discretion. The extent to which the meeting can overturn a decision by the chairman to admit or exclude the Press is untested.

After the meeting

9.9 Frequently there will be some matters to be dealt with after the AGM. These include:

(a) **Transcribing** the **proceedings** and using the transcript to prepare the minutes

(b) **Filing** the **signed accounts** and copies of any special resolutions at Companies House

(c) Making arrangements for the **payment** of any **dividend** which has been approved at the meeting.

10 ICSA GUIDE TO BEST PRACTICE AT ANNUAL GENERAL MEETINGS

10.1 In 1996 the ICSA established a working party whose remit was to set out best practice for the conduct of AGMs and the rights of shareholders. The working party produced *A guide to best practice for Annual General Meetings* in September 1996.

10.2 The main recommendations of the working party were as follows.

(a) The company should **actively communicate** with all shareholders.

(b) Shareholder correspondence should receive a **full reply** from the **chairman**, another director, the secretary or a senior official.

(c) **Communication** with shareholders should be **handled sensitively** but appropriately in accordance with the company's communication policy.

(d) The notice of the AGM and accompanying documents should be circulated at least **20 working days** in advance of the meeting. This is a requirement of the Combined Code, and good practice for other companies.

(e) The **venue** for the AGM should be **accessible** for attendees with disabilities, including those with poor hearing.

(f) Each item of **special business** included in the notice to the meeting should be accompanied by **full** and **detailed information.**

(g) The **Notice** and **form of proxy** should **specify** the **directors** who are **standing** for **re-election**.

(h) The details given of directors standing for re-election should include their **ages**, relevant **experience** possessed, the **dates** they were first appointed to the board and details of **other directorships** they hold.

(i) All directors of public companies should be subject to **retirement by rotation.**

(j) All directors should, if possible, **attend** the **AGM** and should be seated with the Chairman, facing the shareholders.

(k) The Chairman should **not propose** his **own election** or re-election or any resolution in which he has an interest.

(l) Different items of business should be dealt with by **separate resolutions**; in particular the approval of dividends should be kept separate from the receipt or adoption of the accounts.

(m) **Adequate time** should be provided for shareholder **questions** at the AGM.

(n) Shareholders should be able to **raise questions** on **any item** concerning the company's past performance, its results and its intended future performance (subject to restrictions on revealing commercially sensitive or price-sensitive information).

(o) Before each resolution is put to the vote, the chairman should **explain** its **effect** and purpose and invite **shareholders** to **speak.**

(p) If a shareholder raises concerns at the AGM and the chairman promises to look into them, that shareholder should later receive a **full report on** the action taken.

(q) Unless the company agrees at the outset to absorb all costs of circulation, **shareholder requisitions** under s 376 should be **accompanied** by **another resolution** giving shareholders the chance to decide whether the company or the requisitionists should bear the costs.

(r) The **announcement** of a **decision** on a **poll** should include the **total number of votes** cast in favour of and against the resolution.

(s) The chairman should indicate that the **number of proxies** means the **number of proxies lodged** before the start of the meeting (some members who have nominated proxies may in fact be attending the meeting.)

(t) All **proxy forms** should **provide** for **voting** or **abstention** on any matter which may come before the meeting, as well as the business specified in the notice.

(u) All companies should provide an **updated trading statement** at the AGM unless they have just published one or are about to publish one.

(v) One or more of the executive directors should make a **statement** at the **AGM** on the areas of the **company's operations** for which he has responsibility.

(w) All companies should establish procedures for dealing with **disturbances** at their AGM.

(x) The Chairman should seek the **meeting's consent for proxies speaking** and **participating in debates.**

Chapter roundup

- A meeting must have a **chairman** in order to be properly constituted.
- The powers and duties of a chairman are derived from common law not from the Companies Act 1985. However, Table A makes certain provisions with regard to adjournment and voting which you should be aware of.
- A meeting generally requires the presence of **at least two persons**. The articles may fix two or a higher number to constitute a quorum.
- If a meeting is **inquorate** it must be **adjourned**.
- In a company which has a share capital any member entitled to attend and vote at a meeting may appoint another member or non-member as a **proxy** to attend and vote for him.
- In respect of voting, Table A states that on a **show of hands**, every person **present** in person is to have **one vote**. On a **poll he** will have **one vote** for **every share** held. Some shares, however, carry **weighted voting rights**.
- A poll may be demanded by a **minimum number of members**, in which case it replaces the result of a vote on a show of hands.
- The company secretary has various practical matters to consider with regard to the conduct of meetings.

Test your knowledge

1 How is the chairman of a company general meeting appointed? (see paras 1.1 - 1.2)

2 State three of the general duties of the chairman in presiding over a general meeting. (1.6)

3 What is the quorum for a general meeting (a) if the articles are in Table A form and (b) if the articles do not fix a quorum? (3.2 - 3.3)

4 How may a company be represented at the general meeting of another company of which it is a member? (3.8)

5 What statutory rights has a proxy (a) to speak and (b) to vote at a general meeting? Are there any exceptions? (4.3, 4.6)

6 What is a 'two-way' proxy card? Which companies are required to issue them? (4.11)

7 When must proxy cards be returned to the company? (4.18)

8 What are the standard methods of taking a vote at a general meeting? (5.2)

9 What statutory rights are given in respect of a demand for a poll? How far does Table A grant more extensive rights? (6.2 - 6.4)

10 What does Table A provide in respect of the arrangements for the conduct of a poll? (6.6)

11 How may voting on a poll be carried out? (6.11)

12 What paperwork must be prepared by the company secretary for an annual general meeting? (9.5)

Now try illustrative questions 6 to 9 at the end of the Study Text

Chapter 8

RESOLUTIONS AND MINUTES

This chapter covers the following topics.

Introduction

A meeting may be held merely to allow speakers to express their views and others to respond to them, without anyone seeking formal collective decisions. Sometimes, however, it is necessary for a meeting to reach decisions: this is usually so at general and at directors' meetings of companies. Then the discussion should be related to specific proposals, which the meeting may approve or reject.

Company law does not usually make the distinction between:

(a) A 'motion', a proposal made to a meeting for discussion
(b) A 'resolution', a proposition approved by the meeting

Instead it uses the term 'resolution', both for the proposal and for the final approved version.

It does, however, classify resolutions into four categories:

(a) Ordinary
(b) Extraordinary
(c) Special
(d) Elective (private companies only)

These are distinguished mainly by the period of notice required and the majority needed to carry each type of resolution.

Private companies can also conduct business by written resolution, obviating the need for general meetings.

The 'results' of a meeting are recorded in minutes, which set out the resolutions carried and other transactions effected by the meeting.

Recently regulations have come into force allowing single member private companies. Special considerations apply to meetings of such companies.

1 DRAFTING RESOLUTIONS 12/99

1.1 A resolution is a formal decision taken at a general, class or board meeting of a company. In your study of meetings you will find that while it is a proposal under discussion, it is sometimes referred to as a 'motion'. It becomes a 'resolution' only when it has been carried and should demonstrate that the company has reached a clear-cut decision on the matter being discussed.

Matters to be considered

1.2 The secretary has to anticipate the administrative aspects of the proposal and make them clear before putting them into effect.

1.3 For example, for a resolution for the payment of a final dividend to be proposed at an AGM, it is necessary, for practical reasons, to decide the following.

(a) **How much dividend** is to be paid in respect of each share?

(b) **To whom** is the **dividend** to be **paid** if the registered ownership of any of the shares changes between the declaration and the payment of the dividend?

(c) **When** is the **dividend** to be **paid**?

(d) In respect of **which financial year** of the company is the dividend to be paid?

1.4 The following meets the above requirements.

That a first and final dividend in respect of the year ended 30th June 20X9 of 5p per £1 ordinary share be declared payable on 30 November 20X9 to holders of the said shares on the register at the close of business on 15 September 20X9.

Drafting a resolution 12/99

Consideration of powers of meeting

1.5 In determining the wording of any resolution, it is always necessary to consider what the meeting can effectually do.

Simplicity

1.6 If a resolution does not require to be filled out with incidental detail, it is best to **keep it simple**:

'That John Smith be re-elected a director of the company'.

1.7 It is **unnecessary** to **state** in the resolution that the director has **retired by rotation** and is now being re-elected for a further term of office (Table A Articles 72 and 80). His retirement and the period of his tenure on re-election are fixed by the articles, to which the resolution is subject.

Specific references

1.8 A resolution may **refer** to, or **alter**, some **existing document**.

'That the contract for the purchase by the company of 1,000 of its ordinary shares from Henry Jones at a price of £10 per share pursuant to section 164 of the Companies Act 1985, a copy of which has been initialled by the chairman for identification, be approved'.

As there is more than one procedure for the purchase of shares, it is preferable to specify s 164, and that section requires that, as part of 'the terms' (which must clearly include the price), the name of the vendor shareholder must be given in the contract. It is prudent to disclose it also in the resolution, since the vendor may not vote on it: s 164(5).

1.9 Alteration of another document, by reference to it, often arises from an alteration of the objects clause, or of the articles.

Wording

1.10 Resolutions begin with the word 'That' because in origin a resolution is a proposal ('Proposed that ...'), and if passed it is a decision ('Resolved that ...'). The operative part of the resolution is usually a verb in the passive ('be altered', in the example below). Unless otherwise stated, a resolution is an immediate decision.

Type of resolution

1.11 In drafting a resolution for a general meeting, the secretary should be clear as to what type of resolution is required. A **special** or an **extraordinary** resolution must always be **described as such** in the notice convening the meeting (s 378), and imports specific requirements as to the majority required to pass and the period of notice).

1.12 To sum up, drafting a resolution requires a clear understanding of what is to be decided, and how that decision is to be implemented. On the whole, it is better to include optional detail rather than omit it, but reasons and general considerations need not be given. If, for example, the declaration of a dividend reflects an increase in the profits, it would be wrong to make any reference to that fact in the formal resolution; it may influence the voting but it is not part of the actual decision.

1.13 The secretary should also think of what has to be done **after** the resolution has been passed. Is it a case where a signed copy of the printed resolution must be delivered to the registrar: s 380? Does some document, such as the memorandum or articles, have to be reprinted in altered form? Some resolutions have to be implemented by subsequent action, such as the payment of a dividend; others are merely a formal acceptance by the meeting of information laid before it, for example the accounts.

1.14 When a resolution is passed at the instance of a third party, he will usually ask to be provided with a 'certified copy'. The secretary may as part of his duties provide the copy, once the resolution has been passed:

> 'Certified a true copy of the original resolution of the board of directors of XYZ Ltd passed on .... 20X9.
>
> Signed .... Secretary'

2 ORDINARY RESOLUTIONS

2.1 Any resolution which is not 'extraordinary' or 'special' is an ordinary resolution. There can be no doubt about the matter, since a resolution is only extraordinary or special if it is so described in the notice of the meeting: s 377.

2.2 The ordinary resolution is the basic and general purpose means of securing approval in general meeting. It may be used for purely formal, routine business, as is often the case at an AGM, but may also suffice as approval of important or contentious business.

2.3 Unless the relevant section of the Companies Act 1985 specifies that an extraordinary or special resolution is required for a particular item of business, an ordinary resolution will suffice.

2.4 The articles of a company may **provide** that a **special** or **extraordinary resolution** shall be **required.** However in some contexts the Act expressly overrides the articles in providing that an ordinary resolution is sufficient. Thus the power to remove a director from office is to be exercised by ordinary resolution 'notwithstanding anything in the articles': s 303(1).

2.5 As a general rule it is not necessary to deliver a signed copy of an ordinary resolution to the Companies Registry (as it is with an extraordinary resolution) though there are a number of exceptions to the rule (as discussed later).

2.6 A member has a statutory right to inspect the minutes of general meetings, so he can discover the terms of an ordinary resolution passed at a meeting which he did not attend.

2.7 An ordinary resolution, following common law principles, may be carried by a **simple majority** of votes cast at the meeting.

Notice of an ordinary resolution

2.8 Unless 'special notice' procedure applies, the period of notice to be given of an ordinary resolution is determined by the **nature** of the **meeting** at which it is to be proposed, that is by the notice ordinarily required to convene that type of meeting.

(a) If it is business of an AGM, **21 days** notice is required - to convene the AGM.

(b) An ordinary resolution may be passed at an EGM convened by **14 days**' notice (unless the business of the meeting also includes a special resolution): s 368.

Special notice of an ordinary resolution **6/00**

2.9 In some circumstances an ordinary resolution is sufficient but the Companies Act 1985 requires that 'special notice' must be given of intention to propose the resolution. Note that 'special notice' is given *to* the company - *not by it*. This is so in the case of any resolution:

(a) **To remove a director from office** (under the **statutory** power, s 303(1)) or to appoint someone else in his place at the same meeting. To avoid special notice procedure, companies sometimes include in their articles an additional power to remove a director by extraordinary resolution (of which special notice need not be given). As stated below, members can only include a resolution to remove a director if they possess a certain percentage of voting rights or number of shares: s 376. Hence a resolution to remove a director is generally moved by substantial shareholders, maybe in a company with a small number of shareholder - directors when disagreement has arisen.

(b) **To re-elect a director who has attained the age of 70** in companies to which s 293 (age limit for directors) applies, that is public companies and subsidiaries of public companies, unless the articles provide otherwise.

(c) **To remove an auditor before the expiration of his term of office**, to appoint any auditor other than the retiring auditor, to fill a casual vacancy or to re-appoint an auditor originally appointed to fill such a vacancy: ss 388(3) and 391(a). This scenario may arise because the relationship between the company and the auditor has broken down and the next audit is due before the auditor's term of office expires. The company may wish to appoint different auditors for that audit, or the auditors may cause a casual vacancy by **resigning**.

2.10 The procedure for special notice (s 379) is as follows.

(a) Notice of intention to propose the resolution must be given to the company **at least 28 days** before the meeting at which it is to be moved, or the resolution is not effective. Notice would usually be given by the proposer of the motion, but may be given by someone else.

(b) The company must give **notice to members** of the receipt of special notice in addition to any action appropriate to particular situations. If practicable, this information should be included in the notice which is issued to convene the meeting; otherwise it should be given by newspaper advertisement, or by any other means the articles provide for, at least 21 days before the meeting.

(c) If special notice has been received, and the company then calls a meeting for a date which is only 28 days or less from its receipt, the special notice will not have been given in the time required. It is nonetheless deemed to have been **properly given**: this is to prevent directors from frustrating a special notice resolution by advancing the date of the meeting to exclude it.

2.11 You should be aware that special notice procedure imposes a 21 day notice requirement on any ordinary resolution to which it relates, **even if the meeting is an EGM**, for which only 14 days' notice is normally required.

2.12 In a case of a resolution to remove a director or to remove an auditor (or to replace an auditor who has retired or resigned):

(a) The company must 'forthwith' on receipt of special notice **send a copy** of it to the **director** or to the **auditor**, as the case may be.

(b) The individual concerned is then entitled to require the company to **circulate a memorandum** putting his case to members (if it is of reasonable length and not defamatory) *or* to have such a statement read out at the meeting.

(c) The individual is also **entitled** to **address** the meeting in person.

2.13 When giving members notice that the company has received special notice of a resolution, the company must give them certain other relevant information, for example:

(a) That it has received the kind of statement described above
(b) In the case of a director proposed for re-election, his age: s 293(5)

Requisition of business by members **6/99**

2.14 The members may require the company, at the members' expense:

(a) To **include** a **resolution** in the business of the next AGM, and to give appropriate notice of it

(b) To **circulate** a **statement**, with a notice of any meeting, not exceeding 1,000 words in length (and not defamatory) about the business referred to in the resolution: s 376

2.15 S 376 confers rights on members if, and only if:

(a) They represent at least **1/20th** of the voting rights at general meetings.

(b) They are at least **100 in number** and hold shares on which there is an average amount paid up of at least **£100 per member**: *Pedley v Inland Waterways Association 1977*.

2.16 In fact, s 376 itself is rarely used. If members represent a tenth or more of the voting share capital, they can in any case requisition an EGM for business of their choice under s 368 before the next AGM is due to take place.

2.17 Members who wish to issue a circular on the business of a forthcoming general meeting (at their own expense) would do better:

(a) To obtain a list of members (s 356)

(b) To print their statement privately

(c) To distribute it to the members without letting the directors have advance notice (as required under s 376) of its contents

3 EXTRAORDINARY RESOLUTIONS

3.1 An extraordinary resolution is one which:

(a) Is **specifically described** in the notice of a general meeting as one which is to be proposed as an extraordinary resolution

(b) Is carried at the meeting (on a show of hands or on a poll) by **a majority of at least three quarters of the votes actually cast**: s 378(1)

3.2 **No period of notice** is prescribed, so an extraordinary resolution, if proposed at an EGM, requires only the usual 14 day notice.

3.3 A **signed copy** of an extraordinary resolution must be **delivered** to the **Companies Registry** within 15 days of its passing, for enclosure in the company's file at the registry: s 380(4)(d). It must be a 'printed' copy (or in another durable form approved by the registrar) and it must be signed by hand ('autographically') by the chairman of the meeting at which it is passed.

3.4 The two most important occasions on which an extraordinary resolution must be passed are:

(a) **Winding up**. When a company resolves that it is advisable for it to be wound up, being unable to carry on its business because of its liabilities.

(b) **Variation of rights.** At a meeting of the holders of a class of shares, to approve a variation of the rights attached to those shares.

Comparison with other resolutions

3.5 An extraordinary resolution differs from an *ordinary* resolution in respect of both requirements (a) and (b) in paragraph 3.1 above.

3.6 It differs from a *special* resolution in that it **does not** in itself **require more than 14 days' notice** of the meeting. For this reason, it is particularly convenient as a commencement of insolvent liquidation, where even a saving of 7 days (14 instead of 21 days' notice) may be vital to stave off immediate financial collapse and heavy losses.

4 SPECIAL RESOLUTIONS

4.1 A resolution is a special resolution when it is:

(a) **Described** as such in the notice

(b) **Carried** by a **three quarters majority** of votes cast at a meeting called by 21 days' notice: s 378(2)

4.2 A signed copy of the resolution must be **delivered** to the Companies **Registry**: s 380(4)(a).

4.3 Special resolutions are required for most major decisions affecting the structure of the company, including among other things:

(a) An alteration of the objects clause in the memorandum: s 4

(b) An alteration of the articles: s 9

(c) A reduction of capital: s 135

(d) Various alterations of the company's status by re-registration (for example from a private to a public company)

(e) A change of name: s 28

(f) Purchase of own shares: s 164

(g) Private company financial assistance for purchase of own shares: s 155

(h) Disapplication of pre-emption rights s 95

(i) Exempting a dormant company from appointing auditors: s 250

Exercise

Explain the principles relating to notices of special resolutions.

Solution

A resolution is special when it is described as such in the notice of the meeting, and may only be carried by a three-quarters majority of votes cast at a meeting called by 21 days' notice: s 378(2).

Special resolutions are required for most major decisions affecting the structure of the company. These include alterations of the objects clause or articles, reduction of capital, various re-registrations and the change of a company's name.

Although 21 days' notice is required for special resolutions by s 378, there are provisions for accepting short notice. With the consent of a ninety-five per cent majority (in voting shares in the case of a limited company, or in number of members otherwise) a special resolution may be proposed and passed on short notice (at a meeting of members of which less than 21 days' notice has been given).

The notice of the meeting must also describe the resolution to be passed as a special resolution, and it is general practice to reproduce the full text of the resolution in order to avoid disputes as to whether sufficient information on the nature of the business to be transacted has been given.

5 ELECTIVE RESOLUTIONS **Specimen paper, 6/98, 6/99**

5.1 **Only private companies** can pass elective resolutions which disapply certain company law requirements. An elective resolution must be passed by *all* the members entitled to attend and vote at meetings of the company: s 379(A)(2)(b). In all other respects the procedure is the same as for a special resolution. There must be a minimum of 21 days' notice in writing unless all the members entitled to attend and vote waive this requirement. The notice must state the terms of the elective resolution and describe it as such, and it must be registered.

5.2 At present, five cases are dealt with by this procedure, though it is expected that this may be expanded in the future.

(a) **Authority to issue shares** must be given to the directors by the members. Under s 80, this may be for a maximum of five years. S 80A, however, allows a private company to pass an elective resolution under which such authority may be indefinite, or for a finite period in excess of five years.

(b) **Laying accounts before a general meeting** may be dispensed with (unless the auditor or a member requires the company to do so): s 252.

(c) The **annual general meeting** may be dispensed with unless a member requires one to be held: s 366A.

(d) **Consent to short notice** may be given by less than the 95% majority required by s 369(4) provided the majority required is not less than 90%.

(e) **Appointment of auditors annually** may be dispensed with under s 386, so that the incumbent auditors are automatically deemed to be reappointed.

5.3 **Revocation** of an elective resolution can be **achieved** by **ordinary resolution**, but this must also be registered: s 380(4)(bb).

5.4 You should note that, for each of the five cases listed above, a **separate elective resolution** is required. Thus if for example, a company decides by elective resolution to dispense with the requirement to hold an Annual General Meeting, it must nevertheless still hold a general meeting to lay accounts and approve the appointment of auditors unless it passes the relevant elective resolutions.

5.5 A further feature is that the election to dispense with the laying of accounts has effect in relation to the accounts and reports of the financial year in which the *election is made* and subsequent financial years. Thus if the election is made in April 2001, for a company with a 31 December year-end, then it applies to the 31 December 2001 year and subsequent years. If the AGM is held in May 2001, accounts for the 2000 year still have to be laid at that AGM. This problem does not arise with the other types of elective resolution.

6 SHORT NOTICE

6.1 Although 14 days' notice is normally required for meetings to pass extraordinary resolutions, and 21 days for special resolutions, there are provisions for accepting short notice.

6.2 Since the 21 days' notice of a special resolution is specified in s 378(2) it is expressly provided that, with the consent of a **95 per cent** majority (in voting shares, or - if there are no shares - in number of members), a special resolution may be proposed and passed on short notice, that is 'at a meeting of which less than 21 days' notice has been given': s 378(3). This percentage may be reduced (but not below 90 per cent) by a private company under s 369(4).

7 AMENDMENT TO RESOLUTIONS 6/98

7.1 There are general principles which limit the amendment of resolutions while they are under debate. These apply to the proceedings of company general meetings as much as to any others. In addition, the stringent rules on notice and resolutions, peculiar to company law, impose further restrictions.

7.2 An **ordinary resolution** may be amended, even if the text has been set out in the notice of the meeting. However, the resolution as amended must still be **within the scope** of the notice.

7.3 If an **extraordinary or special resolution** is required, it must, as we have noted, be set out as such in the notice convening the meeting: s 378. This means in effect that there can be **no substantial amendment** of these resolutions, since the amended resolution would no longer be the same one of which notice had to be given.

> *Re Moorgate Mercantile Holdings Ltd 1980*
> *The facts:* The notice of the meeting set out the text of a special resolution to cancel the balance of £1,356,900.48 standing to the credit of share premium account. In the interval between the issue of the notice and circular, and the date of the meeting, it was discovered that a small sum of £321.17 in the balance on share premium account represented assets which had not been lost. At the meeting it was proposed that the resolution be amended to provide for a reduction from £1,356,900.48 to £321.17 (instead of total cancellation of the balance) since this would correctly fulfil the *intention* of the proposal. It was considered that as the resolution, when amended, would effect a reduction of *smaller* amount than had been indicated by the original resolution contained in the notice, the amended resolution was within the scope of the notice.
>
> *Decision:* S 378 does not permit a special or extraordinary resolution, as carried, to be anything other than **the resolution of which notice is given in convening the meeting.** The resolution, carried in its amended form, was invalid.

7.4 The court in the above case commented that:

(a) A clerical error might be corrected by amendment.

(b) The wording might be improved.

(c) No amendment of substance (even if very small in effect, as in this case) was possible.

8 REGISTRATION OF RESOLUTIONS

8.1 We have already mentioned that certain categories of resolution must be **registered:**

(a) The resolution must be delivered to the Registrar within 15 days of its passing
(b) It must be 'printed'.
(c) It must be signed by the chairman.

8.2 If the company registered its articles (so that it has not adopted Table A in its entirety), a copy of all resolutions requiring registration must be attached to any copy of the articles issued.

8.3 The main resolutions and agreements which must be registered (under s 380) are:

(a) **Special resolutions**

(b) **Extraordinary resolutions**

(c) **Resolutions** or agreements **agreed** to by **all members of the company**, which would otherwise have required special or extraordinary resolutions

(d) An **elective resolution** or a resolution revoking such a resolution

(e) Resolutions or agreements:

(i) **Agreed** to by **all members of a class** of shareholders, which would otherwise have required a particular size or type of majority

(ii) All resolutions or agreements which are *not* agreed to by *all* members, but are nonetheless **binding** on **all members** of the class

Typically these are agreements for the variation of class rights, as an alternative to passing a resolution by a required majority at a separate class meeting;

(f) A resolution passed by the directors to **change the name** of the company to include the word 'limited', if the Department of Trade and Industry directs the change

(g) A resolution to **give, vary** or **revoke** the **authority** of directors to **allot shares** under s 80

(h) A resolution of the directors under s147(2) to **alter the memorandum** of a public company, when it ceases to be a public company through the acquisition of its own shares

(i) A resolution to **give, vary, revoke** or **renew** the company's **authority** under s 166 for the market purchase of its own shares. (This only in fact affects public companies.)

8.4 In addition, the procedure for an increase of authorised share capital (s 121) requires the company to send a copy of the resolution to the registry with the notice of the increase (Form 123). This must be done within 15 days of the resolution being passed: s 122.

9 UNANIMOUS AGREEMENTS

9.1 The elaborate procedure for convening, constituting and conducting a company meeting is intended to safeguard a minority of members, who may disagree with the resolutions passed at a meeting or who may not be able to attend the meeting.

9.2 If, however, **every member** of a company who is entitled to attend and vote is in agreement with a proposal, it is pointless to invalidate it because of some technical flaw in procedure. This is illustrated by the *Express Engineering Works* case, where a unanimous decision of a board meeting (all the members of the company being directors) was accepted **in place of a resolution in general meeting**.

9.3 In addition to the *Express Engineering Works* case, the courts have recognised that even:

(a) **Informal** but **unanimous agreement**
(b) An **irregular general meeting** which produced unanimous agreement

will be accepted as a binding decision instead of a resolution duly passed at a general meeting (the **assent principle**).

> *Parker & Cooper Ltd v Reading 1926*
> *The facts:* A debenture had been issued by the two directors in circumstances which made it invalid, though it was an *intra vires* transaction which might have been ratified by a resolution passed in general meeting. There was no such meeting, but at various times the four shareholders had discussed the matter, though there had not been a single gathering of all four of them. It was clear that they all approved what had been done. The company went into liquidation and the liquidator denied that the debenture was valid.
>
> *Decision:* As the debenture had been issued 'with the assent of every shareholder', it was valid.

9.4 In *Re Horsley & Weight Ltd 1981*, where a pension had been purchased for a retired director with the informal approval of all shareholders, though no board or general meeting had approved it.

9.5 It is likely that the assent principle also applies to a resolution to which all members agreed by telephone, say in a conference call. However, in such a case adequate precautions would need to be implemented to avoid the risk of impersonation.

Signed resolution procedure

9.6 The assent principle is given recognition in the articles (Table A Article 53):

> 'A resolution in writing executed by or on behalf of each member who would have been entitled to vote upon it if it had been proposed at a general meeting at which he was present shall be as effectual as if it had been passed at a general meeting duly convened and held and may consists of several instruments in the like form executed by or on behalf of one or more members.'

9.7 This procedure is most convenient for companies which have a small but scattered membership, who cannot easily gather in one place.

9.8 If it is expected that all the members will sign, say after consulting them by telephone (though this is not essential) a copy of the resolution may be sent by post to each member, for signature and return (or a single copy may be circulated for signature by everybody).

9.9 The signed resolution should be preserved in the **minute book**, since it serves in place of a resolution passed at a meeting.

9.10 There has been some doubt as to whether this procedure is an adequate substitute for a special or extraordinary resolution, since s 378 specifies that such resolutions must have been 'passed .... at a general meeting'. However the courts have accepted it on occasion: *Cane v Jones 1981.*

9.11 Special resolution procedure is a safeguard to a dissenting minority - which should not exist in a 'signed resolution' situation. The courts have, however, warned (*Re Barry Artist Ltd 1985*) that if the court is asked to approve a transaction (such as a reduction of capital) for which a special resolution in general meeting is expressly required by statute (s 135), the company should convene a general meeting for this purpose: the court is otherwise free to withhold its approval, unless there are strong reasons why the signed resolution procedure should have been used.

10 WRITTEN RESOLUTIONS

Specimen paper, 6/99, 12/99

10.1 In the case of **private** companies the principle of unanimity is now embodied in statute, following the Companies Act 1989. Anything which a private company may do by a resolution of a general or class meeting may now be done by written resolution: s 381A(1). It is specifically stated that the procedure is available in respect of any sort of resolution - ordinary, extraordinary or special. The procedure is available regardless of the provisions of the memorandum and articles: s 381 (c)(1).

10.2 The written resolution must be signed by all the members (or on their behalf) who, at the date of the resolution, would be entitled to attend and vote at a general or class meeting. This can be achieved using a number of different documents, so long as each sets out in identical fashion the terms of the resolution. The resolution is passed on the day that the last member signs. If the resolution would have required **filing** if passed at a general meeting (eg a special resolution), a copy must be filed at Companies House.

10.3 It is best practice to pass a 'resolution in writing', adding that it is to have effect as a special resolution rather than to pass a 'special resolution in writing.'

10.4 Written resolutions can be used in more situations than can Article 52. In particular, Article 53 does not cover class meetings, whereas written resolutions do. More importantly, perhaps, the legislation extends to cases where the Companies Act 1985 would have prevented a particular end being achieved by the broader power to agree resolutions in writing.

10.5 Where information must be given with the notice of the meeting, or with documents supplied or information made available at the meeting, it will be sufficient if this is given along with the resolution when it is supplied for signature: Schedule 15A.

10.6 The auditors must be supplied with a copy of any written resolution. Failure to do that will be a criminal offence, but will not affect the validity of the passing of any written resolution.

10.7 An example of a written resolution is given below.

Specimen copy of a written resolution for filing at Companies House

Company Number: ??????

THE COMPANIES ACT 1985
AND THE COMPANIES ACT 1989

RESOLUTION OF ABCD LIMITED

On the day of 2000, the following RESOLUTION IN WRITING (such resolution to have effect as a Special resolution) was duly passed by all the members of the Company entitled to attend and vote at a general meeting of the Company pursuant to section 381A, Companies Act 1985 (as amended);-

THAT the name of the Company be changed to 'WXYZ Limited'

??????????????
Secretary

11 CONTENTS AND SECURITY OF MINUTES

12/98

11.1 General requirements for recording the decisions and transactions of meetings are covered in your *Administration of Corporate Affairs* syllabus. The main points about the form of minutes are however set out below.

11.2 Every company is required to keep **minutes** of the proceedings of its general meetings and of the meetings of its directors and managers. If it fails to do so, the company and every officer who is in default is liable to a fine: s 381.

Contents of minutes

11.3 There is no legal prescription as to the content of minutes. As a matter of secretarial practice, the minutes of a meeting of any kind generally comprise two or three elements, as explained below.

11.4 There is usually a **heading** on the following lines.

Minutes of the 25th Annual General Meeting of XYZ Ltd held at [*place*] on ...... 20X1.

Present

Chip N Dale	Chairman
I M Bossere	Director
Shareholders	as per attendance sheet

In attendance

F R Vessent ACIS	Secretary

These particulars are a necessary record which serves to show where and when the meeting was held, who took the chair, and that a quorum was present, made up of identified persons. The secretary is there in purely an administrative capacity, principally to record the meeting; he does not vote and therefore is only 'in attendance'.

11.5 The second element of the minutes is the **minutes of resolution**, that is a formal record of the resolutions passed. It is unnecessary and incorrect to record the following:

(a) A summary of the discussion leading up to the vote of a resolution passed

(b) A statement as to who proposed and seconded the resolution when it was put to the vote

(c) The names of those who voted for and against, or even the numbers of votes cast, if the resolution was put to a vote and carried only by a majority

It suffices to record:

'It was resolved that John Smith be re-elected a director of the company.'

11.6 If, however, a person expressly asks that his abstention from voting, or his vote against a resolution, be minuted (which usually only arises at board meetings), it is correct and indeed obligatory to comply with his request.

11.7 The third possible element of the minutes are **minutes of narration**. Sometimes, more especially in minutes of a board meeting, it is helpful to put a resolution in its context by a brief reference to the preceding discussion as follows.

'The directors discussed the impending expiry of the lease of the company's premises at 20 High Street, Town, Shire, on 31 December next. It was resolved that the chairman be authorised to instruct estate agents to find alternative premises to which the company may move its business.'

It would, however, be incorrect to enter into details of the discussion. The outcome of the discussion is the important information, not how it was reached.

11.8 Minutes of narration are sometimes a necessary part of the record of the meeting as they serve to record information received. If no decision was taken in consequence, no resolution can be recorded. For example:

'The statement of cash and funds as at 30 June 20X8 was considered.'

11.9 As explained earlier, it is standard practice to supply to the chairman of a meeting a double-page agenda, with the right hand side blank. He may, if he wishes, enter a record of the proceedings 'Considered', 'Resolved', against each item on the agenda, by way of note. These notes have no legal effect, but they serve as a useful record and reminder after the meeting; the secretary may rely on them to supplement his own notes of the discussion when he writes the minutes afterwards.

Minutes style

11.10 In order for the minutes to fulfil their purpose, they should be:

(a) **Concise**, but sufficiently detailed to make the sense of the meeting clear

(b) **Precise** and unambiguous; factually accurate and fair in implication

(c) **Impersonal**, impartial and uniform in style - not 'coloured' by the 'author'

(d) Written in the **past tense** (with reported speech as appropriate ie: 'X requested that his abstention be minuted', rather than 'X said: "I wish my abstention to be minuted"')

(e) **Clearly laid out**, paragraphed and cross-referenced. They should be serially numbered, with headings for each point

Form and security of minutes

11.11 The minutes (like other company registers and records covered by s 722) may be kept:

(a) In a **bound book**

(b) In **some other manner**, typically a loose-leaf folder into which typed sheets can be inserted as the record of each successive meeting

11.12 If the minutes are *not* kept in the form of a bound book, 'adequate precautions shall be taken for safeguarding against falsification, and facilitating its discovery': s 722(2). These safeguards may include the following.

(a) The **pages** are **numbered**. The chairman signs the final page of the minutes of each meeting anyway, but his initials should be added to each of the other pages, to any manuscript alteration of the typed minutes (only minor ones) which he makes, or permits to be made, before signing them.

(b) The loose-leaf folder in which the minutes are enclosed should have a **locking device**, the key to be kept by the secretary, preferably in the office safe or a locked drawer.

(c) The **minute book** itself should be kept under **lock and key** when not in use.

(d) The pages which are used for adding to the minute book might also be of a **distinctive type** (eg with a watermark). The stock of unused pages should be kept securely.

11.13 S 723 does allow the 'records' of s 722 to be kept in non-legible form, that is on computer disc etc.

12 MINUTES AS EVIDENCE

12.1 Minutes of a meeting which have been signed by the chairman of the meeting (or the next meeting) are evidence of the proceedings of the meeting: s 382(2).

12.2 S 382(2) uses the simple word 'evidence': the implication is that further proof may be needed, and other evidence may be adduced to rebut or correct the minutes.

12.3 To prevent subsequent dispute on a matter which cannot be proved or disproved afterwards, the articles may provide that the minutes are '**conclusive evidence**' in certain circumstances: *Kerr v John Mottram Ltd 1940*.

12.4 The topic most likely to give rise to dispute is whether the chairman's declaration of the result of a vote on a show of hands was correct, say that the resolution was carried or not carried, or that a required three quarters majority was or was not obtained. Table A Article 47 provides that unless a poll is duly demanded at the time, a declaration by the chairman of the result of a vote on a show of hands, once recorded in the minutes of the meeting shall be conclusive evidence without further proof.

12.5 As regards special and extraordinary resolutions, the safeguard against misrepresentation or confusion after the event is statutory: s 378(4).

> 'A declaration by the chairman that the resolution is carried is, unless a poll is demanded, conclusive evidence of the fact without proof of the number or proportion of the votes recorded in favour of or against the resolution.'

12.6 A member may, however, challenge the minutes, even if they have been declared to be 'conclusive evidence', if:

(a) He can show that they are a **false record** fraudulently prepared.

(b) The chairman's **declaration** is **incorrect** by its own terms and are in conflict with the result which it purports to verify.

Re Caratal (New) Mines Ltd 1902
The facts: On a show of hands the chairman declared his count as 6 votes for and 23 against, but added 'there are 200 voting by proxy and I declare the resolution carried'. This was obviously wrong, since proxies do not vote on a show of hands and there had been no poll.

Decision: The chairman's declaration, although recorded in the minutes was, by its own terms, incorrect and therefore invalid.

Inspection of minutes

12.7 Members (but no one else) have a statutory right:

(a) To **inspect** the **minutes** of general meetings - no charge for this

(b) To be **supplied** with a **copy** within seven days of requesting one. If the company fails to comply, it and its officers in default are liable to a fine: s 382

12.8 The company is required to keep the minutes of its general meetings at its **registered office** (and nowhere else) and to make them available for inspection by members, without charge.

12.9 The rights are not always of much practical value, since the minutes of general meetings are usually only a terse, formal record of resolutions passed.

12.10 Note that the rights are confined to minutes of general meetings: members do not have the right to inspect the minutes of board meetings. It is therefore common practice to keep board meeting minutes separate from general meeting minutes.

13 MINUTES OF WRITTEN RESOLUTIONS

13.1 If a written resolution is agreed by a private company in accordance with the requirements set out earlier in this chapter, a record of the resolution and of the member's signatures to it must be entered in a book in the same way as the minutes of general meetings: s 382A(1).

13.2 The point which is reflected in these rules is that written resolutions **take the place** of some decisions made in general meetings; it therefore follows that they should be recorded in the same way.

13.3 The record of written resolutions acts as evidence of the proceedings conducted in agreeing to the resolution, provided they are signed by either a director or the company secretary. Unless the contrary is proved, the statutory requirements relating to those proceedings are deemed to have been complied with.

14 SINGLE MEMBER PRIVATE COMPANIES **Specimen paper**

14.1 Following s 382B, if the sole member takes any decision that could have been taken in general meeting, that member shall (unless it is a written resolution) provide the company with a **written record** of it. This allows the sole member to conduct members' business informally without notice or minutes.

14.2 Filing requirements still apply, for example, in the case of alteration of articles.

14.3 The single member company must hold an annual general meeting unless it has opted out by elective resolution.

14.4 If the single member company has passed an elective resolution dispensing with holding an AGM and has also dispensed with the laying of accounts before a general meeting, the effect will be that no meetings of members will be required. Board meetings, along with resolutions and minutes, are still required, although the **written resolution procedure** may be used.

14.5 Single member companies may conduct member business by written resolution provided they follow the formalities of s 381A.

14.6 Written resolutions cannot be used to remove a director or auditor from office. The 'written record' procedure under s 382B would appear to be available for this purpose. However, while the regulations do not explicitly prohibit this, case law suggests that where company law requires special procedures, an informal decision is not sufficient, for example, in reduction of share capital: *Re Barry Artist 1985*.

Chapter roundup

- You must be clear in your mind about the distinctions as to **function**, **notice** and **voting** regarding ordinary, extraordinary, special and elective **resolutions**. In particular distinguish between ordinary resolutions and ordinary resolutions of which special notice to the company is required, such as a motion to remove a director under s 303.
- Unanimous agreement of members by conference call, in **writing** or by means of written resolutions is also very important.
- Writing the **minutes** of company meetings falls to the company secretary, so make sure to learn the rules.
- Special considerations apply to **single member private companies**. These must be learnt.

Test your knowledge

1 Draft a resolution to be passed in general meeting for the payment of a final dividend. (see paras 1.3, 1.4)

2 Explain how resolutions may be expressed to relate to, or alter, existing documents, giving examples (1.8, 1.9)

3 Contrast the four different types of resolution which may be passed at a company general meeting. (2.1, 2.3, 2.7 - 2.9, 3.1 - 3.3, 3.5 - 3.6, 4, 5.1)

4 In what circumstances is it necessary to give special notice of an ordinary resolution? (2.9)

5 In what situations are (a) extraordinary and (b) special resolutions usually required? (3.4, 4.3)

6 When may an elective resolution be passed? (5.1, 5.2)

7 To what extent is it possible to amend a special or extraordinary resolution of which notice has been given in convening the meeting? (7.3, 7.4)

8 State three types of resolution (or agreement) of which a copy must be delivered to the Companies Registry. (8.3, 8.4)

9 How may binding decisions of members of a company be achieved without holding a general meeting? (9.6, 10.1)

10 In what form may minutes of a general meeting be kept and how should they be kept safe? (11.11, 11.12)

11 What records need to be kept of written resolutions? (13.1)

12 Do single member private companies need to have meetings? (14.4)

Now try illustrative question 10 at the end of the Study Text

Chapter 9

BOARD MEETINGS

This chapter covers the following topics.

Introduction

The same general principles apply to meetings of directors as to class and general meetings of members of the company: a quorum must be present, there must be minutes as a record of the proceedings etc. However there are also a number of special features of board meetings which require separate consideration in this chapter.

The general differences between board and general meetings include the following.

(a) A board of directors is a form of management committee, so it transacts a different kind of business from the matters of routine or policy which are submitted to a general meeting.

(b) The directors are usually a small group, who meet often and know each other well, so they can transact business with less formality. It is unusual, for example, to take a formal vote at a directors' meeting, while many decisions are taken by consensus (general agreement).

(c) The legislation does not require a company to hold board meetings, although the company's Articles may. Provided directors comply with the latter it is not necessary to hold board meetings face-to-face; it would be possible, for instance, to conduct them by conference call or via satellite. This contrasts with the rule on general meetings of the company (see Chapter 5).

(d) A board meeting often deals, at one sitting, with many more separate items than a general meeting. Hence the agenda is more complicated and detailed.

(e) A member of a company may usually cast his vote at a general meeting to suit his own interests. However a director is often prevented from voting at all, at a board meeting, on any matter in which he has a personal interest.

A very large board may find it convenient to appoint standing (continuing) or special *committees* from among the directors:

(a) To deal with particular business, of a routine or special nature

(b) To meet frequently and at short notice when it may be impossible to convene a full meeting of the board

We will look briefly at committees of the board at the end of the chapter.

1 THE NATURE OF A BOARD MEETING

1.1 One of the basic principles of company law is that the powers which are delegated to the directors under the articles (Table A Article 70) are given to them as a collective body. The **board meeting** is the proper place for the exercise of those powers (unless they have been validly passed on, or 'sub-delegated', to committees or individual directors).

Re Portuguese Consolidated Copper Mines Ltd 1889
The facts: The power to allot shares was vested in the directors, of whom there were four. Two directors met, without proper notice of a meeting given to the other two. The two directors present decided that a quorum should be two and allotted shares in response to an application. On a later occasion these two directors and one of the others met, approved the allotment and also the quorum of two. The fourth director sent in a letter, which arrived later still, giving his agreement.

Decision: As there had been no board meeting, properly convened and held, the allotment was invalid.

1.2 However, an irregularity in convening or holding a board meeting may often be remedied by subsequent ratification or the mere acquiescence of all concerned in what has been done.

Face-to-face board meetings

1.3 One of the debatable points about the nature of a board meeting is how far the presence of all the directors in one place is required to constitute the meeting.

(a) It is considered that if all the directors are **in communication**, usually by telephone, though not assembled together, this suffices to constitute a board meeting. Some companies have begun to include in their articles a provision for a 'board meeting' of this kind.

(b) It is also clear (*Barron v Potter*) that even if all the directors are present in one place, there can be no board meeting if **proper notice** has **not** been **given**, and if any of the directors object to holding the meeting in those circumstances.

Signed resolution as a substitute for a board meeting

1.4 As with general meetings, there is a 'signed resolution' procedure (Table A Article 93). Any resolution signed by *all* the directors who are entitled to notice of a board meeting (including alternate directors, on behalf of their 'appointor' directors) will be 'as valid and effectual as if it had been passed at a meeting of directors... duly convened and held.'

2 CONVENING A BOARD MEETING **Specimen paper, 6/00**

2.1 There are no legal requirements as to when or how often a board meeting shall be held, nor as to the notice which is required to convene a meeting.

2.2 Most companies follow Table A Article 88 (or 1948 Table A Article 98) in providing that:

(a) 'A director may, and the secretary at the request of a director shall, call a **meeting of directors**'.

(b) 'It shall **not** be **necessary** to **give notice** of a meeting to a director who is absent from the United Kingdom'. Among other things, this means that a resolution signed by 'all' the directors (entitled to notice of the board meeting), instead of passing it at the meeting, is valid without the signature of a director absent from the UK.

2.3 If the board has previously agreed to meet at **fixed dates**, and at the same place, it is **unnecessary** to give directors **notice** of each meeting. It is in any case usually necessary to send them an agenda, which serves as a reminder.

BPP PUBLISHING

Content of the notice

2.4 Although there are dicta to the contrary (in connection with proceedings which were not proper meetings at all such as the *Portuguese Consolidated* case above), it seems that there is no legal requirement for a notice issued to convene a board meeting to specify the business which it is to transact.

> *La Compagnie de Mayville v Whitley 1896*
> *The facts:* The business set out in the notice did not include the appointment of an additional director, which was in fact made at the meeting.
>
> *Decision:* The appointment was valid since a board must be left free to discuss whatever matters of business the directors consider pertinent, without restricting it to items of which notice has been given.

2.5 There are however, practical reasons why notice of the business, in the form of an **agenda**, is usually given. Some items of business are discussion of lengthy papers, such as management reports or proposals for new projects. Directors cannot usually discuss such matters adequately without having read the papers before the meeting. Hence it is good - and certainly common - practice to issue an agenda in advance.

Period of notice

2.6 The period of notice given to convene a board meeting need be no longer than is **reasonable** to enable directors to attend. Even five minutes' notice has been held reasonable, where the director in question was free to attend and close at hand: *Browne v La Trinidad 1887*.

2.7 This flexibility over notice must not be abused, however.

> *Re Homer District Consolidated Gold Mines 1888*
> *The facts:* There were five directors. Two called a board meeting on three hours' notice, knowing that one of the directors could not attend until an hour after the time appointed for the meeting, and without knowing whether a fourth director could attend or not. The fifth director was abroad and no notice was sent to him. The notice issued did not specify the business to be transacted. The two directors who had called the meeting, and who sufficed as a quorum, met at the appointed time.
>
> *Decision:* 'What was done on that occasion was not the act of the board', and was invalid.

2.8 If no prior notice is given, the mere presence of all the directors does not permit a meeting to be held, should any of them object: *Barron v Potter 1914*.

3 QUORUM FOR A BOARD MEETING

3.1 In order to constitute a board meeting, as any other a **properly appointed chairman** must **preside,** and a **quorum** must be **present**.

3.2 Most companies have articles in common form (Table A Article 89) which provide that:

> 'The quorum for the transaction of the business of the directors may be fixed by the directors and unless so fixed at any other number shall be two.'

3.3 Exceptionally, a decision of the directors to fix a quorum may be deduced merely from their practice at past meetings. However it is much more satisfactory to pass a resolution, duly minuted, fixing the quorum.

3.4 It has been said that even if there are two or more directors, a quorum may be defined to require the presence of one or more named directors, for instance if they are, or represent, major shareholders.

3.5 If the articles permit the appointment of **alternate directors**, an alternate director present in place of his appointor may be reckoned in the quorum. However if a director appoints another director to be his alternate, to vote for him in his absence, that director may only be counted once, as one member of the board and not two (Table A Article 89).

Loss of quorum

3.6 Table A Article 90 provides for a fall in number of directors to less than quorum level.

> 'The continuing directors or a sole continuing director may act notwithstanding any vacancies in their number but, if the number of directors is less than the number fixed as the quorum, the continuing directors or director may act only for the purpose of *filling vacancies* or of *calling a general meeting*.'

You should note these two purposes for which an inquorate board meeting may continue to act.

3.7 Note also that on each item of business, any director who is **disqualified** from voting by having a personal interest may have to be **excluded** in reckoning the quorum for that item. (More will be said about personal interest below.)

4 AGENDA FOR A BOARD MEETING 12/98

4.1 The agenda will vary according to the type and formality of the meeting and the particular business to be discussed. A typical agenda might include the following.

(a) **Membership**: an optional item allowing the chairman to introduce new members or allude to retirements or resignations

(b) **Apologies for absence**

(c) **Minutes of the last meeting**: read out, or previously circulated

(d) **Matters arising** from the minutes

(e) **Business of the present meeting**: presentation of reports, resolutions etc. as appropriate. Examples include:

   (i) Consideration of progress reports, financial statements and management accounts

   (ii) Proposals for acquisition or disposal of assets or businesses, and public announcements to be made

(f) **Any other business**

(g) **Date of the next meeting**

4.2 The **chairman's agenda** is slightly different from that circulated to everyone else.

(a) Each item on the agenda is followed by **brief notes**: information updates, background detail, explanations, reminders of when an item was previously discussed, any problems that might arise between members and need sensitive handling etc.

(b) **A wide right hand margin** or blank facing page, for the chairman to make notes as the meeting progresses.

This means that the chairman is fully prepared to provide all necessary information to the meeting, and can conduct the proceedings with tact and authority.

5 AGENDA FOR THE FIRST BOARD MEETING

Specimen paper, 6/99

5.1 The first board meeting of a newly formed company is of a rather different character, since there are a number of non-recurrent items of business which must be dealt with before the company can begin to conduct its business.

Starton Nowt Limited

Meeting of the directors at [address] on [date] at [time]

AGENDA

1. Table certificate of incorporation dated .... and printed copy of memorandum and articles of association as registered
2. Table copy of Form 10 as registered and note (i) the appointment of the directors and secretary and (ii) the address of the registered office
3. Lay statutory books of company
4. Elect a chairman of the board
5. Appoint Messrs Ballants, Sheet & Co, Chartered Accountants, auditors of the company
6. Appoint Berkeley Bank plc as company bankers (Bank's standard form of resolution attached)
7. Appoint Messrs Loyer & Co to be the company's solicitors
8. Adopt a common seal (impression to be marked in the margin for identification)
9. Resolve that the accounting reference date of the company be 31st December of each year, pursuant to s 224 of the Companies Act 1985, and authorise the secretary to give notice thereof to the Companies Registry
10. Allotment of shares
11. Elective resolutions
12. Declaration of directors' interests
13. Dates of future board meetings
14. Any other business.

5.2 There may, of course, be other items of business, according to the circumstances of the company, such as approval of service agreements of managing director and/or other senior employees or execution of a contract to acquire another business.

5.3 Many of the items on the above agenda are self-explanatory, but the following notes may be helpful. They follow the sequence of the agenda itself.

1/2 These are **matters of record**. The directors should take formal note that the company has been formed (with the effective date), and that they have been appointed its directors by virtue of s 13.

3 The purpose of this is to **remind directors** of the records the company must keep.

4 Once satisfied on these matters, the directors should **appoint** one of themselves to be **chairman**, as provided by the articles. Without a chairman the meeting could not proceed.

5 It is **not essential** to **appoint auditors** at this point: some time will elapse before the first annual accounts are audited. However it is useful to have them in office in case accounting records etc have to be discussed with them, so that the audit of the first accounts may proceed smoothly later on.

6 The company must open a **bank account** in order to carry on its business. The bank will insist that the resolution is in its own standard form of mandate, covering such

matters as: authorised signatories of cheques; who may withdraw company property deposited with the bank for safekeeping etc.

If any of the directors are to sign cheques drawn on the account, their **specimen signatures** will be added to the copy of the resolution supplied to the bank.

7 It is **not essential** to make a **formal appointment** of **solicitors** to the company, but a continuing relationship tends to produce better advice.

8 By convention a **company seal** has the **full name** of the company round the edge, with 'Limited' in the middle, and nothing else. It is the company's signature. Although the Companies Act 1989 removes the requirement that a company should have a common seal, in practice most will still do so since it is a requirement of many foreign jurisdictions that company documents be sealed.

9 The company's accounting reference date will automatically be the **last day** of the **month** in which the **anniversary** of the **company's incorporation** falls unless changed by the directors. It is as well to get this formality, which determines the date to which the annual accounts are to be made up, considered - before it is overlooked.

10 The company will need to raise **permanent capital by allotting shares**. It is assumed that the articles give directors the required authority to allot shares (s 80). If not, no shares may be allotted until authority is given at a general meeting. Written applications for shares, and cheques payable to the company, will be produced (or their receipt reported). Restrictions on allotment of ordinary shares for cash to non-members (s 89) should be remembered.

11 The company may wish to simplify the way it does business by using **elective resolutions** (discussed in Chapter 8).

12 This will be the first time directors have to **declare interests** in **contracts** with the company under s 317.

6 CONDUCT OF BOARD MEETINGS

6.1 There are some aspects of procedure which should be strictly observed.

(a) The discussion should follow the **sequence** of the **agenda**, and be confined at each stage to the item currently under discussion.

(b) Although it is not usually necessary to take a vote, the chairman should sum up 'the **sense** of the **meeting**', so that a suitably worded decision or conclusion may be formulated for inclusion in the minutes.

(c) If a vote does appear to be necessary, it will be along the lines of a **show of hands** or **voice vote**. The usual procedure is to 'go round the table' inviting each member of the board to declare his vote for or against. If any member abstains, perhaps because a personal interest does not allow him to vote, this should be noted and recorded.

(d) Each member of the board, including the chairman, has **one vote**. The articles may provide otherwise, say by weighted voting or a veto given to a particular member (*Salmon v Quin & Axtens* in Chapter 4). The chairman may also be given a casting vote, with which to resolve a tied issue.

(e) Although the chairman's notes on his agenda are not recognised as evidence, it is good practice for him to note the outcome of each discussion as the debate proceeds.

7 THE ICSA CODE OF GOOD BOARDROOM PRACTICE **Specimen paper, 6/00**

7.1 The ICSA published a code of good boardroom practice in March 1991 which is intended to be a guide for company secretaries and directors to the principles and practice required by formal boardroom procedures.

7.2 The aim of the code is not to prescribe a set of procedures but rather to communicate basic principles of universal applicability.

7.3 The code also recommends that directors should periodically review their boardroom procedures so as to ensure that they meet the standards of the code.

7.4 Thirteen principles are listed in the code.

Written procedures

(a) Written procedures should be **authorised** by the board on all matters covered in the code; each director should have a copy of these procedures, and the audit committee of the board (if there is one) should have responsibility for monitoring their operation.

Guidance to directors

(b) Guidance should be given to each director on appointment as to how his or her **duties** should be **performed**. Non-executive directors should be told:

- How to find out information about the company
- How to requisition a board meeting

Information

(c) Each director should be given the **same information** at the **same time** before or at a board meeting, and each should have **sufficient time** to consider it.

Matters requiring the board's approval

(d) The board should identify those matters or transactions which require **prior board approval**. There should also be procedures laid down as to how to handle a decision which must be made in the interim between two board meetings; ideally, written resolutions of the entire board should be obtained.

Material contracts

(e) **All material contracts**, and contracts outside the scope of the company's ordinary business, should have **prior board approval**.

(f) Definitions of '**material**' and '**ordinary**' **business** should be agreed by the board.

(g) If there is any uncertainty as to whether a contract falls into either of the two categories in (e) and (f), it should be assumed that the contract should be brought before the board.

Agenda

(h) The chairman, in consultation with the company secretary, should decide the **content** and **presentation** of the agenda.

Conduct of the meeting

(i) The company secretary is responsible to the chairman for the meeting's proper administration. To fulfil this task the **secretary** should be **present at all meetings** and prepare the minutes of them.

(j) Even though there may not be a formal agenda item, any director or the company secretary should be permitted by the chairman to raise any matter concerning the company's compliance with:

- The code of practice
- Its articles and memorandum of association
- Any other legal or regulatory requirement

Minutes

(k) **Decisions** taken at meetings, and the **background** to them, should be **recorded** in the **minutes.** Papers presented at the meeting should be identified in the minutes and retained. Procedures are required for the circulation and approval of minutes.

Board committees

(l) If the board is permitted by the articles to delegate powers to a committee, the board should give **prior approval** to:

- The membership and quorum of the committee
- The committee's terms of reference

- the extent of its delegated powers

(m) **Board committee minutes**, or a summary of the minutes, should be **circulated** to the **full board** before its next meeting; at that meeting there should be an opportunity to ask questions relating to the committee's minutes.

8 SOLE DIRECTOR AND BOARD MEETINGS

8.1 The questions was raised in *Re Neptune Vehicle Washing Equipment Ltd 1995* whether a sole director had to comply with s 317 and if so how. It was held that a sole director could **hold a meeting** with a company secretary or by himself. Even if holding a meeting alone a director had to make and minute a declaration of interests in contracts, pausing for thought over potential conflicts of interest.

9 MINUTES OF BOARD MEETINGS 12/98, 6/99

9.1 The Companies Act 1985 s 382 imposes the same requirements on **keeping** minutes of board as of general meetings. Remember however that the right of **inspection** by members is confined to minutes of general meetings: s 382. Thus there is no prescribed place at which minutes of board meetings are to be kept.

9.2 Every director has a right to **inspect** the **minutes** of board meetings, and he may bring a professional adviser with him when he does so.

9.3 The auditor has a **statutory right** of **access** to the company books for the purpose of his audit: this entitles him to inspect the board minutes.

9.4 The significance of minutes as evidence of the proceedings is the same for board as for general meetings - see Chapter 8.

Content of the minutes

9.5 The records of decisions of board meetings are often less formal in style than the minutes of general meetings, since boards usually proceed by consensus, after discussion of each topic, rather than by formal resolution.

9.6 However, the minutes of a board meeting should always record clearly:

(a) **What was done**, for instance if a particular document was discussed

(b) **What was decided**, usually in the form of a minute of resolution: 'It was resolved that...'

9.7 Other basics of minute writing apply equally to annual general meetings and board meetings. These include the need for minutes to be **concise and complete**, written in the **past tense**, record which directors were present (and when) and who else was in attendance, and be **headed** and **serially numbered**. Board minutes may however contain more details of discussions that take place than the minutes of annual general meetings would.

9.8 We have already noted that directors have a number of obligations, such as to disclose interests, to abstain from voting etc. They may also decide to abstain from voting for other reasons, or request that their vote against a resolution be minuted.

10 DRAFT AND CERTIFIED RESOLUTIONS

10.1 In some contexts, the law attaches particular importance to a formal resolution passed at a board meeting.

10.2 In certain situations, a third party would want to ensure that the resolution passed is set out in terms which are satisfactory to him. He may supply his own **draft resolution**, in accordance with legal advice which he has received, to be considered by the board and, if approved, duly minuted as the board's decision.

10.3 If it is agreed that the resolution is to be in the proposed form, the third party will usually ask for a **certified copy** of the resolution.

> 'Extract from the minutes of a meeting of the board of directors of ABC Ltd on ... 20X1.
>
> *Bank debenture*
> It was resolved that..... [*text as proposed by the bank*].
>
> Certified a true copy
> Signed ....
> *Secretary*'

11 BOARD COMMITTEES 6/99

11.1 The directors as a board have various extensive powers to manage the company, which are delegated to them by the articles of association (Table A Article 70). In principle, people to whom powers are delegated in this way may not delegate them to anyone else, but should exercise them personally. However, it is often convenient for a board to delegate powers, usually in relation to specific matters, to a **committee**. The articles (Table A Article 72) therefore provide for delegation of powers to committees, (the membership of which must include, but is not confined to, directors) including a possible committee of one: *Re Fireproof Doors Ltd 1916*.

11.2 A board might appoint a **remuneration committee**, consisting of the (non-executive) chairman and another non-executive director, to review the salaries paid to working (full-time) directors, and to recommend increases for approval by the board.

11.3 In the case of a listed company, the Stock Exchange requires that:

(a) Any committee of the board shall have a **majority** of members who are **directors** (although co-option of others may be permitted).

(b) No decision of a mixed committee shall be valid unless a majority of those present are directors.

11.4 In appointing a committee it is usual to lay down terms of reference, including:

(a) A specification of any powers the committee may have to take **executive action**

(b) A quorum for the meetings of the committee. Unless a quorum is fixed at a specified number, it is to be **all the members of the committee.**

11.5 The board will want to be kept informed of the actions taken by committees which have been given executive powers. Normal practice is to table at each meeting of the full board the minutes of committee meetings which have been held since the last full board meeting.

11.6 Note that where a director is required to disclose his interests in a company contract to the board under s 317, and he does so only to a committee of the board, that disclosure is not effective to relieve him of his obligations to avoid a conflict of interests: *Guinness plc v Saunders & Another 1990.*

11.7 As far as the procedure of committees of the board is concerned, Table A Article 72 provides that:

> 'the proceedings of a committee with two or more members shall be governed by the articles regulating the proceedings of directors, so far as they are capable of applying.'

12 DUTIES OF THE SECRETARY

12.1 The secretary is the link between the company staff and the board, which is the source of decisions on matters of policy. He should give adequate time and attention to the important part of his working duties comprised in ensuring that relevant board decisions are communicated to the people who will implement them.

Exercise

The two directors of Able Ltd, a small private company, have been involved in a serious accident. One has just died as a result. The survivor, Quentin, wishes to pass a board resolution very urgently. Advise him of the various ways, if any, in which he can achieve this.

Solution

A quorum for a meeting of the board of directors is two: Table A Art 88. As there is now only one surviving director, there is no readily available means of achieving a quorum, which is required to pass the proposed resolution.

However, the articles (Table A Art 90) also provide that if the number of directors is less than the fixed quorum, the surviving director(s) *may* act as a board for the purpose of filling the vacancy, or calling a general meeting.

Quentin's best course is to hold a board meeting for the purpose of co-opting another director, as provided by Art 90. The power to appoint directors (up to the limit of the number of vacancies) is given by Art 79. Quentin may choose whomever he considers suitable, even someone who is not a shareholder of the company: Table A articles do not fix a directors' share qualification. After appointing a second director, who may be present at the time, the board consists of two directors, who may proceed to pass the urgent resolution.

Quentin might convene a board meeting, for the purpose of convening a further *general* meeting. But this would take time to arrange, if indeed there are sufficient surviving shareholders to provide a quorum at a general meeting. There is no advantage in resorting to that alternative.

The new director co-opted by Quentin would hold office until the next annual general meeting. He would then retire, but might offer himself for re-election: Table A Art 79.

Chapter roundup

- **Board meetings** are the **forum for** many of the most important decisions affecting a company. You need to be aware of the nature and functions of directors, and in particular the rules relating to their interest in contracts.
- As with other types of meeting, the **chairman** of a board meeting has a very important role.
- The rules as to convening and conducting a board meeting, including those as to quorum, are often the topics of exam questions and so you should be sure to know them thoroughly. The ICSA's code of good boardroom practice has effects in this area.

Test your knowledge

1 Give the facts, and explain the significance, of the *Portuguese Consolidated Copper Mines* case. (see para 1.1)

2 How may directors reach a formal decision without meeting as a board? (1.4)

3 What are the provisions of Table A on convening board meetings? (2.2)

4 What quorum is set by the articles for board meetings? (3.2)

5 If the number of directors is reduced to less than the quorum level, what remedial action may be taken? (3.6)

6 Specify two items of business likely to be done at the first meeting of a board of directors of a newly formed company. (5.1)

7 State six of the thirteen principles set down by the ICSA code of good boardroom practice. (7.4)

8 Who is entitled to inspect the minutes of board meetings? (9.1 - 9.3)

9 How may a third party make sure that a board resolution has been passed in terms satisfactory to him? (10.1 - 10.3)

10 What is the quorum for a meeting of a committee appointed by a board? (11.4)

11 What is the effect of a director disclosing a personal interest to a committee rather than to the full board? (11.6)

Now try illustrative question 11 at the end of the Study Text

Part B

Incorporation and corporate compliance

Chapter 10

COMPANY FORMATION

This chapter covers the following topics.

1 The process of incorporation
2 Procedures for registration of a company
3 Procedures for re-registration of a company
4 Other types of UK company
5 Oversea companies
6 Company searches

Introduction

In Part B of this Study Text we turn our attention to formation of a company and compliance matters. A company secretary will have an important role to play in day to day compliance work.

Most of the topics in this section will be familiar to you from your *Corporate Law* studies. However, as you will, see the emphasis is different. Instead of being concerned with legal principles, we are concerned with practical and procedural matters.

1 THE PROCESS OF INCORPORATION

1.1 As you will remember from company law, the single most important aspect of incorporation is that the company is a separate legal person unlike a partnership. It is separate and distinct from its owners who hold shares in the company. This principle was established in 1897 in the famous case of *Salomon*. This can lead to many advantages for a trading concern, such as limited liability, perpetual succession and being able to raise capital outside its membership.

1.2 With these advantages there are however, corresponding disadvantages. On incorporation the company becomes subject to considerable regulation and disclosure requirements under the Companies Act.

Choosing a type of company **6/98, 12/99**

1.3 In deciding which type of company to form the choice lies between the following:

(a) A limited or unlimited company
(b) If limited, between a company limited by shares and a company limited by guarantee
(c) If limited by shares, between a public and a private company

1.4 If an **unlimited company** goes into **insolvent liquidation**, its members are liable to contribute to its assets whatever amount is required to enable the company to pay its debts in full: s 74 Insolvency Act 1986. This is suitable for a company intended merely to hold property, without incurring liabilities.

1.5 A **company limited by guarantee** may not issue share capital: s 1(4) and must be a private company. This type of company is best suited to a non-trading company, formed to provide services to members, for example a trade association: they pay for those services as received. It is also the only type of company, formed for specified purposes such as art, charity or education, which may omit the word 'limited' from its name, if it complies with certain conditions preventing it from paying dividends or returning capital to members: s 30. By the memorandum of association every member is liable, if the company goes into insolvent liquidation, to contribute to the payment of its debts up to a specified amount, which need not be large: s 74(3) Insolvency Act 1986.

1.6 The key characteristics of a **private company limited by shares** are the following.

(a) Each member is **liable to contribute** a **fixed amount** for his shares to the company. If he, or a previous holder of the shares, has paid that amount in full he has no further liability for the debts of the company.

(b) Its name **ends** with the **word 'Limited'** (which may be abbreviated to 'Ltd'). This is the only visible sign that it is not a public limited company (designated 'plc').

1.7 The characteristics of a **public company** are described in greater detail later. They must have a minimum authorised share capital of **£50,000**: s118.

1.8 The main advantage of a public over a private company is that it may raise capital by the offer of its shares or debentures to the public (as described in a later chapter).

2 PROCEDURES FOR REGISTRATION OF A COMPANY **Specimen paper, 6/99**

Preliminary considerations

2.1 Certain documents are required to obtain registration, but before completing them it is advisable to consider the following.

Time available

2.2 It takes time to complete the documents, in particular the memorandum and articles of association, and the registrar will usually issue his certificate about a fortnight after they are delivered to him. If there is not enough time for all this, it may be better to buy and adapt an existing **'off the shelf' company** from a registration agent. Such a company will already have been registered, providing a ready-made memorandum, articles and name - which can later be changed, if the new owners desire.

Name of company

2.3 The name of the company must be decided on, since it must appear on the documents. Factors affecting the choice of name are discussed in the next chapter. The registrar will reject the document if the name is unacceptable.

Registration fee

2.4 Generally on submission of documents to the registrar a fee (for administrative costs) will be payable. The amount of fee may change from time to time and it is recommended to check with Companies House what fee is payable.

Submission of documents to registrar

2.5 A company is formed by submitting certain documents to the Registrar of Companies. These documents must comply with legal requirements and contain details appropriate to the particular type of company to be formed.

Memorandum of association

2.6 This should theoretically follow Table B, set out in the Companies Act as closely as possible. The substance of the memorandum is considered in the next chapter. The following practical requirements apply.

(a) It must normally be **signed** by at **least two subscribers**, each of whom thereby agrees to take at least (generally only) one share and to pay the amount due on it. On incorporation they become the original members of the company.

(b) It must have the **subscribers' signatures witnessed** by adding the signature of another person as witness, and a date inserted: s 2(6). Typed names below signatures are useful for identification.

(c) It must be **'printed'** on **paper of A4 size**. 'Printing' for this purpose includes electrostatic (xerox) and other permanent methods of reproduction, but not typescript.

Articles of association

2.7 The most usual practice is to adopt **Table A** subject to specified modifications. The subscribers to the memorandum should also sign the articles, their signatures are witnessed and a date inserted.

Form 10 (particulars of first directors and secretary)

2.8 This should include the directors' signed **consent accepting appointment** and the **intended address** of the **registered office** on incorporation.

Form 12 (declaration of compliance)

2.9 This form is a **statutory declaration** by a solicitor engaged in the formation of the company, or one of the directors or secretary, to the effect that the Companies Act **requirements** that apply to the formation of the company have been **obeyed**.

Other documents

2.10 A number of other documents may be necessary in certain circumstances.

(a) **Form 225**. This form should be delivered if the date of the company's accounting period is not the last day of the month in which its anniversary of incorporation falls.

(b) **Form 88(2)** which contains returns on allotments of shares issued for cash, shares issued wholly or in part for a consideration other than cash or as bonus share issues.

FORM 10	Statement of first directors and secretary and intended address of registered office. See Appendix 1.
FORM 12	Statutory declaration of compliance with requirements on application for registration of a company. See Appendix 2.
FORM 225	Notice of accounting reference date. See Appendix 3.
FORM 88(2) (new style)	Return on allotments of shares. This covers shares issued for cash, shares issued wholly or in part for a consideration other than cash, or as a bonus share issue. See Appendix 4.

2.11 If the documents are in order the registrar issues his **certificate of incorporation**, which gives the name of the company, the date of incorporation and the fact that it is a private company.

Forming a public company

2.12 The same four documents as were described earlier are delivered to obtain the incorporation of a public company. The memorandum differs in certain respects, and the name and certificate of incorporation will indicate that it is a public company.

Form 117

2.13 Although a public company exists from the date of incorporation, it may not commence business or exercise its borrowing powers until it has obtained an additional certificate, under s 117, from the registrar. The company applies for this trading certificate using **Form 117**, which is a statutory declaration by a director or by the secretary of the company which states that share capital of a nominal value of **not less** than **£50,000** has been allotted. On allotment of its shares, at least one quarter of the nominal value and the whole of any premium must be paid up, so a **minimum** of **£12,500** must have been **subscribed** and **paid for**: s 101(1).

FORM 117	Application by a public company for certificate to commence business and statutory declaration in support. See Appendix 5.

2.14 If the company commences business or borrows before it has obtained a s 117 certificate, the transaction is valid - but the company and the officers are at fault, and liable to a fine. In this situation, the Department of Trade and Industry (DTI) may call on the company to comply with s 117 within 21 days; failure to do so makes them liable to the other party to the transaction for any loss which he may have suffered.

Forming other types of company

2.15 The statutory form of memorandum and articles for a company limited by guarantee is **Form C** and, for an unlimited company, **Form E**. Companies of these types are required to comply with the following.

(a) They must be **private companies**.

(b) They must **register articles**: they cannot simply adopt the relevant statutory model: s 7. *Only* Table A (and in future Table G) can be adopted.

Other points on formation of a company

2.16 As soon as convenient after the receipt of the certificate of incorporation, it is usual (and in the case of a new public company, essential) to set up a **first board meeting**, so that the arrangements for commencement of business may be completed. This is dealt with in the chapter on board meetings.

2.17 It is possible, if sufficient notice is given, to arrange for the certificate of incorporation to be issued on a specified future date, when that is required.

2.18 A company is required to print certain **particulars** on its **letterheads** and some other business stationery. It is a little risky to print stocks before it is known that the company will be formed with the name selected. However it is a necessary preliminary to doing business, and should be effected as soon as prudently possible.

Exercise

Florence, Dougal and Zebedee have operated as a partnership for five years trading in domestic carpets. The business has been successful and they are now considering expanding the business operations by opening three new shops and an additional wholesale unit. The partners are aware that the expansion will require new business capital. They are considering the formation of a company rather than continuing as a partnership.

What types of company may be formed under the Companies Act 1985? Which type of company is suitable for this business?

Solution

The main categories of companies which may be formed under the Companies Act 1985 are a public company, limited by shares, and a private company, which may be limited by shares or by guarantee or be an unlimited company.

A private company limited by shares is the most suitable type for a small business venture of this kind. It offers the advantages of being a corporate entity separate from its members, giving them the protection of limited liability.

The main restriction on a private company is that it may not offer its shares or debentures to the public. It is however subject to fewer restrictions than a public company in respect of dividends and loans to directors. It may use capital to finance the purchase of its own shares and it may give financial assistance for the purchase of its shares. If the company ranks as a small or a medium-sized company for purposes of its annual accounts, the accounts delivered to the registrar need not contain all the material required in the accounts of a public company. The 'elective regime' of the Companies Act 1989 allows further elements of new flexibility to a private company in respect of the AGM, share allotment, auditors, accounts and required majorities for authorisation of meetings at short notice.

3 PROCEDURES FOR RE-REGISTRATION OF A COMPANY

Re-registration of a private as a public company

3.1 There are two stages involved.

- The passing of a **special resolution** by the company in general meeting
- **Application** to the **registrar**, with supporting documents

The change only becomes effective when the registrar issues his certificate of re-registration under s 47.

3.2 The company should check it fulfils the Companies Act requirements for registration as a public company. These include having available for registration the documents listed below, and also the following.

(a) The company should have a **minimum** of **two directors**: s 282(1).

(b) The company should have a **suitably qualified company secretary**: s 286.

(c) The company should fulfil the **minimum authorised share capital requirements**: ss 45 and 118.

General meeting

3.3 As a preliminary to the general meeting, there should be a meeting of the board of directors. The directors approve the issue of the notice to convene the general meeting for the following purposes (to be effected by passing a **special resolution**).

CERTIFICATE OF INCORPORATION OF A PRIVATE LIMITED COMPANY

NO.2589887

I hereby certify that
DEKOY LIMITED

is this day incorporated under the Companies Act 1985 as a private company and that the Company is limited.

Given under my hand at the Companies Registration Office, Cardiff, the 8 March 2000

A.M. Evans
A. M. Evans
an authorised officer

(a) That the company be **re-registered** as a public company.

(b) That the **memorandum** and (if necessary) **articles be altered** to conform to public company requirements. The minimum changes to the memorandum include the following.

(i) **Changing** the **name,** to omit 'Limited' and to substitute 'public limited company' (abbreviated if desired to 'plc')

(ii) **Adding** to the memorandum a **clause declaring** the company to be a **public limited company**: s 43(2).

(c) It may also be necessary to **approve** an **increase** in the company's authorised share capital if the nominal value is less than £50,000.

Documents to be filed

3.4 A signed copy of the special resolution, together with the revised memorandum and articles, must be filed within 15 days after it is passed, to comply with s 380. The following documents must also be submitted to the registrar.

Form 43(3)

3.5 Application (Form 43(3)) for re-registration will be required.

The auditors' written statement

3.6 This should state that in their opinion the company's **balance sheet** shows that the amount of its **net assets** is not **less than** the **aggregate of its called-up share capital and reserves.**

Relevant balance sheet

3.7 The balance sheet must have been prepared at a date **not more than 7 months** before the application which it supports. It is then a 'relevant' balance sheet: s 43(4). An 'unqualified' auditors' report is elaborately defined by s 46 (s 46). If the auditors do make some reservation which is not material, their report is 'unqualified' for the purposes of re-registration.

Valuation report

3.8 If the company has allotted shares for a **non-cash consideration,** between the date of the balance sheet and the passing of the special resolution, there must also be included in the documents a valuation report on that consideration.

Form 43(3)(e)

3.9 The **statutory declaration** is that the following has occurred.

(a) The **special resolution** has been **passed**.

(b) **No shares** have been **allotted** since the date of the balance sheet or, if they have been, a valuation is produced.

(c) Shares of a **nominal value** of at least **£50,000** have been allotted and paid up as described above.

The registrar is entitled to accept the declaration and other documents as sufficient evidence, without conducting his own enquiry. If he is satisfied that the documents are in order, he issues his certificate of re-registration, which is conclusive.

FORM 43(3)	Application by a private company for re-registration as a public company. See Appendix 6.
FORM 43(3)(e)	Declaration of compliance with requirements by a private company on application for re-registration as a public company. See Appendix 7.

Re-registration of a public company as private

3.10 In some circumstances this change is **compulsory**, for example if the capital of the company is reduced by court order to less than the required minimum of £50,000 under the procedure prescribed by ss 135-8. The procedure described below applies only when re-registration is applied for as the **voluntary** act of the company. It is rare, but it has happened, in the case of a listed company deciding to leave the Stock Exchange and go private again.

3.11 There must be a **general meeting** to pass a special resolution to effect the changes. In particular, the name is changed to end with 'Limited' and the 'public company clause' is omitted from the memorandum: s 53(2).

3.12 A copy of the special resolution must also be delivered to the registry within 15 days to comply with s 380. The following should also be submitted:

(a) **Application** (Form 53 signed by a director or by the secretary) for re-registration

(b) A copy of the **special resolution**

(c) A printed copy of the **memorandum** (if applicable) and the articles in their altered (private company) form

(d) Payment of a **fee**

A public company may only apply for re-registration as a private company *limited* by shares or by guarantee; it may not become an unlimited company.

FORM 53	Application by a public company for re-registration as a private company. See Appendix 8.

3.13 The registrar takes no action until the expiry of a period of **28 days** from the passing of the special resolution. Within that period application for cancellation of the special resolution may be made to the court by:

(a) Holders of at **least 5 per cent** (measured by nominal value) of the issued shares of the company, or of any class of shares

(b) **Not less than 50 members**

The applicants must all be persons who did *not* vote for the resolution.

3.14 If any application to the court is made, the company must give immediate notice (Form 54) to the registrar. As the applicants have no duty to give the company notice of their application to the court, the company should keep a watchful eye for such developments.

3.15 If the documents are in order and no application to the court has been made (or the application has been withdrawn or a court order made to confirm the resolution) the registrar issues his **certificate** of **re-registration** and the company then becomes a private company. Forward planning will be necessary here too.

Re-registration of limited to unlimited company

3.16 A company which was originally incorporated as limited may re-register as unlimited (ss 49-50), and a company which was originally incorporated as unlimited may register as limited (ss 51-52). But only **one** such change is possible; it cannot be reversed.

3.17 To change from limited to unlimited, application is made to the registrar by submitting the following:

- Applications (Form 49(1)) for re-registration
- A statutory declaration made by the directors of the company
- The memorandum (and if necessary articles) in altered form
- The signed consent (Form 49(8)(a)) of *all* members to the change
- A special resolution to make the necessary changes
- Payment of a fee

3.18 A copy of the special resolution must also be delivered to the registry within 15 days to comply with s 380.

Re-registration of the unlimited to limited company

3.19 To change from unlimited to limited, the application is made to the registrar by submitting the following documents:

- Application (Form 51) for re-registration
- A special resolution to make the change
- The memorandum (and if necessary the articles) in altered form

3.20 If the documents are in order the registrar issues his certificate of re-registration which effects the change.

3.21 Note the contrast: in the change from limited to unlimited status *unanimous consent* is required, but in the change from unlimited to limited a *special resolution* suffices.

FORM 49(1)	Application by a limited company to be re-registered as unlimited.
FORM 51	Application by an unlimited company to be re-registered as limited.

4 OTHER TYPES OF UK COMPANY

4.1 Incorporation and re-registration, as described above, are based on the issue of a certificate by the registrar as the final and decisive step in a sequence of procedure. There are a number of other types of company whose special status is determined by other means.

4.2 The relationship of **holding** (H) and **subsidiary** (S) company exists when the definition in ss 736, 736A and 736B are met.

4.3 Under s 736 a company is the **subsidiary company** of another company, its *holding company* if:

(a) H holds the **majority** of the **voting rights** in S.

(b) H is a member of S and in addition has the right by voting control to remove or **appoint** a **majority** of S's **board** of directors.

(c) H is a member of S and **controls** a majority of the **voting rights**, pursuant to an agreement with other members or shareholders.

(d) S is a **subsidiary** of a company which is itself a **subsidiary** of H.

A company (A Ltd) is a **wholly-owned subsidiary** of another company (B Ltd) if it has no other members except B Ltd and its wholly-owned subsidiaries, or persons acting on B Ltd's or its subsidiaries' behalf.

4.4 There are other **corporate bodies**, such as companies formed by special Act of Parliament or by Royal Charter. It is possible for certain types of company, not originally incorporated under the Companies Acts, to register under those Acts.

4.5 A **Welsh** company is one whose memorandum states that the registered office is to be situate **in Wales**: s 21. It may then deliver its memorandum and articles to the registrar in Welsh (but with a certified translation in English if necessary). It may also use Welsh equivalents of 'Ltd', 'plc', etc in its name.

5 OVERSEA COMPANIES

5.1 An **oversea** company is one which is incorporated outside Great Britain with a place of business in Great Britain: s 691. A place of business has been defined as a **permanent physical presence** and not the carrying on of business through an agent or by a salesman transacting business from a hotel or other temporary accommodation. The holding of property in Great Britain with no other business activity will not require registration. An oversea company must, within one month of becoming such a company, deliver to the registrar the originals and a certified copy in English of the following documents together with a £20 filing fee.

Statutory documents

5.2 These will be the memorandum and articles or equivalent.

Form 691

5.3 This will contain:

(a) Particulars of its **directors**

(b) Name and address of at least **one person resident** in **Great Britain** who is authorised to accept services of legal notices etc delivered to the company

(c) A **statutory declaration** stating when the place of business was established

Form 701(a)

5.4 This notifies the **accounting reference date** of the company.

Form 694(a)

5.5 This form will be required if the company is to carry on business under a **different name** from its registered name.

Property forms

5.6 Notice on the relevant form will be required of any property subject to a charge owned by the company in Great Britain.

5.7 The company must update the information as and when appropriate.

Form 691	Return and declaration delivered for registration by an oversea company.
Form 701a	Notice of accounting reference date by an oversea company.

Form 694a	Statement of name other than corporate name under which an oversea company proposes to carry on business in Great Britain.

6 COMPANY SEARCHES

6.1 On a practical note it is often necessary for a company secretary to find out about other companies with which he deals. Searches to obtain certain information may be made direct from the registry or through an agent.

6.2 The information obtained from such a search is as follows:

- Annual returns
- Most recent accounts
- Memorandum of Association
- Articles of Association
- Liquidator's/receiver's statement of account
- Mortgage register
- Capital documents
- Documents confirming changes to directors, secretaries and registered office addresses

6.3 Searches will be made as follows:

- By fax - one hour service
- By post - same day despatch by first class post
- By courier - to account members

6.4 The following can be ordered at a charge:

- Paper copies
- Microfiche record
- Certified copies

Chapter roundup

- Decide on **type** of company: limited or unlimited; by shares or guarantee; public or private.
- To form a company the following should be **sent** to the **registrar**:
  - Memorandum of association
  - Articles of association
  - Form 10
  - Form 12
  - Fee
- Characteristics of private company limited by shares:
  - May have only **one member**
  - Name ends with **Limited** (Ltd)
  - Members' **liability** for company debts are **limited** to their share contribution
- Characteristics of public limited company:
  - **Minimum** share capital of **£50,000**
  - At least **two members**
  - At least **one quarter** of **£50,000** and the whole of the **premium** on shares must be **paid up**
- **Re-registration** of **private** company as **public**: the following should be sent to the registrar:
  - Special resolution (file within 15 days)
  - Form 43 (3)
  - Form 43 (3)(e)
  - Written statement by auditors
  - Copy of balance sheet and unqualified auditor's report
  - Fee
- **Re-registration** of **public** as **private** company: the registrar should be sent:
  - A special resolution (file within 15 days)
  - Form 53
  - A copy memorandum and articles
  - Fee
- **Re-registration** of **limited** as **unlimited**: the registrar should be sent:
  - Form 49(1)
  - A statutory declaration
  - Memorandum and articles
  - Signed consent by *all* members
  - Fee
- **Re-registration** of **unlimited** as **limited**: the registrar should be sent:
  - Form 51
  - A special resolution to make the change
  - The memorandum in altered form
  - Fee
- Remember all form numbers are the same number as the section number in the CA to which they refer.
- A company making changes fundamental to its structure must pass a **special resolution** to show the registrar that the members approve of such changes. A special resolution requires a **75% majority vote** approving the resolution and must be filed with the registrar within **15 days** of the vote: s 380.

Summary of documents

FORM 10	Statement of first directors and secretary and intended address of registered office
FORM 12	Statutory declaration of compliance with requirements on application for registration
FORM 225	Notice of accounting reference date
FORM 88(2)	Return of allotments of shares
FORM 117	Application by a public company for certificate to commence business and statutory declaration in support
FORM 43(3)	Application by a private company for re-registration as a public company
FORM 43(3)(e)	Declaration of compliance with requirements by a private company on application for re-registration as a public company
FORM 53	Application by a public company for re-registration as a private company
FORM 49(1)	Application by a limited company to be re-registered as unlimited
FORM 51	Application by an unlimited company to be re-registered as limited
FORM 691	Return and declaration delivered for registration by an overseas company
FORM 701a	Notice of accounting reference date by an overseas company
FORM 694a	Statement of name other than corporate name under which an overseas company proposes to carry on business in Great Britain

Test your knowledge

1 What is the obligation to contribute to the assets of the company of (a) a member of an unlimited company; and (b) a member of a guarantee company? (see paras 1.4, 1.5)

2 What are the statutory rules on share capital of (a) a company limited by guarantee; and (b) a public company? (1.5, 1.7)

3 What are the documents which are presented to the Companies Registry to obtain the incorporation of a company? (2.6 - 2.10)

4 What are the formalities of signing the memorandum of association of a company about to be formed? (2.6)

5 How does the formation of a public company, ready to commence business, differ from that of a private limited company? (2.12 - 2.14)

6 How may a private company obtain re-registration as a public company? (3.1 - 3.9)

7 What changes are made in the memorandum of association of a public company in order that it may re-register as a private company? (3.11)

8 In what major respect does the procedure for re-registration of a limited company as unlimited differ from a change in the opposite direction? (3.17, 3.19)

9 In what circumstances is one company the holding company of another (its subsidiary)? (4.3)

Now try illustrative question 12 at the end of the Study Text

Chapter 11

THE MEMORANDUM AND ARTICLES

This chapter covers the following topics.

1 The content and alteration of the memorandum of association

2 The company name

3 The registered office

4 The content and alteration of the objects clause

5 The liability and share capital clauses

6 The articles of association

Introduction

The memorandum and articles are important in the context of incorporation, and are referred to throughout this Study Text, so their substance, and procedures related to them, are dealt with in some detail in this chapter.

The memorandum and articles together form the written constitution of a company, by which its structure is determined, the powers of the company and of the directors are defined, and the procedure for issue and transfer of shares, conduct of meetings, appointment of directors and payment of dividends (among other things) laid down.

If there is any conflict between them, the memorandum prevails over the articles.

A company has general power to alter its articles, by passing a special resolution in general meeting. There are special procedures for altering clauses of the memorandum, *except* the clause which fixes the country in which the registered office is to be situated, which is unalterable except by promoting a private Act of Parliament. The reason for this is that the company's domicile dictates the jurisdiction to which a company is subject; the law in Scotland and in England and Wales differs in substance and procedure.

1 THE CONTENT AND ALTERATION OF THE MEMORANDUM OF ASSOCIATION

12/98

1.1 To form a company it is necessary to include among the documents delivered to the registrar a memorandum of association, as described in the previous chapter, containing the information prescribed by s 2.

Content of the memorandum

1.2 The content of the obligatory clauses in the memorandum is as follows.

(a) The **name** of the company

(b) Whether the **registered office** is to be situated in England and Wales, or (in the case of Scottish company) in Scotland

(c) The **objects** of the company

(d) The **limited liability** of members (by shares or by guarantee) unless it is an unlimited company (In that case, the mere absence of a limited liability clause establishes that it is unlimited.)

(e) The amount of the **authorised share capital**, unless it is an unlimited company or (as a company limited by guarantee) has no share capital: s 2

1.3 If it is to be a public company, an additional clause to that effect is placed second in the sequence.

1.4 It is permissible to include **additional clauses** in the memorandum, which would otherwise be part of the articles. It is more difficult to alter clauses contained in the memorandum than in the articles, so this is a way of restricting alteration: s 17.

1.5 At the end of the memorandum there is an '**association clause**' by which the subscribers state their wish to form a company on this basis and, if there is a share capital, they agree to subscribe for at least one share (by convention never more than one): s 2(5)(c). These subscribers' signatures are dated and witnessed.

1.6 In form the memorandum must be 'as near as circumstances permit to the relevant statutory model, that is Table B (private company limited by shares), Table C (company limited by guarantee with no share capital), Table E (unlimited company) and F (public company): s 3. In practice the objects clause has developed to be much longer than the model, as we will see later.

Alteration of the memorandum

1.7 If a company alters its memorandum or articles, it is **required** to **deliver** to the registrar, within 15 days, a **printed copy** of the **resolution** by which the alteration is made, and also a copy of the memorandum or articles in their altered form: s 18.

1.8 The resolution has to be **filed** if it is a special resolution (s 380) or in some cases an ordinary resolution, ie 'any document making or evidencing an alteration in the company's memorandum or articles: s 18.

1.9 If the objects clause is altered, the copy of the memorandum as altered is delivered later, to allow time for objections.

1.10 Any copy of the memorandum or articles delivered to the registrar must be '**printed**' (as explained in the previous chapter). In practice a xerox copy of the altered memorandum (with the alteration typed on to the original for copying) will be accepted. Following major alterations, it is usual to produce a stock of copies of the altered text, together with copies of the resolutions by which the alterations were made, so that the sequence of alterations can be traced if necessary.

1.11 Any member may, on application, be supplied by the company (on payment of a fee not exceeding 5p if demanded) with a copy of the memorandum and articles of the company: s 19. Whenever a company issues to anyone a copy of its memorandum, the copy must incorporate all alterations made up to that time: s 20.

2 THE COMPANY NAME — **Specimen paper**

2.1 The choice of name is regulated by ss 25-34. The main purpose of these rules is to ensure that each company has a **distinctive name**, and that it does not include in its name certain words which might be misleading or objectionable. If the registrar considers that there has been a breach of the rules, he refuses to register the company with the proposed name.

2.2 The rules applicable are as follows.

(a) The name of public company must end with the words '**public limited company**' (or the abbreviated form 'plc' or Welsh equivalent 'cwmni cyfyngedig cyhoeddus' for a Welsh company). The name of a private company limited by shares or guarantee (unless exempt - as specified later) must end with the word '*limited*' (or 'Ltd' or the Welsh equivalent): s 25. It is a criminal offence to carry on business under a name which ends with 'limited' or 'plc' unless the trader is a company with limited liability: s 34. A limited company may not have the word 'limited' elsewhere in its name than as described above: s 26(1)(a).

plc = cwmni cyfyngedig cyhoeddus (ccc)

(b) A company may not adopt the **same name** as an existing company already on the register. For this purpose some minor differences are disregarded in deciding whether the names are the same: s 26(1)(c) and (3).

(c) A company may not adopt a name which in the opinion of the DTI would constitute a **criminal offence or be offensive**: s 26(1)(d) and (e).

(d) The use of certain words in a name requires **official permission** and no name may suggest a connection with a government department or local authority without such permission: s 26(2).

Restricted words and expressions

2.3 The following words require the Secretary of State for Trade and Industry's consent before use in a company (or business) name.

(a) *Words which imply national or international pre-eminence*

International
European
National
United Kingdom
Great Britain
English
England
Scottish
Scotland
etc.

(b) *Words which imply governmental patronage or sponsorship*

Authority
Board
Council
etc

(c) *Words which imply business pre-eminence or representative status*

Association
Federation
Institute
Society
etc

(d) *Words which imply specific objects or functions*

Assurance
Insurance
Building Society
Trust
Fund
Group
Holdings
Chartered
Registered

Co-operative
Trade Union
etc.

Other words require approval from the relevant body concerned (for example Dentist, Optician or Bank), or from other government departments. Use of Royal, Queen, Prime and other terms implying connection with royalty is sanctioned by the Home Office.

2.4 At the time of writing, Companies House was discouraging the use of symbols outside the standard alpha-numeric series. In particular there had been many attempts at requesting existing names with the addition of the @ prefix used on the Internet. Legal advice was being sought by Companies House.

Change of name

2.5 A change of name might be compulsory, directed by the registrar, or voluntary, if the company chooses to be re-registered under a new name.

2.6 The registrar may require a company to change the name by which it has been registered in the following cases.

(a) If the name is the **same** or is considered to be '**too like**' that of another company. The time limit for giving a direction on this ground is 12 months from the date on which the name, which is now to be altered, was registered.

(b) If the name was registered on the basis of information or assurances which were **misleading** or have **not been observed**. In this case the time limit for directions to change the name is 5 years: s 28.

(c) If the name is considered to be so **misleading** about the company's **activities** as to be likely to cause harm to the public. In this case there is no time limit and if directions are given, the company has 3 weeks in which to appeal to the court to set them aside: s 32. In practice directions are not given under s 32, as this power was foisted on the registrar by Parliament in 1967 against advice.

2.7 If the DTI does give directions for a change of name to the company, the directions include a period for compliance. A special resolution should be used.

2.8 A change of name takes effect only when the registrar issues his certificate of change of name.

2.9 The most likely occasion of a direction for a change of name is when an **existing company** makes a protest to the registrar that a second company has been incorporated (or has voluntarily replaced its name) with a name which is 'too like' its own, so that confusion results. The 12 month time limit for directions sets a limit on the period of uncertainty. It is reckoned that if there *is* likely to be confusion between the two companies, signs of it will have come to light within that period. Companies House are planning to make the key test whether a member of the public would be confused by the similiarity.

2.10 A company may **of its own initiative** change its name, by passing a special resolution and obtaining re-registration with the new name. It takes effect only when the new certificate of incorporation, with the altered name, is issued: s 28(6). The same restrictions apply to the adoption of a new name when the company is first formed.

2.11 It is possible to obtain an up-to-date copy of the registrar's index of names of existing companies, and to make a search in it to see whether there is an existing company on the register with the same or a very similar name. There are company agents who hold a copy of the index and will make a search for a fee. It is also possible to examine a microfiche of company names at some of the better libraries.

Procedure for changing the name

2.12 A change of name requires much preparation, for which a timetable should be prepared at the outset. Matters to be considered are as follows.

(a) A check should be made of the **index of company names** and of the list of words which, if included in a company name, require official permission, as discussed above.

(b) A **board meeting** will be required to convene an **Extraordinary General Meeting** which can pass a special resolution to change the name. If the company's shares are listed on the Stock Exchange, there are various SE requirements to comply with (as explained in a later chapter dealing with general meetings).

(c) The **special resolution** will have to be printed for submission to the Registrar (and copies made for insertion in the stocks of memorandum and articles). The company will also require new stocks of **letterheads and other business stationery** bearing the new name for use as soon as the change takes effect.

(d) In applying to the registrar for his certificate of incorporation under the new name, a **registration fee** of £20 has to be paid.

(e) The new name must be **displayed** outside every office or place in which its business is carried on, in a conspicuous position and legible: s 348. Signboards and company equipment, such as its vehicles, may have to be repainted to show the new name.

(f) The board must be asked to adopt a **new seal** bearing the new name (if the company has one, the CA 1989 makes the company seal optional).

(g) The **identity** of the company is **not altered** by a change of name: s 28(7). However its bank and others who have business relations with it may wish to see the certificate of incorporation in the new name.

(h) A copy of the resolution by which the name is altered should also be sent to the company's **advisers** (solicitors, accountants etc) and to the **bank** for inclusion in their reference copy of the memorandum and articles. They may also need a copy of the registrar's certificate of re-registration of the new name.

2.13 Again good secretarial practice will require some forward planning so that the company is prepared for the change, for instance with printed business stationery.

Omission of 'limited' from the name: s 30

2.14 Only companies limited by **guarantee** can omit limited from their name by satisfying the conditions set out below: s 30.

(a) The **objects** of the company must be the promotion of commerce, art, science, education, religion, charity or any profession, and anything incidental or conducive to any of those objects.

(b) The memorandum or articles must comply with the following conditions.

  (i) They must require all **profits** or other income to be **applied** in **promoting** the company's **objects**.

  (ii) They must **prohibit** the payment of **dividends** to members.

  (iii) They must require that on liquidation of the company the **assets** of the company, otherwise available to members (after payment of debts), shall be **transferred** to another company with **similar objects** or to a **charitable body**.

2.15 A company which wishes to omit the word 'limited' from its name must apply to the registrar **(Form 30)** by a statutory declaration, stating that the company complies with the above conditions. It may be a company about to be formed, or an existing company which seeks to change its name. The registrar may accept the declaration as sufficient evidence of compliance.

2.16 In addition to the right to omit the word 'limited' from its name, the company is not required to comply with the rules (discussed later) on display of company names nor to send a list of its members to the registrar with its annual return. However it must state that it is a limited company on its business letters and order forms: s 351(1)(d).

2.17 A company which has these privileges must at all times comply with the conditions set out above. If it fails to do so the DTI may direct it to change its name, adding 'limited' to the end: s 31.

FORM 30	Declaration on application for registration of a company omitting 'limited' from company name

Business names

2.18 A company must always comply with the legal rules on the use of company names, in particular the display of the name. However no company is prohibited from carrying on business under a name which is not its official registered name. If it does so, it is said to use a 'business name' or 'trading name' and becomes subject to the requirements of the **Business Names Act 1985** ('BNA').

2.19 The same list of words for which official permission is required applies to business as to company names. Before a company adopts a business name, it should check whether permission is required and obtain it, if necessary, by either of the following methods:

(a) **Immediate application** to the registrar

(b) **Application** to a **designated body** for preliminary clearance (for example to the Charity Commissioners for the word 'charitable') and then to the registrar

There is also a ban on the use of words which suggest connection with a government department or local authority without permission from the Secretary of State.

2.20 If the company proposes to use a business name which does not include a regulated word of any kind, it need not seek official permission to do so. The following, however, should be borne in mind.

(a) There is no **exclusive right** to the use of a business name, since the 'same or too like' rule does not apply to a business name. There are many teashops trading as 'Ann's Pantry'. But a company may find itself liable to a common law '**passing off action** if, by its own business name, it damages the business goodwill of a competitor with a similar name.

(b) Official permission for a regulated word in a business name gives no exclusive rights nor does it afford a defence to a passing off action.

2.21 A company which uses a business name is required to do the following.

(a) To **state** in legible characters on all **business letters**, written orders for goods or services, invoices, receipts and written demands for payment:

(i) The **registered name** of the company

(ii) An **address** in Great Britain at which legal documents may be validly served on the company: BNA s 4(1)

(b) To **display**, in a **prominent position** at **business premises** to which customers and suppliers have access, the particulars in (a) above

(c) To **supply**, on demand by any person with whom the company is doing business, **written particulars** as described in (a) above

2.22 Failure to comply with these requirements is punishable by fine and may expose the company to being sued in certain circumstances: BNA ss 5 and 7.

Publication of the name and other company particulars 12/98

2.23 The company is obliged to display its name and registered office address. Different legal requirements have accumulated in this area, and the result is rather confusing. The following is a summary (grouped by reference to the document, or other place of display).

(a) **Letterheads** must, to comply with s 351 unless otherwise stated, give the following information:

(i) The registered name of the company: s 349

(ii) The 'place of registration' ie usually 'England'

(iii) The registration number of the company at the Companies Registry (as shown on the certificate of incorporation)

(iv) The address of the registered office, which should be described as such, for example 'registered office: 52 Gracechurch Street, London EC3'

In addition the circumstances of a particular company may require that:

(v) It be described as either (1) an investment company or (2) a limited company, if it is permitted to omit 'limited' from its name

A company need not show the names of its directors though many in fact do so. If any director is named (otherwise than by typing his name in the letter or beneath his signature) the names of *all* the directors must be given: s 305.

A company may also include particulars of its capital (though this is unusual). If it does so, the figure must be the paid-up share capital. By reason of (i) and (iv) above, such a letterhead will also comply with BNA, if applicable.

Companies should regard a communication by e-mail as equivalent to one issued via letterhead; as good practice therefore, e-mails should include the same details as letterheads.

(b) **Order forms** of the company must also comply with the compulsory items (i) - (v) of (a) above.

(c) **Financial documents**, such as bills of exchange and cheques, invoices, receipts etc and also company notices and 'official publications' must bear the name of the company: s 349.

(d) **Offices and places of business** must display the company name and, if the company trades under a business name, the address of the registered office: s 348 and BNA s 4.

Company seal 12/99

2.24 A company may have a '**common seal**' for general use on documents, such as debentures, which it executes as deeds. Under s 36A(3), this is no longer mandatory, although it will be inconvenient not to have one since many foreign jurisdictions still require the use of seals. If a company does not have a seal (or has not used it), s 36A(4) provides that 'a document signed by a director and the secretary of a company or by two directors of the company, and expressed (in whatever form of words) to be executed by the company has the same effect as if executed under the common seal of the company'. If it states on its face that it is intended to be a deed executed by the company, then it takes effect as a deed on delivery.

Use of the seal

2.25 If the company does have a seal it must have the **name** of the company **engraved** upon it in legible characters: s 350.

2.26 The secretary will normally have custody of the seal. The secretary should as a matter of good practice also maintain a register of sealings, which details all documents to which the seal is affixed.

2.27 Companies vary in how the use of the seal is authorised, who can witness the use of the seal and who can sign documents that have been sealed.

(a) Regulation 101 of the 1985 Table A requires that the seal should only be used on the **authority** of the **directors** or a **committee** of the directors authorised by the board as a whole. If Regulation 101 is followed, reference should be made in the board or committee minutes to the use of the seal. If Regulation 101 is not in the articles, the company can elect to delegate authority for use of the seal to various officers of the company.

(b) 1985 Table A does not require the physical presence of two directors, or one director and the secretary when the seal is affixed to the document.

(c) The directors may determine **who should sign** any instrument to which the seal is affixed. Unless they determine otherwise, the instrument should be signed by two directors or one director and the secretary.

Securities seal

2.28 Companies which have a common seal can have an **official seal**. This seal is a facsimile of the common seal with the addition on its face of the word '**security**'. It can be used to seal certificates relating to the securities of the company: s 40. Such seals are useful in larger companies where the register of members is maintained by an external registrar.

Seal for use abroad

2.29 Companies which operate abroad can, if authorised by their articles, have an official seal for use abroad. This seal should be a facsimile of the common seal with the name of every territory, district or place where it is to be used on its face. Its use can be delegated to an agent abroad, who should certify in writing on the document on which the seal is used the date when and place where it is used: s 39.

Signing of incorrect name

2.30 A secretary or other company officer, such as a director, is liable to a fine if he purports to sign, or authorises the issue of, company documents on which the company name is not given, or appears in incorrect form. If it is a bill of exchange or a cheque or other financial document, he is also **personally liable** to the holder of the document if the company defaults on it: s 26 Bills of Exchange Act 1881.

Penrose v Martyr 1858
The facts: A company secretary signed a bill of exchange drawn on the company, on which the company name had been written without the final word 'limited'. The company defaulted.

Decision: The secretary was personally liable on the bill, as it did not bear the complete name of the company.

2.31 However, if the error is introduced into the bill by the person who presents it for signature in that defective form, he cannot hold the company signatory liable for the mistake which the former has made: *Durham Fancy Goods Ltd v Michael Jackson (Fancy Goods) Ltd 1968.*

2.32 Particular care should be taken to ensure that company cheque books, prepared by the bank for use in drawing on the company bank account, show the pre-printed company name (below the signature space) in its correct form.

Exercise

Dennis is acting as a promoter of a private limited company which wishes to use the name 'The British Tyre Company'. Are there any difficulties for the company in selecting this name?

Solution

A company's name must be contained in the name clause of its memorandum of association: s 2 Companies Act 1985. Because Dennis's company is described as 'private, limited', the name must end with the words *Limited* or *Ltd*, unless he is permitted to omit this from the name: s 25. He will only be permitted to do so if the company is limited by guarantee and fulfils certain strict criteria: s 30. As a trading company, it will not do so. Hence the company may not be called 'The British Tyre Company'; it must (all other things being equal) be called 'The British Tyre Company Limited'.

No company may have a name which is the same as that of any existing company appearing on the statutory index at the registry. Two names are treated as 'the same' in spite of minor differences. If there is already a company called, say, 'British Tyre Company', Dennis may not use the same name with 'the' at the front: s 26(3).

The registrar will not allow a name which he considers to be a criminal offence or offensive: s 26(1). This does not appear to be at issue here. But he may also prevent use of a name which he believes to suggest a connection with a government body or which is subject to control: s 26(2).

In this case, he may consider that the word 'British' carries pretensions to size and standing which are not warranted by a new, private company. He may feel that, by its use, Dennis is misleading the public.

If Dennis does use the name 'The British Tyre Company Limited' as registered at the registry, he may still find that he is ordered to change the name within 12 months if it is too like another on the index. If he misled the registrar, the time limit is 5 years.

He may find that a person who believes his rights have been infringed by the use of the name applies to the court for an order to restrain it, because it suggests that Dennis is carrying on the complainant's business. But the plaintiff will not succeed if he lays claim to exclusive use of a word (such as 'tyre') which has a general use. He must show that he lays claim to something distinctive and that confusion is intended or likely to result: *Aerators Ltd v Tollitt 1901.*

He may also be subject to a common law 'passing off' action by another trader with a similar name, if his conduct is causing confusion in the public's mind between the goods they sell. This may result in an injunction preventing his use of the name: *Ewing v Buttercup Margarine Co Ltd 1917.*

3 THE REGISTERED OFFICE — Specimen paper, 12/99

3.1 Another item which must appear in the memorandum is the **situation** of the 'registered office': that is, in England, Wales and Scotland.

3.2 The address of the registered office, identified as such, must be shown on all business letters and order forms: s 351. It also appears in the annual return.

3.3 After registration, the directors may at any time resolve to alter the address of the registered office, provided that it is **within** the **country specified** in the memorandum for that purpose. Notice of any such change of address (Form 287) must be given to the registrar. Under s 287 the change of address takes effect from when notice is registered by the registrar. However, there is a period of 14 days from the time of registration during which a person may validly serve any document on the company at its previous registered office.

FORM 287	Notice of change in situation of registered office. See Appendix 9.

3.4 The registered office is important in two main respects.

(a) It is the place where **registers** and other documents which a company is required to **keep** and to make **available** for **inspection** are normally held, though for some of them alternative addresses are allowed.

(b) A **legal document**, such as a notice or a writ to commence legal proceedings, is '**served**' ie effectually delivered to a company, if it is left at or posted to the company at its registered office: s 725. In addition many sections of the Companies Act provide for delivery of a formal document, such as a requisition of a general meeting (s 368), to the registered office.

3.5 The registered office of the company is often also its main place of business and where the company secretary has his office. If the registered office is elsewhere, adequate arrangements should be made to ensure that any document delivered to the registered office is promptly sent on to the secretary, or another officer competent to deal with it. It is not uncommon to have the registered office at the place of business of, say, the company's solicitors or auditors.

3.6 The secretary should also ensure that if there is a **change of address** of the registered office, the new **address** is **shown** on letterheads etc as required by law. If this is not done, the company will be deemed to have received documents which have been delivered to the old registered office, unless the person who delivers the document is otherwise informed of the change. It is also an offence to breach these legal requirements.

4 THE CONTENT AND ALTERATION OF THE OBJECTS CLAUSE

4.1 The objects clause states the objects of the company's activities, beyond which the company may not venture. The well-known perils of the **ultra vires** doctrine, diluted by the CA 1989, should already be familiar to you from your study of *Corporate Law*. The following paragraphs relate to the practical aspects of the objects clause under the Companies Act.

4.2 It is unusual, under the 1985 legislation, to follow the narrow drafting of the statutory model objects clauses (Tables B to F) in defining by a single short sentence the business which the company has legal capacity to conduct.

4.3 Company solicitors, as much as company secretaries if the task falls to them, usually frame an objects clause by taking one of the model forms, or precedents, which are available from law stationers, and completing and adapting it to the circumstances of the company.

4.4 It is possible and usual to widen the effect of an objects clause by declaring that:

(a) Each paragraph is to be read as an **independent object**: *Cotman v Brougham 1918*.

(b) The company has capacity to enter into **additional business activities** which the directors may consider advantageous: *Bell Houses Ltd v City Wall Properties Ltd 1966*.

4.5 The courts are reluctant to deny a company the capacity to enter into a transaction covered by an express power in the objects clause: *Re Horsley & Weight Ltd 1982*. There can, however, be an unexpected *ultra vires* situation when the directors are, with the knowledge of the other party, exercising company powers for an irregular purpose.

4.6 If the company or other party to a proposed transaction realises, before the matter is set in train, that there is the slightest doubt about the company's capacity as defined by its existing objects clause, the clause may be altered under the wider statutory power given by s 3.

4.7 Section 3A provides that it is now possible to register a company with objects which merely state that the company's object is to 'carry on business as a **general commercial company**'. S 3A specifically states this to mean that:

(a) The object of the company is to carry on any trade or business whatsoever.

(b) The company has power to do all such things as are incidental or conducive to the carrying on of any trade or business by it.

Alteration of objects

6/99

4.8 S 4 states that 'a company may by special resolution alter its memorandum with respect to the statement of the company's objects: s 4(1). The effect of this is to allow a company to alter its objects for any reason whatsoever.

4.9 A company may 'alter' its objects clause by resolving to delete it entirely and replace it with a completely new clause. The secretary should of course seek competent legal advice on the alteration to be made. No objection to its validity can be raised after the expiry of a 21 day period referred to below: s 6(4).

4.10 The sequence of procedure, which should be planned in advance, is as follows.

(a) A **board meeting** approving the documents and authorising the issue of a notice to convene an **Extraordinary General Meeting** ('EGM') is held. Unless the company is listed, it is not obligatory to issue an explanatory circular to shareholders, but it may be advisable. If the company's shares are listed, the documents will have to be submitted to The Stock Exchange for its approval.

(b) At the EGM a **special resolution** is passed to alter the objects clause. A printed copy of the resolution, signed by the chairman, must be delivered to the registrar within 15 days: s 380.

(c) Within the period of 21 days following the general meeting, the **holders of not less than 15 per cent of the issued shares**, or of a class of shares (or, in very special circumstances, of debentures carrying the right of objection),who did not vote in favour of the special resolution, may apply to the court for a cancellation of the alteration. Objections of this type are very rare. If, however, objection to the merits of the alteration is made by a 15 per cent minority, the court has powers to impose a compromise: s 5.

(d) If no application is made to the court, the company may proceed at the expiry of the 21 day period. If application is made, the company **gives notice** *(Form 6)* to the registrar and awaits the outcome. Unless the application is successful, the company may proceed when it is dismissed or withdrawn. In any such case there is a period of 15 days to complete the final stage.

(e) Within the 15 day period (usually within 15 days after the 21 day period allowed for objections), the company delivers a **printed copy of the memorandum**, as altered, to the registrar. The company also prints a stock of the memorandum and articles, in their altered form, for immediate distribution to those who hold copies of the previous version, and for issue as required thereafter.

5 THE LIABILITY AND SHARE CAPITAL CLAUSES

Limited liability clause

5.1 A fourth item in the memorandum is the limited liability clause. If the company is limited by shares, the clause merely states that the liability of members is limited. If however it is limited by guarantee, there is an additional clause by which members agree to **contribute**, up to a specified amount, to the assets of the company, if it is wound up and unable to pay its debts in full from its existing assets. (A past member is liable within a year of selling his shares in respect of debts incurred while he was a member.) If the company is unlimited, there is no limited liability clause at all.

Authorised capital

5.2 A fifth item is a statement of the amount of authorised share capital. The amount to be specified is fixed by reference to the expected needs of the company when it is formed, though the limit may be increased, as described in a later chapter. The model clause in Table B reads:

> 'The company's share capital is £50,000 divided into 50,000 shares of £1 each.'

It is essential that the shares should be 'of a **fixed amount**', called 'the **nominal** (or par) **value**' since that fixes the minimum consideration for which they may be allotted.

5.3 If the company has no share capital, which is now the situation with a newly formed company limited by guarantee, there is no capital clause.

Additional clauses

5.4 If the company has more than one class of shares, there may be a clause in the memorandum to define the rights of each class. However it is more usual, and convenient, to include such clause(s) in the articles. If the company is limited by guarantee and entitled to omit the word 'limited' from its name, the relevant restrictions may be contained either in the memorandum or in the articles.

5.5 Any clause included in the memorandum which could have been included in the articles may be altered by the company by **special resolution**, and subject to the same rights of minority objection. But the power to alter such a clause (s 17) cannot be exercised to:

(a) Vary the rights of a class of shares, for which there is a special procedure, as described in a later chapter

(b) Alter a clause which provides its own procedure for alteration, or is expressed as unalterable

Statutory model of Memorandum of Association

5.6 Set out below is Table B of the Companies (Tables A-F) Regulations 1985 which is the model memorandum of association for a private company limited by shares.

MEMORANDUM OF ASSOCIATION

1 The company's name is 'The South Wales Motor Transport Company cyfyngedig'.

2 The company's registered office is to be situated in Wales.

3 The company's objects are the carriage of passengers and goods in motor vehicles between such places as the company may from time to time determine and the doing of all such other things as are incidental or conducive to the attainment of that object.

4 The liability of the members is limited.

5 The company's share capital is £50,000 divided into 50,000 shares of £1 each.

We, the subscribers to this memorandum of association, wish to be formed into a company pursuant to this memorandum; and we agree to take the number of shares shown opposite our respective names.

Names and Addresses of Subscribers	Number of shares taken by each subscriber
1 Thomas Jones, 138 Mountfield Street, Tredegar.	1
2 Mary Evans, 19 Merthyr Road, Aberystwyth	1
Total shares taken	2

Dated 20.

Witness to the above signatures,

Anne Brown, 'Woodlands', Fieldside Road, Bryn Mawr.

6 THE ARTICLES OF ASSOCIATION 12/98

Content of the Articles of Association

6.1 A company must have articles of association. Table A of the Companies (Tables A-F) Regulations 1985 provides model articles, with regulations on the following areas.

(a) Share capital

(b) Share certificates

(c) Lien

(d) Calls on shares and forfeiture

(e) Transfer and transmission of shares

(f) Alteration of share capital

(g) Purchase of own shares

(h) General meetings:
- notice
- proceedings
- votes of members

(i) Directors:
- number
- alternate directors
- powers
- delegation of powers
- appointment and retirement
- disqualification and removal
- expenses
- appointments and interests
- gratuities and pensions

(j) Secretary

(k) Minutes

(l) The Seal

(m) Dividends

(n) Accounts

(o) Capitalisation of profits

(p) Notices

(q) Winding up

(r) Indemnity

Table A articles under the 1985 regulations are summarised in an appendix to this text.

6.2 A company limited by shares may adopt the model articles of Table A, with or without alteration, or it may adopt 'special' articles. It is advisable to make an *explicit* choice, by providing in the company's articles that Table A:

- Shall apply
- Shall apply with modifications as defined
- Is entirely excluded and replaced by the special articles which follow

It is unsatisfactory to leave the position to be deduced, by considering how far the company's articles do in fact substitute for Table A.

6.3 A company limited by guarantee or an unlimited company must be registered with **special articles**. Statutory models (Tables C and E) are provided which are suitably modified versions of Table A, and the company may, in its special articles, use the models in altered form as it may prefer. S 8A of the Companies Act 1989 envisages an additional Table G containing articles appropriate for 'partnership companies'.

6.4 Unless it has special needs, a private company limited by shares will generally adopt Table A with modifications, to avoid the expense of drafting and printing full length special articles. A public company, if its shares are listed on the Stock Exchange, must in practice adopt **special articles** to incorporate the many alterations and additions to Table A which Stock Exchange requirements impose.

6.5 The articles must be 'printed' and divided into numbered paragraphs. The articles with which a company is registered on incorporation (though not any later articles adopted as a substitute) must be signed by the subscribers to the memorandum, dated and witnessed, as described in the previous chapter.

Alteration of the articles

6.6 A company may by special resolution alter its articles: s 9. In your study of *Corporate Law* you will have considered some overriding principles affecting this general power. It is also worth noting here some specific limitations.

(a) The articles may not be altered so as to **conflict** with the **Companies Acts** or with the memorandum.

(b) If the articles define the rights of a class of shares, the **consent** of the holders of the shares of that class must be obtained (under the appropriate procedure) before the articles may be altered in that respect.

(c) No alteration of the memorandum or articles may, without the consent of a member, **compel him** to **subscribe** for additional shares or to pay more for the shares which he holds than was agreed at the time of allotment: s 15.

(d) Articles cannot be made unalterable, members cannot fetter their future rights to alter the articles. Remember however that the existence of a separate contract (for example a director's contract of service) does **not** limit the company's right to alter its articles. Damages may however be payable if articles are altered and a contract therefore breached.

6.7 In preparing for alteration of the articles, the company management should consider whether to adopt a complete new set of articles in place of existing ones, or whether to make specific but limited alterations to the existing articles. For these purposes special resolutions might be as follows.

(a) **New articles**

'That the regulations contained in the printed document submitted to the meeting and for purposes of identification signed by the chairman shall be adopted as the articles of association in substitution for and to the total exclusion of the existing articles of association.'

(b) **Specific alteration**

'That the articles of association of the Company be altered by:

(i) deleting Article 31 and substituting therefore the following new Article

'31 ....' [text of new article];

(ii) inserting in Article 73, after the words 'any director' the words 'or alternate director'.

6.8 A copy of the **complete articles**, as altered, must be submitted to the registrar under s 18. If only minor alterations are made, it may be possible to paste amendment slips to appropriate places in the existing articles and then make a xerox or photographic 'printed' copy for delivery to the registrar. However, if there are numerous alterations, or they cannot be dealt with by the method just described, a complete reprint may be unavoidable. In that case, it is just as convenient to adopt **new articles**, with the amendments in the printed text, as to make piecemeal alterations and then reprint the articles which incorporate them.

6.9 These requirements make it expensive to alter the articles. Apart from printing costs, it will usually be advisable to obtain legal advice. Alterations should therefore only be made when there are sufficient reasons for them, usually at intervals of several years.

6.10 A signed copy of the special resolution (within 15 days) and a complete copy of the articles as altered have to be delivered to the registrar, duly signed by the chairman for identification. A stock of copies of the altered articles is also required for distribution to banks, professional advisers, members (if they request them) and, if the company is listed, to the Stock Exchange.

Chapter roundup

- Obligatory clauses to be included in the **memorandum**:
  - Company name
  - Registered office in England and Wales (or Scotland)
  - Objects of company
  - Limited liability (if appropriate)
  - Amount of authorised share capital
  - Plc status (if appropriate)
  - Association clause
- May adopt or adapt statutory models for the memorandum and articles from the Companies (Tables A-F) Regulations 1985.
- The **alteration** of the memorandum is generally by **special resolution**, to be filed with a copy of the printed memorandum and articles in altered form within 15 days (if the objects clause is altered a copy of the memorandum can be delivered later).
- The company name must:
  - End in **plc** or Ltd as appropriate
  - **Not** be the **same** or so similar as to cause confusion with the name of an existing company
  - **Not constitute** a **criminal offence** or be offensive
  - Have **official permission** where appropriate

  Business or **trading names** are governed by BNA but are subject to similar regulations as above.
- The situation of the **registered office** must be stated in the **memorandum** and the address must be specified on all business letters; this identifies location of records of the company and the address for service. Notice of change of registered office should be filed on Form 287 with the registrar; within the following **14 days** from the time of registration of change a person can validly serve any document on the old registered office.
- The company must show on its **letterheads**:
  - Its registered name
  - Its place of registration
  - Its registration number
  - Its registered office address
  - *Either* the names of *all* its directors *or* the names of *none* of them
- The company may **alter its objects clause** for any reason (s 4) by **special resolution** at an EGM to be filed within 15 days. Objections can be made within 21 days following the EGM: s 5.
- The **articles** of association usually state the **procedures** and **workings** of the company and not the substance of the company. Articles are generally in the form of Table A of the Companies (Table A-F) Regulations 1985 or as adapted.
- Alteration of **articles** is done by **special resolution** and must not conflict with the CA nor the memorandum.

Summary of documents

FORM 30	Declaration on application for registration of a company omitting 'limited' from company name
FORM 287	Notice of change in situation of registered office
TABLE A	Regulations for management of company limited by shares: articles of association
TABLE B	A private company limited by shares: memorandum of association
TABLE C	A company limited by guarantee and not having a share capital: memorandum and articles of association
TABLE D:	
PART I	A public company limited by guarantee and having a share capital (memorandum of association)
PART II	A private company limited by guarantee and having a share capital (memorandum of association)
PART III	A company (public or private) limited by guarantee and having a share capital (articles of association)
TABLE E	An unlimited company having a share capital (memorandum and articles of association)
TABLE F	A public company limited by shares (memorandum of association)
TABLE G	A partnership company

Test your knowledge

1 What are the obligatory clauses found in the memorandum of a public company? (see para 1.2)

2 What is meant by the statutory requirement (s 18) that a printed copy of the memorandum or articles shall be delivered to the registrar after any alteration is made? (1.7)

3 What are the restrictions on the choice of a company name? (2.2)

4 In what circumstances (a) *must* and (b) *may* a company change the name with which it is registered until then? (2.5, 2.10)

5 Outline the programme of action by a company in connection with a change of name. (2.12)

6 Subject to what conditions may a limited company omit the word 'limited' from its name? (2.14 – 2.15)

7 What is meant by a 'business name'? (2.18) What additional requirements fall on a company which uses such a name? (2.21)

8 What details about a private limited company would be found on its printed letterheads? (2.23)

9 What is the importance of the registered office of a company in the conduct of its affairs? (3.4)

10 Describe how modern objects clauses are drafted so as to have wide effect. (4.4, 4.7)

11 Is there any right of objection to the alteration of the objects of a company? (4.10 (c))

Now try illustrative question 13 at the end of the Study Text

Chapter 12

SHARES

This chapter covers the following topics.

Introduction

Shares, types of capital and variation of class rights are all topics covered in your *Corporate Law* studies. They are not specifically mentioned in your *Company Secretarial Practice* syllabus. However, a knowledge of these topics underpins your studies for nearly all of the following chapters. This chapter therefore serves as a revision exercise. You should look back to your *Corporate Law* study material if you want further information.

In the next chapter we move from share capital to loan capital. It is important that you understand the differences between the two.

1 THE PURPOSE OF SHARES

1.1 The total share capital of a company is divided into shares of specified value: s 2(5)(a).

1.2 Shares are the fixed capital of a company which, unless repaid, purchased or redeemed in the manner described in the previous chapter, will continue until the company is liquidated.

1.3 In many companies, especially small ones, all the shares may be uniform, ie shares of one class, designated '**ordinary shares**'. However the capital structure of a company can include two or more distinct classes of shares, with different rights.

1.4 If the company has only one class of shares, it is sufficient to state (in the memorandum) their nominal value.

1.5 Forthcoming legislation will allow all companies to denominate their share capital in any currency, not just sterling (therefore allowing companies to denominate their capital in euros). If companies wish to change the currency in which their share capital is denominated, they can do so by an ordinary resolution (or a directors' resolution if the translation was to **euros** during the transitional period leading to membership of the single currency). Companies will have to convert at the level of total nominal value of each class of share. Individual par values would be derived by dividing the converted share capital in each class by the number of shares in that class.

1.6 Individual par values could subsequently be rounded up or down, with a corresponding change being made in the company's undistributable reserves. An ordinary resolution would be required if there was an overall increase in share capital, a special resolution if there was a decrease. Companies would not need to issue new share certificates as there would be no new issue of shares.

1.7 The **voting rights** attached to each class of share, and entitlement to dividend, are usually **specified** in the **articles** (Table A Article 54 and Article 104). If the articles are silent, each share or £10 of stock confers one vote: s 370(6). With only one class of share, the rights of shareholders are based on the principle that each share has the same rights and obligations as any other: there is equality on all points unless otherwise stated.

1.8 A share is personal property: s 182. In more technical terms it is a '**chose in action**': its holder must enforce his rights by legal action, since he cannot take possession of it. Although it is an abstract thing, a share is deemed to exist for legal purposes where the company has its register of members (and their shareholdings).

2 TYPES OF CAPITAL

2.1 We now turn to consider the different possible types of capital, particularly shares, in more detail, together with the various rights and obligations conferred on their holders.

Preference shares 12/98

2.2 The essential characteristic of **preference shares** is that they carry a right of priority, up to a specified limit, to whatever profits the company may decide to distribute in each year. For example, 6% preference shares of £1 nominal value each carry a right up to 6p per share in priority (to other different class shareholders), to whatever profits the company may decide to pay out as dividend in each year. Unless each preference share receives dividend of 6p out of profits, no dividends can be payable on other classes of shares.

2.3 The preference shareholders' right is usually set out in any of three ways:

- The articles
- The memorandum
- The resolution by which the shares, with that right, are created

2.4 In defining the rights attached to preference shares, the following points should be considered and, where necessary, clearly expressed.

(a) In normal circumstances, when the holders of preference shares have received dividends at the specified priority rate, they have **no further right to participate** in any profits which the company may decide to distribute. In the example, above, of 6% £1 preference shares, holders of preference shares would be entitled to a priority dividend of 6p per share out of profits, but no more than that, unless their shares were **participating preference shares**.

(b) The right is to receive dividends up to the specified rate, **before any dividends may be paid on ordinary shares**. If the company has no profits, or decides not to distribute profits as dividend, the preference shareholders cannot compel it to do so: *Bond v Barrow Haematite Steel Co 1902*.

(c) If preference dividends are 'passed' (not paid at all or not paid at the full rate) it is implied, unless the contrary is stated, that the **priority is carried forward** (is cumulative). Thus, if a 6% dividend, say, is not paid in Year 1, the shares carry a double (12%) priority in Year 2, and so on. Although this is 'implied unless expressly excluded', it is better to be explicit. Preference shares should be described as 'cumulative' or 'non-cumulative' so that the position is clear.

(d) Where preference shares are cumulative, their **entitlement to dividend arrears passes** with the shares to the registered holder for the time being: if arrears are later paid off, it is the holder at the time of payment who receives the extra amount. The entitlement ends, unless otherwise stated, if the company ceases to be a going concern.

(e) It is common practice to define the rights of preference shares to include a **priority in repayment of capital in winding up**. However this right is not implied and, if it is to be given, it should be expressly conferred.

(f) It is also common practice to **restrict the voting rights** of preference shares to specific situations, for instance to voting on a resolution to liquidate the company, or on a resolution to vary the rights attached to preference shares, or to make the shares non-voting altogether. Again, if that is intended it should be expressly stated; if it is not, the shares carry the same voting rights as ordinary shares.

Redeemable preference shares

2.5 Redeemable preference shares hold **dual rights** as redeemable shares and preference shares.

Participating preference shares

2.6 We have seen that preference shares of the normal type carry no entitlement to dividend **beyond** the priority rate. It is possible, however, to confer on preference shares a right to **participate**, usually on the basis of equality, with ordinary shares, after the latter have received a **dividend equal** to the preference dividend. For example, with 6% participating preference shares, the holders of those shares receive a 6% dividend out of the first profits distributed, then the next slice is applied in a 6% dividend to ordinary shareholders, and thereafter any further distribution is made at the same rate on both classes of shares.

Rights of preference shareholders on the company's liquidation

2.7 Preference shares usually carry a **priority** right to the **return of capital** paid up on the shares, if the company goes into liquidation. The general principle is that the rights, as expressly defined, are 'exhaustive' (nothing more is implied in favour of the shares once their explicit entitlement has been satisfied).

2.8 For example, if a company which has, say, £100,000 in preference shares and £900,000 in ordinary shares has net assets of £2 million when it goes into liquidation, the liquidator, after paying the company's debts, repays the first £100,000 to the holders of preference shares in complete satisfaction of their entitlement. The remaining £1,900,000 is allocated to the ordinary shares, whose holders therefore receive a surplus; the preference shareholders get nothing more.

2.9 Of course, if the preference shares do not carry a priority entitlement to repayment of capital, they participate equally in any surplus, or suffer the same deficiency as the ordinary shares, in the example above they would receive £200,000.

2.10 An additional consequence of giving preference shares a priority in the return of capital is that the company may, by an authorised reduction of capital, **pay off** the **preference shares entirely,** and continue with ordinary shares alone. Preference shares may of course be given an express safeguard against this situation.

Deferred shares

2.11 Deferred shares are no longer common. Typically, the promoter(s) of a new public company would agree to take part of the payment for assets or services supplied to the company in the form of deferred shares, on which **no dividend** was to be **paid** until the **ordinary shares** had **received dividends** of a **specified level.** In return, the promoters might attach to their deferred shares a larger number of votes per share, to secure a greater influence on the management.

Non-voting shares

2.12 Apart from the common practice of providing that preference shares shall carry no, or restricted, voting rights, it is possible to create ordinary shares with no voting rights but which rank equally with other (voting) ordinary shares. Such non-voting ordinary shares are by convention usually distinguished as **'A Ordinary Shares'**. The company may also attach different levels of votes to distinct classes of ordinary shares.

Loan capital

2.13 The point which must be emphasised is that a **lender is a creditor whose rights against the company are created and defined by a contract**, usually in the form of debentures or a debenture trust deed. His claim as a creditor to interest at the agreed rate and repayment of capital takes priority over any claims of shareholders. Since the basis of the lender's position is a contract with the company, it is essential that the terms should be clearly expressed. It is usual that the terms are set out in detail in the form of debentures. Chapter 13 covers loan capital in greater detail.

Exercise

Explain the distinction between preference shares and debentures from the points of view of both the company and the holder of the securities.

Solution

The main distinction between debentures and share capital for both company and the holders is that debentures are normally secured by a fixed or floating charge on the assets of the company.

(a) *Debentures*

For the company, debentures may restrict free trading of assets which are encumbered by a fixed charge. It has also assumed a long-term liability which, unless irredeemable, must be repaid. Funds should therefore be set aside.

Irrespective of whether profits are made, debenture interest must be paid, and so reduce profits further, although it is deductible for Corporation Tax as a charge on income.

Failure to pay interest, or to fulfil some other term of the debenture trust deed, will lead to crystallisation of the charge.

The investor has security for his loan and a guaranteed source of income. Unlike shares, however, debentures confer no rights to attend and vote at company meetings, since a debenture-holder does not own the assets; he is not a member.

(b) *Preference shares*

For the company, preference shares are treated as part of capital and hence no provision need be made for them to be repaid.

Usually they take priority for both dividend and return of capital over ordinary shares, but the dividend may only be paid out of profit. Hence, if no profits are made, no dividends can be paid.

Preference shares can be cumulative, which means that all arrears of dividend must be paid out before ordinary shareholders get their dividends. They can also be participating, meaning that once ordinary shares are paid a dividend, any excess may be shared out.

The investor is normally assured of a priority dividend and return of capital. However, depending on the terms of the issue, he generally may not vote at general meetings, nor participate in excess profits. No restriction exists on his right to vote at and attend class meetings.

3 VARIATION AND REGISTRATION OF SHARE RIGHTS

3.1 If the company has only one class of share, a variation of their rights can be effected by altering the memorandum or articles, which define the rights. Even then, a dissenting minority may be able to appeal to the court on grounds of equity. However such disputes are essentially legal and not within the scope of secretarial practice.

Variation of rights

3.2 If the company has different classes of shares (if some shares form a distinct class, because they have different rights attached from those attached to other shares), the company may only vary the rights of the class if it obtains the **consent** of the holders of that class of shares, before altering its memorandum or articles to that effect. If *all* the shareholders of the class give their formal consent, that obviously suffices. However company law also recognises that a binding decision for the whole class may, in certain circumstances, follow from a mere majority decision.

3.3 If there is a clear proposal to vary class rights, the first step is to refer to the articles (or possibly the memorandum), which will usually contain a clause providing a procedure by which the binding consent of the class may be obtained. If there is no provision in the articles or memorandum then the standard procedure is now contained in s 125 and states that either of the following must be satisfied.

(a) The company must **obtain consent**, **in writing**, of the holders of at least three quarters of the shares of the class.

(b) The company must hold a **meeting** of the holders of the shares of the class at which an **extraordinary resolution** is passed by the required three quarters majority. In this case, the **quorum** (ie the necessary attendees) at the meeting is **at least two persons**, holding or representing by proxy at least one third (in nominal value) of the issued shares of the class: s 125(6)(a). If all the shares are held by one person it is better to obtain his consent in writing thereby satisfying (a) above. But s 125(6)(a) also provides that, at an adjourned meeting of the class, a quorum of one suffices. Hence if there is only one member, or only one who has one third or more of the shares attends, the meeting may be briefly adjourned, to resume with a quorum of one.

Requirement (b) is less demanding than (a), but (a) entails less formal procedure.

3.4 If the memorandum or articles provides a different formula, that procedure must be followed. However, if the variation involves an authority to the directors to issue shares (s 80) or a reduction of capital (s 135), the conditions set out above - consent by a three quarters majority - must be satisfied in addition to the specific requirements of the memorandum or articles.

3.5 It may be that the class rights of a particular class of share are not expressed as variable under the memorandum or the articles, and so there will be a specified procedure for their variation contained in the memorandum or articles. In this event the following applies.

(a) If the rights of the class of shares are defined in the memorandum, the **consent required** to **vary them** is that of **all the members** of the company.

(b) If the **rights** are **defined** in the **articles**, the formula described earlier applies.

Any change in the variation procedure itself, or the insertion of such a procedure into the articles for the first time, is treated as a variation to which the above rules apply.

3.6 Where the rights of a class of shares are to be varied under a procedure contained in the memorandum or articles, the **holders** of **not less than 15 per** cent (in nominal value) of the shares of that class may, within 21 days of consent being given by a majority of that class, **apply** to the **court** to disallow the variation on grounds of unfair prejudice to them: s 127.

Registration of class rights

3.7 The company must, within one month of allotting any of the new class of shares (unless they are uniform with shares previously allotted), give notice (Form 128) of the rights to the registrar, so that the information is made available for inspection in the company's file.

FORM 128(1)	Statement of rights attached to allotted shares.
FORM 128(3)	Statement of particulars of variations of rights attached to shares.
FORM 128(4)	Notice of assignment of name or new name to any class of shares.

4 SPECIAL RIGHTS AND TRANSACTIONS RELATING TO SHARES

Lien on shares

4.1 A lien is effectively a form of **equitable mortgage** on shares by which, if the articles so provide (Table A Articles 8 to 11), a company may assert rights over the shares to enforce payment of any debt owed to it by the registered holder of the shares.

4.2 Private companies sometimes have a widely drawn lien in their articles, applying even to fully paid shares and to any debt owed to the company by the shareholder. It is always necessary to examine closely the wording of the relevant articles. Table A Article 8 is confined to a lien on partly paid shares, to secure money due on those shares.

4.3 If the company has a valid lien and occasion to enforce it, the company may withhold dividends and/or sell the shares as a means of recovering its debt.

4.4 If the company receives notice, even informally, that a third party has an interest in the shares, eg as purchaser or mortgagee, and the company later enforces a lien as security for a debt created after that notice was received, the **third party interest will take priority over the company's lien**.

5 CONSOLIDATION AND SUBDIVISION OF SHARES

5.1 The share capital of a company may be consolidated if the Articles give authority Consolidation means that the shares of the company will be divided into shares of a larger nominal value, eg ten shares of 10p each consolidated into one share of £1 each.

5.2 The procedure is similar to increasing authorised capital but certain further matters have to be addressed. For example the **register of members** will have to be **rewritten** so as to show the holdings of each member in the new denomination.

5.3 A company does not need to file with the Registrar a copy of the resolution passed at the general meeting if it is an ordinary resolution. However, Companies Form No 122 '*Notice of consolidation, division, sub-division, redemption or cancellation of shares, or conversion, re-conversion of stock into shares*' must be sent to the Registrar within one month of the resolution being passed.

5.4 Some holdings of members will not consolidate into an exact number of new shares. The directors should be given authority to deal with such **fractions** as they believe appropriate. For a listed company the directors would sell such fractional shares on the market and distribute the proceeds to the member subject to a minimum distributable amount of, say, £5 which would be retained by the company.

5.5 Share certificates may be called in to be amended. Alternatively members can be sent a notice that the consolidation has taken place.

Subdivision of shares

5.6 Subject to provision in the articles an ordinary resolution of the company in general meeting may be passed subdividing (also known as splitting) the company's shares into shares of a smaller nominal amount, for example when the shares have risen to a very high value.

5.7 The procedure for effecting a subdivision of shares is similar to the procedure for the consolidation of shares, except that fractions of shares cannot arise. **Companies Form 122** must be filed within one month of the resolution.

FORM 122	Notice of consolidation, division, sub-division, redemption or cancellation of shares, or conversion, re-conversion of stock into shares. See Appendix 10.
FORM 123	Notice of increase in nominal capital. See Appendix 11.
FORM 169	Return by a company purchasing its own shares. See Appendix 12.
FORM 173	Declaration in relation to the redemption or purchase of shares out of capital. See Appendix 13.

Chapter roundup

- Shares are a source of **capital** to the company and **personal property** of the shareholder.
- Types of share include:
  - **Preference** shares
  - **Ordinary** shares
  - **Deferred** shares; dividends are paid after dividends are paid to ordinary shareholders
- Other ways to raise money include **loan capital**, **debenture** issues and **bank loan/overdraft**.
- Loan capital is a contractual loan, by which the lender is a **creditor** of the company. The lender's return on investment is generally by way of **fixed interest** payable as an expense of the company. As a creditor the investor of loan capital will effectively take priority over preference shareholders on liquidation.
- To **vary class rights** the terms of the **articles** must be referred to or, if there is no provision, consent must be obtained, in **writing**, from at least **three quarters** of the class members; alternatively, an extraordinary resolution by a three quarters majority could be passed: s 125.

Summary of documents

FORM 128(1)	Statement of rights attached to allotted shares
FORM 128(3)	Statement of particulars of variation of rights attached to shares
FORM 128(4)	Notice of assignment of name or new name to any class of shares
FORM 122	Notice of consolidation, division, sub-division, redemption or cancellation of shares, or conversion, re-conversion of stock into shares
FORM 123	Notice of increase in nominal capital.
FORM 169	Return by a company purchasing its own shares.
FORM 173	Declaration in relation to the redemption or purchase of shares out of capital.

Test your knowledge

1 How may the rights of ordinary shares be ascertained? (see para 1.7)

2 What rights are normally given to preference shares? (2.2, 2.4)

3 Distinguish loan capital from share capital. (2.13)

4 What is the standard procedure for obtaining consent for a variation of rights of a class of shares? (3.3)

Now try illustrative question 14 at the end of the Study Text

Chapter 13

LOAN CAPITAL AND CHARGES

This chapter covers the following topics.

Introduction

The advantages of raising some part of the company's capital by borrowing were listed in an earlier chapter, in connection with capital structure. Borrowing is usually in the form of either *overdraft facilities* provided by the company's bank, or *debentures* issued by the company as the basis of borrowing for a fixed period, often many years.

Debentures (or debenture stock) are loan contracts by which the lenders provide money to the company, to be repaid eventually and meanwhile bearing interest at an agreed rate. Debentures may be secured, say on property, but they need not be.

Any type of borrowing is a contract by which the company binds itself to repay the capital and meanwhile to pay interest. Hence it is necessary to consider first the limits on the borrowing powers of a company and its directors.

1 DEFINITION OF BORROWING

1.1 A company whose objects are to carry on a trade or business has an implied power to borrow for **purposes incidental** to the **trade or business**. Traditionally the objects clause always contained an express power to borrow. It may well be that objects clauses will continue to state this explicitly despite the provisions of the CA 1989, to ensure that the situation is covered.

1.2 In the case of a non-trading company it was essential to have an express power to borrow since it was not implied. Again the CA 1989 has potentially changed the emphasis.

1.3 It is usual not to impose any maximum amount on the company's capacity to borrow (though it is possible to do so). In delegating the company's power to borrow to the directors it is usual (and essential in the case of a company whose shares are listed on the Stock Exchange) to impose a **maximum** on the **borrowing arranged** by **directors.**

1.4 A contract to repay borrowed money may therefore be unenforceable in principle in either of the following cases.

(a) It is money borrowed for an **ultra vires** purpose.

(b) The directors **exceed** their **borrowing powers** or have **no powers** to borrow at all.

In either case however, the lender should be able to enforce the contract if he is acting in good faith under ss 35(1) or 35A.

1.5 Moreover, if the contract is within the capacity of the company but beyond the delegated powers of the directors the company may ratify the loan contract or may be bound by the contract under the rule in *Royal British Bank v Turquand 1856* which is explained later in connection with directors' powers.

1.6 If there is a power to borrow there is also a power to **create charges** over the company's assets as security for the loan.

1.7 A public company initially incorporated as such cannot borrow money until it has obtained a certificate under s 117. Only a public company may offer its debentures to the public and any such offer is a prospectus; if it seeks a listing on the Stock Exchange then the rules on listing particulars must be followed.

Limits on directors' borrowing powers

1.8 Most companies include in their articles a **limit on** the amount directors may borrow (without obtaining the sanction of a general meeting), by adapting the formula found in the 1948 Table A Article 79 (since there is no article of this kind in the 1985 Table A); the limit is set at an amount equal to the nominal value of the issued share capital plus reserves, or a multiple of that figure.

1.9 The following two points should be noted in connection with this formula.

(a) Company borrowing is defined to include the liability (if any) of the company as **guarantor** of a debt owed by a third party, such as an associated company.

(b) In reckoning the amount actually borrowed 'temporary loans obtained from the company's bankers in the ordinary course of business' are to be excluded from the total. Because of the **continuing nature** of **overdraft facilities**, however, the banks themselves do not consider that this exclusion can safely be applied even to an overdraft; it may not be 'temporary' in the required sense. Hence the banks insist that a company shall include its overdraft in the total of its borrowing (within the limit set by the articles).

2 THE CHARACTERISTICS OF DEBENTURES AND HOW THEY ARE ISSUED

2.1 Any document which states the terms on which a company has borrowed money is a **debenture**: s 744. It may create a charge over the company's assets as security for the loan. However a document relating to an unsecured loan is also a debenture in company law (though often called an unsecured loan note in the business world to distinguish it from a secured debenture).

2.2 It is usual, but not essential, for a company to issue debentures under the **common seal**, if the company has one. If it is a secured debenture and sealed (or appropriately signed and expressed) it is a mortgage created by deed which under the law of property gives power to the mortgagee to enforce his security, if necessary.

2.3 A debenture is usually a formal legal document, often in printed form. Broadly, there are three main types as follows.

(a) **A single debenture**

If, for example, a company obtains a secured loan or overdraft facility from its bank, the latter is likely to insist that the company seals the bank's standard form of debenture creating the charge and giving the bank various safeguards and powers.

(b) **Debentures issued as a series and usually registered**

A company may, for example, raise loan capital from its directors or members. Different lenders may provide different amounts on different dates.

Each transaction is a separate loan but the common intention is that the lenders should **rank equally** (*pari passu*) in their right to repayment and in any security given to them. Each lender receives a debenture in identical form in respect of his loan and the debentures are expressed to form a series (by which a global sum is raised) ranking *pari passu*.

The debentures are transferable securities and the normal conditions require the company to maintain a register of debentureholders. The debenture-holder's title to his loan then depends on the entry of his name as original allottee or as transferee in the register. A trust deed (see below) may be issued.

(c) **The issue of debenture stock subscribed to by a large number of lenders**

This is the method by which a public company raises loan capital from the **public at large**. Each lender has a right to be repaid his capital at the due time and to receive interest on it until repayment. For convenience this form of borrowing is treated as a single global loan 'stock' in which each debenture stockholder has a specified fraction (in money terms) which he or some previous holder contributed when the stock was issued.

Debenture stock is transferable in multiples of, say, £1 or £10 etc. as stipulated in the conditions of issue (thus the holder need not dispose of all his holding at once). There is again a register of debenture stockholders maintained by the company in which the names of the persons currently entitled are entered as evidence of their ownership.

The terms of the debenture stock are expressed in a trust deed, and a trustee for the debenture stockholders is appointed to represent their interests and to enforce their rights. Each debenture stockholder receives a debenture stock certificate which records (like a share certificate) that he is the registered holder of £X of debenture stock subject to the terms and conditions of the trust deed.

2.4 It is possible to vary or to combine features from these basic types.

Debenture trust deed 12/98

2.5 A **debenture trust deed** is usually a long and elaborate legal document whose main elements are as follows.

(a) The appointment of a **trustee** for prospective debenture stockholders is set out. The first trustee is formally appointed by the company (as the other party to the deed). Any replacement trustee is to be appointed by the debenture stockholders. The trustee is usually a bank or other institution, but may be an individual.

(b) The **nominal amount** of the debenture stock is defined, which is the maximum amount which may be raised then or later. The date or period of repayment is specified, as is the rate of interest and half yearly interest payment dates.

(c) If the debenture stock is secured, the deed **creates** a **charge** or **charges** over the assets of the company.

(d) The trustee is **authorised** to **enforce** the **security** in case of default and in particular, to appoint a receiver with suitable powers of management.

(e) The company enters into **various covenants,** eg to keep its assets fully insured or to limit its total borrowings; breach is a default by the company.

(f) There are elaborate provisions for a **register** of **debenture stockholders,** for transfer of stock, for issue of stock certificates and meetings of debenture stockholders. At these meetings extraordinary resolutions passed by a three quarters majority are decisions binding on *all* debenture stockholders.

2.6 The main advantages of the use of a debenture trust deed are as follows.

(a) The **trustee** with appropriate powers can **intervene promptly** in case of default.

(b) **Security** for the debenture stock in the form of charges over property can be **given** to a **single trustee** (a mortgage could not be given to a numerous and changing body of debenture holders).

(c) The company can **contact** a **representative** of the debenture **stockholders** with whom it can **negotiate,** say for consent to sell an obsolete asset and to replace it, as security, by another.

(d) By calling a **meeting** of debenture stockholders, the trustee can **consult** them and obtain a decision which is binding on them all.

(e) The debentureholders will be able to enjoy the benefit of a **legal mortgage** over the company's land. This would not be possible without trustees since under the Law of Property Act 1925, a legal estate in land cannot be vested in more than four persons.

Register of debentureholders

2.7 There is no general rule of law which requires a company to maintain a register of its debentureholders. However, it is common practice when debentures are issued as a series or when debenture stock is issued, to impose on the company, an obligation to maintain a register as a record of the current ownership of its loan capital. Clearly also a company has to have some means of knowing whom to pay when the loan capital is redeemed.

2.8 When there is a **register of debentureholders** the following applies.

(a) The company is required by law to keep the **register** in the **same country** as its registered office, either at that office or if the register is made up elsewhere at an address of which notice is given to the registrar: s 190.

(b) The register of debentureholders must be **open to inspection** by any person. Any person may obtain a copy of the register or part of it. A holder of debentures issued under a trust deed may require the company (on payment) to supply him with a copy of the deed: s 191.

(c) The register should be properly kept in accordance with the following rules:

(i) The register may be kept in **bound books** or by recording the matters by any other method, care being taken to guard against falsifications: s 722.

(ii) The register may be kept in an **otherwise than legible form** provided it can be reproduced in a legible form: s 723. Hence it can be maintained on computer.

2.9 The holder of a debenture, whether it is a single debenture or one of a series, will generally have the full conditions of the loan set out on that document. If, however, he has a certificate of his registered holding of a debenture stock the following applies.

(a) A **summary** of the more important terms of the trust deed is printed on the back of the certificate. This is always required if the stock is a listed security.

(b) He may, on application to the company, obtain a copy of the **entire printed deed,** on payment of a fee: s 191(3). The company should, in arranging for the printing of the deed, obtain a number of copies to meet such demands.

Shares and debentures compared — **Specimen paper, 12/99**

2.10 The position of debentureholder and shareholder has, at first sight, a good deal in common as follows.

(a) Both **own transferable company securities** which are usually long-term investments in the company.

(b) The **issue procedure** is much the same. An offer of either shares or debentures to the public is a prospectus as defined by the Financial Services Act 1986.

(c) Both usually **derive** their **title** to their securities from an **entry** in a **register** kept by the company. The procedure for transfer of registered shares and debentures is the same.

2.11 There are however important and more fundamental differences including the following.

(a) A shareholder is a proprietor or **owner** but a debentureholder is a **creditor** of the company.

(b) A shareholder as a member may **vote at general meetings**; a debentureholder has no such right as a member, though exceptionally he may have votes if the Articles and the deed allow.

(c) In liquidation, **debentures** like other debts must be **repaid in full** before anything is distributed to shareholders.

(d) **Interest** at the agreed rate must be **paid** on debentures even if it is necessary to pay out capital in doing so. A shareholder, even if he holds preference shares on which dividends at a specified rate at fixed dates are due, receives dividends only if they can be paid out of distributable profits and the company decides to declare a dividend.

(e) A company has **no statutory restriction** to **redeeming** or **purchasing** its debentures (unless prohibited by the terms of the debenture). It may usually reissue debentures which have been redeemed. There are elaborate rules to regulate the redemption or purchase by a company of its own shares.

(f) The company's relationship with the **shareholders** is governed by its **articles**, with its **debentureholders** by the **debenture trust deed**.

2.12 From the investor's standpoint debenture stock is often preferable to preference shares since the former offers greater security and yields a fixed income. Many companies have in recent years issued debenture stock to replace preference capital because they prefer debenture stock for the reasons listed below.

(a) The advantages of **security** and **regular fixed interest** mean that debentures can usually be issued at a lower rate of interest than that required to attract buyers of preference shares.

(b) As debenture holders are **loan** creditors, the raising of money by debentures does **not extend** the **company's membership**.

(c) **Debenture interest** is **deductible** when calculating taxable profits.

2.13 From the company's viewpoint the main **advantages** of debentures are as follows.

(a) A debenture is **easily traded**, and as the company issuing it is a public company, the trading will take place on the Stock Exchange.

(b) Its **terms**, as set out in the trust deed, are **clear** and **specific**, so that the company can be certain of its obligations.

(c) The debentureholder has **no say** in the **running** of the company; his status is as creditor, not member, as he would be had a share issue been made. The 'balance of power' in the company is thus not altered by the issue of debentures.

(d) **Debentures secured** by **floating charges** are **popular** instruments. They give holders the security of a charge, but mean from the company's viewpoint that the assets charged can be freely traded.

(e) The debenture offers potential investors the **security** of a **guaranteed income**, and thus from the company's viewpoint an issue of debentures may be more popular than an issue of preference shares.

(f) **Interest payable** on debenture stock is **deductible** when **computing taxable profits**, whereas **dividends** are **not**.

(g) The Companies Act requirements that affect debentures are more relaxed in a number of ways than those that affect shares. There are no restrictions on a company purchasing its own debentures, and debentures can be issued at a discount, unlike shares.

2.14 The main **disadvantages** of debentures for the company are as follows.

(a) The company may have to offer a **relatively high rate of interest** in order to make the debenture attractive. This particularly applies in times of inflation where the real value of fixed interest payments will decline.

(b) **Payment of debenture interest** is **mandatory** not discretionary (as, for example, payment of dividends on shares is discretionary). The company must consider whether this liability can be met.

(c) If interest payments result in cuts in dividend yield, this may lead to pressure from shareholders, and **cause share prices** to **fall**.

(d) Debentureholders' **remedies** include the **appointment of liquidators** or receivers, which may have **disastrous** consequences for the company.

(e) **Crystallisation** of floating charges can mean the **security** is **swiftly enforced**. Given that the security will often be over trading assets, enforcement would cause major problems for the company.

Notice of trust

2.15 There is no rule of law which prevents a company from accepting notice given by a third party that he has an interest in a debenture which is not registered in his name but in the name of someone else. However contrast the rule relating to beneficial interests in shares under s 360 which provides that no notice of any trust etc must be entered in the register. In practice however the same rule is applied to debentures as to shares by making it a contractual term of the issue of debentures. However a person who wishes to protect an equitable interest in debentures may do so by serving a stop notice on the company.

Unsecured loan stock

2.16 The essential terms of issue of an unsecured loan stock (apart from the absence of security, by way of charge on the company's assets) are much the same as those of a secured debenture stock. However there are the following differences.

(a) It is always (as is obligatory for a listed security) expressly described in all relevant documents as an 'unsecured loan stock' or 'unsecured loan notes'. The term '**debenture**' is in practice (not law) reserved for **secured loans**.

(b) To make an unsecured loan more attractive to investors, it is more likely than a secured debenture to carry an **option** to convert into shares.

(c) The **terms of** issue are likely to **prohibit** the company from issuing any secured **debentures**, since these would rank ahead of the unsecured loan.

Except as regards questions of security, what is written in this chapter with reference to 'debentures' is applicable to unsecured as well as secured loans.

Transactions in debentures

2.17 The main features of transactions in debentures are as follows.

(a) Debentures are issued under the **same procedure** as shares. **Application** is made to the company, and the directors **allot debentures** to applicants, who must pay for them the agreed amount at the agreed time (usually on application or issue). An invitation to the public to apply for debenture stock is a **prospectus** and is regulated by the FSA.

(b) **Debentures** may be issued at a **discount**; they may also be issued on terms that they are to be repaid at a premium. For example, a company may issue £100 (nominal) debentures for £95 in cash, or for £100 cash with an undertaking to repay £105 at maturity (the contractual date for repayment).

(c) It is legally possible to issue **bonus debentures** to shareholders, but tax rules make it unwise to do so.

(d) A **registered debenture**, or debenture stock, is **transferred** by completing and delivering to the company the **same form of transfer** as is used for the **transfer** of **shares**. The debenture or debenture stock certificate is surrendered to the company (for issue of a new one or, in the case of a separate debenture, endorsement of the name of the new holder on the debenture).

(e) The **terms of repayment** are set down on issue, as one of the conditions of the debenture. They are simply a **matter of contract** to be settled by the company and its debenture holders. Debentures may be issued on terms that they are not to be repaid for a long period of years, or are 'irredeemable', ie not to be repaid until the company either defaults or goes into liquidation (when all its debts must be discharged).

Secured debentures

2.18 A secured debenture is a **form of mortgage** which is subject to general mortgage law (except that the date for redemption may be postponed for a long period): s 193. This allows debentures to be issued as perpetual or irredeemable.

2.19 A secured debenture is, however, subject to the principle of general mortgage law that on redemption the company must **recover** its property free of any **unfair advantages** secured by the lender. But this rule does not prohibit a lender from securing commercial advantages to continue after repayment provided that is a reasonable arrangement: *Kreglinger v New Patagonia Meat Co 1914.*

2.20 An order for specific performance may be obtained by a company to enforce a contract to subscribe for debentures. This is an exception to the general rule that specific performance is not available in contracts for the lending of money: s 195.

Convertible debentures

2.21 A debenture, especially an unsecured loan stock, may be issued on the basis that at fixed dates, and at fixed prices, the holder may at his option convert his holding into shares. The legal theory of 'conversion' is a two-stage operation as follows.

(a) The **loan is** to be **repaid.**

(b) The money due on repayment is then applied in **paying** the **capital** to be subscribed for shares, at a prearranged issue price. If debentures are issued at a discount (for less consideration than their nominal value), the right of conversion may have to be restricted to ensure that, on conversion, the shares are not issued at a discount: *Moseley v Koftyfontein Mines 1904.*

2.22 More recently imposed restrictions include the following.

(a) The directors may not allot shares unless **authorised** by the **articles** or by the members in general meeting: s 80.

(b) The shareholders have **pre-emption rights** in respect of ordinary (and participating preference) shares, if allotted for cash: s 89.

These rules also apply to the issue of convertible loans.

2.23 Finally, the company should always ensure that it has sufficient unissued shares to satisfy the conversion rights, if and when they are exercised.

2.24 If there is more than one optional conversion date (it being common to space them out at yearly intervals over several years), it is usual to encourage early conversion by providing that at each successive option date, the number of shares obtainable on conversion is slightly reduced. In effect, the issue price of the shares is being raised by stages.

3 PROCEDURE FOR THE CONVERSION OF DEBENTURES

3.1 Conversion of debentures has two stages; **approval** as appropriate and the process of **conversion.**

3.2 The **articles of association** should be checked for permission to convert the debentures, and a **board meeting** should pass a resolution to recommend the conversion to shareholders.

3.3 An **Extraordinary General Meeting** will be required. The business will be to pass an **ordinary resolution** specifying the number of shares that are to be created by the conversion and to approve the circular to be sent to members giving reasons for the conversion. The circular together with a two-way proxy should be sent out with the notice of the meeting. For listed companies, two copies of the proxy cards should be sent to the Stock Exchange Listing Department, and six copies of the notice and circular and proxy cards should be sent to the Company Announcements Office.

3.4 Once passed, copies of the resolution should be sent to the Registrar (one certified copy), and, for listed companies to the Company Announcements Office (six copies). Copies of the updated memorandum and articles, should also be filed with the Registrar and if appropriate, the Company Announcements Office (two copies).

Conversion procedure

3.5 The main stages are as follows.

(a) As each conversion date approaches, a notice is issued to holders of the convertible loan:

(i) To remind them of their **right of conversion** and its terms

(ii) To explain that if they wish to have shares allotted to them, they have only to complete and return the **conversion form** on the reverse of the loan stock certificate

(iii) To explain that if they wish to have shares allotted to some other person, they should complete a **nomination form** (enclosed with the notice) and return it with their certificate

If the loan is a listed security, the notice etc. must be submitted to the Stock Exchange for approval. Time should be allowed for this stage.

(b) When the documents are received, they should be checked to ensure that they have been correctly completed; it is also good practice to record each stage of the ensuing action on a **progress sheet** (for each holder who exercises his option).

(c) At the expiry of the period for notice of exercise of the option, an **announcement** should be made to the Stock Exchange, if the loan is listed, and to the debenture trustee (if any).

(d) Shares should be **allotted**, and **share certificates** prepared (and the particulars noted in the progress sheets). If there are fractions, that is small sums which do not suffice to subscribe for one more share, a cheque should be issued for repayment in cash of these sums.

(e) If the company's shares are **listed**, **application** is **made** to the **Stock Exchange** for listing of the newly allotted shares.

(f) **Appropriate entries** are made in the **register of members** and a return of allotments is sent to the registrar, with Form 88(2) (see Appendix 4).

4 PROCEDURE FOR THE REDEMPTION OF DEBENTURES

4.1 Debentures may be issued as 'irredeemable': s 193. This means that there is no fixed date when the company is required to redeem them (though it may have the option to do so). However, if the company defaults on the terms of the debenture or eventually goes into liquidation, even irredeemable loans are repayable.

4.2 The terms of issue may also provide for the following.

(a) **Annual appropriations** to build up a sinking fund (which accumulates interest until sufficient cash has been gathered to redeem the debt)

(b) **Selective redemption** by **purchase** in the **open market** or drawing lots at intervals

(c) **Redemption** at a **premium**, that is at a price in excess of the nominal value of the debentures

These are contractual obligations binding on the company.

Purchase in the open market

4.3 It will be necessary to instruct the company's stockbrokers to buy the amount of stock required. The amount of stock to be purchased will depend on the market price. It should be made clear to the brokers that the stock is being purchased for redemption so that no instrument of transfer will be necessary.

As the debenture stock is listed, the Stock Exchange would be notified of the amount of stock purchased and the amount remaining outstanding.

Holding a drawing

4.4 The main procedures are as follows.

(a) The **record date** and the **date** of the **drawing** should be **agreed** with the debenture trustees.

(b) If the stock is listed, the **Stock Exchange** should be **notified** of these dates and the amount to be drawn.

(c) Immediately following the record date, the **register** of debenture stockholders should be **balanced** and from it a **complete list** of the holders showing their holdings **prepared** in triplicate. This task can be completed quickly if the register is kept on computer.

(d) **Holdings** should be **progressively numbered** in blocks of say £100. Those holdings for less than the block figure or any fractional amounts over that figure should be aggregated into composite blocks which will also be numbered.

(e) Discs or **tickets individually numbered** to correspond with the numbered blocks will be prepared and thoroughly mixed in a suitable container in the presence of at least three persons, say a representative of the company, a representative of the trustees and a notary public. Each will have a copy of the list.

(f) As each disc or ticket is drawn by the notary, the **holdings** or partial holdings will be **marked off** on the lists.

(g) The drawing will be complete when **sufficient discs** or **tickets** have been **drawn.** A list of the drawn holdings will be extracted and appropriately certified.

(h) If the debenture stock is listed, the **Stock Exchange** would be **notified** that the drawing has duly taken place, confirming the amount drawn and stating the amount still in issue for listing purposes.

(i) **Notification** of the drawing would then be given to the **holders** concerned as follows.

> **Trumpington Oil Traders plc**
>
> **address**
>
> Dear Sir or Madam
>
> *Annual Redemption of 6% Debenture Stock 20X0-20X3*
>
> In accordance with the provisions of the Trust Deed dated ...., constituting and securing the above named debenture stock, there has been drawn for redemption and the company will redeemed at par on .... (date), £X of the debenture stock held by you with interest to that date.
>
> A further letter will be sent to you in due course enclosing a form of discharge for completion and return with your stock certificate(s).
>
> Yours faithfully
>
> Company Secretary

4.5 About three weeks before redemption date, **forms of discharge** are sent to the relevant holders for completion and return with stock certificates. In the meantime redemption and final interest warrants will be prepared for issue. A board minute will record the drawing.

Final redemption

4.6 **Notice** would be given to every debenture stockholder of the company's intention to redeem the stock on a specified date. This will be followed by a letter enclosing a **payment authority** and **form of discharge** for signature. The letter would be as follows.

> **Trumpington Oil Traders plc**
>
> **address**
>
> Dear Sir or Madam
>
> *Final Redemption of 6% Debenture Stock 2020X0-2020X3*
>
> Further to the letter sent to you on .... (date) notifying you that £X of the above mentioned debenture stock will be redeemed at par on .... (date) next, I enclose payment authority and form of discharge for your signature.
>
> Please complete the form and return it together with the relevant stock certificates not later than .... (date).
>
> In exchange, a cheque for the value of this stock together with an interest warrant will be posted by return.
>
> Yours faithfully
>
> Registrar

4.7 As some stockholders will not respond, for example because they have changed address and have not notified the registrar and others do not present their cheques for payment, there will be **balances outstanding** on the **redemption** account and the **interest account**. In due course these balances will be handed over to the trustees who will then deal with any further payments in respect of unclaimed money. The Stock Exchange will be notified of the final redemption if the company is listed.

4.8 For accounting purposes, if the debentures are redeemed at a premium, the premium can be **set off** against the company's **share premium account**, if it has one: s 130.

4.9 At the time for redemption, if a date is fixed (usually it is a period, within which the company may select a date for redemption), a **notice** is sent to **every holder** inviting him to send in his certificate in exchange for the sum due to him.

4.10 If a secured debenture stock or series of debentures is redeemed, the company should clear the registration of the charge from its file at the Companies Registry, and make a corresponding alteration in its own register of charges, held at the registered office. Form 403a should be used.

FORM 403 (a)	Declaration of satisfaction in full or in part of a mortgage or charge. See Appendix 14.

5 FIXED AND FLOATING CHARGES AS SECURITY FOR A LOAN 6/98

5.1 A charge over assets of a company gives to a creditor a prior claim (over other creditors) to payment of his debt out of those assets. Charges are of two kinds.

(a) **Fixed or specific charges** which attach to the relevant asset as soon as the charge is created. By its nature a specific charge is best suited to **fixed assets** which the company is likely to retain for a long period. If the company does dispose of the asset it will either repay the mortgage debt out of the proceeds of sale so that the charge is discharged at the time of sale, or pass the asset over to the purchaser still subject to the charge.

(b) **Floating charges** which do not attach to the relevant assets until the charge crystallises. The nature of a floating charge has been defined in *Re Yorkshire Woolcombers Association Ltd 1903* as:

- (i) A **charge** on a **class** of assets of a company, present and future . . .
- (ii) Which **class is,** in the ordinary course of the company's business, **changing** from time to time and . . .
- (iii) Until the **holders enforce** the charge the **company may** carry **on business** and **deal** with the **assets charged.**

A floating charge is not restricted however to current assets such as book debts or stock in trade. A floating charge over 'the undertaking and assets' of a company (the most common type) applies to fixed as well as to current assets. But it does not attach to any assets (point (iii) above) *until* crystallisation.

Fixed charges

5.2 A fixed charge may be:

(a) A **legal mortgage** of, say, land or shares, in which case appropriate procedures must be followed for its creation

(b) Over **other property** such as book debts (*Siebe Gorman v Barclays Bank Ltd 1979*), ships, aircraft and other chattels

(c) An **equitable (or informal) mortgage,** usually created by deposit with the lender of the borrowers' title deeds to property to which it attaches from the time of creation

5.3 If a fixed charge is created to secure a debt within six months before a company becomes insolvent then it *may* be invalid as a preference: s 239 IA. There is also a risk that when he comes to enforce the charge, the holder of the charge may find that the value of the asset does not fully discharge the debt. In a liquidation, the unpaid balance then falls to be an **unsecured debt**.

Floating charges **6/00**

5.4 A floating charge is often created by **express words**; for example a debenture may be expressed to create 'a floating charge over the undertaking and assets' etc. However no special form of words is essential. If a charge is by nature a floating charge, calling it a fixed charge will not convert it into a fixed charge: *Re Double S Printers Ltd 1998*.

5.5 The same rules on preference apply to a floating as to a fixed charge. Additionally a floating charge, if created within **12 months** before liquidation, may become void automatically on liquidation: s 245 IA.

5.6 Crystallisation of a floating charge means that it is converted into a fixed equitable charge; that is, a fixed charge on the assets owned by the company at the time of crystallisation. Events causing crystallisation are as follows:

(a) The **liquidation** of the company

(b) The **cessation** of the company's business

(c) **Active intervention** by the chargee, generally by way of appointing a receiver over the assets of the company subject to the security or exercising a power of sale

(d) If the charge contract so provides, when **notice** is given by the chargee that the charge is converted into a fixed charge (on whatever assets of the relevant class are owned by the company at the time of the giving of notice): *Re Brightlife Ltd 1987*

(e) The **crystallisation** of **another floating charge** if it causes the company to cease business

Automatic crystallisation

5.7 Floating charge contracts sometimes make provision for '**automatic crystallisation**': the charge is to crystallise when a specified event - such as a breach of some term by the company - occurs, whether or not:

- The chargee learns of the event.
- The chargee wants to enforce the charge as a result of the event.

5.8 Such clauses have been accepted by the court if they state that, on the event happening, the **floating charge is converted** to a fixed one: *Re Brightlife 1987*. In *New Bullas Trading 1994* contracting parties were allowed to provide that future book debts should be subject to a fixed charge while they were uncollected, and the proceeds should be subject to a floating charge once paid into a specific bank account. Clauses which provide only that the company is to cease to deal with charged assets on the occurrence of a particular event have been rejected.

Fixed and floating charges compared

5.9 A fixed charge is usually the more satisfactory form of security since it confers **immediate rights** over identified assets. A floating charge has some advantage in being applicable to current assets which may be easier to realise than fixed assets subject to a fixed charge. If for example a company becomes insolvent it may be easier to sell its stock in trade than its empty factory premises. However the holder of a floating charge cannot be certain what assets will form his security until the company fails.

5.10 A second disadvantage to the holder of a floating charge is that even when his charge has crystallised over an identified pool of assets he may find himself postponed to the claim of other creditors as follows.

(a) A **judgement creditor** or landlord who has seized goods and sold them may retain the proceeds if received before the appointment of the debentureholder's receiver: s 183 IA.

(b) **Preferential debts** may be paid out of assets subject to a floating charge unless there are other uncharged assets available for this purpose: ss 40 and 175 IA.

(c) The **holder** of a **fixed charge** over the same assets will usually have priority over a floating charge on those assets even if that charge was created before the fixed charge (see below).

(d) A creditor may have sold goods and delivered them to the company on condition that he is to retain legal ownership until he has been paid (a **Romalpa** clause).

6 PRIORITY OF CHARGES

6.1 If different charges over the same property are given to different creditors it is necessary to determine their priority. If, for example, charges are created over the same property to secure a debt of £5,000 to X and £7,000 to Y and the property is sold yielding only £10,000 either X or Y is paid in full and the other receives only the balance remaining out of £10,000 realised from the security (he then claims for the amount unpaid as an unsecured creditor of the company but there may be insufficient assets to pay those claims in full).

6.2 Leaving aside the question of registration, the main points to remember in connection with the priority of any charges are as follows.

(a) **Legal charges** rank according to the **order of creation**. If two successive legal charges over the same factory are created on 1 January and 1 February the earlier takes priority over the later one.

(b) An **equitable charge** created **before** a **legal charge** will only take priority over the latter if, when the latter was created, the **legal chargee** had **notice of** the equitable charge.

(c) A **legal charge** created **before** an **equitable one** has priority.

(d) **Two equitable** charges take priority according to the **time of creation**.

It is always possible to vary these rules by agreement of both creditors.

6.3 If a floating charge is created and a fixed charge over the same property is created later, the fixed charge will rank first since it attached to the property at the time of **creation** but the floating charge attaches at the time of **crystallisation**. Once a floating charge has crystallised it becomes a fixed charge and a fixed charge created subsequently ranks after it.

6.4 A creditor to whom a floating charge is given may seek to protect himself against losing his priority by including in the terms of his floating charge a prohibition against the company creating a fixed charge over the same property which would otherwise take priority (sometimes called a '**negative pledge clause**'). If the company breaks that prohibition the creditor to whom the fixed charge is given nonetheless obtains priority unless at the time when his charge is created he has actual knowledge of the prohibition imposed by the floating charge: *Wilson v Kelland 1910*.

6.5 If a company sells a charged asset to a third party the following rules apply.

(a) A **chargee** with a **legal charge** still has recourse to the property in the hands of the third party - the charge is automatically transferred with the property.

(b) **Property only** remains **charged** by an **equitable charge** if the third party had notice of it when he acquired the property.

6.6 A charge may become void against any creditors and a liquidator following failure to register it or, in some circumstances, if the company goes into liquidation. A charge which is void is no charge at all and obviously carries no priority over a valid charge. However the debt which it secured still exists as an **unsecured debt** of the company, and if the charge is void because of a relevant event following failure to register it then the money secured becomes repayable immediately.

7 REGISTRATION OF CHARGES 6/99

7.1 The Companies Act 1989 set out changes to the regulations governing the registration of company charges. However the 1989 Act changes were opposed by banks and other financial institutions. The DTI has indicated that the 1989 Act will not come into complete force in this area. The DTI is considering various options for reform, as well as leaving the pre-1989 provisions alone.

7.2 For the moment then the pre 1989 provisions remain in force. These are set out below together with indications of the changes the new legislation would have made.

The registration process

7.3 Certain types of charges created by a company should be registered within **21 days** with the registrar: s 395 (1) and s 399 (1).

7.4 Charges securing a debenture issue and floating charges are specifically registrable: s 396 (1).

7.5 Other charges that are registrable include charges on:

(a) Uncalled share capital or calls made but not paid

(b) Land or any interest in land, but not charges on rent or other periodical sums from the land

(c) Book debts

(d) Goodwill or any intellectual property

(e) Ships or aircraft or any share in a ship (this category was not included in the 1989 Act): s 396

7.6 In addition the current legislation requires registration of a charge created or evidenced by an instrument which, if executed by an individual, would require registration as a bill of sale.

7.7 The company is responsible for registering the charge but the charge may also be registered as a result of an application by another person interested in the charge.

7.8 The registrar should be sent **copies of the instrument** by which the charge is created or evidenced: s 395(1).

7.9 The registrar also has to be sent **prescribed particulars of the charge.**

(a) The date when the charge was created
(b) The amount of the debt which it secures
(c) The property to which the charge applies
(d) The person entitled to it

Additional particulars may be included but this does not make them known by constructive notice to anyone unaware of them (see *Wilson v Kelland* above).

7.10 The registrar files the particulars in the companies charges register which he maintains (s 401) and notes the date of delivery. He also issues a certificate which is **conclusive evidence** that the charge had been duly registered.

Re C L Nye Ltd 1971
The facts: A company created a charge in favour of a bank in February. The necessary documents were executed but left undated and the solicitor acting for the bank did not register them. In June he realised his mistake, wrote a June date into the documents and proceeded to register them within 21 days of that date. A certificate of registration was issued. The company went into voluntary liquidation in July and the liquidator challenged the validity of the charge on the grounds that it was not registered within 21 days of creation.

Decision: The charge was valid and enforceable as the registrar's certificate was conclusive evidence that the charge had been registered within 21 days of creation (although the date was not correctly stated).

(The Companies Act 1989 would have changed this position. Since the original of the charge would no longer have been submitted to the registrar, and he would merely have filed the particulars when submitted, the registrar would only have issued a certificate stating the date on which they were submitted.)

Delivery of inaccurate particulars

7.11 The current legislation does not deal with this problem since the registrar's certificate carries a warranty that the registered particulars are accurate.

(The new legislation did consider the effect of delivery of inaccurate particulars. Where they were not complete and accurate, the charge would have been void to the extent that it conferred rights which would have been disclosed by full and accurate particulars, subject to certain conditions.)

Delivery of further particulars

7.12 Under the current legislation, a mistake in registered particulars can only be ratified by **court order**, with the subsequent registration of a memorandum of satisfaction if this involves a reduction in the amount secured or the registration of a completely new charge if the amount secured was increased or the property charged changed: s 404.

(The new legislation would have allowed these alterations to be made by the filing of supplementary particulars, signed by both the company and chargee.)

Time period for delivery of particulars

7.13 The 21 day period for registration runs from the creation of the charge, or the acquisition of property charged, and not from the making of the loan for which the charge is security: s 395(1). The exception to this rule is a charge created abroad in respect of property situated aboard. Here the 21 days run from the date when the instrument creating the change or a copy of it would in due course of post have been received in the UK. Creation of a charge is usually effected by execution of a document. However, it may result from informal action.

Re Wallis & Simmonds (Builders) Ltd 1974
The facts: The company deposited title deeds to secure a loan.

Decision: The purpose of the deposit was to create a charge. As it had not been registered the charge was void.

The effect of non-delivery

7.14 We have seen that the duty to deliver particulars falls upon the company creating the charge and if no one delivers particulars within 21 days, the company is liable to a fine, as are its officers: s 399(3).

7.15 Non-delivery in the time period results in the **charge** being **void** against an administrator, liquidator or any creditor of a company.

(Under the new legislation a charge would only have become void on the expiry of 21 days and a relevant event occurring (a relevant event being the acquisition of another interest or right in that property, or the onset of insolvency proceedings)).

7.16 Non-delivery of a charge means that the sum secured by it is **payable forthwith** on demand: s 395 (2).

Late delivery of particulars

7.17 The rules governing late delivery in the current legislation are the same as governing registration of further particulars, ie a **court order** is required for registration.

7.18 A charge can only be registered late if it is registered '**without prejudice to the rights of parties acquired prior to the time when the charge is actually registered**'. Therefore if a fixed charge is created but not presented for registration until nine months after it should have been, a fixed charge created and registered correctly during that nine month period will have priority over the earlier created charge: *Re Monolithic Building Co 1915.*

(Under the proposed legislation, if the charge had not been registered within 21 days, but a relevant event had **not** yet occurred, it would have been possible to perfect the charge by late delivery under s 400(1). Such late delivery would not however have had a *retrospective* effect to defeat a creditor's rights which had been acquired by the occurrence of a relevant event.)

Memorandum of charge ceasing to affect the company's property

7.19 A company *may* deliver to the registrar a '**memorandum of satisfaction**', signed on behalf of both the company and the chargee (s 403(2)), stating that the debt has been satisfied, or part of all of the property has been realised from the charge or is no longer part of the company's property.

Register of charges

7.20 Every company is under an obligation to keep a copy of **documents creating charges**, and a **register** of other charges, at its registered office: s 406 (1) and 407 (3).

Exercise

Distinguish 'fixed' and 'floating' in relation to charges created by a company.

Solution

In company law a 'charge' of any type gives to the holder of the charge a priority claim to payment of what is owing to him out of the value of the property subject to the charge. As such the charge gives an advantage over the other creditors of the company who are postponed to the claim of the holder of the charge.

A *fixed charge* attaches at the moment of its creation to the relevant property. From then on the company cannot dispose of the property except subject to the charge. Few purchasers are willing to buy property if in doing so they also accept the burden of the existing charge, the liability to pay the company's debt. It normally happens that if the company wishes to sell property which is subject to a fixed charge it repays its debt out of the proceeds of sale and the creditor on receiving payment releases the property from his charge so that it passes unencumbered to the ownership of the purchaser.

This procedure is workable in connection with fixed assets which are not often sold. It would not generally be practicable to create a fixed charge over current assets which by their nature are constantly 'turned over', sold and replaced in the course of the company's business.

A company may however create a *floating charge* over any kind of asset, including current assets. A floating charge does not attach to the charged property at once and the company is free to dispose of the property unencumbered to a purchaser and also to create subsequent fixed charges over it (if the property subject to the floating charge is a fixed asset - as it may be).

The floating charge attaches to the property in various circumstances such as cessation of normal business, commencement of liquidation or default by the company in its obligations to the holder of the charge followed by intervention on his part. The floating charge is said to 'crystallise' in these cases and thereupon it attaches to whatever property of the type charged the company may then own.

A floating charge may be postponed to a subsequent fixed charge if the latter charge is created before the floating charge crystallises. A floating charge is also postponed to those unsecured debts of the company which are 'preferential' unless there are uncharged assets from which preferential debts can be paid: s 40 Insolvency Act 1986.

The advantage of a floating charge is its potentially wide scope as it commonly extends to all property of the company. Its disadvantage is the uncertainty as to what property will remain when it crystallises and the risk that it will be postponed to other claims.

---

8 DEBENTUREHOLDERS' REMEDIES

8.1 Any debentureholder is a creditor of the company with the normal remedies of an unsecured creditor. To reclaim his investment where the company is in default he could:

(a) **Sue** the company for debt. If he gets judgement for the debt, under the court's direction, he may apply to seize the company's property to enforce the court's judgement

(b) **Present** a **petition** to the court for the **compulsory liquidation** of the company

(c) **Present** a **petition** to the court for an **administration order** *

* "Admin. order": Orders that, during period in force, affairs, business & property of a co. to be managed by a court-appointed administrator. (s8(2) IA 1986)

8.2 A **secured debentureholder** (or the trustee of a debenture trust deed on behalf of secured debentureholders) may **enforce the security**. He may take the following actions.

(a) **Take possession** of the asset subject to the charge if he has a legal charge (if he has an equitable charge he may only take possession if the contract allows)

(b) **Sell it** (provided the debenture is executed as a deed)

(c) **Apply** to the **court** for its transfer to his ownership by a foreclosure order (rarely used and only available to a legal chargee)

(d) **Appoint** a **receiver**

8.3 The appointment of a receiver is usually the first step. The secured creditor may need an order of the court in some circumstances to enforce these remedies. But they arise from his contractual rights as a secured creditor with a priority claim to be paid out of the relevant assets.

Chapter roundup

- A company may borrow provided it is permitted to do so by the memorandum or articles and the procedure stipulated therein is followed. A company generally **borrows on overdraft** or by issuing debentures (fixed term loan accounts from investors other than banks).
- Debentures may be **secured** or **unsecured**, single or issued as a **series** (usually registered). A debenture stock issue is subscribed by a large number of members, whether it is convertible, redeemable or irredeemable.
- The **debenture trust deed** sets out the **terms** of the loan and provides **procedures** to be followed. Care should be taken to follow the terms carefully and keep a record of those terms.
- There are fundamental differences between debentures and shares:
  - **Shareholders own** part of the company, whereas **debentureholders** are **creditors of** the company.
  - **Debentureholders** are paid as **creditors** on liquidation.
  - **Interest is** paid at an **agreed rate** as an expense of the company whereas **dividends** on shares are **not always paid** and amounts vary.
  - There are **no statutory restrictions** on a company **redeeming** or **purchasing** its own debentures.
  - **Debentures** may be **issued** at a **discount** or **repaid** at a **premium**; shares may not.
- Debentures are issued in the same way as shares.
- There are two forms of charges which may be given by a company as security for a debenture:
  - A **fixed charge** over property which may be legal or equitable
  - A **floating charge** over various property which may be dealt with by the company and **crystallises** only on the happening of certain events which fix the charge over the property at the time of crystallisation
- Both fixed and floating charges *must* be **registered** in order to be valid and binding. Charges must be registered within **21 days** of creation: if they are not so registered they are void and unenforceable.
- In general **legal fixed charges** take priority over **equitable fixed charges** which both take priority over **floating charges**, but at all times it is the time of creation of the fixed charge or time of crystallisation of a floating charge which determines the priority.

Summary of documents

FORM 403a	Declaration of satisfaction in full or in part of mortgage or charge.
FORM 395	Particulars of mortgage or charge.

Test your knowledge

1. What are the limits on borrowing by companies? (see para 1.4, 1.7 - 1.9)
2. Describe the different kinds of debenture. (2.3)
3. Give the main contents, and also the advantages, of a debenture trust deed. (2.5, 2.6)
4. How does an unsecured company loan document differ from a secured debenture? (2.16)
5. To what extent do the rules on the issue of debentures correspond with, or differ from, those applicable to shares? (2.17)
6. What legal restrictions affect the issue of debentures carrying conversion rights? (2.21 - 2.22)
7. Describe the procedure for: (a) conversion; and (b) redemption of debentures. (3.1 - 3.5, 4.3 - 4.7)
8. What are the different kinds of charge over its property which a company may create? (5.1)
9. In what circumstances will a charge created subsequently to a floating charge take priority over the floating charge? (6.3)
10. Describe the procedure for registration of a charge. (7)
11. What is the effect of failure to register a registrable charge? (7.14 - 7.16)
12. What remedies are available to a debentureholder who has not been paid capital and/or interest? (8.1)

Now try illustrative questions 15 and 16 at the end of the Study Text

Chapter 14

STATUTORY REGISTERS AND INFORMATION

This chapter covers the following topics.

Introduction

A company is required to maintain a number of registers and great importance is attached to the need to maintain these registers and records properly.

The maintenance of registers is one of the most important administrative tasks of the company secretary. It is sometimes a tedious job, but it cannot be done well without prompt and careful attention to detail, based on a sound grasp of the relevant legal requirements.

In this chapter we are concerned with the upkeep of statutory registers. Various voluntary registers must also be maintained, and these are dealt with elsewhere in the text: the sealings register in Chapter 19, the register of transfers in Chapter 20 and the directors' attendance register in Chapter 7.

1 THE LEGAL FRAMEWORK OF STATUTORY REGISTERS

Specimen paper, 6/98, 12/98, 12/99

1.1 A company is required to maintain certain registers and other records, containing prescribed information. To make inspection of the registers reasonably easy for persons who are entitled to have access to them, the company must keep them at specified places. To remove difficulties that arose over inspection under previous legislation s 723A removes many of the previous details which were provided, and gives the Secretary of State wide powers to make discretionary rules by statutory instrument. The statutory registers (with the relevant sections) are as follows.

To be kept at the registered office:

- The register of directors and secretaries: s 288
- The register of charges: s 411
- The minutes of general meetings of the company: s 382
- The register of written resolutions: s 382A

To be kept at the registered office or at certain other places:

- The register of members: s 352
- The register of directors' interests in shares and debentures of the company: s 325
- Minutes of directors' meetings: s 382
- Minutes of managers' meetings (if any): s 382

- The register of substantial interests in shares (public companies) s 211.
- Accounting records: s 221

1.2 In addition, there are legal requirements in respect of documents in the following categories, if they exist.

To be kept at the registered office:

- Contracts for the purchase of the company's own shares: s 169(4)
- Instrument creating a registrable charge: s 411(s 406)

To be kept at the registered office or at certain other places:

- Register of debentureholders: s 190
- Directors' service agreements: s 318

Form of registers and other records

1.3 A company has the choice of keeping its statutory records in one of three forms:

(a) In **bound books.** This will often satisfy the needs of a small company

(b) In **more flexible loose-leaf or other non-bound** form. In any such case adequate precautions must be taken against falsification and to facilitate its discovery

(c) In **computer storage media**, so that the information is not in immediately legible form. In this case the company must supply a printout to a person who has a right to inspect or to have a copy of the record

1.4 The basic requirements for keeping the statutory records (ss 722-3) are supplemented by regulations dealing mainly with records in non-legible form (the Companies (Registers and Other Records) Regulations 1985 and s 723A.

1.5 There are company forms which give notice to the registrar of the place where a register is kept and in general can be available for inspection. Where a register may contain numerous entries an alphabetical index may be prescribed, unless the entries are arranged alphabetically, eg in card index form. There are also requirements, in some cases, that old registers or documents shall be preserved for a minimum period of time. The ICSA publication '*A Short Guide to the Retention of Documents*' gives further details.

2 REQUIREMENTS FOR EACH REGISTER 12/98

2.1 Requirements for the register of members are described in the next chapter. Each of the other documents listed above is dealt with in more detail below.

Register of directors and secretaries 6/99, 12/99

2.2 This is a register giving details about the directors and shadow directors of the company, and about the company secretary. In outline, the register should show the following in respect of each individual director:

- Name
- Usual residential address
- Nationality
- Business occupation
- Other directorships
- Date of birth (note that this is not required for the secretary)

2.3 It is unnecessary to show the maiden name of a married woman, the personal name of a peer (if his title is given), or a former forename or surname if it has not been used for 20 years or more, or if it was changed or disused before the age of 18: CA 1989 Sch 19.

2.4 Under point (d) above 'company director' is only an appropriate 'business occupation' if the individual is a director of several companies. His other directorships must include **directorships held within** the **previous five years**, even though they may now have been relinquished, but exclude directorships of dormant companies and wholly owned subsidiaries of the same company group.

2.5 If the director is another company, its company name and its registered office or principal office should be shown.

2.6 If the **secretary** is an individual, his **present name** (and any former name used within the past 20 years) and his **usual residential address** are required.

2.7 The '**name**' of an individual means his full name, usually his surname and forenames.

2.8 The Forms 288 have to be filed with the Registrar on appointment or removal of a director or the secretary, or change in their particulars.

2.9 The register may only be held at the registered office. It must be open for inspection at reasonable times. Any person who is not a member of the company may be required to pay an inspection fee, that is 'such fee as may be prescribed': CA 1989 s 143(6).

FORM 288a	Appointment of director or secretary. See Appendix 15.
FORM 288b	Resignation of director or secretary. See Appendix 16.
FORM 288c	Change of particulars for director or secretary. See Appendix 17.

Register of directors' interests **6/99, 12/99**

2.10 The current law places on every director the duty to **give notice** to the company, on his appointment and thereafter as changes occur, of any '**interest**' in the shares or debentures of the company and of any other company of the same group: s 324. The company has a duty to enter the information which it receives in the register of director's interests in shares or debentures: s 325.

2.11 'Interest' is elaborately defined by Sch 13 Pt 1. It is also extended so that the duty to notify and to enter in the register includes interests of the director's spouse or children (under the age of 18): s 328.

2.12 The responsibility for deciding whether Sch 13 Pt 1 or s 328 applies rests upon the director himself. He must give notice to the company within five days of becoming aware of the interest, and of the obligation to give notice of it: Sch 13 Pt 2. The company then has three days in which to comply with its duty to make an entry in the register Sch 13 paragraph 22. The director may merely give notice that he has an 'interest' (unspecified) in shares or debentures. However, if he requires that the 'nature and extent' of his interest is to be entered in the company's register, the company must comply: Sch 13 paragraph 23.

2.13 In determining the period of days, Saturdays, Sundays and bank holidays are excluded.

2.14 In general, the company has no duty to enter in its register a director's interest, or an event relating to it, until the director himself **gives notice** to the company. However, by way of exception, if the company grants to the director a **right to subscribe** for shares or debentures, the **company** itself has the duty to register particulars of the date, duration, consideration (if any) and the securities to which the right relates. It is still the director's duty to give notice to the company of a similar right granted to his spouse or minor children, and also of any **disposal** of such a right granted to him or his family.

2.15 If the company's shares or debentures are listed on the Stock Exchange, information received must not only be entered in the company's register, but must also, and not later than the following day, be **passed** on to the **Stock Exchange**, which may publish it: s 329. The interests that must be disclosed under Stock Exchange rules are wider than under the Companies Act; therefore the Stock Exchange also requires companies to ensure that each director furnishes particulars of all notifiable dealings and interests.

2.16 The DTI has made regulations granting exemption from these requirements in certain cases. In particular, only the holding company of a group of companies is required to make entries in its register; a subsidiary of which a holding company director is also a director of the subsidiary need not do so.

2.17 The entries made against each name must be in chronological order and, unless the names are in alphabetical order, there must be an index. The register is held with the register of members, ie at the registered office, or elsewhere if the register of members is elsewhere. The right of inspection is as stated earlier. In addition the register must be made available at the AGM: Schedule 13, paragraph 29. Any person may have a copy, on payment of such fee as may be prescribed.

Register of charges

2.18 This register, which must be kept by the company at its registered office, is not to be confused with the registration of charges on company property at the Companies Registry. A limited company is required to enter in its register the following: s 411.

(a) All **charges** specifically **affecting** its **property**, and also floating charges

(b) **Particulars** of the **property charged**, the amount of the charge and the persons entitled to it (unless it is a bearer security)

Even if there are no charges to enter in the register, the latter must exist so that its blank pages will afford evidence of the position to anyone who may inspect it.

2.19 There are the same rights of inspection as described earlier, except that a creditor or member may inspect the register free of charge: s 412.

Minutes of general meetings

2.20 The minutes of general meetings must be **held** at the **registered office**, and must be available for **inspection by members** (and no one else) free of charge: s 383. A member may have a copy within seven days on payment of the appropriate charge.

Minutes of directors' meetings

2.21 A company is required to keep minutes of board meetings: s 382. However there are **no statutory rules** as to where the minute book is to be kept, nor have members (or other persons) any right of inspection, or to have copies. In practice the minutes should be available to directors (though they are likely to have their own copies of board minutes) and to the auditors, if required for their duties. Similar considerations apply to minutes of the meetings of any managers of the company, although in practice this is normally taken to relate only to its directors who actively manage the company's affairs.

Register of substantial interests in shares 12/99, 6/00

2.22 This register is governed by ss 198-220, and applies only (a) to **public companies**, and (b) in respect of interests in shares carrying **unrestricted voting rights**. It is designed to reveal if a group of members are together controlling a significant section of the voting rights. Such groups ('**concert parties**') can exercise considerable influence; for example, a concert party with in excess of 25% of the voting rights could block a special resolution, or it may have built up a powerful secret holding from which to launch an unexpected takeover bid.

2.23 As with the register of directors' interests, the primary duty is placed on other persons to give notice to the company, which then has the duty to enter the received information in a register. The register must be maintained even if it contains no entries. The company has certain powers (not duties) to investigate and call for information, which once obtained is entered in the register.

2.24 The obligation to give notice to the company arises if a shareholder acquires **3%** of the **voting shares** of a **public company**: ss 198-201. The company must then register the shareholder's interest within two days: s 202.

2.25 For this purpose there are very complex rules, designed to disclose the following:

- The interests of a spouse or minor children
- Interests existing through indirect means, such as control of other companies
- The interests of 'concert parties'

2.26 The basic duty is to give notice to the company of the following circumstances:

(a) When the interest first reaches 3%, and when it falls below that level (in respect of the issued voting shares or any class thereof)

(b) When the interest changes by **at least one percentage point** (s 200). In calculating the position before and after an event, fractions of one per cent are disregarded:

There are a number of exceptions, where interests do not have to be notified: s 209 (and statutory regulations).

2.27 The obligation to give notice to the company arises when the person concerned is knowingly involved in the notifiable event or becomes aware of his interest, he must then give notice to the company within two working days. The notice must specify the following:

(a) The **number of shares** in which the person now has an interest: s 202(2)(a)

(b) The number and identity of **registered holders** of these shares

(c) The **number held** by each of those registered holders: s 202(3)

(d) That he is **party** to a '**concert party**' agreement (should this be the case) (He should then give the names and addresses of the other parties, and the number of shares in which he is deemed to be interested by virtue of the agreement: s 205(4).)

2.28 If the person concerned is required to give notice that he *no longer* has a notifiable interest, he merely gives notice of that fact: s 201.

2.29 The company has two days in which to enter in its register the information received: s 201. If, as is likely, the shares are listed, there is an obligation to pass the information on to the Company Announcements Office.

2.30 The notice given to the company may involve some other person as being interested (say because two or more persons are acting in concert) and each in giving notice is required to specify the names and addresses of the others so acting with him. On receiving such a notice, the company is required within 15 days to inform the other person(s) named in the notice: s 217. The other person(s) may then, if they wish, seek to persuade the company that the information relating to them is inaccurate, so that the entry may be corrected.

2.31 The register is to be kept with the register of directors' interests, and with the register of members. The register must be open to inspection to any member free of charge and anyone may have copies on payment of 'such fee as may be prescribed': s 219, as amended by CA 1989 s 143.

S 212 investigation **Specimen paper**

2.32 Under s 212, a *public* company may require anyone who the company knows or has reasonable cause to believe is interested in its shares or was interested within the past three years, to **confirm** this **interest** together with any other interest held during the past three years. Where the interest is a past interest, the former holder should give, if he can, details of the person who obtained the interest once he ceased to hold it. Details should also be given of any concert party arrangements in which the person holding the interest is or was involved.

2.33 If the person fails to provide the requested information, the company can apply to the court for **restrictions** to be imposed under Part XV of the Act, including stopping dividend payments and the exercise of voting rights. The person asked for information will also be subject to imprisonment or a fine for failing to provide it, or for making a false statement knowingly or recklessly.

2.34 In addition a public company may be required by its members to undertake a **s 212 investigation**. The members must hold at least one tenth of the company's issued share capital, and they must specify that they require a s 212 investigation, the manner in which it is to be undertaken, and reasonable grounds for asking for it.

2.35 Details of the findings of a s 212 investigation should be entered in the company's register of substantial interests: s 213.

2.36 It has been suggested that a company's power to investigate shareholdings has become more significant as a result of the advent of CREST and the increased use of nominee accounts.

Distinction between material holdings and aggregate holdings

2.37 From September 1993 the law changed to require additional disclosure. The change came about as a result of the Disclosure of Interest in Shares (Amendment) Regulations 1993, prompted by an EU directive.

2.38 A new distinction is made between **material holdings** and **aggregate holdings**.

2.39 A **material holding** is **any shareholding** other than:

(a) Shares held by an investment manager

(b) Shares held by a unit trust or other collective investment scheme

(c) Those held by people who are already exempt because of restrictions on their voting rights

2.40 An **aggregate shareholding** is any shareholding **held** by a **person** whether for his beneficial interest or not, plus any shareholdings held by a **related person**, ie a close relative or company where he controls the board or has greater than one third of the shares.

2.41 The new disclosure rules require disclosure of **material holdings** from **3%** (as before) and of **aggregate holdings** from **10%.**

Accounting records

2.42 The secretary will only be concerned with the statutory requirements relating to accounting records if he is also the company's officer responsible for its accounts.

(a) The accounting records must contain information of the **company's transactions.**

(b) They must be preserved for at **least three years** (six years for a public company): s 222(5).

(c) They may be kept **wherever** the directors think **fit** but, if held outside the UK, information from them must be sent to the UK.

(d) The records are **open to inspection** by the company's **officers**, but not to members, creditors or the public.

The penalties for not keeping proper accounting records can be severe: in *Re Firedart Ltd, Official Receiver v Fairall 1994* the main reason for disqualifying a director was failing to keep proper accounting records.

Register of debentureholders

2.43 If a register is maintained (it is not compulsory), the same general rules apply to its location as to that of the register of members; it may be held **either** at the **registered office** or at **some other place** (where it is made up) in the **country** where the registered office is situated: s 190. The registered holder of the debenture or of shares has a right to inspect the register free of charge and to have copies on payment of 'such fee as may be prescribed'. A person who is neither a shareholder nor a debenture holder may be required to pay 'such fee as may be prescribed': s 191.

Instruments creating a registrable charge

2.44 Not every charge is created by a written document. A mere deposit of title deeds or of share certificates if, for example, intended to constitute a security for a loan may create a charge without any written agreement.

2.45 If there is a document (called an '**instrument**' in legal terminology) creating or evidencing a charge over company property, the company must keep a copy of it and a register of such charges at its registered office: s 411. The register must give a short description of the property subject to the charge, the amount of and the parties to, the charge.

2.46 The copies and the register must be open to inspection to:

(a) **Any creditor** or member **free of charge**
(b) **Any persons** on **payment** of 'such fee as may be prescribed' by the company

2.47 Any other person may request:

(a) **Copies of entries** of the register on payment of 'such fee as may be prescribed' to the company

(b) **Copies of the instrument** (under the wording of the Act there is no mention of a fee payable, but logic would suggest that 'such fee as may be prescribed' will be payable, if demanded by the company.)

Refusal of inspection rights may lead to a fine and the court has the right to compel inspection or to direct that a copy be sent: s 412.

3 ACCESS TO STATUTORY REGISTERS

3.1 Several of the registers and other documents, to which there is a right of access, may be held at the registered office, but may alternatively be held elsewhere, for various practical reasons. In particular the register of members is often held by a specialist firm of registrars; the board and management minutes are typically held at the principal place of business. To prevent attempts to frustrate the statutory right of inspection, the following rules are laid down.

(a) The alternative place must be within the **same country** as the registered office.

(b) Registers which relate to **interests** in the company's capital must be **held together**, that is the register of members, of directors' interests and of substantial interests in the voting shares of public companies.

(c) If the register of members (and by implication the other registers listed in (b) above), or the register of debentureholders, or the copies of directors' service agreements, are not held at the registered office, the company is required to **notify** the **registrar** of the address at which they are held and may be inspected, so that the information is on file at the Companies Registry.

(d) As regards the registers of members and of debentureholders, the address at which they are held and may be inspected also appears in the **Annual Return**.

4 LOCATION OF STATUTORY REGISTERS AND OTHER DOCUMENTS **12/99**

4.1 Simplicity and commonsense suggest that all the registers and records described in this chapter should be held at the registered office, unless there are sufficient practical reasons for putting them in another place.

4.2 If the registered office is not also the company's head office or principal place of business, the secretary will find it more difficult to discharge his administrative task of supervising those registers and records which can only be held at the registered office. For that reason, among others, it is usually better to have the registered office at the same place as the head office being the same as the office of the secretary.

4.3 If any of the registers or records whose location is regulated by law are *not* to be held at the registered office, the secretary should consider whether the alternative location is permissible, and what **notice** (if any) has to be given to the **registrar** of the alternative location.

4.4 As regards the choice of alternative location, there should be a positive reason for it. This is enforced by law in respect of the registers of members or of debentureholders (if any) which, if not held at the registered office, may only be located where the work of maintaining the registers (and dealing with transfers) is done, that is at the premises of professional registrars: ss 353 and 190.

4.5 A **move** of the register of members to an alternative address entails a similar transfer of the registers of directors' interests and of substantial interests in shares of a public company. The register of members and the register of debenture holders, however, need not be at the same address; they may be in the hands of different registrars, or be at the registered office in one case but not the other. They must always be in the same country as the registered office, say England and Wales.

5 THE ANNUAL RETURN **Specimen paper, 12/98, 6/00**

5.1 Every company is required to deliver to the registrar once a year an annual return in the prescribed form **(Form 363a)**, as a summary of essential information about the company, its members and officers. Apart from specific notices which a company is also required to deliver, as occasion arises, and the need to register or re-register in certain circumstances, the annual return, with the annual accounts, is the most important source of information about the company available to anyone who may search the company's file at the registry.

5.2 Section 363 lays down that the annual return should be made up to date, up to the company's 'return date', which is either the anniversary of incorporation or the anniversary of the date of the previous return (if this differs). Delivery to the registrar must be **within 28 days** of the return date. Failure to comply renders the company liable to a fine, and/or a daily default fine. The return must be signed by a director or a secretary. All the directors and the secretary are liable to be fined if the regulations are broken, unless they can show that all reasonable steps were taken to avoid the commission or continuation of the offence. Officers of a company who are persistently in default may be disqualified by court order from being a director or concerned (in various capacities) in the management of *any* company: s 3 CDDA.

Completing the annual return

5.3 The paragraphs which follow deal with the correct completion of the **annual return form**. You might wish to refer to the copy of Form 363a in Appendix 18. In outline the form comprises the following.

(a) The **name** (and registry serial number) of the company

(b) The **date** of the return

(c) The **address** of the **registered office** of the company: s 364

(d) The **address** (if not the registered office) at which the **register of members** or any register of debentureholders is kept: s 364

(e) The **type** of company it is and its **principal business activities**: s 364

(f) The **total** number of **issued shares** of the company up to the date on which the return was made up, and their **aggregate nominal value**: s 364A

(g) In respect of each **class** of shares, the **nature** of that **class** and the **total value** of **issued shares** to the date of making up of the annual return, and their nominal value

(h) The **names** and **addresses** of **members** of the company at the date of the return, and those who have ceased to be members since the last return. This list should be indexed or alphabetical: s 364A. If this has been fully covered in either of the preceding two returns, only changes in membership and share transfers need be noted

(i) The **number** of **shares** of **each class held by members** at the return date, along with details of shares of each class transferred since the date to which the last return was made up, and the dates on which the transfers were registered

(j) If (h) and (i) have been fully covered in either of the preceding two returns, only changes in membership and share transfers need be noted: s 364A

(k) **Names** and **addresses** of the **directors** and secretary and, in the case of each indexed director, his **nationality, date of birth, previous occupation**: s 364. (See 5.6 below.)

(l) Where shares have been converted into **stock, corresponding particulars** are required as for shares: s 364A

5.4 The name and address of the person who presents the return is inserted (as with most prescribed forms) so that if the return is incorrect or incomplete it may be returned to him in the first instance. Under s 363, the signature of a director or the secretary is required. A fee of £18 must be sent.

5.5 The registrar will also pre-print capital and shareholder information on shuttle annual returns sent to companies which have 20 members or less and have previously made an annual return. For companies with more than 20 members (except large companies with dynamic share capital) aggregate share capital information will be printed.

FORM 363a	Annual Return of a company. See Appendix 18.

6 RETURN OF ALLOTMENTS

6.1 Following a rights issue s 88 Companies Act 1985 requires the company to deliver to the Registrar of Companies a return of the allotments in the prescribed form (Form 88(2)). The purpose of the return of allotments is to ensure that the company file held at Companies House accurately records up-to-date details of the company's shareholdings.

6.2 The return of allotments should contain the following information:

- **Number** of shares allotted
- **Nominal amount** of the allotted shares
- **Names** and **addresses** of the allottees
- **Amount paid** on the shares or the amount due and payable

6.3 If the shares are allotted either fully or partly paid up for non-cash consideration the following documents should also be sent to the registrar:

(a) The **contract** for the **sale** of the shares **duly stamped**

(b) A **contract** which **constitutes** the **title** of the allottee to the shares

(c) A **return stating** the **number**, **nominal amount** of the allotted shares, the consideration for the shares and the **extent** to which they are to be treated as **paid up**

6.4 When renounceable allotment letters are issued, the **return** is by **concession** sent in after the renunciation period has expired to show the names of the persons entered in the register as holders of the new shares.

6.5 If the company fails to comply with s 88 Companies Act, ie fails to deliver the return of allotments within one month of the allotment, then **liability** for that **default falls on** the **officers** of the company (ie the directors, secretary and managers). Every officer in default is liable to a fine and, if there is continuing contravention, to a daily default fine.

FORM 88(2)	Return of allotments. See Appendix 4.

Exercise

What does an annual return contain?

Solution

Look back at Para 5.3.

7 ELECTRONIC COMMUNICATIONS

7.1 Certain forms can now be filed electronically with Companies House. The new service allows companies to send Email messages in an approved format. To use the service companies need to notify Companies House of a code it will use to authenticate documents, and of a Presenter who will transmit documents on its behalf.

7.2 The documents that can be filed in this way are as follows:

(a) Form 287 Change of registered office address

(b) Form 288a Appointment of a director/secretary

(c) Form 288b Resignation of a director/secretary

(d) Form 288c Change of director/secretary details

(e) Form 363 Annual return

7.3 There are a number of advantages of electronic filing, including less paperwork, fewer delays and electronic acknowledgement of all electronic filings.

Electronic Communications Act 2000

7.4 The Electronic Communications Act 2000 allows ministers to amend other laws to permit or facilitate the use of electronic communications or storage. The Department of Trade and Industry has issued a draft Order that would, if enacted, enable companies to use electronic communication instead of paper in the situations listed below if they so wished. ICSA has issued a consultative document on best practice in this area (a copy of the consultative document is available on the ICSA website).

(a) **Incorporation** and **re-registration** as a different type of company. Forms could be sent electronically.

(b) **Sending reports, accounts** and **notices** of meetings to members. This applies to full and summary accounts. Either the accounts and notices would themselves be sent electronically, or notice be given that they were published on a website. If notice is given, ICSA suggests that a hyperlink to the appropriate website pages should be provided, and notification on the website of details of meetings should indicate special business.

(c) **Appointment of proxies** by members. A company's articles may already enable voting instructions to be given electronically to the proxy, even though the proxy's appointment has to be lodged in writing. The legislation will clearly state that proxy forms can be delivered **to members** by electronic means; return of proxy forms to the company would have to be to a valid electronic address specified by the company.

(d) **Submission of documents** to the registrar of companies. This can be in any electronic form.

7.5 The ICSA code suggests that companies should send a letter to shareholders explaining what is happening when they first decide to use electronic means of communication. The letter should make clear that use of electronic means will not result in certain shareholders being treated more favourably than others. If electronic mail indicates that the message sent to a shareholder is undeliverable, the company should automatically send a paper copy.

7.6 A key ICSA recommendation is that members should make a **positive decision** to opt for electronic means of communication; if the company hears nothing from members, it should continue to send them paper copies.

7.7 Shareholders may have problems receiving certain documents because the documents are too large or because they lack the appropriate software. Companies should therefore **supply free** certain types of software, (or provide hyperlinks to where such software can be downloaded on the internet) for example Adobe Acrobat™ if members need it to open documents but may not have it.

7.8 ICSA suggests the use of a **unique identification code** for each shareholder to maintain security.

7.9 ICSA expects that in the short-term the principal users of electronic communications will be **professional** and **institutional investors** and overseas shareholders.

Chapter roundup

- The company is required to keep records of certain particulars, transactions and instruments to which the company or its officers are a party.
- **Inspection** is generally available at all reasonable times to **members**, free of charge; to third parties and the public they are available on payment of 'such fee as may be prescribed' CA 1989 ss 143, 212 and Sch 23.
- The company is required by legislation to make certain registrations with Companies House, as well as keeping its own registers.
- 'Other places' where certain registers may be kept are governed by the following.
  - Such places must be within the **same country** as the registered office.
  - Registers relating to the **company's capital** must be **kept together**.
  - Notice of the **location** of certain registers must be given to the registrar.
- The company must complete an **annual return** which gives yearly up-to-date particulars of the company. This is held at the registry and is available for inspection: s 362.

Summary of documents

FORM 288a	Appointment of director or secretary.
FORM 288b	Resignation of director or secretary.
FORM 288c	Change of particulars for director or secretary.
FORM 363a	Annual return of a company.
FORM 88(2)	Return of allotments.

Test your knowledge

1 Give three registers or other documents which a company is required to hold at its registered office (and nowhere else). (see para 1.1)

2 In what forms may statutory registers be kept, and subject to what conditions? (1.3)

3 What particulars of an individual director are entered in the register of directors and secretaries? (2.2)

4 Explain the general nature of the statutory requirements for disclosure of a director's interest in shares or debentures of his company. (2.10)

5 What particulars are entered in the company's register of charges, and where is the register to be found? (2.18)

6 How far does the law impose rules on the minute book of directors' meetings? (2.21)

7 What events impose a duty to give notice to the company of an interest in its shares? (2.26)

8 Who may inspect (a) a register of debentureholders; and (b) an instrument creating a registrable charge? (2.43, 2.46)

9 Which statutory registers are always to be held together at the same place? (3.1(b))

10 What information is submitted on a company's return of allotments? (6.2)

Now try illustrative question 17 at the end of the Study Text

Chapter 15

THE REGISTER OF MEMBERS

This chapter covers the following topics.

Introduction

The register of members (in this chapter 'the register') is the most important of all the statutory registers which a company is required to maintain and to make available for public inspection.

Unless the company has no share capital (usually because it is limited by guarantee), the register of members is also the register of shareholders, since among other particulars it must show the number of shares held by each member.

Entry in the register is the critical test of membership: s 22. The share certificate, to which each shareholder is entitled, is only *prima facie* evidence of his title to the shares: s 186.

1 THE CONTENTS OF THE REGISTER

1.1 The register of every company must show the following.

- The name and address of each member
- The date on which he was registered as a member
- In due course, the date on which he ceased to be a member: s 352(2)

1.2 If the company has a share capital the following must also be entered.

(a) **A statement of the shares held by each member.** If the shares have identifying serial numbers, those numbers must also be shown.

(b) **The amount paid** (or, if the consideration has been provided in non-cash form, the amount credited as paid) **on the members' shares.** If, as is common, all the issued shares are fully paid, no separate entry is made of the amount paid or credited to each shareholding.

(c) If the shares have been converted to stock (and notice has been given to the registrar pursuant to s 122) the **amount of stock held by each member**. It is usual, as stock is transferable in units of specified value (eg £1 or £10), to show the number of stock units rather than the total amount (in nominal value) of stock held. The page in the register should then be headed appropriately, say 'Stock units of £1'.

1.3 If the company has more than one class of shares and/or of stock, **holdings of each class** should be **distinguished.** It is usually convenient to open a separate account for each class of shares or stock held by a member, as separate holdings, rather than to combine them in a single statement, which may be confusing.

1.4 If a company which has no share capital has more than one class of members, eg some who have votes and some who do not, the class to which each member belongs must be shown.

Updating the register

1.5 When a company first issues shares, the initial register will be drawn up. When new shares are issued, or when a person acquires existing shares in the company, the following statutory details should be entered in the register:

- The name and address of the new member(s)
- The date of entry in the register
- The number of shares acquired by the member(s)
- The amount paid

1.6 If a company issues a **share warrant** to a member, it removes from the register the name of the member and holder of the shares comprised in the warrant (since he is not a member in respect of those shares) and records the issue of the warrant: s 355.

1.7 When a member ceases to be a member, the date is entered on the register, but the entry relating to the member may only be removed from the register **20 years later**: s 352(6).

Closing the register

1.8 The company may **close the register** (after giving notice by local newspaper advertisement) for **not more** than **30 days** in the year: s 358. The effect of closing the register is that transfers are not entered during the closure period and the public may not inspect the register during that period. This enables a company to make its register static while it prepares, for example, dividend warrants from the register as it stands. However most companies select a record date and declare a dividend payable to members on the register at that date. They extract a list of members at that date and continue with current transfer registration to avoid building up a backlog. The date for payment is later than the 'record date'. A listed company must give notice to the Stock Exchange of both closure and selected record date.

Rectification or amendment of the register 12/99

1.9 There is a procedure by which the court may order rectification of the register: s 359. In any case of importance or where dispute has arisen, the company should in its own interests seek a court order before making an alteration in a record of ownership of its shares. The company should check that the order specifies the shareholding, and the shareholding referred to is completely identical to a registered shareholding.

1.10 In working practice, however, it is sometimes necessary to make a **minor** and '**non-controversial**' change, such as correction of an initial or recording of a new address, and this may be done without legal formality. Legal backing was given for this in *Michaels v Harley House Marylebone Ltd 1997* when the judge ruled that if an entry was clearly mistaken, the company could and should rectify it without a court order. The following safeguards should be observed if a change is made.

(a) An **existing** entry should **never** be **erased** so that it can no longer be read. A line should be neatly ruled through it.

(b) An **insertion** should be **clearly written**, or if possible typed, alongside the former entry.

(c) The person who makes the alteration should write **his initials** against it, to show who made it and to remove any doubt about its authority.

1.11 The ICSA Registrars' Group has issued a best practice statement on how companies should deal with requests from brokers to correct mistakes in the register that arose from mistakes in particulars of transferees recorded on stock transfer forms.

1.12 The guidance draws a distinction between **minor** and **major** alterations.

Minor alterations

1.13 For minor errors which **do not affect** the **identity** of the transferee, the register may be altered if the company receives a **rectification form** which, together with the incorrect stock certificate:

(a) **Identifies** the **transfer** by reference to the amount of stock and other relevant details

(b) **Authorises** and requests the company's registrar to **amend** the register

(c) **Confirms** that the alteration is for the **sole purpose** of **correcting** a minor mistake

(d) **Carries** the signature of an authorised signatory of the broker firm; the signature acts as an **indemnity**

1.14 Examples of minor alterations include:

1 Watkins Road	5 Watkins Road
1 Watkins Road	1 Watkins Avenue
1 Watkins Road	1 Wattkyns Road
Katharine Cook 1 Watkins Road Guildford Surrey GU3 7SH	Katharine Cook 5 MacQueen Street Warnham West Sussex RH11 2ST
Katharine Sarah Cook	Katharine Sara Cook
Katharine Cook	Katharine Sara Cook
K Cook	Katharine Cook Katharine Sara Cook
Designation 123WAT	WAT123

Major alterations

1.15 Major alterations are principally those that **affect** the **identity** of the transferee. The register may be altered if the company receives a rectification form which, together with the incorrect stock certificate:

(a) **Identifies** the **transfer** by reference to the amount of stock and other relevant details

(b) **Authorises** and requests the registrar to **amend** the register

(c) **Warrants** that the **alteration** is for the purpose of **correcting** a **mistake**, and is not the result of a sub-sale or change of mind of the broker or client as regards the names in which the stock is registered, or where monies from the client are not forthcoming

(d) **Carries** the signature of an authorised signatory of the broker firm; the signature acts as an **indemnity**

(e) Includes the **guarantee** of a bank, insurance company or trust corporation unless the broker is one

1.16 The rectification form for major alterations includes on its reverse side a form of indemnity which must be used, otherwise the transfer will be rejected.

1.17 Examples of major alterations include:

Mr K Cook	Mrs Katharine Cook
Mr James Cook	Mr Jonathan Cook
Mr Peter Stewart	Mr Kumar Guha

1.18 If there is doubt about the rectification being sought, a **court order** may be required or, ultimately, a **stock transfer form** completed.

1.19 A company should not normally allow rectification if:

(a) The **original certificate** was issued **more than three months** before the receipt of the request for rectification.

(b) If a **dividend** has been **paid** or accepted, or the company has other evidence that the transferee has accepted the shares.

Index

1.20 If the register itself is not self-indexing (for example, with the names of members in alphabetical order), a company of **more than 50 members** is required to maintain an index, which is to be kept with the register. Any alteration incidental to a change in the register is entered in the index within 14 days of that change: s 354.

2 THE FORM OF THE REGISTER

2.1 As explained in the earlier chapter on statutory registers and records, a register may be kept in the form of a bound book, in some loose-leaf form such as a card index, or on computer.

2.2 Although a simple book (which may include the other statutory registers as well as the register of members) is usually sufficient for a small company with a small and static membership, larger companies would find this impractical.

2.3 Large companies will therefore adopt one or both of the following methods:

(a) Keeping their register of members in a **loose-leaf form**, or possibly on **computer**

(b) **Contracting out** the maintenance of the register to professional registrars, who will use a computer

2.4 With a loose-leaf system the entries can always be kept in alphabetical order; new entries can be inserted and obsolete ones removed from the card sequence. If a large job is to be done on the register, it can be split temporarily so that more than one person can work on it at the same time. It is also easier to microfilm.

2.5 If either a loose-leaf form or a computer file is used as a register, certain safeguards are required to prevent falsification of data, and to safeguard public access to the information: s 722. The most obvious safeguard against falsification of a loose-leaf register is to keep the sheets in **strong covers** with a **locking device** (the keys being held by a responsible officer, such as the secretary). In addition, or as an alternative, the stock of blank sheets for insertion in the register may be numbered or otherwise controlled, and bear the company's printed name or other means of identification.

2.6 Where a register is kept in computer format the company must ensure that it can be printed out in legible form as required: s 723.

Additional information in the register

2.7 The only legal prohibition on entering information in the register (for English, but not Scottish, companies) is that a company may not enter on its register a **notice** of a **trust** 'express, implied or constructive': s 360. It would, for instance, be quite wrong to make an entry such as 'Cher Holder, trustee for Benny Fichery' at the request of either Holder or Fichery. The entry in the register would have to be Cher Holder: the fact that she is trustee for Benny Fichery is irrelevant.

Register does not recognise trustees: s 360.

2.8 If a notice of a trust is received, it should be returned to the presenter with an explanatory letter, referring to s 360. The company may nonetheless retain a copy of the notice among its working papers for record.

2.9 A person who claims an interest in shares registered in the name of some other person, say as beneficiary under a trust, purchaser or mortgagee of the shares, *may* serve on the company a **stop notice** obtained from the court under the Charging Orders Act 1979. Receipt of such a notice is entered on the shareholder's account in the register, where it can be noted whenever the record is updated. The stop notice imposes a delay before any transfer may be registered or dividend paid to the registered holder (whichever is specified). During this period, notice of the proposed action must be given to the server of the stop notice, who can then apply to the court to protect his rights, if necessary. He has only fourteen days to do so, however.

2.10 Some companies use their register as a working record of information or instructions which they have received from members. For example:

(a) The company may note on the relevant page of the register a member's instruction to credit his dividends direct to his bank account (a **dividend mandate**, described in the chapter on 'dividends').

(b) the company may accept a member's instructions to **divide** his **holding** by making separate entries in his name, so as to identify nominee holdings and to make the record of his shareholding a 'designated account' by adding some identifying letter or number ('A Account' or 'No 1 Account').

2.11 If a person demands a copy of the register, the copy supplied should certainly **omit** any **non-statutory information**. This makes it more difficult to supply a copy of the register, since it will have to be edited rather than simply reproduced by mechanical means.

2.12 Finally, if the register is kept on computer, it is exempt from the elaborate requirements of the Data Protection Act 1984 if its entire contents are available for public inspection. The exemption is lost if the register includes particulars which the public is not entitled under s 356 to inspect.

3 LOCATION OF THE REGISTER AND PUBLIC RIGHT OF INSPECTION 12/98

3.1 The register must be kept either at the **registered office** or at the **place** where the **work** of making up the register is done, usually the premises of a professional registrar, or another office of the company: s 353. It must *always* be kept at an address within the same country as the registered office, say England and Wales, or Scotland for a Scottish company.

3.2 If the register is held elsewhere than at the registered office, notice must be given (Form 353) within 14 days of removing it from the registered office, or any subsequent change of the address. The index (if any) must be kept with the register: s 354.

3.3 If the register is held on computer elsewhere than at the registered office, notice must be sent to the registrar of the place at which it may be inspected in legible form, and of any subsequent change of address (Form 353a).

3.4 S 356 states that except where the register of members is closed for transfers, the register and any index of members' names shall be open to the **inspection** by any **member** of the company without charge and any other person on payment of such fee that may be prescribed. **Any person** may require the company to **provide** him with a copy of all or any part of the **register**, **within 10 days** beginning from the day following the receipt of the request. The company may require him to pay 'such fee as may be prescribed': s 356.

3.5 Under the regulations all the statutory records that are available for inspection and copying should be available for not less than two hours between 9 am and 5 pm on every business day.

3.6 Under the Companies (Inspections and Copying of Registers, Indices and Documents) Regulations 1991, a company is not obliged to present the register of members for inspection nor extract information from it in a manner that groups members by geographical area, nationality, size of holding, gender or whether they are a natural person (The same provisions apply to the register of debentureholders if the company maintains one).

3.7 The Takeover Code requires a target company to provide a copy of its share register within **two business days** of a request from the offeror. ICSA guidance requires the target company's registrar to try to provide the copy register in the format required by the offeror's receiving agent, and also other information that will enable the offeror to assess whether ultimately it does receive all the necessary documentation.

3.8 A request for a copy of the register usually indicates a hostile intention, for instance to make a takeover bid, or to issue a circular soliciting support in opposition to the directors. The company is not entitled to demand an explanation before supplying the copy, nor to refuse it if it knows or suspects that some unwelcome move is impending.

FORM 353	Notice of place where register of members is kept or of any change in that place. See Appendix 19.
FORM 353a	Notice of place for inspection of a register of members which is kept in a non-legible form, or of any change in that place. See Appendix 20.

3.9 The location of the register if shares are held in electronic form in CREST is discussed further in Chapter 20.

4 JOINT HOLDERS OF SHARES

4.1 The articles may impose a maximum on the number of joint holders of a share or shares who may be entered on the register. The first named holder is always (Table A Article 55 on votes, and Article 12 on notices) treated as the representative of the group, with priority over the others, unless they jointly instruct otherwise.

4.2 Joint holders may not find it convenient to have all notices etc from the company sent only to the first named of them. There are two main methods of getting over this difficulty if it arises.

(a) The company may accept a written request, signed by all the joint holders, for the **splitting** of their total holding into two or more distinct holdings. The same names are registered, but in different orders, so that different individuals appear first among the registered holders of each of the new divided holdings (if the register of members is kept in alphabetical order, this arrangement may involve some reshuffling).

For example, if Juan Olda and Anne Uddhur are joint holders of 500 shares in ABC plc, they can ask the company, in writing, to split the holding into 250 shares, say, held jointly by J Olda and A Uddhur, and 250 shares held jointly by A Uddhur and J Olda: each would then receive notices relating to one set of these shareholdings.

(b) The company may at the joint request of the holders **divide** their **holding** into **designated accounts**, and accept their instructions that the notices etc issued in respect of each joint account shall be sent to a different holder.

In the previous example, Olda and Uddhur might ask for their 500 shares to be divided into a 'J Olda and A Uddhur No 1 Account' (250 shares), and a 'J Olda and A Uddhur No 2 Account' (250 shares). They would ask for notices etc. issued by the company to its members to go out to Olda for the No 1 account, and Uddhur for the No 2 account.

In either case the company should ask the applicants to confirm that the proposed arrangement does not reflect any sale or disposition of beneficial ownership.

5 NOMINEE ACCOUNTS 6/98, 12/98

5.1 These arise where the beneficial owner of the shares does not want the shares registered in his own name. The shares may be registered instead in the name of a nominee. The nominee can be an individual, group of people or a company. All communications will be addressed by the company to the nominee. Under s 360 the company's register of members cannot refer to the beneficial owner, because, a company is not permitted to recognised any trust affecting any of its shares.

5.2 An example of when a nominee can arise is when there is a **wholly-owned subsidiary** company whose articles require two or more shareholders, or the company is a public limited company. In this situation one or more shares may be registered in the name of a nominee, often a director of the holding company.

5.3 Another example is when an adult holds shares as the **nominee** of a **minor**. This situation arises because a minor cannot normally compel a company to register him as a holder of fully paid shares, although there is no prohibition as such on a minor holding shares.

5.4 The nominee should provide a **dividend mandate** (see Chapter 22) requesting that all dividends be paid to the beneficiary. A short declaration of trust should also be executed, stating that the share is held as a nominee, and that the nominee has no beneficial interest in it. The **declaration of trust** would often include the following provisions.

(a) The nominee will pay any dividends as the beneficial owner may direct.

(b) The nominee will transfer or deal with the shares as the beneficial owner may direct.

(c) The nominee will vote at general meetings as the beneficial owner may direct, and carry out other directions from the beneficial owner.

5.5 Appropriate arrangements are needed for transfer of a nominee shareholding. In a wholly-owned subsidiary situation a **blank transfer** should be executed. The name of the transferee and the date should be left blank so that if the director leaves the company, it should be possible for his nominee share to be transferred to another director. The declaration of trust should contain provisions empowering the directors to take appropriate action.

6 OVERSEAS BRANCH REGISTERS

6.1 A company limited by shares, whose objects include the transaction of business in any country which is or was a British overseas territory may also keep a branch register of members resident in that country: s 362.

6.2 An overseas branch register is essentially a section of the register of members **kept** in a **different country**, appropriate to the members whose shares are registered in it. A company has no legal obligation to maintain such a register in a particular country and, if it does so, it is optional for a member resident in that country to hold his shares on the branch register.

6.3 The company must give notice to the registrar within 14 days if it establishes, discontinues or changes the address at which the overseas branch register is kept (Form 362). The regulations for such registers are contained in Sch 14 Pt II.

6.4 A duplicate of the branch register is kept with the company's main register of members. There is a legal duty imposed on the company to transmit to its registered office a copy of every entry made in the branch register 'as soon as may be' after the entry is made. The normal practice is to make up 'transmission sheets' with the particulars of entries to be made in the duplicate register in England the branch register and its duplicate should be reconciled at intervals.

6.5 Shares registered on a branch register must be **distinguished**, usually by a letter or other prefix which appears before the serial number of every share certificate relating to such shares.

6.6 All the rules applicable to the main register on inspection, supply of copies, closing the register, rectification etc also apply to the branch register. The company may include in its articles suitable supplementary rules, for example about transfer of shares from the main register to the branch register and so on. The usual procedure is as follows.

(a) A member who wishes to have his shares transferred from the main register to a branch register sends in a **form of application,** with his existing share certificate. If the applicant appears to be resident in the country where the branch register is located, the company may, without investigation, accept and comply with his request.

(b) The **relevant entry** on the **main register** is **deleted**, and the share certificate cancelled.

(c) The company sends a **schedule of requests** for transfer to the local registrar in charge of the branch register. He makes an entry in the branch register and issues a new share certificate with a distinguishing prefix, sealed with the official seal held for that purpose.

(d) Any person whose shares are entered on a branch register may apply to the local registrar for **transfer** of his holding to the **main register,** by the same sequence of action (though obviously in the opposite 'direction') as described above.

6.7 The advantage of opening an overseas branch register is that it encourages investment in the company's shares in the country where the register is held. It may follow from a listing of the shares on the local stock exchange, at the request of that exchange. A transfer of shares held on a register outside the UK does not attract UK stamp duty, though it may be subject to a similar local tax.

FORM 362	Notice of place where an overseas branch register is kept, of any change in that place or of discontinuance of any such register.

Exercise

What particulars must be entered in the register of members of a company which has a share capital?

Solution

See paragraphs 1.1 – 1.4.

Chapter roundup

- The **register of members** will show at any one time:
  - The name and address of a member
  - The date he was registered as a member
  - The date he ceased to be a member within the last 20 years
  - The number of shares held and amount paid on each share by each member (if company has a share capital)
  - The amount of stock held by each member (if shares are converted to stock)
  - The distinguished classes of shares and stocks held by each member
  - The share warrants issued, on which dates and the shares comprised in them
  - Any stop notices issued by the court
- **No notices** of **trusts** are entered.
- **Court orders** may be **obtained** to **rectify** or **amend** the register.
- A register containing **50 members** or more must be **indexed**. The index must reflect changes in register within 14 days of the change.
- The register may be a **bound book**, in **loose-leaf** form, a card **index** or on **computer** but necessary **precautions** should be taken to avoid the opportunity to falsify information.
- The register must be **available for inspection** (except for a 30 day period: s 358) in the country of the registered office, either at the registered office or where it is made up. Notice must be given to the registrar of its location: Form 353.
- Any person may obtain all or part of the register, **within 10 days** of the request, subject to paying a prescribed fee set by the company: s 356.
- The company can **restrict** the number of **joint holders** identified in the register. The first named holder receives all notices unless other arrangements have been made (splitting the shareholding).
- **Nominee shareholdings** may be necessary if a company is required to have two or more shareholders.
- Part of the register may be kept in a **separate country** (where necessary). A copy of it must be kept with the main register. Notice of its location and existence must be given to the registrar within 14 days of locating or creating it. A **branch register** reflects **resident shareholders** of the country in which it is located: s 39.

Summary of documents

FORM 353	Notice of place where register of members is kept or of any change in that place.
FORM 353a	Notice of place for inspection of a register of members which is kept in a non-legible form, or of any change in that place.
FORM 362	Notice of place where an overseas branch register is kept, of any change in that place or discontinuance of any such register.

Test your knowledge

1 To what extent may a company close its register for the preparation of a dividend list and what alternative procedure is available? (see para 1.8)

2 What are the procedures for making a correction to an entry in the register? (1.9 - 1.10)

3 In what different forms may the register of members be kept and what safeguards should be taken to prevent falsification? (2.1, 2.5)

4 What additional optional information may a company enter on its register and what is prohibited? (2.7 - 2.10)

5 How does a person protect his rights in shares registered in the name of some other person? (2.9)

6 Where may the register of members be kept? (3.1)

7 What is the procedure if more than one joint holder of shares wishes to receive notices etc from the company? (4.2)

8 What is the procedure for the transfer of a shareholding from the main to the overseas branch register? (6.6)

Now try illustrative question 18 at the end of the Study Text

Chapter 16

REGULATION OF LISTED COMPANIES 1

This chapter covers the following topics.

1 The structure of the City

2 Dealings on the London Stock Exchange

3 Regulation of the investment industry

4 Admission to listing and trading

5 Continuing obligations

6 Overseas companies

7 Admission and disclosure standards of the Stock Exchange

8 Insider dealing

Introduction

We turn our attention now to the regulations which operate once a company is listed. These are contained in the Listing Rules.

Some of the rules, such as the Model Code (see Chapter 2) have been examined or will be examined in their context. Some have been classed as 'Continuing Obligations'.

The chapter concludes with a discussion of the legislation on insider dealing, contained in the Criminal Justice Act 1993. This subject was first introduced in Chapter 2 of this Study Text on directors.

1 THE STRUCTURE OF THE CITY

1.1 The Securities Industry is the term used to describe a number of different financial services to investors, provided by firms and companies based mainly in the City of London; hence it is referred to as 'the City'. There are some outlying centres in the larger provincial cities such as Birmingham, Manchester and Glasgow.

1.2 From the standpoint of company secretarial practice, the most important of these organisations is the **Stock Exchange**. The Stock Exchange and its associated markets provide an organised market place for sellers and buyers of stocks, shares and derivative instruments of companies, and loan stocks of the UK government and local authorities.

1.3 By this means an intending seller or buyer of a particular security should be assured of finding a buyer or seller at the prevailing market price - without having to search him out, or accept a discount or surcharge as an inducement to a bargain. The ruling price reflects the market assessment of the balance of supply and demand, and the inherent value of the security.

1.4 As well as the London Stock Exchange, other **Recognised Investment Exchanges** also operate, or are considering operation in the UK. Tradepoint is one such, whilst NASDAQ, the US screen-based stock market, is planning to operate in London.

1.5 There are also institutions, notably **merchant banks**, which act as financial advisers to companies, for example in raising new capital by the issue of shares, bonds, derivatives and debentures, or in promoting or resisting proposed amalgamations (takeover bids) and reconstructions.

2 DEALINGS ON THE LONDON STOCK EXCHANGE

2.1 Membership of the London Stock Exchange has in the last 10-15 years undergone major changes. This was one of the features of the so-called Big Bang.

2.2 Big Bang occurred on 27 October 1986:

- Membership of the Stock Exchange was opened up.
- Fixed commission rates were abolished.
- The distinction between 'stockbrokers' and 'stockjobbers' was removed.

2.3 As a consequence of this last change, member firms are allowed to trade in the dual capacity of agent and principal.

(a) They may have an **agency broking arm** which charges commission to clients when selling or buying securities on their behalf.

(b) They may also have a **market making arm** which is registered to make prices in certain securities. This means that, for their registered stocks, market makers are obliged to quote firm prices at which they are committed to buying and selling the stocks. They always act as principals, making their profit on the turn between their higher selling ('offer') price and their lower buying ('bid') price.

2.4 Market makers are very similar to the old stockjobbers, being required to quote ('make') firm prices in their stocks during 'SEAQ time' - that is, during the time when the SEAQ system is live - and being obliged to sell and buy at the prices they quote. However, they may also sell directly to members of the public: it is no longer obligatory go through an agent. Market makers are exempt from stamp duty.

SEAQ

2.5 Only **market makers** are allowed to display share prices on SEAQ, which is the share price quotation system introduced following Big Bang. The Stock Exchange Automated Quotations is at the heart of the Stock Exchange's 'high-tech' character. Dealing is conducted through computer terminals located in offices in London and abroad, and linked to a central exchange. Private investors are also be able to look at SEAQ information via Prestel. This gives dealers abroad access to the system. As a result, there is no longer a 'face to face' market on the floor of the Stock Exchange.

Order driven trading

2.6 The **Stock Exchange Trading Service** (SETS) automatically matches buy and sell orders for shares in the largest FTSE companies entered by brokers on computer screens. Under SETS, buying and selling orders are matched with each other without the need for a market-maker; SETS allows automatic execution of trading on an electronic order book.

2.7 Orders can contain limitations on price or quantity, or can be for unspecified quantities at the best possible price. Orders must also be on standard settlement terms. Orders are prioritised as follows:

- **Best price** (i.e. highest buys and lowest sells)
- Within orders at the same price, **oldest orders** being put through first

2.8 Only Exchange members can enter orders into the system. Automated transactions are reported to the market immediately, although the identities of the buyer and seller are not revealed. Market makers can also view orders to buy or sell a specified quantity at the best possible price which have not been executed fully but are not told of the person making the order.

2.9 Automated trading is suspended by the Exchange if there are significant price movements or if there are system problems.

2.10 The Financial Times has reported that the new system has suffered initial teething troubles; it has been blamed for volatility in share trading, and the new system has also suffered from a lack of liquidity at the start and finish of trading on certain days.

2.11 Proposals for the introduction in 2001 of a central counterpary for SETS have recently been published. All stocks that can currently be traded on SETS or in SEAQ auctions will be cleared via the central counterparty service.

3 REGULATION OF THE INVESTMENT INDUSTRY

Historical background

3.1 The Financial Services Act 1986 established a new legal framework for investor protection and introduced a new range of criminal offences.

3.2 The Act gave overall responsibility to the Treasury for regulation in the investment industry, with operational powers delegated to the Securities and Investment Board (SIB).

Statements of Principle

3.3 The SIB issued a number of Statements of Principle which the Board expects to be applied by *all* authorised persons however authorised. The principles were not exhaustive, and individuals and organisations were expected to obey the other requirements that apply to them.

3.4 The statements are summarised below.

Integrity

3.5 An authorised firm should observe high standards of integrity and fair dealing.

Skill, Care and Diligence

3.6 A firm should act with due skill, care and diligence.

Market Practice

3.7 A firm should observe high standards of market conduct and should comply with any standard that applies to it.

Information about Customers

3.8 A firm should obtain enough information from its customers about their circumstances and investment objectives to enable it to act for them properly.

Information for Customers

3.9 A firm should give customers comprehensible and timely information to enable them to make a balanced and informed decision, and should be prepared to give customers a full and fair account of how it has fulfilled its responsibilities to them.

Conflicts of Interest

3.10 A firm should either avoid conflicts of interest or deal with them by disclosure, confidentiality rules, declining to act or other means. A firm should not unfairly place its own interests above its customers, and where a well informed customer would expect a firm to place his interests above its, the firm should do so.

Customer Assets

3.11 If a firm has control over, or has custody of customer's assets, those assets should be safeguarded by proper segregation and identification arrangements.

Financial Resources

3.12 A firm should maintain adequate financial resources to meet its commitments and to combat risks.

Internal Organisation

3.13 A firm should control its own affairs responsibly. It should keep proper records, have well-defined compliance procedures and should employ suitable staff or agents who are properly trained and supervised.

Relations with Regulators

3.14 A firm should deal openly and co-operatively with the Regulator and promptly inform the Regulator of all relevant information.

The Financial Services Authority

3.15 In May 1997 the new Labour Government announced plans to reform the financial services regulatory regime under a single regulatory organisation, subsequently named the Financial Services Authority.

3.16 The major objectives of the Authority are as follows:

- **Maintaining confidence** in the UK financial system
- **Promoting public understanding** of the financial system
- **Consumer protection**
- **Fighting financial crime**

3.17 The Authority is required to take account of:

- How its resources can be used in the most efficient and economic way
- The responsibilities of the managers of authorised persons
- The principle that a burden or restriction should be proportionate to its benefit
- The need to encourage innovation in regulation of economic activities
- The international character of financial services and markets and the desirability of maintaining the UK's competitive position
- Value of competition between financial firms

- The principle that competition in the sector should not be distorted unnecessarily

3.18 The Financial Services Authority brings together a number of existing regulatory organisations. Its wide-ranging role will encompass the regulation of banks, investment firms, insurance companies, building societies, friendly societies, credit unions, exchanges and clearing houses and collective investment schemes. The Authority will also be responsible for external regulation of the Lloyd's insurance market, including managing agents and members' agents. It will also regulate professional firms offering investment business.

3.19 The Authority's remit may be extended in future if felt necessary to cover for example the marketing of mortgages.

3.20 The Authority sees two major reasons for regulating financial markets:

(a) Supervision of institutions so that they are less vulnerable to market shocks

(b) The lack of availability of information which make it difficult for individuals to assess the risks and returns of their transactions, particularly their long-term contracts, regulation is required to give consumers assurance about the terms on which contracts are offered, the quality of advice and the safety of the assets

Standard setting

3.21 The Authority has proposed in October 1999 eleven **Statements of Principle** to replace the SIB's ten principles. These require a regulated firm to do the following areas:

- Conduct its business with integrity
- Show due skill, care and diligence
- Organise and control its affairs effectively with adequate risk management systems
- Maintain adequate financial resources
- Observe proper standards of market conduct
- Pay due regard to the interests of its customers and treat them fairly
- Pay due regard to the information needs of customers and communicate with them in a clear and non-misleading way
- Manage conflicts of interest fairly, both between itself and customers, and also between customers themselves
- Keep the trust of any customer entitled to rely on its judgement
- Arrange for the adequate protection of customer assets
- Deal with its regulators in an open and co-operative way

3.22 The Authority will be concerned with five types of standard:

- **Rules** applicable to regulated firms
- **Principles** applicable to approved persons
- **Evidential provisions** demonstrating observance or breach of binding requirements
- **Endorsement** of **codes** or standards issued by other regulators
- **Guidance** on **interpretation** of the new rules, and on compliance and best practice

3.23 The standards will encourage firms to integrate compliance into their operations and **actively manage** their **risks**. The standards will be contained in a **handbook**, and the Authority will try to see that the standards are appropriate, clear and flexible. The approach to regulation will be built around a number of key processes:

- Standard setting
- Authorisation, not only of firms but also appointed representatives, and key employees
- Supervision, with the emphasis being that the senior management of authorised firms should ensure compliance

- Education and training
- Enforcement; this includes the power to bring civil and criminal proceedings and to prohibit the employment of certain individuals
- Redress

3.24 In early 1999 the Financial Services Authority published a consultative paper *Financial Services Regulation: Enforcing the New Regime*. In the paper the Authority sets out proposals on how it intends to use its new powers. The Authority will be able to intervene to correct non-compliance with laws or regulations, or to contain continuing loss or risk of loss to consumers, secure compensation for clients, and impose civil or criminal sanctions for market abuse or other offences. The panel's operation will be overseen by an impartial enforcement committee including practitioner and public interest representatives.

3.25 Each year the Authority will carry out a number of **focused theme projects**. This will be chosen on the basis that they represent a significant **risk** that is best dealt with on a pan-Authority basis rather than by an individual division. Regulated firms should be able to take their own steps to **deal** with the **risks**, and the project should deliver measurable outcomes.

3.26 Pilot theme projects are likely to include:

(a) **E-commerce**, its domestic and international implications for legitimate business and the enforcement challenges in respect of potential criminal activity

(b) **The implications of a low-inflation environment** including how the FSA's objectives can be met

(c) **Money laundering**, including best approaches when customers are taken on and subsequently, and also the approach in different market sectors

(d) **Treating customers fairly after point of sale** in line with expectations that regulations should not just be concerned with the initial purchase

Financial Services and Markets Act

3.27 The Financial Services and Markets Act 2000 received Royal Assent on 14 June 2000. The act will replace not just the Financial Services Act 1986, but other acts relating to specific institutions. The Government has stated a target of about a year for completion of the necessary subsidiary legislation, and other preparations for the implementation of the Act.

3.28 The bill sets out the powers of the Authority to authorise, regulate, investigate and discipline authorised persons. Its investigation and disciplinary roles will be kept separate, and everyone will be able to have their case heard by an independent tribunal. There will also be an ombudsman and a compensation scheme for investors. The Authority will have powers to impose financial penalties on those who abuse financial markets, by insider dealing or market manipulation.

3.29 Although under the bill there is a general principle that consumers should take responsibility for their own decisions, there is also the requirement that investors' needs for advice and accurate information should be taken into account.

Exercise

Watch out for developments in this area. Concerns have been expressed about the wide scope of the new Authority's responsibilities, and its alleged lack of accountability. You should watch to see to what extent these concerns are addressed, or if other significant problems arise with the new arrangements.

4 ADMISSION TO LISTING AND TRADING

4.1 The role of **Competent Authority for Listing** was transferred from the London Stock Exchange to the Financial Services Authority on 1 May 2000. The reasons for this were that the London Stock Exchange has moved away from mutual status towards a more freely-transferable share structure, and rival listing markets such as NASDAQ and Tradepoint will be operating in London; hence the London Stock Exchange can neither be both one of the markets and regulator of all the other markets (recognised investment exchanges).

4.2 As **UK Listing Authority**, the Financial Services Authority will control **admission to listing**. This means that the Authority:

(a) **Controls** the **admission of securities** to the UK's **Official List**

(b) **Makes** the **Listing Rules**, covering the initial **admission** to listing, and the **continuing obligations** of companies that are listed

(c) **Polices compliance** with those Rules

4.3 The recognised investment exchanges, including the London Stock Exchange, will control **admission to trading**. This raises a number of issues about the balance between the rules set by the Financial Services Authority (who will be setting the minimum acceptable standards) and the recognised investment exchanges (who are likely to be subject to certain constraints when setting their own rules, but also will be allowed some flexibility to promote competition between them). These issues will be debated over the next few years.

4.4 The listing rules published by the Financial Services Authority differ from those previously published by the Stock Exchange only inasmuch as they now reflect the transfer of the role of Listing Authority.

4.5 A more cosmetic change is that the Stock Exchange previously published its Listing Rules in a Yellow folder; hence the rulebook colloquially became known as the Yellow Book. The Financial Services Authority has published its rules in a purple folder; hence no doubt its regulations will become commonly known as the **Purple Book**.

4.6 Some of the regulations contained in the Listing Rules are as follows.

(a) The company should have published or filed accounts which cover at least **three years**.

(b) Whenever a company goes public, the Stock Exchange will require that a **sufficient number of shares** should be **made available** to the investing public so that a ready market exists, and there is no shortage of supply for would-be investors. It is therefore generally ruled that an offer for sale will only be allowed if at least 25% of the company's equity is subject to the offer.

(c) **Enough shares** must be **available** on the Stock Exchange launch to create a free market. Thus it is more appropriate to issue 2 million shares with a nominal value of £1 each than to issue only 2,000 shares with a nominal value of £1,000 each.

(d) The company's listed securities would be expected to have a **minimum total value**, currently at least £700,000. In addition to the size qualification, a company must have a satisfactory trading record and be in a financially stable position.

(e) The company must undertake to **obey** the **rules** of the Listing Authority and Recognised Investment Exchange, for example about the provision of information such as the announcement of half year (interim) results. (When an application is made for a listing, the board of directors must adopt as a resolution the terms and conditions of the Stock Exchange Listing Agreement.)

(f) Shares in the company must be traded on the Stock Exchange by **market makers**.

(g) A company must take all reasonable care to ensure that any statement or forecast or other information notified to, or made available through, the Company

Announcements Office is **not misleading, false or deceptive** and does not omit anything significant.

5 CONTINUING OBLIGATIONS

5.1 The requirements of the Financial Services Authority as UK Listing Authority are, as mentioned above, set out in the Listing Rules.

5.2 A 'Checklist' for the continuing obligations appears in Appendix 22.

Information to be supplied

5.3 The Listing Rules impose various requirements, the aim of which is to make available to the market information which may affect investors' views on the value of company securities. The information given by companies should be promptly and widely disseminated.

5.4 Although as listing authority the Financial Services Authority has overall responsibility for the mechanism of company announcements, the old regime operated by the Stock Exchange remains in place at the time of writing. Companies make announcements to the **Companies Announcement Office** (CAO) which releases the information through its **Regulatory News Service** (RNS). The RNS ensures that company announcements are published promptly and in a controlled fashion.

Company Announcements Office

5.5 The requirements for supplying **information** to the Company Announcements Office may be summarised as follows.

(a) A company must give notice of any **information** necessary to enable holders of its securities and the public to appraise the ability of the company to meet its commitments. The company should notify information about a change in its financial condition, in the performance of its business or the company's expectation of its performance, if knowledge of that change would substantially affect the share price. This is to avoid a false market in those securities.

(b) Any **decision on dividends** must be notified as soon as it has board approval.

(c) If the company has listed loan capital, it must notify any **new issue of capital** of this type (or the giving of security or a guarantee in respect of such capital).

(d) **Changes in capital structure** must be notified, also changes in the rights attaching to securities and the effect of issues on conversion rights. The results of new issues must be disclosed.

(e) If there has been an offer of securities to the public for subscription in cash, the **basis of allotment** must be announced before dealings commence.

(f) The results of a **redemption** or **drawing** of listed securities must be notified.

(g) Any extension in the **time granted** for the currency of temporary documents of title must also be notified.

(h) If a listed company purchases its **own listed securities** it must give notice to the Stock Exchange.

(i) Persons who have significant interests in shares of public companies, and also directors of any company, are required to give notice to the **company** of changes in their **interests in securities**. The company (if listed) is required to pass such information on to the Stock Exchange.

5.6 There are various time limits and other detailed requirements in connection with these disclosure rules.

Approval of company documents

5.7 The basic requirement is that no circular may be circulated or made publicly available until it has been approved in final form by the UK Listing Authority. Related documents including letters from sponsors and statements of adjustments have to be filed prior to approval as appropriate. Three copies of the circulars and related documents must be submitted to the Listing Authority at least 10 clear business days prior to the intended publication date of the circular.

5.8 Circulars of a **routine nature** do not need to be sent to the UK Listing Authority prior to being issued, provided they are clear, contain full information about voting and other specific information depending on the type of circular. The circulars must have no unusual features, and must not qualify as advertisements under the Financial Services Act. Circulars of a routine nature are circulars which cover one of the following matters.

- Authority to allot shares
- Disapplication of pre-emption rights
- Increase in authorised share capital
- Reduction of capital
- Capitalisation issue
- Scrip dividend alternative
- Scrip dividend mandate schemes
- Purchase of own securities
- Convening of company meetings at which ordinary business is to be discussed
- Adoption or amendment of memorandum and articles, trust deeds, employee share schemes, long-term incentive schemes and discounted option arrangements
- Early redemption of listed debt securities
- Reminders of conversion rights

5.9 In any event the company must forward to the UK Listing Authority two copies of all circulars, at the time they are issued.

5.10 In addition two copies of the following documents must be lodged if they are issued or amended. They must be sent no later than the date of despatch of the notice convening the meeting at which they are to be discussed, the date they are sent to members or the date they are issued or amended. The documents are:

- Memorandum and articles of association
- Trust deeds
- Employees' share schemes, long-term incentive schemes and discounted option arrangements
- Temporary documents of title
- Definitive documents of title
- Proxy forms
- Circulars relating only to (a), (b), or (c) above.

Registration procedure in connection with share transfers etc

5.11 The procedure for transfer of listed securities will be described in a later chapter. The continuing obligations require companies to have appropriate settlement arrangements for their listed securities. This includes settlement by electronic means, discussed further in the section on CREST in Chapter 20.

Protection of shareholder interests

5.12 The requirements listed above are in part intended to protect the interests of members of a listed company. There are a number of other requirements which have a similar effect, including the following.

(a) There shall be **no restriction** on the **registration** of **transfers** of fully paid shares.

(b) An '**open offer**' of securities to shareholders, that is an offer not limited to their entitlement under a rights issue, must not enable securities to be purchased by the directors except in exceptional circumstances.

(c) The annual accounts must be **issued within six months** of the end of the financial year; a number of disclosure requirements are imposed (in addition to the statutory requirements of the CA 1985). The company must send to the Company Announcements Office its preliminary announcement of annual results and dividends **within 120 days** of the **period-end**. The statement must include as a minimum a balance sheet, profit and loss account and cash flow statements.

(d) The **accounting policies** and **presentation** of half-year accounts must be consistent with those applied to the last annual accounts. The report must be published within 90 days of the end of the period to which it relates.

(e) If a notice is issued to convene a general meeting which is to transact any business other than routine AGM business, the notice must be accompanied by an **explanatory circular**.

(f) A **recommendation** from the **directors** should be included in all circulars where shareholders are required to vote. The directors must indicate whether the proposal is in the best interests of the members as a whole.

(g) With the notice convening any general meeting the company must issue '**two way**' **proxy cards**, so that members may vote 'for' or 'against' each item of business without attending the meeting in person.

(h) If shareholders have **registered** an **address outside** the **EU**, any communications sent to them by the company must be despatched by airmail or equivalent service. Members in the UK and the EU should be sent accounts by first class mail or equivalent service.

(i) As explained in the chapter on directors, there are rights of inspection of **directors' service agreements**, safeguarded by requirements relating to the AGM notice and the availability of the agreements. A more detailed listing of Continuing Obligations is given in Appendix 22.

5.13 Some other safeguards of a general nature require a mention.

(a) A listed company must adopt a code of conduct for the **securities transactions** *of its directors* (as explained in the chapter on directors).

(b) The Listing Rules regulate **significant transactions** with **related parties**. Related parties are defined as **directors, substantial (>10%) shareholders**, anyone who **exercises significant influence over the company,** and their associates. Prior approval must be given by members, who have been informed by a circular of the details of the transaction. The company must ensure that the related party abstains from voting on the resolution approving the transaction, and takes steps to ensure that its associates abstain from voting on the resolution. The UK Listing Authority should also be given details of the transaction. Listed companies should also have arrangements in place to ensure relationships between itself and a controlling shareholder are at arms length and on a normal commercial basis (a **controlling shareholder** is a shareholder who has 30% of voting rights or rights to control a majority of the votes of the directors).

(c) The Listing Rules also regulate **transactions** (purchases and sales) in **assets** by listed companies. The procedure to be followed is designed according to the size of the transaction in relation to the company; the more material the transaction, the more information must be given to shareholders. To this end, transactions are ranked by 'class' as described below.

5.14 Briefly, the categories of transaction described by the Listing Rules, and the disclosure requirements related to them, are as follows.

(a) **Class 3**. A transaction where all percentage ratios are **less than** 5%. The Company Announcements Office must be notified.

<5% shares have been acquired by one individual. ⇒ tell CAO.

(b) **Class 2.** A transaction where any percentage ratio is **5% or more** but each is **less than 25%.** The Company Announcements Office must be notified, giving more detail than required for Class 3.

(c) **Class 1.** A transaction where any percentage ratio is **25% or more**. The CAO must be notified and an explanatory circular sent to shareholders. The circular is more detailed than for Class 2 and requires prior Stock Exchange approval.

(d) **Reverse takeover.** An acquisition by a listed company of a business, an unlisted company or assets where any percentage ratio is 100% or more or which would result in a fundamental change in the business or in a change in the board or voting control of the listed company. Requirements as for Class 1 plus listing particulars.

5.15 The percentage ratios relate to:

(a) Assets in the transaction and total gross assets

(b) Profits attributable to the assets in the transaction and total profits

(c) Turnover attributable to the assets in the transaction and total turnover

(d) Consideration of the transaction and the total market value of all ordinary shares

(e) Gross capital of the company or business being acquired divided by the gross capital of the listed company

5.16 The transaction categories and regulations, and in particular reverse takeover rules, apply to takeover and merger transactions. There are also elaborate statutory and other regulations for takeovers and mergers.

6 OVERSEAS COMPANIES

6.1 Overseas companies (companies registered outside the United Kingdom) are subject to certain modifications of the Listing Rules, set out in Chapter 17. Some of these modifications apply to all overseas companies, others depend on whether the overseas company has a primary or **secondary listing** in London. A primary listing is defined as 'a listing of a security by a competent authority, equivalent regulatory body or stock exchange by virtue of which the issuer is, as respects the security, subject to the full requirements applicable to listing of the competent authority, equivalent regulatory body or stock exchange'. The primary listing will normally be in the country of incorporation, the country in which a majority of the company's shares are held.

Modifications applying to all overseas companies

6.2 The modifications which relate to all overseas companies are as follows.

(a) When a company is incorporated in a country that is not part of the EU, and its shares are not listed either in its country of incorporation or the country in which a majority of its shares are held, the shares will not be admitted to listing unless the UK Listing

Authority is satisfied that the absence of such a listing is not due to the need to **protect investors**.

(b) Where the Authority is satisfied that the accounts are appropriate to investors' needs, it will accept an **accountant's report** and **accounts** which are not prepared in accordance with UK requirements subject to requirements on consolidation, reserves and asset valuation.

(c) **Documents** which **accord** with **foreign regulations** may with consent be included in listing particulars. The Authority may also allow certain information to be omitted from listing particulars, depending on the standards of the market on which the overseas company conducts its business, and the regulations governing the company in its country of incorporation.

(d) **Half yearly reports** prepared by a company incorporated outside the EU, and published in its country of incorporation may be acceptable if the information is **equivalent** to what is found in UK half-yearly reports.

(e) An overseas company is **not required** to **comply** with the **pre-emption** rules of the Companies Act.

(f) Information sent to shareholders and to the Companies Announcement Office must be in English.

Overseas companies with a primary listing on the Stock Exchange

6.3 Overseas companies who have or are seeking a primary listing must comply **with all the listing rules** if the information available enables it to do so, and provided compliance would not be contrary to the rules in the country of incorporation. The only exceptions are that the overseas company does not have to comply with the disclosure requirements that were introduced as a result of the corporate governance reports, apart from those concerning directors' service contracts. The details notified about new directors must be adjusted to take account of the laws that the overseas company must obey.

Overseas companies with a secondary listing

6.4 Overseas companies who have or are seeking a secondary listing are subject to the following modifications.

(a) Its sponsor does **not** have to **report** on **working capital**.

(b) Where the country in which the overseas company has a primary listing requires a statement to be included which constitutes a profit forecast, its inclusion will be allowed in UK listing particulars without the need for a report by the issuer's sponsors and auditors or reporting accountant, provided the company confirms that the forecast has been **properly compiled** on a basis consistent with the accounting policies of the company, and has been made after due and careful enquiry.

(c) Listing particulars must generally contain **three years' annual accounts**, but the most recent may be up to twelve months old.

(d) The 20% limit on warrants and options to subscribe does not apply to overseas companies.

(e) A new applicant must be in, and **confirm, compliance** with the requirements of any **overseas stock exchange** on which it has securities listed and any authority or regulatory body to which it is subject.

(f) The requirement for an **indebtedness statement** in **listing particulars** may be fulfilled by a consolidated capitalisation and indebtedness statement prepared in accordance with the Yellow Book requirements relating to specialist securities.

Continuing obligations relating to overseas companies with a secondary listing

6.5 The Listing Rules list separately the continuing obligations which apply to overseas companies with a secondary listing. Certain provisions relating to UK companies do not apply.

6.6 However this type of overseas company is subject to the general requirement that it must notify to the Company Announcements Office equivalent information to what is notified to the stock exchange on which the company has its primary listing, or, if earlier, to any other stock exchange on which its securities are listed. Information communicated to the Companies Announcement Office or made available through the UK Listing Authority must not be misleading, false or deceptive, and must not omit anything significant.

6.7 Specific information that the overseas company must relay to the Companies Announcement Office includes the following.

- Business developments that significantly affect the price of securities
- Changes in capital structure
- Acquisitions and disposals
- Directors' and other significant interests in shares
- Changes in directors
- Dividends
- Copies of circulars published overseas

6.8 There are also rules governing the content of preliminary statements of annual results and half-yearly reports.

6.9 The overseas company's annual report and accounts must be prepared to a standard necessary to protect the interests of investors. It should be **independently audited**, be **published within six months** of the end of the accounting period, be in consolidated form if appropriate, and explain reasons for any departure from a true and fair view.

6.10 There are also general requirements which aim to ensure fair treatment (including the giving of sufficient information) to all shareholders. Information should be sent by first class mail to members in EU member states, and airmail to members in non-EU states.

7 ADMISSION AND DISCLOSURE STANDARDS OF THE STOCK EXCHANGE

7.1 In May 2000 the London Stock Exchange published its admission and disclosure standards for entry into trading. An application is required not only when a company first comes to market, but also whenever it issues any new traded securities or makes a further issue of existing trading securities.

7.2 The standards emphasise the importance of **communication** with the Exchange. New applicants, along with their professional advisers, have to meet with Exchange representatives before applying for admission to trading, and have to nominate a named contact for the Exchange to liase with during the admission process.

8 INSIDER DEALING 6/98

8.1 The facts of the following case are an example of what is now called insider dealing. Note that the directors purchased the shares when they (as directors) knew and the vendor shareholders did not know that there was the possibility of a takeover bid at a higher price. The case also demonstrates that the law offered no remedy to shareholders in such a situation.

Percival v Wright 1902

The facts: The plaintiffs asked the company whether it could find buyers for their shares which they valued at £12.50 each. The directors purchased the shares at that price. At the time the directors knew that a third party was interested in buying the entire issued share capital at a higher price than £12.50. In fact nothing came of these negotiations. But the plaintiffs demanded that their sale to the directors should be rescinded for non-disclosure of the possibility of re-sale by the directors at a higher price.

Decision: The directors owed no duty to members individually which obliged the directors to disclose what they knew.

8.2 Part V of the Criminal Justice Act 1993 introduced new rules governing insider dealing. The following points provide a summary of the Act's section on insider dealing.

(a) **The offence**

S 52 describes the offence as dealing in securities while in possession of inside information as an insider, the securities being **price-affected** by the information.

The prosecution must prove that the possessor of inside information:

- **Dealt** in **price affected securities**
- **Encouraged another** to **deal** in them
- **Disclosed** the **information**

(b) **Dealing**

S 55 defines dealing as **acquiring or disposing** of or **agreeing** to **acquire** or **dispose** of relevant securities whether **directly** or **through an agent** or nominee or a person acting according to direction.

(c) **Encouraging another to deal**

An offence is also committed if an individual, having information as an insider, **encourages another person** to deal in price-affected securities in relation to that information, **knowing** or having reasonable cause to believe that **dealing** would **take place.**

It is irrelevant whether:

(i) The **person encouraged realises** that the **securities** are **price-affected** securities.

(ii) The **inside information is given** to that person; for example, a simple recommendation to the effect that 'I cannot tell you why but now would be a good time to buy shares in Bloggs plc' would infringe the law.

(iii) **Any dealing takes place**, the offence being committed at the time of encouragement.

(d) **Disclosing information**

It is also an offence for an individual who is considered an insider to **disclose** the **information** to another person otherwise than in the proper performance of the functions of his employment, office or profession.

(e) **Securities covered by the Act**

S 54 states that the securities include shares, debt securities and warranties.

(f) **Inside information**

S 56 defines inside information as '**price sensitive information**' relating to a **particular issuer** of **securities** that are price-affected and not to securities generally. It must, if made public, be likely to have a **significant effect on price** and it must be **specific or precise.** Specific would, for example, mean information that a takeover bid would be made for a specific company; precise information would be details of how much would be offered for shares.

"Specific" ⇒ why share price is likely to be affected.

"Precise" ⇒ share price info.

(g) **Insiders**

S 57 states that a person has information as an insider if it is (*and* he **knows** it is) inside information; and if he has it (*and* **knows** he has) from an inside source:

(i) Through being a **director, employee** or **shareholder** of an issuer of securities

(ii) Through **access** because of **employment, office** or **profession**

(iii) If the **direct** or **indirect source** is a **person within these two** previous **categories**

(h) **General defences**

S 53 gives a general defence where the individual concerned can show that:

(i) He did **not expect** there to be a **profit** or avoidance of loss.

(ii) He had **reasonable grounds** to **believe** that the **information** had been **disclosed widely.**

(iii) He would have **done** what he did **even** if he had **not had** the **information**, for example, where securities are sold to pay a pressing debt.

Defences to disclosure of information by an individual are that:

(i) He **did not expect** any person to **deal.**

(ii) Although dealing was expected, **profit** or **avoidance of loss** was **not expected.**

(i) **'Made public'**

S 58 defines this term, but not exhaustively, leaving final determination to the Court. Information **is** made public if:

(i) It is **published** under the rules of the regulated market, such as the Stock Exchange.

(ii) It is in **public records**, for example, notices in the *London Gazette.*

(iii) It can **readily be acquired** by those likely to deal.

(iv) It is **derived** from **public information.**

Information **may** be treated as made public even though:

(i) It can **only** be **acquired** by **exercising diligence** or expertise (thus helping analysts to avoid liability).

(ii) It is **communicated only** to a **section** of the **public** (thus protecting the 'brokers' lunch' where a company informs only selected City sources of important information).

(iii) It can be **acquired** only by **observation.**

(iv) It is **communicated only** on a **payment of a fee** or is **published only outside the UK.**

(j) **Penalties**

Maximum penalties given by s 61 are **seven years' imprisonment** and/or an **unlimited fine.** Contracts remain valid and enforceable at civil law.

(k) **Territorial scope**

S 62 states that the offender or any professional intermediary must be **in the UK** at the time of the offence or the market must be a UK regulated market.

Chapter roundup

- The City comprises **Recognised Investment Exchanges**, the merchant banks, clearing banks (both UK and foreign), and institutional and individual investors.
- The conduct of business of the City is monitored by the **Financial Services Authority**.
- The Stock Exchange now works with dual capacity firms acting as agency brokers and market makers as opposed to single capacity stockbrokers and jobbers. The firms buy and sell securities on their own account 'as principal' and on behalf of clients 'as agent'.
- The Stock Exchange is now computerised on SEAQ.
- The Listing Rules impose **continuing obligations** on a company with listed securities which include:
    - Information to be supplied initially and updated
    - Approval of company documents
    - Disclosure requirements for the protection of shareholders
- The application of the Listing Rules to **overseas companies** partly depends on whether they have a primary or secondary listing.
- **Insider dealing** is prohibited by the Model Code and by the Criminal Justice Act 1993.

Test your knowledge

1 Describe the types of financial institution which make up the City. (see paras 1.2 - 1.5)

2 Indicate briefly the changes resulting from the Stock Exchange reorganisation known colloquially as 'the Big Bang'. (2.2 - 2.3)

3 Give three examples of organisations which will be regulated by the Financial Services Authority (3.18)

4 In broad terms what types of obligation does a listed company accept by reason of its listed status? (5.3)

5 Give two examples of events of which a company must inform the Company Announcements Office. (5.5)

6 Give three examples of circulars of a routine nature which do not need to be sent to the UK Listing Authority in advance of being issued. (5.8)

7 Give three examples of safeguards to members of listed companies resulting from the UK Listing Authority Continuing Obligations. (5.12)

8 What is a reverse takeover? (5.14)

9 How are the Stock Exchange Listing Rules modified: (a) for all overseas companies; (b) for overseas companies with a secondary listing? (6.2, 6.4 - 6.6)

10 What is 'inside information'? (8.2)

When you have worked through Chapter 17 try illustrative questions 19 to 20 at the end of the Study Text

Chapter 17

REGULATION OF LISTED COMPANIES 2

This chapter covers the following topics.

1 Public issues
2 Raising capital in the market
3 Different types of public issue
4 Initial considerations before an issue
5 Legal requirements for listing particulars
6 Offers of unlisted securities and the Alternative Investment Market
7 Contravention of rules on listing particulars and prospectuses
8 Drafting issue documents
9 Action at and after the time of issue

Introduction

Having considered the general framework of regulation, we now consider how companies can raise capital on the London Stock Exchange and how the listing regulations impact upon this process.

Practical matters relating to issue documents, always of importance to the company secretary, are dealt with in Sections 8 and 9.

1 PUBLIC ISSUES

1.1 'Public issue' is not a technical term, but it is generally used to describe the **issue** of shares or debentures to investors from among the **general body** of the **public** (or to financial institutions in the City of London) who have applied for them. If a company makes a public issue of its securities for the first time, the process is sometimes called a 'flotation'. On most points the same procedure applies to the issue of debentures and other forms of company loan capital as to shares. The term 'securities' is generally used in this chapter to embrace both categories.

"Securities" ⇒ shares, debentures & other loan capital.

2 RAISING CAPITAL IN THE MARKET

2.1 The main advantage of being a public company is that there is a wider market for its securities. Private companies' shareholders tend to be its managers, employees, founders and their relatives. Whilst this system may assist a company in its early years, lack of capital for expansion will often necessitate public company status.

2.2 Securities may be bought and sold on recognised investment exchanges or 'over the counter'. To assist this trade there are 'brokers' who can put investors in touch with 'market makers' who, since the Big Bang in October 1986, *must* trade at the price they display on a computer screen, known as the Stock Exchange Automated Quotation System (SEAQ). There are also 'matching' or 'inter dealer' brokers who *will attempt* to buy or sell when asked to do so.

The Listed Market

2.3 An official listing on this market can be obtained by large public companies with a minimum market value of securities of **£700,000** (£200,000 for debt securities). Directors and major shareholders (and their associates) may only retain a maximum of 75% of the equity shares.

The Alternative Investment Market

2.4 The Alternative Investment Market (AIM) is the London Stock Exchange's public market for small, **young and growing companies** enabling them to raise capital and see their shares more widely traded.

2.5 Having a public market in shares has disadvantages as well as advantages. As a way of raising new finance, making securities attractive as consideration in takeovers, enhancing status and benefiting shareholders by allowing them to sell securities easily, 'going public' is advantageous. However, the procedures required for admission are lengthy and expensive, and the company may find itself victim of a takeover, prey to disgruntled shareholders and hostages to short-term policy making for dividends as a result.

3 DIFFERENT TYPES OF PUBLIC ISSUE 6/98

3.1 There are various ways in which a public company can make a 'public' issue of shares.

Offer to the public

eg. Orange float.

3.2 A public company can make an invitation to the public to apply for securities which the company intends to issue. For this purpose the company publishes 'listing particulars', or for non-listed securities, a prospectus.

3.3 The offer to the public may take various forms, including the following.

(a) A **rights issue** of new securities to existing shareholders or debenture holders, in proportion to their existing holdings, with a right to renounce in favour of other persons, as discussed in the previous chapter (because of the unrestricted right of renunciation, the effect is to give existing members first refusal (as required by s 89) of the new shares, but also the opportunity of passing the offer over to any member of the public.)

(b) An **open offer to members**, by which they may apply for whatever number of new shares they may wish to obtain in proportion to their existing holdings, but no renounceable letter of allotment is made available

(c) **A direct offer to the public** to apply for new securities

3.4 The choice between these three methods must depend on factors incidental to the nature of the offer. If an existing company with securities already listed on the Stock Exchange is raising more capital, it is likely to make a rights issue; indeed, it would have some difficulty in justifying an alternative choice to members. If on the other hand the company is being floated for the first time, as has been the case with the recent 'privatisation' issues, the whole object is to get large numbers of shares directly into the hands of new members.

Offer for sale

3.5 The other main means of offering securities to the public generally is an 'offer for sale'. This entails the **acquisition** by an **issuing house** of a large block of shares of a company, with a view to offering them for resale to the public.

3.6 An issuing house is usually a merchant bank (or sometimes a firm of stockbrokers). It may acquire the shares either as a direct allotment from the company or by purchase from existing members. In the latter case the company may first increase its issued capital by an allotment of shares, on renounceable allotment letter, to existing members; they then renounce their new shares to the issuing house. In either case the issuing house publishes an invitation to the public to apply for shares, either at a fixed price or on a tender basis, as described later in this chapter.

3.7 The advantage of an offer for sale over a direct offer by the company to the public is that the issuing house **accepts responsibility** to the public, and gives to the issue the support of its own standing. It is a method often used when a flourishing unlisted company is 'floated' by an offer of its shares (for which a listing will be sought) to investors generally.

Placing

3.8 The third major method of effecting a public issue is a placing, to which much the same legal rules apply, since it is contemplated that the securities which are 'placed' in the first instance will later be re-sold to the public. Under a placing, a number of **major institutions** are **allotted securities** in large blocks which they may hold or resell, wholly or in part. This method is only considered suitable for comparatively small issues.

3.9 The Stock Exchange has laid down a number of guidelines for these 'selective marketings', especially when the securities involved are ordinary shares. The upper limit is £15 million (in market value) and a minimum proportion must be disposed of, by a sufficiently widespread distribution, on re-sale.

Intermediaries offer

3.10 An 'intermediaries offer' is a **marketing of securities** already or not yet in issue by means of an offer by or on behalf of the issuer to intermediaries for them to allocate to their own clients.

Introduction

3.11 An 'introduction' is not a new issue, but an arrangement by which **existing** securities are **admitted** to the official list **for the first time**. This is only permitted if the securities are, widely enough held to make a real market after listing.

Capitalisation issue

3.12 A capitalisation, 'bonus' or 'scrip' issue does not bring money into the company, but, like a rights issue, the new shares are usually issued on a **renounceable letter of allotment**. Where the members decide to dispose of their new shares, they pass into the hands of buyers who may not be members of the company.

Vendor placing

3.13 In a vendor placing the company arranges to **purchase property** at a price which the vendor wishes to receive in cash. If it does not suit the company to raise the required cash by a rights issue to its members, it may arrange with the vendor to fulfil the arrangement as follows:

(a) To allot **shares** to the vendor on a renounceable letter allotment, in satisfaction of the price of the property

(b) To **find a buyer**, at an agreed price, for all the consideration shares which the company will allot under (a)

In these transactions the buyer is often the merchant bank, which acts for the purchaser company. The bank resells the shares by placing them among its clients.

3.14 This type of transaction has sometimes been abused by companies which do not wish to make a rights issue, say because the company wishes to increase the proportion of its shares held by **friendly** interests. The property transaction is then merely a pretext for the issue of a large block of shares which are destined to end up in the hands of pre-selected buyers. This could not be effected under a rights issue since, in that case, each member would be free to keep his new shares or to sell them through the market to the highest bidder. To counter this practice there may be a '**vendor rights issue**' by which the vendor must first offer the shares to members of the acquiring company before it may sell them to others.

3.15 A vendor consideration placing is a marketing, by and on behalf of vendors of securities that have been allotted as securities for an acquisition.

Other methods and techniques of raising cash by issuing securities

3.16 Another method of raising cash without going through the rights issue procedure is to **make a takeover bid**, on the basis of shares for shares (to which the statutory members' pre-emption rights do not apply), thereby acquiring the whole capital of a company, such as an investment trust, whose assets are marketable securities. After the acquisition has been completed, the target company is put into liquidation; its investments are sold and the cash comes through to the company which is now its holding company.

3.17 Chapter 19 describes a variety of rights to subscribe for securities (usually shares), such as option certificates, warrants, etc., often issued in connection with a larger transaction. The grant of such rights is of course subject to the statutory pre-emption rights of members. Moreover the company which grants the rights, as an option, cannot be sure that the holders of the rights will elect to use them.

4 INITIAL CONSIDERATIONS BEFORE AN ISSUE

4.1 A new issue requires careful planning, and should be implemented according to a timetable. In modern practice, a company never makes a public issue without seeking the advice and services at all stages of a merchant bank, as issuing house. In a large transaction the merchant bank will also retain its own professional advisers, such as accountants and solicitors. The company on its side will be advised by its accountants, solicitors, brokers and perhaps valuers.

4.2 The fees for all these services, plus Stock Exchange fees, advertising and printing expenses, and perhaps a fee payable to the receiving bank which is employed to process the applications for shares, will often run into very large sums. Hence it is not economic to undertake a small scale new issue.

4.3 When a decision is taken to make a public issue, and the size and method of issue have been selected, there are several other preliminary matters to resolve.

The issue price

4.4 One of the major 'strategic' points for consideration between the company and its advisers is the issue price of the new securities, and the manner in which the price is to be fixed and paid.

4.5 It is not possible to fix a price until just before the issue is made. This is because the price must be fixed in relation to prevailing market conditions, which fluctuate from day to day. Even so, a company will have a rough idea from an early stage of the issue price that it might expect to obtain.

4.6 In fixing an issue price, the company and its advisers are steering a course between opposite errors.

(a) If the price is **too low** the issue will be heavily **oversubscribed**; the company then obtains less than the full value of its shares. The applications will be scaled down so that all but the applicants for small numbers, receive fewer shares then they actually applied for. In the consequent active market following the issue, speculators ('stags') will be able to sell shares, which they never intended to keep, at a profit to themselves.

(b) If the price is fixed **too high**, there will be **insufficient applications** for the securities on offer and a number of shares issued will be left in the hands of the **underwriters**. The market price in the period after the issue may be less than the issue price, with a depressing effect on the company's standing and on the value of the shares allotted.

4.7 Generally the aim is to err on the side of too low a price, though only by a modest margin, rather than suffer a 'flop' which will embarrass the merchant bank.

Offer for sale by tender

4.8 In modern practice it is sometimes advantageous, instead of hazarding a fixed issue price, to offer securities at a price to be tendered by the applicant as follows.

(a) In inviting subscriptions a **minimum tender** price is fixed, below which securities will not be issued.

(b) In applying for shares, each applicant states **how much more** than the minimum price he is prepared to pay to obtain the specified number of shares.

(c) When the applications are all in, a '**striking price**' is set which is just low enough to bring in applications for all the securities on offer. The applications made at prices below the striking price are rejected, and the money, if sent with the applications is returned. A simple example may illustrate this.

4.9 Walter Wall Carpets Ltd wishes to issue 250,000 shares. It has invited subscribers to submit tenders with a minimum price of £0.80. The tenders received can be analysed as follows.

Tender price per share	*No of shares applied for*	*Cumulative total*
£2.00	10,000	10,000
£1.50	15,000	25,000
£1.25	50,000	75,000
£1.10	75,000	150,000
£1.00	100,000	250,000
£0.90	110,000	360,000
£0.80	80,000	440,000

The highest price at which the issue is fully subscribed is £1.00. Subscribers who submitted tenders at or above this price will receive the full number of shares they applied for at the striking price of £1. Those subscribers who tendered prices in excess of £1 will only have to pay that price per share. The subscribers who submitted tenders of £0.90 and £0.80 will not be allotted any shares.

4.10 In practice this method has drawbacks, and is used mainly when uncertainty about a suitable fixed price is especially acute.

Underwriting

12/98

4.11 There is always a danger that the issue price will be too high, with the consequence that the issue will be under-subscribed. To remove the risk of under-subscription by ensuring that the whole amount of securities offered is in fact subscribed (and so issued), it is standard practice to have the issue 'underwritten'. It is not a compulsory requirement to have an issue underwritten for the following reasons.

(a) It is unnecessary to underwrite a **placing** since a purchaser for the shares is arranged in the issue process.

(b) An **offer for sale by tender** only needs underwriting if there is a **risk** that there will be **under-subscription** even at the minimum price.

(c) A **rights issue,** in theory, should not require underwriting, since new shares are being offered to existing shareholders. However, the underwriting of rights issues is common practice.

4.12 A main underwriter (often the company's merchant bank) agrees, by letter, with the company or the issuing house, as follows.

(a) The underwriter will **purchase any securities** which are **not subscribed** for by the investing public.

(b) He is to pay the **fixed issue** price or **minimum tender price** for those shares as the case may be.

(c) A director or other representative of the company is authorised, as his representative, to complete a **formal application** for whatever part of the underwritten securities he may become obliged to take.

(d) The issue is to proceed upon the **basis** of the **listing particulars**, or other document which is the basis of the offer to the public.

4.13 The underwriter makes an **underwriting charge** or fee, fixed at perhaps 2.25% of the issue value (the finance to be raised). The underwriter may also offset his risk by '**sub-underwriting**' with a variety of banks and pension funds etc. The underwriting contract is between the company and the main underwriter. The arrangement with the sub-underwriters is of no direct concern to the company, nor need it be disclosed.

4.14 Alternatively, a main underwriter may merely undertake to the company that he will find a sufficient number of persons to act as underwriters by direct arrangement with the company. The main underwriter is then entitled to an 'overriding commission' for his services in arranging the underwriting.

4.15 Finally, an underwriter may '**underwrite firm**', meaning that it may undertake to subscribe for securities (of a specified amount) regardless of the level of response to the issue by the general investor public.

4.16 There are a number of company law disclosure requirements in respect of underwriting, and in particular commissions/fees to underwriters. It is not usual to settle the underwriting arrangements until just before the date of the issue, when the issue price has been fixed and the proposed underwriter can assess the risk which he is asked to undertake.

Deep discount

4.17 As an alternative to underwriting an issue, a company could choose to issue its shares at a 'deep' discount, meaning at a price **well below** the **current market price**. This ensures the success of the issue. A major disadvantage of issuing shares at a 'deep' discount is that, since companies try to avoid reducing the dividends paid out per share, the total amount required for dividends in future years will be that much higher, since *more* shares would have to be issued at the lower price in order to raise the amount of finance required.

The issue date

4.18 The approximate date for the new issue must be set so as to allow time to prepare the relevant documents and advertise the issue. Obviously it must be at around the time the company has need of the cash. Finally for a large issue, set to take large amounts of funds away from banks and building societies, the Bank of England and the Stock Exchange need to be consulted.

Possible need for an EGM

4.19 It may be necessary to plan an extraordinary general meeting to give the directors the following authorisations:

(a) To **allot shares** (s 80)

(b) To **increase** the **authorised capital** by the creation of new shares: s 121

(c) To **obtain** the **shareholders' consent** to a waiver of their statutory pre-emption rights (s 89), if there is not to be a rights issue

5 LEGAL REQUIREMENTS FOR LISTING PARTICULARS

5.1 Listing particulars for admissions to listing on the main Stock Exchange market are required by the financial services legislation. These rules are contained in the Listing Rules book.

5.2 Listing particulars so prepared must be:

- **Submitted** to and **approved** formally by the UK Listing Authority
- **Published** (they must not be circulated beforehand unless clearly marked as a draft)
- **Delivered** to the **registrar** of companies on or before the date of publication

Contents of listing particulars

5.3 The Listing Rules set out the content required, but there is also a general requirement to disclose all such information as investors and advisors may *reasonably* require so as to make an informed assessment of:

- The issuer's assets and liabilities, its financial position, profit and loss, and prospects
- The rights attaching to the securities

5.4 To decide what may be 'reasonably required', those responsible should consider the following factors:

- The nature of the **securities** and their issuer
- The nature of the **persons** likely to consider acquisition
- The fact that professional advisors consulted by the public may reasonably be expected to **know certain things**
- The **general knowledge** available to the issuer since listed companies have continuing obligations to give information

5.5 The contents required by the Listing Rules for a company include the following details:

- The persons responsible for listing particulars, the auditors and other advisors
- The securities for which application is being made
- General information about the issuer and its capital
- The group's activities
- The issuer's assets and liabilities, financial position and profits and losses
- Management
- The recent development and prospects

5.6 In limited circumstances, **the competent authority may allow** information to be omitted which would otherwise be included in listing particulars; such as where disclosure would be seriously detrimental to the issuer, or if summary listing particulars are permitted.

5.7 Once listing particulars are prepared, approved, registered and published, the issuer's obligations are not yet over. If, between registration and the commencement of dealing, a **significant change** in matters originally included in the listing or a significant new matter arises, supplementary listing particulars must undergo the same procedure (including registration).

Advertisements on listing

5.8 All advertisements issued in the UK relating to the listing must be authorised. Advertisements in this context include 'mini prospectuses' issued in major flotations when the full particulars are very complex. They also include advertisements in the following:

- A publication
- A notice, sign, label or showcard
- An exhibition of pictures, photographs or film
- A broadcast or recording

5.9 Companies with a full listing have continuing obligations to provide all information necessary, after listing, to protect investors and maintain an orderly market.

Summary listing particulars

5.10 Summary particulars may be circulated to shareholders whenever listing particulars are required. There is no list given of detailed contents in the Listing Rules, to discourage the provision of too much detailed information.

5.11 Full listing particulars must nevertheless still be published. The summary particulars must contain a statement about the availability of full particulars.

6 OFFERS OF UNLISTED SECURITIES AND THE ALTERNATIVE INVESTMENT MARKET

6.1 Offers of unlisted securities are governed by the Public Offers of Securities Regulations 1995 (POOS).

6.2 Under the POOS Regulations, if shares which are not admitted to official listing are offered to the public, then a prospectus must be prepared, published and registered. Provision is also made for a prospectus to be prepared, scrutinised and approved in accordance with the Listing Rules. There are certain exceptions set down by Regulation 7.

Contents of prospectus **6/00**

6.3 A prospectus to which these rules apply is defined as:

> 'any prospectus, notice, circular, advertisement or other invitation offering to the public for subscription or purchase any shares or debentures of a company: s 744 CA.'

6.4 Strictly, a prospectus is not an offer but an **invitation** to the public to make offers by applying to the company in response to the prospectus. The company accepts the applications wholly or in part by allotting shares or debentures. This produces a contract to which ordinary rules of contract law, such as rescission for misrepresentation in the prospectus, apply. Special rules of company law also apply.

6.5 Except where the securities have been admitted on an approved exchange, the content of the prospectus is laid down in the POOS. The regulations contain general requirements for the information to be clearly presented, and for the prospectus to contain all the information that the investors would reasonably require or reasonably expect to find there.

The detailed requirements relating to prospectuses on the Alternative Investment Market are considered below.

The Alternative Investment Market (AIM) **Specimen paper, 6/00**

6.6 AIM is open to all companies regardless of where they are incorporated and is suitable for a broad range of companies - from young businesses to management buy-outs and family concerns. AIM provides the opportunity to:

- **Raise capital** to fund further growth
- **Determine** the **market value** of the business
- **Enhance** the company's **visibility** and public profile

6.7 The requirements for admission to AIM are straightforward. The company does not have to have reached a particular size or demonstrate a lengthy trading history. In addition, it is not required to have a certain percentage of its shares in public hands.

6.8 AIM is operated by the London Stock Exchange and managed by its own team within the Exchange.

6.9 Any type or class of security issued by a company can be admitted to AIM. Although ordinary shares are most commonly traded, a company may also have its preference shares and debt securities traded on the market.

6.10 Companies and other market participants will have to comply with relevant legislation. In particular, companies will have to meet the requirements of the **POOS**. In addition the Exchange has introduced a number of extra requirements to ensure fair trading and a proper level of protection for investors.

6.11 The application process for companies wishing to join AIM has been made as simple as possible.

- There are few rules, making it easy for a company to know what is required.
- The rules are clearly set out.
- They are tailored for small and growing companies.
- Information is available from the Exchange's AIM team.

6.12 To join AIM it is necessary to appoint a **nominated broker** and a **nominated adviser** to assist in the admission procedure and compliance with ongoing requirements. The role of the advisers and the other steps required to join AIM are set out below.

The nominated adviser

6.13 The nominated adviser's first job is to help the company with the **application process** by ensuring that the directors have been guided and advised on their responsibilities and obligations under the market's rules. The adviser must be drawn from the register of firms kept by the Exchange. The adviser is likely to be a stockbroker, banker, lawyer, accountant or other financial professional experienced in corporate finance.

6.14 The directors are responsible for compliance with the market's rules. It is essential that they are confident, they understand their responsibilities and have taken the steps required to ensure the **information** in the admission document - the prospectus - is **complete** and **correct**. At the time of admission, the nominated advisers will confirm to the Exchange that the company has complied with the relevant rules. Once the company has been admitted to the market, the nominated adviser should be available at all times to guide and advise the board and provide any further assistance required.

The nominated broker

6.15 As well as a nominated adviser, companies are required to appoint a firm which is a member of the London Stock Exchange to act as the nominated broker. A single firm may fill the role of nominated broker and adviser. The broking firm appointed will have an important role to play in bringing buyers and sellers of the company's shares together. Investors wanting to buy or sell shares in the company will know that at least one firm is ready to trade or do its best to match transactions in the shares.

Duration of employment

6.16 The company will be required to retain the services of a nominated broker and adviser at all times.

Relations with the investment community

6.17 Although it is not an Exchange requirement, companies wish their nominated adviser or broker to become the point of contact for information between the company and the investment community. The firm performing this role is generally known as the corporate broker.

Admission to AIM

6.18 The main requirements for companies wishing to access and remain on the market are set out in the following sections.

Conditions to be satisfied at all times

6.19 Companies traded on AIM must meet the following criteria at all times. These conditions are designed to ensure that there is orderly trading in the shares and to protect the integrity of the market. The company needs to:

(a) Appoint and retain a **nominated adviser** and **broker**

(b) Have **published accounts** that **conform** to the UK, US Generally Accepted Accounting Principles or International Accounting Standards

(c) Ensure that appropriate arrangements are in place for the **settlement** of its securities

(d) Adopt by board resolution a code equivalent to that set out in the **Model Code** for AIM companies relating to trading while in possession of unpublished price sensitive information (discussed below)

(e) **Publish annual audited accounts** within six months of the year-end

(f) **Prepare a half-yearly report** within four months of the year-end

(g) **Make copies** of any document they send to shareholders **available** to the public

(h) **Forward** to the Companies Announcement Office **six copies** of all announcements and six copies of all circulars, notices, reports or other documents at the same time that they are issued to shareholders

6.20 The Model Code for AIM companies requires that the companies impose restrictions, beyond those imposed by law, on the freedom of their directors and certain employees to deal in the company's shares in certain circumstances. For example, directors must refrain from dealing in their company's shares for **two months** preceding the announcement of the annual results. These conditions must be met at all times once the company's shares have been admitted to AIM. The board must be satisfied before joining the market that the directors are willing and able to meet the conditions on an on-going basis.

6.21 If the main activity of the company has been generating revenue for less than two years, admission to AIM will be subject to an additional condition designed to reassure investors of the commitment of its directors and employees to the company.

(a) Directors and employees must agree **not to sell** any **interests** they may have in the company's securities for at least one year from the date of joining AIM.

(b) The nominated adviser may recommend that investor confidence in the company's shares would be enhanced if the **restriction** was **extended** to other parties concerned, for example major shareholders.

Admission procedures

6.22 Every application to AIM needs to be supported by:

- A prospectus which contains the information required for admission to AIM
- An application form signed by the directors
- A declaration by the nominated adviser
- A letter from the company's nominated broker confirming its appointment

6.23 The application and supporting documents should be submitted to the Exchange at **least five business days** before the company requires its shares to be admitted to AIM. Applications may be submitted directly by the company or its advisers to the Exchange's London office or to any of its regional offices. If submitting documents through the regional network, one additional day should be allowed for transfer.

6.24 Recent changes have imposed upon companies the requirement to make an official announcement containing details of their business, directors, shareholders and advisers at least ten business days before joining AIM.

The prospectus

6.25 The prospectus is an essential document. Without it potential investors cannot make an informed decision about the company's shares. The directors are responsible for ensuring that it contains accurate and full information and that there are no material omissions. The information in the prospectus will consist of the details required by the **POOS** regulations, supplemented with additional information which the Exchange believes is **essential for investor protection**.

6.26 The prospectus must contain all such information as investors would reasonably expect to find there, for the purpose of making an **informed assessment** of the assets and liabilities, financial position, profits and losses, and prospects of the issuer of the securities and the rights attaching to those securities. This must include:

(a) A description of the **securities** to be traded on AIM

(b) A full description of the **company**, its principal activities and its capital

(c) **Financial information** about the company, its trading history and performance in recent years

(d) Details of the **management**, **administration** and **supervision** of the company

(e) **Recent developments** and prospects

6.27 In addition the Exchange requires:

(a) Details of all **directors**, including their directorships over the past five years, any unspent convictions and all bankruptcies, receiverships or liquidations of companies where they were directors at the time or within the 12 months preceding these events, and any public criticisms by statutory or regulatory authorities

(b) Details of the company's **promoters**

(c) Names of **substantial shareholders** and the percentage that each holds, ie anyone entitled to exercise or control the exercise of 10 per cent or more of the votes able to be cast at general meetings

(d) A confirmation that the company is satisfied there is **sufficient working capital** in place to meet the present requirements of the company

(e) A notice on the first page of the prospectus drawing investors' attention to the fact that **AIM** is a **different market** from the Official List, being a market for small emerging companies. This notice should include a warning about the risk of investing in AIM companies

Methods of issuing shares

6.28 There are no rules governing the method of issuing shares. There are several ways of distributing shares in the market, depending on the type of investor and how much money the company wishes to raise.

6.29 Once the shares have been traded on AIM for at least two years, the company can apply to join the Official List without producing full listing particulars. However, information beyond that already disclosed under the AIM rules will be required to fulfil the listing requirements.

Ongoing obligations

6.30 The company's involvement with the market must continue once its shares have been admitted to AIM. For this reason companies are required to meet certain ongoing requirements, designed to be straightforward and to keep costs to a minimum. The company will be required to notify the Exchange immediately of any developments which could have an impact on the price of its shares. This information is known as **'price sensitive' information**. The company will need:

(a) To notify details of:

(i) Major developments in activities that may have a significant effect on prices

(ii) Directors and connected persons' interests in securities

(iii) Substantial shareholdings

(iv) Changes in directors or directors' details

(v) Publication of annual audited accounts and change in accounting reference date

(vi) Dividends

(vii) Issue of new securities or cancellation of existing securities

(viii) Substantial transactions (those reaching at least 10% of the percentage ratios of the company, see Chapter 17)

(ix) Transactions with related parties where the ratio is 5% or more

(x) Material differences between actual and forecast performance

(b) To advise the Exchange promptly of the resignation, dismissal or appointment of a nominated adviser or nominated broker.

6.31 If the company makes an acquisition or disposal, it will need to decide whether it could have an effect on the price of the shares. If so details should be notified. Shareholder approval is only required if the company wishes to make an acquisition which would result in a reverse takeover. If it goes ahead, the company will need to reapply for admission to AIM.

6.32 If any transaction by the company involves a related party (eg a substantial shareholder, director or an associate) the announcement will need to contain details of the **nature** and

extent of the **interest** of the related parties and a statement from the directors that the terms and transactions are fair and reasonable.

The trading on AIM

6.33 Liquidity in the shares of small companies tends to be less than for larger companies as there are often fewer shares available for the public to acquire. For this reason the company needs to consider carefully with its advisers the implications of any decision on distribution of the company's shares and the number of shares in public hands.

6.34 The Exchange promotes the liquidity of smaller company shares through the use of the Stock Exchange Alternative Trading Service, **SEATS PLUS**, which supports AIM securities. SEATS PLUS is a service which enables buyers and sellers to trade shares with each other through the Exchange's central trade system. Information on this service is carried by leading news distributors, the larger investors and market intermediaries.

6.35 The service has the benefit of providing an **order board** through which orders to buy and sell shares can be displayed and matched. There is also the facility for **competing quotations** allowing one or more market makers to display prices in the company's shares throughout the day. A market maker is an Exchange member firm which offers to buy and sell shares in which it is registered. In addition, details of the latest trades in a company's shares are available.

6.36 SEATS PLUS also carries key background information about the company and its shares including accounting details, date of announcement of annual and interim results, number of shares in issue, percentage of shares in public hands, and monthly and annual share trading volumes.

Supervision of trading

6.37 Orderly and fair trading in the company's shares according to the AIM rules is monitored by the Exchange's Market Supervision and Surveillance departments.

Settlement

6.38 An **orderly stock market** also requires a timely and reliable method of settlement. Transactions in the shares of the company must be settled between the trading parties. Details of market transactions will be posted to the Exchange each day, to effect settlement through the Exchange's central service CREST providing there are no restrictions in the company's own constitution.

Issues not dealt on approved exchanges

6.39 Even though a security is not dealt on any exchange it is still possible to issue an advertisement for one, provided a prospectus (relating to the securities and expressed to be in respect of the offer)is or will be published, and gives a UK address from which it is or will be available: reg 12 POOS.

7 CONTRAVENTION OF RULES ON LISTING PARTICULARS AND PROSPECTUSES

7.1 An issuer of securities is duty-bound to disclose changes and new matters in supplementary documents. Any person responsible for the particulars who knows of any changes or new matters must notify the issuer, who must publicise it. Failure to do so or failure to include all information will lead the issuer and those other persons to pay compensation to anyone who suffered loss. A defence is to prove a reasonable belief that the supplement is unnecessary. Failure to register listing particulars before publication leads the issuer and any person knowingly a party to a fine on conviction.

7.2 As regards the POOS different penalties exist, according to whether an advertisement was issued by an authorised or unauthorised person.

(a) An **authorised person** who breaches the POOS (issues advertisement without prospectus or fails to register prospectus) will have breached his body's conduct of business rules. He may as a result be de-authorised or otherwise restricted, or have to pay damages. It would be a civil offence.

(b) An **unauthorised person** in breach commits a criminal offence.

In either case a person who suffers loss can sue for damages for breach of statutory duty. No offence is committed if a prospectus is issued with omissions, but any such person may still be liable for damages.

Persons responsible for the listing particulars and prospectus

7.3 The following persons are responsible for the issue documents:

- The issuing company
- Its directors
- Anyone who authorised himself to be named as a director
- Anyone who is named as accepting responsibility
- Any other person who is responsible

Directors will not be responsible if the particulars/prospectus was published/registered without their consent and they gave notice of this fact. In addition, persons in category (a) to (c) are not responsible if the offer is a secondary offer of unlisted securities which they did not authorise.

Misrepresentation and omission

7.4 The most important ground, for which penalties are available, for contravening the regulations is where there is **misrepresentation** and/or **omission**. Any person responsible for information is liable to compensate anyone who has acquired the securities and suffered loss as a result of any untrue or misleading statement, or of any omission from both the main and supplementary documents, or under the general duty of disclosure.

7.5 An omission of any matter required to be included or of matters that do not apply, is a statement that there is no such matter and so may be a misrepresentation.

7.6 Therefore a person need not have subscribed on the faith of the document to be able to claim for compensation, they can rely on the omission as a misrepresentation. Even a subsequent purchaser within a reasonable time may claim compensation. This extends the old s 67 CA, which allowed compensation only to subscribers on the faith of a prospectus which contained misleading information.

7.7 The measure of loss will normally be the difference between the purchase and sale price.

Defences to misrepresentation and omission

7.8 Generally, directors are held to be responsible for issuing **false** or **misleading information**, and to this end their **names and addresses** and **declaration of responsibility** is included in listing particulars and prospectuses. However, the relevant exchange may certify that he should be excluded for whatever reason.

7.9 The defences available to responsible persons are similar to those under the old s 68 CA, but have moved more towards persons **notifying** investors of any change rather then merely **withdrawing consent**. Beyond the defence that omissions were permitted under statute, the following may be successful defences for a responsible person.

(a) The person had a reasonable belief, after enquiries, that the statement was true and not misleading, or that the omission was justified and that either

(i) He **continued** to **believe** this until the securities were acquired.

(ii) It was **not reasonably practicable** to notify potential investors of the correction.

(iii) He had taken **all reasonable steps** before they were acquired to notify investors

(iv) He **continued** in the **belief** until **dealings commenced**, or until such a long time after securities were acquired that he should be excused.

(b) For loss arising out of a statement made by an expert, he can prove he reasonably believed in the **expert's competence** and **consent**, and he can prove one of the four conditions in (a).

(c) He took reasonable steps to bring a **correction**, or notice of an expert's incompetence or lack of consent, to the attention of investors.

(d) A statement or document by an official person is **reproduced accurately** and **fairly**.

(e) The party challenging him knew the statement to be **false, misleading, incomplete** or **out-of-date**.

(f) He reasonably believed that the change or new matter in question was not such as to call for a **supplementary prospectus**.

7.10 'Expert' in this context means any engineer, valuer, accountant, or other person with relevant qualifications, experience or professional status.

Criminal liability

7.11 Criminal offences are committed in this general area if **false listing particulars** or **false prospectuses** are issued. This covers statements, promises and forecasts known to be false, misleading or deceptive, concealment of facts, and reckless statements made to induce an investment agreement. It is also an offence under this section to create a false or misleading impression as to the value of an investment.

7.12 Either offence has a **maximum penalty** of **seven years in prison** and/or a fine.

7.13 A criminal offence is committed under if a private company issues an **unauthorised advertisement.** The maximum penalty is two years in prison and/or a fine. An offence makes any agreement unenforceable. Hence unlisted offer advertisements issued by an unauthorised person will also lead to an unenforceable contract.

Common law remedies

7.14 If listing particulars or a prospectus are misleading, the common law remedies available to a subscriber for shares or debentures are **rescission** of the contract of allotment on the ground of misrepresentation or an action for damages for **deceit** against those who issued the prospectus.

Rescission

7.15 An allottee may be entitled to rescind the contract with the company and recover his subscription money if he can show all the following.

(a) The prospectus included a **material false statement** of fact.

(b) The prospectus was issued by or on behalf of the **company** and he was one of the persons to **whom** it was **addressed**.

(c) The false statement **induced him** to **subscribe**.

7.16 A statement of fact is usually contrasted with a statement of opinion which does not suffice as grounds for rescission; for example, 'in my opinion the business has excellent prospects' is not an assertion that the prospects are in fact excellent. However it is an assertion that the opinion is genuinely held: *Edgington v Fitzmaurice 1885*.

7.17 If the prospectus cites a report by an expert in such a way as to adopt his remarks as part of the company's case and the report is untrue, that is a misrepresentation by the **company**: *Re Pacaya Rubber & Produce Ltd 1914*.

7.18 Finally, in claiming the right to rescind, the allottee must show not only that the untrue statement was **material** (an objective test) but also that he personally was **induced** to **subscribe** by it. If he knew the true facts or made his own enquiries and relied on them, he cannot rescind. He has no duty, however, to investigate and does not lose the right to rescind if he accepts the prospectus without taking up opportunities to investigate: *Central Railway of Venezuela v Kisch 1867*.

7.19 In an action for rescission it is **no defence** that the **misrepresentation** was made in the honest belief that it was **true** and with **reasonable grounds** for that belief. Even an innocent misrepresentation can be grounds for rescission (though honest and reasonable belief is a defence against other remedies claimed by an allottee). If the statement can be read ambiguously, the allottee can claim rescission on the basis of what he took it to mean even though the company intended to convey something different.

7.20 As explained earlier in this text, a company in issuing a **renounceable letter of allotment undertakes** to **allot shares** to a renouncee to whom the letter has been transferred. The contract of allotment (performed by entering his name in the register) is with him and so he can claim rescission. However, a purchaser of shares from the allottee (after registration), if he buys in reliance on the prospectus, cannot have rescission since there was never a contract between him and the company for the allotment of shares.

7.21 If the misrepresentation is made through an **offer for sale** the subscriber who takes his shares from the issuing house may **rescind** the **contract** and **return** the **shares** to the issuing house, with which the contract was made. He has no right to rescind the issue of shares by the company in the first place (nor is he affected if the company goes into liquidation). He returns his securities to the issuing house which becomes the holder in his place.

7.22 As a remedy, rescission is of little value, since the right to rescind is lost in any of the following situations.

(a) If the allottee **discovers** the **true facts** and then by his conduct affirms the contract even if it was not his intention to do so. This can result if he exercises members' rights, say by attending a meeting or attempting to sell the shares as his property.

(b) If, on discovering the truth, he **fails** to **rescind promptly**. He may, however, have a short time in which to make enquiries without thereby losing the right to rescind.

(c) If it is **no longer possible** to **restore both parties** to their pre-contract position.

(d) If the company has meanwhile gone into **liquidation** so that its creditors have the first claim on its remaining assets.

However he does not lose his rights merely because he fails to make enquiries.

Claim for damages for deceit

7.23 Those who issue an untrue prospectus may be liable to pay damages. An action for deceit is based on the same essential points as rescission except that:

(a) The claim is **against** the **directors** etc. who issued the prospectus and not usually against the company.

(b) **Fraud** on their part must be **proved.** An untrue statement is made fraudulently if it is made knowingly, without belief in its truth or recklessly (careless whether it be true or false). It is difficult for an allottee to show how much the directors actually know at the time and for that reason an action for deceit is not often successful.

Derry v Peak 1889
The facts: A private Act of Parliament was passed to authorise the company to run trams in Plymouth. The Act permitted horse-drawn trams and, with the consent of the Board of Trade, steam trams. The need to obtain this consent arose from an amendment made to the original Bill after it was first submitted to Parliament. The directors, who attached no importance to this change, assumed that the consent would be granted on application and stated in the prospectus merely that the company had statutory authority to run either horse-drawn or steam trams. They were sued for damages for deceit.

Decision: There was no deceit (the formula above was laid down as the definition for fraud) since the directors, however careless, honestly believed that their statement was true.

7.24 As a general rule only the person who has been **entered** in the **register of members** as the allottee can sue for deceit. However if a purchaser of the securities from the allottee can show that the prospectus was itself, or formed part of, a plan to deceive and defraud investors generally, he can recover damages for deceit on the basis that the prospectus was intended to deceive him: *Andrews v Mockford 1896.*

7.25 An action for deceit is against those who were responsible for the issue of a prospectus with intent to defraud:

(a) The **directors** (and possibly experts or promoters if parties to the fraud)

(b) The **issuing house** if the prospectus was an offer for sale.

As it is, the directors who actually prepare the prospectus they will usually be jointly liable. The issuing house is only liable for their fraud if it is aware of the facts which made it a case of fraud.

(c) The **company,** since the directors are its agents in issuing the prospectus

7.26 As a result of *Hedley Byrne v Heller & Partners 1964* it may now be possible to recover damages for **negligent mis-statement** in circumstances such as arose in *Derry v Peak*. The Misrepresentation Act 1967 also gives the right to recover damages for negligent misrepresentation - an untrue statement made without reasonable grounds. However, the statutory remedy given by the FSA, as described above, is a much more effective remedy in cases where rescission is no longer possible and compensation for loss is claimed instead. The claimant has only to show that the prospectus contained an untrue or misleading statement, or an omission. He is not concerned with the intricate rules on liability for negligence or misrepresentation.

8 DRAFTING ISSUE DOCUMENTS

8.1 Much work will be required. The company secretary should, as soon as the plan for the issue has been agreed, prepare his own schedule of things to be done, including documents to be drafted.

8.2 As a summary illustration of the work arising from a simple issue, the following is a list of the documents which may be required.

(a) **Financial**

- Accountants' reports on working capital and profit forecast figures
- Bank confirmation (to be provided by the bank) of existing company indebtedness to the bank, and promised facilities to the company

- Estimate of expenses (itemised)

(b) **Issue arrangements**

- Underwriting agreement
- Letter of allotment
- Share certificate
- Listing particulars (in compliance with the Listing Rules)

(c) **Internal company procedure**

- Minutes of board meeting(s)
- Notice of EGM
- Proxy card
- Circular to members
- Documents for Companies Registry as appropriate
- Adoption as a resolution by the board of directors of the Listing Agreement

(d) **Stock Exchange/UK Listing Authority**

- Application for listing (and supporting documents)
- Letter regarding working capital
- Declaration (of compliance) at completion

(e) **Publicity**

- Press advertisements
- Press announcements
- Documents (if any) for inspection by public

This list is not exhaustive, as circumstances vary, but will indicate the range of what has to be planned and prepared. Consent will also be needed from other parties - solicitors, brokers, bank and auditors to their names appearing in the listing particulars.

8.3 Listing particulars may involve much time and effort. At an early stage the draft, in printers' proof form, is submitted to the UK Listing Authority, which is likely to make comments (usually requests for clarification or additional detail) which will entail further revision. It is not uncommon for this basic document to go through as many as a dozen successive revisions. Once it has been submitted to the underwriters, the text is virtually 'frozen'; for that reason underwriting cannot be arranged until the end of the process.

8.4 Even if there is a rights issue, for which only abbreviated listing particulars, or none at all, are required, it will be necessary to draft the following documents.

(a) An **explanatory circular** to shareholders, giving the reasons for the issue, an explanation of the details of the issue (so that shareholders may understand the options available to them and what they have to do) and the prospects of the company.

(b) The **provisional allotment letter**, or other **document of title** to be issued to members, including forms for renunciation and registration, the timetable and amounts due for payment of subscription money. The Stock Exchange has guidance notes ('*Temporary Documents of Title*') on the required form and content of these documents.

All such documents will of course have to be submitted to and approved by the Stock Exchange, so adequate time should be allowed for this.

8.5 In preparing documents, the secretary should take the utmost care to protect the confidential information which they may contain. In the early stages it is often wise to omit from the draft a key figure, such as the projected issue price, and insert it only in the final drafts or proofs.

Role of the broker

8.6 The UK Listing Authority requires a company applying for listing to deal with the authority through the company's broker or '**sponsor**'. The broker will also advise on Listing Authority requirements, and may be concerned in the underwriting arrangements.

8.7 He may also assist in consulting with officials on making the issue at the impact date. Many major financial institutions, such as insurance companies, have only so much **cash** for **investment** over a period. An orderly market is best secured if investment opportunities, through public issues, take their turn 'in the queue'.

Role of the bank

8.8 Neither a company nor its usual registrars are likely to be equipped to cope with the demands of a public issue. It is usual to contract the work out to the new issue department of a '**receiving bank**' which is doing this kind of work for different companies all through the year. The board's authority will be required for the decision of whom to use.

8.9 The bank should be involved throughout the **issue process**. There should be liaison at an early stage on the title and operation of the accounts, and to reach agreement on general procedures. The bank should receive copies of the draft issue documents.

Role of allotment committee

8.10 The board will normally delegate authority to an allotment committee who will supervise the issue. The committee usually comprises the company secretary, company registrar and (one) director. The full board will however be responsible for approving the circular and listing particulars.

Other specialist services

8.11 Many companies retain the services of press and public relations firms who arrange with newspapers to reserve space for advertisements (listing particulars, if at full length, can take several pages of space), press announcements, etc.

Timetable prior to issue of particulars

8.12 At least **10 clear business days** before the date of publication of listing particulars (in lieu of a prospectus) a large number of documents are submitted to the UK Listing Authority, including (among many other things) the following:

- The listing particulars
- Circulars and formal notices
- Application form
- Letters of allotment
- Share certificates etc

In practice the draft documents would be submitted much more than 10 days in advance of publication, since alterations will almost certainly be required in order to obtain approval.

8.13 **Two days** before the application for listing is considered, the formal application for **listing** must be submitted to the **UK Listing Authority**, and the formal application for **admission to** trading must be submitted to the Stock Exchange, together with two copies of any listing particulars and other prescribed documentation. At this stage the listing particulars will have been advertised but no new shares will have been allotted. Unless there is some utterly unexpected hitch of a serious nature, the grant of listing will follow. However, it is at the final, formal stage that listing is granted. On the proposed publication date the company must pay the listing fee and the first year's annual fee.

9 ACTION AT AND AFTER THE TIME OF ISSUE

9.1 What has to be done at the time of issue depends on the type of issue. If there is a rights issue, the first step is the **despatch of provisional allotment letters** to members (or debenture holders, as the case may be) on the register. Thereafter the receiving bank, with which the company secretary must be in constant touch, will be processing requests for split letters of allotment, payment of sums due, requests for registration etc.

9.2 If the issue takes the form of an offer of new securities to the public, or an offer for sale, one of the major tasks is to consider the **number of applications** (and the total of securities applied for) on the appointed day for 'the opening of the lists', usually the third clear day after the publication of the relevant advertisements. The board of the company will have to decide, if the issue is **oversubscribed**, the basis on which securities are to be allotted; the receiving bank will then issue letters of allotment, and deal with the subscription moneys.

9.3 It is important that the result of an issue is made public in an **orderly fashion** and at the earliest possible time. If it is necessary to scale down the allotment, as a result of the issue being oversubscribed, the **Companies Announcement Office** and the press should be notified of the basis of allotment, the date when letters of allotment will be posted, and the date for despatch of letters of regret (with returned application moneys). It sometimes happens that an applicant relies on this information and proceeds to sell his allotted securities before he receives his letter of allotment. If so, he has acted at his own risk, if he finds that he misunderstood his position.

9.4 The Listing Rules have requirements as to the documents to be furnished to it 'as soon as practicable' after the grant of listing. These include, as appropriate:

(a) In an intermediaries offer, from each intermediary the names and addresses of its **clients** with whom it placed securities and details of securities allocated to each client

(b) Where securities are offered with a cash alternative, a statement of the **total amount of securities** issued; where different from the number of securities which were the subject of the application, the aggregate number of securities in issue

(c) A **formal notice** where only a final draft has been lodged and a document of title where a draft document has been lodged

(d) If securities have been issued as consideration for the compulsory acquisition of listed shares, under Companies Act 1985 s 429, a certified copy of the **statutory notice** (of intention to acquire), given under s 429

(e) In an introduction a statement of the **opening market price** of the listed securities (plus payment of any additional fee due to The Stock Exchange, if the price exceeded the issue price)

(f) If there are **bearer documents of title**, a statement from **security printers** (as to safeguards required by Chapter 7 of the Listing Rules)

(g) A written request for **re-imbursement of listing fees** if the number of such securities issued is less than the number which was the subject of application

(h) A **comprehensive declaration** (in the form of Schedule 6) by a director or by the Secretary, concerning due compliance of the company in connection with various legal and Listing requirements incidental to the listing and related transactions

Other documents **if necessary** such as agreements, documents of title and accounts may also be requested.

9.5 Once the allotment has been made, and payment received, the normal formalities will be required to complete the issue: entry in the register of members, issue of share certificates, and filing of a return of allotments on form G88(2) with the registrar.

Shelf documents

9.6 This system was introduced in 1999. It allows issuers who have been listed for at least 12 months to publish a shelf document on an annual basis, containing much of the information required in listing particulars. If during the next 12 months the issuer wishes to issue and list further shares, all it will need to publish is a short issue note containing the information required to complete and update the shelf document.

Exercise

What documents are likely to be required when a new issue is made?

Solution

Look back at paragraph 8.2

Chapter roundup

- A **public issue** may take the form of an offer to the public, an **offer for sale**, a **placing**, an **intermediaries offer**, an **introduction**, a **capitalisation issue** or a **vendor placing**.
- Before a public issue is made, it is important to decide on: the issue **price**, the necessity for **underwriting**, the issue (or impact) **date** and the **date** for an extraordinary general meeting.
- The **contents** of listing particulars are determined by Part (IV) FSA and the Listing Rules; those of a prospectus for a non-listing issue are contained in Public Offers of Securities Regulations.
- The company secretary has a very important role to play before, at the time of and after the issue date.

Test your knowledge

1 What is the normal basis of offering securities in a rights issue? (see para 3.3)
2 What is (a) an introduction and (b) a vendor placing? (3.11, 3.13)
3 By whom is a company likely to be advised in preparing to make a public issue? (4.1)
4 Explain how the system of tender prices is operated. (4.8)
5 Explain the terms on which an issue is usually underwritten. (4.12)
6 Why might an extraordinary general meeting be required prior to a public issue? (4.19)
7 What must be contained in a set of listing particulars? (5.5)
8 What criteria must companies trading on AIM satisfy at all times? (6.19)
9 Which people are responsible for a publicly quoted company's listing particulars? (7.3)
10 What is the role of the company's broker or sponsor in connection with a new issue? (8.6)

Now try illustrative questions 19 to 20 at the end of the Study Text

Part C
Share registration function

Chapter 18

ALLOTMENT AND ISSUE OF SHARES

This chapter covers the following topics.

Introduction

The basic legal rules on the allotment of shares are much more restrictive on an issue by a public than by a private company. When a public company issues shares, usually to a large number of persons through the market, there is a much more elaborate issue procedure.

The issue of a series of debentures or of a debenture stock follows much the same procedure as an issue of shares, but the legal rules which regulate the issue of shares do not apply to the issue of debentures, except as regards prospectuses.

1 DEFINITION OF ALLOTMENT AND ISSUE OF SHARES

1.1 **Allotment** occurs when 'a person acquires the **unconditional right** to be entered in the register of members' in respect of the shares allotted to him: s 738.

1.2 Allotment is a form of **contract** in which an application (the offer) is made to the company for its shares and the allotment (acceptance of the offer) follows. The moment of allotment is usually when the directors consider the application and formally resolve to allot shares in response to it, with the result that authority is given for entering the name of the allottee in the register of members as the holder of the shares. If the directors impose some condition, such as the receipt of subscription moneys not yet paid, the allotment follows when the condition is satisfied.

1.3 **Issue**' is a wider concept, which is not defined by statute. Shares are said to be issued when the formalities are completed and the allottee has received a share certificate or other evidence of his title to the shares. It is the common and convenient practice to use the word 'issue' to cover the whole process by which the ownership of new shares passes to a shareholder.

2 PRELIMINARY CONSIDERATIONS 12/98, 6/99, 12/99, 6/00

2.1 In planning the allotment of shares by any company, private or public, there are a number of basic questions to consider as follows.

(a) Has the company **sufficient unissued shares** to make up the issue now proposed? In other words, would the proposed issue of shares exceed the authorised share capital?

(b) Has the board of directors the **authority required** to allot shares in the manner proposed?

(c) What does the company wish to do about **pre-emption rights**?

(d) Will the company **receive consideration** of a value at least equal to the nominal value of the shares to be allotted?

We will look at each of these points in detail.

Unissued shares

2.2 The memorandum fixes a limit on the amount of share capital (the authorised share capital) which the company may issue: s 2(5), although this may be increased through the procedure laid down by s 121 and by the articles (Table A Article 32).

2.3 The secretary should refer to the memorandum and to the articles, to discover whether the company has **sufficient unissued shares** of the appropriate class. If necessary a general meeting must be called to increase the authorised share capital by the creation of new shares, or to reorganise the existing capital. Under the normal form of articles (Table A Article 32) both of these changes would require only an ordinary resolution.

2.4 If the authorised share capital is to be increased the following is necessary.

(a) **Form G123** (see Appendix 10) and a signed copy of the ordinary resolution must be sent to the registrar within 15 days.

(b) A note of the change should be appended to the **capital clause** of the memorandum, and a copy sent to the registrar within 15 days.

(c) Other action will be taken in connection with **alterations** to existing copies of the memorandum, as explained in the earlier chapter.

2.5 If unissued share capital is to be subdivided into shares of smaller denomination the following applies.

(a) The **articles** should first be **reviewed** to ensure that they contain appropriate provisions (voting, dividends etc) for shares of smaller amount.

(b) **Form 122** (see Appendix 15) must be delivered within a month.

(c) A **note of the change** should be appended to the capital clause of the memorandum, and a copy sent to the registrar within 15 days.

(d) Action will be taken to **alter existing copies** of the memorandum.

Authority to allot **12/98, 6/99**

2.6 Under Section 80 and Section 80A of the Companies Act the directors may be given the power to allot shares either by the articles or by ordinary resolution in general meeting. (which must be filed within 15 days).

2.7 The authority to allot shares must specify the following.

(a) The **maximum number** of shares that the directors are permitted to allot

(b) A **date no more** than **five years** from the grant of the authority, on which the authority will expire: s 80(4)

Authority to allot: ss 80 and 80A

2.8 **Relevant securities**, to which ss 80 and 80A relate, comprise the following.

(a) **All shares** other than those of the original subscribers to the memorandum and shares allotted pursuant to an employees' shares scheme.

(b) Any **right** to subscribe for, or convert any security into, shares (unless to be allotted under an employees' shares scheme). This prevents evasion by the issue of convertible debentures or the grant of options to take up shares: both are of course permissible if duly authorised under s 80.

2.9 A private company may pass an **elective (100%) resolution** conferring authority to allot shares for an **indefinite period**, or for **a fixed period** of more than **five years**: s 80A. If an election under s 80A ceases to have effect and it was given five years or more before this time, then the authority expires forthwith. Otherwise, it has effect as if it had been given for a fixed five year period. Such an authority may be revoked, varied or renewed by the company in general meeting.

2.10 If the shares are allotted without the authority required by ss 80 or 80A, the allotment is still valid, but any director who has knowingly and wilfully been in contravention is liable to a fine.

2.11 If the authority is about to expire the directors can, provided that they act in good faith, make an offer or enter into an agreement to allot shares; they are then authorised to do so after the expiry of their authority.

2.12 If the ordinary resolution is passed to give, vary or revoke authority under ss 80 or 80A, a printed copy signed by the chairman must be delivered to the registrar within 15 days: s 380(4)(f).

2.13 The authority may be given either **generally** or for a **specific allotment**. Once given a general authority the directors can exercise it without needing to consult the general meeting. But a **general meeting** will be needed (unless a private company uses the new written resolution procedure of s 381A-C):

(a) If **no authority** has been **given in advance** or if it has been given subject to conditions or restrictions which deny to the directors authority to make the allotment which they now propose

(b) If **general authority** given previously has **expired** by lapse or time or has been fully used by previous allotments made under it

Pre-emption rights: s 89

2.14 Pre-emption rights are given to shareholders by s 89. This provision requires:

(a) A company who proposes to allot **equity securities** must first offer them to **each existing shareholder**. This is the right of pre-emption or right of first refusal.

(b) The company must make the offer on the **same terms** or as favourable terms as it would to third parties, so not to prejudice the existing shareholders.

(c) The company must offer a **proportion** of those securities so as to maintain that shareholders proportionate holding in the company.

Such an offer is known as a **rights issue**.

2.15 **Equity securities** are defined as either of the following.

(a) Any **relevant shares**, with the exclusion of two categories.

(i) Subscribers' shares, which they agreed to take by signing the memorandum

(ii) Bonus shares (which will be discussed later)

(b) **Rights** to subscribe for, or to convert securities into, **relevant shares** in the company.

2.16 'Relevant shares' in this context are defined (s 94) as shares **other than** the following.

(a) Shares which as respects dividends and capital carry a right to participate only up to a specified amount in a distribution. This means that shares, typically preference shares, which carry limited rights in respect both of dividends and return of capital are not relevant shares, and therefore not equity securities for the purposes of s 89. However, participating preference shares, as described in an earlier chapter, are equity securities, since they have an **unlimited** right to participate in dividends.

(b) Shares which have been, or are to be, allotted in **pursuance** of an **employees' share scheme**. There is a separate definition of 'relevant employee shares' (shares which would be relevant in all respects but that they are held by a person who acquired them through an employees' share scheme). 'Relevant employee shares' *are* included in pre-emption rights.

2.17 For example if a company with four million shares already in issue wants to issue a further one million shares to raise cash, the company must first offer the new shares to existing shareholders in proportion to their shareholding. In this example the rights issue should be of one new share for every four shares currently held.

2.18 The company may not allot those securities to any other party until it has complied with the provisions set out above and the offer has been accepted, refused or the time to accept the offer has expired: s 89(1)(b).

2.19 The company secretary must ensure **compliance** with the **delivery of offer** provisions. It should be noted that close attention should be paid, at all times, to provisions regarding service of notices, offers etc. If proper service is not made then the transaction may be subject to dispute for that reason alone; see later for the appropriate procedure.

2.20 The memorandum or articles may make special provision regarding rights of pre-emption. Close attention must be paid to these terms.

2.21 Under the statutory procedure s 89, any shares which members may acquire in this way are disregarded in calculating entitlements and making any subsequent **statutory offer** of shares under s 89.

2.22 If no provision is made or under the specified terms of the memorandum or articles the company does not allot all the shares it wishes to allot, then the **statutory pre-emption rights** apply but only to allotments of **equity securities**.

2.23 The right of pre-emption, however, 'does not apply to a particular allotment of equity securities if these are, or are to be, wholly or partly paid up otherwise than in cash': s 89(4). This is an important point. It means that a takeover bid in which the bidder offers its own shares in exchange for **shares** of the target company, and an allotment of shares in payment of the price of **property** which the company is to acquire, are *not* subject to s 89.

Disapplication of pre-emption rights

6/99

2.24 If the directors are given general authority to allot shares under s 80 they may at the same time and for the same period be authorised to allot shares without regard to the standard pre-emption rights of members: s 95(1). That authority may be given by the **articles** or by **special resolution**. When shares are issued for cash to 'outside' buyers in this way, existing shareholders forfeit their pre-emptive rights to the new shareholders.

2.25 Special statutory provision is made providing that a **private company** may, by its memorandum or articles **exclude** the statutory pre-emption rights **permanently**, once and for all: s 91. Any such exclusion should be explicit, and preferably refer to s 89 as excluded. For example the articles may provide as follows.

> 'In accordance with Section 91(1) of the Act, Section 89(1) and 90(1) to (6) (inclusive) of the Act shall not apply to the company.'

2.26 As explained in connection with s 80, it is common practice to pass a resolution at each annual general meeting to authorise the directors to allot shares. If desired, it may be (or be followed by) a **special resolution** which at the same time **disapplies** the **pre-emption** rights generally.

2.27 If the **directors** have authority to allot shares but currently lack authority to override s 89 on pre-emption rights, the necessary authority may be given to them by **special resolution** relating to a specified allotment.

2.28 In that event, together with the notice convening the meeting to consider the special resolution, the directors must issue a **statement to members** giving three items of information:

- Their reasons for the proposal
- The amount which an allotment in disregard of pre-emption rights will raise
- Their justification of that amount: s 95(5)

2.29 If the directors allot shares or grant rights in breach of the statutory pre-emption rights of members, they are liable to compensate the members for their loss, provided that the claim against them is made within two years: s 91.

The Stock Exchange rules on disapplication of pre-emption rights

2.30 A disapplication of pre-emption rights is effective so long as the authority to allot under s 80 is effective, which may be for up to **five years**.

2.31 The significance of the relaxation of the Stock Exchange rules is that companies can issue shares for cash without having to bear the high costs of a rights issue - they can place shares for cash at a higher price than they might have been able to obtain from a rights issue.

Exercise

(a) Define and explain the term 'pre-emption rights'.
(b) Is it possible to exclude pre-emption rights?

Solution

(a) If a company issues ordinary shares for cash, it has a statutory obligation to offer those shares to holders of similar shares in proportion to their holdings: s 89. If, for example, a company has an issued ordinary share capital of 400,000 £1 shares and it intends to issue 100,000 ordinary shares for cash, it should first offer the new shares to the existing shareholders in the ratio of one new share for every four shares already held. The shares must be offered on terms at least as favourable as they would be offered to third parties.

(b) A private company may by its memorandum or articles permanently exclude these rules so that there is no statutory right of first refusal: s 91.

Any company may, by special resolution, resolve that pre-emption rights shall not apply: s 95. Such a resolution to 'disapply' the right may either:

(i) Be combined with the grant to directors of authority to issue shares under s 80. It is then restricted to a maximum duration of five years; or

(ii) It may simply permit an offer of shares to be made for cash to a non-member (without first offering the shares to members) on a particular occasion.

In case (ii) the directors, in inviting members to 'disapply' the right of first refusal, must issue a circular setting out their reasons, the price at which the shares are to be offered direct to a non-member and their justification for that price.

Consideration for shares

6/00

2.32 **No company** may allot shares at a **discount** (for a consideration of **less value** than the **nominal value** of the shares): s 100. In other words, a company cannot allot shares with a nominal value of £1, say, for a consideration of less than £1 per share.

2.33 Any consideration may be paid in **money or money's worth**, which includes goodwill or know-how: s 99. However, shares which the subscribers to the memorandum agree to take must be paid up in cash: s 106.

Private companies

2.34 A **private company** is free to allot shares as **partly-paid** to any extent (even nil paid), and to **value non-cash** consideration **for shares** at whatever amount the directors, if acting in good faith, deem appropriate: *Re Wragg Ltd 1897.*

2.35 In spite of the decision in *Wragg's* case, directors who do not value assets (acquired for shares) in the company's books at the purchase price risk being reproached with bad faith, and so made liable.

Public companies

2.36 A **public company** which allots shares for a non-cash consideration must have the consideration **professionally valued,** unless in a takeover, in which the consideration is the shares of the target company. It is relatively easy to evade this procedure if the company purchases the property for cash and the vendors then apply the money in paying for the shares which the company allots to them.

2.37 A valuation is also prescribed (subject to some exceptions) when a **public company** acquires assets in excess of one tenth of the nominal value of its issued capital from the following persons:

(a) The **subscribers** to the memorandum, within two years of obtaining a certificate under s 117 (that is, a certificate to commence business as a public company)

(b) From **members, within two years** of **re-registration** of a private as a public company: s 104.

This procedure too is of little practical importance since there are ways of avoiding it.

2.38 If a public company allots shares, the time of receipt of the consideration is regulated by law.

(a) At the time of allotment the company must receive consideration equal to **at least one quarter** of the **nominal value** of the shares, plus the **whole** of any **premium**: s 101.

(b) If the consideration includes an **undertaking** to be performed at a later date, the time fixed for performance and the actual performance must be within the ensuing five years: s 102.

2.39 A **public company** may not at any time accept as consideration for its shares an **undertaking** to do work or perform services: s 99. **Past services** are **no consideration** at all, hence (b) above applies mainly to contracts for the delivery of property, including goodwill or know-how, at a future date. However, if past services resulted in a valid and acknowledged debt which the company discharges by allotting shares then this is valid.

Share premium

2.40 A company whose shares have a market value in excess of their nominal value will usually find it advantageous to issue new shares at a **premium** over the nominal value; by this means it maximises the ratio of new assets to increased share capital (to be serviced by dividend payments etc.).

2.41 If the shares are allotted in the first instance to existing members on a rights issue basis, it is generally held that the company and its directors have no duty to obtain the maximum premium, or any premium at all. It is argued that there is nothing wrong in permitting existing members to obtain new shares at a price below their market value (provided that it is at least equal to the **nominal value** of the shares).

2.42 If the shares are issued at a premium, whether in terms of a cash issue price, or the excess value of assets acquired over the nominal value of shares issued in payment for them, the premium so obtained must be **credited** (except in a few, very limited types of reconstruction) to the **share premium account**, as fixed capital: s 130.

3 ALLOTMENT PROCEDURES — 12/98

3.1 The procedure for allotting shares may be very simple or, in a public issue as mentioned above, very complicated. The procedure should always be adapted to the needs of the company and of the particular issue. In outline, the possible stages are as follows.

(a) An **invitation** (a prospectus) may be issued to attract applications for shares from the public.

(b) The company receives **completed applications**, which may be accompanied by cheques for the whole or part of the subscription money on the shares applied for.

(c) The directors (if duly authorised under s 80) **resolve to allot** shares to the applicants; this is minuted.

(d) **Letters of allotment** (alternatively 'letters of acceptance') or letters of regret (with a refund of prepayments) are sent to the applicants.

(e) The **names** of the allottees and **particulars** of the shares allotted to them are **entered in** the **register of members**.

(f) **Share certificates** are later **issued** to the allottees.

(g) A **return of allotments** is delivered to the registrar (Form G88(2)). If shares are to be allotted for non-cash consideration, the written agreement setting out the terms should be filed with the Registrar. Alternatively if there is no written agreement, the terms should be set out and submitted to the Registrar on Form G 88(3).

3.2 However, in the simplest case it suffices to have a board resolution to allot, an entry in the register of members, and (usually) the issue of a share certificate; plus, of course, payment for the shares, and a return of allotments. The documentation is merely an optional means of providing evidence of what is done.

An invitation to subscribe

3.3 This stage should be handled with care. Any written invitation or particulars distributed beyond the immediate circle of directors, existing members and employees of the company may well be a **prospectus**: s 744. Prospectuses and listing particulars are covered in detail in a later chapter.

Applications for shares

3.4 If there are to be written applications (essential, if the applications are numerous), it is convenient for the company to provide **standard letters**, which may be very simple, or

printed application forms. These standard application forms can be used by investors wishing to subscribe for shares.

Allotment

3.5 A suitable resolution would be as follows:

> 'That 1,000 shares of £1 each [numbered ... to ...] be allotted at par fully paid to the persons listed below in the proportions set opposite each name respectively, the subscription moneys in respect thereof having been received, and that the Secretary is authorised to make the appropriate entries in the register of members and to prepare share certificates for issue to the said persons.
>
> *Name* *Number of shares allotted*

3.6 If the allottees are too numerous for inclusion individually in the resolution, it should refer to allotment sheets initialled by the Chairman for identification. If the shares have identifying serial numbers, a column should be added for the serial numbers of the shares allotted to each person.

3.7 As mentioned earlier, a company can allot shares without receiving the full amount due on them at that stage, but a **public company** is subject to the **minimum amount** to be paid at this stage: s 101. If the shares are allotted at a premium (as explained later) the issue price should be specified.

Allotment letters

3.8 There is no legal requirement for the issue of letters to inform the allottees that shares have been allotted to them. If allotment letters are issued, pending the issue of share certificates, they may be no more than a simple statement that so many shares have been allotted and that share certificates will be issued by a given date.

3.9 However, in a **public issue**, it is standard practice to send out elaborate **renounceable letters of allotment**, mainly to provide successful applicants with the means of selling all or part of their new shares, in the interval between allotment and the despatch of share certificates, usually some weeks later.

3.10 The same is true of rights issues, as well as issues to the investing public in general. Offers of securities by way of a rights issue are **normally** required (by the Stock Exchange) to be made by means of a renounceable letter or some other similar negotiable document, which the shareholder can sell on, if he wishes, to someone else.

3.11 Accordingly a letter of allotment may include additional pages or parts of pages, which may be completed by inserting a signature and some brief but essential particulars. The basic elements are as follows.

(a) **Renunciation Form** ('Form X') by which the allottee renounces his right to the shares allotted to him in favour of the person who presents the form below.

(b) **Registration Application Form** ('Form Y') by which the holder of the 'renounced' allotment letter (see above) applies for registration of the shares in designated name(s).

3.12 If the allottee (or a subsequent holder of the renounced letter) wishes to divide the shares allotted, for purposes of sale in smaller numbers, he applies to the company for the issue of **'split' letters** (with specified numbers of shares in each) in exchange for the original letter, which is surrendered.

3.13 The explanatory part of the letter provides information of the **procedure** to be followed to complete these steps, together with a **detailed timetable** and information of the due **dates for payment** of instalments (if any) of the total amount due on the shares. In the context of the Listing Rules, a renounceable allotment letter is 'a **temporary document of title**' and its content and layout is prescribed in detail to meet Listing requirements.

3.14 It is common practice for companies to retain the services of the 'new issue department' of a bank as its agent in the work.

3.15 The timetable set out in the letter specifies a **closing date** by which any renouncee must deliver the letter (with the Forms X, Y duly completed) for registration. If the letter is not returned, the company enters the name of the original allottee in its register at the closing date for renunciation.

3.16 The advantage to the company of providing a facility for transfer of new shares without registration is that, when the register is made up to include the new shares at the expiry of the renunciation period (usually six weeks), the ownership of the shares will have reached a normal degree of stability after the initial flurry of adjustment.

4 BONUS ISSUES 12/99

4.1 A **capitalisation (or 'bonus' or 'scrip') issue** is also an allotment of shares to existing members in ratio to their present holdings. It differs from a rights issue as follows.

(a) The company merely **increases** the **nominal value** of its issued share capital by allotting unissued shares, say in the ratio of one new share for each share held, which will double the issued and paid up capital.

(b) No extra funds are raised by the issue.

4.2 In a **bonus issue** the new shares are fully paid up by applying company reserves to the payment of shares which are then allotted to members. The reserves which are capitalised may either be distributable profits or non-distributable reserves, such as share premium account or capital redemption reserve.

4.3 The purpose of a bonus issue is usually to bring the issued capital of the company more into line with its underlying asset value. If, for example, the company has an issued capital of, say, £100,000 in £1 shares, and its profits and assets suggest that it has a market value as an entity of about £1 million, the market value of the shares may be £10 each. The balance sheet will include substantial reserves. If there is a bonus issue of 1 for 1, each shareholder will have twice as many shares as before but their market value will be about £5 per share. This change may make them easier to buy and sell, and it will probably enhance the company's commercial standing, since the issue is a mark of confidence in its position and prospects.

Preliminary considerations

4.4 A bonus issue can only be made if the company's articles allow, which they usually do.

4.5 The company must also consider:

- Whether it has **sufficient unissued** shares for the issue
- Which **reserves** will be **applied for** the capitalisation
- What is the most **convenient ratio** of new shares to existing shares

Unless the new shares are to be allotted on the basis of 1 for 1, or some multiple (in new shares) of each existing share, say 5 for 1, there may be problems over fractions. The usual procedure for dealing with this problem is to provide that fractional entitlements to shares will be sold (in complete shares) and the proceeds, in cash, distributed to the members entitled to the fractions.

4.6 The company must also ensure that the directors have **authority** to **allot** the relevant shares under s 80.

4.7 Providing the above matters have been considered, the bonus issue can be approved. This is done by an ordinary resolution of members in general meeting.

4.8 An appropriate ordinary resolution is rather lengthy but its sense is not difficult to grasp. It should cover the following points.

(a) The **decision** to **capitalise** should be stated.

(b) **Specified amount(s)** from specified balances in the latest balance sheet should be stated, to be applied in paying up (usually in full) a specified number of unissued shares.

(c) These unissued shares should be **allotted** to members **in a specified ratio** to their existing holdings (on the register at a 'record date').

(d) There should be provision for **sale** of **any fractions** and the distribution of the proceeds in cash.

(e) A **named person** (often a director or the secretary) should be authorised to enter into a contract with the company, on behalf of members, for the allotment to them of the shares to which they will be entitled.

Non-renounceable and renounceable allotments

4.9 Members can be allowed to renounce all or some of the shares to be issued.

4.10 If the shares are not renounceable, the procedures are straightforward.

(a) The directors **resolve** to allot the shares.

(b) The **share certificates** will be **prepared and issued**, and the register of members amended.

(c) A **return of allotments**, Form 88(2) must be filed with Companies House within one month of allotment, together with Form 88(3) because the issue is not for cash.

4.11 If the shares are renounceable, a written renounceable letter of allotment would normally be dispatched to each member, together with a draft letter of verification and registration application form. These documents must give a **time limit** for **renunciation**. Unless appropriate other restrictions are put on renunciation (for example renunciation only allowed to existing members), the offer may qualify as an offer to the public, not allowed for private companies.

4.12 After the renunciation the directors will meet to allot shares either to the member or to the renouncees.

4.13 Once shares have been allotted, the administrative procedures listed above for non-renounceable shares will also be required.

4.14 If the company has more than one class of shares, the issue of new shares on a rights or bonus issue basis to the class of shares entitled (always ordinary) may alter the balance of voting rights and possibly dividends between classes. It is established that this is *not* a 'variation' of the rights of the class which suffers a diminution of its influence. However it is a point for consideration and possibly for some change in the articles to preserve the existing balance.

5 RIGHTS ISSUES

6/99, 12/99

5.1 As mentioned above, s 89 requires that existing shareholders must have pre-emption rights unless the articles or a special resolution dictate otherwise.

5.2 Assuming the shares are to be allocated according to the requirements of s 89, an ordinary resolution will not normally be required for the issue. However a resolution in general meeting will be required if the articles make provision or if the articles lay down a detailed pre-emption procedure which is not suitable for the current issues. **Resolutions** will also be **required** if the company lacks sufficient **authorised share capital** or the **directors lack authority** to make the allotment, as with other issues.

Procedures for a rights issue

5.3 When meeting to discuss the rights issue, directors will have to decide whether members will be permitted to **renounce** the offer in favour of other people or will only be allowed to **accept** or **reject the offer themselves**. They will also need to decide the offer price, which will as an inducement generally be below what the market price would be if the shares were offered directly to outsiders.

5.4 The directors should also draw up a timetable in conformity with the time limits set for the statutory procedure.

5.5 A '**record date**' is then selected; this should be not more than 28 days before the date on which the offer will be made. Every member as at that date is entitled to participate in the offer in respect of his '**relevant shares**', including '**relevant employee shares**' held under an employees' share scheme. The following do *not* participate.

(a) Members who hold **only preference shares** (other than participating preference shares, which because of their unlimited right to dividend are 'relevant').

(b) Persons who hold **convertible debentures**, or options to subscribe for shares, which they have not converted into actual shareholdings at the record date. They are not 'members'.

5.6 The offer must conform to the following regulations: s 90.

(a) It must be **in writing**, and in the form specified by the Listing Rules, if the company is listed.

(b) It must be **delivered personally** or by **post**. In particular cases, such as joint holdings, the same rules apply as are contained in Table A Articles 111-116 for sending notices to members. If there are holders of share warrants, or members who have no registered address in the UK, a notice must be published in the *London Gazette* giving an address where a copy may be obtained or inspected.

(c) It must specify a period of **not less than 21 days** within which the offer may be accepted and should also give details about payment. There should be a statement that failure to reply will cause the offer to lapse automatically.

(d) It must be an offer on a '**rights basis**' in proportion to the member's holding, as a fraction of the holdings of all members eligible to receive the offer. It should state the number of shares provisionally allotted, the issue price, and that the shares will rank equally for future dividends.

5.7 In the normal course the company must wait until the period of the offer has expired. But if, before its expiry, the offers made have been accepted or expressly refused by **every member**, the company may then allot the shares to outsiders, or in different proportions between members. A member has no **right** to be offered shares which other members have not accepted.

5.8 Once the offer has expired, the directors will meet to consider the results and approve any renunciations. The remaining procedures are as for a bonus issue.

6 REQUIREMENTS FOR LISTED COMPANIES 6/99

6.1 The basic requirements as regards listing particulars, documents to be filed etc are summarised in Chapter 17.

Bonus issues

6.2 No new **listing particulars** need to be published for a bonus issue. A circular must be sent by the company to the shareholders giving information on the issue and the rights of the new shares including dividends.

Rights issues

6.3 Where shareholders entitled to a rights issue do not sell their rights and do not subscribe to the shares, their **rights** are **aggregated** and sold on the Stock Exchange in nil paid form. The proceeds less expenses are distributed to the provisional allottees.

7 GRANTING RIGHTS TO ALLOTMENT

7.1 There are a number of devices by which a company may grant to others the right to have shares allotted to them, at their option and usually on pre-arranged terms. These include the following:

- Convertible debentures (as described in the later chapter on loan capital)
- Warrants to subscribe for shares
- Option certificates or subscription rights attached to other company securities

7.2 The common feature of these types of security, which may in appropriate cases be dealt with on the Stock Exchange, is that in issuing them the company does not immediately allot the shares to which they relate. However, from the time of issue the company is contractually bound to allot the shares if later called upon to do so, on the terms agreed. As indicated in the earlier part of this chapter, the statutory restrictions on allotment of shares, and the statutory shareholders' pre-emption rights, are defined to prevent the use of these devices to evade statutory rules. Subject to that, and if the articles make proper provision for their issue, there is no objection to their use.

7.3 In all three categories the investor who exercises his rights has to pay for his shares.

(a) In the case of convertible debentures, his money is already in the **hands** of the **company**; by exercising his right of conversion, under the terms agreed, the following occurs (in theory):

eg. Xerova ⇒ warrants.

(i) He calls on the company to repay the debenture.

(ii) He authorises the company simultaneously to retain the money and use it to pay for the shares for which he is now applying.

(b) Warrants and option certificates are usually issued in support of, and in association with, some other transaction, such as a **takeover bid**, as an additional inducement. The holder who exercises his rights has to pay the agreed subscription price for the shares to be allotted to him; but it is an **option**, and he has no obligation to take up the shares unless, in the light of the company's commercial success, he judges it advantageous to do so.

7.4 The terms on which these rights are granted will often prescribe a **system of registration**, like the register of members, to be operated by the company. On transfer, the name of the transferee is entered in the register. The document on which the terms are set out is surrendered if the rights which it gives are exercised.

7.5 A company which has granted rights to subscribe for its shares by any of these means should **maintain** its **authorised capital** at such a level that it has unissued shares available to allot if called upon to do so. The grant of these rights is regulated by ss 80, 80A and 89, as described above; the actual allotment of shares is in pursuance of an existing commitment (authorised when it was undertaken) and does not require fresh authorisation.

7.6 The same procedural steps apply to allotment of shares in these cases as in a normal allotment in response to an original application for shares. The company secretary must remember the following points:

(a) The shares must be **allotted.**

(b) **Entries** made in the **register of members.**

(c) **Share certificates** must be **issued.**

(d) A **return of allotments** must be **made** to the Companies Registry: Form 88(2). (See Appendix 3.).

Restrictions on allotment in a prospectus issue

7.7 In a general offer of shares (or debentures) to the *public*, which is the essence of a 'prospectus', there are incidental restrictions on allotment, relating to the timetable, minimum subscription and Stock Exchange listing (if any). These are features of public issues by public companies, which are described in the next chapter.

8 FORFEITURE AND CANCELLATION OF ISSUED SHARES

8.1 If, as is usual (Table A Article 20), the articles give a suitable power, a company may forfeit shares (or accept a surrender of them) if a call has been made for money due on the shares, and the holder has defaulted. Any such action is very rare and may be avoided altogether if the whole amount due on the shares is required before allotment. It is advisable to obtain **professional legal advice** before seeking to forfeit shares, as there are many technical points which, if not properly observed, may make the action invalid (see below) and result in the member suing for damages. If the shares of a member are forfeited, his name should be **removed** from the register of members. He will not be liable for future calls but will be **liable** for any amounts **called** or **due and unpaid** at the time of forfeiture.

8.2 If shares have been forfeited, the company may reissue or transfer them to some other person. A public company is required to **cancel** forfeited shares, unless they have been disposed of within the ensuing three years (reduced to one year in certain circumstances). Cancellation **reduces** the amount of the **issued share capital**. If it is thereby reduced to less than the £50,000 required of a public company, the company must re-register as a private company under the relevant procedure: s 146-8.

Procedure

8.3 Again it must be kept in view that a company may only forfeit shares for unpaid calls if the articles give it power to do so, and the power must be exercised strictly in accordance with the articles.

8.4 If forfeiture is contemplated, **letters of reminder** should be followed by a **final warning notice**, with a time limit for payment, sent through the post by recorded delivery. Table A Article 18 provides that such a final and formal demand must give at least **14 clear days**' notice, with particulars of the amount unpaid, the interest (if any) which has accrued, the place for payment, and a warning that the shares may be forfeited for non-payment of the call. This is an example of the detailed procedure which must be meticulously observed.

8.5 On the expiry of the notice given, the directors should resolve (Table A Article 20) whether to sell, re-allot or otherwise dispose of the shares to be forfeited, with particulars of the person(s) to whom those shares are to be transferred. If the articles so provide, the directors may if necessary authorise some person to execute a transfer of the shares. They may be sold at a price less than the amount paid up prior to forfeiture, but the **transferee** will become liable for **remaining amounts unpaid** and due to the time of purchase.

8.6 The shareholder in default should be asked to **surrender** his **share certificate** for cancellation. The shares should be transferred in the register of members from his name to a 'forfeited shares account', pending disposal. The articles (Table A Article 22) may provide that if the member whose shares have been forfeited lays claim to them, a **statutory declaration** of their forfeiture by a director or by the secretary shall be conclusive evidence that the new holder of the shares has good title to them.

Chapter roundup

- On **allotment**, the allottee obtains the **unconditional right to** be registered as a member of the company. Shares are said to be **issued** where all formalities are completed, that is, when **share certificates** are **issued**. To allot shares there must be **sufficient authorised share capital** unissued.
- S 80 empowers directors to allot all shares and rights to subscribe for, or convert into, shares (except subscribers' shares) provided the necessary **authority** is given, in general meeting or by the company's articles. This authority must specify the **maximum number** of shares authorised to be allotted and a **date**, not more than five years from the grant of the authority, on which the **authority** will **expire**. S 80A allows private companies to be relieved of the requirements.
- S 89 (unless excluded) ensures that the company shall **first offer existing shareholders** the right to purchase a proportion of a proposed equity securities allotment equal in proportion to their existing shareholding on similar terms to an offer to third parties. S 89 should be applied with close reference to the provisions of the memorandum and articles; similar **rights** are conferred under the Stock Exchange regulations.
- No shares can be sold at a **discount**, that is at a price below the nominal value per share. Care should be taken at all times to ensure that shares are priced accurately in accordance with statutory provisions; they should be professionally valued to avoid reproach.
- **Share premium** is the amount in **excess** of the **nominal value** of the share for which a purchaser is prepared to buy that share. A strong company will have high premiums as the investment is safer and more likely to reap good returns by way of dividends.
- A **rights issue** is an **allotment** to **existing shareholders** in ratio to their present shareholding.
- A **bonus issue** is the same as a rights issue but **no shares** are actually **paid for**, so no funds are received. The company merely increases the nominal value of its existing share capital by allotting unissued shares to existing shareholders in ratio to their present holding, thereby diluting the value of each share but maintaining the value of each shareholding.
- If a shareholder has **defaulted** on a **call for money** due on **shares**, the shares may be **forfeited** provided the appropriate procedure is followed and the articles give the power to do so.

Test your knowledge

1 Define (a) an allotment; and (b) an issue of shares. (see paras 1.1, 1.3)

2 How can a company set about increasing its authorised share capital? (2.4)

3 How may a company obtain the power to allot ordinary shares for cash to a non-member? (2.25, 2.27)

4 In what circumstances must the consideration for shares always be provided in cash? (2.33)

5 In what situation is a public company entitled to allot shares for a non-cash consideration without having it valued? (2.36)

6 State in outline the sequence of action in an allotment of shares. (3.1)

7 How may shares provisionally allotted or offered to members of a public company be made available to other persons? (3.11)

8 Explain briefly the nature and purpose of (a) a bonus issue; and (b) a rights issue. (4.1, 5.1)

9 What procedures should be followed in the case of forfeiture of shares? (8.4 - 8.6)

Now try illustrative question 21 at the end of the Study Text

Chapter 19

SHARE CERTIFICATES AND SHARE WARRANTS

This chapter covers the following topics.

1 The issue of share certificates
2 The legal status of share certificates
3 Form and content of share certificates
4 Procedures for issue and replacement of share certificates
5 The form of share warrants
6 The issue of share warrants
7 Replacement of share warrants
8 Warrant holders' and members' rights

Introduction

A member of a company which has a share capital is entitled to a copy of the essential particulars of his holding as they appear on the register of members.

(a) The *share certificate* is that formal extract from the register. It is not a document of title, but it must be produced when ownership of shares is transferred.

(b) By contrast, a *share warrant* is a bearer document of title, whose transfer effects a change of ownership by the mere act of delivery of the document.

1 THE ISSUE OF SHARE CERTIFICATES

1.1 Every company which allots or registers the transfer of shares (or debentures) has a legal duty (s 185) to issue a certificate in respect of the shares (or debentures) registered in the name of the holder. The statutory duty must be performed within certain time limits:

(a) **Within two months of allotment** (unless the issue otherwise provides); or

(b) **Within two months** of the **presentation** of the transfer to be registered in the name of the transferee

The Stock Exchange requirements for a listed company are much more stringent.

2 THE LEGAL STATUS OF SHARE CERTIFICATES 6/00

2.1 A share certificate is only **prima facie evidence** of title to the security, so other evidence may be brought forward to show that it is incorrect, or has become invalid by reason of subsequent events. Subject to that, however, the company is **'estopped'** ie prohibited from denying, against a person who has innocently relied on a share certificate, that the certificate is a correct copy of the relevant particulars in its register: s 186. However the principle does not apply when:

(a) The certificate is a **forgery**

(b) It has been issued **without authority**

(c) The person claiming on it has **not relied upon** it, say in the case of a transferee who fails to obtain the certificate (or other evidence) at the time of transfer.

2.2 The practical effect of this is (for example) that if A buys 1,000 shares from B, B shows A his share certificate for 1,500 shares. A therefore arranges with B for the preparation of a stock transfer form, and sends the old share certificate and the stock transfer form to the company to be registered. If the company now claims that B doesn't have 1,500 shares any more, but only 700 (so that A can't buy 1,000 shares from him), it cannot simply say 'too bad' to A, who has innocently relied on B's certificate. The company would be liable for A's losses. Most public companies take out insurance against such liabilities in respect of share certificates.

2.3 Listed companies are permitted to have shares which are held without any certificate being issued, in **uncertificated** or **dematerialised** form, on CREST (discussed further in Chapter 20).

3 FORM AND CONTENT OF SHARE CERTIFICATES

3.1 There is no prescribed legal form of share certificate, but by custom they are always issued in a standard format. A specimen appears on the following page which is in the form used by almost all private companies and available from any law stationers or suppliers. Listed public companies normally have their own versions printed. These must be of a uniform size of 9" × 8" (22.5 cm by 20 cm) and normally in a computerised form. The second specimen provided is typical but may vary slightly from company to company.

In designing or revising the company's form of share certificate, the first step is to refer to the articles. Table A Article 6 provides the relevant rules.

(a) **Every certificate shall be sealed.** Every document to which the seal is applied must also bear the signatures of a director and of the secretary, or of two directors (Article 101). Where however the number of shareholders runs into tens of thousands, the articles may dispense with these formalities. Where they apply, the words '*Given under the Common Seal of the said Company*', followed by spaces for the date of issue and the two necessary signatures, will appear in the lower part of the certificate.

(b) **The certificate shall specify the number, class and distinguishing numbers (if any) of the shares to which it relates, and the amount(s) paid up thereon.**

3.2 The **particulars** of the shareholder's name should **correspond exactly** with those on the register of members at the time when the share certificate is issued. If the holder is a company, its full company name in the correct form should be shown both on the register and of course on the certificate.

3.3 Unless the company issues a large number of certificates in the course of transfer work (which is the normal situation of a public company), it may obtain its supply of certificates in book form, each page comprising three parts as follows:

(a) A counterfoil to record the issue

(b) The certificate itself

(c) A detachable receipt issued with the certificate, which the recipient is asked to sign and return

Where large numbers are required, however, it is more convenient to obtain stocks of loose certificates which can be more readily processed for issue.

SHARE CERTIFICATE (referred to in paragraph 3.1)

Certificate no. ________ ________ of ________
shares ________ nos. ________ to ________ dated ________
No. of transfer ________ Old certificate ________

No of Certificate

________ Limited

Incorporated under the Companies Act

No. of shares

CAPITAL: DIVIDED INTO SHARES OF EACH

This is to Certify that ________
of ________
is (are) the registered holder(s) of ________
shares of ________ each fully paid, numbered
________ to ________ inclusive, of the Company, subject to the
Memorandum and Articles of Association of the Company

Given under the Common Seal of the said Company
on the ________ day of ________ 20__

________ Director ________ Director ________ Secretary

NO TRANSFER OF THE WHOLE OR ANY PORTION OF THE ABOVE SHARES CAN BE REGISTERED WITHOUT THE PRODUCTION OF THIS CERTIFICATE

No. of CERTIFICATE

THE SPECIMEN PLC

(Incorporated under the Companies Act, 1985)

This is to Certify that the undermentioned is/are the holders of

SHARE OF ONE POUND EACH

fully paid, in the capital of THE SPECIMEN PLC

subject to the Memorandum and Articles of Association of the above-named Company

Name(s)	Transfer No.	Account No.	Date	No. of shares

Given under the Common Seal of the Company on the above stated date

Esd____________

No transfer of any portion of the above Shares will be registered without the product of this certificate at the offices of the Registrars

3.4 Both specially printed share certificate forms and standard blank forms are likely to conform in essentials to Stock Exchange requirements, which are as follows.

(a) The **date** of the certificate must be shown.

(b) Under the name of the company at the head of the certificate is given the '**authority**' (the statute), under which it is constituted: for example, 'Incorporated under the Companies Act 1985'. If it is a foreign company, its country of incorporation (and registered number) is given; its authorised capital (divided into shares) may also be given.

(c) The **number of shares** (or amount of stock) comprised in the certificate is shown in the top right hand corner (with the serial number of the certificate in the left hand corner).

(d) At the foot of the certificate is printed a **sentence**, such as:

> *'No transfer of the whole or any part of the above shares can be registered without the production of this certificate.'*

If it relates to stock, there will be an additional notice of the minimum amount (or multiple) in which the stock is transferable, eg: 'Transferable in units of £10 or a multiple thereof'.

(e) Certificates (usually pre-printed) for preference shares or debentures carry information of the **rights** of those securities, for example dividend/interest payments, return of capital etc.

Sealing of certificates

3.5 A certificate must either bear the company's **common seal** or, under the new procedure of s 36(4), it must be **signed** by a director and the secretary, or by two directors, and be expressed to be executed by the company. A company may use 'an official seal which is a facsimile of the common seal' with the addition of the work 'securities' (s 40).

4 PROCEDURES FOR ISSUE AND REPLACEMENT OF SHARE CERTIFICATES

4.1 There should always be an effective system of checking new certificates before they are issued.

4.2 When shares are allotted in a new issue, there are two bases upon which the new certificate can be prepared as follows:

(a) On the **allotment list**

(b) If the company has issued renounceable allotment letters, on the **particulars** entered in the register of members at the end of the renunciation period

4.3 The time limit for issuing of a certificate and the need for careful checking have already been mentioned.

4.4 When the certificates are ready, the board of directors or a committee of the board should be asked to resolve that they are to be issued. If the seal is used, a record of the sealings should be entered in the company's **sealings register**. (A company should keep a register giving details of the use of the company seal).

4.5 A certificate arising from a non market transaction (for example the transfer of shares in a private company) is sent to the **lodging agent**, commonly the solicitor, bank or accountant of the transferee, who will then send it to their client or hold it according to their client's instructions. Where there is no lodging agent involved the certificate is sent to the registered address of the shareholder.

4.6 No charge is made for the share certificate if it relates to the entire new allotment. If, however, the shareholder asks for two or more certificates for split parts of his holding, he may be asked to pay 'a reasonable sum' (Table A Article 6).

Replacement of certificates **6/99**

4.7 The articles (Table A Article 7) usually provide that a member may have a new certificate to replace one which has been defaced, worn out, destroyed or lost.

4.8 In the case of a defaced or worn out certificate, the holder is required to give up the old certificate, which should be carefully examined to ensure that it is genuine, and then marked '**cancelled**'. If there is any doubt about it, such a certificate should be treated as if it had been lost. The surrendered certificate should be preserved in case some question about it should arise later. The issue of the new certificate should be noted in the register of members, or accompanying record of dealings with members. Under the articles, the company may have the right to demand an indemnity or guarantee, but it is unusual to do so in these cases.

4.9 In case of reported loss, the member should first be asked to make another thorough **search** for his certificate. In case of reported destruction, he should be asked to explain how this occurred: the articles permit the company to ask for 'evidence'.

4.10 As regards safeguards against fraud, the company may call for any or all of the following:

(a) A **letter of indemnity**, whereby the member agrees to recompense the company for any losses it may sustain, through fraud in connection with the 'lost' certificate

(b) A **guarantee** of the indemnity by a bank or other financial institution

(c) A **statutory declaration** by the member stating the circumstances of the loss

4.11 The company should refer to its record of Stop Notices and should not register the transfer of the shares or other securities until 14 days after sending notice thereof, by ordinary first class post to the person on whose behalf the notice was filed. There are complex rules of the court (Rules of the Supreme Court, Order 50) and the company may well be advised to take legal advice.

4.12 The minimum precaution is to obtain a suitable **indemnity** preferably in the standard form approved by the ICSA a specimen of which appears on the next page. This would normally be given by the member himself, but if the original certificate was lost in transit between the member and a third party, an indemnity from the third party is acceptable. The indemnity will only be needed if the member is dishonest, probably due to financial difficulties, in which case the indemnity itself may prove to be worthless: that is the argument for demanding a guarantee in support of it.

4.13 In preparing a duplicate certificate, the company should mark it plainly and indelibly with the word '**Duplicate**'. A note of the loss of the original certificate and of the issue of a duplicate should be recorded in the register of members, or related records, so that the issue cannot be overlooked if the member or some other person later presents the 'lost' original certificate. It is advisable to note the loss also in the 'stop list'.

INDEMNITY FOR LOST CERTIFICATE (referred to in paragraph 4.12)

INDEMNITY FOR LOST CERTIFICATE

(Above this line for Registrar's use only)

To the Directors of ....

The original certificate(s) of title relating to the undermentioned securities of the above-named company has/have been lost or destroyed.

Neither the securities nor the certificate(s) of title thereto have been transferred, charged, lent or deposited or dealt with in any matter affecting the absolute title thereto and the person(s) named in the said certificate(s) is/are the person(s) entitled to be on the register in respect of such securities.

I/We request you to issue (a) duplicate certificate(s) of title for such securities and, in consideration of your doing so, undertake [jointly and severally]* to indemnify you and the company against all claims and demands (and any expenses thereof) which may be made against you or the company in consequence of your complying with this request and of the company permitting at any time hereafter a transfer of the said securities, or any part thereof, without the production of the said original certificate(s).

I/We undertake to deliver to the company for cancellation the said original certificate(s) should the same ever be recovered.

[*Applicable only to joint accounts.]

PARTICULARS OF CERTIFICATE(S) LOST OR DESTROYED

Particulars of certificate	Amount and class of securities	In favour of

Dated this .... day of .... 20 ....

Signature(s) ....

We. .... hereby
join in the above indemnity and undertaking

4.14 The articles generally permit the company to recover from the member its **expenses incurred** in investigating the reported loss; it may for example be necessary to refer the matter to the company's solicitor. The articles may also provide for a small fee for the issue of a duplicate certificate. The Stock Exchange Listing Rules require, however, that a listed company, in issuing a duplicate certificate for any reason, shall not demand any payment except reimbursement of expenses.

5 THE FORM OF SHARE WARRANTS — 6/00

5.1 The form and content of a share warrant are similar to those of a share certificate, except where differences must arise because of their nature.

5.2 Attached to the warrant is a sheet of **numbered coupons** (called the 'coupon sheet') which are used to obtain dividends. At the top or bottom of this sheet of coupons is a document called a talon which is exchanged for a fresh coupon sheet when all the existing coupons have been used. The warrant number and the number of shares should be clearly printed on the talon.

6 THE ISSUE OF SHARE WARRANTS — 6/00

6.1 A company which is limited by shares, and which has authority in its articles, may issue warrants under its **common seal** relating to **fully paid shares**: s 188. The statutory model Table A does not contain any such provision, so a special article would be required.

6.2 A share warrant attracts **stamp duty** at the time of issue at the rate of £1.50 per £100 of market value, rounded up.

6.3 The effect of a share warrant is to make the person in possession of the warrant the owner of the shares. A bearer warrant is a **negotiable instrument**, the value of which (ownership of the shares) is transferable by simple delivery to another person. As a negotiable instrument, it will be regarded by banks as stale if it is more than six months old. If it is that old, the bank will contact the company to see if the warrant should still be paid.

6.4 Thus, if a shareholder has a share **certificate**:

(a) His name will be on the share certificate and also on the register of members.

(b) If he sells all or some of his shares, he must apply for the transfer to be registered and new share certificates to be issued.

In contrast, if a person holds a share **warrant**:

(a) His name will not be on the warrant, nor on the register of members.

(b) Ownership of the warrant can be transferred simply by giving it to someone else.

6.5 As you can imagine, warrants carry the risk of forgery and fraud. If a listed company wishes to issue share warrants, it is required to submit for approval a proof of its form of share warrant to the Stock Exchange. As a further security measure, the actual warrants must be printed by 'recognised security printers' and be printed on watermarked paper, such as is used for printing banknotes or bonds.

Company records relating to warrants

6.6 A company which issues share warrants should maintain adequate records, including:

(a) A record (with the identifying serial numbers) of **warrants issued**, or surrendered for cancellation

(b) A record of **coupons surrendered** to obtain dividends etc

(c) The original **applications** by former **members** for the issue to them of warrants, with the consequent removal of the shares from the members' registered holdings

The procedure for issuing warrants

6.7 If the company has due authority in its articles, the procedure for the issue of warrants comprising fully paid shares *may* be as follows.

(a) A member **completes an application form** (supplied by the company on request) and sends it in with his share certificate, the sum required to pay stamp duty on the warrant and the fee (if any) payable to the company for the warrant.

(b) The company checks the application and share certificate against the register of members and issues an **interim receipt**. This receipt should preferably be issued for unspecified 'documents', so that if the receipt is stolen, it will not be obvious that later presentation of it will obtain a warrant; since no names need be recorded to transfer ownership of the warrant, it will be impossible to trace the thief later.

(c) A **warrant** or warrants is **prepared**; it is usual to hold stocks of warrants for various fixed numbers of shares ie 100, 500, 1,000 etc. The member's share certificate should be cancelled. If any of the coupons which are attached to the warrant(s) to be issued relate to dividends paid before the date of issue, these coupons should be detached from the warrant(s) and cancelled.

(d) The warrant(s) is/are **submitted** to the **Stamp Office** for stamping, with evidence of the market value of the shares, since stamp duty is calculated as a percentage of market value, not nominal value.

(e) The member's name is **removed** from the **register of members**, as the holder of the shares to be held on warrant. A note is made in the register that the warrant has been issued with the date of issue and the particulars of the shares comprised in the warrant (including identifying numbers, if any).

(f) A careful **check** is made of all the particulars entered in the appropriate records, notably the register of warrants issued. If warrants are issued in more than one denomination (see (c) above) it is useful to keep separate records of stocks held, and issues made, of warrants of each denomination (in number of shares).

(g) At the appropriate stage the board is asked to **authorise** the **issue** of warrant(s), to be sealed and witnessed in the same way as share certificates.

(h) To facilitate balancing the 'shares issued' account, shares comprised in share warrants are credited to a **'share warrants issued'** account which is added to the total of shares shown on the register of members, in calculating the issued capital of the company.

(i) The **completed warrant(s)** is/are **issued against** the **surrender** of the interim receipts (see (b) above); warrants should be sent by registered post, if posted.

In the case of listed companies the whole procedure must be completed so that the warrants are ready within 14 days of the deposit of share certificates.

The procedure for surrendering warrants in exchange for a share certificate

6.8 The holder of a share warrant may apply to surrender his warrant, and to be entered in the register of members as the holder of the shares comprised in the warrant. The procedure is as follows.

(a) The holder of the warrant completes and returns a **form of application** obtained from the company. With the application he sends in the warrant(s) to which the application relates.

(b) A **temporary receipt** is **issued**. The company checks the particulars against its register of warrants issued.

(c) The **surrendered warrant(s)** is/are **cancelled**. Before this, a check is made to ensure that all the coupons not yet used to obtain dividends declared to date are still attached to the surrendered warrant(s). If any are missing, the applicant is told that until he produces them, no further action can be taken on his application; in the last resort his indemnity is taken.

(d) The cancellation of the warrant(s) is/are marked '**cancelled**' and filed safely away.

(e) A **new share certificate** in the name of the applicant is **prepared** and his application is submitted to the board for approval and authorisation of the sealing and issue of the certificate.

(f) An **entry** is **made** in the **register of members**, and the 'share warrants issued' account is debited with the number of shares now added to the register of members.

(g) The **share certificate(s)** is/are issued in exchange for the receipt.

In this case also, a listed company must complete the whole procedure within 14 days.

Dealings with warrant holders: dividend payments, bonus issues and rights issues

6.9 The conditions of issue of share warrants provide for the *payment of dividends* to warrant holders. The procedure is usually as follows.

(a) The company advertises that it will **pay dividends** (on the relevant number of shares) on presentation (often by the holder's bank) of **coupon** No. X at the company's bank, on or after a specified date. The advertisement should be published in newspapers in all countries where there is reason to believe holders of warrants may reside. Those countries are sometimes listed in the conditions of issue of warrants.

(b) On receipt, the **coupons** are **checked against** the company's records of **warrants issued** (with the number of shares comprised in each such warrant). It is usual, when a warrant is issued, to add its particulars to a standing list of dividend warrants outstanding, on which the company is liable to pay dividends in future. It is removed from the list whenever the warrant is surrendered.

(c) After checking, the **coupons** are **cancelled** and filed in serial order of the warrants to which they relate.

(d) **Dividends** are **paid** by **cheque**, together with a UK tax credit certificate.

6.10 There will come a time when all the coupons issued as part of outstanding share warrants have been used. The company then prints a sufficient number of new coupons and advertises that **new** sets of **coupons** will be **issued** in exchange for the **talons** of the original issue of coupons. The new coupons should be numbered serially in continuation of the old, to avoid confusion. If, for example, the original sets of coupons were numbered 1-30, the new set would begin at 31.

6.11 The coupons attached to share warrants may also be used, on due advertisement by the company, for other purposes - such as giving holders an entitlement to **participate** in a **bonus** or **rights issue**, by surrendering the next coupon in the numbered series.

7 REPLACEMENT OF SHARE WARRANTS

7.1 The articles usually provide that the company may issue a replacement for a share warrant said to have been lost on **terms similar** to those which apply to replacement of **lost share certificates**. If the warrant has merely been defaced or is worn out, the applicant must pay the cost of the replacement (including any stamp duty payable) but, if the surrendered document appears genuine, no additional requirements need be imposed.

7.2 The replacement of a share warrant said to have been lost or destroyed, so that no original warrant is available to be surrendered, obviously requires extreme caution. In the case of a listed company, the Stock Exchange stipulates that the company must be '**satisfied** beyond **reasonable doubt** that the original has been destroyed'. This is not an easy requirement to satisfy in respect of a missing document.

7.3 Basic safeguards (as were described for replacement share certificates) are available: an **indemnity**, **guarantee** of the **indemnity** and **statutory declaration** of the circumstances of loss etc. The risk of fraud is much greater and the company should require all three as a condition of issuing a new share warrant.

7.4 The same principles apply if it is the **strip** of dividend coupons which has been **detached** from the warrant and **then lost.**

8 WARRANT HOLDERS' AND MEMBERS' RIGHTS

8.1 The holder of a share warrant is **not a member of the company**, since his name is not on the register of members. However the articles and the terms of issue of warrants usually provide that the holder of a warrant, on depositing his warrant at the registered office, may exercise **specified rights** of a **member**, such as attending a general meeting (or appointing a proxy to do so), or requisitioning a meeting.

8.2 For convenience, companies which have issued share warrants do not require their temporary deposit with the company, but undertake to recognise a letter, written by a bank or other agent of good standing, to the effect that a **named person** has **deposited** a **specified warrant** with the bank or agent for safekeeping. On production of the letter, the holder can then exercise rights as described above.

8.3 It is usual to advertise (as in connection with impending dividends) that holders of warrants may exercise their rights in this way. In the case of a final dividend, to be declared at an annual general meeting, the same advertisement may serve to give notice both of the **dividend payment**, and of the **method** of **attending** the **meeting**.

8.4 The company has no record of an address to which it may send a copy of its annual report and accounts to each holder of warrants. Here again, the advertisement of the AGM and final dividend may announce that copies may be obtained on request.

Exercise

What is the effect of a share warrant?

Solution

The effect of a share warrant is to make the person in possession of the warrant the owner of the shares. A warrant is a negotiable instrument, the value of which (ownership of the shares) is transferable by simple delivery to another person. Thus, if a shareholder has a share *certificate* his name will be on the share certificate and also on the register of members, and if he sells all or some of his shares, he must apply for the transfer to be registered and new share certificates to be issued. In contrast, if a person holds a share *warrant*, his name will not be on the warrant, nor on the register of members, and ownership of the warrant can be transferred simply by giving it to someone else.

Chapter roundup

- **Share certificates** are not documents of title; they merely **evidence title**, but they must be issued within two months of allotment or presentation of transfer: s 185.
- Share certificates are generally in a **standard form** as provided by the articles, detailing the **number** of the certificate, the **number** of **shares** to which it relates, and **naming** the **company** and the **type of share**. They should be sealed by the company or alternatively the procedure in s 36A(4) needs to be followed.
- Stock Exchange requirements for the form of share certificates will dictate further the **form** and **content** of the share certificate as to size, authority under which the company is incorporated, number and any details of rights attached.
- Again the articles will provide **procedures for issue** and **replacement** which should be followed carefully. At all times the company must guard against fraud by obtaining necessary indemnities and insurance cover.
- **Share warrants** are **documents of title** which are registered at the company without noting ownership. Ownership changes by mere **delivery** of the warrant document.
- **Coupons** are issued and attached to the warrant and on presentation they entitle the holder to receipt of dividends under the terms of the warrant.
- A **warrant holder** is **not a member** of the company but may have similar rights if so provided by the articles and/or terms of the warrants.

Test your knowledge

1. In what circumstances may a company deny that the particulars shown in a share certificate are correct? (see para 2.1)
2. Give three items which would appear on a share certificate. (3.4)
3. Explain the usual procedure for sealing share certificates. (3.5)
4. What safeguards may a company take in dealing with a request for the issue of a replacement share certificate? (4.10)
5. What marks or records should be made in the course of issuing a share certificate to replace one which has been lost? (4.13)
6. Give the main stages of procedure in the issue of share warrants. (6.7)
7. How does the holder of a share warrant obtain any dividend declared on the shares comprised in his warrant? (6.9)
8. Is it possible (and if so, how) for the holder of a share warrant to attend a general meeting? (8.1)

Now try illustrative question 22 at the end of the Study Text

Chapter 20

TRANSFER AND TRANSMISSION OF SHARES

This chapter covers the following topics.

Introduction

The registration of share transfers, and the work incidental to it, form part of the basic skills of a company secretary. This is so even if, as is common among large companies, the registration work itself is delegated to professional registrars, who keep the register of members on computer: the secretary will be in regular contact with the registrars and must be able to deal with their queries.

Transfer of shares means relinquishing ownership of shares to someone else, by sale, gift etc.

Transmission of shares is the term applied to change of ownership or control, by operation of law - usually on the death, bankruptcy or mental incapacity of a member.

The Stock Exchange procedure is based on the same principles as company share transfer work, which is described in the first part of this chapter. It is rather more complex, however; this is explained in Sections 3 and 4. The most significant recent development in this area is the introduction of CREST, and you should follow the financial press for details of the development of CREST.

The same procedures are followed on the transfer of registered debentures or debenture stock, but with some minor modifications.

1 THE STATUTORY FRAMEWORK OF SHARE TRANSFER

1.1 A share is personal property 'transferable in the manner provided by the company's articles, but subject to the Stock Transfer Act 1963': s 182. The articles always impose certain procedural requirements and they may confer on the directors power to **reject a transfer**, even of fully paid shares, and this is often the case in a private company. Stock Exchange regulations, however, do not permit a listed company to impose any restrictions on a transfer of fully paid shares.

1.2 Table A Article 24 permits the directors to refuse to register a transfer of shares in the following circumstances:

(a) The shares are **not fully paid.**

(b) The shares are **subject to a lien.**

(c) The transfer is **not accompanied** by the **transferor's share** certificate and **delivered** to the **transfer office**. A right is reserved to demand evidence of the transferor's entitlement to transfer the shares.

(d) By Article 23, the transfer is not 'in the usual form', or such other form as the directors may approve.

(e) A **stop notice** is in place and the person who lodged the stop notice has to be given notice of the proposal transfer (see Chapter 21).

1.3 Articles (Table A Article 30) usually extend the regulations on share transfers to 'a person becoming entitled to a share in consequence of the death or bankruptcy of a member', being either the **personal representatives** of a **deceased member**, or the **trustee** of a bankrupt member. This is transmission. Such person(s) may apply to be entered as holder of the shares on the register, or may present a transfer of the shares to a third party. The representative of a deceased member has a **statutory right** to effect a transfer under s 183, but Article 30 makes it clear that this is only the **same right** as the deceased had in his lifetime.

1.4 The articles may also include the power to **refuse** an **application** for registration by the holder of a renounced letter of allotment. Stock Exchange rules would not permit such a power to be invoked, however, so if the company's shares are listed there is little point in the articles providing for such an event.

Transfer of fully paid shares

1.5 The Stock Transfer Act 1963 sought to set up a more efficient system of transferring securities in the UK for the purpose of reducing delays to the investor. Two new forms were introduced.

(a) The **Stock Transfer Form** for general use

(b) The **Brokers Transfer Form** to be used when a single holding of stocks or shares was to be broken up among several purchasers

1.6 The main procedural changes introduced by the 1963 Act were:

(a) The **signature** of the transferee is **not required**.

(b) The transferor, unless itself a company, need not execute the transfer by sealing it as a deed. A simple **signature** of an individual suffices.

(c) A share transfer document which **omits** to **state** the **amount paid** for the shares is still a **valid** document.

Transfer of partly paid shares

1.7 If the shares are only *partly* paid, the 1963 Act does not apply. The procedure instead is as follows:

(a) The transfer must be **executed** as a **deed.**

(b) The transferee must **sign.**

(c) The transfer must be in the **form prescribed** by the articles.

(d) The **serial numbers** of the shares must be given, since partly paid shares cannot be 'denumbered' under s 182(2).

1.8 It is unlawful for a company to record a change of legal ownership of shares in its register, unless a '**proper instrument of transfer**' has been delivered to it, so the stock transfer form (shown on the following page) has an important legal status.

Re Greene 1949
The facts: A deceased shareholder had signed (as subscriber to the memorandum) the original articles which provided that at his death his shares should be transferred to his widow. At his death it was argued that the articles constituted a signed form of transfer.

Decision: This was not a 'proper' form of transfer. Moreover it did not identify the transferee (the widow) since the deceased member might have remarried after signing the articles.

2 TRANSFER REGISTRATION PROCEDURE 12/98, 6/99

2.1 The following relates to a transfer of shares on sale by private negotiation, and not through the Stock Exchange.

(a) Before the company secretary receives the transfer, the registered holder should have completed a **standard form of transfer**, leaving the name of the transferee blank.

(b) The transferor hands the **completed transfer**, with his share certificate (if the transfer comprises all the shares to which the certificate relates) to the **transferee** in exchange for the **agreed price**. (Additional procedures will be required if the transfer does not relate to the entire shareholding; this is described later under 'certification'.)

(c) The transferee inserts on the transfer form the **name** and **address** of himself or his nominee, dates the transfer and **presents** it to the **Stamp Office** to be stamped. Stamp duty may be payable at the *ad valorem* rate, that is 50p per £100 of market value, rounded up if necessary to the next higher multiple of £100. There is a £5 minimum charge for transfers between nominee shareholders without changes in the beneficial ownership.

(d) The Stamp Office will either **accept** the **consideration** declared on the transfer form or **require other evidence** of the true value of the shares (in place of the declared price). (Generally this would only happen for private companies where no market prices could be checked).

(e) Finally, the transferee **presents** the **completed transfer**, with the old share certificate, to the company for registration.

2.2 The company secretary then has a maximum period of two months in which to deliver a new share certificate to the transferee (s 185), or to give him notice that his transfer has been rejected: s 183(5). The action to be taken in that period is as follows.

(a) The transfer should be carefully examined with the following points in mind.

(i) Is the transfer in the **correct form**?

(ii) Does the **transferor's name correspond** with that which appears in the register of members and on the share certificate? Does his address (if any is given on the transfer) differ from that recorded in the register of members?

(iii) Does the **transferor's signature correspond** (for instance in respect of initials) with his name as given on the transfer form? Is the transferor a corporate body, and if so has it executed the transfer under its seal?

(iv) Has the **transferee's name** and **address** been **legibly entered**, so that it may be accurately copied into the register of members?

(v) Do the **particulars** of the share shown on the form **tally** with those in the register of members and the share certificate? (If the transferor is transferring shares of different classes, he should execute a separate transfer for each class of shares.)

(vi) Is the price given as '**consideration**' (the total amount of money to be paid for all the shares to be transferred) **reasonable** in relation to what is known of the market value of the shares? (The transfer is still valid if it does not show the consideration.)

(vii) Has the transfer been **stamped**?

(viii) Has the **transfer passed through** the hands of an **agent** of the transferor or of the transferee, such as a bank, stockbroker or solicitor? If so, the agent should have put his stamp against his client's name or signature; in the case of the transferor, the agent's stamp is usually taken as confirmation that the signature is genuine. It should be noted that if an agent is acting for the transferee, they will usually lodge the transfer.

(ix) If the signature is executed by **power of attorney** then the power should be produced for registration and a copy kept in the company's register of documents.

(b) In checking the transfer against the register of members, the secretary should also ensure that there is **no apparent impediment** to the transfer, such as a stop notice or a lien.

EXAMPLE OF A STOCK TRANSFER FORM

CON 40 (1963)

STOCK TRANSFER FORM

(Above this line for Registrars only)

Consideration Money £	Certificate lodged with the Register **(For completion by Registrar / Stock Exchange)**

Name of Undertaking		
Description of security		
Number or amount of Shares, Stock or other security and, in figures column only, number and denomination of units, if any	Words	Figures (units of)
Name(s) of registered holder(s)should be given in full: the address should be given where there is only one holder. If the transfer is not made by the registered holder(s) insert also the name(s) and capacity (eg Executor(s)) of the person(s) making the transfer.	In the name(s) of	

I/We hereby transfer the above security out of the name(s) aforesaid to the person(s) named below. Signature(s) of transferor(s) 1.. . . . . 2 . . . . 3 . . . . 4 . . . . A body corporate should execute this transfer under its common seal or otherwise in accordance with applicable statutory requirements.	**Stamp of Selling Broker(s) or, for transactions which are not stock exchange transactions, of Agent(s), if any, acting for the Transferor(s)** *Date* . . . .

Full name(s), full postal address(es) (including County or, if applicable, Postal District number) of the person(s) to whom the security is transferred. **Please state title, if any, or whether Mr, Mrs, or Miss** **Please complete in typewriting or in BLOCK CAPITALS**	

I/We request that such entries be made in the register as a necessary to give effect to this transfer

Stamp of Buying/Broker(s) (if any)	**Stamp or name and address of person lodging this form (if other than the Buying Broker(s))**

Reference to the Registrar in this Form means the registrar or registration agent of the undertaking NOT the Registrar of Companies at Companies House.

FORM OF CERTIFICATE REQUIRED WHERE TRANSFER IS EXEMPT FROM STAMP DUTY

Instruments executed on or after 1st May 1987 effecting any transactions within the following categories are exempt from stamp duty-

A The vesting of property subject to a trust in the trustees of the trust on the appointment of a new trustee, or in the continuing trustees on the retirement of a trustee.

B The conveyance or transfer of property the subject of a specific devise or legacy to the beneficiary named in the will (or his nominee). Transfers in satisfaction of a general legacy of money should not be included in this category (see category D below).

C The conveyance or transfer of property which form part of an intestate's estate to the person entitled on intestacy (or his nominee). Transfers in satisfaction of the transferees entitlement to cash in the estate of an intestate, where the total value of the residuary estate exceeds that sum, should not be included in this category (see category D below)

D The appropriation of property within section 84(4) of the Finance Act 1985 (death: appropriation in satisfaction of a general legacy of money) or section 84(5) or (7) of that Act (death: appropriation in satisfaction of any interest of surviving spouse and in Scotland also of any interest of issue).

E The conveyance or transfer of property which forms part of the residuary estate of a testator to a beneficiary (or his nominee) entitled solely by virtue of his entitlement under the will.

F The conveyance or transfer of property out of a settlement in or toward satisfaction of a beneficiary's interest, not being an interest acquired for money or money's worth, being a conveyance or transfer constituting a distribution of property in accordance with the provisions of a settlement.

G The conveyance or transfer of property on and in consideration only of marriage to a party to the marriage (or his nominee) or to trustees to be held on the terms of a settlement made in consideration only of the marriage. A transfer to a spouse after the date of marriage is not within the category, unless made pursuant to an ante-nuptial contract.

H The conveyance or transfer of property within section 83(1) of the Finance Act 1985 (transfers in connection with divorce etc)

I The conveyance or transfer by the liquidator of property which formed part of the assets of the company in liquidation to a shareholder nor any consideration referred to in section 57 of the Stamp Act 1891 (conveyance in consideration of a debt etc.)

L The conveyance or transfer of property operating as a voluntary disposition *inter vivos* for no consideration in money or money's worth nor any consideration referred to in section 57 of the Stamp Act 1891 (conveyance in consideration of a debt etc)

M The conveyance or transfer of property by an instrument within section 84(1) of the Finance Act 1985 (death: varying disposition).

(1) Delete as appropriate

(2) Insert "(A)", "(B)" or appropriate category

(3) Delete second sentence if the certificate is given by the transferor or his solicitor

(1) I/We hereby certify that the transaction in respect of which this transfer is made is one which falls within this category(2) above. (1) I/We confirm that (1) I/We have been duly authorised by the transferor to sign this certificate and that the facts of the transaction are within (1) my/our knowledge.(3)

Signature(s) *Description ("Transferor", "Solicitor", etc)*

Date 20

NOTES

(1) If the above certificate has been completed, this transfer does not need to be submitted to the Controller of Stamps but should be sent directly to the Company or its Registrars.

(2) If the above certificate is not completed, this transfer must be submitted to the Controller of Stamps and duly stamped. (See below.)

FORM OF CERTIFICATE REQUIRED WHERE TRANSFER IS NOT EXEMPT BUT IS NOT LIABLE TO *AD VALOREM* STAMP DUTY

Instruments of transfer, other than those in respect of which the above certificate has been completed, are liable to a fixed duty of 50p when the transaction falls within one of the following categories.

(a) Transfer by way of security for a loan or re-transfer to the original transferor on repayment of a loan.

(b) Transfer, not on sale and not arising under any contract of sale and where no beneficial interest in the property passes: (i) to a person who is a mere nominee of, and is nominated only by, the transferor; (ii) from a mere nominee who has at all times held the property on behalf of the transferee; (iii) from one nominee to another nominee of the same beneficial owner where the first nominee has at all times held the property on behalf of that beneficial owner. (NOTE - This category does not include a transfer made in any of the following circumstances: (i) by a holder of stock, etc., following the grant of an option to purchase the stock, to the person entitled to the option or his nominee; (ii)to a nominee in contemplation of a contract for the sale of the stock, etc. then about to be entered into; (iii) from the nominee of a vendor, who has instructed the nominee orally or by some unstamped writing to hold stock, etc., in trust for a purchaser, to such purchaser.)

(1) Delete as appropriate

(2) Insert "(a)", "(b)"

(3) Here set out concisely the facts explaining the transaction. Adjudication may be required

(1) I/We hereby certify that the transaction in respect of which this transfer is made is one which falls within this category(2) above. (1) I/We confirm that (1) I/We have been duly authorised by the transferor to sign this certificate and that the facts of the transaction are within (1) my/our knowledge. (3)

Signature(s) *Description ("Transferor", "Solicitor", etc)*

Date 20

(c) If the shares are **partly paid**, the form of transfer may be different; it must be **signed** by the transferee and include the **serial numbers** of the shares (corresponding to those on the share certificate and the register). Enquiries should be made about the transferee to ensure that he has **sufficient means** to meet the amount unpaid on the shares, if called upon, and that he is not a minor who might repudiate the shares and the consequent liability.

(d) Some companies keep a **transfer register** but there is no legal obligation to do so. They may otherwise imprint a rubber stamp or affix an adhesive label to the transfer, with a sequence of 'boxes' (spaces in which each stage of the registration process may be recorded).

(e) The **old share certificate** is **cancelled**, and **marked as such**, (but kept generally with the register of members, with a note of the disposal of the shares endorsed thereon). A new share certificate is prepared in the name of the transferee.

(f) The **transfer is submitted** to a meeting of the **board**, or of its transfer committee (if any), for approval and authority to seal the new share certificate.

(g) **Entries** are **made** in the **register of members**; ie the transferor's account is debited with the shares transferred out, and the transferee's account is credited with the shares transferred in.

(h) The **new share certificate is sent by post** to the transferee, or to his agent if the agent presented the transfer.

2.3 A few companies send to the transferor a **written 'transfer advice'**. However it has been established by court cases that a transferor who does not respond to a transfer advice may still claim against the company and have his name restored to the register, if the signature on the transfer is a forgery. Now most companies no longer issue a transfer advice.

2.4 Both the transfer and the old share certificate should be carefully preserved by the company.

2.5 If the transfer is not approved by the company, **notice of refusal** must be sent to the person who presented it, **within two months** of presentation. Unless the articles otherwise provide, no reason need be given; the company may simply return the transfer, stating that the board declines to approve it.

Certification 12/98

2.6 Certification is a procedure, recognised by law (s 184), by which the transferor sends the transfer to the company to be certified before he delivers it to the transferee. Certification is necessary if:

(a) The transferor's share certificate comprises shares when he wishes to transfer **more than one transferee.**

(b) The transferor wishes to **retain part** ('the balance') of his holding, for instance where he has a single certificate for 100 shares, of which he sells 50 and retains the balance of 50.

(c) The transferor has only a **temporary document**, such as a letter of allotment, relating to the shares entered on the register which he wishes to transfer.

(d) The **share certificate** is **not in order**.

(e) There is a **discrepancy** between the **name** and **address** given on the certificate and on the stock transfer form.

2.7 In any such case the following action is necessary, for verification by the company.

(a) The transferor **sends** his **share certificate** (or temporary document of title) to the company with the relevant transfer(s).

(b) The **company's registrar endorses each transfer** with a rubber stamp to the following effect.

> *XYZ Ltd*
> Certificate for .... shares has been lodged at the Company's Office.
> Date............ ....
> Secretary

(c) The company's registrar then **endorses** the **particulars** of **certification** on the back of the share certificate. The share certificate is retained, having been marked 'cancelled'.

(d) The **certified transfer** is **returned** to the **transferor**, who hands it over to the transferee, who must accept the certification as a *substitute* for a share certificate of the transferor.

(e) When the transferee has completed his or her part of the transfer procedures (described earlier) and submitted the completed transfer to the company for registration, the company will obviously **accept the transfer** - since it has been certified - without the need for the transferor's share certificate, which is already cancelled and in the company's possession.

2.8 If the reason for certification is that the transferor is to retain part of the holding comprised in his certificate, the company will, in the course of registration of the transfer, make out a 'balance certificate' for the shares retained, and send this to the transferor at the same time as it sends a certificate to the transferee.

Forged transfers **Specimen paper**

2.9 The legal effect of certification is a topic covered by the *Corporate Law* syllabus. The possibility of a transfer being presented for registration with a forged signature purporting to be that of the transferor represents an area of potential liability for the company regardless of certification. Briefly the situation is as follows.

(a) **Forgery confers no title** on the transferee. If the name of the true owner has been wrongfully removed from the register the member can insist on its restoration and on the payment of any missed dividends with interest: *Barton v London and North Western Rail Co 1889.*

(b) If as a result of the undetected forgery a certificate is issued in favour of the fraudulent transferee and a subsequent **innocent purchaser relies** on the certificate to acquire the shares, then the company is **estopped** from **denying ownership** of the shares to the innocent purchaser who holds the certificate and is liable in damages to the holder.

(c) A person such as a bank or solicitor who presents a certificate for registration does not represent to the company that the transferor is entitled to the shares. The presenter does represent, however, that the document is a **genuine document** duly executed by the transferor and if the document is accepted by the company there is an implied contract that the transfer is genuine. If it is a forgery and the company is compelled to make good the loss sustained by a person relying on the certificate, the company is entitled to be **indemnified** under this implied contract in respect of its liability: *Sheffield Corporation v Barclay 1905.*

(d) The modern practice is to **insure** against any liability of the company arising from a forged transfer (including payment of dividends to persons not entitled). The company should be clear as to the cover obtained. The insurers may impose various conditions, for instance that claims must be notified within a limited period after discovery of the forgery.

Certification by the Stock Exchange

2.10 Where securities are traded on the London Stock Exchange a certification service is provided by the Exchange Certification Office which deals with a considerable volume of certifications in the following manner.

(a) If there is only **one buyer** the stock transfer form will be **certified by the** Exchange and the cancelled certificate sent to the company.

(b) If the number of shares on the certificate is greater than those sold according to the transfer form a **balance ticket** in respect of the unsold portion will be sent as soon as practicable to the transferor's broker. This will normally have an expiry date allowing time for a new balance certificate to be issued.

(c) If the shareholder intends to sell the remaining balance of shares the broker can instruct the secretary to **hold** the **balance certificate 'to order'**, that is pending further instructions. In these circumstances a balance certificate will not normally be prepared and issued until a **further transfer** is lodged for the balance. A balance ticket will be issued immediately after certification as usual.

(d) Where stock or shares are being sold to two or more buyers a **broker's transfer form** will be used, the amount of each broker's transaction being noted. The transfer form itself will act as advice of certification and will be lodged with the company with the old certificate(s).

After checking that the form is in order the Secretary will then retain the certificate(s) until individual transfer forms are received from the various brokers for registration and the issue of new certificates to the transferees.

Non-market transfers 12/98

2.11 A transfer does not always result from a sale, mortgage, or other commercial transaction. It may merely be a means of **rearranging legal ownership** of shares in the course of, for example, trust administration (a change in trustees). Another example is where the executors of a deceased person transfer shares from his estate to the beneficiaries under his will.

2.12 Non-market transfers are subject to the same procedures as a commercial sale of shares. However they are often transfers by joint holders to joint holders (or transfers by or to a corporate trustee), and they are often prepared and presented by solicitors, accountants or banks. In dealing with such transfers the company secretary should give attention to the following points, should they arise.

(a) Any **transfer** by **joint holders** should **bear** their **names** in the **same order** as is found in the register of members and on the share certificate. Two or more joint holdings are sometimes distinguished by the order of names, which differs although the names are the same.

(b) Trustees who hold **different investments** for **different beneficiaries** (eg 1,000 shares of the company for X and 2,000 shares for Y) may have arranged to have their accounts in the register of members **designated**, eg 'X Account', 'Y Account' etc. A request for the designation or redesignation of an account should be submitted to the company on the form approved for the purpose by the Institute of Chartered Secretaries and Administrators and The Stock Exchange. It should be signed by the holder or by all the holders, if more than one, and lodged with the company or its registrar, accompanied by the appropriate share certificate. The certificate will then be cancelled and replaced by a new certificate bearing the designation on its face. Any transfer should bear the distinguishing letter or number of the holding to which it relates.

(c) If a transfer is made to joint holders, a check should be made to see whether the **articles impose** a **maximum** on the number of joint holders (usually four) who may be registered as such.

(d) Professional agents who present transfers should add their '**stamp**' to the transfer. If they do so the company has greater security against the risk of forgery or fraud, since a person presenting a transfer warrants that it is correct.

Shares transferred to partnerships or clubs

2.13 The transferee may not be a named individual (or named individuals within the permitted maximum number) or corporation sole, but some 'collective' or official body. If so, the company should satisfy itself that the transferees are competent to hold the shares.

(a) A partnership or a club (unless incorporated) has no collective existence and cannot usually hold property. The proper course is to register shares in the **names of individual partners** (as trustees for the firm - but this should not appear on the register), or in the names of **individuals** (also as undisclosed trustees). It is then for the registered holders and those for whom they hold the shares to deal with the trust aspect, in which the company should not get involved.

(b) An **office holder**, such as 'The Treasurer, Fulham Glee Club', is **not a satisfactory** registered holder of shares, since there may be difficulty in identifying or contacting the person who happens to be the office-holder, especially since from time to time different individuals will hold the office. Again the correct course is for the body or group to appoint a *named* person to act as undisclosed trustee of the shares registered in his name.

Representatives of deceased members

2.14 The shares of a deceased member remain in his name until such time as the personal representatives have the shares registered in their own names or present a transfer of the shares to a third party by the appropriate procedure (described in the next chapter). It is not correct in the meantime to register the shares in the names of the personal representatives in that capacity. If, without going on the register as shareholders in their own right, they present a transfer of the shares, the transfer should describe them as 'personal representatives' of the deceased member.

3 STAMP DUTY AND STAMP DUTY RESERVE TAX 12/98

3.1 As mentioned above, transfers of shares attract stamp duty. Stamp duty is currently charged at 50p per £100 or part £100 of the consideration.

Exemption from stamp duty

3.2 A number of transfers of shares are however potentially exempt. These include:

- Gifts between living individuals
- The vesting of property in new trustees on a change of trustees
- The transfer of property from trustees to a beneficiary
- The transfer of property from a deceased's estate to his heirs
- The transfer of property between spouses in connection with their divorce

3.3 In order to be exempt, such transfers have to be appropriately **certified**, and a company presented with such a transfer should check that it has been certified (or that it has been stamped).

3.4 The standard form of certificate is 'I/we hereby certify that this instrument falls within category ... in the Schedule to the Stamp Duty (Exempt Instruments) Regulations 1987'. The categories are referred to by the letters A to N. The certificate should be included in, endorsed on or attached to the instrument, and should be signed by the transferor or by his solicitor or other duly authorised agent.

3.5 Certain other non-market transfers attract a fixed 50p **stamp duty**. These include transfers to and from nominees of the beneficial owner, and transfer by way of security for a loan.

Stamp duty reserve tax

3.6 Stamp duty reserve tax was introduced to deal with situations where there were a number of agreements for the sale of shares and securities, but an instrument of transfer from the first seller direct to the last purchaser. Stamp duty would only be charged once, based on the price paid by the last purchaser. All the intermediate sale agreements would escape duty under the Stamp Act. This meant that dealings could take place in shares during a Stock Exchange period without paying stamp duty if the securities concerned had not yet reached the final purchaser.

3.7 Stamp duty reserve tax is a separate charge from stamp duty and is levied on the **intermediate sale agreements**. The tax applies to agreements to **transfer chargeable securities**, and does not, unlike stamp duty, need the execution of a written transfer instrument for a charge to be levied. The tax is charged at 50p per £100 of the price paid by the intermediate purchaser, and is payable by the intermediate purchaser. The tax must be paid by the accountable date which is the last day of the month following the month in which the charge arises.

3.8 Liability arises at the **date** of the **agreement**, or, for a conditional agreement, the date the condition is satisfied. For transactions via an exchange (CREST transactions), the tax is payable on a date agreed with the Inland Revenue (or, if there is no agreed date, the fourteenth day after the transaction). For other transactions, the tax is payable on the seventh day of the month following the date of the transaction.

3.9 Chargeable securities that will be subject to stamp duty reserve tax include **renounceable letters of allotment** and **acceptance** where the rights are renounceable not later than six months after the issue of the letter.

3.10 A share transfer which has been stamped as exempt from stamp duty is treated as a duly stamped instrument and no charge for stamp duty reserve tax will arise. Likewise transfers that attract a fixed 50p stamp duty will not be charged stamp duty reserve tax. There is a £5 minimum charge for transfers between **nominee** shareholders without changes in the beneficial ownership.

Exercise

Explain the circumstances in which certification is necessary.

Solution

Look back at paragraph 2.6 if you are unsure.

4 CREST

12/99

4.1 A totally new system was introduced on 15 July 1996 to replace the old TALISMAN system as a means of settling transactions in shares and other securities. The purpose of the change is to bring the UK up to the best international standards by making settlement faster and more secure. CREST will be run for the benefit of the market as a whole by CRESTCo and will own and operate the service.

4.2 Anyone dealing on the stock market will be able to hold shares in **electronic form**, rather than on paper. Electronic holdings can be quickly, cheaply and safely exchanged for money in CREST when shares are bought or sold. Shareholders are not compelled to change to CREST but will be encouraged to do so. Apart from faster settlement the shareholder's name will appear on the register the same day. Under CREST, investors will still receive a contract note from their broker to confirm their purchase. In addition, brokers will be sending a list of clients' stock held in the CREST system, much as they do now for nominee-based accounts.

4.3 Stock Exchange rules require companies to make all their securities eligible for electronic settlement, apart from certain debt securities and in other circumstances where the Exchange agrees.

4.4 The key figure in CREST for the company is the **registrar**. The Listing Rules state the company must appoint a registrar, unless it provides financial services and has an in house registration function.

Sponsored membership of CREST for the private investor

4.5 Active shareholders might like to consider being a **sponsored member** of CREST.

4.6 As a sponsored member, they will authorise a CREST user (their sponsor - perhaps a broker or bank) to operate their membership on their behalf. Their sponsor will act on their instructions. Sponsored membership gives the benefits of electronic settlement without the need to spend money on a computer link to CREST.

Electronic communications with CREST

4.7 Users will communicate with CREST over electronic networks to input their instructions and to receive information.

(a) The CREST system has procedures for **encrypting** messages.

(b) The accuracy and completeness of messages is ensured by all messages entering the CREST gateway being encrypted with a **Message Authentication Code** which is re-computed by the CREST central system when the message is received.

(c) All messages sent to CREST must have a **user identifier** attached. When the message is transmitted the CREST gateway also attaches a gateway identifier, and both the user and gateway identifiers are subsequently checked by the CREST central system.

(d) Each user is assigned a single operator ID, the **MASTER ID.** The MASTER ID has full access to the user's data through CREST. It can also be used to create new operator IDs or set the access rights of operators. Each additional operator will need an operator ID and a password, and there are a number of rules governing the format of passwords.

Becoming eligible for CREST

4.8 The Uncertificated Securities Regulations 1995 provide that companies can make their shares eligible for CREST by means of a simple **Board resolution**. In practice, this route is likely to be suitable only in relation to ordinary shares and some types of preference shares (in particular, non-redeemable and non-convertible preference shares).

4.9 The resolution has the effect of disapplying company articles which are inconsistent with CREST, such as articles requiring written instructions of transfer. However, should this course be adopted without changing the company's articles to permit CREST membership the company's members may by **ordinary resolution resolve** to **revoke** or reverse the directors' decision (Regulation 16(6)).

4.10 A resolution of the directors to allow title to securities of a particular class to be transferred through CREST (a 'directors' resolution') **overrides** any provision of the **articles** relating to that class of share which are inconsistent with the holding of the shares of that class in uncertificated form, that transfer of title to the shares through the CREST system, or the provisions of the regulations (Regulation 16(3)).

4.11 **Notice** of the directors' resolution is required to be given, in accordance with the company's articles, either before it is passed or within 60 days of its being passed, to **every member** of the company. This notice should be sent to all members irrespective of whether the directors' resolution relates to the class of shares held by those members.

4.12 A copy of the **directors' resolution** must be **filed** at Companies House within 15 days of being passed and must be embodied in or annexed to any copies of the articles of association issued thereafter (Regulation 40(3)).

4.13 Where shares are held in **bearer warrant** form, they must be treated as a **separate class** for the purposes of the Regulations (Regulation 17).

Overturning a directors' resolution

4.14 Unless and until the company's articles are modified so that they are consistent with the company's shares being transferred through CREST, members could by ordinary resolution:

(a) If a directors' resolution has not been passed, resolve that directors shall **not pass** such a resolution

(b) If a directors' resolution has been passed but not yet come into effect, resolve that it shall **not come into effect**

(c) If a directors' resolution has come into effect but the shares concerned have not yet been admitted to CREST, resolve that it shall **cease to have effect**

(d) If a directors' resolution has been passed, has come into effect and the shares concerned have been admitted to CREST, resolve that the shares shall **cease to be transferable** through CREST

4.15 There is no provision in the Regulations requiring the company to put a resolution to the members or to call a meeting for that purpose. Thus in order to propose any such resolution, members would need to **requisition** an **extraordinary general meeting** or put forward a members' resolution at the annual general meeting.

Admission of company securities other than ordinary shares

4.16 CREST can settle all types of UK and Irish registered or constituted corporate securities. Holders of securities not eligible for CREST are outside the mainstream and find dealing and settlement slower and more expensive. It will also be more risky since only CREST can provide delivery versus payment protecting shareholders against potential loss of stock and cash if the purchaser defaults.

4.17 It should be noted however that the Regulations do not allow the same Board resolution route for the dematerialisation of other than ordinary shares. Companies will need to look at the particular document (eg loan stock trust deed) which constitutes a security in order to determine whether it contains provisions such as those requiring a written certificate or instrument of transfer, which would make it ineligible for CREST.

4.18 If, as is likely, there is such wording, companies will need to consider **amending** the particular document to permit the security to be held and transferred in dematerialised form.

The CREST settlement process

4.19 The CREST system **matches instructions** from the seller and buyer and holds them until the settlement date. The settlement process, which runs continuously, checks whether the settlement date has been reached.

4.20 On the settlement date, CREST checks for each pair of instructions that the purchaser has **sufficient credit**, and the buyer **holds enough stock**. If they do, CREST debits the seller's and credits the purchaser's stock accounts with the securities, and debits the purchaser's and credits the seller's cash account with the consideration.

4.21 CREST then gives the company's **registrar** an **instruction** to update the register of members. This should be done within two hours of settlement.

4.22 To settle more complex arrangements involving a series of mutually dependent transactions, CREST operates what is known as **circles processing**. This initially involves calculating the settlement position if all remaining transactions were to settle (ignoring stock and credit limits) and then taking these limits into account. Circles processing is run on occasions throughout each day, and other settlement activity temporarily ceases while circles processing occurs.

4.23 The amounts payable are settled through each member's **clearing bank**; at the end of every settlement day CRESTCo sends the Bank of England a schedule listing the amounts to or from each bank, and these are settled by a Bank of England debit or credit. The bank settles with the members outside the CREST system.

Alteration of register of members

4.24 The Uncertificated Securities Regulations contain provisions on the alteration of a CREST user's share register, and legal responsibilities should fraud or other problems occur. A separate section of the register will apply to the CREST environment. Regulation 23 sets out rules governing the alteration of a participating company's share register.

(a) Instructions to alter the share register of companies participating in CREST will only come from the **system operator**, except in circumstances such as a court order or instruction under legislation.

(b) The company's registrar is **obliged to obey** the instructions of the systems operator within two hours of settlement (as mentioned above), and must acknowledge to the systems operator that the transfer has been completed. However a transfer should not be registered:

(i) In breach of a court order

(ii) If the company knows that the transfer will be to a deceased person, minor or someone who is not a natural person

(iii) If the company knows that there is an irregularity (transfer instruction made with inaccurate information, not made on proper authority or not sent by systems operator)

(c) The company's registrar can initiate adjustments to the register by sending an **adjustment message** to the systems operator to correct errors or to deal with company actions such as bonus issues.

4.25 The company will be liable for damages under Regulation 37 if it **registers a transfer without instructions** from the systems operator, or **fails to obey an instruction** to transfer and does not inform the systems operator. The systems operator will be liable under Regulation 30 if it sends to the company an instruction to transfer as a result of:

(a) A dematerialised instruction not sent by a computer within the system

(b) An act other than a dematerialised instruction or an act that results in a dematerialised instruction

4.26 The systems operator may be relieved of liability if it can identify the person who was responsible for the forged instruction or other act, or demonstrate that the company should not have registered the transfer.

Change in securities

4.27 Once securities join CREST, all market transactions go through the system whether they are certificated or uncertificated.

4.28 A member of CREST who wants to move certificated securities into an uncertificated CREST account should lodge the **share certificates** and a **completed dematerialisation request form** with the CREST Courier and Sorting Service (CCSS). The CCSS will then pass the documents on to the company's registrar for entry in the company's register.

4.29 If a client of a CREST member sells certificated securities, the client will execute a **CREST transfer form** in favour of the CREST member. The transfer form and share certificates will be sent to the CCSS, and from the CCSS to the company's registrar for action. The registrar will transfer the securities from the certificated account of the client and credit them to the uncertificated account of the CREST member so that they can subsequently be settled through CREST. No stamp duty or stamp duty reserve tax will be payable as a result of the transfer from certificated to uncertificated form.

4.30 A CREST member may on the other hand want securities held on its uncertificated account to be held in **certificated form**. If so, the member will transmit through CREST a **stock withdrawal request** to the company's registrar. The registrar will move the securities into an account in the certificated part of the register of members and issue a certificate which is sent to the CREST member via the CCSS. Again this procedure will not itself attract stamp duty or stamp duty reserve tax.

The initial operation of CREST

4.31 CREST had a number of initial problems during the latter part of 1996. There were a number of reconciliation failures resulting from CREST users failing to set up member accounts. CREST was also working very slowly due to the volume of transactions. A number of FTSE companies were asked to delay their entry into CREST until the early part of 1997.

4.32 Since the start of 1997 the situation has improved and in particular CREST has successfully handled floatations of various of the major building societies. Further improvements are planned, including reducing the standard settlement period to match international standards.

4.33 CREST has already proved to have a number of implications for a company's share registration function.

(a) **Bed and breakfasting situations**. Bed and breakfasting is the sale of a security on one day and its repurchase the next day in order to establish a capital gain or loss. Under CREST, unlike the previous systems of market settlement, two entries will be required in the share register, and this has resulted in a significant increase in transfers processed by company registrars.

(b) **Notices of meetings**. Regulation 34 of the Uncertificated Securities Regulations allows CREST users to specify a time in the notice of company meetings for calculating attending and voting entitlements. This time may not be more than 48 hours before the meeting. It is necessary to specify a time since under CREST, the part of the register that relates to CREST shareholdings could be altering up to the start and even during the course of the meeting. Indications are that the time preferred by companies is close of business of the day which is two days before the meeting day (for example for a meeting on Friday, close of business on the previous Wednesday). Regulation 34 also allows companies to specify a date for determining entitlement to receive notice of a meeting. This must be not more than 21 days before the date on which the notice is sent out. The date should be expressed in terms of the close of business and should be included in the board resolution approving notice of the meeting.

(c) **Nominee members**. The introduction of CREST and in particular the development of sponsored membership has meant many new nominee accounts have been opened, and companies are not aware of the shareholders using these accounts. It has become more difficult for companies to keep track of their underlying shareholders and hence it is important for companies to obtain confirmation in accordance with s 212 CA 85 of who is interested in their shares.

(d) **Administrative problems**. Because some shareholders will continue to hold their share in paper form, registrars will have to operate two systems rather than one. CREST also demands that the registrar's working day starts early; 6.30 a.m. has been proposed.

(e) **Rights issues.** CREST can be used to facilitate a rights issues relating to shares held in uncertificated form by treating nil and fully paid rights as a separate class of CREST securities. The use of CREST can hasten the receipt of cash by the company and enable those taking up the rights to obtain their shares more quickly.

5 TRANSMISSION OF SHARES

5.1 The transmission of shares by **operation of law** may require entries in the register of members. In such cases (death, bankruptcy or mental incapacity of a member) the company requires that the person to whom legal control of the shares has passed shall produce the appropriate evidence of his authority. This aspect of is considered in more detail in the next chapter.

6 AMERICAN DEPOSITORY RECEIPTS (ADRs)

6.1 As the above has shown, the business of transferring shares is administratively complicated. American Depository Receipts are a way round these complications.

6.2 Instead of trading in shares of British companies as such, Americans may buy and sell ADRs which confer ownership rights to the shares. The shares themselves are held on deposit with a bank. Trading in ADRs avoids the necessity to register changes in ownership of shares and obviates the need to pay stamp duty.

Chapter roundup

- Transfer of shares involves **change** of **ownership** by **sale** or **gift** etc; transmission involves change of ownership/control by operation of law such as bankruptcy, on death etc.
- Close attention should be paid to the **provisions** of the **articles** with regard to transfer and transmission of shares, as well as statutory provisions.
- A company may **refuse**, if the articles provide, to **register** a **transfer** and therefore acknowledge the transferor as the registered shareholder if shares are not fully paid up.
- The document of transfer which is usually used is the standard form set out in the Stock Transfer Act 1963 which requires the following details to be completed.
  - Consideration for all shares
  - Name of company in whose shares the party is dealing
  - Type of shares to be transferred, such as ordinary shares of £1 each
  - Share details in words and figures
  - Transferor's name and address
  - Signature of transferor(s)
  - Transferee's name and address
  - Date and stamp of agent

  Attached to the forms is the share certificate(s) of the shares transferred.
- On transfer of **partly paid shares** a different procedure applies.
- All transfer forms should show that **stamp duty** has been paid as appropriate.
- The company should take particular care to check all the **details** of the transfer to avoid fraud, for which the company may be held liable if loss is suffered by a third party in consequence of that fraud. Insurance cover is often taken out to protect the company in such instances. The extent of cover should be considered.
- If a shareholder wishes to sell off part of his shareholding, or all of it, to two or more parties, then he may obtain **certification** from the company. This is an endorsement effectively certifying the transfer proposed.
- Recent developments for Stock Exchange listed companies include the introduction of a **rolling settlement** and the implementation of the **CREST** system, the system of electronic settlement of transactions in securities. You should be aware of how CREST operates.

Test your knowledge

1 On what grounds may the directors of a company whose articles follow the model of Table A refuse to register a transfer of shares? (see para 1.2)

2 What changes in the execution of a share transfer of fully paid shares were introduced by the Stock Transfer Act 1963? (1.5)

3 Describe the basic procedure for preparing a transfer of the shares comprised in the transferor's share certificate. (2.1)

4 Give five points to which attention should be given in the scrutiny of a transfer presented for registration. (2.2)

5 In what circumstances is certification of a share transfer appropriate? (2.6)

6 What is the legal effect of registration of a forged transfer? (2.9)

7 For what points should a company watch in dealing with a transfer of shares by or to joint holders? (2.12)

8 What are the essential features of the CREST system of transferring shares? (4)

Now try illustrative question 23 at the end of the Study Text

Chapter 21

REGISTRATION OF DOCUMENTS

This chapter covers the following topics.

Introduction

Apart from a straightforward transfer there are other situations which give rise to changes to the share register as follows.

(a) If a member dies, his 'personal representatives' have authority to deal with his shares.

(b) If a woman member changes her name on marriage, her name on the register will have to be changed.

(c) If a member becomes insolvent, the company may have to deal with his trustee in bankruptcy, or respond to a variety of court orders which may be issued at the behest of his creditors.

(d) A member may go off on a long trip abroad and issue a power of attorney by which an agent can deal with his shares.

The common element of these, and some other events with which this chapter is concerned, is that the company must see and note in its records an appropriate *document* as evidence of the information given to it.

In all cases where the proper procedures have been completed, the share certificate should be produced to the company for endorsement of the change and returned to the newly named member.

1 DEATH OF A MEMBER AND ITS CONSEQUENCES 6/98, 6/00

1.1 The death of a member is a matter with which the Secretary frequently has to deal. In acknowledging the notification the Secretary will normally express sympathy and condolences on behalf of the company and then proceed to outline the formalities.

1.2 The formal evidence of his death is his '**death certificate**' issued by the Registry of Births, Deaths and Marriages. A company may always accept as genuine a death certificate which bears the official seal of the registry. Problems may arise, however, if what is produced is a xerox or photocopy of a certificate which could hide an attempted fraud.

1.3 If a death certificate is produced the company may enter the fact and date of death in its register of members, against the member's name. The most accurate way of preserving a record of the information is to make a facsimile copy of the certificate, ie a xerox or photographic copy, before returning it. The copy should be filed where it can be found if needed. There is no need to call in the share certificate(s) to endorse them with the fact of the member's death, but there is no objection to doing so.

1.4 Although a deceased member is no longer a member, his shareholding is still part of the company's issued capital on its register. The legal effect differs according to whether the deceased member was the sole shareholder, or one of two or more joint holders.

(a) If he was the sole registered holder, the shares form part of his '**estate**' and will be dealt with as described below.

(b) If he was one of **joint holders**, the **survivors** become **the legal owners** of the holding; the company deals with them alone, after deleting the name of the dead member from the holders of the shares.

In either case there may be underlying 'trust' interests, but the company is prohibited (s 360) from taking note of a trust; it need not and should not concern itself with such matters.

Grant of representation

1.5 The law requires that the property of a deceased person, which includes shares registered in his sole name, shall be properly administered by a person or persons duly authorised to do so. In English law, that authority is given by a '**grant of representation**' (to the estate) from the court to one or more persons called 'personal representatives'. These may be 'executors' or 'administrators'.

(a) If the deceased person **made a valid will,** appointing one or more **executors,** they may obtain legal authority to act under the will, by presenting it to the court for approval. (This is called 'obtaining probate' or 'proving the will'.) In a straightforward case, they simply apply to the Registry of the Family Division of the High Court, which issues to them a 'grant of probate' under the seal of the court. That document is the necessary evidence of the executor's authority.

(b) If the deceased **did not make a will,** (died intestate) or if the executor(s) named in his will cannot (for example because he is dead) or will not apply for probate, the next of kin of the deceased (or beneficiaries under the will) apply to the court (as in (a)) for 'letters of administration', giving them authority under the seal of the court. Again this is the evidence of authority, given in this case to '**administrator***(s)*' of the estate.

1.6 It is common practice to obtain a number of '**office copies**' of these grants, each of which is legally equivalent to the original, since it is issued by the court registry under its seal. Office copies should be distinguished from mere xerox or photocopies made privately, which do not have the same legal effect and should not be accepted. A copy of the document should be filed on the company's register of documents and the original office copy should be returned to the sender.

1.7 A company is required to accept 'as sufficient evidence of the grant' a **probate** or **letters of administration** issued by the court registry: s 187. In other words, if an executor or administrator of an estate presents a probate or letters of administration to a company, the company must accept this as evidence that the executor or administrator has been given a grant of representation to act as personal representative of the deceased member's estate. The company may also accept the grant as evidence of the member's death (without seeing his death certificate), since the grant will, among other things, record the death and its date.

Confirmation

1.8 If the deceased person died when he or she was domiciled in Scotland, there is a similar (but not identical) system of issuing a '**confirmation**' (instead of a probate) of a will by the court. Confirmation is granted to the executors named in the will, the '**executors nominate**'. If there are no surviving executors or if there was no will, the Court makes a grant to a person to administer the estate. These are the '**executors dative**' (the English equivalent are administrators).

1.9 The chief difference between English probates and letters of administration is that Scottish confirmation has annexed to it an **inventory** of the deceased's property to which the executors have been confirmed. They may only deal with the property listed. Therefore companies must confirm that the list includes the securities of the company. If not included, the Court can add in the securities.

1.10 An English company may (under the Administration of Estates Act 1971) accept a Scottish confirmation without further formality, unless its terms do not confer authority to deal with the shareholdings of the deceased. S 187 also refers to a 'confirmation' as sufficient evidence of the grant. A Northern Ireland grant is also recognised in England.

1.11 Most other countries have similar systems of making a 'grant' of some sort in connection with the estate of a deceased person. However these documents are not valid authority in England unless **'re-sealed'** or a **fresh transfer** made. If any such document is presented by the personal representatives of a now deceased member the company should not recognise it until the appropriate English procedure, giving it legal effect in England, has been carried through (and evidence of it produced). Only Commonwealth grants can be 're-sealed' in the English High Court. Grants emanating from the Channel Islands and Isle of Man are not acceptable and fresh grants will be required.

Death of a personal representative

1.12 The administration of a large estate may take years to complete, and it often happens that a person to whom a grant has been made dies before his work is finished.

(a) If he was one of two or more personal representatives, the **survivor(s)**, after producing his death certificate, may be **accepted** by the company as still authorised to represent the estate.

(b) If he was a sole executor (or sole surviving executor) and he made a will which has been admitted to probate, **his executor(s)** on producing their probate may be **recognised** as his successor(s).

(c) In any other case, including one where the original grant was by letters of administration, (the deceased did not make a will), the death of the sole surviving representative must be followed by action to obtain a **new grant** to another person; that other person will then produce his grant to the company and be treated as successor to the deceased representative.

Action by the company on receiving a grant of representation

1.13 When the grant is produced to the company, it should be examined to ensure that the **deceased person** to whom it relates (whose full name and address are given) is indeed the **shareholder** whose name is on the company's register. The **share certificate** should accompany the grant. It provides confirmation of identity if the name is a common one. The grant should also be examined to ensure that it is an original or 'office copy'.

1.14 The company must then act as follows.

(a) **Add** the word **'deceased'** after the shareholder's name in the **register** of members, with the **date of death.** The sheet in the register relating to this holding should not be removed from the register, since it still relates to an existing holding. A similar endorsement to the **share certificate**(s), when returned, will also have to be made.

(b) **Record** the **names** and **addresses** of the **representatives** named in the grant, and the particulars of the grant (what type etc):

- In the register of members
- On the share certificate(s)
- In any other relevant company records

(c) **Impress** a **company stamp** on the back of the grant, to record that it has been registered with the company.

(d) **Return** the **grant** to the person who presented it, with the share certificate(s) and also a dividend mandate and letter of request in appropriate cases.

Letter of request

1.15 The registration of the grant gives the **personal representatives** the **power** to present a transfer of the deceased member's shares for registration, subject to any relevant provisions of the articles. Table A Article 30 permits a person to have the share registered either in his own name or in that of another on providing such evidence that the directors properly require (usually the grant of probate). If he then wishes to transfer the shares(s) to another person he must do so by completing a stock transfer form.

1.16 If the personal representatives wish to be registered as the named holders of the shares, Table A Article 30 provides that they may give 'notice' rather than presenting a transfer. This notice, called a **'Letter of Request'**, is addressed to the company and should be signed by *all* the personal representatives. A letter which is properly signed needs no other formality, such as witnessing.

1.17 Companies generally prefer that the personal representatives **hold the share(s)** in their own name and are **entered** on the **register as members,** without reference to their trustee status. On receiving a Letter of Request, the company should record a transfer out of the name of the deceased member (so that his account is closed) and open a new account in the name of the personal representative(s) as normal members.

1.18 1985 Table A Article 31 provides that personal representatives not registered as members shall have the **same rights** as a **registered shareholder,** except that they may not attend or vote at general meetings: they are, however, still entitled to receive notice of meetings (Table A Article 38).

1.19 If, after the member's death, the company pays a dividend which relates partly to a financial year or other period *before* his death, it is the responsibility of the personal representatives, not the company, to **apportion** it between the periods (before and after death) for tax and other purposes.

Grants of representation and small estates

1.20 Although there are simplified procedures for obtaining a grant in respect of a small estate, it always entails expense and some formality. Companies often receive applications from a deceased member's close relatives for informal acceptance (without production of a grant) of a transfer of the shares into the name of the applicant, as the person entitled to the shares. A company has no legal obligation to comply with any such request, and should certainly refuse it unless it is reasonably clear that the whole estate of the deceased does not **exceed,** say, **£5,000**; some companies adopt a lower or higher figure.

1.21 If it does appear to be a genuine case of a small shareholding comprised in a small estate, the company may at its discretion agree to register a transfer without seeing a grant, if the following procedure is adopted.

(a) The applicant presents both the following:

(i) The **death certificate**

(ii) A **statutory declaration** (sworn statement) of his or her identity, relationship to the deceased and grounds for claiming to be entitled to the shares

(b) It is desirable, though companies do not always insist on it, that the applicant obtains a letter from the Capital Taxes Office to the effect that on the information given, the Office does not consider that any liability to Inheritance Tax arises in connection with the shareholding.

(c) In any event, the applicant should supply an **indemnity** to the company against any liability which the company may incur as a result of permitting the transfer of the shares without seeing a grant or clearance from the Capital Taxes Office. The indemnity should also include an undertaking that the applicant will obtain and produce to the company a grant of representation, if the company should later require it. The indemnity should be joined by a bank, insurance company or guarantee society.

1.22 In the majority of cases these precautions suffice, and no further problems arise. But there is the risk to the company that the applicant is withholding material facts, or is unaware that the deceased made in his lifetime substantial gifts which, when added to his estate at his death, will attract a liability to Inheritance Tax. Also if the deceased was resident abroad at the time of his death, a different procedure may be required, since the tax position is likely to be much more complicated.

Death of a joint holder of shares

1.23 As indicated earlier, legal ownership of shares in joint names is in the survivors, on the death of one joint holder. The following points may arise.

(a) The company should preferably **see the death certificate**, but a grant in respect of the estate of the deceased, although not otherwise relevant, will suffice as evidence of his death.

(b) If the deceased was the first named joint holder, the **second name** now becomes the **first**. If the register is in looseleaf, alphabetical form, the record of the holding may have to be moved to a new position; the index (if any) may also require alteration.

(c) The **surviving joint holder(s)** should **produce** their **share certificate(s)** for appropriate alteration, ie by endorsement of a note of the death.

(d) **Dividend mandates** and other instructions **remain in force** unless the survivor(s) elect to issue new ones.

Bona vacanta

1.24 If a person dies domiciled in England and Wales without having made a will and no persons remain with the lawful rights of succession which apply in such cases, the High Court will issue a grant of administration (known as **bona vacanta**) appointing the Treasury Solicitor or officers of the Duchy of Lancaster or the Duke of Cornwall to administer the estate. The procedure for registration is the same as in the case of a probate. In such cases the shareholding would usually be disposed of forthwith and consequently no letter of request would be issued.

Ultimus Haeres

1.25 **Ultimus Haeres** is a Scottish process roughly equivalent to the English **bona vacantia**. Where in Scotland a person dies without having made a will and there are no relatives entitled to succeed to the intestate estate, it falls to the Crown as *ultimus haeres* and the Queen's and Lord Treasurer's Remembrancer takes possession of the estate.

1.26 The Scottish rules of succession apply to the moveable estate of a person who dies domiciled in Scotland and to the devolution of heritable property situated in Scotland whatever the domicile of the deceased.

1.27 The company should check that the deceased named is the registered shareholder. Details of the death and the Queen's and Lord Treasurer's Remembrancer should be included in the register of members. The register should show that the shareholder is deceased; legally the deceased is still the registered shareholder. The share certificate should be enclosed with details of death and of the court order to be endorsed by the company; the endorsement should be validated by the company's registration stamp. The registration stamp should also be impressed on the back of the order which should be returned together with the endorsed share certificate.

2 INSOLVENCY OF A MEMBER

2.1 Individual insolvency (bankruptcy) is regulated by the **Insolvency Act 1986** *and the* **Insolvency Rules 1986**.

2.2 A member becomes bankrupt when the court makes a **bankruptcy order** against him: s 278 IA. The effect of the order is that the Official Receiver of the DTI assumes control of the estate of the bankrupt, pending the appointment of a trustee. The trustee must be an **authorised insolvency practitioner**. If no trustee is appointed the Official Receiver acts in that capacity.

2.3 The bankrupt member remains a member until such time as the trustee exercises his power to re-register the shares in the name of the trustee, by **Letter of Request** (to which the same considerations apply as on the death of a member). On receipt of a vesting order, vesting the shares in the trustee, the company should require a trustee (if not the Official Receiver) to produce evidence of his appointment. Once appointment has been confirmed the bankruptcy should be noted in the register of members.

2.4 A trustee is usually appointed by **resolution** passed at a **meeting of creditors**. The chairman of the meeting signs a formal certificate of the appointment. In certain cases a trustee (other than the Official Receiver) may be appointed by the **court**, or by the **DTI**. The required evidence of his appointment is either a **certificate** signed by the chairman of the creditors' meeting, or by an official of the DTI or an order of the court.

2.5 It is provided (Insolvency Rule 6.123) that a **copy certificate** (duly authenticated) or a **sealed court order** is sufficient evidence of the appointment for all legal purposes. As the trustee will be an insolvency practitioner, a professional man recognised by the DTI, the company may elect to deal with him on a less formal basis, once they have seen evidence of his appointment.

2.6 The trustee will usually sell the shares to raise money for the benefit of the bankrupt person's creditors. He may present a transfer of shares to another person (in which he is described as trustee) without going on the register as a member.

2.7 The trustee may also by formal notice (s 315 IA) **'disclaim'** the shares as 'onerous property' (that is property which is not readily saleable, or 'such that it may give rise to a liability to pay money', or otherwise a burden on the trustee). A disclaimer under s 315 IA 'discharges the trustee from all personal liability in respect of that property as from the commencement of his trusteeship'.

2.8 Insolvency Rule 6.178 provides that such a disclaimer shall be submitted to the court for **sealing** before it becomes effective; the company may of course accept the sealed disclaimer as sufficient for its purpose. The name of the member (or of the trustee) should then be removed from the register.

2.9 If the bankrupt member is a joint holder, his **interest** in the holding passes to the **trustee** and not to the other joint holders.

2.10 Problems arise where the bankrupt member holds **partly paid shares**. The trustee (like the personal representative) does not usually apply to become the registered holder of shares to which a liability attaches. It is partly paid shares which are most likely to be **disclaimed**; even if fully paid shares are worthless, the trustee secures no advantage by disclaiming them.

Liquidation of a company member

2.11 'A company member' means a company who is a member (shareholder) of another company. The liquidator of the company member, who must be an insolvency practitioner, should produce copies of either of the following documents.

(a) The **court order** (in case of compulsory liquidation)

(b) The **resolution** by which the company went into liquidation and appointed him its liquidator (or by which the creditors' meeting appointed him: s 100 IA)

In either case there will also be notices in the **London Gazette**, which may provide confirmation if required.

3 MENTAL INCAPACITY OF A MEMBER

3.1 Under the Mental Health Act 1983, the Court of Protection may appoint a receiver (with defined powers) over the estate of a mentally disordered person. A **copy of the court order** is sufficient to establish the status and powers of a receiver seeking to deal with such a member's shares. It is not usual for the Court to issue an order giving *general* powers over the property (as distinct from the income) of the 'patient', and so the terms of the order should be scrutinised carefully.

4 CHANGE OF MEMBER'S NAME 6/00

4.1 The most frequent occasion of a change of name is the marriage of a female shareholder. She should be asked to produce two documents.

(a) Her official **marriage certificate** (though some companies will accept a photocopy, if presented by a solicitor or other professional agent)

If she cannot or will not produce the certificate, the company may (in the absence of suspicion) accept a statutory declaration.

(b) Her **share certificate**, for endorsement and return.

4.2 Any person may change his or her name, either informally or by deed poll ('poll' simply indicating that only the member is a party to the deed instead of there being two parties to a deed, as is usual).

4.3 If the change is made informally, the member should produce to the company either of the following:

(a) A **statutory declaration**

(b) A **written declaration** of identity (under the old and new names) by some person of professional or public standing, such as a solicitor or a bank manager

The company may then alter its entry in the register of members (and amend the share certificate).

4.4 The more formal procedure is a **deed poll**, duly stamped, and a notice in the *London Gazette*. The company should see one or other of these documents.

4.5 If a company member changes its name it should produce its **certificate of re-registration**, obtained from the Companies Registry.

5 CHANGE OF MEMBER'S ADDRESS

5.1 If a member sends a notice of change of address on a printed card, it should be returned with a polite request that he should add his **personal signature**, since it would be unwise for the company to rely on an impersonal notification. A notification by a professional agent, such as a solicitor, accountant or bank, is generally acceptable. If in doubt, **acknowledgement** of the notice should be **sent** to both the **old** and **new address**. It is unwise to accept notice of change of address from a relative or any other private individual purporting to act for the member; the opportunities for fraud are obviously too great.

5.2 On receiving the notice, the company should **alter** the **register of members** accordingly. It is not usually necessary to call in the share certificate, since in modern practice the holder's address is not given on the certificate.

6 MEMBER'S POWER OF ATTORNEY

6.1 A Power of Attorney is the **written appointment** of an **agent** (called 'the attorney', or 'the donee' of the power) by a principal ('the donor'), giving the agent **power** to **enter** into **transactions** on behalf of the principal. The basic law on this subject is contained in the Powers of Attorney Act 1971 (extended by the Enduring Powers of Attorney Act 1985). A Power of Attorney should be executed as a deed. A typical situation giving rise to a Power of Attorney would be where a member goes off on a long trip abroad, and issues a Power of Attorney to an agent.

6.2 When someone presents to a company a Power of Attorney authorising him to act for a member (as principal), say in signing a transfer of shares, the company should check it to ensure that it displays the following features:

- It is genuine.
- It is correct in form.
- It confers the requisite powers.
- It is still in force.

6.3 In the normal case, the donor **signs** the **document** (as a deed) and the **signature** of a **witness is added**. If the company has a specimen of the member's signature, it should compare the two. It is also possible (for the convenience of donors who are infirm) for another person to execute the power, provided that this is done in the presence of the donor and by his direction (which should be recorded in the document); in this case there should be two witnesses to the signature.

6.4 A Power of Attorney must be **executed** as a **deed**. This requires that the donor should sign below or alongside the formula 'Signed sealed and delivered by'. A corporate donor, should always impress its seal on the document (if it has one) and have it witnessed, as required by its articles or other regulations; it is generally witnessed by two directors or a director and the secretary of the company.

6.5 A corporate body, such as a company member, may execute a Power of Attorney (in accordance with the provisions of its articles), but this is not often done by English companies, unless they are appointing an attorney to act in another country.

6.6 It is possible to appoint more than one attorney, to act **jointly**, or **jointly** and **severally**. If it is joint all the attorneys must act together. If joint and several, the attorneys can act individually. In any event an attorney may not delegate his power to some other person.

6.7 Schedule 1 to the Power of Attorney Act 1971 ('PA') provides a standard form of '**general power**' which gives the attorney power to do whatever the donor is competent to do (through an agent). A general power suffices to authorise the attorney to sign a transfer, or other document relating to the donor's shares or interest in the company.

6.8 Sometimes however the power is limited, by its terms, to **specified transactions** or even to a **single act**. This is likely to be the case if the donor is a company or a trustee (for whom there are limited possibilities of delegation under the PA).

6.9 On receiving a power which is specific, the company should consider whether the **power is wide enough** to authorise the attorney to act as he proposes. Specific powers are strictly construed in a limited, rather than an extended, sense. It may be necessary to repeat the process on each occasion when the attorney presents his power, seeking recognition from the company for a particular purpose.

Revocation of a Power of Attorney

6.10 A Power of Attorney is often expressed to be **irrevocable** for a period of a **year**, so the date of the power may be material. However the PA gives protection to a third party (the company), if it deals with the attorney in ignorance of the fact that his power has been revoked.

6.11 There is no problem for a company with **express revocation** (a deliberate act by the donor to take away an agent's Power of Attorney), since a donor who revokes will usually recover (take back into his own hands) the power from the donee, and perhaps give notice to the company.

6.12 **Revocation** is **automatic** on notice of death, insanity or insolvency of the donor: a company which receives notice of the death etc of a member should remember that, with this knowledge, it can no longer accept as operative any Power of Attorney, apart from powers of attorney validated by the Court of Protection (see below).

Action by the company on receiving a Power of Attorney

6.13 Apart from considering, and where necessary checking, the above points, a company on receiving a Power of Attorney should take the following action.

(a) It should be checked to ensure the following.

(i) It is in the **correct form**, ie complies with the Powers of Attorney Act 1971 (as amended) and is **executed** as a **deed** by the donor of the power. The power is executed as a deed if the donor signs alongside the words, 'Signed sealed and delivered by'. The donor's signature should be witnessed.

(ii) It is the **original document** or a photocopy which has been certified as original and as genuine (by checking the donor's signature against the member's signature).

(iii) It is **still in force**, ie was originally expressed to be permanently irrevocable or irrevocable for a limited period of time, in which case check to ensure the period has not expired.

(iv) It **confers powers** on the donee to do what is required; if, for example, the power appears to be limited or specifies what the donee can do on behalf of the donor, check whether it will allow the donee to act on behalf of the shareholder for example to attend and vote at company meetings.

(b) A **photocopy** of the power should be taken for the company's records.

(c) The **original power** should be **stamped** with the company's registration stamp.

(d) The **original power** should be **returned** to the person who sent it to the company (often the donor).

6.14 If the power was not executed by the donor personally but by someone on his behalf, (a likely instance of fraud), send to the donor a '**protective notice**' that the power has been lodged, and that the company will take action on it as a valid authorisation of the attorney, *unless* the donor replies to the company, within a certain period of time, instructing it not to do so.

6.15 Under the Enduring Powers of Attorney Act 1985 ('EPA'), however, if the power is made in a **special form** and is presented to the Court of Protection for validation (after proper enquiry) it continues **in force** despite the donor's subsequent incapacity. A company which receives such a power should ensure that it bears the authorisation of the Court of Protection, or that the donor is at that point still mentally capable.

6.16 If the power is presented while validation by the Court of Protection is still in process, the company may, subject to conditions, accept it. Remember also that unless a company is at the time **aware** of a member's incapacity, it is entitled to assume that he is mentally capable: the company is shielded from liability by its unawareness.

Exercise

What action should a company register take on receipt of a photostat copy of a power of attorney given by Mr Peter Scott, a registered shareholder in favour of Mr Charles Smart? The document has been certified a true copy by an accountant.

Solution

A Power of Attorney is the written appointment of an agent - the attorney or the donee of the power - giving the agent power to enter into transactions on behalf of the principal. The basic law is contained in the Power of Attorney Act 1971, as extended by the Enduring Power of Attorney Act 1984.

When a Power of Attorney is presented to a company, it must check that the document is genuine, that it is in correct form, that it confers the requisite powers, and that it is still in force.

Normally, the Power is signed by the donor (the document is a deed) and the signature of a witness is added. If the company has a specimen of the member's signature, it should obviously compare the two. It is also possible for another person to execute the Power, for instance where the donor concerned is infirm, provided that this is done in the presence of the donor and by his or her direction. This should be recorded in the document, and the number of witnesses is increased to two.

As mentioned above, a Power of Attorney is a deed. This requires that the donor should sign below or alongside the formula 'signed sealed and delivered by...' although the use of a seal or wafer is no longer necessary.

In addition to checking these points, the secretary should also satisfy himself that it is either the original power or a copy duly certified. It is here that problems arise in respect of the Power given by Mr Peter Scott. The 1971 Act recognises only photocopies certified by a stockbroker, solicitor or the transferor.

Since the Power is only certified as a true copy by an accountant, the secretary should return it, explaining the reasons why.

When the secretary receives a properly certified copy (or the original if this is necessary), the procedure is as follows.

A photocopy of the Power of Attorney is made for the company records, then the document should be stamped with the company's registration stamp and returned to the person by whom it was presented. Since the Power here has been executed by the donor himself, there will be no need for the use of a protective notice, as there would be where it has been executed by someone on his behalf (with the consequent possibility of fraud).

---

7 OTHER DOCUMENTS PRESENTED FOR REGISTRATION

7.1 Other documents which might be presented to a company for registration include court orders, such as 'stop notices'.

7.2 To enable a third party to protect his interest in shares not registered in his name, he is permitted to apply to the court registry, with an affidavit* setting out the nature of his interest and the notice which he wishes to serve on the company. He obtains from the court a sealed copy of the notice, and of his own affidavit; these documents he then delivers to the company. This procedure is prescribed by the Charging Orders Act 1979, and the rules of the Supreme Court.

* A statement (written) sworn on oath.

Stop notice

7.3 A 'stop notice' may relate only to a **transfer** of the **specified shares**, or it may in addition relate to **payment of dividends** on those shares as well. On receiving the documents, the company should check that the **stop notice** is **sealed** by the court and relates to a shareholding in the register of members. **No note** should be made in the register of members of the **nature** of the claim, but there should be a note in the register of members that restrictions have been **placed** on the holding. The stop notice and copy affidavit should be carefully filed. It is common practice to place a code number or letter on the register of members to indicate to staff that there is a stop on the account.

7.4 If the stop notice is limited to a transfer of the shares, and does not cover payment of dividends, no action is required unless a transfer of those shares is presented. In that case the company's duties are as follows.

(a) **Give notice in writing** of the presentation of the transfer to the person who lodged the stop notice. He then has 14 days in which to obtain an injunction (court order) directed to the company to prohibit the transfer.

(b) **Inform the person** who presented the transfer that 'stop notice' procedure has been taken.

If at the end of **14 days** no injunction has been served on the company, it may and should proceed to deal with the transfer in the normal way.

7.5 If the stop notice is expressed to cover payment of dividends, similar action must be taken, and a 14 day interval observed, before the dividend may be paid.

Charging and garnishee orders

7.6 There are other legal proceedings which may result in a court order addressed to a company.

(a) A person who has been awarded a court judgement as creditor of a member may, under the Charging Orders Act, obtain a **charging order** in respect of the debtor's assets, including his shares.

(b) The creditor may alternatively obtain a '**garnishee order**' which prohibits the company from making a payment, for example of a dividend, to a member and instead making it to the creditor. This applies only to sums already due for payment when the order is received. However a **garnishee order** cannot prevent a transfer of shares. The procedure is that an **order nisi** is obtained, requiring the company to attend court. If the debt is settled prior to the date of the court hearing, the order will be discharged; if the shareholder does not pay the debt, the order will be made absolute and the company required to pay the dividend to the creditor in partial or full settlement of the shareholder's debts.

See "Mareva injunctions"

7.7 There can be no doubt whether a court order is genuine or not. When presented, it bears the **seal** (in fact a rubber stamp) of the court. The only question which can arise is whether the person who obtained the order, by application to the court, asked for it to be issued in appropriate terms. It is best for the company to consult its legal advisers in such matters. If in doubt, comply with the notice, give notice to the member, and let the member seek a declaration in respect of the order.

Vesting order

7.8 A vesting order is an order of the court under which property passes as **effectually** as it would under a **conveyance**.

Registration of documents in general

7.9 As indicated above, a company should always consider whether the document presented to it is **genuine** and **sufficient** for its purpose. However, by presenting it to the company the presenter warrants (guarantees) that it is genuine. If the document comes from a presenter of high standing and professional status, such as a solicitor or a bank, this fact is itself a considerable safeguard.

7.10 If there are discrepancies, over names, addresses etc., it may suffice to obtain a **formal declaration** from a presenter of good standing to resolve the matter.

7.11 If an entry or alteration is made in the register of members, the **relevant share certificate** should be **called in** to alter it so as to correspond with the register. In making any alteration or addition to a share certificate, the company should stamp the alteration so that any change to the certificate not made by the company can be repudiated as unauthorised.

7.12 The company should maintain comprehensive and exact records of all documents which it has inspected, even if the originals are returned to the presenter (as is done with a grant of representation of a deceased member's estate, or a Power of Attorney). The usual procedure is as follows.

(a) To **maintain a register** (or separate registers, for important categories of documents) in which particulars of each document, including the date of registration, are entered at the time.

(b) To make, and file for easy access, a **copy** of any document the original of which is to be returned. This is much safer than making notes of the contents of the document.

Chapter roundup

- A company must record all changes of membership in registers, and either endorse or issue a new share certificate.
- On death of a member the following rules apply.
  - **Proof of death** (the production of the death certificate) is required.
  - Shares vest in **personal representatives** (PRs) or joint holders (depending on the terms of the shareholding).
  - PRs either have a **grant of probate** (where a valid will was written) or a **letter of administration** (where there is no valid will) issued by the court, empowering PRs to deal with the deceased's estate. Once the grant or letter is produced to the company this is sufficient evidence of the PR's right to deal (s 187).
  - PRs are entitled to produce a **letter of request** instructing a transfer of the shares to themselves or a Stock Transfer Forum to a third party. The company should comply.
  - The company has discretion on how it may be satisfied that a member is actually dead and on its procedures on death. If need be the company should get an indemnity.
- If a member is mentally incapacitated then the Court of Protection can appoint a **receiver** to deal with his affairs.
- A **change** of **name** and/or **address** of a member requires **proof of change** and possibly an **indemnity**.
- Powers of Attorney give the right to the donee to act in the **capacity** of the **donor**. Care should be taken as to the scope of its terms, and the continuing existence of the power.
- The court is permitted to grant a '**stop notice**' to an individual who is to have the right to be notified on any instrument of transfer lodged for registration with the company.
- The **Stock Exchange Document Service** ('SEDS') acts as a centre to hold original documentation and make this available as necessary for inspection. The certified copies can be used instead of the originals.

Test your knowledge

1 How may a company be satisfied as to (a) the death of a member; and (b) the legal authority of other persons to deal with his shares? (see paras 1.2, 1.7)

2 How is a grant of representation given outside England made valid for use in dealings with an English company? (1.10, 1.11)

3 Describe the action to be taken by a company to which the probate of the will of a deceased member has been produced. (1.13)

4 Does the executor of a deceased member become himself a member of the company, and, if so, how? (1.15)

5 Who is competent to deal with the shares of a bankrupt member, and how does he demonstrate his authority to the company? (2.4 – 2.5)

6 Give two examples of change of name by a member and how it may be established to the satisfaction of the company. (4)

7 What is a Power of Attorney? (6.1)

8 How are the limits of the powers given by a Power of Attorney determined? (6.7, 6.8)

9 What is (a) a stop notice; (b) a charging order; and (c) a garnishee order? (7.3, 7.6)

10 How may a company keep adequate records of documents produced to it? (7.12)

Now try illustrative questions 24 to 26 at the end of the Study Text

Chapter 22

DIVIDENDS

This chapter covers the following topics.

1 Distributable profits
2 Infringement of dividend rules
3 Declaration and payment of dividends
4 Dividend warrants and mandates
5 BACS system
6 Scrip dividends
7 Dividend re-investment schemes
8 Special dividends and capital repayments

Introduction

Shareholders are induced to invest in a company by the prospect of obtaining a return on their money. Whilst this return may be in the form of an increase in the value of the shares themselves, it is normal to provide a *regular* return on the investment in the form of dividends.

Dividend payments should be clearly distinguished from the payment of interest on loan capital of debentures or debenture stock. The *administrative* aspects of both payments are often very similar, but it should be remembered that the liability to pay interest is a liability arising from a *contract*, and must be discharged even if the company had made no profits. Dividend payments, however, are made if the company's financial situation allows it, and not always then if it is not in the interest of the company. Largely, the question is of the level of *distributable profits*.

1 DISTRIBUTABLE PROFITS

1.1 Distributable profits are the profits which may be distributed as dividend, being:

> 'accumulated realised profits, so far as not previously utilised by distribution or capitalisation, less accumulated realised losses, so far as not previously written off in a reduction or reorganisation of capital duly made: s 263(3).'

1.2 The word '**accumulated**' requires that any losses of previous years must be included in reckoning the current distributable surplus.

1.3 A profit or loss is deemed to be **realised** under s 262(3) if the profit or loss falls to be treated as realised in accordance with generally accepted accounting principles at the time the accounts are prepared. Hence accounting standards in issue, plus generally accepted accounting principles (GAAP) should both be taken into account when determining realised profits and losses. Furthermore, Schedule 4 paragraph 12 provides that:

(a) Only **profits realised** at the balance sheet date shall be included in the profit and loss account.

(b) Losses which have **arisen**, or are likely to arise, in respect of the **current accounting period** *and* any **previous accounting period** should be **taken into account**. In addition, losses which arise between the balance sheet date and the date the accounts are signed should also be taken into account.

Valuation of assets

1.4 Insofar as **depreciation** relates to the **historical cost** of the asset it must be treated as a realised loss, and debited against profit, in determining the amount of distributable profit remaining.

Dividends of public companies - 'full net worth'

1.5 The above rules on distributable profits apply to all companies, private or public. A public company is subject to an additional rule (s 264) which may diminish but cannot increase its distributable profit as determined under the above rules.

1.6 A public company may only make a distribution if its **net assets are**, at the time, **not less** than the **aggregate** of its **called up share capital** and **undistributable reserves**. The dividend which it may pay is limited to such amount as will leave its net assets at not less than that aggregate amount.

1.7 Undistributable reserves are defined in s 264(3) as:

(a) Share premium account

(b) Capital redemption reserve (eg. "sinking fund" - sum of money used to repay debenture).

(c) any surplus of accumulated unrealised profits over accumulated unrealised losses (often known as a revaluation reserve)

(d) Any reserve which the company is prohibited from distributing by statute or by its memorandum or articles

1.8 The dividend rules apply to every form of distribution of assets of the company to its members except the following: s 263.

(a) The **issue of bonus shares** whether fully or partly paid

(b) The **redemption or purchase** of the **company's shares** out of capital or profits

(c) A **reduction of share capital** by cancelling liability for unpaid capital or by repaying share capital to members

(d) A **distribution of assets** to members in a winding up

1.9 As stated above, companies may make bonus issues of shares which are not subject to dividend distribution rules.

Relevant accounts

1.10 The question whether a company has profits from which to pay a dividend is determined by reference to its '**relevant accounts**' which are generally the latest audited annual accounts: s 270. Relevant accounts must be **properly prepared** in accordance with the requirements of the Companies Acts. If the auditors have qualified their report on the accounts they must also state in writing whether in their opinion, the **subject matter** of their qualification (if it relates to statutory accounting requirements) is **material in** determining whether the dividend may be paid: s 271.

1.11 A company may produce **interim accounts** if the latest annual accounts do not disclose a sufficient distributable profit to cover the proposed dividend. It may also **produce initial accounts** if it proposes to pay a dividend during its first accounting reference period or before its first accounts are laid before the company in general meeting. These accounts may be unaudited.

1.12 A private company's interim or initial accounts must suffice to permit a **proper judgement** to be made of amounts of any of the relevant items.

1.13 If a public company has to produce initial or interim accounts, which is unusual, they must be **full accounts** such as the company is required to produce as final accounts at the end of the year. They need not be audited though the auditors must, in the case of initial accounts, satisfy themselves that the accounts have been 'properly prepared' to comply with the Acts. A copy of any such accounts of a public company (with any auditors' statement) must be delivered to the registry for filing: s 271.

Exercise

What are the main rules that determine what profits can be distributed?

Solution

Look back at paragraphs 1.1 – 1.3

2 INFRINGEMENT OF DIVIDEND RULES

2.1 If a dividend is paid otherwise than out of distributable profits the company, the directors and the shareholders may be involved in making good the **unlawful distribution**.

2.2 Any member of a company may apply to the court for an **injunction** to restrain the company from paying an unlawful dividend. A resolution passed in general meeting to approve the dividend is invalid and it does not relieve the directors of their liability.

2.3 The company is entitled to **recover** an **unlawful distribution** from its members if at the time of receipt they knew or had reasonable grounds for knowing that it was unlawful: s 277. If only part of the dividend is unlawful, that is if it exceeds the distributable profits by a margin, it is only the excess which is recoverable. If a member knowingly receives an improperly paid dividend a derivative action cannot be brought by him against the directors.

2.4 The initiative in payment of dividends rests with the **directors** since it is they who either recommend to members in general meeting that a dividend or interim dividend should be declared (if authorised to do so). Moreover the accounts sent to shareholders are prepared by or under the supervision of directors and are approved and signed by them. Accordingly the directors are **liable** to make good to the company the amount unlawfully distributed as dividend if they caused an unlawful dividend to be paid.

2.5 The directors may however **honestly rely** (in declaring or recommending a dividend) on **proper accounts** which disclose an apparent distributable profit out of which the dividend can properly be paid. They are not liable if it later appears that the assumptions or estimates used in preparing the accounts although reasonable at the time were in fact unsound.

2.6 If members receive a dividend which they *know* (at the time of receipt) is paid out of capital and the directors are required to make good to the company the unlawful payment of dividend, the directors are entitled to an **indemnity** from the shareholders: *Moxham v Grant 1900*. Members who are unaware of the irregularity are not liable.

3 DECLARATION AND PAYMENT OF DIVIDENDS 12/99

3.1 Except in the case of a company which has only a very small number of members, the payment of a dividend requires thorough planning. It involves the following.

(a) Consideration of the **articles**

(b) A **board meeting** to declare or recommend the amount of the dividend; if the company is listed, advance notice must be given to the Stock Exchange and an announcement made before the end of the day on which the board meeting is held (If the directors merely recommend a dividend, the final declaration requires a decision in general meeting; usually it is a final dividend for the year, declared at an AGM.)

(c) **Finding the money** for payment of the dividend and making arrangements with the bank

(d) Selecting a '**record date**'

(e) Preparing a **dividend list** from the register of members as at the close of business on the 'record date'

(f) Drafting and printing **dividend warrants** and **counterfoils** (tax vouchers) for distribution individually or by bulk payment, in accordance (in either case) with members' mandates for payment to their banks

(g) **Distribution of warrants and vouchers** at the appropriate time and liaison with the company's bank as the warrants are presented for payment.

(h) Action in connection with **unclaimed dividends**

These points are considered in more detail below.

Consideration of the articles 6/00

3.2 The articles of most companies follow the standard provisions of Table A Articles 102-8, the main points of which are as follows.

(a) The company in general meeting may declare dividends not **exceeding** the **amount recommended** by the directors, and in accordance with the rights of members. Hence preference dividends must always be paid before any dividend is paid to ordinary shareholders.

(b) The directors may declare **interim dividends** 'if it appears to them that they are justified by the profits of the company available for distribution'. Again preference dividends, including any arrears, must take priority.

(c) Unless special terms apply, dividends are payable according to **the amount paid up on the shares** of each member. Thus a 50p per share dividend would be 50p on a £1 share fully paid, 25p on a £1 share 50p paid.

(d) Dividends may be paid in the form of **non-cash assets**. For example, a company may offer new shares as an alternative to a cash dividend.

(e) Dividends may be paid by **cheque** sent through the post to each member at his registered address and, in case of joint holdings, to the **first named holder** on the register, unless directions to the contrary have been given by them all.

(f) **No interest** is **payable** on dividends not paid at a due date (which might happen if preference dividends payable half yearly fell into arrears).

(g) An **unclaimed dividend** is **forfeited** after a period of **12 years**, and is no longer payable by the company.

(h) A member may request in writing to have **dividends** paid to **someone else** (her husband for example).

The procedure for deciding what dividends to pay

3.3 The normal procedure for deciding what dividends to pay is as follows.

(a) In the second half of the company's financial year, the directors will consider an unaudited statement of the company's trading profit for the **first half** of the year, and possibly a forecast of the likely out-turn of the second half. On the basis of those figures they declare an **interim dividend** and, where applicable, a half year's fixed dividend on preference shares.

(b) When the accounts for a financial year have been completed (in the first half of the following year), they are laid before the directors, usually as part of the business for the forthcoming Annual General Meeting. The directors then decide what **final dividend** to recommend for approval at the general meeting. If there is a preference dividend the directors may declare it for payment on the due date, or merely include it in their recommendations to shareholders.

Preliminary announcements by listed companies

3.4 The Stock Exchange attaches great importance to the **prompt** and **accurate disclosure** of the financial information and dividends described above. The market value of the shares will be affected by this information, and it should be published for the guidance of the market (and the avoidance of 'insider dealing') as soon as possible. This has led to a formalised procedure for listed companies.

3.5 A company should give **advance notice** to the Company Announcements Office (CAO) of the date of a board meeting at which the decision of interim or final dividends is to be made. At least three days' advance notice should be given. The market is then aware that up-to-date financial information will be forthcoming on a given future date. The information is sent out through the Regulatory News Service (RNS).

3.6 The time of the board meeting should be so arranged that an announcement can be delivered to the CAO without delay and not later than 7.30am on the day following the board meeting.

3.7 The content of the statement to be made (through the CAO) should include the following.

(a) **Profits** for the half year or full year, as the case may be, with an explanation in the former case

(b) Turnover, taxation, minority interests (in subsidiaries), profit attributable to shareholders, dividend declared or recommended, earnings (in pence) per share, and comparative figures for the previous corresponding period

(c) A **balance sheet**

(d) A **cash flow statement**

(e) Any significant **additional information** necessary for assessing the results

The report of the auditors, including any qualifications, must be reproduced in full.

Finding the money for dividend payments

3.8 It does not follow that because there are available profits, there is a corresponding sum of cash at the bank; the profits may be partly absorbed in outstanding trade debts, increased stocks, or discharge of previous indebtedness to the bank or to trade creditors. In deciding what dividend to declare or recommend, the directors should always take into account the effect, in dividend and advance corporation tax, on the company's liquid resources.

3.9 Directors are usually also concerned about the company's prospects of maintaining an increased dividend in future years. In general it is prudent to withhold some part of the year's profits to finance future expansion, and incidentally to provide a '**cushion**' against the inherent risk of a fall in profits. It is an unfortunate fact of life that the despondency created by a reduction in dividend is always greater than any gratification of shareholders at an increase.

3.10 As a matter of administration, the company should instruct its bank to open a **special account** for each dividend, and transfer to it sufficient funds to meet dividend payments to individual members.

Record date **6/98**

3.11 Although a company may close its register of members, to avoid changes while the dividend list is prepared (s 358 and Table A Article 26), it is not usually satisfactory to resort to that procedure. A backlog of unregistered transfers builds up while the register is closed; this creates an extra burden of work when the register is opened again.

3.12 The modern practice is to select in advance a '**record date**', on which the company endeavours to clear all outstanding transfers etc., so that the register is fully up to date at that point. This means, for example, that a company's final dividend for 2000 may be made payable to all shareholders who were on the register as at, say, 20 September 2000.

3.13 A copy of the register is made by photocopy or print-out, if it is on computer, at the close of business on the 'record date'. This copy provides the basis for compiling a dividend list, showing the amounts due and to whom they are payable.

Buying and selling shares 'ex div' and 'cum div' **12/98**

3.14 A company which is listed should select the most convenient of the 'record dates' proposed by the Stock Exchange (which publishes those dates each year for the coming year). In this way, dealings in the company's shares on the Stock Exchange go over to an **ex div** basis (the seller keeps the dividend, even if received after the sale) at a convenient moment. The aim is to reduce to a minimum the number of transactions in which the buyer has to recover a dividend, to which he is entitled (having bought **cum div**), from the seller, who was on the register at the record date.

3.15 The chosen record date is included in an announcement of a forthcoming dividend, and dealings are on an *ex div* basis from the start of the next Stock Exchange dealing period.

3.16 The principles underlying these arrangements are simple, though their application may be complicated.

(a) The company always pays the dividend to the person who was on the **register** at **close of business** on the record date. The position is not altered if, in the interval between record date and payment of dividend (some weeks later), the shares have been registered in the name of a different holder.

(b) To avoid doubt, dealings in shares are always expressly made on the basis of a *cum div* (buyer takes the dividend) or *ex div* (seller keeps the dividend) sale. *Ex div* dealings are always more convenient since they avoid any need for the seller to pay over to the buyer a dividend received after the date of sale. Dealings *ex div*, however, cannot begin until it is known what dividend the company will later pay; that information affects the market price of the shares.

Preparation of dividend lists

3.17 A large company makes use of computers or other machines to prepare (from the register of members as at the record date) the required dividend list(s). The advantage of a computer is of course that it stores, as well as produces, information. The register of members on the other hand will not produce the correct information for dividends paid under mandate to a bank or other third party.

Distribution of warrants and vouchers and payment by the company's bank

3.18 The form of dividend warrant and voucher should be prepared as printers' proofs (with suitable **security precautions** - the amount of the dividend cannot be inserted until it has been determined what the dividend is to be).

3.19 Unless window envelopes are used, it is also necessary to produce a set of **envelopes**, addressed by machine, for the posting of the warrants and vouchers. If the bulk payment system is used, much of this work can be avoided.

3.20 Although transfers received after the record date do not alter the position, different considerations may arise if, in the interval before payment, the company registers a probate (with the names of the personal representatives), or is informed of a **change of name** or **address** of a member. If possible, the company should withdraw the mechanically printed warrant and voucher, and either replace it or alter it by hand (authorised by the company officer concerned initialling) before despatch.

3.21 The **dividend warrant** authorises the company's bank to pay the dividend, when the warrant is presented by the member's bank (effectively it is a form of cheque). When a large number of warrants have to be issued, it is usual to use printed instead of handwritten signatures. This procedure is permissible only if sanctioned by the articles. In any event, the bank should be supplied with a specimen of the completed form of warrant before the payment date, to facilitate checking.

3.22 As the warrants are paid, the company's bank sends them to the company with a covering schedule. The **warrants** should then be **checked** against the dividend list and filed, in case any need to refer to them as evidence of payment later arises.

3.23 If a warrant is presented more than six months after the date of issue, the bank would probably refer it to the company as a 'stale' cheque, for confirmation that it is still in order to pay it. The warrant may give warning of this.

3.24 If the company opens a new account for the payment of each successive dividend, it should **close** that **account** after a suitable interval, and transfer out of it any balance representing unclaimed dividends. It is not satisfactory to have small sums lying in dormant accounts for long periods.

Unclaimed dividends **6/99**

3.25 Some dividend warrants may be **returned** through the post by the Post Office or by the present occupier of premises at which the shareholder is no longer to be found (after moving without leaving a forwarding address). In such cases the company should write to the bank through which the untraceable shareholder previously collected his dividend.

3.26 In other cases, the dividend warrant may be neither returned nor presented for payment. It may have been lost in the post, or have reached an address at which the shareholder is no longer to be found, where the present occupier simply throws it away. The procedure in these cases is to **write to the member** (at the same address if no other is known), to point out that at the expiry of six months the warrant, if still unpresented for payment, may be queried before it is eventually paid.

3.27 The shareholder may respond by saying that the warrant did not reach him, or has been lost from his possession. In such cases the company would issue a **duplicate warrant**. Unless the amount was very small, however, it would first obtain an **indemnity** against the risk that the missing warrant would subsequently be presented by another person, who has good title to it; **dividend warrants**, remember, are **negotiable instruments**.

3.28 If enquiries on these lines produce no response or explanation, a company whose articles are in standard form faces the prospect of continuing to issue dividend warrants, which evidently do not reach the person entitled to them. After 12 years the company ceases to be liable to pay the dividend, should the relevant warrant be presented.

3.29 It is not satisfactory to allow uncertainty (and possible liability) to continue in this fashion. Some companies therefore include in their articles a provision that if **two successive dividend warrants** are **not presented** for payment, the company may **withhold** the issue of dividend warrants to the member until he appears to claim them. Companies do not generally refuse to pay dividends in these circumstances, when the member makes his claim.

3.30 Unclaimed dividends also indicate that the company has lost touch with the member. Some companies therefore include in their articles a power to **sell** the **shares** of untraceable shareholders after **12 years**; the proceeds of sale are still held for them. The Stock Exchange requires certain safeguards to be observed, in the exercise of such powers by a listed company.

4 DIVIDEND WARRANTS AND MANDATES **6/98, 6/00**

4.1 The most basic procedure for paying dividends, which would be suitable for a small private company, is to despatch to each shareholder a cheque, with a statement of the 'tax credit' on the dividend, which he can submit with his individual tax return. This aspect of company distributions falls within the syllabus of the *Corporate Finance, Regulation and Taxation* paper.

4.2 There is always a risk that the **dividend warrant** will go astray in transit either between the company and the individual member, or between the latter and his bank. That risk is reduced, and the whole procedure for payment of dividends improved, if each member will issue to the company standing instructions (a **dividend mandate**) for the payment of his dividends direct to his bank, for credit to his account. Specimen copies of a dividend warrant and dividend mandate appear on the following pages.

4.3 There is an ICSA standard form of mandate, which members should be encouraged to use (*Request for Payment of Interest or Dividends*). Note the following.

(a) Although the mandate specifies a particular **branch of a bank** into which dividend payments to the shareholder should be made, it is so worded that if the member's account is switched to another branch, the bank will route it to the branch where the account now is.

(b) The mandate does not designate the particular **account** to which the bank is to credit the payment; it merely **names the shareholder**, who must make his own arrangement with the bank if he has more than one account. The company has no control over the account to which the bank credits the payment, and should not accept instructions on this point.

(c) Each mandate should relate to **one shareholding only**. If the member has more than one holding, such as preference and ordinary shares, or designated accounts in the register, he should issue a **mandate** for each holding. Otherwise there may be confusion.

4.4 The mandate should be **signed** by the **member** who issues it; if there is a joint holding, it should be signed by all holders. If any person presents a mandate on behalf of a member, the presenter should produce to the company his authority from the member to act on his behalf.

4.5 A member should be advised to submit his mandate through his bank, after he has signed it, rather than send it direct to the company. If necessary, a mandate sent direct should be returned with a polite request to that effect. A mandate which passes through the hands of the bank will bear the stamp of the branch; this affords the company greater protection, since the banks accept liability for payments made on mandates which bear their stamp. In handling the mandate, the bank will check, or insert the following details:

(a) The **address** and **title** of the branch

(b) The **sorting code** number by which the dividend will be correctly routed through the electronic credit clearing system, to the branch identified by that number

(c) The **number** of the **account** to which the member has instructed the bank to credit his dividends

Registration of mandates

4.6 A dividend mandate, when received, should be **registered** in the same way as other documents delivered to the company providing information or instructions. If the company sends dividend warrants by post to individual banks, it should add the particulars (bank - by name, address, sorting number - and shareholder by name) to the list used in distributing dividends.

Changing or revoking mandates

4.7 On a registration of change of name, for instance on the marriage of a female shareholder, it is wise to ask for **confirmation** that any **existing mandate** given in the previous name is **still in force**. If a member presents to the company a Power of Attorney, this does not of itself cancel any mandate previously given by him. However if the Power covers receipt of dividends (as a general one would), the donee of the Power may issue a new mandate if he has good reason.

4.8 There is no legal objection to the receipt and acceptance of a **mandate** which requests payment to any other **type of agent** other than a bank, such as a building society, or a professional firm.

4.9 A mandate may be **revoked** by **written notice** to the company, signed by the person(s) who gave it. The death of a sole shareholder revokes any mandate he has given, but his personal representatives, on producing their grant, may issue a new mandate.

4.10 On the **death** of one of two or more **joint holders**, the **mandate** continues **in force**. If there is only one surviving shareholder, and he also has a holding in his sole name, with separate mandates for the two holdings, they will normally continue to be treated as two distinct holdings - unless he gives instructions to merge them. If they are to remain separate, though in the name of the same holder, the accounts should be designated, to distinguish them.

4.11 The bankruptcy of a member does not automatically revoke a mandate which he has given, but if his **trustee revokes** the **mandate**, or issues a new one, the **company** must accept and **comply** with those instructions.

4.12 If a member's **account** in the register of members is **closed**, typically because his entire holding has been transferred out of his name, any **mandate** which he has given **lapses**, and does not revive if he later becomes a shareholder again. He should then, if he wishes, issue a fresh mandate.

4.13 If a member moves his bank account from one branch to another of the same bank, the **bank from** which the account is moved will send a **'change of branch'** notice to the company. Unless some special problem arises, the wording of the mandate suffices to permit the company to pay future dividends to the branch of the bank which now has the member's account. A change of branch notice should be registered by the company, under the same procedure as applies to original mandates.

4.14 If a member **closes** his account at Bank A and **opens** an account at Bank B (different banks - not different branches of the same bank), the **mandate** to pay dividends to Bank A **lapses**; a new mandate, if required, should be issued for future payments to the appropriate branch of Bank B.

DIVIDEND WARRANT

ORDINARY SHARE DIVIDEND WARRANT

X-XX-XXT

........................p.l.c.

PAYMENT NUMBER
....

REFERENCE No.
....

.... 19.....

.... BANK p.l.c.
....

£ ....

Pay .... [Amount in words]

OR ORDER

TO: (Name) ....
(Address) ....
....

For .... p.l.c.

....
Secretary

IF NOT PRESENTED WITHIN SIX MONTHS THIS WARRANT MUST BE VERIFIED AT THE COMPANY'S OFFICE

XXXXX 00000 0 0000000

DIVIDEND MANDATE

REQUEST FOR PAYMENT OF INTEREST OR DIVIDENDS

(Above the line for Registrar's use only)

Name of undertaking	
Please complete in typewriting or in block capitals Full name and address of first named or sole holder Full name(s) of joint holder(s) (if any) Any change of address should be notified by quoting former and present address	Account designation (if any)
Full name and address of the Bank Branch, Firm of Person to whom Interest and Dividends are to be sent	Please forward until further notice, all Interest and Dividends that may from time to time become due on any Stock or Shares now standing, or which may hereafter stand, in my (our) name(s) or in the name(s) of the survivors of us in the Company's books to: or, where payment is to be made to a Bank, to such other Branch of that Bank as the Bank may from time to time request. Your compliance with this request shall discharge the Company's liability in respect of such interest or dividends.

PLEASE SIGN HERE

1. 2.
 3.
Date 4.

NOTES
(i) Executors or administrators must insert the name of the deceased holder
(ii) This form must be signed by ALL the registered holders
(iii) A Body Corporate should sign by means of Authorisd Signatory(ies) whose capacity must be stated
(iv) Directions to credit a particular account MUST be given to the bank direct and NOT INCLUDED in this form
(v) Where instructions are in favour of a Bank, this form should be sent direct to the Bank Branch concerned for completion of the section below.

Bank's reference number and details	STAMP OF BANK BRANCH
(1) Sorting code number [— —] (2) Name of bank Title of Branch Please quote all digits including zeros (3) Account number (if any) [| | | | | | | |]	

Marketing of mandates

4.15 An article in *Chartered Secretary* in December 1997 stated that in 1996 only 30% of the dividends processed by the major bank-owned registrars were mandated. Companies are thus trying to market mandates in various ways by use of **promotional literature**, and in one case running a prize draw for shareholders. Companies are also seeking **bank branch authentication** of account details, and are providing freepost or reply-paid envelopes to make mandating easier for their shareholders.

5 BACS SYSTEM

5.1 A significant number of registrars now use the Bankers Automated Clearing System (BACS), the banks' electronic payment system. Details of dividends (to be paid in the form of credit transfers, bank/building society sort codes and account numbers are transmitted to **BACS in electronic form**, by tape disk or computer terminals connected by telephone directly to BACS, at least three working days ahead of the dividend payment date. If this system is used, the company must post the tax vouchers to each shareholder.

5.2 Use of the BACS system does **remove the risks** of using the cheque system, and also leads to cost savings in printing and storing cheque stationery. The shareholder's funds are cleared for use on the due date with there being no need to pay in the cheque or arrange for the tax voucher to be posted. Bank charges will be reduced.

5.3 The system **reduces** the **opportunity** for **fraud** by alteration of cheque details. The BACS system enables tax vouchers to be issued on an annual basis, covering all the payments made in one year. The system also means that shareholders' accounts **receive** the **dividends** on the **day of payment**, rather than being delayed in the post, and by shareholders having to go to bank or building society to pay in the warrants.

5.4 Problems can be caused if a payment cannot be applied to a particular account and if details cannot be matched to the rejected payment being returned to the Registrar. In addition the articles of some companies contain a requirement that dividends have to be paid by cheque or warrant. However the BACS system does bypass other problems which may prevent dividends being paid in, for example being lost in the post or shareholder failure to notify the company of a change of address.

6 SCRIP DIVIDENDS

6.1 Some companies allow shareholders to choose whether to receive dividends in the form of shares instead of in cash. This is effected by the issue of **fully paid shares** to equity shareholders in lieu of cash dividends. Authority to do this must be contained in the company's articles.

6.2 The shareholder is able to **build up** his **shareholding** in the company without incurring brokerage expenses and stamp duty expenses. The company can **retain** the **money** which would be distributed in cash as dividends in the business for the benefit of the company. However, the value of the shares issued is still taxed as a distribution of income in the same way as a cash dividend.

6.3 An **ordinary resolution** is **required** allowing the board to offer shareholders the right to choose to receive new ordinary shares instead of cash for all or any part of any dividends. When the board declares an interim dividend or recommends a final dividend on the company's shares it should also resolve to make the offer of new shares to shareholders as an alternative to the cash dividend.

TAX VOUCHER

PAYMENT No.
001

ISBN CODE
GB0001234567

TAX VOUCHER

.... PLC

ORDINARY SHARES OF £1 EACH FULLY PAID

14 - SEPT- 00
WARRANT No
123456

HOLDING	TAX CREDIT	DIVIDEND PAYABLE
	£	£

FINAL DIVIDEND ON
ORDINARY SHARES
RATE: 7.0 PENCE PER SHARE
YEAR TO 31-DEC-00
TO HOLDERS
REGISTERED ON 30-APR-00

HECTOR
KEEP IT

This voucher should be kept. It will be accepted by the Inland Revenue as evidence of a tax credit

6.4 The price of the new shares will be determined by taking the **average** of the **middle market quotations** for the company's shares derived from The Stock Exchange Daily Official List for the five business days commencing on the date when the company's shares were first quoted ex dividend on The Stock Exchange.

6.5 A circular letter is sent to shareholders **giving the price** of the new shares and **explaining the action** they should take if they wish to receive new shares instead of the whole or any part of the cash dividend to which they are entitled. The circular should make clear that shareholders who do not wish to receive any new shares need not take any action and that their dividend will be paid in cash in the usual way. The Stock Exchange imposes further disclosure requirements.

6.6 A form of election, which must be signed by the shareholder(s), will accompany the circular letter. This will give the following information:

(a) **Number of shares** held on dividend record date

(b) **Maximum number of shares** on which **election** may be made (this number will be an exact multiple of the number of shares required to be elected to receive one new share)

(c) **Number of shares** on which the **dividend** will be **paid** in cash if the maximum number of shares is elected as in (b) above (ie the balance of the shares being less than the multiple required for one new share)

(d) The **maximum number** of **new shares** to be **issued** if the maximum number of share is elected as in (b) above

(e) The **number of shares** which the shareholder wishes to **elect for new shares** if he wishes to elect fewer than the maximum in (b) above

6.7 **Special dividend warrants** will be prepared with boxes to show the number of elected shares and the number of non-elected shares on which the normal full cash dividend will be paid. On these dividend warrants the pence per share, tax credit and amount payable boxes will be shown in the normal way.

6.8 New share certificates will be prepared for each member for the number of shares issued in lieu of cash dividend. These certificates should have a counterfoil attached showing the following information:

(a) The **number** of **shares** on which a valid share **election** was **made**

(b) The **number** of **new shares** allotted

(c) The total **cash equivalent** of new shares allotted (ie the cash dividend multiplied by the number of shares allotted)

(d) The **notional tax** (ie what would have been the tax credit if the dividend on the elected shares had been paid in cash)

(e) The **number of shares** on which the full **cash dividend** is being **paid** for which a separate tax counterfoil with the dividend warrant attached will be received. (An explanatory note explaining how the figures in the counterfoil have been determined is usually attached.)

6.9 A sum equal to the aggregate nominal amount of the new ordinary shares allotted will be capitalised out of any amount standing to the credit of any reserve or fund as decided by the directors.

6.10 **Application** will be made to **The Stock Exchange** for the new shares issued as scrip dividends to be listed.

6.11 Some companies have introduced **scrip dividend mandates**. If the shareholder signs a scrip dividend mandate, all his **future dividends** (except for any part of his dividend which is paid in cash in respect of any balance of his holding of shares which does not make up the multiple required for a new share) will be in the **form of shares** until he cancels the mandate.

6.12 This is known as an 'evergreen scrip dividend scheme'.

7 DIVIDEND RE-INVESTMENT SCHEMES 12/99

7.1 Under dividend re-investment schemes, a shareholder instructs the company to pay his dividends to the company itself or to its registrar and use them to **purchase additional shares** for him on the **stock market**. The significant difference between dividend re-investment schemes and scrip dividends is therefore that with a dividend re-investment scheme, the shareholder is receiving shares that are already in issue, whereas with scrip dividends new shares are issued to the shareholder.

7.2 The shares are purchased at the **current market price** on the day the dividend is paid. Thus dealing costs will be lower since a bulk purchase is being made; however **stamp duty** will be **payable.** If there is an amount of dividend left over that is insufficient to purchase a share, the amount is carried forward and added to the next dividend. The shareholder subsequently receives a certificate for the additional shares and a tax voucher for the dividend paid.

7.3 Dividend re-investment schemes are used more by investment trusts than by commercial companies.

8 SPECIAL DIVIDENDS AND CAPITAL REPAYMENTS

8.1 Special dividends in the form of capital repayments or issues of redeemable shares have recently been used by a number of companies.

8.2 Reasons for using these procedures include making the **company less attractive** to bidders seeking cash-rich targets. Special dividends have also been used in **contested take-overs** to win over reluctant holders of target shares. Recently companies have also trying to replace some of their share capital with borrowing to increase gearing and reduce the company's cost of capital. Borrowing is seen as more attractive because interest is tax deductible.

8.3 A repurchase of shares usually takes place through the market at market prices.

8.4 A special dividend or an issue of redeemable shares is likely to **reduce** the value of the **existing equity shares** because of the loss of assets involved. If the share price is affected, the terms of options may have to be revised.

8.5 At the time of each capital repayment, companies try to **consolidate** their **ordinary shares** so that each shareholder will hold a smaller number of shares with each share having a greater nominal value. The consolidation will be in such a ratio so that the market value of each of the consolidated shares will be roughly equal to the value that each share had prior to the special dividend, the shareholder holding fewer shares.

8.6 The payment of a special dividend can be authorised by the board as an **interim dividend**. Some companies have allowed shareholders to use the special dividend in subscribing for bonds, which are similar to loan stock. These are attractive to institutional investors, as the tax regime for interest-bearing investments has recently become relatively more favourable. These instruments will be even more attractive if there is also an option to convert into equity.

8.7 If capital is returned by issue of redeemable shares in exchange for ordinary shares, the issue of the shares will **not be** treated as a **distribution** for tax purposes, but will be treated as a part disposal possibly giving rise to a capital gain.

Chapter roundup

- Dividends are payable out of **distributable profits**, being **accumulated realised profits** (not yet used by distribution or capitalisation) **less accumulated losses** (not yet written off in a reduction or reorganisation of capital).
- Dividends are generally payable by reference to the **last audited annual** (or unaudited interim) **accounts** (relevant accounts); provision must be made for depreciation and an increase on revaluation of assets should not be included.
- A plc can only make a distribution if its **net assets** are **more** than the **aggregate** of its **called up share capital** and **undistributable reserves** (share premium account, capital redemption reserve, surplus accumulated unrealised profits over accumulated unrealised losses and other statutory undistributable reserves).
- Dividend rules apply to all forms of distribution of assets to members except:
  - Bonus shares
  - Redemption or purchase of own shares
  - Reduction of capital by the company
  - Distribution on a winding up
- Directors and shareholders may be liable to account for an **unlawful distribution**: this depends on their knowledge and good faith at the time of distribution.
- At all times close attention should be paid to the articles to determine the company's power to pay and the procedure to follow on payment.
- The Stock Exchange requires **prompt disclosure** of dividends, which reduces the likelihood of insider dealing and encourages an open market responsive to fluctuations in the value of shares.
- A company may have strong accounts showing high distributable profits but this may not be available to pay as cash. Care should be taken to assess the **liquidity** of the company to assess whether or not it can actually pay the dividend.
- Paying dividends is generally achieved by issuing **dividend warrants**, which entitle the holder of the warrant to payment of the dividend. Other methods include a **mandate** giving instructions to pay dividends straight to the investor's account. Such mandates should be adequately recorded by the company. Procedures have also been developed for bulk payment of dividends.
- On the Stock Exchange, dividends are declared at **record dates** set by the Exchange. This enables investors to buy and sell shares in the knowledge of whether the shares are sold with or without the dividends then payable (**cum div or ex div**).
- Where dividends are not claimed, the company is still liable to pay them until they have been **unclaimed** for 12 years. Such unclaimed dividends are generally kept on a separate account.
- **Scrip dividends** are dividends where the shareholders **elect** to **receive dividends** in the form of new shares rather than cash.
- **Dividend re-investment schemes** involve shareholders electing to receive shares purchased on the open market rather than cash.

Test your knowledge

1 What are distributable profits? (see para 1.1)

2 What special rules apply to public companies under s 264? (1.6)

3 What does s 264 define as 'undistributable reserves? (1.7)

4 In what circumstances are directors liable to make good the amount of an unlawful dividend distribution? (2.4)

5 Under the Table A form of articles, who may declare a dividend? (3.2)

6 Explain the nature of a 'preliminary announcement' of financial results by a listed company. (3.7)

7 Explain the significance of a 'record date' for the purpose of payment of dividends. (3.12, 3.13)

8 What action (if any) should be taken if, after the record date and before issuing dividend warrants, the company receives (a) a transfer of shares to a new holder; and (b) a notice of change of a member's address? (3.20)

9 What action should a company take if a dividend warrant is: (a) returned as undeliverable by the Post Office; or (b) not presented for payment within six months of issue? (3.25, 3.26)

10 What is the effect of a dividend mandate? (4.2)

11 What particulars are inserted on a dividend mandate to ensure that the member receives his dividend in the manner intended? (4.5)

12 What happens if a member who has issued a mandate in the usual form (a) transfers his account to a different branch of the same bank; or (b) closes his account and opens a new one at a different bank? (4.13, 4.14)

13 How do companies use the BACS system to pay dividends? (5.1)

14 What are the advantages to members and the company of scrip dividends? (6.2)

Now try illustrative question 27 at the end of the Study Text

Chapter 23

EMPLOYEE PARTICIPATION IN PROFITS AND SHARES

This chapter covers the following topics.

1 Employees' share schemes
2 Profit-sharing schemes and all-employee share plans
3 Savings related share option schemes
4 Company share option plans
5 Employee share ownership trusts

Introduction

A company may encourage its employees to acquire shares of the company (or of its holding company), and make special arrangements for that purpose. For example, when a company issues new shares to the public, it is common to reserve a proportion of the issue for priority allotment to employee applicants, to whom application forms of a distinctive colour are provided.

By way of exception to the general prohibition against giving financial assistance for the purchase of its own shares, a company may lawfully promote an 'employees' share scheme' providing financial assistance for that purpose: s 153(4).

1 EMPLOYEES' SHARE SCHEMES

1.1 An employees' share scheme is defined as a scheme for encouraging or facilitating the holding of shares or debentures of the company by the following groups:

(a) *Bona fide* **employees** or former employees of the company, or of another company of the same group

(b) The **close relatives** (including children under 18) of employees or former employees: s 743

(c) **Trustees**, for the benefit of (a) or (b)

1.2 Before establishing an employees' share scheme, the company should also ensure that it has suitable express powers in its objects clause.

1.3 The Stock Exchange Listing Rules require that a listed company shall obtain the approval of its shareholders for any employees' share scheme before making such allotments, and must disclose the following information:

(a) The **full text** of the scheme or details of its most important terms

(b) Details of **directors** who are trustees

(c) A statement that the **provisions** relating to who can participate in the scheme, limitations on the cash, securities or other benefits subject to the scheme, the maximum entitlement for any participant and the basis of determining a participant's entitlement **cannot be altered** without the **prior approval** of **shareholders**

(d) Whether the **benefits** are **pensionable** and why

(e) If the scheme is not circulated to shareholders, details of where it will be **available** for **inspection**

1.4 There are a number of remissions of company law rules, in relation to shares held under an employees' share scheme, including the following.

(a) The requirement that the directors shall have authorisation for the **allotment of shares** does not apply to allotment under an employees' share scheme which would be separately approved in general meeting: s 80(2).

(b) Shareholders' **pre-emption rights**, in respect of ordinary shares allotted for cash, do **not apply** to shares allotted under an employees' share scheme: s 89(5).

Types of scheme **Specimen paper**

1.5 The types of scheme described in this chapter are designed to give employees opportunities of acquiring shares on favourable terms. The first of the schemes considered below is a combination of profit sharing and subscription for shares. The others are based on the grant of options to employees to acquire shares, on such a basis that the benefit of the option, if exercised, does not become subject to income tax (as it would, if made otherwise than under an approved scheme acceptable to the Inland Revenue). If an employee who has acquired shares in any of these ways later disposes of them, the disposal may attract a liability to capital gains tax on the realised gain in the usual way.

1.6 Any scheme of this kind has to be carefully administered, which entails keeping proper records. It often falls to the company secretary to ensure that this is done.

1.7 The examiners have pointed out a tendency amongst students to confuse **profit sharing** schemes with **savings related share option** schemes. It is as well, therefore, to emphasise that these schemes are entirely distinct, and are treated separately in this text.

2 PROFIT-SHARING SCHEMES AND ALL-EMPLOYEE SHARE PLANS 6/98

2.1 Apart from employee participation in share schemes, a company may establish a profit sharing scheme as part of the conditions of employment either for the employees generally, or of individuals. Payments made under these arrangements are normally treated as part of their remuneration for income tax purposes.

2.2 Schemes of this type were introduced under the Finance Act 1978, the provisions of which have now been consolidated in the Income and Corporation Taxes Act 1988.

2.3 The main feature of these schemes is that the **company** sets aside a proportion of each year's profits and pays it over to trustees, **to be applied in subscribing for shares of the company** which are then held for individual employees.

2.4 The limits and conditions of such schemes are as follows.

(a) For tax purposes, the maximum amount which may be allocated in any tax year to buy shares for any individual employee is **£3,000 or, if higher, 10% of salary** (excluding benefits) subject to a **maximum of £8,000**. 'Salary' is the salary of the current or preceding year, whichever is higher. Each employee is notified of the amount allocated to him.

(b) **All full time employees** of the company (or of the group, as the case may be) within general qualifying limits must be entitled to participate on similar terms; selection of individual participants is not permitted. If a minimum period of service is imposed as a qualification, it must not exceed five years.

(c) The scheme is not open to a shareholder who owns **over 25%** of the shares in, or controls, a '**close company**'.

(d) **Dividends** on the shares held for each employee are paid to him and are **taxable income**.

(e) If, as is usual, the trustees subscribe for new shares instead of purchasing existing shares of the company, the **issue price** is fixed by reference to the **average price paid** in dealings in the existing shares, on the three Stock Exchange dealing days following the announcement of the company's results. There are in fact two quoted prices - a lower price for a sale, and a higher price for a purchase. As is usual in this type of share valuation, the price for scheme purposes is the *lower* price, plus one quarter of the difference between the two prices (averaged over the three dealing days).

2.5 The statement sent to each participating employee informs him of the **number of shares** allocated to him, the **date of allocation**, the **value** (for tax purposes) and the **Release Date**, after which a sale of the shares will not attract income tax liability. Although he is not a member, since the shares are held by the trustees, the employee is provided with a **proxy card** (for each general meeting), by which he may instruct the trustees how to vote on his behalf, in respect of his shares.

2.6 A variant form of this scheme operates as follows.

(a) The employee **advances** his **own money** to enable the trustees to purchase shares, or he transfers shares which he already owns to the trustees. He must leave them with the trustees for a minimum of two years, but pays no income tax if he then sells them.

(b) The company **allocates** an equal number of **shares** (to match those provided as in (a)), and these 'additional shares' are subject to the conditions set out below.

Disposal of shares acquired in a profit sharing scheme

2.7 The following timescale operates for the disposal of the shares.

(a) The employee agrees that the **trustees** shall **retain** the shares for a **minimum of two years**, unless he dies, reaches pensionable age, ceases work because of injury or disability, or becomes redundant meanwhile. On a **disposal within the three years** after the shares are allocated to the employee (unless a relief is available), there is **liability** to **income tax** on:

(i) The shares' market value when appropriated to the employee
(ii) The sale proceeds

(b) If the employee leaves because of injury, disability, redundancy or reaching pensionable age, the charge is only **50%** of the **market value**, or proceeds. "Good leaver"

(c) After **three years** there is **no income tax liability**, but the disposal attracts **capital gains tax** on any realised gain (sale proceeds less original value); the employee's gains may well be covered by the annual allowance on his capital gains.

Bonus shares and rights issues: effect on profit-sharing schemes

2.8 If the company makes a **bonus issue** while shares are held by the trustees, the bonus shares are added to those held by the trustees for each participant employee. If there is a **rights issue**, the employee has a choice as follows.

(a) **Take up** the **additional shares** offered to him, by providing cash for that purpose.
(b) **Sell** his **rights**. In this case, there is a capital receipt to be dealt with as above.

Register of participants in a profit sharing scheme

2.9 As the trustees generally have no administrative organisation of their own, it usually falls to the company secretary to maintain a register of participants in the scheme, showing, year by year, the number of shares held by the trustees for each participant, and the original value ('the locked in value'). On the basis of this register the company sends direct to the participant the following:

(a) Dividend warrants

(b) Copies of the annual reports and accounts, and other company announcements and notice to members

All-employee share plans

2.10 Following the publication of detailed proposals in 1999, the Chancellor announced in the 2000 Budget details of a new all-employee share plan (ESOPs) to replace approved profit-sharing schemes. Employers have until April 2002 to transfer existing approved profit-sharing schemes into ESOPs. Tax relief on profit-sharing schemes will be discontinued after that date.

2.11 Under ESOPs employers can give up to **£3,000** of 'free shares' a year to employees with no tax or national insurance contributions payable

2.12 Employees can buy '**partnership shares**' with their pre-tax salary up to the following limits:

(a) Maximum of **10%** of **gross earnings,** subject to an upper limit of **£1,500** per tax year

(b) Maximum monthly contributions of **£125**

(c) Any **minimum** monthly contributions as specified in the plan but this minimum cannot be more than **£10**

2.13 Purchases do not affect pension contribution limits. Employers can give up to 2 free '**matching shares**' for each partnership share purchased. The matching shares, up to a maximum of **£3,000** are in addition to the £3,000 of free shares and must be provided on the same basis for all employees. The maximum ESOP value during any one year is therefore £7,500 (ie £3,000 free shares, £1,500 partnership shares and £3,000 matching shares).

2.14 Employers offering free shares must offer a **minimum** amount of free shares to each employee on '**similar terms**'. Between the minimum and the maximum of £3,000, the employer can offer shares in different amounts and on different bases to different employees. This means that employers can reward either individual or team performance. Employers can set performance targets subject to the overriding requirement that a plan must not contain any features that concentrate rewards on directors and more highly paid employees.

2.15 Free and matching shares must normally be held in a plan for at **least three years**. If shares are withdrawn within three years (because the employee leaves) there is a **charge** to income tax and national insurance on the market value of the shares at the time of withdrawal.

2.16 If shares are taken out of the plan **after three years** but **before five years,** there is a charge to income tax and national insurance based on the **lower** of the **initial value** of the shares - and their **value** at the **date of withdrawal**. Any increase in value is free of income tax and national insurance. If one of the specified reasons applies eg redundancy or retirement, there is no tax or national insurance charge. Once the shares have been held for **five years** there is **no income tax or national insurance**.

2.17 **Partnership shares** can be taken out at any time. If the shares are held for less than **three years,** there is a charge to income tax and national insurance on the **market value** at the time the shares are removed. If the share are removed **after three years** but **before five years,** the charge to income tax and national insurance is based on the **lesser** of **salary** used to buy the shares and the **market value** at the date of removal. Once the shares have been held for **five years** there is **no income tax or national insurance**.

2.18 **Dividends** of up to **£1,500** on shares in the plan are **tax-free** provided the dividends are used to **acquire additional shares** in the company, which are then **held** in the **plan** for **three years**. These 'dividend' shares do not affect entitlement to partnership or matching shares.

2.19 A plan may provide for **free** and **matching** shares to be **forfeited** if the **employee leaves within three years**, unless the employee leaves for **specified reasons** such as retirement or redundancy. All shares have to come out of a plan if an employee leaves his job.

2.20 Provided they were held in the plan for at least **three years**, there is **no charge** to **capital gains tax** on shares taken out of a plan and sold immediately. A charge to capital gains tax will arise on sale to the extent that the shares increase in value after they are withdrawn from the plan.

2.21 The plan must be operated through a **UK resident trust**. The trustees acquire the shares from the company or, if the plan incorporates partnership shares, from the employees. The existence of arrangements to enable employees to sell shares held in a new plan trust will not of itself make those shares readily convertible into cash and require employers to operate PAYE and national insurance. There is also a form of **'roll over' relief** for individuals who dispose of shares to the trustees

2.22 A deduction in computing profits of the company is given for:

(a) The costs of setting up and administering the plan

(b) The gross salary allocated by employees to buy partnership shares

(c) The costs of providing shares to the extent that the costs exceed the employees' contributions

(d) The market value of free and matching shares when they are acquired by the trustees

(e) Interest paid by the trustees on borrowing to acquire shares where the company meets the trustees' costs

2.23 Shares used in the plan must be fully paid up irredeemable ordinary shares in a company either:

(a) Listed on a recognised stock exchange (or in its subsidiary); or

(b) Not controlled by another company

2.24 A plan established by a company that controls other companies, may be extended to any or all of these other companies. Such a plan is called a **group plan**.

2.25 A plan need not include all the components – it is possible to have a plan with only free shares.

2.26 Companies must offer **all employees** the opportunity to participate in the plan, whether they work full or part time. A **minimum qualifying period of employment** may be specified, but not more than 18 months.

2.27 Companies will be able to obtain approval for these plans under a fast track process. Plans may provide for the award of free shares for performance periods prior to the Finance bill being enacted.

2.28 The new plans will allow good performance to be rewarded with shares, and partnership shares bought with employee's pre-tax earnings to be matched by the company. The major drawback may be the period for which employees are locked into retaining shares; they are vulnerable to falling share prices during that time.

2.29 Shareholder approval of plan rules is required by a listed company where newly issued shares are to be used to satisfy awards under ESOP.

3 SAVINGS RELATED SHARE OPTION SCHEMES "Sharesave" 6/98, 6/00

3.1 Another type of employee participation scheme is a savings related share option scheme which for the time being will be run in addition to the ESOP, (see above). Essentially, an employee enters into a contract by which he undertakes to **save**, either with the Department of National Savings or with a building society, over a period of **three** or **five years**. He is then entitled to the total amount which he has saved, plus a tax-free bonus.

3.2 At the time of entering into the savings contract he is granted an **option** (at a price fixed at that time) to apply the money at the end of the period, in subscribing for shares of the company. Alternatively, he may **extend** the **period**, leaving his money where it is until the end of the **seventh year**; he does not make any further contributions after the fifth year but receives a doubled bonus at the end. He may then withdraw the money to subscribe for shares, at the same pre-arranged price. It is merely an option; he may withdraw his money without subscribing for shares.

3.3 If he *does* take up shares and later sells them, there is **no income tax liability**, though there may be **capital gains tax** on the surplus of the proceeds over the option price (unless his annual capital gains tax exemption suffices to offset the gain in full).

3.4 In setting up the contract, the limiting conditions are as follows.

(a) The maximum amount which may be saved under the contract is **£250 per month** and the employer may also set a minimum, which may **not exceed £5 per month**.

(b) The scheme is **not open** to any employee of a '**close company**' (for tax purposes) who **controls more than 25%** of its shares. All other full-time employees with a qualifying period of service (which must not exceed five years) must be eligible to participate.

(c) The **option price** fixed for acquiring the shares may **not be less than 80%** of the '**middle market price**' on the last Stock Exchange dealing day before the grant of the option.

(d) As the SAYE contract bonus is fixed in advance, it is known at the outset how much the employee will be entitled to at the completion of the three of five year savings period. Applied to the option price, this **fixes** the **number of shares** in respect of which the option is granted.

(e) If the employee opts to leave his money where it is until the **end of the seventh year**, the **option is increased correspondingly** to cover as many more shares as the additional bonus will buy at the same option price. It is open to employing companies to grant at the outset an option related to the proceeds of the whole period, if the employee prefers to commit himself to that alternative from the start.

3.5 The tax position of the employee is as follows.

(a) He is **not a shareholder** until he exercises his option to subscribe for shares. In consequence, he receives no dividends during the five (or seven) year period of the savings contract. The bonuses which accrue on his savings are free of income tax and also (when the money is withdrawn) of capital gains tax.

(b) If he exercises his option and later sells the shares, there is a **normal realised capital gain** on the difference between option price and sale price (less capital gains tax indexation allowance, reliefs and exemptions).

3.6 If he leaves the scheme before the end of **five years**, he will normally be liable for **income tax** on the amounts involved. If however, during the period of the savings contract the employee becomes disabled, retires, or is made redundant, he will have **six months to use** the **savings** at the date of leaving to purchase shares at the price determined on commencement.

3.7 In the event of the employee's **death** (a) during the period of the savings contract, or (b) within six months after it (but before exercising his option), his personal representatives have a period of **12 months** in which to decide whether to exercise his option, and take up the shares. (The period is calculated from the date of death or the completion of the contract, whichever is the earlier.)

3.8 The structure of the scheme provides for saving *either* a bank or a building society; the employer may decide to relate the scheme to one or the other, or to give employees the choice between them. When the contract matures, the employee has a period of six months in which to decide whether to exercise his option and acquire shares, or to withdraw the money for his own use.

The administration of savings related share option schemes

3.9 The administration of savings related share option schemes involves the following:

(a) The issue of an **option certificate** to each employee when the option is granted;

(b) A **register** of employee participants, with dates when the contracts will be completed and the price at which each may acquire a specified number of shares;

(c) **Deductions** from monthly or weekly pay, duly recorded, and the proceeds remitted to the Department of National Savings or the building society;

(d) **Obtaining payment** of the accumulated savings (with bonus) for each employee, when the contract matures;

(e) Inviting the employee to decide whether he wishes to **exercise his option** to take shares (in which case he completes an option form on the reverse of his certificate).

If the employee does exercise his option, the company carries out the normal procedure for allotment of shares (to which the restrictions of ss 80 and 89 do not apply). If he decides not to take shares, the money is paid over to him against a receipt. He may exercise the option in respect of part, but not all, of the money.

3.10 While the options are outstanding, the employees to whom they have been granted are not members of the company, and no question of membership rights arises at that stage. The company may, however, **decide to distribute copies** of its annual reports and accounts, so that the option-holders may be kept informed.

4 COMPANY SHARE OPTION PLANS 6/99

4.1 An employee can be granted options to buy shares under an approved scheme, and there is no income tax on the grant of an option or on the profit arising from the exercise of an option between three and ten years after the grant. Capital gains tax will, however, arise on the gain made when an employee eventually sells his shares.

4.2 To obtain Inland Revenue approval schemes must satisfy the following conditions.

(a) The shares must be **fully paid shares** not subject to special restrictions.

(b) The **price** of the shares must **not** be **less** than their **market value** at the time of the grant of the option.

(c) **Participation** in the scheme must be **limited** to **employees** and **full-time directors**. Options must not be transferable. However, ex-employees and the personal representatives of deceased employees may be able to exercise options; personal representatives must generally do so within one year after the death. The scheme need not be open to all employees and full-time directors.

(d) No options may be granted which take the **total market value** of shares for which an employee holds options above **£30,000**. Shares are valued as at the times when the options on them are granted.

(e) If the issuing company has more than one class of shares, the majority of shares in the class for which the scheme operates must be held other than by:

(i) Persons acquiring them through their positions as **directors** or employees (unless the company is an employee controlled company)

(ii) A **holding company** (unless the scheme shares are quoted)

(f) Anyone who has within the preceding 12 months held over **10%** of the **shares** of a **close company** which is the company whose shares may be acquired under the scheme, or which controls that company either alone or as part of a consortium, must be excluded from the scheme.

4.3 The tax exemption is lost in respect of an option if it is exercised **earlier than three years** or **later than ten years** after grant, or within three years after the employee last exercised an option on which the tax exemption was obtained. However, neither of these three year waiting periods need be observed when personal representatives exercise the options of a deceased employee (but the ten year rule still applies).

4.4 Schemes may be altered so that in the event of the company concerned being taken over, employees may exchange their existing options for equivalent options over shares in the acquiring company.

4.5 There is no income tax charge on:

(a) The occasion of the **grant** (except to the extent that the sum of the cost of the option and the exercise price is below the market value at the time of grant)

(b) The **increase in value** between the grant date and the exercise date

Any capital gain will however be chargeable to capital gains tax, with any amounts charged to income tax under (a) above treated as allowable expenditure

(c) The **disposal** of the shares

4.6 The costs of setting up approved share option schemes (both savings related and executive schemes) are deductible in the same way as the costs of setting up profit sharing schemes.

Administration of schemes

4.7 The administrative records etc of these schemes are essentially similar to those of the savings related share option schemes. The exercise of an option is a straightforward matter; the holder of the option **presents** his **option certificate** (duly completed), with the money due for the option price. The company **allots** the **shares**, and **applies** for a **Stock Exchange listing** for those shares. There must, of course, also be a return of allotments (for cash).

5 EMPLOYEE SHARE OWNERSHIP TRUSTS

5.1 Companies may set up **employee share ownership trusts**. Such arrangements give tax advantages to companies, but not to employees. A company can obtain a deduction in computing its taxable profits for money given to the trust to buy shares in the company. The trust must make the purchase within **nine months** of the end of the period of account in which the company provides the funds, and the trust then distributes the shares to the employees.

5.2 The following conditions apply.

(a) The **trustees** must all be **UK resident**, must be at least three in number and must include a trust corporation or a solicitor or other professional.

(b) Most of the trustees must be **employees**, and must be chosen by a majority of employees or by their elected representatives.

(c) All **full-time employees** and **directors** who have worked for a **qualifying period** of between one and five years must be beneficiaries of the trust. For trusts set up after 29

April 1996, the period is between nought and five years. Anyone who owns more than 5% of the shares is not eligible.

(d) The shares acquired must be **fully paid up, non-redeemable ordinary shares,** and not subject to any restrictions not attaching to all shares of the same class.

(e) The trustees must **not acquire shares** at **greater** than their **open market value,** or at a time when the company is under the control of another company.

(f) Shares must be **transferred** to **employees** within seven years of their acquisition by the trustees. For trusts set up after 3 May 1994, the time limit is 20 years.

(g) All beneficiaries must **receive shares** on **similar terms.** Adjustments for levels of remuneration and length of service are allowed.

5.3 Where the trust is set up after 3 May 1994, there are two alternatives to the trust structure described above.

(a) **A paritarian trust structure.** There must be at least three UK resident trustees. At least one must be a professional trustee (a trust corporation, solicitor or other professional who is not a director or employee of the founding company and who is chosen by the non-professional trustees). At least two UK resident trustees must not be professional trustees. At least half of the non-professional trustees must be employees, elected by employees or their elected representatives.

(b) **A UK resident corporate trustee** which is controlled by the founding company and which has directors composed in the same way as the trustees of a paritarian trust.

Exercise

What are the main conditions which apply to:

(a) A profit-sharing scheme
(b) A savings-related share option scheme
(c) A company share option plan
(d) An employee share ownership trust

Answer

See the following paragraphs.

(a) Paragraphs 2.4 and 2.7
(b) Paragraph 3.4
(c) Paragraph 4.2
(d) Paragraph 5.2

Chapter roundup

- A company may encourage employees to purchase shares in the company and thereby take a closer interest in the success and performance of the company. Company and tax law both encourage and make allowance for such employee participation schemes.
- **Employee share schemes** encourage holding of shares or debentures by employees, ex-employees, employees of the same group, and close relatives of employees.
- The company must have the express power under the memorandum objects clause permitting such employee participation. Always look to the memorandum and articles to check the company's powers and rules with which it has to comply.
- There are four types of scheme as follows:
  - Profit-sharing schemes
  - Savings related share option schemes
  - Company share option plans
  - Employee share ownership trusts

  The law governing these schemes can generally be found in the Income and Corporation Taxes Act 1988 (as amended by later Finance Acts).
- Distinctions between each type of scheme must be identified. The following distinctions apply.
  - **Profit sharing.** Some profits are kept aside to be applied in the purchase of some of the company's own shares to be held by the individual employees.
  - **Saving related share option**. The employee contracts to save over a period of three or five years (subject to extension) and at the end he may purchase the company shares at a pre-arranged price (fixed by the contract) or withdraw the money. As the money sits in the savings accounts it earns a tax-free bonus.
  - **Company share option plans**. Employees are given an option to purchase shares in the company, giving them a priority in buying shares.
  - **Share ownership trust**. The company obtains tax savings by transferring funds to a trust which can buy shares for the benefit of employees.

Test your knowledge

1. How are company law rules modified for employee share schemes? (see para 1.4)
2. What is the main feature of profit sharing schemes? (2.3)
3. What is the tax position of an employee in a savings related share option scheme? (3.5)
4. How does an employee participant under a savings related share option scheme or a company share option plan exercise his option? (3.9, 4.7)
5. What are the main tax implications for the employee of participation in a company share option plan? (4.5)

Now try illustrative question 28 at the end of the Study Text

Chapter 24

TAKEOVERS, MERGERS AND SCHEMES OF ARRANGEMENT

This chapter covers the following topics.

Introduction

An *acquisition* is the purchase of a controlling interest in one company by another company. These transactions are generally referred to as 'takeovers'.

An *amalgamation* is a merger between two separate companies to form a single company.

In practice, the distinction between amalgamations and takeovers is not always a clear one, when a large company 'joins' with another company that is not quite so large. The methods of merging are often the same as the methods used to make a takeover.

A proposed acquisition might be one of the following:

(a) The takeover of a private (unquoted) company by another private company
(b) The takeover of a private (unquoted) company by a plc
(c) The takeover of a plc by another plc
(d) The takeover of a plc by a private company (known as a reverse takeover)

The reasons for making a distinction between these categories of takeover are chiefly as follows.

(a) Public limited companies will have their shares quoted on a stock market (the Stock Exchange, AIM etc.) whereas private companies do not have a marketplace for their shares. This means that when a takeover is considered, the shares of an unquoted company must be 'valued' subjectively, without the benefit of an 'objective' market price as a guideline.

(b) Public companies with shares quoted on the main stock market or AIM must follow the City Code on Takeovers and Mergers. The City Code is explained in general terms later in this chapter.

The other main category of transaction with which this chapter is concerned is a scheme of arrangement. This is a flexible procedure which can be used to effect an arrangement with members or creditors by for example varying share or debenture rights, or re-organising the capital structure of the company.

1 PROCEDURE FOR THE TAKEOVER OF A PUBLIC COMPANY **6/99**

1.1 For convenience, the company which wishes to acquire the share capital of another is referred to below as 'the bidder' and the other company as 'the target company'. These are not recognised technical terms.

1.2 The bidder's opening move may be an approach to the board of the target company, with a view to securing the latter's consent and recommendation to the shareholders of the target company that they should accept the bid.

1.3 However, it is also common practice, if the target company is a public company, with shares traded on a stock exchange, for a bidder first to purchase some shares of the target company, as they become available over a period of time and without disclosing its intention to gain control. In this way it hopes to strengthen its bargaining position and to reduce the possibility of a rival bid from some other company, which may be called in by the target company to defeat the original bidder. Hence the other bidder is sometimes colloquially called a '**white knight**', or a rescuer.

1.4 If a company builds up a shareholding in another company, with a view to taking it over eventually, s 198 CA 1985 requires it to **disclose** its shareholding once it reaches **3%.** Shareholding in these circumstances includes shares held by nominees and shares held as part of concert party arrangements. Once that level is reached, any **increase** (by 1% stages) must also be **notified** to the target company and, if it is a listed company, the latter will disclose these transactions to the Stock Exchange. This means that if one company does build up a shareholding in another, the target company's management will be aware of the predator's build-up of shareholding.

1.5 In the early stages of building up a shareholding by market purchases, the bidder and any associates usually proceed slowly, in order not to force up the market price, and in consequence the price at which the takeover bid itself must later be made. In the later stages before making the bid, however, the bidder may seek to acquire a much increased holding very rapidly, by the manoeuvre known as a '**dawn raid**', a simultaneous approach to every known holder of a substantial number of shares of the target company. In this way the bidders position is greatly strengthened before the market can react by the inevitable sharp price rise.

1.6 To check this abuse the Takeover Panel administers *Rules governing the Substantial Acquisition of Shares (SAR)*, which restrain the speed at which shareholdings may be increased in the range between **15% and 30%.** (30% is another critical level, at which the City Code imposes an obligation to make a general offer to acquire the remainder of the shares of the target company.)

The rules governing the substantial acquisition of shares **6/98, 12/99**

1.7 The SAR and the City Code apply rules to the acquisition of shares in public companies with the following effects.

(a) When a bidder acquires 3% or more of the shares in the target company, the **target company must be notified,** and any increase in holding by 1% or more (ie. to 4%, 5%, 6% etc.) must also be notified.

(b) When the bidder's shareholding reaches **15%,** the rules of the **SAR** begin to apply.

(c) When the bidder wants to increase his holding to **30% or more**, the rules of the **City Code** begin to apply.

1.8 The general effect of the SAR is to require any person who seeks to acquire 10% or more of the voting shares, with the result that his shareholding increases to a level between 15% and 30%, to make an **advertised offer** to *all* shareholders. He invites tenders for their shares, up to the amount he wishes to acquire:

(a) At a **fixed price**

(b) if the tender is over-subscribed, at the **ceiling price** of the lowest-priced range of offers that will enable the bidder to acquire the desired number of shares, all tenders at or below the 'ceiling' receive that price.

2 THE TAKEOVER CODE (THE CITY CODE)

2.1 When the bidder wants to increase his shareholding to 30% or more, he is required by the City Code to make a full takeover bid. The general sequence of events in a takeover bid, which is regulated by the **City Code on Takeovers and Mergers,** is administered by the Takeover Panel.

2.2 The City Code on Takeovers and Mergers (the 'Blue Book') is a non-statutory code of practice, which applies to take over bids made for shares of public companies listed on the Stock Exchange. The Code is observed on the basis of voluntary agreement among merchant banks, stockbrokers and other financial institutions in the City of London.

2.3 The operation of the Code is supervised by a **Panel** to which takeover bidders, directors of companies subject to takeover bids and their advisors may refer for guidance.

2.4 The nature and purpose of the City Code is described within the Code itself.

> 'The Code and the Panel operate principally to ensure fair and equal treatment of all shareholders in relation to takeovers. The Code also provides an orderly framework within which takeovers are conducted. The Code is not concerned with the financial or commercial advantages or disadvantages of a take over. These are matters for the company and its shareholders. Nor is the Code concerned with those issues, such as competition policy, which are the responsibility of government.
>
> Those who do not so conduct themselves may find that, by way of sanction, the facilities of those markets are withheld.

2.5 Companies subject to the Code include all public companies (listed or unlisted) and some classes of private company, including those whose shares are or have been traded on AIM.

2.6 The Code, which is revised from time to time, sets out the following:

(a) Ten general principles

(b) 38 rules which lay down more detailed instructions on conduct in the course of takeover bids

(c) Practice notes which are specific rulings (often arising from decided cases) on particular matters

2.7 In broad outline, its main purpose is to ensure that, in a takeover bid, all shareholders are as far as possible treated in the same way. Information put forward to influence them in deciding whether to accept or reject an offer for their shares should be accurate and equally available to all concerned.

Summary of the City Code: takeover bid procedure — **Specimen paper, 12/99**

2.8 Briefly summarised, the City Code's rules and other laws and practises are as follows.

(a) P plc must make an **initial approach** to Q plc, announcing its intentions. P plc will probably be advised by a merchant bank.

(b) Q plc must **check** P plc's **financial ability** to make the bid. An independent advisor to Q plc will be appointed (probably another merchant bank).

(c) If any other company is intending to acquire Q plc, the information about P plc's offer should be **made known** to its **management**.

(d) When talks are proceeding between P plc and Q plc, **insider dealing** in the shares of P & Q is **not permitted**.

(e) P plc will **formally notify** Q plc of its intention to bid. The offer must be **kept open** for at **least 21 days** and then P plc must state its holdings and its intentions. If the offer is revised, the revised offer must be kept open for at **least 14 more days** after notification of the revision. A formal offer cannot be withdrawn during this period without permission from the Takeover Panel. A formal offer cannot be made unconditional without at **least 50% acceptance** by the shareholders of Q plc.

(f) When P plc has made formal notification to Q plc, Q plc's directors must make a **press release** and **notify it's shareholders** of the identity of the bidder and the terms and conditions of the bid. Announcements must be made when there is an obligation to make an offer in circumstances where the offeree is the subject of rumour and speculation, or when negotiations are about to be extended outside a very restricted circle.

(g) An **offer document** is issued to shareholders stating the terms of the bid, whether there is agreement between the boards of P plc and Q plc, information about P plc, its stake in Q plc and its future intentions, a profit forecast of Q plc together with material changes since the date of the last balance sheet etc.

(h) If P plc has built up a **30% stake** in the (voting) equity of Q plc, it is generally obliged to make a bid to the remaining shareholders at the highest price paid for any of its acquired shares during the preceding year. This is because 30% or so of voting shares concentrated in one hand will often give **effective voting control**, if the remaining 70% is widely dispersed among shareholders who will find it difficult to take concerted action. 30% has therefore been selected as a 'trigger' which sets the City Code rules into operation.

(i) Q plc's directors may **not now issue new shares, nor institute changes** to its balance sheet (for example, selling off a major fixed asset or buying a major new asset for which no contract to purchase had been made prior to the takeover bid) so as to **affect** the likely success of the **takeover bid**, without agreement at a general meeting. For example, by making a bonus issue of shares, the bidding company would have to buy up more shares to gain control.

(j) P plc may **not try** to **sway** the **decisions** of some of Q plc's shareholders by offering preferential terms.

(k) **'Arm's length' dealing** in shares - on the stock market - is permitted, subject to daily disclosure to the Takeover Panel, the Stock Exchange and the press.

(l) However, it is **illegal** for a company to **support** or **influence** the **market price** of its shares during a takeover bid by providing finance (or financial guarantees etc) for the purchase of its own shares - for example an offeror company that is making a share exchange bid, or an offeree company whose directors are trying to fight off a bid.

2.9 For the company secretary, the main features of a takeover bid are as follows.

(a) The first step is an approach by the bidder to the board of the target company, usually for the purposes of:

   (i) **Expressing an interest** in buying the target company

   (ii) **Finding out** whether the **latter** is willing to **recommend** an offer, if one is made, to shareholders of the target company

   (iii) **Exchanging information** in confidence about the financial and commercial advantages and consequences of a merger of the two companies

   As soon as the bidder has shown a firm intention to make an offer, the board of the target company must inform its members and make an announcement. A formal offer document is then prepared and issued.

(b) A person who acquires **30 per cent** of the issued shares of a company by other means (by purchase in the market or a private negotiation) must then make an offer for the **remainder** of the shares.

(c) The directors of the target company may decide to **recommend the offer** to their shareholders or on the other hand to **resist the offer**, to defend against the takeover bid.

(d) If a bidder, or the directors of the target company, introduce a forecast of profits into the statements issued to shareholders, the basis of such a **forecast** must be **examined** by the auditors and by the merchant bank concerned. Both must state whether they consider the basis on which the forecast is made to be reasonable.

(e) A takeover bid must be open for acceptance for at least **21 days**. The bid will usually be **conditional**, which means that the bidder will only undertake to buy the shares in the target company from shareholders who accept the offer, provided that there is a minimum level of acceptances. Typically, an offer will be conditional on enough acceptances being received to take the bidders' total shareholding in the target company to more than 50% - ie enough to give the bidder control of the target company.

(f) If the offer is made conditional on obtaining a **minimum level of acceptance** (eg 51 per cent, or 90 per cent), and the required level of acceptance is achieved, the offer is declared **unconditional**, and is extended for at least 14 days so that shareholders who have so far held back and refused to accept the offer may, if they wish, then accept.

(g) There are elaborate rules which require disclosure of information, eg concerning dealings in the shares by directors, the takeover bidder etc.

2.10 The City Code does not permit an offer to be declared unconditional at a level of acceptance below 50 per cent. In most cases, the bidder declares his intention of acquiring the entire share capital, and states that he will resort to acquisition under s 172 and Schedule 12, if he obtains 90 per cent acceptance or more: such a compulsory acquisition is described later in the chapter.

3 GENERAL CONSTRAINTS ON A TAKEOVER BID

3.1 A takeover bid for the shares of a listed company, made by a bidder which is itself a listed company, is subject to a series of constraints *in addition* to the rules of the City Code, as follows.

(a) The relevant parts of the legislation make it almost unavoidable that the formal bid shall be made by a **merchant bank**, acting on behalf of the bidder. The bank and its professional advisers will take the leading part in drafting the offer document, but will require much information and assistance from the directors and secretary of the bidder.

(b) It may be necessary to convene an EGM of the bidder company to obtain approval for various actions.

(i) **The allotment of shares** as the consideration for the shares of the target company, if it is a 'shares for shares' offer

(ii) **An increase in the authorised capital.**

A company which needs to issue shares to raise cash to pay for the target company, or for a shares for shares offer, may need to increase its authorised share capital in order to be able to issue enough new shares to meet its needs.

(iii) **To give general approval to the offer,** in view of its size

(c) Where the offer, if successful, would produce a merger of two leading companies in the same field, there may have to be a reference to the **Competition Commission** for investigation and report. This will happen when the Office of Fair Trading believe that the merger will result in a significant reduction in competition in the market, to the detriment of customers.

3.2 The CA 1989 introduces provisions (by insertions into the Fair Trading Act 1973) designed to streamline pre-merger consultation procedures.

3.3 A **pre-clearance procedure** is available for merger proposals which are to be publicly announced. Notification must be made to the Director General of Fair Trading, after which a waiting period of 20 days applies (with the possibility of extensions of 10 and 15 days). Generally, if no action is taken within this period, the merger is able to proceed, but must be completed within six months.

3.4 The Director General of Fair Trading is empowered, where a merger is viewed as having potentially adverse effects on the public interest, to accept **undertakings** from the interested parties to divest or separate part of the business in order to remedy the situation. The acceptance of these recommendations by the Secretary of State prevents referral of the merger to the Competition Commission.

3.5 After a reference of the merger has been made to the Competition Commission, the parties concerned are prevented from acquiring any interest in shares in any of the companies involved unless permission is given by the Secretary of State.

3.6 The effect of EU competition rules should also be considered if the takeover is likely to have international complications.

3.7 The CA 1989 also contains measures making the provision of false or misleading information a criminal offence, and enabling fees to be charged by the Director General or the Secretary of State in respect of qualifying mergers.

4 THE OFFER DOCUMENT

4.1 The **offer document** is an elaborate printed letter setting out the terms of the offer and procedures for acceptance and for declaring the offer unconditional. It will include various important pieces of information:

(a) **The shares to be acquired**, for example information on their quoted market value at intervals over the six months preceding the publication of the bidder's intention to make the offer

(b) **The bidder**, for example details of its financial and trading prospects

(c) **The consideration offered**, which may be shares in the bidder company (for example, two shares in the bidder company for every three shares in the target company), cash, a mixture of shares and cash or, sometimes, other securities as well, such as convertible loan stock of the bidder company

4.2 With the offer document (and its detailed appendices giving information) will be sent a form of **acceptance and transfer,** which each shareholder of the target company is invited to sign and return with his share certificate. He will be informed that if his share certificate is not immediately available, he may send in his acceptance and deliver the certificate later. The document should make special provisions if the securities are held in dematerialised form through CREST.

4.3 If the board of the target company has decided to recommend the offer to its shareholders, a **letter of recommendation** will be sent, if possible with the offer document.

4.4 There is, of course, a clear explanation in the offer document of the timetable of impending events, such as the closing date for receipt of acceptances. The offeree is advised to seek professional advice on the offer, and on his personal tax position arising from acceptance.

4.5 Finally, the offeree will be informed that, if the offer is accepted by holders of at **least 90%** of the shares, the bidder may resort to **compulsory acquisition** of the remaining shares under s 428.

Preparing the offer document

4.6 Among practical points requiring attention in preparing the offer document are the following.

(a) If the offeree receives **dividends** on his shares of the target company through his bank account by dividend mandate, the mandate will, unless he expresses a contrary intention, be treated as applicable to dividends to which he may become entitled in future, if he accepts shares of the bidder company in exchange for his existing shareholding.

(b) If the offeree has **recently acquired shares**, which are in course of registration by the target company, he may **accept** by **showing** that he is **in the course of becoming** the **registered holder**.

(c) If the articles of the target company require its directors to hold **qualification shares**, and it is intended that they should remain in office after the bid takes effect, they should retain the required qualification shareholding in their names for the time being, but declare themselves nominees of the bidder in respect of them.

(d) With the offer document, and form of acceptance and transfer, there should be a **printed pre-addressed envelope** to be used in sending the completed acceptance and share certificate to the bidder's agent, for example the merchant bank acting on behalf of the bidder.

(e) The target company should do its best to **clear all outstanding transfers**, received for registration up to the time of the issue of the offer, and should provide the most current list of members possible.

(f) It was mentioned earlier that there is a possibility that an EGM of the bidder company or the target company may have to be called to pass one or more resolutions to allow the takeover to go ahead. If there is to be an **EGM** of either company, the **required notice** and **circular** should be prepared. The timetable may not require that the EGM should be convened, unless the offer is accepted by a decisive majority and declared unconditional.

(g) If the offer is a cash payment or includes cash as an alternative to shares, the money should be made available in a **separate bank account**. A **'cash alternative'**, however, is often in the form of a separate offer made by the merchant bank, acting for the bidder, to acquire the bidder's own shares (which have in theory been accepted by the offeree, in a share-for-share exchange) for cash at a specified price. In other words, the offeree acquires shares in the bidder in exchange for his shares in the target company, but then sells them to the merchant bank, ending up with a cash sum for the value of his original shares. The merchant bank then sells the shares through the market or, more usually, places them with institutions to avoid depressing the market price by a bulk sale on the market. It may be required to offer the shares first to shareholders of the bidder (a vendor rights issue, as explained in an earlier chapter).

Role of the company secretary

4.7 The secretary of a bidder or a target company in a situation such as this will obviously be extremely busy for many weeks.

(a) He will have to **attend meetings** to settle the terms of documents and discuss questions of strategy.

(b) It is likely that most of the documents will be **drafted** by **professional advisers** to the merchant bank or to the company, since they are extremely technical. The experts will, however, call on and rely on the secretary - as better informed about his own company - for information and for the most careful checking of the documents which they have drafted.

(c) **Announcements** will have to be made from time to time of the progress of the bid; these require prompt and careful drafting. In the eyes of the City and the Stock Exchange in particular, the most heinous of all 'innocent' defaults is the supply of inaccurate information of any kind.

Compulsory acquisition of shares in a takeover bid 12/98

4.8 If acceptances of a takeover bid reach the level at which the bidder will control more than half the voting shares of the target company, the bidder will (by the terms of the offer) have the right - but not the obligation - to **declare** the **offer unconditional**. The bidder is then bound to acquire. The accepting shareholders are bound to sell the shares in respect of which acceptances have been lodged. However, the object is usually to raise the level of acceptances to **90%** or more. If acceptances are in the range between 50% (plus one share) and 90%, strenuous efforts will be made, by extending the period of the offer and inviting non-accepting shareholders to send in acceptances, to reach the 90% level before the offer expires. If 90% is obtained, the offer will undoubtedly become unconditional and binding.

4.9 Any person (an individual or persons acting jointly) may make an offer for the issued shares, or the shares of a class, of a company which it does not already own. If the statutory code is to apply, the offer must be for **all the shares,** not just part of them. Any shares which the offeror, or his associates, may acquire by market purchase while the bid is outstanding are excluded from the offer (for the calculation of 90% acceptances). The offer may also be expressed to include any new shares which the target company may allot during the period of the offer.

4.10 Any **variation** of the offer, such as an increase in price, is treated as the **same offer** in **varied form** and not as a new offer. The offer itself may include alternatives, to give the offeree a choice, but the same terms must be offered to all holders of shares of the same class. By way of exception, if some shareholders reside in a foreign country the offer to them may be modified to suit the local circumstances of their country of residence, such as tax or exchange control.

4.11 If the offeror makes an offer for **two classes** of shares, such as ordinary and preference shares, this is treated as **two separate offers**; one may, of course, be made conditional on the success of the other.

4.12 If **within** a period of **four months** from making his offer, the bidder obtains at least 90% acceptance (in terms of shares to which the offer relates), he need not wait for the expiry of the permitted four month period. He may immediately **serve notice,** on shareholders who have not accepted, of his **intention** to **acquire** their **shares 'compulsorily'** on the terms of the offer (including any 'cash alternative').

4.13 There are various procedures which a company secretary should note.

(a) The notice must be in the **prescribed form** (Form 428).

(b) It must be sent **within two months** of the date on which the 90% acceptance is reached (*not* the expiry of the four months' period allowed for reaching that level).

(c) When the bidder serves the first such notice, he must also send the target company a **copy** of the notice, with a statutory declaration by a director that the conditions (90% acceptance) for operating the procedure have been satisfied.

4.14 The person on whom the Form 428 is served has the right, **within six weeks** of receiving it, to **apply** to the **court** for an **order** to **cancel** or vary the terms of the compulsory purchase. If the offer comprises alternatives, he also has the same period of six weeks in which to select the alternative which he prefers, and to give notice of it.

4.15 On the expiry of the six week period the bidder sends the target company the following.

(a) A **copy** of the **notice of intention** to **acquire** the **shares**

(b) A **transfer** of the **shares** to the **bidder**, (signed by a person authorised by the bidder) for registration "Global Transfer"

(c) The **money** or **other consideration** to be held in trust for the former owner of the shares

4.16 A bidder is not bound to acquire the shares of a non-accepting shareholder because he has obtained 90% acceptances, but if he elects to serve notice, he is then bound to complete the acquisition. If he decides not to give notice to acquire the shares, he must instead give notice to the non-accepting shareholder(s) stating that:

(a) He has obtained **90% acceptance.**

(b) The shareholder(s) may **within three months** by notice **require him** (the bidder) to acquire the shares on the terms of the offer.

Exercise

What role does the company secretary have to play in a takeover bid?

Solution

Look back to paragraph 4.7.

---

5 PURCHASE OF OWN SHARES

5.1 The City Code states that when a public company redeems or purchases its own voting shares, a resulting increase in the shareholdings of the directors and people acting in concert with the directors will be treated as an acquisition.

5.2 The Takeover Panel may grant exemption from any need to make a general offer which results from the purchase of own shares if there is a **vote of independent shareholders,** and the **waiver procedure** set out in the City Code is otherwise followed (this includes a circular to shareholders and prescribed announcements). The directors and their associates must not acquire shares at any time between the posting of the circular to shareholders prior to the meeting and the meeting itself, and should in any event not acquire shares knowing that the company intended to gain permission from its members to redeem or purchase its own shares.

5.3 An important part of the waiver procedure is consultation with the Takeover Panel, and the Code states that the **Takeover Panel** must always **consulted** if it appears likely that a general offer will be required as a result of a purchase of own shares.

5.4 Any shareholder who is independent of the directors and those in concert with the directors will not have to make a general offer if as a result of the purchase of shares, his shareholdings are above the limits specified in the City Code (unless he has purchased shares believing a purchase or redemption by the company will occur). Any subsequent acquisition of shares by anyone will be subject to the rules of the City Code in the normal way, calculated on the new amounts of issued share capital.

5.5 There must be appropriate disclosure if a redemption or purchase takes place during an offer.

Listing Rules

5.6 Listed companies are also subject to Chapter 15 of the Listing Rules when they wish to purchase their own shares.

(a) The Companies Announcement Office must be notified of the **board resolution** to propose purchase, copies of the relevant general meeting resolutions, details of the outcome of the vote and details of the purchase.

(b) **Approval** must be given not only by a meeting of shareholders of the class of equity shares which the company is intending to purchase, but also **any class** which has **conversion rights** into the class of equity shares from which the purchase is made.

(c) If shareholder approval is sought of a purchase of **15% or more**, the circular must include inter alia a working capital statement and details of future prospects. When 15% or more will be purchased within a year on a general authority to purchase, the purchase must be made either by **tender** or **partial offer** to all shareholders of that class of shares. If a series of purchases within a year amounts to more than 15%, only the purchase that takes the aggregate above 15% need be by tender or partial offer.

(d) When the company intends to make a purchase of less than 15% within a year other than by tender or partial offer to all shareholders in that class, the purchase may be made through the market only if the price paid is **not more than 5%** of the average of the **market values** for the **five business days prior** to the purchase being made.

(e) Purchases of a **company's own shares** are **prohibited** during periods where directors would be **prohibited** from dealing in its securities under the Listing Rules.

(f) More limited rules apply to purchases of securities other than equity shares.

6 SCHEMES OF ARRANGEMENT 12/98

6.1 A scheme of arrangement, under s 425, is a different sort of arrangement, which may be used for either a takeover (in some circumstances) or a reconstruction scheme. A reconstruction scheme, you may remember, is a scheme which is likely to alter the rights of shareholders, or a class of shareholders or of creditors of the company.

6.2 The following sequence of action is necessary.

(a) **Application** is made to the **court** (usually by the company itself) for an order that one or more meetings of members and/or of creditors (if the scheme will affect the rights of creditors) shall be held. With the application, the company submits a document setting out in detail the terms of the scheme of arrangement, and also an explanatory statement to be issued with the notice(s) convening the meeting(s).

(b) If the court is satisfied that the scheme is generally suitable for consideration as a '**scheme of arrangement**', it will **order** that a **meeting** or meetings be held to consider it. The court is not at this stage concerned with the details of the scheme, nor the issue (which may arise later) of whether there are conflicts of interest, which require that more separate meetings should be held. The court merely looks at the outline of the scheme and, if it seems suitable, orders that meeting(s) be held.

(c) A **meeting**, or **several meetings**, is/are held as the court has ordered. A substantial quorum, for example members (present in person or by proxy) holding one third of the shares, is required. The scheme must be **approved** by **members** (or as the case may be, creditors) voting at each meeting. They must comprise both a majority in numbers, and must represent three quarters in value of the shares (or at a creditor's meeting, of the amounts owing).

(d) Following approval of the scheme at meeting(s), **application** is made to the **court** for an order to approve and implement the scheme. At this stage any minority which opposes the scheme may state its objections for consideration by the court.

(e) A **copy** of the court order approving the scheme is delivered to the registrar, and the scheme then **takes effect** (the changes are made automatically as soon as this is done).

6.3 A scheme of arrangement is very flexible, since it may be used to effect any 'compromise or arrangement' with members or a class of members, or with creditors or a class of creditors.

6.4 It is generally considered that it is legally permissible to resort to a scheme of arrangement as a means of acquiring the shares of a company by **compulsory means**, even though s 428 provides a specific alternative procedure. A scheme of arrangement only requires approval by a **75% majority** of votes cast at a meeting, which is a less effective safeguard to a minority than the 90% of all shares prescribed for a takeover by statute. In a scheme of arrangement, however, the final decision always rests with the court, to which the minority may express their objections.

6.5 Apart from the lower level of approval required in a scheme of arrangement, the main advantage of promoting a takeover by this means is that it may thereby **save substantial sums in stamp duty**; under a scheme of arrangement, the shares acquired are not transferred but cancelled (by virtue of the court order). The disadvantage of a scheme of arrangement is the substantial expense arising from the need to make two applications to the court at different stages.

6.6 A scheme of arrangement is also sometimes useful in **acquiring** the **outstanding minority** shareholding of a partly owned subsidiary, where the minority who object have more than one tenth, but less than one quarter, of the outstanding shares. There must of course be a meeting of the holders of the outstanding minority as a group; the holding company may not use its control of its existing holding (even if held by a nominee) to achieve the required majority.

6.7 There is a particular pitfall to avoid in promoting a scheme of arrangement: **failure to distinguish** the **'classes'**, each of which must be given the opportunity to vote on the scheme at a separate meeting. The holders of each class of shares (preference or ordinary shares, for example) must obviously be called to separate meetings. But members holding shares of the *same* class may also have to be distinguished, if their 'interest' in the transaction is identifiably different: *Re Hellenic & General Trust Ltd 1975*.Stamp duty

6.8 Certain kinds of reconstruction are eligible for exemption from stamp duty. The company secretary should obtain expert advice on the tax effects of what is proposed.

7 DEMERGERS

7.1 Demerging is the splitting of a company or group. It can take place by either of two methods.

(a) A holding company **distributes** to its shareholders **shares** in its subsidiary.

(b) A holding company **distributes** the **assets** and trade of, or shares in, its subsidiary to its shareholders. A new company then issues shares to the shareholders of the holding company in consideration for the assets or shares.

7.2 Demergers potentially attract a number of tax concessions. Therefore an application for Inland Revenue clearance needs to be made at least 30 days before the proposed date of the demerger. A formal demerger agreement will be required.

7.3 The procedures when a demerger involving a new company takes place are as follows.

(a) The **position of various shareholders** should be **considered**, also the assets and liabilities that may be transferred.

(b) The **consent** of the **bank** may be **required** if the bank has taken security over the assets of the company.

(c) A **new company** will have to be set up as **appropriate**. Normal registration procedures will be required.

(d) **Board meetings** will be needed of the holding company and the new company to approve the demerger agreement and convene extraordinary general meetings.

(e) The holding company will need to hold an **extraordinary general meeting** for any necessary alteration of articles (for example to allow dividends in specie) and also perhaps approve substantial property transactions by directors. The new company will need to hold an extraordinary general meeting primarily to authorise directors to allot shares and remove statutory pre-emption rights.

(f) **Dividends** will be distributed to the shareholders of the holding company in the form of **assets or shares.**

(g) The new company will **obtain the assets** of, or **shares in**, the **subsidiary** by accepting them as **consideration** for **shares in itself**.

Chapter roundup

- An **acquisition** (takeover) is the purchase of a controlling interest in one company by another example.
- An **amalgamation** is a merger between two separate companies to form a single company.
- The main reasons for a takeover or amalgamation are as follows:
  - Operating economies
  - Diversification
  - To bolster asset backing
  - To improve the quality of earnings
  - Growth
  - Entering a market at lower cost
  - Acquiring the products of a competitor.
- There must be **unanimous consent** to the takeover (effected by an amalgamation or reconstruction agreement or acquisition by private treaty) or, if not, then the dissenting minority must be less than **10%** of the shares of the target company before it can be a permissible takeover.
- The takeover may be '**friendly**', by a direct approach to the directors and full disclosure of intent at the beginning, or '**hostile**' which means purchasing shares on the open market and building a shareholding alone or with other friendly institutions (however, where 3% shareholdings are acquired disclosure must be made to the shareholders; Substantial Acquisition rules must be observed when at least 15% of shares are acquired).
- The **City Code** imposes other regulations when 30% or more of shares are acquired: the company buying must make a full takeover bid administered by the Takeover Panel.
- In addition to the Code legislation imposes a number of **statutory constraints** as follows.
  - The 'formal offer' (which must set out clearly the details of the offer) shall be made by a merchant bank.
  - The Listing Rules control and regulate the offer document.
  - An EGM must be called by the bidder to approve the allotment of any shares and any increase in authorised capital and to give general approval of the offer.
  - Referrals may be made to the Competition Commission.
  - Notification procedures and proper pre-merger consultations are required.
- **Schemes of arrangement** can be used as a means of takeover, as well to vary class rights or reorganise a company's capital structure.
- A scheme of arrangement requires approval by **75% majority** in general meeting.

Test your knowledge

1 What is the significance and effect of acquiring (a) 3%; (b) 15%; and (c) 30% of the voting shares of a listed public company? (see para 1.4, 1.7 – 1.8)

2 How might a takeover bid affect the bidder's secretary? (2.9)

3 What general constraints regulate the conduct of a takeover bid? (3.1)

4 What should be sent, as additional enclosures, with an offer document issued in the course of a takeover bid? (4.2 - 4.5)

5 What is the basic timetable for acquisition of shares of non-accepting shareholders, after obtaining acceptance from holders of 90% or more of the shares? (4.12 - 4.16)

6 What are the requirements of the Listing Rules on a listed company wishing to purchase its own shares? (5.6)

7 Describe the general nature of a scheme of arrangement, and the procedure (a) for ascertaining the views of shareholders; and (b) for making the scheme effective. (6.1 - 6.2)

8 In what ways can a demerger take place? (7.1)

Now try illustrative question 29 at the end of the Study Text

Appendices 1 to 20 Prescribed forms

[Note that the numbers given to the prescribed forms are derived from the section number of the Companies Act which prescribes them]

COMPANIES HOUSE

10

Please complete in typescript, or in bold black capitals.

Notes on completion appear on final page

First directors and secretary and intended situation of registered office

Company Name in full

F010001H

Proposed Registered Office
(PO Box numbers only, are not acceptable)

Post town

County / Region — Postcode

If the memorandum is delivered by an agent for the subscriber(s) of the memorandum mark the box opposite and give the agent's name and address

Agent's Name

Address

Post town

County / Region — Post code

Number of continuation sheets attached

Please give the name, address, telephone number and, if available, a DX number and Exchange of the person Companies House should contact if there is any query.

Tel

DX number — DX exchange

Companies House receipt data barcode

When you have completed and signed the form please send it to the Registrar of Companies at:
Companies House, Crown Way, Cardiff, CF4 3UZ DX33050 Carfiff
for companies registered in England and Wales
or
Companies House, 37 Castle Terrace, Edinburgh, EH1 2EB
for companies registered in Scotland **DX235 Edinburgh**

Form revised March 1995

Company Secretary (see notes 1-5)

Company name

NAME *Style/Title — *Honours etc

*voluntary details

Forename(s)

Surname

Previous forename(s)

Previous surname(s)

Address

Usual residential address
For a corporation, give the registered or principal office address.

Post town

County / Region

County — Postcode

Country

I consent to act as secretary of the company named on page 1

Consent signature — **Date**

Director (see notes 1-5)

Please list directors in alphabetical order

NAME *Style/Title — *Honours etc

Forename(s)

Surname

Previous forename(s)

Previous surname(s)

Address

Usual residential address
For a corporation, give the registered or principal office address.

Post town

County / Region

County — Postcode

Country

Date of birth Day Month Year — **Nationality**

Business occupation

Other directorships

I consent to act as director of the company named on page 1

Consent signature — **Date**

Director (continued) (see notes 1-5)

Please list directors in alphabetical order

NAME *Style/Title ______ *Honours etc ______

*Voluntary details

Forename(s) ______

Surname ______

Previous forename(s) ______

Previous surname(s) ______

Address ______

Usual residential address
For a corporation, give the registered or principal office address.

Post town ______

County / Region ______

County ______ Postcode ______

Country ______

Date of birth Day Month Year ______ **Nationality** ______

Business occupation ______

Other directorships ______

I consent to act as director of the company named on page 1

Consent signature ______ **Date** ______

This section must be signed by
Either
as an agent on behalf of all subscribers — Signed ______ Date ______

Or the subscribers (i.e. those who signed as members on the memorandum of association).

Signed ______ Date ______

Signed ______ Date ______

Signed ______ Date ______

Signed ______ Date ______

Signed ______ Date ______

Signed ______ Date ______

Notes

1. Show for an individual the full forename(s) NOT INITIALS and surname together with any previous forename(s) or surname(s).

If the director or secretary is a corporation or Scottish firm - show the corporate or firm name on the surname line.

Give previous forename(s) or surname(s) except that:

- for a married woman, the name by which she was known before the marriage need not be given.

- names not used since the age of 18 or for least 20 years need not be given.

A peer, or an individual known by a title, may state the title instead of or in addition to the forename(s) and surname and need not give the name by which that person was known before he or she adopted the title or succeeded to it.

Address:

Give the usual residential address.

In the case of a corporation or Scottish firm give the registered or principal office

Subscribers:

The form must be signed personally either by the subscriber(s) or by a person or persons authorised to sign on behalf of the subscribers

2. Directors known by another description:

- A director includes any person who occupies that position even if called by a different name, for example, governor, member of council.

3. Directors details:

- Show for each individual director, the director's date of birth, business occupation and nationality.
The date of birth must be given for every individual director.

4. Other directorships:

- Give the name of every company of which the person concerned is a director or has been a director at any time in the past 5 years. You may exclude a company which either **is, or** at **all times during the past 5 years,** when the person was a director, **was:**

- dormant,

- a parent company which wholly owned the company making the return,

- a wholly owned subsidiary of the company making the return, or

- another wholly owned subsidiary of the same parent company.

If there is insufficient space on the form for other directorships you may use a separate sheet of paper, which should include the company's number and the full name of the director.

5. Use Form 10 continuation sheets or photocopies of page 2 to provide details of joint secretaries or additional directors and include the company's number.

COMPANIES HOUSE

12

Declaration on application for registration

Company Name in full

F012001J

I,

of

+ please delete as appropriate

do solemnly and sincerely declare that I am a [Solicitor engaged in the formation of the company] [person named as director or secretary of the company in the statement delivered to the Registrar under section 10 of the Companies Act 1985] + and that all the requirements of the Companies Act 1985 in respect of the registration of the above company and of matters precedent and incidental to it have been complied with.

And I make this solemn Declaration conscientiously believing the same to be true and by virtue of the Statutory Declarations Act 1835.

Declarant's signature

Declared at

the day of

One thousand nine hundred and ninety

[1] Please print name

before me[1]

Signed **Date**

A Commissioner for Oaths or Notary Public or Justice of the Peace or Solicitor

Please give the name, address, telephone number and, if available, a DX number and Exchange of the person Companies House should contact if there is any query.

Tel

DX number DX exchange

Companies House receipt date barcode

Form revised March 1995

When you have completed and signed the form please send it to the Registrar of Companies at:
Companies House, Crown Way, Cardiff, CF4 3UZ **DX33050 Cardiff**
for companies registered in England and Wales
or
Companies House, 37 Castle Terrace, Edinburgh, EH1 2EB
for companies registered in Scotland **DX235 Edinburgh**

BPP PUBLISHING

COMPANIES HOUSE

Change of accounting reference date **225**

Please complete in typescript, or in bold black capitals

Company Number

Company Name in full

F2250010

NOTES

You may use this form to change the accounting date relating to either the current or the immediately previous accounting period.

a. You **may not** change a period for which the accounts are already overdue.

b. You **may not** extend a period beyond 18 months unless the company is subject to an administration order.

c. You **may not** extend periods more than once in five years unless:

1. the company is subject to an administration order, or
2. you have the specific approval of the Secretary of State, (please enclose a copy), or
3. you are extending the company's accounting reference period to align with that of parent or subsidiary undertaking established in the European Economic Area.
4. the form is being submitted by an oversea company.

	Day	Month	Year
The accounting reference period ending			
is shortened/extended+ so as to end on			

Subsequent periods will end on the same day and month in future years

If extending more than once in five years, please indicate in the box the number of provision listed in note c. on which you are relying.

Signed **Date**

+a director/secretary/administrator/adminstrative receiver / receiver and manager/ receiver (Scotland) / person authorised on behalf of an oversea company

+ Please delete as appropriate

Please give the name, address, telephone number and, if available, a DX number and Exchange of the person Companies House should contact if there is any query.

Tel

DX number DX exchange

Companies House receipt date barcode

April 1996

When you have completed and signed the form please send it to the Registrar of Companies at:
Companies House, Crown Way, Cardiff, CF4 3UZ **DX33050 Cardiff**
for companies registered in England and Wales
or
Companies House, 37 Castle Terrace, Edinburgh, EH1 2EB
for companies registered in Scotland **DX235 Edinburgh**

Please complete in typescript, or in bold black capitals

88(2)

Return of Allotment of Shares

CHFP041

Company Number

Company Name in full

Shares allotted (including bonus shares)

	From			To		
Dates or period during which shares were allotted *(If shares were allotted on one date enter that date in the 'from' box)*	Day	Month	Year	Day	Month	Year

Class of shares *(ordinary or preference etc)*			
Number allotted			
Nominal value of each share			
Amount (if any) paid or due on each share *(including any share premium)*			

List the names and addresses of the allottees and the number of shares allotted to each overleaf

If the allotted shares are fully or partly paid up otherwise than in cash please state:

% that each share is to be treated as paid up			

Consideration for which the shares were allotted (This information must be supported by the duly stamped contract or by the duly stamped particulars on Form 88(3) if the contract is not in writing)	

When you have completed and signed the form send it to the Registrar of Companies at:

Companies House, Crown Way, Cardiff, CF4 3UZ **DX33050 Cardiff**
for companies registered in England and Wales
or
Companies House, 37 Castle Terrace, Edinburgh, EH1 2EB
for companies registered in Scotland **DX235 Edinburgh**

Companies House receipt date barcode

Form revised September 1999

Names and addresses of the allottees *(List joint share allotments consecutively)*

Shareholder details	Shares and share class allotted	
Name Address UK Postcode	Class of shares allotted	Number allotted
Name Address UK Postcode	Class of shares allotted	Number allotted
Name Address UK Postcode	Class of shares allotted	Number allotted
Name Address UK Postcode	Class of shares allotted	Number allotted

Please enter the number of continuation sheet(s) (if any) attached to this form

Signed ______________________ **Date** ______________________

A director / secretary / administrator / administrative receiver / receiver manager / receiver

Please delete as appriopriate

Please give the name, address, telephone number and, if available, a DX number and Exchange of the person Companies House should contact if there is any query

	Tel
DX number	DX exchange

COMPANIES HOUSE

117

Please complete in typescript, or in bold black capitals.

Application by a public company for certificate to commence business

Company Number

Company Name in full

F117001P

applies to a certificate that it is entitled to do business and exercise borrowing powers, and, for that purpose.

I,

of

[1] [a director] [the secretary] of the above company do solemnly and sincerely declare that:-

1. the aggregate nominal value of the company's allotted share capital is not less than £50,000
2. the aggregate amount paid up on the allotted share capital of the company at the time of this application is £
3. the [1][estimated] amount of the preliminary expenses of the company is £

[2]

[1] Please delete as appropriate

[2] Please insert the name(s) of person(s) by whom expenses paid or payable

Please give the name, address, telephone number and, if available, a DX number and Exchange of the person Companies House should contact if there is any query.

Tel

DX number DX exchange

Companies House receipt data barcode

When you have completed and signed the form please send it to the Registrar of Companies at:
Companies House, Crown Way, Cardiff, CF4 3UZ DX33050 Carfiff
for companies registered in England and Wales
or
Companies House, 37 Castle Terrace, Edinburgh, EH1 2EB
for companies registered in Scotland **DX235 Edinburgh**

[1] [4a. no amount or benefit has been paid or given or is intended to be paid or given to any of the promoters of the company]
[1] [4b the amount or benefit paid or given or intended to be paid or given to any promoter of the company is:]
[1] Please delete as appropriate

Promoter No 1;
The amount paid or intended to be paid £
Any benefit given or intended to be given
The consideration for such payment or benefit

Promoter No 2;
The amount paid or intended to be paid £
Any benefit given or intended to be given
The consideration for such payment or benefit

Promoter No 3;
The amount paid or intended to be paid £
Any benefit given or intended to be given
The consideration for such payment or benefit

And I make this solemn Declaration conscientiously believing the same to be true and by virtue of the Statutory Declarations Act 1835

Declarant's signature

Declared at

the day of

One thousand nine hundred and ninety

before me[1]

[1] Please print name

Signed **Date**

A Commissioner for Oaths or Notary Public or Justice of the Peace or Solicitor

COMPANIES HOUSE

43(3)

Please complete in typescript, or in bold capitals.

Application by a private company for re-registration as a public company

Company Number

Company Name in full

F043301Q

applies to be re-registered as a public company by the name of: [1]

and for that purposes delivers the following documentation for registration:

1. A declaration on form 43(3)(e) by a director or secretary, according to section 43(3)(e) of the Companies Act 1985
2. A printed copy of the memorandum and articles as altered in pursuance of the special resolution under section 43(1)(a) of the above Act.
3. A copy of the auditors written statement in relation to section 43(3)(b) of the above Act.
4. A copy of the relevant balance sheet with the auditors unqualified report
5. [2] A copy of any valuable report

[1] Please insert full name of company amended to make it appropriate for this company as a public limited company

2 Please delete if section 44 of the Act does not apply

Signed **Date**

+a director/ secretary

+ Please delete as appropriate

Please give the name, address, telephone number and, if available, a DX number and Exchange of the person Companies House should contact if there is any query.

Tel

DX number DX exchange

Companies House receipt date barcode

Form revised March 1995

When you have completed and signed the form please send it to the Registrar of Companies at:
Companies House, Crown Way, Cardiff, CF4 3UZ **DX33050 Cardiff**
for companies registered in England and Wales
or
Companies House, 37 Castle Terrace, Edinburgh, EH12EB
for companies registered in Scotland **DX235 Edinburgh**

COMPANIES HOUSE

43(3)(e)

Declaration on application by a private company for re-registration as a public company

Please complete in typescript, or in bold capitals.

Company Number ____________

Company Name in full ____________

F043E011

I, ____________

of ____________

[1]. [a director][the secretary] of the company do solemnly and sincerely declare that:

1. the company passed a special resolution on [Day Month Year] that the company be re-registered as a public company
2. the conditions of sections 44 and 45 of the Companies Act 1985 (so far as applicable) have been satisfied
3. between the balance sheet date and the application for re-registration, there has been no change in the company's financial position resulting in the amount of its net assets becoming less than the sum of its called-up share capital and undistributable reserves.

And I make this solemn Declaration conscientiously believing the same to be true and by virtue of the Statutory Declarations Act 1835

Declarant's signature ____________

Declared at ____________

the ____________ day of ____________

One thousand nine hundred and ninety ____________

before me[2] ____________

Signed ____________ **Date** ____________

A Commissioner for Oaths or Notary Public or Justice of the Peace or Solicitor

[1] Please delete as appropriate

[2] Please print name

Please give the name, address, telephone number and, if available, a DX number and Exchange of the person Companies House should contact if there is any query.

	Tel
DX number	DX exchange

Companies House receipt date barcode

Form revised March 1995

When you have completed and signed the form please send it to the Registrar of Companies at:

Companies House, Crown Way, Cardiff, CF4 3UZ **DX33050 Cardiff**
for companies registered in England and Wales
or
Companies House, 37 Castle Terrace, Edinburgh, EH1 2EB
for companies registered in Scotland **DX235 Edinburgh**

COMPANIES HOUSE

53

Please complete in typescript, or in bold black capitals

Application by a public company for re-registration as a private company

Company Number

Company Name in full

F0530010

applies to be re-registered as a private company by the name of [1]

1. Please insert name of company amended to make it appropriate for the company as a private limited.

and for that purpose delivers the following documents for registration

2. Please delete if previously presented for registration.

1. [2] [A copy of the Special Resolution that the company be re-registered as a private company]
2. A printed copy of the memorandum and articles as altered by the Special Resolution that the company be re-registered as a private company.

Signed **Date**

† Please delete as appropriate

† a director/secretary

Please give the name, address, telephone number and, if available, a DX number and Exchange of the person Companies House should contact if there is any query.

Tel

DX number DX exchange

Companies House receipt date barcode

Form revised March 1995

When you have completed and signed the form please send it to the Registrar of Companies at:
Companies House, Crown Way, Cardiff, CF4 3UZ **DX33050 Cardiff**
for companies registered in England and Wales
or
Companies House, 37 Castle Terrace, Edinburgh, EH1 2EB
for companies registered in Scotland **DX235 Edinburgh**

Companies House
for the record

287

Please complete in typescript, or in bold black capitals.
CHFP000

Change in situation or address of Registered Office

Company Number

Company Name in full

New situation of registered office

NOTE:

The change in the situation of the registered office does not take effect until the Registrar has registered this notice.

For 14 days beginning with the date that a change of registered office is registered, a person may validly serve any document on the company at its previous registered office.

PO Box numbers only are not acceptable.

Address

Post town

County / Region

Postcode

Signed **Date**

+ Please delete as appropriate

+a director/secretary/administrator/adminstrative receiver / liquidator/ receiver manager/ receiver

Please give the name, address, telephone number and, if available, a DX number and Exchange of the person Companies House should contact if there is any query.

Tel

DX number DX exchange

Companies House receipt date barcode

Form revised March 1995

When you have completed and signed the form please send it to the Registrar of Companies at:
Companies House, Crown Way, Cardiff, CF4 3UZ **DX33050 Cardiff**
for companies registered in England and Wales
or
Companies House, 37 Castle Terrace, Edinburgh, EH1 2EB
for companies registered in Scotland **DX235 Edinburgh**

G

COMPANIES FORM No. 122

Notice of consolidation, division, sub-division, redemption or cancellation of shares, or conversion, re-conversion of stock into shares

122

Please do not write in this margin

Please complete legibly, preferably in black type, or bold block lettering

***insert full name of company**

Pursuant to section 122 of the Companies Act 1985

To the Registrar of Companies
(Address overleaf)

For official use

Company number

Name of company

*

gives notice that:

‡ Insert Director, Secretary, Administrator, Administrative Receiver or Receiver (Scotland) as appropriate

Signed　　Designation‡　　Date

Presentor's name address and reference (if any):

For official Use General Section	Post room

G

COMPANIES FORM No. 123

Notice of increase in nominal capital

123

Please do not write in this margin

Please complete legibly, preferably in black type, or bold block lettering

Pursuant to section 123 of the Companies Act 1985

To the Registrar of Companies
(Address overleaf)

For official use

Company number

Name of company

*insert full name of company

*

gives notice in accordance with section 123 of the above Act that by resolution of the company dated ______________ the nominal capacity of the company has been increased by £______________ beyond the registered capital of £______________

A copy of the resolution authorising the increase is attached.†

†the copy must be printed or in some other form approved by the register

The conditions (eg voting rights, dividend rights, winding-up rights etc.) subject to which the new shares have been or are to be issued are as follows:

Please tick here if continued overleaf ☐

‡ Insert Director, Secretary, Administrator, Administrative Receiver or Receiver (Scotland) as appropriate

Signed　　Designation‡　　Date

Presentor's name address and reference (if any):

For official Use
General Section　　Post room

BPP PUBLISHING

G

COMPANIES FORM No. 169

Return by a company purchasing its own shares

169

Please do not write in this margin

Please complete legibly, preferably in black type, or bold block lettering

Pursuant to section 169 of the Companies Act 1985

Please do not write in the space below For Inland Revenue use only

To the Registrar of Companies
(Address overleaf)

For official use

Company number

Name of company

*insert full name of company

*

Shares were purchased by the company under section 162 of the above Act as follows:

Note
The return must be delivered to the Registrar within a period of 28 days beginning with the first date on which shares to which it relates were delivered to the company.

φ A private company is not required to give this information

Class of shares			
Number of shares purchased			
Nominal value of each share			
Date(s) on which the shares were delivered to the company			
Maximum prices paid for each share φ			
Minimum prices paid for each share φ			

The aggregate amount paid by the company for the shares to which this return relates was:	£
Stamp duty payable pursuant to section 66 of the Finance Act 1986 on the aggregate amount at 50p per £100 or part of £100	£

‡ Insert Director, Secretary, Administrator, Administrative Receiver or Receiver (Scotland) as appropriate

Signed Designation‡ Date

Presentor's name address and reference (if any):

For official Use
General Section | Post room

G

COMPANIES FORM No. 173

Declaration in relation to the redemption or purchase of shares out of capital

173

Please do not write in this margin

Please complete legibly, preferably in black type, or bold block lettering

Pursuant to section 173 of the Companies Act 1985

To the Registrar of Companies
(Address overleaf)

For official use ______ Company number ______

Name of company

*insert full name of company

Note Please read the notes on page 2 before completing the form

ø insert name(s) and address(es) of all the directors

I/Weø ____________________

† delete as appropriate

[the sole director][all the directors]† of the above company do solemnly and sincerely declare that:

δ delete whichever is inappropriate

The business of the company is:

(a) that of a [recognised bank][licensed institution]† within the meaning of the Banking Act 1979δ
(b) that of a person authorised under section 3 or 4 of the Insurance Companies Act 1982 to carry on insurance business in the United Kingdom.δ
(c) that of something other than the above.δ

The company is proposing to make a payment out of capital for the redemption or purchase or its own shares

The amount of the permissible capital payment for shares in questions is £__________ (note 1)

Continued overleaf

Presentor's name address and reference (if any):

For official Use
General Section | Post room

I/We have made full enquiry into the affairs and prospects of the company, and I/we have formed the opinion:

(a) as regards its initial situation immediately following the date on which the payment out of capital is proposed to be made, that there will be no grounds on which the company could then be found unable to pay its debts (note 2), and

(b) as regards its prospects for the year immediately following that date, that, having regard to my/our intentions with respect to the management of the company's business during that year and to the amount and character of the financial resources which will be in my/our view be available during that year, the company will be able to continue to carry on business as a going concern (and will accordingly be able to pay its debts as they fall due) throughout that year. (note 2)

Please do not write in this margin

Please complete legibly, preferably in black type, or bold block lettering

And I/we make this solemn declaration conscientiously believing the same to be true and by virtue of the provisions of the Statutory Declarations Act 1835.

Declared at ____________________ Declarant(s) to sign below

the ________ day of ____________
one thousand nine hundred and ____________

before me ____________________

A Commissioner for Oaths, or Notary Public, or Justice of the Peace, or Solicitor having the power conferred on a Commissioner for Oaths.

Notes

1 'Permissible capital payment' means an amount which, taken together with
(i) any available profits of the company; and
(ii) the proceeds of any fresh issues of shares made for the purposes of the redemption or purchase;
is equal to the price of redemption or purchase.
'Available profits' means the company's profits which are available for distribution (within the meaning of section 172 and 263 of the Companies Act 1985).
The question whether the company has any profits so available and the amount of any such profits is to be determined in accordance with section 172 of the Companies Act 1985.

2 Contingent and prospective liabilities of the company must be taken into account, see sections 173(4) & 517 of the Companies Act 1985.

3 A copy of the declaration together with a copy of the auditors report required by section 173 of the Companies Act 1985, must be delivered to the Registrar of Companies not later than the day on which the company publishes the notice required by section 175(1) of the Companies Act 1985, or first publishes or gives the notice required by section 175(2), whichever is the earlier.

4. The address for companies registered in England and Wales or Wales is:-

The Registrar of Companies
Companies House
Crown Way
Cardiff
CF4 3UZ

or, for companies registered in Scotland:-

The Registrar of Companies
Companies House
100-102 George Street
Edinburgh
EH2 3DJ

M

COMPANIES FORM No. 403a

Declaration of satisfaction in full or in part of mortgage or charge

403a

Please do not write in this margin

Please complete legibly, preferably in black type, or bold block lettering

Pursuant to section 403(1) of the Companies Act 1985

To the Registrar of Companies
(Address overleaf)

For official use

Company number

Name of company

*insert full name of company

*

I, ____________________

of____________________

† delete as appropriate

‡ insert a description of the instrument(s) creating or evidencing the charge, eg 'Morgage' 'Charge' 'Debenture' etc

θ the date of registration may be confirmed from the certificate

φ insert brief details of property

[a director][the secretary][the administrator][the administrative receiver] of the above company, do solemnly and sincerely declare that the debt for which the charge described below was given has been paid or satisfied in **[full][part]** †

Date and Description of charge‡ ____________________

Date of Registrationθ ____________________

Name and address of [chargee][trustee for the debenture holders] ____________________

Short particulars of property chargedφ ____________________

And I make this solemn declaration conscientiously believing the same to be true and by virtue of the provisions of the Statutory Declarations Act 1835.

Declared at ____________________

Declarant to sign below

the ________ day of ________

one thousand nine hundred and ________

before me____________________

A commissioner for Oaths or Notary Public or Justice of the Peace or Solicitor having the powers conferred on a Commissioner for Oaths.

Presentor's name address and reference (if any):

For official Use Mortgage Section	Post room

Companies House
for the record

288a

Please complete in typescript, or in bold black capitals.
CHFP000

APPOINTMENT of director or secretary
(NOT for resignation (use Form 288b) or change of particulars (use Form 288c))

Company Number [ ]

Company Name in full [ ]

Appointment form

Date of appointment — Day | Month | Year

†Date of Birth — Day | Month | Year

Appointment as director [ ] as secretary [ ] *Please mark the appropriate box. If appointment is as a director and secretary mark both boxes.*

NAME *Style / Title [ ] *Honours etc [ ]

Forename(s) [ ]

Surname [ ]

Previous Forename(s) [ ] Previous Surname(s) [ ]

Usual residential address [ ]

Post town [ ] Postcode [ ]

County / Region [ ] Country [ ]

†Nationality [ ] Business occupation [ ]

Other directorships (additional space overleaf) [ ]

I consent to act as ** director / secretary of the above named company

Consent signature [ ] **Date** [ ]

* Voluntary details
† Directors only
** Delete as appropriate

A director, secretary etc must sign the form below.

Signed [ ] **Date** [ ]

(** a director / secretary / administrator /administrative receiver / receiver manager / receiver)

Please give the name, address, telephone number and, if available, a DX number and Exchange of the person Companies House should contact if there is any query.

Tel

DX number DX exchange

Companies House receipt date barcode

Form revised July 1998

When you have completed and signed the form please send it to the Registrar of Companies at:
Companies House, Crown Way, Cardiff, CF4 3UZ **DX33050 Cardiff**
for companies registered in England and Wales
or
Companies House, 37 Castle Terrace, Edinburgh, EH1 2EB
for companies registered in Scotland **DX235 Edinburgh**

BPP PUBLISHING

Company Number

† Directors only † Other directorships

NOTES

Show the full forename, NOT INITIALS. If the director or the secretary is a corporation or Scottish, show the name on surname line and registered or principal office on the usual residential line.

Give previous forenames or surname(s) except:

- for married woman, the name by which she was known before marriage need not be given.
- for names not used since the age of 18 or for at least 20 years

A peer or individual known by a title may state the title instead of or in addition to the forenames and surname and need not give the name by which that person was known before he or she adopted the title or succeeded to it.

Other directorships.

Give the name of every company incorporated in Great Britain of which the person concerned is a director or has been a director at any time in the past five years.

You may exclude a company which either is, or at all times during the past five years when the person concerned was a director, was

- dormant
- a parent company which wholly owned the company making the return, or
- another wholly owned subsidiary of the same parent company.

Companies House
for the record

288b

Please complete in typescript, or in bold black capitals.
CHFP000

Terminating appointment as director or secretary
(NOT for appointment (use Form 288a) or change of particulars(use Form 288c))

Company Number

Company Name in full

	Day	Month	Year
Date of termination of appointment			

as director ☐ as secretary ☐ *Please mark the appropriate box. If terminating appointment as a director and secretary mark both boxes.*

NAME *Style / Title *Honours etc

Please insert details as previously notified to Companies House

Forename(s)

Surname

	Day	Month	Year
†Date of Birth			

* Voluntary details
† Directors only
** Delete as appropriate

A serving director, secretary etc must sign the form below.

Signed **Date**

(** serving director / secretary / administrator /administrative receiver / receiver manager / receiver)

Please give the name, address, telephone number and, if available, a DX number and Exchange of the person Companies House should contact if there is any query.

Tel

DX number DX exchange

Companies House receipt date barcode

Form revised 1999

When you have completed and signed the form please send it to the Registrar of Companies at:
Companies House, Crown Way, Cardiff, CF4 3UZ **DX33050 Cardiff**
for companies registered in England and Wales
or
Companies House, 37 Castle Terrace, Edinburgh, EH1 2EB
for companies registered in Scotland **DX235 Edinburgh**

Companies House
for the record

288c

Please complete in typescript, or in bold black capitals.
CHFP000

CHANGE OF PARTICULARS for director or secretary *(NOT for appointment (use Form 288a) or resignation (use Form 288b))*

Company Number

Company Name in full

Complete in all cases Date of change of particulars — Day Month Year

Changes of particulars form

Name *Style / Title — *Honours etc

Forename(s)

Surname

Date of Birth — Day Month Year

Change of name *(enter new name)* Forename(s)

Surname

Change of usual residential address
(enter new address)

Post town

County / Region — Postcode

County

Other change *(please specify)*

* Voluntary details
† Directors only
** Delete as appropriate

A serving director, secretary etc must sign the form below..

Signed — **Date**

(** director / secretary / administrator /administrative receiver / receiver manager / receiver)

Please give the name, address, telephone number and, if available, a DX number and Exchange of the person Companies House should contact if there is any query.

Tel

DX number — DX exchange

Companies House receipt date barcode

When you have completed and signed the form please send it to the Registrar of Companies at:
Companies House, Crown Way, Cardiff, CF4 3UZ **DX33050 Cardiff**
for companies registered in England and Wales
or
Companies House, 37 Castle Terrace, Edinburgh, EH1 2EB
for companies registered in Scotland **DX235 Edinburgh**

Form revised July 1998

Companies House
for the record

363a

Please complete in typescript, or in bold black capitals.
CHFP000

Annual Return

Company Number ______________________

Company Name in full ______________________

____

____

Date of this return
The information in this return is made up to

Day Month Year
__ __ / __ __ / __ __ __ __

Date of next return
If you wish to make your next return to a date earlier than the anniversary of this return please show the date here. Companies House will then send a form at the appropriate time.

Day Month Year
__ __ / __ __ / __ __ __ __

Registered Office
Show here the address **at the date of this return.**

____

____

*Any change of registered office **must** be notified on form 287.*

Post town ______________________

County / Region ______________________

UK Postcode __ __ __ __ __ __ __

Principal business activities

Show trade classification code number(s) for the principal activity or activities.

______________ ______________

______________ ______________

If the code number cannot be determined, give a brief description of principal activity.

____

____

Companies House receipt date barcode

Form revised September 1999

When you have completed and signed the form please send it to the Registrar of Companies at:
Companies House, Crown Way, Cardiff, CF4 3UZ **DX33050 Cardiff**
for companies registered in England and Wales
or
Companies House, 37 Castle Terrace, Edinburgh, EH1 2EB
for companies registered in Scotland **DX235 Edinburgh**

Register of members

If the register of members is not kept at the registered office, state here where it is kept.

Post town

County / Region | UK Postcode

Register of Debenture holders

If there is a register of debenture holders or a duplicate of any such register or part of it, which is not kept at the registered office, state here where it is kept.

Post town

County / Region | UK Postcode

Company type

Please tick the appropriate box

- Public limited company ☐
- Private company limited by shares ☐
- Private company limited by guarantee without share capital ☐
- Private company limited by shares exempt under section 30 ☐
- Private company limited by guarantee exempt under section 30 ☐
- Private unlimited company with share capital ☐
- Private unlimited company without share capital ☐

Company Secretary

Details of a new company secretary must be notified on form 288a.

(Please photocopy this area to provide details of joint secretaries)
**Voluntary details*

If a partnership give the names and addresses of the partners or the name of the partnership and office address.

Name

*Style/Title

Forename(s)

Surname

Address

Usual residential address must be given. In the case of a corporation or a Scottish firm, give the registered or principal office address.

Post town

County / Region | UK Postcode

Country

Directors

Please list directors in alphabetical order.

Details of new directors must be notified on form 288a

Directors in the case of a director that is a corporation or a Scottish firm, the name is the corporate or firm name.

Name

*Style/Title

Date of birth Day / Month / Year

Forename(s)

Surname

Address

Usual residential address must be given. In the case of a corporation or a Scottish firm, give the registered or principal office address.

Post town

County / Region UK Postcode

Country **Nationality**

Business occupation

* Voluntary details

Directors in the case of a director that is a corporation or a Scottish firm, the name is the corporate or firm name.

Name

*Style/Title

Date of birth Day / Month / Year

Forename(s)

Surname

Address

Usual residential address must be given. In the case of a corporation or a Scottish firm, give the registered or principal office address.

Post town

County / Region UK Postcode

Country **Nationality**

Business occupation

	Class *(e.g. Ordinary / Preference)*	**Number of shares issued**	Aggregate Nominal Value *(i.e. Number of shares issued multiplied by nominal value per share, or total amount of stock)*
Issued share capital Enter details of all shares in issue at the date of this return.			
	Totals		

List of past and present shareholders
(Use attached schedule where appropriate)
A full list is required if one was not included with either of the last two returns.

There were no changes in the period ☐

	on paper	in another format
A list of changes is enclosed	☐	☐
A full list of shareholders is enclosed	☐	☐

Certificate

I certify that the information given in this return is true to the best of my knowledge and belief.

Signed **Signature** ______________ **Date** ______________

†Please delete as appropriate

†a director / secretary

When you have signed the return send it with the fee to the Registrar of Companies. Cheques should be made payable to **Companies House.**

This return includes ______ continuation sheets
(enter number)

Please give the name, address, telephone number, and if available, a DX number and Exchange, for the person Companies House should contact if there is any query.

____

____

______________ Tel ______________

DX number ________ DX exchange ______________

Companies House
for the record

353

Please complete in typescript, or in bold black capitals.
CHFP000

Register of members

Company Number	
Company Name in full	

F353001R

NOTE
The register **MUST** be kept at an address in the country of incorporation.

This notice is not required where the register has, at all times since it came into existence (or in the case of a register in existence on 1 July 1948 at all times since then) been kept at the registered office.

The register of members is kept at:

Address	
Post town	
County / Region	Postcode

Signed **Date**

** Delete as appropriate

(** a director / secretary / administrator /administrative receiver / receiver manager / receiver)

Please give the name, address, telephone number and, if available, a DX number and Exchange of the person Companies House should contact if there is any query.

	Tel
DX number	DX exchange

Companies House receipt date barcode

Form revised 1999

When you have completed and signed the form please send it to the Registrar of Companies at:
Companies House, Crown Way, Cardiff, CF4 3UZ **DX33050 Cardiff**
for companies registered in England and Wales
or
Companies House, 37 Castle Terrace, Edinburgh, EH1 2EB
for companies registered in Scotland **DX235 Edinburgh**

G

COMPANIES FORM No. 353a

Notice of place for inspection of a register of members which is kept in a non-legible form, or of any change in that place

353a

Pursuant to the Companies (Registers and Other Records) Regulations 1985

Note: For use only when the register is kept by computer or in some other non-legible form

Please do not write in this margin

Please complete legibly, preferably in black type, or bold block lettering

*insert full name of company

† delete as appropriate

To the Registrar of Companies
(Address overleaf)

For official use

Company number

Name of company

*

gives notice, in accordance with regulation 3(1) of the Companies (Registers and Other Records) Regulations 1985, that the place for inspection of the register of members of the company which the company keeps in a non-legible form is [now]†

Postcode

Signed [Director][Secretary] † Date

Presentor's name address and reference (if any):

For official Use General Section	Post room

Appendices 21 to 24

THE STATUTORY MODEL ARTICLES OF ASSOCIATION (TABLE A)

A summary of the 1985 Table A

1 The Companies Act 1985 contained a new model Articles of Association (Table A). This is summarised below, but note that many companies incorporated before 1st July 1985 may not have adopted this yet. At any rate, most companies have their own individual Articles, or tailor Table A to suit their needs. Every company is required to have articles. It may either adopt special articles in substitution for Table A or it may adopt Table A in its entirety or with modifications. Most public and some private companies adopt full length special articles. The majority of private companies are subject to Table A with a few modifications expressed in short articles which begin:

'The articles of association of the company are Table A of the Companies Act (date) except as expressly provided by these articles'.

Then follow a few clauses which modify the Table A wording or exclude a complete passage.

2 Unlike the previous versions the 1985 Table A is not printed as part of a schedule of the Act. It is promulgated by statutory regulations (The Companies (Alteration of Table A etc) Regulation 1984 - S1 1984/1717) and it came into effect on 1 July 1985.

3 Although the 1985 version of Table A was made by statutory powers given to the Secretary of State for Trade and Industry its content is in most respects in accordance with the advice of the Law Society, which undertook a comprehensive review of the earlier (1948) Table A and put forward a draft for consideration by the DTI. Apart from updating Table A the aim was to make it no longer duplicate some (but not all) provisions of the Companies Act. Where the Act gives a power which the company may exercise without any corresponding provision in its own articles, Table A omits all reference to it.

4 One such case is the procedure for variation of rights attached to a class of shares. Section 125(2) confers a general power to vary class rights, *unless* the articles vary or exclude it. The 1985 Table A, unlike the previous versions, is therefore silent on this subject. Where the articles are in Table A form the company simply resorts to the unfettered power of variations given by the Act.

5 The remaining paragraphs of this note are a summary of the provisions of the current (1985) Table A. In answering examination questions it should be assumed, unless the question itself gives information to the contrary, that the company's articles are in this form. It is not necessary - or possible - to memorise *all* the provisions of Table A but a general knowledge of the more important articles of Table A is certainly required. Table A itself is sometimes referred to as 'regulations' but in this note (and elsewhere in the text) we refer to 'articles' of Table A since that is essentially what they are.

Share capital and shares (Articles 2 - 35)

6 The company may issue shares with whatever rights or restrictions as the company by ordinary resolution may determine. This includes the issue of redeemable shares of any type (Art 2 and 3). The company may pay commission as authorised by the Companies Act. This may be made partly or wholly by shares (Art 4).

7 The company is prohibited from recognising the interest of a third party in shares registered in the name of a member; the company deals only with members in connection with rights to shares (Art 5). The register of members will not, therefore, make note of the fact that shares are held on trust.

8 A member is entitled to one or more share certificates for his shares and may obtain replacement for a lost certificate (Art 6 and 7).

9 The company has a lien on partly paid shares for sums still outstanding on those shares (Art 8). There is power to sell shares if the holder defaults in payment of calls (Arts 9 - 11). There is a procedure for making calls and forfeiture in case of non payment (Arts 12 - 22).

10 The procedure for transfer and transmission of shares (Arts 23 - 31) is described later, in the chapter on shares. There is no discretionary power to refuse to register a transfer for a fully paid share. If the company needs such a power it must adopt a special article to that effect.

11 The power to alter share capital follows ss 121 (alteration) and 135 (reduction) of the Act since those powers are only available if the articles authorise them (Arts 32 - 34). There is no longer a power to convert shares into stock but a company may adopt a special article covering it (s 121(2)(c) permits it).

12 The company may purchase its own shares in accordance with the statutory provisions (Art 35 and ss 159 - 181).

Meetings (Articles 36 - 63)

13 The procedure for convening and conducting general meetings is set out in detail later in this text.

14 Article 37 requires that, when members requisition an Extraordinary General Meeting, the directors shall set a date for it within 8 weeks. S 368(8) now overrides this article and provides that a requisitioned EGM must be held within 28 days of issuing the notice of the meeting.

15 The notice convening a meeting no longer distinguishes between ordinary and special business. In all cases the requirement is that the notice shall specify 'the general nature of the business to be transacted'. Here the overriding requirement of the Act (s 378) is, as before, that the full text must be given of any special or extraordinary resolution (this is not mentioned in Table A). If a meeting is an annual general meeting the notice must state it to be such.

16 A meeting may only transact business if 'a quorum is present' (Article 40). The quorum requirement is no longer limited to the number present at the outset; under Article 41 if a quorum ceases to be present the meeting is adjourned.

17 If a meeting is adjourned for 14 days or more, seven clear days notice of the adjourned meeting must be given (Article 45).

18 In arranging a poll the chairman has power to appoint scrutineers, who need not be members (in practice it is usual to appoint the auditors) (Article 49).

Directors (Articles 64 - 98)

19 The minimum number of directors is two. There is no maximum (Article 64). Many companies find it convenient to fix a maximum by a special article to that effect.

20 A director may appoint as his alternate (to vote for him in his absence) another director or any other person of his choice whom the other directors may approve. An alternate director is declared to be a 'director' for all purposes including the many provisions of the Act (Articles 65 - 69).

21 The directors have delegated authority to exercise all the powers of the company except where restricted by (a) the Act (b) the memorandum or articles or (c) a special resolution. These restrictive provisions cannot be exercised retrospectively to invalidate what the directors have already done under their existing powers (Article 70). A meeting of directors at which a quorum is present may exercise all the powers exercisable by directors.

22 The above general power of management includes (though it is not expressly stated) the company's power to borrow money. If, as will often be the case, the company decides to impose a limit on the amount which the directors may borrow without obtaining sanction in general meeting the company must adopt a special article to that effect.

23 Article 71 specifically allows directors to appoint agents, who may, if authorised, delegate.

24 There are articles on appointment and retirement of directors, disqualification, interest in transactions of the company, and board meetings. The substance of these provisions is described in the sequence of chapters on directors in the main text. There are some differences of detail as compared with the 1948 Table A articles.

Dividends, accounts, bonus issues (Articles 102-110)

25 These are straightforward provisions, mainly on procedure, which are somewhat simpler than in the previous Table A because the Table A articles no longer reproduce the requirements of the Act, for instance on maintaining accounting records (Article 109, which is now concerned with the right of members to inspect records). The company must of course comply with the Act: since the Act is very detailed in its requirements on accounting records it is unnecessary to reproduce it all in the articles.

26 Article 110, on capitalisation of profits, allows directors:

(a) To capitalise undistributed profits, share premium account or capital redemption reserve

(b) To apply profits to paying up amounts unpaid on shares, or to paying up and allotting shares as fully paid

(c) To authorise any person to enter the company into an agreement that shares or debentures should be treated as fully paid. Such agreement would be binding on all members

Notices (Articles 111-116)

27 These articles set out how the company may validly deliver notices to its members, for example to convene general meetings.

Winding-up and indemnity (Articles 117-118)

28 The liquidator is authorised, with the sanction of an extraordinary resolution passed in general meeting, to distribute assets in specie to members - he need not sell them in order to distribute their value in cash (Article 117). Officers are indemnified by the company against the expenses of a successful defence against legal proceedings in which negligence is alleged against them (Article 118).

The Combined Code principles of good governance and code of best practice is discussed in Chapter 3, Section 1.

Directors

The board

All listed companies should be led by an effective board. The board should meet regularly and have certain matters reserved for its decision. Directors should be able to obtain independent professional advice and have access to the services of the company secretary. The company secretary is responsible for ensuring that board procedures and relevant regulations are followed. The whole board should be responsible for removing the company secretary. Every director should use independent judgement when making decisions. Every director should receive appropriate training.

Chairman and Chief Executive

There are two leading management roles; running the board and running the company. A clear division of responsibilities should exist so that there is a balance of power, and no-one person has unfettered powers of decision. Combination of the roles of chairman and chief executive should be justified publicly. There should also be a strong and independent body of non-executive directors with a recognised senior member other than the chairman.

Board balance

The board should have a balance of executive and non-executive directors so that no individual or small group is dominant. The non-executive directors should be of sufficient calibre and number to have a significant influence and should comprise at least one third of the board. The majority of non-executive directors should be independent.

Supply of information

The board should be promptly supplied with enough information to enable it to carry out its duties. Information volunteered by management will sometimes need to be supplemented by information from other sources. All directors should be properly briefed.

Appointment of directors

There should be a clear, formal procedure for appointing new directors. A nomination committee should make recommendations about all new board appointments.

Re-election

All directors should submit themselves for re-election regularly, and at least once every three years.

Directors' remuneration

Remuneration policy

Remuneration levels should be sufficient to attract directors of sufficient calibre to run the company effectively, but companies should not pay more than is necessary. A proportion of remuneration should be based on corporate and individual performance. Comparisons with other companies should be used with caution. When designing performance-related elements of remuneration, the remuneration committee should consider annual bonuses and different kinds of long-term incentive schemes.

Service contracts and compensation

Boards' ultimate objectives should be to set notice periods at one year or less. Directors should consider whether to include compensation commitments in the contracts of service.

Procedure

Companies should establish a formal and clear procedure for developing policy on executive remuneration and for fixing the remuneration package of individual directors. Directors should not be involved in setting their own remuneration. A remuneration committee, staffed by independent non-executive directors, should make recommendations about the framework of executive remuneration, and should determine specific remuneration packages. The board should determine the remuneration of non-executive directors

Disclosure

The annual report should contain a statement about remuneration policy and details of the remuneration of each director. The report should give details about all elements of the remuneration package, share options, pension entitlements and service contracts or compensation in excess of one year. Shareholders should approve all new long-term remuneration schemes. The remuneration report need not be a standard AGM item, but the board should consider whether the report needs to be approved.

Relations with shareholders

Institutional shareholders

Companies should be prepared to communicate with institutional shareholders.

Use of the AGM

The AGM should be a means of communication with private investors. Companies should count all proxies and announce proxy votes for and against on all votes on a show of hands. Companies should propose a separate resolution on each substantially separate issue, and there should be a resolution covering the board and accounts. The chairmen of the audit, nomination and remuneration committees should be available to answer questions at the AGM. Papers should be sent to members at least 20 working days before the AGM.

Accountability and audit

Financial Reporting

The board should present a balanced and understandable assessment of the company's position and prospects in the annual accounts and other reports such as interim reports and reports to regulators. The directors should explain their responsibility for the accounts, and the auditors should state their reporting responsibilities. The directors should also report on the going concern status of the business.

Internal Control

A good system of control should be maintained. The directors should review effectiveness annually and report to shareholders that they have done so. The review should cover all controls including financial, operational and compliance controls and risk management. Companies who lack an internal audit function should regularly consider whether they need one.

Audit committees and auditors

There should be formal and clear arrangements with the company's auditors, and for applying the financial reporting and internal control principles. Companies should have an audit committee consisting of non-executive directors, the majority of whom should be independent. The audit committee should review the audit, and the independence and objectivity of the auditors. In particular the committee should keep matters under review if the auditors supply significant non-audit services.

Shareholder voting

Institutional shareholders should use their votes carefully and disclose how they have voted to their clients. They should also enter into a dialogue with companies, and should give appropriate weight to all relevant criteria when considering corporate governance arrangements.

The Continuing Obligations of listed companies are set out below as a checklist for revision. Not all of the obligations are shown here, and some are described in a slightly simplified form. Nevertheless, they should give you a good idea of what obligations a listed company has, and of which the company secretary should be aware.

General

1 As a general rule, a listed company must continue to provide any information which is necessary to keep shareholders and the public aware of the company's position, and to prevent the creation of a false market in the company's shares. This information includes its financial condition, in the performance of its business or the company's expectation of its performance.

(a) 'Insider information' which can give some people or groups of people a 'privileged trading position' must not be divulged outside the company and its advisers. It is particularly important that price-sensitive information - ie. information which, if disclosed, might affect the share price - must not be given in advance to people outside the company or its advisers.

(b) If some price-sensitive information has to be given to a third party, it must be released simultaneously to the Stock Exchange, through the Stock Exchange's Company Announcements Office (CAO) and its Regulatory News Service (RNS).

2 A listed company must ensure equality of treatment for all shareholders who are 'in the same position'.

A listed company must also ensure equality of treatment for all holders of its listed debt securities, for securities of the same class, in respect of all rights attached to the securities (eg redemption rights, conversion rights etc).

Public announcements

3 There are several rules which require a listed company to notify the Stock Exchange of events that will happen or have happened so that the Stock Exchange can make a public announcement through its Regulatory News Service.

4 A listed company must inform the Stock Exchange of any major new developments which are not public knowledge, but which may affect the share price or the company's ability to meet its debt commitments. The Stock Exchange will then decide whether to make the information public.

5 When the board:

(a) Decides to pay or make any dividend

(b) Approves a preliminary announcement of profits or loss for the half year or year

(c) Approves a change in capital structure, such as a new issue of listed debt securities or a change of rights

(d) Decides to redeem some debt capital

(e) Decides to submit a proposal to shareholders that the company should be authorised to purchase its own shares

(f) Decides to change the general character or nature of the company's business

The Stock Exchange must be notified after the board meeting when the decision or approval takes place

6 The company must also notify The Stock Exchange about various other matters, such as:

(a) When the company allots shares for cash, other than by a placing ('selective marketing') it must provide details of the basis on which the allotment has been made

(b) All information which must be disclosed under the rules of the City Code on Takeovers and Mergers

(c) Details of shareholders whose shareholding reaches 3% of all the voting shares, and details of any shareholders whose holding reaches 4%, 5%, 6% etc.

(d) Details of any purchases by the company of its own shares

(e) Results of new issues other than specialist securities or a public offer of existing securities

Annual accounts

7 A listed company must issue an annual report and accounts within six months of the end of the financial period to which they relate.

Certain information must be included in the accounts. A full list of items which must be included is not given here, because it would be unnecessary detail: as examples, however, the items include:

(a) An explanation of why trading results have differed materially from any forecast made (and publicised) previously by the company, in the event that this situation arises

(b) Changes in interests of directors in share capital and other securities of the company, including share options

(c) Details of shareholders who hold 3% or more of any class of voting shares in the company

(d) Details of any contract of significance between the company or its subsidiaries, and any of its directors or controlling shareholders

(e) Details of the company's policy on, and details of directors' remuneration

(f) Details of compliance with the combined corporate governance code

Foreign companies

8 There are certain additional requirements, mainly relating to the annual accounts, which apply to foreign companies whose share are listed on the Stock Exchange.

Half yearly reports and preliminary profits statements for the full year

9 A listed company must prepare a half-yearly report on its activities and profit or loss for the first six months of the financial year.

The report must appear no later than 90 days after the end of the period to which it relates and must either be (a) sent to security holders or (b) inserted as a paid advertisement in at least one national daily newspaper. A copy must also be sent to the Company Announcements Office of the Stock Exchange.

Note: the Accounting Standards Board has also published guidance on interim reports, which listed companies are strongly recommended to follow. The guidance recommends the interim report should treat the interim period as a distinct accounting period. The interim reports should contain the following details:

(a) Management commentary
(b) A profit and loss account
(c) A statement of total recognised gains and losses
(d) A balance sheet
(e) A cash flow statement

10 The half yearly report must consist of:

(a) Certain accounts items, such as net turnover, profit or loss before tax, tax on profits, interim dividend, earnings per share, comparative figures for the corresponding previous period etc. These figures need not be audited, but there must be a statement that they are unaudited, if this is the case; if they have been audited or reviewed the report must be included.

(b) An explanatory statement about the group's activities and profit or loss for the six month period.

11 When a listed company makes a *preliminary* profit statement for the full year - before its accounts are finally published - the statement must include the same accounting information as in a half yearly report.

12 A company must ensure that it has appropriate settlement arrangements for its listed securities.

Communications with holders of listed securities

13 The Listing Rules emphasise that companies must ensure that the necessary information and facilities are available to enable holders of securities to exercise their rights. Companies must:

(a) Send to shareholders details of holding of meetings which they are entitled to attend

(b) Enable shareholders to exercise their voting rights

(c) Publish or distribute information on the allocation and payment of dividends and interest, the issue of new securities, and redemption or payment for securities

14 A company must send to the UK Listing Authority:

(a) *Six* copies of all circulars, notices, announcements etc. as soon as they are issued

(b) *Six* copies of all resolutions passed by the company at a general meeting (excluding resolutions on routine business at an AGM)

15 When a company sends out a notice of meeting, it must also send out proxy forms, which include provision for shareholders to vote either for or against each resolution to be proposed at the meeting.

16 One of the Continuing Obligations is for the company to respect the pre-emptive rights of its shareholders. 'Unless shareholders otherwise permit, a company proposing to issue equity securities for cash must offer those to existing equity shareholders ... in proportion to their existing holdings; only to the extent that the securities to be issued are not taken up by such persons may they then be issued to others or otherwise than in proportion as mentioned above.'

17 Similarly, unless shareholders permit otherwise, a listed company must obtain the prior consent of its shareholders before any of its major subsidiaries issues equity shares for cash so as to 'materially' dilute the percentage equity interest in the subsidiary of the company and its shareholders.

Directors

18 Any change in the directors of a listed company must be notified immediately to the Stock Exchange.

19 Copies of directors' service contracts (for contracts of over 12 months' duration) must be made available for inspection by *any* person:

(a) At the registered office of the company, or in the case of an overseas company, at the offices of any paying agent in the United Kingdom during normal business hours on each business day

(b) For at least 15 minutes before the AGM and during the AGM, at the place of the meeting

20 The company's rules governing dealings by directors in securities of the company must be at least as stringent as the rules of the Stock Exchange's model code for securities transactions by directors of listed companies.

The list of publications below can be obtained from ICSA.

Corporate Sector

The Company Secretary (The Company Secretaries Group's monthly magazine)

A Guide to Best Practice for Annual General Meetings

Duties of a Company Secretary

Duties of a Company Secretary in Ireland

The Appointment and Induction of Directors

Reporting Lines for the Company Secretary

Implementing Cadbury Matters Reserved for the Board

Implementing Cadbury Terms of Reference of a Nomination Committee

Good Boardroom Practice – A Code for Directors and Company Secretaries

Role of the Secretary to the Trustees of a Retirement Benefits Scheme

The ICSA Compendium of EU Corporate Bodies

Retention of Documents

Model Board Resolution on Independent Professional Advice

A Guide to the Statement of Compliance

Terms of Reference – Nomination Committee

Terms of Reference – Audit Committee

Terms of Reference – Remuneration Committee

Not-for-profit sector

An Introduction to Practical PR – a guide for the voluntary sector

The Appointment and Induction of Charity Trustees

Guide to Guarantee Companies

Charities and Meetings (Joint ICSA / Charity Commission Publication)

Public sector

Business Planning – a practitioners guide

Marketing for the Public Services – a practical guide

The Public Service Ethos in Local Government

The Local Authority Secretary

Local Authority Propriety – Members' Interests

Powers of Persuasion (Local Government)

Good Councillor Guide (Local Government)

Matters Reserved for the Board (NHS)

Good Boardroom Practice (NHS)

The role of the Secretary to the Board of a NHS Trust

Cross sector

Establishing a Whistleblowing Procedure

Illustrative questions and suggested answers

1 DUTIES OF SECRETARY

Explain in detail the duties of the secretary of a company at a meeting of the board of directors.

2 VACANCY IN OFFICE OF DIRECTOR

What would be the procedure for declaring a vacancy in the office of director in each of the following circumstances and when would each vacancy be deemed to occur?

(a) Mr George Watson dies.

(b) Mr Harry Webb has been absent from board meetings without permission beyond the period stipulated in the articles as grounds for disqualification.

(c) Mr Nigel Smythe-Watson has written to the Chairman expressly resigning from office.

(d) Sir James Kimberley, as a director of a public limited company, has reached the age of 70.

3 SHAREHOLDER CONTROL

Explain the powers of the general meeting in relation to the management of the affairs of a company, and describe the procedures which must be followed for the exercise of these powers.

4 ADVICE ON MEETINGS

You have been appointed as company secretary to a public company which has a new and relatively inexperienced board of directors. The directors require your advice on several matters relating to company meetings.

You are required to advise the board on the following issues.

(a) Can a company director be removed from office at a general meeting by a resolution put by members at that meeting without prior notice?

(b) When is a company compelled to call an extraordinary general meeting?

5 NOTICE OF MEETING

B, C and D are the directors of Alpha Ltd. B holds 200 shares, C holds 300 shares and D holds 250 shares. The shareholdings of the other members of the company are: X 100 shares, Y 100 shares and Z 50 shares.

Notice of the company's Annual General Meeting is posted on 2 June calling the meeting for 12 noon on 22 June. The notice simply states the meeting is to be held at the time and place specified and that a resolution is to be proposed in favour of Alpha Ltd giving Gamma Ltd financial assistance for the purchase of shares in Alpha Ltd. By mistake, notice is not sent to X but to S, the previous holder of his shares. Z returns a proxy form appointing Y as his proxy and directs her to cast his votes against the resolution.

At the meeting, B is appointed Chairman. Y requests an inspection of the directors' declaration and auditor's report but is refused by B on the basis that they are not available. Y and D then demand a poll on the special resolution. The votes are as follows:

Y used both her own shares and Z's proxy to vote in favour of the resolution; C abstains; B and D vote in favour of the resolution, and B declares the resolution carried by the required majority.

Advise the shareholders on the validity of the above proceedings. (Alpha Ltd's Articles of Association are in the form of Table A).

6 CONDUCTING A POLL

The annual general meeting of Oldman Industries plc is likely to be highly contentious and a poll may be demanded.

Advise on an adequate procedure for conducting the poll both before and during the meeting.

7 PROXIES AND RIGHTS TO VOTE

(a) What are the statutory requirements in regard to the appointment of proxies?

(b) When has a proxy the right to speak at a meeting?

(c) Under what circumstances may a chairman refuse to count a member's votes at a company meeting?

8 POLL AND PROXIES

Leonidas is the managing director of a large and prosperous family company, Classics Ltd. He also owns 30% of the ordinary voting shares. He wishes to sell his shares to the company and retire. At a meeting of the board attended by Leonidas and one other director, the meeting discusses a proposal that Classics Ltd purchases the shares of Leonidas. The meeting resolves that this proposal be recommended to the company in general meeting.

At the general meeting called for this purpose Aunts Agatha and Roxana, who between them hold 20% of the company's voting shares, wish to challenge the proposal fearing that it will affect their dividends. They demand a poll but Leonidas who is acting as chairman refuses on the basis that he holds proxies from his family (who are members of the company) in favour of the proposal and that this would render a poll pointless. These proxies had simply been taken to the meeting by Leonidas without first being deposited with the company. The minutes of the meeting declare the resolution in favour of the purchase of Leonidas's shares carried. The Articles of Classics Ltd are in Table A form.

Discuss the correctness of these events from a legal and procedural point of view.

9 EXTRAORDINARY GENERAL MEETING

Draft the notice, agenda and minutes of an extraordinary general meeting of a company at which the directors intend to propose an increase in the company's share capital.

10 ENGINEERS LTD

Engineers Ltd is a successful engineering company. Its Articles are in Table A form. Fixit Ltd is not currently a wholly owned subsidiary. Fixit Ltd is proposing to give financial assistance to Engineers Ltd for the purchase of Fixit's shares.

You are asked:

(a) To draft the necessary resolution

(b) To advise on any difficulties arising, if any, should an amendment to the resolution become necessary

11 BOARD MEETINGS

(a) Write a full account of the business conducted at the first meeting of the board of directors and at subsequent meetings of the board.

(b) What constitutes good conduct of board meetings?

12 INCORPORATION

As a chartered secretary in public practice, you are approached by your clients Messrs Smith and Wilson, grocers, intimating that they are considering converting their firm into a private company. Report to them outlining the principal advantages and disadvantages of such a conversion.

13 MEMORANDUM

As a chartered secretary in public practice you are instructed by a client to draft the memorandum of association of a prospective private company. What information would you require to know before you can proceed?

14 VARIATION OF CLASS RIGHTS

Where would you expect to find the rights attaching to different classes of your company's shares, and how may these be varied?

15 ISSUE OF PREFERENCE SHARES OR DEBENTURES

Write a memorandum to your directors advising on the relative merits of raising fresh capital by an issue of preference shares or debentures.

16 DEBENTURE TRUST DEED

Your directors have decided to finance a programme of expansion by the issue of debenture stock. What matters would you expect to find covered by the trust deed?

17 STATUTORY BOOKS

State what are the statutory books and briefly summarise their contents.

18 REGISTER OF MEMBERS

Explain the function of the register of members, give the information which must be entered therein and state the methods of becoming a member of the company.

19 LISTING

You are the secretary of a public limited company which has recently been granted a listing. Set out in a memorandum to your board of directors the procedure required by the Listing Rules after a listing has become effective.

20 CONTINUING OBLIGATIONS

As secretary of a listed company, prepare a memorandum listing the continuing obligations imposed upon the company by the Listing Rules that relate to public announcements, share certificates and general meetings.

21 RIGHTS ISSUE

You are the secretary of a public company. The board is considering raising further capital by means of a rights issue. In the form of a memorandum to your board, set out in paragraphs the various stages that are required to effect such an issue. (You may assume the issue is not taking place through CREST.)

22 SHARE CERTIFICATES

As the secretary of a listed company you receive a letter from a shareholder informing you that his share certificate for 1,000 ordinary shares and his dividend warrant for £100 have been lost. He requests that duplicates be issued to him. Explain in detail the procedure to be followed and draft a reply to the shareholder.

23 SHORT NOTES

Write short notes on the following:

(a) The CREST system
(b) The Alternative Investment Market
(c) Non-market transfers

24 STOP NOTICE

As the company secretary you receive an official stop notice restraining the transfer of a specified shareholding.

Explain in detail the procedure you would adopt.

25 REGISTRATION OF TRANSFER

How would you deal with a transfer lodged for registration purporting to be signed by:

(a) The attorney of a shareholder
(b) The executor of a deceased shareholder?

26 DEATH OF A SHAREHOLDER

Mr A Jones and Mr B Brown have a joint holding of 500 ordinary shares in the public limited company of which you are the secretary. You receive a letter from Mrs Brown informing you that Mr Jones died on 31 March 20X1 and that her husband, Mr Brown, died on 25 May 20X1. She states that her husband appointed her as the sole executrix by will and that as she will not be engaging a solicitor to deal with the shareholding, she would be grateful if you would advise her how to proceed.

(a) Draft a letter of reply to Mrs Brown.
(b) Outline the share registration procedure when the required documents have been received.

27 UNCLAIMED DIVIDENDS

Explain in detail the procedure the company secretary should adopt for dealing with unclaimed dividends.

28 SAVINGS RELATED SHARE OPTION SCHEME

You are the secretary of a company which has recently introduced a savings related share option scheme. Set out in a memorandum to your finance director the information that it will be necessary to give in the option certificate.

29 COMPULSORY SHARE PURCHASE

What are the rules governing compulsory purchase of the shares of a minority?

1 DUTIES OF SECRETARY

> **Tutorial note**. Much of the work of a company secretary arising from meetings of the board is done before and after the meetings - but those subjects are outside the scope of the question.

Unless it is the company's practice (now generally obsolete) to maintain a directors' attendance book, which each director signs at the start of the meeting, the secretary notes who is present (and, if it arises, who arrives or leaves during the meeting, and from which parts of the agenda he is absent). This material should be incorporated in the minutes.

The secretary should ensure that there is a quorum before the meeting proceeds to business, and that the quorum is maintained. Apart from directors being absent for part of the meeting, the effective quorum may be reduced if the business includes items on which directors may not be counted as part of the quorum (Table A Article 95). If the secretary notes any difficulty of this kind, he should bring it to the notice of the chairman. It is not for the *secretary* to rule that the meeting is, or has become, inquorate.

The main duty of the secretary is to take notes of the proceedings of the meeting. In addition to matters which will be recorded formally in the minutes, he may have need to note some point on which he is required to take action (or request a colleague to do so) after the meeting. If, as is usual, the chairman has been supplied with a full agenda, with a blank right-hand sheet for notes of decisions, the secretary should ask to have it for reference at the end of the meeting. It is a useful check on his own notes, which he should keep in any event. Unless the secretary is also a director, he should not speak at the meeting, unless invited to do so. It is however usual for the secretary to sit alongside the chairman, to whom he may speak quietly or pass a note, if he (the secretary) wishes to draw the chairman's attention to some point of procedure, such as a requirement of the articles relevant to the board's discussions.

If members of the company management are called to be in attendance for some particular item of business, (for instance the chief accountant, while the board is discussing papers which he has prepared), the secretary should warn him to be ready when required, and go out to call him in to the meeting at the appropriate moment.

Finally, at the end of the meeting the secretary should gather up any papers which have been left on the table; this is particularly important if such papers are confidential. The secretary himself often brings a pile of working files to the meeting, for reference as required. All this material should be removed and returned to its proper place (or destroyed, as the case may be).

2 VACANCY IN OFFICE OF DIRECTOR

> **Tutorial note**. Examiner's comments have emphasised the importance of knowing the Table A provisions relating to this area.

(a) The board should, at its next meeting, formally note with regret the death of Mr Watson. The vacancy occurs at the date of his death.

(b) Much depends on the exact wording of the articles. It has been held that the words 'absents himself' limits disqualification (on the ground of absence) to voluntary absence, and not to cases such as absence through illness. It has also been held that this expression causes the prescribed period to run from the first board meeting which the director fails to attend, and not from the last meeting which he did attend.

The 1985 Table A, Article 81 provides for disqualification if the directors 'shall have been absent' without leave for more than the permitted period. It is thought that these words would cover involuntary absence, and would also cause the period of reckoning of absence to run from the date of the last meeting which the director has attended. Moreover, the Table A formula does not make the disqualification automatic, but merely provides that after such a period of absence the other directors 'may resolve that his office be vacated'. Under this formula, the directors should pass a resolution; the absent director vacates his office from the date of the resolution.

(c) The effect of a letter of resignation is immediate. It takes effect as soon as the letter reaches the company. It is not necessary to *accept* the resignation (unless the articles provide that it shall not be effective until accepted). At the next board meeting, the board should note the resignation with effect from the date when the letter reached the chairman, unless the letter itself was expressed to make the resignation effective from the next board meeting.

(d) It is possible that the articles of the company expressly exclude retirement of directors on attaining the age of 70: Companies Act 1985 s 293(7). However, it is assumed that in the present case there is no such exclusion.

S 293 provides that the director shall vacate office at the conclusion of the annual general meeting next following his 70th birthday. It is, however, possible for the director to offer himself for re-election, provided that special notice is given of intention to propose a resolution for that purpose. The special notice, and the notice issued to convene the meeting, should in this case disclose his age.

3 SHAREHOLDER CONTROL

Tutorial note. There are two separate but related questions here - how the company in general meeting may arrive at valid and binding decisions on matters within the competence of a general meeting, and how far, if at all, a general meeting can intervene in matters within the delegated powers of management given to the directors. A methodical and thorough approach to answering the question is required, dealing with key points and not getting bogged down in details.

Decisions in general meeting

Under the rule in *Foss v Harbottle 1843* a decision of the company in general meeting taken by the appropriate majority is a valid decision of the company binding on the company and all its members, insofar as the matter is within the competence of a general meeting to decide it.

However a majority decision in general meeting is only valid if it is intra vires the company and lawful, and if the meeting is properly convened and conducted. Moreover a majority decision is not valid if it amounts to a fraud on the company: *Cook v Deeks 1916*.

The first requirement of a meeting is that it shall be properly convened. The power to call meetings is generally exercised by the directors, under powers given by the articles. In special circumstances however it may be convened by members, by the court or by the DTI.

To convene the meeting notice of 21 or 14 days is required according to the nature of the meeting and of the business. There is a procedure by which all or a large majority of members may waive these periods of notice.

The notice issued to members must give adequate information of the business to be conducted; in particular, the text of any special or extraordinary resolution must be set out in full: s 378. For the removal of a director and the removal of an auditor or the appointment of a new auditor special notice to the company is also required. If the formal notice convening the meeting does not adequately disclose the nature of the business, additional information must be supplied, usually in an accompanying circular: *Kaye v Croydon Tramways Co 1898*.

At the meeting a quorum must be present and any resolution, if it is to be valid, must be passed by the required majority. For a special or extraordinary resolution a three quarters majority of votes cast is required: s 378.

Powers of a general meeting in relation to the directors

There is complete flexibility as to the extent of the powers of management delegated by the articles to the directors.

The articles usually follow Table A Art 70 in delegating to the directors all the powers of the company, except such as are reserved to the company in general meeting by the Companies Act or by the articles. The articles also reserve to the general meeting power to give instructions to the directors, but not with retrospective effect, by passing a special resolution.

The general meeting cannot therefore normally override a decision of the directors, taken in the proper exercise of their delegated powers: *John Shaw & Sons (Salford) Ltd v Shaw 1935* (where an instruction to the directors to discontinue a legal action which they had commenced on behalf of the company was held to be invalid).

There are however certain exceptions to this general principle. If there are no directors (*Alexander Ward & Co Ltd v Samyang Navigation Ltd 1975*) or if deadlock among the directors prevents them from exercising their powers (*Barron v Potter 1914*) a general meeting may exercise their powers.

If the directors propose to exercise their powers, usually to allot shares, for an irregular purpose, they require the approval of a general meeting for so doing: *Bamford v Bamford 1970*.

In recent years a number of matters have by statute been reserved to the company in general meeting, though it falls to the directors as managers of the company's business, to execute these decisions. These matters include authorisation of the issue of shares (s 80), purchase by the company of its own shares (s 162), approval of transactions in which the directors are interested, such as long-term service agreements (s 319) and substantial transactions of sale or purchase of assets (s 320).

The underlying power of the company in general meeting to control the directors lies in its statutory power to remove directors from office (s 303) and its reserve power (Table A Art 70) to pass special resolutions binding on the directors in respect of a future transaction.

4 ADVICE ON MEETINGS

(a) There is a procedure under ss 303-304 Companies Act 1985 by which a company may by ordinary resolution remove any director from office.

However, this procedure requires that special notice shall be given to the company at least 28 days before the meeting of the intention to propose such a resolution. Moreover, the directors are not required to include the resolution in the notice of the meeting (and it cannot then be put to the vote) unless the person who intends to propose it has (with any support from other members) a sufficient shareholding as required by s 376: *Pedley v Inland Waterways Association Ltd 1977*.

If a company receives special notice it must forthwith send a copy to the director concerned who has the right to have written representations of reasonable length circulated to members and to speak before the resolution is put to the vote at the meeting.

The above analysis applies if the company's articles are silent on the power of members to remove directors at a general meeting (as Table A is), or if the articles follow s 303. However s 303(5) states that the section does not derogate from any further power to remove a director. Thus a company's articles can disapply the provision that special notice is required; this will mean that a director can be removed not only by resolution at a general meeting, but also by unanimous agreement of members, or, if a private company, by written resolution. However the articles cannot impose conditions stricter than those set out in s 303, since s 303(1) states that a director can always be removed by ordinary resolution notwithstanding any provisions to the contrary in the articles or any agreement with the director.

(b) Members of a company who hold not less than one tenth of the company's paid up share capital carrying voting rights, may requisition the holding of a extraordinary general meeting. As this is a public company it must have a share capital and the alternative qualification does not arise. The directors are then required within 21 days of the deposit of the requisition to issue a notice convening the meeting to transact the business specified in the requisition, for a date not more than 28 days hence: s 368.

An auditor who resigns giving reasons for his resignation may requisition an extraordinary general meeting so that he may explain to members the circumstances of his resignation: s 392A.

If the net assets of a public company are reduced to less than half in value of its called-up share capital, it is the duty of the directors to convene (within 28 days of becoming aware of this situation) an extraordinary general meeting to consider what, if any, steps should be taken: s 142.

The Department of Trade and Industry (s 367) and the court (s 371) have statutory power in certain circumstances to direct that a meeting shall be held.

5 NOTICE OF MEETING

> **Tutorial note.** The question covers a large number of problems that may arise when calling a meeting and voting on resolutions

The first issue which arises from the facts given in this question concerns the validity (or otherwise) of the notice of the meeting. This is open to question for a number of different reasons.

Notice of the meeting

The required period of notice for an AGM is 21 days: s 369. Any attempt to require a shorter period than this is void. The 1985 Table A, which we are told Alpha Ltd has adopted, uses the expression '21 clear days' in Article 38, which indicates that in calculating the period of notice given, the day on which the notice is deemed to be received and the day of the meeting are to be excluded. In addition, where the post is used to serve the notice, Article 115 assumes delivery 48 hours after posting. Relating these principles to Alpha Ltd, it can be seen that the deemed date of receipt of notice will be 4 June, with the meeting to be held on 22 June. The period of notice given is therefore 17 days (since the day of the meeting itself is excluded), four days short of the required period. In principle, the meeting is therefore invalid due to short notice being given.

It is, however, possible that the period of notice will be waived under the procedure set out in s 369. This requires the consent of *all* the members entitled to attend and vote (so it could not have been given at the meeting itself, since X is absent), but it may be given later (as in *Re Pearce Duff & Co Ltd 1960*). The waiver may be oral, though it would be prudent to obtain it in writing.

Another problem arising from the notice is that X, who is entitled to attend and vote is given no notice at all. Article 39 provides that 'accidental omission' to give notice to a member who is entitled to receive it shall not invalidate the proceedings, but it is questionable whether this is a case of accidental omission. *Musselwhite v C H Musselwhite & Sons Ltd 1962* makes it clear that a company must give notice to all those who are on the register of members, without regard to the known interest of a third party (for example, where the shares have been sold, but the register of members has not yet been changed to reflect this). If the company makes the mistake of sending notice to the new (as yet unregistered) owner, then this is *not* an accidental omission for the purposes of Article 39.

Much therefore depends on the relative positions of S and X. If, for instance, S is still on the register of members following a recent sale of the shares, then the notice is properly sent. If, however, X is the registered owner, it is questionable whether a court would hold this to be an accidental omission. If it is not, then the meeting is invalid since notice must be sent to all those entitled to receive it, and this right cannot be waived: *Young v Ladies Imperial Club 1920.*

A final point on the notice relates to its content. A resolution for the company to provide financial assistance for the purchase of its own shares (this is legal in the case of a private company such as Alpha Ltd) must be a special resolution: s 155(4). Where such a resolution is to be proposed, the notice of the meeting must specify this intention: s 378(2). It is arguable whether this requirement has been fulfilled here, particularly in view of the fact that no figures are given concerning the assistance proposed. If the notice is held to be insufficient, the resolution passed will be invalid; the rationale behind this is that the notice of a meeting should give the recipient enough information to decide whether or not to attend the meeting. If the notice is 'tricky' (*Kaye v Croydon Tramways Co 1898*), and the recipient is led into thinking that he need not attend, he should not lose his right to protest when he finds out the true nature of the business which was transacted in his absence.

Inspection of declaration and auditors' report

At the meeting, Y demands an inspection of the directors' declaration and the auditor's report, but is refused by B on the basis that they are not available. This is in contravention of s 157(4)(a), which provides that the directors' declaration and its accompanying auditor's report (required by s 156) must be available for inspection by members at the meeting at which the resolution to provide financial assistance for purchase of the company's own shares is passed. Further, the section provides that if such inspection is not available, the resolution passed is invalid.

Demand for a poll

The demand for a poll made by Y and D is valid, since Table A Article 46 provides that a poll may be demanded by, amongst others, at least two members having the right to vote at the meeting.

Y is a validly appointed proxy, but the validity of her use of the proxy to vote against Z's wishes is open to question. Much depends on the form in which the instructions how to vote are given. If the proxy form is that given by Article 61, it will include written instructions on how to vote, and these must be complied with if the vote is to be valid. If, however, the form is similar to that given by Article 60, which includes no direction on voting, it is doubtful that a mere oral instruction would be enforceable. It is probably worth mentioning that Y has the right to vote as a proxy on a poll, as here, but would not have been able to vote on Z's behalf on a show of hands.

Special resolution

As a final point, the voting on the special resolution should be briefly analysed. A special resolution requires a three-quarters majority of the votes cast at a general meeting in order to be validly passed. At first sight it may appear that the voting was 600 out of a possible 900 votes in favour - a mere two-thirds majority - but it should be remembered that C abstained. His votes are therefore not cast, and are not reckoned into the calculation of whether the necessary majority has been reached. The voting is in fact 600 for and none against.

This total unanimity, it might be argued, brings into play the assent principle (exemplified by cases such as *Parker & Cooper Ltd v Reading 1926* and *Cane v Jones 1981*). The fact that C abstained is not enough to displace the imputation of assent (*Re Bailey Hay & Co 1971*), and it is frequently the case that defects of procedure are held to be immaterial in the face of complete agreement. It can be doubted whether the principle will apply here, particularly in view of X's absence from the meeting (assuming that he ought to have been sent notice) and the great number of other procedural defects which can be seen in the proceedings.

6 CONDUCTING A POLL

> **Tutorial note**. The rules on polls and proxies are very important aspects of procedures at meetings.

It is assumed that the company's articles of association follow the model of Table A as regards proxy voting and the conduct of a poll. References below are to articles of the 1985 Table A.

The purpose of demanding a poll is to permit the casting of proxy votes, to displace the show of hands and determine the result on the basis of votes related to shareholdings. The procedure for issuing proxies will be as follows:

(a) Proxy cards will be prepared in advance and issued to Oldman Industries' shareholders, so that they may be completed and returned during the period up to 48 hours before the meeting: Article 62(a).

(b) As the cards are received, they should be checked against the register of members to ensure that the persons who send them in are in fact entitled to cast the number of votes claimed. They should also be checked for correctness of execution: Articles 60-61.

(c) A list should be compiled of the proxy cards received, with figures of the votes which they represent. In the interval of 48 hours between the closing time for receipt of proxies and the meeting the auditors should be invited to check the proxy cards against the list, to ensure that it is reliable and that the cards are in order.

The chairman has the power to decide how and when the poll shall be taken: Articles 49 and 50. He should consider, perhaps with professional legal advice, whether it will be better to conduct the poll at the end of the meeting, as is usual, or whether it should be postponed to a later date, with the result that additional proxy cards may be deposited with the company up to 24 hours before the poll is held.

There are two main methods of holding a vote on a poll. The simplest is have two tables in the meeting hall, on which are laid out voting lists, suitably ruled. Members and proxies are invited to go up to the table on which the appropriate list ('For' or 'Against') has been placed, and to sign it; to indicate the number of votes cast; and (in the case of proxies) to give the name of the member for whom the proxy is voting.

The other method is to distribute to members (and proxies) individual voting cards, which they sign and hand back, while remaining in their seats. Under this procedure cards should be printed in advance and a sufficient number of stewards should be at hand to give out and collect in the cards. This requires more organisation, but is more orderly: a large number of people jostling each other (especially where the issues are contentious) may pose problems.

Finally, the chairman should decide whether he will appoint the auditors to be scrutineers, to conduct the poll and report the result to him, or whether he will invite each side to appoint a representative to act as scrutineers: Article 49.

At the meeting it is usual to hold a vote on a show of hands (Article 46), even though it will be displaced by a properly demanded poll. When the demand for a poll is made, the chairman should consider whether it is a proper one (Article 46), but in any event he himself may, and should, demand a poll if there is a real divergence of opinion. He may know what the likely result will be, from the proxy cards received, but he should not generally seek to induce a withdrawal of the demand for the poll, by divulging the figures. It is better to hold the poll and achieve an indisputable result.

When the poll is demanded, the chairman should inform the meeting of the procedure which he is to adopt. He might, for example, say that the poll will be held at the end of the meeting, with the auditors as scrutineers and voting by the use of cards. When the time for the poll arrives, the scrutineers take over (with such help from the chairman as they may require). They will examine the voting cards, to ensure that there is no double voting (say, by members voting in person and also by proxy). They report in writing to the chairman their count of the votes cast for and against the resolution. The chairman declares the result to the meeting.

7 PROXIES AND RIGHTS TO VOTE

(a) A member who is entitled to attend and vote at a meeting is entitled to appoint another person, whether a member or not, as his proxy to attend and vote instead of him. However these statutory rights (Companies Act 1985 s 372) do not apply to a company which has no share capital; a member of a private company may only appoint one proxy; and a proxy may not vote except on a poll.

There are a number of subsidiary rights also given by s 372.

(I) Every notice of a meeting of a company which has a share capital must state the right to appoint a proxy, and that the proxy need not be a member.

(II) In fixing the closing date for receipt of proxy forms, the company may not require the forms to be lodged longer than 48 hours before the meeting.

(III) If the company issues proxy cards (which is obligatory for a listed company), it must send them to *all* members.

It is left to companies to prescribe, by their articles, the form in which proxy appointments shall be made. It is usual (and obligatory for a listed company) to issue proxy cards in 'two-way' form (Table A Article 61), so that the member may instruct his proxy how he should vote on each item of business. There is no objection to inviting members to appoint the chairman, or other director(s), to vote on his instructions as his proxy.

(b) A proxy appointed by a member of a *private* company has the statutory right to speak at the meeting. The articles, or the chairman at his discretion, may permit a proxy to speak at a meeting of a public company. The reason for this distinction is to prevent members of public companies from sending professional advocates to meetings, to argue legal points on their behalf.

A proxy has the same right as a member present in person to demand a poll: s 373(4). He may in this way enforce the right to vote, which he does not have on a show of hands.

(c) A member's right to vote is defined by the articles. It is a personal right and if he is wrongly denied the opportunity to vote he may sue the company: *Pender v Lushington 1877.*

The chairman may properly refuse to count a member's votes if the Companies Act or the articles do not give to the member a right to vote on that occasion. Among these occasions are the following.

(i) A proxy may not vote on a show of hands unless the articles so provide: s 372(2)(c). A proxy is merely authorised to vote as agent of the member whom he represents. The member may revoke his proxy's authority by notice to the company (Article 63) or by attending the meeting and exercising his right to vote in person.

(ii) If shares are registered in the names of two or more persons as joint holders the articles provide (Article 55) that the vote of the person who appears first in the list of holders on the register shall be accepted so that the vote of any other joint holder must in these circumstances be rejected. If, of course, the first-named holder does not vote, the vote of the second in order must be accepted - and so on if there are more than two.

(iii) Most companies have an article which follows Table A Article 57 in providing that a member may not cast a vote attached to a share in respect of which (share) he is indebted to the company (say for an unpaid call on the share).

(iv) The articles may provide that a class of shares shall not carry the right to vote. This is normal in the case of preference shares.

8 POLL AND PROXIES

L has a *personal interest* in the proposal and so he cannot vote or be counted in a quorum when the board reaches its decision: Table A Article 94-95. It might be argued that the board merely decides to *recommend* the proposal to a general meeting and so there is no conflict of interest which brings Articles 94-5 into operation. However as the board 'recommends' the proposal, it is doing more than lay it before the general meeting for a decision. If L is disqualified, there is no quorum (of two - Article 89) and the resolution of the board is invalid.

As this is a private company (Classics *Ltd*) and the proposal is to purchase L's shares by private treaty, the 'off-market purchase' procedure (Companies Act 1985 s 164) applies. This requires, among other things, that:

(a) The vendor shareholder shall not vote on a show of hands nor cast the votes attached to the shares which he is to sell if there is a vote on a poll.

(b) The contract shall be approved by a special *resolution*.

The narrative does not state whether any part of this procedure has been applied.

Under s 164 (5)(b) even a single member is entitled (regardless of shareholding) to demand a poll. Moreover the two aunts have a right to demand a poll under the articles - as two members entitled to vote, and as representing more than one tenth of the voting rights: Table A Article 46.

It is not unlawful for a chairman to disclose the number of proxy votes available on a poll as an argument to persuade members to withdraw a demand for a poll. However some authorities consider that it is undesirable for him to use his knowledge of the proxy position in this way.

On the facts given, the chairman's statement is inaccurate and misleading. The articles (Table A Article 62(a)) require that proxy cards shall be deposited with the company *at least 48 hours* before the meeting. As this has not been done, the proxy cards held by L are invalid and could not affect the result of a vote on a poll.

The position is that a poll has been properly demanded: the question does not state (though it implies) that the resolution was approved on a show of hands. The chairman's declaration that the resolution had been carried (on a show of hands) is therefore invalid, as a poll was subsequently demanded. The record of his declaration in the minutes is equally incorrect and invalid: Table A Article 47.

For these various reasons the proceedings at the general meeting do not constitute authority for the purchase of L's shares under s 164. The general prohibition (s 143) against a company's acquisition of its own shares (*unless* it proceeds validly under s 164) remains in force. It would be unlawful for the company to purchase L's shares.

9 EXTRAORDINARY GENERAL MEETING

(a) *Notice*

PQR Limited

Notice is hereby given that an Extraordinary General Meeting of PQR Ltd will be held at [address] on [date and time] for the purpose of considering and if thought fit passing the following ordinary resolution:

Resolution

That the share capital of the company be increased from £10,000 divided into 10,000 shares of £1 each to £20,000 divided into 20,000 shares of £1 each by the creation of 10,000 shares of £1 each ranking *pari passu* with the existing shares.

By order of the board

Dated X December 20X1

J. Smith

Secretary

Registered office

(address)

A member entitled to attend and vote at the meeting is entitled to appoint a proxy to attend and vote instead of him. A proxy need not also be a member of the company.

(b) *Agenda*

Extraordinary General Meeting of PQR Ltd to be held at [*place*] on [*date and time*]

1 The chairman to invite the meeting to take the notice of the meeting as read.

2 The chairman to address the meeting, explaining the purpose of the resolution, and to propose the resolution as follows:

[*Resolution as in EGM notice above*]

Mr X, a director, to second the resolution.

The chairman to invite, and reply to, questions from shareholders.

The chairman to put the resolution to the vote (by show of hands) and declare the result.

3 The chairman to close the meeting.

(c) *Minutes*

Minutes of an Extraordinary General Meeting of PQR Ltd held at [*address*] on [date]

Present

Mr A Chairman
Mr X Director

In attendance

The Secretary

It was resolved that [*Resolution as in EGM notice*]

Signed A

Chairman

10 ENGINEERS LTD

(a) As a general rule it is unlawful for a company to give financial assistance for the purchase of its own shares: Companies Act 1985 s 151. However a private company may do so under the procedure laid down in ss 155-158. This requires, among other things, that a *special resolution* shall be passed, for example:

That the provision by the company of financial assistance to Engineers Ltd for the purpose of acquiring all the issued shares of the company be and is hereby approved.

(b) The draft resolution might well be expanded to specify the details of the financial assistance to be given, say by inserting after 'Engineers Ltd' the words '(by way of an interest free loan of £100,000)'. However it appears from s 157 that this detail is not essential; it suffices to approve the giving of assistance without specifying its nature.

It is not permissible to make any substantial amendment to a special resolution, since Companies Act 1985 s 378(2) requires that the resolution, as carried, shall be the same resolution 'of which notice has been duly given' in convening the meeting: *Re Moorgate Mercantile Holdings Ltd 1980*.

If Fixit Ltd has only a small number of shareholders, all of whom are in favour of the resolution, the best course may be to prepare a new notice to convene a general meeting of Fixit Ltd, setting out the amended special resolution as an original one. Shareholders may then be invited to sign a waiver (s 369) of the statutory period of 21 days' notice so that the revised resolution may be passed on the same day as was fixed for the meeting to consider the original resolution.

It is, of course, possible to convene a second general meeting, the notice of which contains the revised resolution: the 21 day period of notice would not have to be waived. The difficulty would then arise, however, that the resolution would not be passed, as s 157 requires, within seven days of the statutory declaration of solvency made by the directors. In effect, if the whole operation has to be postponed by a 21 day notice to consider the revised resolution, the directors may have to make a new statutory declaration and the auditors will have to make a fresh report on it, to comply with s 156. This change of plan will add considerably to the expense, as well as causing delay.

11 BOARD MEETINGS

(a) The first board meeting of a newly formed company is of rather an individual character, since it handles a number of items of non-recurrent business which must be dealt with before the company can begin to transact its business. These will include the following.

(i) The directors should take formal note that the company has been formed and the effective date of that formation, along with the fact that they have been appointed its directors by virtue of s 13.

(ii) Once satisfied on these matters, the directors should appoint one of themselves to be chairman, as provided by the articles. Without a chairman the meeting could not proceed.

(iii) It is useful (but not essential) to appoint auditors at this point, in case accounting records, etc, have to be discussed with them. This may smooth the audit of the first accounts later on.

(iv) The company must open a bank account in order to carry on business. The bank will insist that the resolution is in its own standard form of mandate, covering such matters as authorised signatories of cheques, who may withdraw company property deposited with the bank for safekeeping, etc.

(v) Company solicitors may be appointed at this point. As in the case of the auditors, appointment at this stage is not essential, but may be desirable; a continuing relationship will tend to provide better advice, for example.

(vi) A common seal may be adopted, generally with the full name of the company round the edge and the word 'limited' in the middle. It is in effect the company's 'signature', although no longer obligatory.

(vii) An accounting reference date is generally chosen at this time. Unless the company gives notice of its accounting reference date to the registrar within nine months, the date is taken to be the last day of the month in which the company's anniversary of incorporation falls: s 224(3). It is as well to get this formality, which determines the date to which the annual accounts are to be made up, completed before it is overlooked.

(viii) Shares should be allotted, thus raising permanent capital. This assumes that authority to allot shares under s 80 is conferred by the articles. If this is not the case, no shares may be allotted until the general meeting confers the authority to do so.

(ix) The dates of future board meetings are decided.

(x) There may be other items of business, depending on the circumstances of the company. The service agreements of the managing director and/or other senior employees may be approved, for example, or contracts to acquire other businesses or leases of premises may be executed.

The subsequent board meetings will be concerned with the day-to-day running of the company, the making of company contracts, consideration of reports from board committees, etc. There may in addition be special items of business, such as the receipt of a disclosure from a director of his interest in a company contract, appointment of a new chairman, acquisition or disposal of assets or businesses, etc. These, however, are the exceptions rather than the rule, and the majority of business transacted will be of a regular and predictable nature in the exercise of the directors' management function.

(b) Board meetings are, by their nature, busy but relatively informal occasions. The Articles (Table A Article 88) provide that the directors 'may regulate their proceedings as they see fit', so there need be no elaborate procedures if the directors are few in number and know each other well. There are, however, some aspects of procedure which should be strictly observed, in order to keep the proceedings fair and orderly, especially if there is a definite rift between directors. This will mainly be the responsibility of the chairman.

(i) The discussion should follow the sequence of the agenda and should be confined at each stage to the item currently under discussion.

(ii) Although it is often not necessary to take a formal vote, the chairman should sum up the sense of the meeting, so that a suitably worded decision or conclusion may be formulated for inclusion in the minutes.

(iii) If a vote does appear to be necessary, it will be along the lines of a show of hands or a voice vote. The usual procedure is to go round the table inviting each member of the board to declare his vote for or against. If any member abstains, perhaps because a personal interest does not allow him to vote, this should be noted and recorded.

(iv) Each member of the board has one vote, unless the articles provide otherwise, perhaps by conferring weighted voting rights (as in *Salmon v Quin & Axtens Ltd 1909*) or by giving the chairman a casting vote to decide tied issues.

(v) Although the chairman's notes on his agenda are not recognised as evidence, it is good practice for him to note the outcome of each discussion as the debate proceeds.

12 INCORPORATION

> **Tutorial note**. The subject matter of this question was also covered in depth in your *Corporate Law* studies, but questions on this area have been asked in CSP.

To: Messrs Smith & Wilson X June 20X1

Dear Sirs,

You have asked for advice on the advantages and disadvantages of transferring your grocery business to a private company, of which you yourselves will presumably be the only shareholders and directors. I will leave the tax and other transitional aspects of this proposal for consideration on a later occasion and confine this letter to the basic commercial considerations.

As you are no doubt aware the main advantage of incorporating a business is that the proprietors may thereby trade with limited liability for the debts of the business, which they do not have if they continue to trade as partners. However you should expect that your bank may seek to obtain some security by way of a charge over the company's assets. You yourselves may be asked to become guarantors of the company's liabilities. Subject to that, by forming a company you limit your losses, if the business becomes insolvent, to loss of the capital invested in the company. You might of course take debentures, with suitable security, in part payment by the company of the value of the business, but both your bank and your trade creditors may on that account be less willing to lend or to supply goods on trade credit to the company.

The other major advantage of incorporation is that your respective interests as shareholders will be more readily transferable than if you continue to trade in partnership. In particular either of you is free, subject to any restrictions imposed by the articles of association, to transfer your shares, for example to a relative. However shares of a small private company are not readily marketable and might be difficult to sell.

As already indicated a company, unlike a partnership, can give security by way of charge over its current assets. This factor may facilitate raising capital to finance the growth of the business.

The management structure of a company is more formal than that of a partnership. Unlike partners, directors and shareholders are not, as such, agents of the company with authority to commit it to contracts. The board of directors will have to decide important commercial matters affecting the business. As a company to make major changes, say in the structure of the company, formal procedures laid down by the companies legislation need be adhered to, requiring records to be kept and made available for inspection and for registration at Companies House.

The same factor of formal procedure is usually regarded as the main drawback of incorporation. As a small company you may deliver simplified accounts to the Registrar of Companies, but accounts which comply with the requirements of the Companies Act 1985 will have to be prepared and laid before the annual general meeting. Moreover the accounts will have to be audited if your turnover is greater than £350,000, which will entail the payment of an audit fee.

Yours faithfully

H. Jones FCIS

13 MEMORANDUM

A memorandum of association of a private company must comply with the requirements of the Companies Act 1985 s 2, including the five basic clauses. It is necessary to obtain the client's instructions for that purpose.

The first clause states the *name* of the company. It would be prudent to check any name selected by the client against the index of names of existing companies to ensure that no objection will be raised to his choice as being the same or very similar to that of some other company. It is also necessary to consider whether the name includes any word which is regulated under s 29 with the result that official permission for its use must be sought.

The second clause states the country within which the company is always to have its *registered office*. This is also the country in which the company is legally domiciled. Generally the country will be stated as England and Wales, (separately stated as Scotland). It is not necessary to have the address of the first registered office for completion of this clause but it will be given in another document (Form 10) to be filed at Companies House to obtain registration of the company.

The client may wish for a lengthy *objects* clause, quite unlike the statutory model. A law stationer will supply a common form clause but it will be necessary for the client to specify the type of business (and related objects) to be described in the opening paragraphs of the clause. If the company is to acquire an existing business, it is usual to state that as the first paragraph of the objects clause. As a result of the Companies Act 1989, however, it is possible to register objects as a 'general commercial company', and the client may prefer the simplicity inherent in this approach.

It is assumed that the *liability* of members is to be *limited*. That basic proposition is the next clause.

The last of the five standard clauses must state the *authorised capital* (if it is to be a company limited by shares) divided into shares of specified value, eg £100 divided into 100 shares of £1 each.

The client may be asked whether he wishes to have *additional clauses*, but it is generally better to deal with all other aspects of the company's constitution in the articles of association, unless the client has good reasons for wishing to 'entrench' any such clauses. In the memorandum they are more difficult to alter if a minority objects.

Subscribers to the memorandum, of whom there must be at least two, add their signatures to an *association clause* by which they agree to form the company and to take a minimum of at least one share each, to be paid for in cash. This is purely formal, but the client should be asked whether he wishes to nominate the subscribers, whose name will appear on the printed memorandum indefinitely. The subscribers' signatures must be witnessed by another person's signature and dated.

14 VARIATION OF CLASS RIGHTS

All the shares of a company may carry uniform rights. If that is so, there are no classes and in consequence no class rights.

It is, however, possible to create shares with different rights, for example to dividends, or to return of capital or to votes at general meetings. In that case all the shares which have uniform rights are grouped as a class. The most common example are preference and ordinary shares.

The definition of the rights of different classes of shares is usually contained in the articles of association, but it may be found in the memorandum or in a resolution passed to create a new class of shares. A statement of the rights of a class of shares must always be found, in one form or another, on the file at the Companies Registry: Companies Act 1985 ss 128-9.

When it is proposed to vary the rights of a class of shares, for instance by increasing the preferential rate of dividend of preference shares, it is necessary to follow the correct procedure, which is often contained in the articles. Alternatively, the memorandum of association may both define the rights and provide a procedure for variation. The 1985 Table A contains no such provision, as it is contemplated that companies should follow the statutory method. If there is a variation procedure it usually requires that the company shall obtain the consent of the holders of the shares of the class, either by:

(a) Securing the passing of an extraordinary resolution by a three quarters majority of votes cast at a separate class meeting; or.

(b) Obtaining the consent of the holders of three quarters of the shares of the class.

Where there is no variation procedure in the company's constitution and the class rights are not contained in the memorandum, the rights may be varied by a three quarters majority as explained above: Companies Act 1985 s 125. If in that situation the class rights are defined in the memorandum, the consent of all members of the company is required (ie if there is no variation procedure in the memorandum or articles: s 125(5)).

It is possible to alter the articles to introduce into them a provision for variation of class rights. However, in that case the alteration is itself treated as a variation of rights for which consent of a three quarters majority is required. When the required consent has been given, the company in general meeting passes a special resolution to alter the memorandum or articles of association to incorporate the variation.

In the last resort variation may be effected by scheme of arrangement approved by the court under s 425.

15 ISSUE OF PREFERENCE SHARES OR DEBENTURES

MEMORANDUM

To: the Directors of XYZ plc X June 20X1

From: the Secretary

Methods of raising additional capital

This memorandum reviews the considerations affecting the decision to be taken by the board on raising the required additional capital by an issue of preference shares or of debentures. It is assumed that the preference shares would not be issued as redeemable.

In either case it is necessary to keep in view the relevant powers. The issue of shares of any kind requires authority, to be given by the members in general meeting, under Companies Act 1985 s 80 (s 80A cannot apply here, as XYZ is a public company). As preference shares (unless they are participating preference shares) are not equity securities, the pre-emption rights given by s 89 do not apply.

If the board decides to issue debentures, that will be a form of borrowing, subject to the limit of twice the issued share capital and reserves (say, £X on the basis of the last audited balance sheet) on the powers of the directors to borrow without obtaining sanction from the members in general meeting. It will also be necessary to create preference shares with suitable class rights, if shares of that type are to be allotted. To sum up, borrowing (depending on the amount) may, and an allotment of shares will, entail the convening of a general meeting as the first step.

The main contrast between preference shares and loan capital is that the company is not required to pay the fixed dividend on the preference shares, if it does not have sufficient distributable profits to cover the dividend. On the other hand interest on debentures is a contractual debt, which must be discharged (if the company is not to default on its obligations) whether or not there are available profits. From the tax standpoint a preference dividend is paid out of taxed profits, while debenture interest is a charge deducted in calculating profits for tax.

Both preference shares and debentures are a fixed capital sum to be discharged in liquidation. The debentures must always, as a debt, take priority over repayment of share capital. Preference shares usually carry a priority entitlement to repayment in liquidation, though there is no legal requirement of general law that they must. It would be difficult to find subscribers for preference shares if they did not carry that conventional priority.

It is suggested that the board should now seek the advice of merchant bankers as to the terms on which preference shares and debentures could be issued in present market conditions and as to the method of issue. It may well be necessary to support an issue of debentures by giving security in the form of a charge on the company's property. Preference shares are not now a popular form of investment. It is likely that the board will be advised that, on balance, an issue of debentures, with or without security, is to be preferred.

J Smith

Secretary

16 DEBENTURE TRUST DEED

A *debenture trust deed* is usually a long and elaborate legal document the main elements of which are as follows.

(a) A trustee for prospective debenture stockholders is appointed. The first trustee is formally appointed by the company (as the other party to the deed); any replacement trustee is to be appointed by the debenture stockholders. The trustee is usually a bank, insurance company or other institution, but may be an individual trustee.

(b) The nominal amount of the debenture stock is defined; this is the maximum amount which may be raised, then or later. The date or period of repayment is specified, with the rate of interest, and half yearly interest payment dates.

(c) If the debenture stock is secured, the deed creates a charge or charges over the assets of the company (and often of its subsidiaries, which are parties to the deed for that purpose). If the security is a floating charge, the creation of subsequent charges with priority is prohibited.

(d) The trustee is authorised to enforce the security in case of default, and in particular to appoint a receiver with suitable powers of management.

(e) The company enters into various covenants, for instance to keep its assets fully insured, or to limit its total borrowings; breach is a default by the company. The remuneration of the trustee is fixed.

(f) There are elaborate provisions for a register of debenture stockholders, transfer of stock, issue of stock certificates, and meetings of debenture stockholders at which extraordinary resolutions passed by a three quarters majority are decisions binding on all debenture stockholders.

17 STATUTORY BOOKS

The statutory registers and books of a company are as follows:

(a) *Register of members*, with particulars of each member, date of becoming and ceasing to be a member, and details of the shares (distinguished by classes) which he holds. A company with a share capital also details the shares held by each member and amount agreed paid on those shares. If shares converted to stock the register will show the amount and class of stock held by each member. If there is no share capital but different classes of members these details are shown in the register: s 352

(b) *Register of directors and secretary*, with particulars of names (and former names) and address and for each director: his nationality, business occupation, date of birth (in some cases) and other directorships, including (with exceptions) those held within the previous five years: s 288

(c) *Register of directors' interests* in shares or debentures, showing the directors' interests, as elaborately defined to include interests of spouse or minor children and interests in securities of other companies of the same group: s 325

(d) *Register of charges on the property of the company*, including particulars of the property charged, in favour of whom, and the amount secured: s 407

(e) *Minutes* includes a copy of all the minutes of the proceedings of general and board meetings: s 382

(f) *Accounting records* sufficient to disclose the trading transactions of the company: s 221

A public company is also required to maintain a register to record information relating to substantial interests in voting shares of which it has been notified in accordance with s 198 to 203: s 211.

18 REGISTER OF MEMBERS

Function. Every company is required by s 352 to maintain a register of members, and to enter the information therein prescribed, as described below. The function of the register is to establish who is a member and to make the information available to the public, since any person may inspect the register and, on payment of such fee as may be prescribed, have a copy of it or of a part of it.

If, as is usual, the company has a share capital, the relevant details of shareholdings are entered in the register, and these are prima facie evidence of the ownership of the shares.

Information. S 352 provides that the following information should be entered in the register of members:

(a) The name and address of every member, the date on which he became a member, and in due course the date on which he ceased to be a member

(b) If the company has a share capital, the shares held by each member, distinguished by their serial numbers (if any), their class (if there is more than one class of shares), and the amount paid (or credited as paid) in respect of each share

(c) If the company has no share capital, but there is more than one class of members (for instance some with and some without voting rights), the class to which each member belongs

Becoming a member. Subscribers to the memorandum of association are deemed to agree thereby to become members, on the formation of the company, and to pay in cash for their subscribers' shares. They should be entered in the register as soon as the company is formed.

Other persons become members if they agree to be members, and their names are then entered in the register: s 22(2). The most common categories are:

(a) Transferees who present transfers of shares for registration in their names

(b) Allottees (or holders of renounced letters of allotment) who have applied for shares, or for registration as holders of the shares comprised in the letters of allotment

(c) Personal representatives of deceased members, if they apply to be registered as holders of the shares of the deceased member whom they represent

In each case, the act described implies agreement to be a member, and the person concerned becomes a member on being entered in the register of members (but not until that is done).

19 LISTING

MEMORANDUM

To:	the Directors of PQR plc	X December 20X1
From:	the Secretary	

Chapters 3 - 7 of the Listing Rules set out in detail the procedure for an application for listing. Chapter 7 specifies what has to be done 'as soon as practicable' after the grant of a listing. The action required is the delivery of a number of documents, marked 'FAO Listing Applications', comprising:

(a) In an intermediaries offer, from each intermediary the names and addresses of its clients with whom it placed securities and details of securities allocated to each client

(b) Where securities are offered with a cash alternative, a statement of the total amount of securities issued, where different from the number of securities which were the subject of the application, the aggregate number of securities in issue

(c) A formal notice where only a final draft has been lodged and a document of title where a draft document has been lodged

(d) If securities have been issued as consideration for the compulsory acquisition of listed shares, under Companies Act 1985 s 429, a certified copy of the statutory notice (of intention to acquire), given under s 429

(e) In an introduction a statement of the opening market price of the listed securities (plus payment of any additional fee due), if the price exceeded the issue price

(f) If there are bearer documents of title, a statement from security printers (as to safeguards required by Chapter 7 of the Listing Rules)

(g) A written request for re-imbursement of listing fees if the number of such securities issued is less than the number which was the subject of application

(h) A comprehensive declaration (in the form of Schedule 6) by a director or by the Secretary, concerning due compliance of the company in connection with various requirements incidental to the listing and related transactions

20 STOCK EXCHANGE CONTINUING OBLIGATIONS

MEMORANDUM

To: the Directors of XYZ plc X December 20X1

From: the Secretary

Continuing Obligations

The Continuing Obligations imposed on listed companies are contained in the Listing Rules. The memorandum below summaries the main obligations.

Public announcements.

The company is required to notify:

(a) Any major new developments in its sphere of activity (unless already known to the public) which may affect the value of its securities

(b) Information about the interests of directors and connected persons in a company's securities

(c) Any decision by the board on dividends, profits etc

(d) Its half-year or end of year financial results as soon as the figures have been approved

(e) A proposed change in share or loan capital structure (this is specified in some detail)

(f) Changes of rights attaching to securities

(g) Redemption or drawing of listed securities

(h) Basis of allotment of listed securities

(i) Effect of issues on conversion rights

(j) Results of new issues

(k) Extension of time for currency of temporary documents of title

(l) Notification of major interests in shares under s 198-212 CA85

Copies of documents

Six copies of any notice or circular to be issued to members must be submitted to the Companies Announcement Office at the same time they are issued. All resolutions passed in General Meeting other than AGM routine must also be submitted without delay.

Share transfers and certificates

(a) A company should ensure it has appropriate arrangements in place for its listed securities.

(b) No fee may be charged for registration of transfers and other documents.

General meetings

The rules emphasises the importance of informing holders of securities of meetings and enabling them to exercise their right to vote. With every notice of a general meeting the company must issue a 'two-way proxy' card.

J Smith

Secretary

21 RIGHTS ISSUE

MEMORANDUM

To: Directors of XYZ plc X December 20X1

From: Secretary

Proposed rights issue

(a) This memorandum written is for the board to enable it to review the main stages of procedures of a proposed rights issue of ordinary shares.

(b) The *authority to allot* required by Companies Act 1985 s 80 was renewed at the last Annual General Meeting. There are sufficient unissued shares of the authorised share capital of the company to make the issue. A rights issue complies with the pre-emption provisions of s 89. There do not appear to be legal problems, but it will be useful to consult the company's solicitors on these points, among others. There will also have to be general discussions with the merchant bank, the company's brokers and auditors.

(c) As the shares are to be listed, it will be necessary to ascertain and to comply with *Stock Exchange requirements* at all stages. As a consequence of the Financial Services Act 1986 Part IV, the whole operation will be subject to Stock Exchange control. The brokers will consult the Stock Exchange over the timetable and will advise the board on the numerous detailed requirements incidental to an issue of listed securities. As the new shares will be uniform with the existing listed ordinary shares, these requirements will be less onerous than if it were an entirely new flotation.

(d) It will be necessary to prepare, and submit to the Stock Exchange for approval, a form of renounceable allotment letter on standard lines, with forms of renunciation and application by renuncees for registration.

(e) Arrangements will be made with A Bank plc to act as *Receiving Bank* under authority given by the board. The bank will deal with the applications for splitting letters of allotment and for registration. The bank will also receive on the company's behalf the subscription moneys on the shares.

(f) A *committee* of the board will have to be established, to meet as necessary to *allot* the shares and to deal with incidental matters, such as the sale of fractions and distribution of the proceeds. The Stock Exchange will have to be fully consulted and informed on these matters.

(g) After the renunciation period has expired, *share certificates* will be prepared by the company's registrars and entries made in the register of members. It will also be necessary to file a *return of allotments*, as required by s 88. By concession, the registrar will permit the company to defer making the return until the entries have been made in the register.

J. Smith

Secretary

22 SHARE CERTIFICATES

The company should note in its register of members, and/or any related register of dealings with members, that the original share certificate has been lost. There should be an explicit 'stop' on any registration of a transfer presented with the lost certificate. The company's bank should be informed at once of the loss of the dividend warrant, and instructed to refuse payment if that warrant is later presented.

In respect of the lost share certificate, a letter of indemnity in the standard form should be prepared, and another in respect of the lost dividend warrant. These are required to safeguard the company against any loss arising from the issue of new documents. Further action appears from the draft letter to the shareholder which follows.

Dear Sir,

Thank you for your letter of (*date*) informing me of the loss of share certificate No.......... in respect of 1,000 ordinary shares, and dividend warrant No.............. for distribution No......... for payment to you of £100.

I have taken action to prevent any subsequent registration of a transfer of shares supported by the lost certificate, and to stop payment of the dividend warrant if presented to the bank. If you later discover either or both documents, would you please immediately surrender them to the company.

I enclose two letters of indemnity for signature and return. You should arrange with your bank, or an insurance or guarantee company, to countersign the letter in respect of the share certificate, in support of your personal liability.

On receiving the two letters duly signed, I will arrange to issue to you a duplicate share certificate, clearly marked as such, and also a replacement dividend warrant and counterfoil, also suitably marked.

Yours faithfully,

J. Smith

Secretary

23 SHORT NOTES

> **Tutorial note**. You should be aware of developments in CREST and AIM; both are regularly covered in the financial press and Chartered Secretary.

(a) CREST is a means of settling transactions in shares and other securities. It is designed to make settlement faster and more secure. It means that anyone dealing on the stock market will be able to hold shares in electronic form, rather than on paper.

A directors' resolution is required for transfer to CREST; this can be overturned by general meeting resolution.

The CREST system matches instructions from the seller and buyer of securities and holds them until the settlement date. The settlement process, which runs continuously, checks whether the settlement date has been reached.

On the settlement date, CREST checks for each pair of instructions that the purchaser has sufficient credit, and the seller holds enough stock. If they do, CREST debits the seller's and credits the purchaser's stock accounts with the securities, and debits the purchaser's and credits the seller's cash accounts with the consideration.

CREST then gives the company's registrar an instruction to update the register of members. This should be done within two hours of settlement

The amounts payable are settled through each member's clearing bank; at the end of every settlement day CRESTCo sends the Bank of England a schedule listing the amounts to or from each bank, and these are settled by a Bank of England debit or credit. The bank settles with the members outside the CREST system.

Once securities join CREST, the system deals with all market transactions. Requests to change the form of securities from certificated to uncertificated form and vice versa (from paper to electronic form and vice versa) are processed by the company's registrar and the CREST Courier and Sorting Service.

(b) The Alternative Investment Market (AIM) is operated by the London Stock Exchange, and is designed for a broad range of companies, to help them raise capital and increase their Market profile. Any type of security can be traded on AIM.

The main regulations governing AIM are the Public Offer of Securities Regulations 1995 governing the content of prospectuses together with certain requirements of AIM itself. Key conditions are that the company needs to appoint a nominated broker and adviser, ensure that its securities are freely transferable, and adopt a code relating to trading while in possession of unpublished price sensitive information.

The company will be required to notify the Stock Exchange of any price sensitive information. Other requirements are imposed regarding information that has to be sent to shareholders and included in the accounts.

Trading on AIM can be carried on through the Stock Exchange Alternative Trading Service, SEATS PLUS, which supports AIM securities.

(c) In the ordinary way, the transfer of a listed security is made under a sale through the market. However there are also occasions for other types of transfer. As examples: the beneficial owner of shares may require his nominee (say his bank), in whose name the shares are registered, to transfer them to him; executors of a deceased member may transfer shares from his name to the beneficiaries entitled under his will.

A non-market transfer of a listed securities is effected by delivery to the company, for registration, of a duly completed standard form of transfer, plus of course the transferor's share certificate.

24 STOP NOTICE

A company is prohibited by Companies Act 1985 s 360 from entering in its register of members any notice of a trust. If therefore any person, a prospective purchaser, or mortgagee, or beneficiary of a trust, sends to the company a communication to the effect that he has an interest in shares registered in the name of some other person, the company should return the notice to him, drawing his attention to s 360.

To enable a third party to protect his interest in shares not registered in his name, he is permitted to apply to the court registry, with an affidavit setting out the nature of his interest and the notice which he wishes to serve on the company. He obtains from the court a sealed copy of the notice, and of his own affidavit; these documents he then delivers to the company. This procedure is prescribed by the Charging Orders Act 1979, and the rules of the Supreme Court.

A 'stop notice' may relate only to a transfer of the specified shares, or it may in addition relate to payment of dividends on those shares as well. On receiving the documents, the company should check that the 'stop notice' is sealed by the court and relates to a shareholding in the register. No note should be made on the register of the nature of the claim, but there should be a record that restrictions have been placed on the holding. The notice and copy affidavit should be entered in the register of documents and carefully filed.

If the stop notice is limited to a transfer of the shares, no action is required unless a transfer of those shares is presented. In that case it is the duty of the company to give notice in writing of the presentation of the transfer to the person who lodged the stop notice. He then has 14 days in which to obtain an injunction (court order) directed to the company to prohibit the transfer. The company should at the same time inform the person who presented the transfer that stop notice procedure has been taken. The company is not involved in any court proceedings between the parties. If at the end of 14 days no injunction has been served on the company, it may and should proceed to deal with the transfer in the normal way.

If the stop notice is expressed to cover payment of dividends, similar action must be taken, and a 14 day interval observed, before the dividend may be paid on the relevant shares.

25 REGISTRATION OF TRANSFER

(a) *Power of attorney*

It is assumed that the Power of Attorney has not been registered in the company's records on a previous occasion. If it had been, it would be necessary to refer to those records which should, if possible, include a photo or xerox copy of the original document.

The transfer should only be registered after it has been established that the attorney has proper authority from the shareholder.

The attorney should present to the company the original Power of Attorney, or a photocopy duly certified. A copy should be made for the company's records before it is returned.

In examining the document, the secretary should note whether:

(i) It names the attorney as authorised to act under it.

(ii) It gives adequate authority either in general terms (as provided by the Powers of Attorney Act 1971) or in specific terms covering a transfer of shares.

(iii) It has been properly executed as a deed by the principal.

(iv) It is stamped or is dated on or after 26 March 1985.

The secretary should also check from his records that no notice has been received of any event, such as the shareholder's death, or the revocation of the power, which would terminate the authority given by it.

If the power appears to be in order the company may register the transfer as duly executed on behalf of the shareholder.

(b) *Executor's transfer*

Again it is assumed that the grant of probate to the executor has not been registered on a previous occasion. If it had been the company should have for reference, if possible, a photo or xerox copy of the original document.

The executor should be asked to produce to the company the grant of probate to him by the court, for inspection, registration (including taking a facsimile copy) and return. The original, or an 'office copy' (bearing the seal of the court), is generally required, though some companies will accept a facsimile copy if duly certified by a responsible person.

If the executor holds a grant of probate to him as the sole proving executor (or if he can produce evidence of the death of any other executor to whom the grant was made jointly with him) the company may, and indeed must, recognise him as vested with statutory power (Companies Act

1985 s 187) to transfer the shares registered in the name of the deceased shareholder, whose executor he is.

There can be complications, in special circumstances which do not appear to exist in the present case.

26 DEATH OF A SHAREHOLDER

Although the information of both deaths has been received at the same time, the deaths were not simultaneous and the relevant action is determined by the order of the deaths.

The death of Jones caused the legal ownership of the shares to pass entirely to Brown. On Brown's death (as sole surviving shareholder) the executrix must establish her authority to deal with the shares.

(a) Dear Mrs Brown,

Thank you for your letter informing me of the successive deaths of Mr A Jones and of your husband. May I express to you on behalf of the company our sympathy on your bereavement.

In order that I may be able to deal properly with this matter could you send me (or arrange with the executor of Mr Jones to send me) a copy of the death certificate of Mr A Jones. The effect of his death on 31 March 20X1 was to constitute your late husband the sole shareholder of the 500 ordinary shares.

That was the position when your husband died on 25 May 20X1. I am obliged by the rules of the Companies Act 1985 to ask to see a grant of probate of your late husband's will, as evidence of your authority to dispose of the shares. I note that you do not intend to employ a solicitor. Perhaps you could obtain competent advice from a Citizens' Advice Bureau or (if the joint holding was trust property) obtain suitable assistance elsewhere. In the meantime would you please send me, for inspection and return, a copy of your husband's death certificate and in due course the probate of his will, granted to you as executrix.

Yours sincerely,

(b) The certificate of Jones' death having been received, it should first be checked to ensure that it relates to the A Jones on the register, and that it is an original certificate issued by the public registry (and not a xerox or other privately made copy). An entry should be made in the register of members of the date of death, and production of the certificate. A record should also be made in the register of documents produced, supported by a xerox copy of the death certificate, which should then be returned.

It would also be wise to make a note that dividends cannot now be paid (as there is no one legally entitled to receive them) until the probate is produced.

On receipt of the probate, the same check should be made as with the death certificate. The name of Mrs Brown as executrix should be entered on the register of members (with the date of Brown's death - of which the probate is sufficient evidence). The probate should be endorsed with a registration stamp (and a copy made for the company's records) before it is returned.

At some stage the company should ask to have the share certificate, in the joint names, in order to endorse it with a note of the two deaths. As Jones was the first-named holder, it is unlikely that Mrs Brown has it among her husband's papers. The presenter of Jones' death certificate might be asked for it. It must of course be surrendered whenever Mrs Brown, after producing the probate, presents a transfer of the shares.

If Mrs Brown argues that, in view of the small size of her husband's estate, it is not reasonable to obtain probate, the company might (on obtaining suitable indemnity) agree to allow her to transfer the shares without producing probate. However, it is not obliged to do so and there is some risk.

27 UNCLAIMED DIVIDENDS

The articles (Table A, Article 106) provide that the company may discharge its obligation to pay a dividend by sending a cheque through the post to each shareholder at his registered address. Nonetheless, it is inconvenient to have unclaimed dividends outstanding as a potential claim on the company (if the warrants are eventually presented), continuing for years after each dividend payment.

As a reminder to shareholders, it is usual to print on the dividend warrant a notice that, unless presented for payment within six months, the warrant will not be paid by the bank unless it is first returned to the company for redating or other authorisation.

Companies also seek to persuade shareholders to issue mandates to the company, for payment of all dividends through their bank account. It is then possible for a company with a large number of shareholders to pay dividends by the 'bulk payment' system, which ensures payment so long as the shareholder has a bank account at the designated bank.

It is good practice - at, say, the end of the fifth month after the despatch of dividend warrants - to write to shareholders who have not yet presented them for payment, reminding them to do so. This may elicit replies from shareholders who have not received, or who have mislaid, their warrants (so that these cases may be dealt with under 'lost dividend warrant' procedure), and prompt others to claim payment before the six months elapses. In the meantime, the bank account opened for the payment of the dividend in question remains open, with funds available to meet outstanding payments.

If the dividend has not been paid at the time when the next dividend is due, a further reminder may be sent with the next dividend warrant.

The articles (Table A Article 108) usually provide that the company may forfeit any dividend which is not claimed within 12 years; the Stock Exchange will not permit any shorter period, if the company is listed. This disposes of the matter after twelve years; the shareholder cannot assert that his right against the company has been extended, by the written acknowledgement of 'unclaimed dividends' in the annual accounts.

However, it is inconvenient to continue to send dividend warrants to shareholders who do not present them, year after year. It is possible to include in the articles a power to *withhold* dividend warrants if, say, two such warrants issued in succession have not been presented for payment, and the company has been unable to trace the shareholder, or the warrants have been returned as undeliverable through the post, since the addressee is not at the specified address. This procedure complies with Stock Exchange requirements.

It is also possible to include in the articles power to sell shares in respect of which dividends have not been claimed for twelve years or more.

28 SAVINGS RELATED SHARE OPTION SCHEME

MEMORANDUM

To: the Finance Director X December 20X1

From: the Secretary

Savings Related Share Option Scheme

Option Certificates

The information to be given on the Option Certificates will include the following.

(a) The period over which the savings related contract with the Department of National Savings will run. It may be a three year or a five year period, or an initial five year period with the choice of extending it to seven years at the end of the fifth year. The precise dates will have to be specified.

(b) The amount of the monthly or weekly instalment which the employee is to set aside over the saving period.

(c) The guaranteed terminal bonus, currently eleven monthly payments in addition to the 60 payments actually made by the employee.

(d) The formula for determining the subscription price of the shares, if the option is exercised, which may not be less than 80 per cent of the middle-market price, on the latest dealing day preceding the grant of the option. This price will of course be ascertained at the time when the option is granted, and may be specified as a precise amount per share (in accordance with the terms of the scheme, approved by the company when it was established).

(e) The period within which the option must be exercised, following the completion of the period specified under (a) above.

It will also be convenient to show on the certificate the relevant provisions for dealing with various contingencies under the scheme.

J. Smith

Secretary

29 COMPULSORY SHARE PURCHASE

If Company A ('transferee company') offers to acquire shares of Company B ('the transferor company') and the takeover bid is accepted by holders of nine tenths of the shares for which the offer is made, Company A may then compulsorily acquire the remaining 10 per cent (or less) of the shares so as to achieve a complete 100 per cent acquisition of the shares: s 428. A takeover bid is usually made by one company but the procedure also applies to a bid by an individual or by persons acting jointly.

It is standard procedure in making a takeover bid to state that if 90 per cent acceptance is attained, compulsory acquisition will follow. Company A may resort to this method whether it offers its own shares for shares of Company B, or cash. The procedure is available if Company A already owns shares of Company B and offers to acquire those which it does not already own; the non-accepting minority may, however, apply to the court to prevent company A from acquiring their shares.

If Company B has two or more classes of share and Company A makes a bid for shares of both classes, this is treated as two separate offers, *each* requiring 90 per cent acceptance. In such cases it is usual (but not legally necessary) for Company A to reserve the right to withdraw its bid for either class if acceptance for the other class does not reach the 90 per cent level.

The takeover bid must (to bring it within s 428) be for all the shares of Company B which Company A and its associates do not already own. In calculating the 90 per cent, any shares acquired on different terms (usually through the market) while the bid is outstanding are disregarded. The bid need not, however, extend to shares held by overseas holders who reside in countries where there are legal obstacles to acceptance of the bid, in the terms in which it is made generally.

The bid must be on the same terms for all shares to which the bid relates, but it may be in the form of alternatives, eg shares of Company A, or cash ('a cash alternative'), or some combination selected by the individual offeree. The cash alternative is often provided by arranging that a third party undertakes to purchase from accepting offerees, at a fixed price, any consideration shares of Company A which they do not wish to retain.

Acceptance, by the holders of 90 per cent of the shares for which the bid is made, must be obtained within four months from the making of the bid. On reaching 90 per cent, Company A has the ensuing two months in which to serve notice on non-accepting shareholders of its intention to acquire their shares compulsorily on the same terms. They in turn then have six weeks, from receiving the notice, in which they may appeal to the court against the proposed acquisition of their shares or, if they are minded to accept the bid, to select which of the alternative terms (if any alternatives are given) they will accept.

Finally, if there is no objection, or if an objection fails, Company B, as trustees for the non-accepting shareholders, transfers their shares to Company A in exchange for the agreed price.

The non-accepting shareholders have a further statutory safeguard. Company A is not obliged to serve notice of intention to acquire their shares, but as soon as Company A's total ownership of shares in Company B reaches 90 per cent (or 90 per cent of a class) it must within one month give notice of that fact to the holders of the outstanding shares. Those shareholders may then within the ensuing three months require Company A to acquire their shares on the same terms as have been accepted by approving shareholders.

Glossary, List of cases and Index

Account day See *account system*.

Administration A procedure under which a moratorium is imposed by the court on creditors' actions against the company while an insolvency practitioner attempts to secure a good resolution. The insolvency practitioner involved is called an *administrator*.

Administrative receiver A person defined by the Insolvency Act 1986 under a *floating charge* to manage or realise the assets which are the security with a view to paying out of those assets what is due to the debentureholders whom he represents.

Administrator Insolvency practitioner in charge of an *administration*.

Allotment letter Letter informing allottees that shares have been allotted to them.

Allotment of shares The allocation to a person of a certain number of shares under a contract of allotment. The intending shareholder applies to the company for shares. This is an offer which the company accepts by allocating shares to him.

Annual general meeting (AGM) Every company is required to hold a meeting of each its members each (calendar) year, at intervals of not more than 15 months, at which it is usual, but not obligatory to transact the 'ordinary business' of the company. Such business may include consideration of the accounts, declaration of a dividend and appointment of auditors. Private companies may dispense with such meetings if they pass an *elective resolution*.

Annual return A form which must be delivered to the registrar once a year, summarising essential information about the company, its members and officers.

Articles of association Rules governing the internal conduct of a company's affairs, such as appointment, powers and proceedings of directors, alteration of capital structure, dividends and so on. Limited companies may draft their own articles or adopt a model format provided by *Table A* of the Companies (Tables A - F) Regulations 1985.

Bona fide In good faith

Bonus issue A bonus issue is made when a company applies its reserves to paying up unissued shares which are then allotted to members. Bonus shares are a substitute for additional dividends which might otherwise be paid.

Business name A name used by a company other than the registered one.

Call A demand made by a company upon a member to pay an amount outstanding on his partly-paid shares. The power of the directors to make calls is defined by the articles.

Called up share capital The aggregate amount of calls for money or other consideration which members are required to pay (or have paid) in applying for shares.

Capital clause A clause appearing in the memorandum of association of a company which specifies the amount of share capital and its division into shares of a fixed amount.

Capitalisation The conversion of profits into capital by the issue of bonus shares.

Caveat emptor Let the buyer beware.

Certificate of incorporation A certificate issued by the Registrar of Companies on the registration of a company. The certificate is conclusive evidence that the company has been registered and that all the requirements of the Companies Act in respect of registration have been complied with.

Certification A procedure recognised by law under which the transferor sends the transfer to the company to be certified before he delivers it to the transferee. The secretary stamps it 'certificate for .... shares lodged'.

Charge An encumbrance upon an asset which gives the holder certain rights over the asset. In particular a charge gives to the creator a prior claim over other creditors for payment of his debt out of the asset.

Charging order An order imposing a charge on a person's assets, including shares.

Class rights Rights attaching to particular types of shares. They are usually specified in the articles.

Compensation for loss of office A sum paid by a director when he ceases to hold office. If a director has a service contract he may be entitled to compensation for its breach by his dismissal as provided by the Companies Act 1985. The Companies Act provides that such compensation must be approved by the company in general meeting and disclosed in the accounts.

Compulsory liquidation A winding up by order of the court. Normally this procedure is adopted where a company is insolvent but will not admit it, so a creditor petitions the court.

Concert party Several persons acting in concert who control a significant part of a company's share capital. Where the joint holding is more than 3% of equity shares in a public company, this holding must be disclosed.

Connected person With regard to directors' loans and substantial property transactions, this includes the director's spouse or child under 18, a company in which the director and connected persons own one fifth or more of the equity share capital.

Consolidation of shares A company combines shares with a low nominal value into fewer shares with a high nominal value.

Constructive notice A person may be deemed in law to know of a certain matter regardless of whether he has actual knowledge of it. In the case of companies this applies to some of the details in company registers, for example the register of charges.

Constructive trust So called because a trust relationship is construed regardless of the wishes or intentions of the parties concerned. Specifically directors are held to be constructive trustees of corporate property. If they misappropriate the property, they are liable to account to the company for any profit and compensate the company for any loss.

Contributory A person liable to contribute to the assets of a company in a winding up. This includes present and certain past members, personal representatives of deceased members and trustees of bankrupt members.

Creditors' voluntary liquidation A liquidation when the directors realise that the company is insolvent.

CREST A system to computerise paper-based functions in the Stock Exchange and to improve the speed and efficiency of the settlement process.

Crystallisation A *floating charge* is converted into a *fixed charge*, for example on liquidation or if the contract so provides.

Cum div The buyer of a share is entitled to recover the dividend.

Cumulative preference share A type of *preference share* where dividends which are not paid in one year are payable the following year.

Debenture A written acknowledgement of a debt.

Debenture trust deed A deed made in connection with a series of separate registered debentures. The deed appoints a trustee to represent the interests of the holders, defines the nominal amount of the debenture stock and specifies the date of repayment, the interest rate and the rights of the trustee to enforce the security.

Derivative action A remedy available to a minority shareholder to redress a wrong done to the company. Such an action is brought where those who have committed the offence control the company, and thus, under *Foss v Harbottle* could prevent it from taking action. Any benefit obtained will accrue to the company since the claim is derived from and made on behalf of the company.

Director A person who takes part in making decisions and managing a company's affairs.

Dividend A distribution of profits to members made in proportion to their shareholdings.

Dividend mandate A standing instruction by a member to a company to pay a dividend into his bank.

Dividend warrant A form of cheque authorising a company's bank to pay a dividend when the warrant is presented by the members' bank.

Employee share ownership trust An arrangement giving tax advantages to the company but not to the employee. A company can obtain a deduction in computing its taxable profits for money given to the trust to buy shares in the company. The trust must make the purchase within nine months of the company providing the funds and the trust then distributes the shares to the employees.

Employees' share scheme A scheme for encouraging or facilitating the holding of shares or debentures of the company by employees or former employees, their close relatives or a trustee for the benefit of the above.

Equity share A share which gives the holder the right to participate in the company's surplus profit and capital. There is no limit to the size of the dividend which may be paid except the size of the profit itself. In a winding up the holder is entitled to a repayment of the nominal value plus a share of surplus assets. The term equity share embraces ordinary shares but it can also include a *preference share* when the terms of issue include either the right to an additional dividend or the right to surplus assets in a winding up.

Ex div The seller of a share keeps the dividend.

Extraordinary resolution A resolution requiring a 75% majority at a general meeting of which 14 days' notice has been given. An extraordinary resolution is required, for example, to put the company into creditors' voluntary liquidation.

Fiduciary duty Duty imposed upon certain persons, such as agents, because of their position of trust and confidence.

Fixed charge A *charge* attaching to a particular asset on creation. The asset in question is usually a fixed asset, which the company is likely to retain for a long period. If the company defaults in payment of the debt the holder can realise the asset to meet the debt. Fixed charges rank first in order of priority in a liquidation.

Floating charge A *charge* on a class of assets of a company, present and future which changes in the ordinary course of the company's business. Until the holders enforce the charge the company may carry on business and deal with the assets charged. It attaches to the assets only on *crystallisation*.

Forfeiture A company may forfeit (accept a surrender of) shares if a call has been made and the holder has defaulted. Power to do so must be given in the articles.

Fraud Obtaining an unfair advantage by making a misrepresentation knowing it to be untrue, or recklessly without caring whether it be true or false.

Fraud on the minority Discrimination by the majority shareholders against the minority. The minority may have a remedy at common law.

Fraudulent trading Carrying on business and incurring debts when there is to the knowledge of the directors no reasonable prospect that these debts will be repaid, ie with intent to defraud the creditors. Persons so acting may be liable for the debts of the company as the court may decide.

Garnishee order A creditor obtains an order prohibiting a company from making a payment.

General commercial company An *objects* clause of a company implying that it can carry on any trade or business whatsoever. This clause may now be used as a result of the reforms of the Companies Act 1989.

Good faith Fair and open action without any attempt to deceive or take advantage of knowledge of which the other party is unaware.

Guarantee A promise to answer for the debt or default of another.

Holding company A company which controls another, its *subsidiary* by holding the majority of its voting rights, being a member of it and having the power to appoint or remove a majority of the board of directors.

Indemnity Security against or compensation for loss.

Indoor management rule The principle which states that the outsider who deals with the directors (or apparent directors) is aware of the requirements or restrictions imposed by the articles but is entitled to assume, unless he knows or should suspect the contrary, that these internal rules have been observed. This is also known as the rule in *Turquand's* case.

Insolvency practitioner Persons acting as a liquidator, administrative receiver, administrator or supervisor of a voluntary arrangement must be insolvency practitioners, authorised by the professional body to which they belong or by the DTI.

Insolvency The inability to pay creditors in full after realising all the assets of a business.

Introduction An arrangement by which existing securities are admitted to the official list for the first time.

Investment company A company which has given notice to the registrar of companies that the business of the company consists of spreading investment risks of members. The distinction between investment and ordinary companies is important because the former have special rules on profits available for distribution.

Issue at a discount An issue of company securities at less than their nominal value. Debentures may be issued at a discount but shares may not, according to the Companies Act 1985.

Issue at a premium An issue of a share at more than its nominal value. There are special rules laid down by the Companies Act governing the treatment of the premium.

Issued share capital The *nominal value* of the shares which a company has issued.

Lien A right to retain possession of property until a debt has been paid.

Lifting the veil (of incorporation) A company is normally to be treated as a separate legal person from its members. 'Lifting the veil' means that the company is identified with its members or directors or that a group of companies is to be treated as a single commercial entity. An example of this is to prevent fraud.

Limited liability Limitation of the liability of members to contribute to the assets of a business in the event of a winding up.

Liquidator A person who organises a company's liquidation or winding up. His task is to take control of the company's assets with a view to their realisation and the payment of all debts of the company and distribution of any surplus to members.

Listed Quoted on a recognised stock exchange.

Loan capital A form of business finance which means that the lender is a creditor of the business either short term (eg a bank overdraft) or long term (eg a debenture redeemable in five years' time). Loan creditors are not the same as members and have no voting rights.

Medium sized company A private company which in both the current and preceding year complies with at least two of the three conditions listed below.

(a) Turnover is not more than £11.2m

(b) Gross assets are not more than £5.6m

(c) Weekly average employees are not more than 250.

Member Shareholder of a company.

Members' voluntary liquidation A method of liquidation adopted when the members *consider* the company has come to the end of its useful life and they wish to share out its property amongst themselves. It must be preceded by a declaration of solvency from the directors.

Memorandum of association Together with the *articles of association*, this defines what the company is and how its affairs are to be conducted. It gives details of the companies name, objects, capital and registered office.

Minimum number of members A public company must be formed with two members. The Companies Act provides that if a public company carries on business without at least two members for more than six months, the remaining member who is aware of this is jointly and severally liable with the company for the company's debts. A *private* company, however, may now be formed and operate with only one member.

Minor A person under the age of eighteen.

Minutes A written, indexed record of the business transacted and decisions taken at a meeting. Company law requires minutes to be kept of all company meetings. Minutes of general meetings should be available for inspection by members.

Nominee shareholder A person whose name appears on a company's register of members but who in fact holds the shares for somebody else. This is important in connection with *concert parties*.

Objects clause A clause in a company's memorandum of association which sets out the 'aims' and 'purposes' of the company.

Offer for sale The acquisition by an issuing house of a large block of shares of a company with a view to offering them for resale to the public.

Ordinary resolution A resolution carried by a simple majority of votes cast. Where no other resolution is specified, 'resolution' means an ordinary resolution.

Ordinary share A share which gives the holder the right to participate in the company's surplus profit and capital. The dividend is payable only when preference dividends, including arrears, have been paid.

Oversea company A company incorporated outside Great Britain which establishes a place of business in Great Britain.

Overseas branch register A section of the register of members kept in a different country appropriate to the members whose shares are registered in it.

Partnership The relation which subsists between persons carrying on a business in common with a view of profit. Every partner is liable without limit for the debts of the partnership. In the absence of any written agreement, matters such as profit sharing are determined by the Partnership Act 1890.

Passing off Carrying on a business in a manner which is likely to mislead the public. This normally relates to using a name which is similar to that of another business.

Perpetual succession The principle by which a change in the membership of a company or the death of a member is not a change in the company itself. A company is a separate legal person which continues unaffected by changes among its members.

Placing A form of public issue whereby a number of major institutions are allotted securities in large blocks which they may hold or resell, wholly or in part.

Poll A method of voting whereby each person entitled to vote does so in writing, indicating the number of votes which he is casting in proportion to his shareholding.

Power of attorney Authority in the form of a deed enabling one person to act on behalf of another.

Pre-emption rights The right of shareholders to be offered new shares issued by the company in proportion to their existing holdings of that class of shares.

Pre-incorporation contract A contract purported to be made by a company or its agent before the company has received its certificate of incorporation. An agent may be made personally liable on such a contract which will be unenforceable against the company.

Preference shares A share which carries a prior right to receive an annual dividend of a fixed amount. There are no other *implied* differences between preference and ordinary shares but there may be express differences, for example preference shares may carry a priority right to return of capital. Unless otherwise stated, preference shares are assumed to be *cumulative*.

Premium The amount by which the payment for a share exceeds its nominal value. The Companies Act lays down detailed rules regarding the treatment of a premium and a *share premium account*.

Prima facie At first sight or on first impressions.

Private company A company which may not offer shares to the public, and which has not been registered as a public company.

Pro rata In proportion to the value.

Promoter Person who undertakes to form a company by making the appropriate business preparations.

Prospectus A notice, circular, advertisement or other invitation offering to the public for subscription or purchase any shares or debentures of a company.

Proxy A person appointed by a shareholder to vote on behalf of that shareholder at a company meeting.

Public company A company registered as such under the Companies Act. The principal distinction between public and private companies is that only the former may offer shares to the public.

Purchase of own shares A company may, subject to detailed rules, purchase its own shares. A private company may finance the purchase out of capital but this is closely regulated.

Quasi loan A payment to a third party on a director's behalf with the company being indemnified later by the director.

Quasi partnership A small, usually private company, where the relationship between the directors is essentially like that of a partnership. The courts have taken into account the existence of such quasi-partnerships when applying the law.

Quorum Minimum number required to be present for a valid meeting to take place.

Quoted company Company whose securities are listed on a stock exchange.

Re In the matter of.

Receiver Person who takes control of the assets of a company subject to a charge as a means of enforcing the security for the benefit of the secured creditors by or for whom he was appointed.

Reconstruction Alteration in the structure of a company's capital or in the rights of individual members, groups of members or debenture holders.

Record date A date selected by a company for the purpose of declaring a dividend. A dividend will be payable to all members on the register of members on a particular record date.

Rectification Putting right. Used in connection with the register of members when an incorrect or forged transfer has taken place.

Reduction of capital A diminution of the share capital of a company, for example to reflect a loss in the value of its assets. The scheme needs to be approved by the court to ensure that the creditors are not adversely affected.

Registered office A business address to which all communication with a company must be sent.

Registration Process by which a company comes into being. Certain documents must be filed with the Registrar of Companies and a Certificate of Incorporation must be issued.

Relevant accounts Accounts used to determine whether or not a company has sufficient profits to pay a dividend. These are usually the latest annual audited accounts.

Relevant company Any public company and any private company which is a member of a group which includes a public company.

Renounceable letter of allotment An *allotment letter* containing a renunciation form by which the allottee renounces his right to the shares allotted to him in favour of the person who completes a registration application form.

Rescission The act of repudiation of a contract. An equitable remedy.

Retention of title clause A clause which states that goods sold on credit remain the property of the seller until they are paid for.

Rolling settlement A system of settlement on The Stock Exchange which replaced the old account system. Transactions become due for settlement five business days after dealing.

Romalpa clause - See *retention of title* clause.

Savings related share option scheme An employee contracts to save for five (or seven) years after which he is entitled to his saving plus a tax free lump sum. At the time of making the contract he is granted an option (at a price fixed at that time) to apply the money at the end of the period in subscribing for shares of the company.

SEAQ The Stock Exchange Automated Quotations. Sophisticated computer system which displays share prices and enables dealing to be conducted.

Secretary An officer of a company appointed to carry out general administrative duties. Every company must have a secretary and a sole director must not also be the secretary.

Securities Company shares and debentures.

SEPON Stock Exchange Pool Nominees Ltd. This is a company managed by the Stock Exchange settlement centre. In the case of transactions which have not been settled, shares appear on the company register in the name of SEPON.

SETS Stock Exchange Trading Service. It automatically matches buy and sell orders in the largest FTSE companies.

Shadow director A person in accordance with whose instructions other directors re accustomed to act.

Share A member's stake in a company's share capital.

Share certificate A formal extract from the register of members. It is only *prima facie* evidence of title, not a document of title.

Share option scheme Scheme under which options are granted to employees giving them a priority in buying shares.

Share premium account An account into which an excess of payment for a share over its nominal value cannot be placed.

Share warrant Bearer document of title whose transfer effects a change of ownership by the mere act of delivery of the document.

Show of hands Method of voting in which each member has only one vote, shown by raising his hand, regardless of the size of his shareholding. This contrasts with a *poll*.

Small company Company which complies with two out of the three conditions below in two successive years.

(a) Turnover does not exceed £2.8m

(b) Gross assets do not exceed £1.4m

(c) Weekly average employees do not exceed 50.

Special resolution Resolution requiring a 75% majority of votes cast and 21 days' notice. A special resolution is required for major changes in the company, such as alteration of the name or articles.

Stop notice Means by which a beneficiary of a trust protects his interest.

Subdivision of shares Dividing shares into a larger number of shares with a lower nominal value.

Subsidiary company A company under the control of another company, its holding company.

Substantial property transaction An arrangement by which the company buys from or sells to a director of the company or of its holding company property which exceeds £100,000 in value or (if less) 10% of the company's net assets subject to a minimum of £2,000. The shareholders' approval is required.

Table A A model form of *articles* for a company limited by shares set out in the Companies (Tables A - F) Regulations 1985.

Title Legal right to possession or ownership of property.

Trust An arrangement by which the legal owner of a property has an obligation to administer it for the benefit of the beneficiary who has an equitable interest in it.

Uberrimae fidei Of utmost good faith. This applies to contracts of insurance and means that all material facts must be disclosed.

Ultra vires Beyond their powers. In company law this term is used in connection with transactions which are outside the scope of the objects clause and therefore, in principle at least, *unenforceable*.

Unenforceable Not actionable in a court

Unfair prejudice to members Treating any part of the membership of a company unfavourably. A member may apply to the court for relief under the Companies Act.

Void Having no legal effect.

Voidable Capable of being rendered void at the option of one of the parties, but valid until the option is exercised.

Waive Give up a claim or right, such as the right to receive notice.

Winding up A process by which a company ceases to exist, otherwise known as a liquidation.

Wrongful trading The term used where directors of an insolvent company knew or should have known that there was no reasonable prospect that the company could have avoided insolvency and did not take sufficient steps to minimise the potential loss to the creditors.

ORDER FORM

To order your ICSA books, you can phone us on 020 8740 2211, email us at *publishing@bpp.com*, fax us on 020 8740 1184, or cut out this form and post it to us at the address below.

To: BPP Publishing Ltd, Aldine House, Aldine Place London W12 8AW **Tel: 020 8740 2211** **Fax: 020 8740 1184**

Forenames (Mr / Ms): ____________________ Surname: ____________________

Daytime delivery address: ______________________________________

____

Post code: ______________ Date of exam (month/year): ______________

	Price (£)		Quantity		Total
	9/00	3/01			
	Text	Kit	Text	Kit	£
Foundation					
Business Economics	18.95	10.95			
Quantitative Techniques	18.95	10.95			
Introduction to English and EU Law	18.95	10.95			
Organisation and the Human Resource	18.95	10.95			
Information Systems	18.95	10.95			
Pre-Professional					
Introduction to Accounting	19.95	10.95			
Business Law	19.95	10.95			
Management Principles	19.95	10.95			
Managing Information Systems	19.95	10.95			
Professional Stage One					
Professional Administration	20.95	10.95			
Management Practice	20.95	10.95			
Corporate Law	20.95	10.95			
Financial Accounting	20.95	10.95			
Professional Stage Two					
Administration of Corporate Affairs	20.95	10.95			
Company Secretarial Practice	20.95	10.95			
Corporate Finance and Taxation (FA 2000) (10/00)	20.95	10.95			
Management Accounting	20.95	10.95			

Postage and packaging:	
UK: Texts £3.00 for first plus £2.00 for each extra	
Kits £2.00 for first plus £1.00 for each extra	
Europe (inc ROI): Texts £5.00 for first plus £4.00 for each extra	
Kits £2.50 for first plus £1.00 for each extra	
Rest of the World: Texts £20.00 for first plus £10.00 for each extra	
Kits £15.00 for first plus £8.00 for each extra	

Total ________

We aim to deliver to all UK addresses inside 5 working days; a signature will be required. Orders to all EU addresses should be delivered within 6 working days. All other orders to overseas addresses should be delivered within 8 working days.

I enclose a cheque for £ ________ or charge to Access/Visa/Switch

Card number | | | | | | | | | | | | | | | | | | | |

Start date (Switch only) ________ **Expiry date** ____________ **Issue no. (Switch only)** ____

Signature ____________________

REVIEW FORM & FREE PRIZE DRAW

All original review forms from the entire BPP range, completed with genuine comments, will be entered into one of two draws on 31 January 2001 and 31 July 2001. The names on the first four forms picked out on each occasion will be sent a cheque for £50.

Name: ______________________ **Address**: ______________________

____

____

How have you used this Text?
(Tick one box only)

☐ Home study (book only)
☐ On a course: college ______________
☐ With 'correspondence' package
☐ Other ______________

Why did you decide to purchase this Text?
(Tick one box only)

☐ Have used complementary Kit
☐ Have used BPP Texts in the past
☐ Recommendation by friend/colleague
☐ Recommendation by a lecturer at college
☐ Saw advertising
☐ Other ______________

During the past six months do you recall seeing/receiving any of the following?
(Tick as many boxes as are relevant)

☐ Our advertisement in *Chartered Secretary*
☐ Our brochure with a letter through the post

Which (if any) aspects of our advertising do you find useful?
(Tick as many boxes as are relevant)

☐ Prices and publication dates of new editions
☐ Information on Text content
☐ Facility to order books off-the-page
☐ None of the above

Have you used the companion Practice & Revision Kit for this subject? ☐ Yes ☐ No

Your ratings, comments and suggestions would be appreciated on the following areas

	Very useful	*Useful*	*Not useful*
Introductory section (How to use this Study Text, etc)	☐	☐	☐
Introduction to chapters	☐	☐	☐
Syllabus coverage	☐	☐	☐
Exercises and examples	☐	☐	☐
Chapter roundups	☐	☐	☐
Test your knowledge quizzes	☐	☐	☐
Illustrative questions	☐	☐	☐
Content of suggested answers	☐	☐	☐
Glossary and index	☐	☐	☐
Structure and presentation	☐	☐	☐

	Excellent	*Good*	*Adequate*	*Poor*
Overall opinion of this Text	☐	☐	☐	☐

Do you intend to continue using BPP Study Texts/Kits? ☐ Yes ☐ No

Please note any further comments and suggestions/errors on the reverse of this page.

Please return to: ICSA Range Manager, BPP Publishing Ltd, FREEPOST, London, W12 8BR

REVIEW FORM & FREE PRIZE DRAW (continued)

Please note any further comments and suggestions/errors below

FREE PRIZE DRAW RULES

1 Closing date for 31 January 2001 draw is 31 December 2000. Closing date for 31 July 2001 draw is 30 June 2001.

2 Restricted to entries with UK and Eire addresses only. BPP employees, their families and business associates are excluded.

3 No purchase necessary. Entry forms are available upon request from BPP Publishing. No more than one entry per title, per person. Draw restricted to persons aged 16 and over.

4 Winners will be notified by post and receive their cheques not later than 6 weeks after the relevant draw date.

5 The decision of the promoter in all matters is final and binding. No correspondence will be entered into.